The Yale Edition of the Complete Works of St. Thomas More

VOLUME 3

PART II

LATIN POEMS

Published by the St. Thomas More Project, Yale University,
under the auspices of Gerard L. Carroll and Joseph B. Murray,
Trustees of the Michael P. Grace, II, Trust,
and with the support of the Editing Programs of the
National Endowment for the Humanities
and the Knights of Columbus

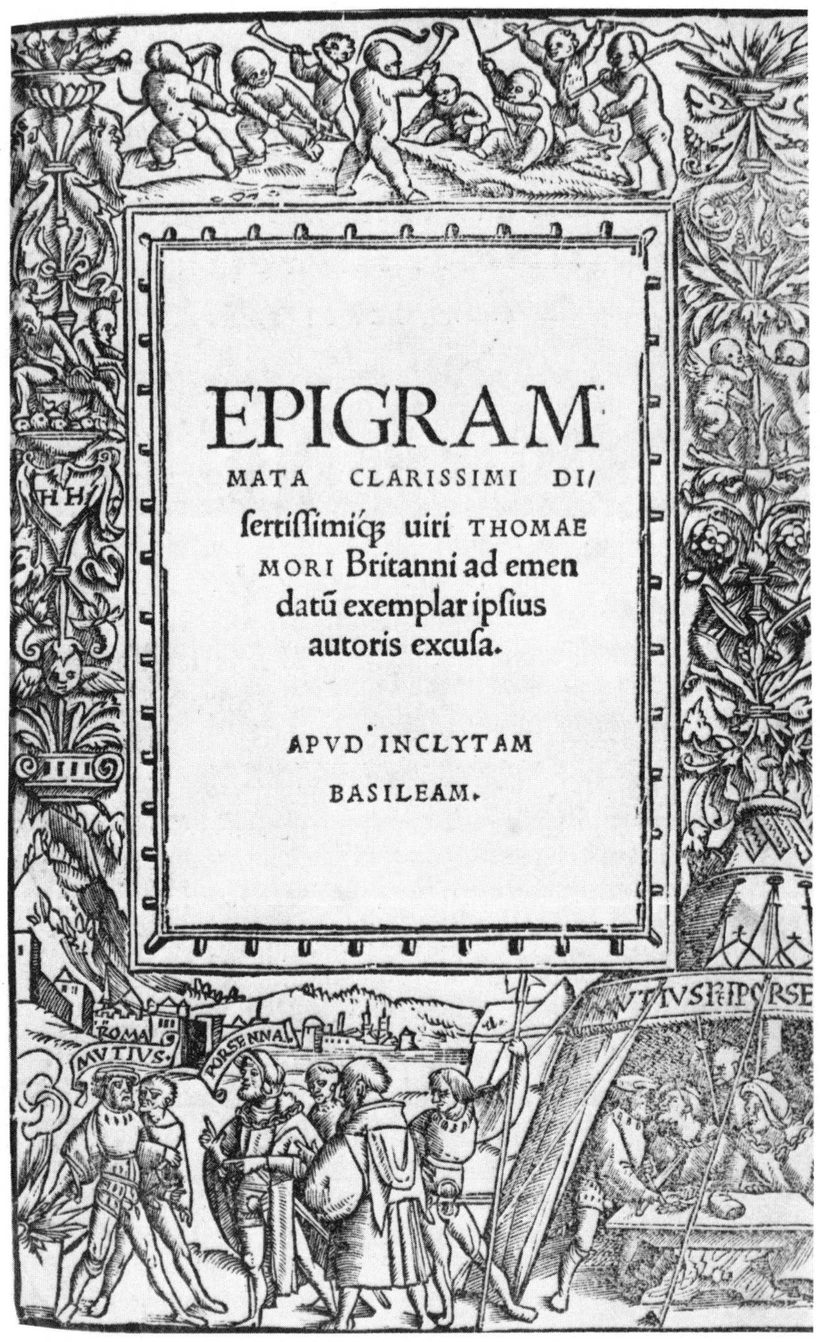

EPIGRAM
MATA CLARISSIMI DI/
ſertiſſimiq́ʒ uiri THOMAE
MORI Britanni ad emen
datū exemplar ipſius
autoris excuſa.

APVD INCLYTAM
BASILEAM.

Title-page, *Epigrammata . . . Thomae Mori,* Basel, 1520 (reduced)

The Complete Works of ST. THOMAS MORE

VOLUME 3

Part II

Edited by

CLARENCE H. MILLER

LEICESTER BRADNER

CHARLES A. LYNCH

and

REVILO P. OLIVER

Yale University Press, New Haven and London

Published with assistance from the National Endowment for the Humanities.

Library of Congress catalogue card number: 63-7949
International standard book number: 0-300-02591-2

Set in VIP Baskerville type.
Printed in the United States of America by The Murray Printing Company, Westford, Mass.

10 9 8 7 6 5 4 3 2 1

In Memoriam
Richardi Sylvestris
Magistri Operum Mori
Qui charitatem eius festivam
Scriptis edendis illuminavit

Lux perpetua luceat ei

ACKNOWLEDGMENTS

The entire Yale edition of Thomas More is a monument to the memory of Richard Sylvester, but it is especially appropriate that this volume should be dedicated to him because he worked on it and worried about it for many years. To him it was rather like a favorite but somewhat wayward child, and he would have been particularly pleased to see it finally full grown and ready to take its place in the world.

This edition is a complete revision and augmentation of the edition of More's Latin poems (Chicago, 1953) by Leicester Bradner and Charles A. Lynch, whose death in 1963 was a serious loss to the new edition. In the first, second, and fourth parts of the introduction, the authors have been identified by initials at the end of each subsection. Clarence H. Miller is primarily responsible for the text. The translation is basically that of Leicester Bradner and Charles Lynch in their edition of 1953, but it has been completely revised by Clarence Miller, with many helpful suggestions from James Hutton. The commentary is primarily the work of Clarence Miller, with much useful information provided by the other editors, by James Hutton, and by Daniel Kinney. Charles Clay Doyle was especially generous in providing full and detailed information about many sources and analogues.

The edition owes much to the labors of the staff at the More Project: Elizabeth D. Coffin, Stephen M. Foley, Shane Gasbarra, Po-chia Hsia, Ralph Keen, Daniel Kinney, Rosemarie P. McGerr, Ardelle Short, and James P. Warren. Maureen MacGrogan of the Yale University Press guided us carefully and patiently along the intricate paths that led to the final goal of a printed book. Ann Hawthorne, undaunted by an anfractuous typescript, copyedited it with great skill and made many rough places smooth. We owe an especially large debt of gratitude to Professor Jozef IJsewijn of the Catholic University of Louvain, who read the whole typescript with meticulous care and inexhaustible patience: his erudition and acumen corrected and improved it in many places.

Finally, we are very grateful to the Knights of Columbus for their generous support of our project.

C. H. M., L. B., R. P. O.

New Haven, Conn.
Providence, R. I.; Champaign-Urbana, Ill.

CONTENTS

ILLUSTRATIONS

INTRODUCTION

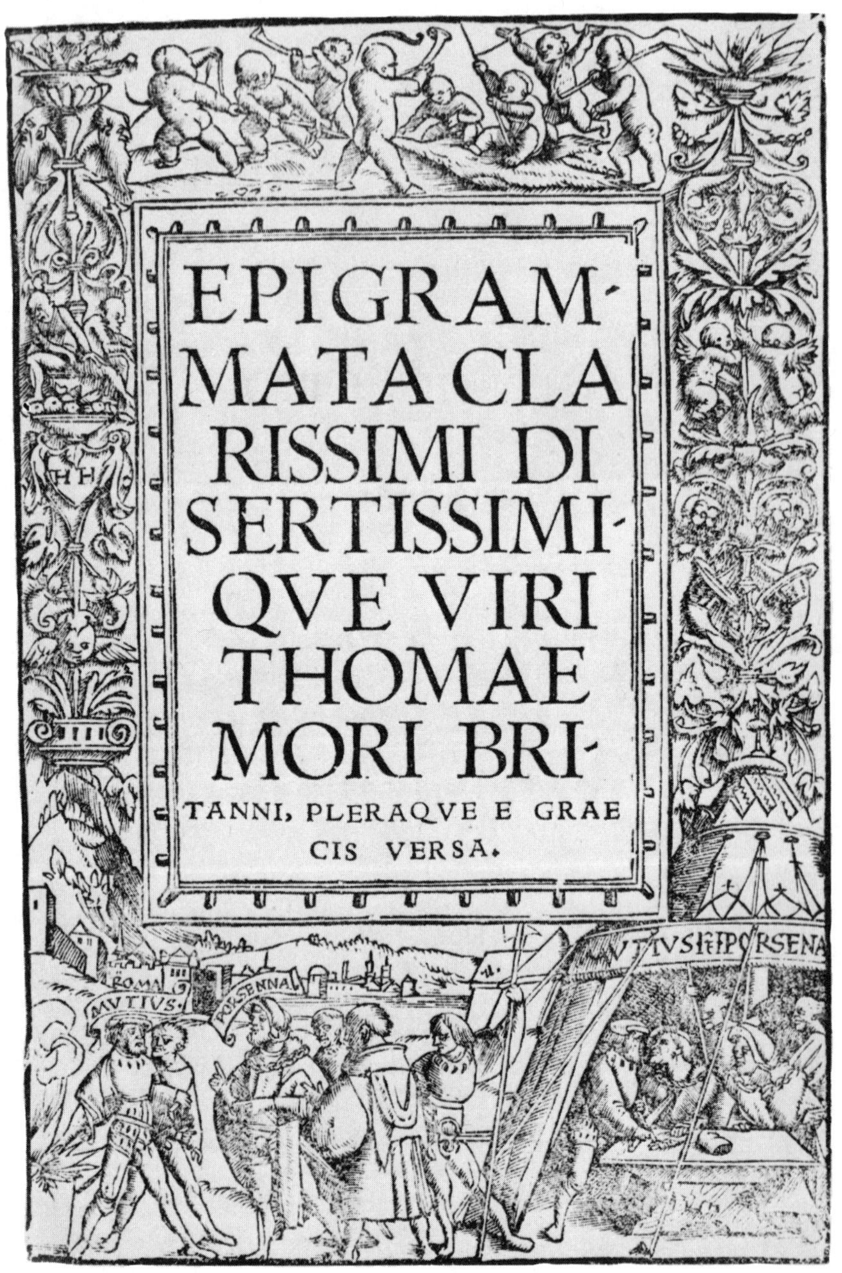

EPIGRAM-
MATA CLA
RISSIMI DI
SERTISSIMI-
QVE VIRI
THOMAE
MORI BRI-
TANNI, PLERAQVE E GRAE
CIS VERSA.

Title-page, *Epigrammata . . . Thomae Mori,* Basel, March 1518 (reduced)

COMPOSITION, EDITIONS, AND SOURCES

Editions and Revisions

Basel, March 1518 (*1518*ᵐ)

DURING THE ENFORCED delays of an embassy in Flanders in the summer of 1515 More wrote the second book of *Utopia* and by September of 1516 had finished the first book as well.[1] When Erasmus arrived in London for a brief visit in August 1516,[2] we may assume that he learned of the story of Hythloday's remarkable commonwealth and urged More to prepare it for the press. As early as June 1516 Erasmus had apparently proposed that he see to the publication of More's Latin poems.[3] At any rate, on September 3 More wrote to Erasmus, then in Antwerp, that he was sending him the manuscript of *Utopia.* In this letter he also refers to his epigrams: "If you later publish my epigrams, consider whether those ought to be printed which I wrote against Brixius, for some of them are rather biting."[4] This implies that the epigrams were already in Erasmus' hands and that plans for printing them had been discussed but not decided upon. It sounds as if Erasmus had been pressing More to establish a literary reputation by putting into print the works which he had on hand.

When More wrote to Erasmus in June 1516 urging him to decide what to do with More's verses,[5] he may have been replying to a suggestion that they be printed with *Utopia,* but they were not in fact included in the first

---

[1]*Utopia,* ed. Edward Surtz, S.J. and J. H. Hexter, The Yale Edition of the Complete Works of St. Thomas More, vol. 4 (New Haven and London, 1965), xv–xvii; the Yale edition of More is hereafter cited as *CW*. Abbreviations and full titles of all works frequently cited in this Introduction will be found in the Bibliography preceding the Commentary.

[2]*Opus epistolarum Des. Erasmi Roterodami,* ed. P. S. Allen, H. M. Allen et al., 12 vols. (Oxford, 1906–58), 2, 288–330; hereafter cited as "Allen."

[3]On June 21, 1516, More wrote to Erasmus: "De versiculis nostris nihil scribo; tu vide quid statuas" (Allen, 2, 261).

[4]"Si edas posthac Epigrammata mea, tu expende tecum an putes ea premenda que scripsi in Bryxium, nempe in quibus sunt quaedam amarulentiora. . . ." (Allen, 2, 340).

[5]See n. 3, above.

two editions of that work (Louvain, December 1516; Paris, 1517).[1] As early as May 30, 1517, Erasmus wrote to More that he had sent *Utopia* to Basel to be reprinted, along with the epigrams and some of his own *lucubrationes.*[2] In a letter of July 1517 he again mentioned to More that he had sent *Utopia,* together with More's epigrams and Lucianic translations, to Basel in the hands of his own trusted servant, Iacobus Nepos.[3] On August 23 he wrote to Beatus Rhenanus urging haste in printing what he had sent and "especially that they be careful to do a good job on More's pieces."[4] On the following day he wrote to Froben's corrector and secretary, Wolfgang Angst, expressing his desire that More's *Utopia* and *Epigrammata* be provided with a prefatory letter of commendation from Beatus Rhenanus. In the same letter Erasmus included his own preface to the *Utopia* and Progymnasmata.[5] In late November and early December Erasmus expressed impatience at the delay in printing.[6] He was especially eager to have the sheets well corrected, and for that reason had tried to get Rhenanus reinstated as Froben's corrector.[7] By December 1517 it seems that Rhenanus had resumed his work at Froben's press, so that he or Angst or both could have read proof for More's *Utopia* and *Epigrammata.*[8] By December Froben was finally ready to issue a joint volume devoted to the works of Erasmus and More. As the table of contents indicates, it was to have included their Lucianic translations, Erasmus' *Querela pacis* and *Declamatio de morte,* More's *Utopia,* and the Latin poems of both men.[9] But, as Froben explained at the end of the December volume (p. 644), it had grown too large, so that *Utopia* and the double set of epigrams were published in a separate volume in March 1518.

The signatures and pagination of *1518*^{m} are continuous throughout *Utopia,* More's epigrams, and Erasmus' epigrams. Though each has its

---

[1]R. W. Gibson and J. Max Patrick, *St. Thomas More: A Preliminary Bibliography of His Works and of Moreana to the Year 1750* (New Haven and London, 1961), nos. 1 and 2; hereafter cited as "Gibson." See also *CW 4,* clxxxiii–clxxxvii, and *CW 3/1,* lxi–lxiii.

[2]Allen, 2, 576.

[3]Allen, *3,* 6.

[4]Allen, *3,* 52.

[5]Allen, *3,* 56–57.

[6]Allen, *3,* 50, 153, 160–161.

[7]Allen, *3,* 160, 163. This last letter (Allen, no. 733) has been redated to early November 1517 (no. 704A) in *The Collected Works of Erasmus,* trans. R. A. B. Mynors and D. F. S. Thomson, ann. Wallace K. Ferguson, James K. McConica, and Peter G. Bietenholz, 5 vols. (Toronto, 1974–), *5,* 186–87; hereafter cited as *CWE.*

[8]*CWE 5,* 2, 228.

[9]Allen, 2, 420–21.

own title page,[1] the book was designed as a unit. The running heads THOMAE MORI ET GVIL. | LILII PROGYMNASMATA. (sigs. x_4v–y_4)[2] and THOMAE MORI | EPIGRAMMATA. (sigs. z_1–K_6)[3] stress the division between those two parts of the work.

The correspondence between More and Erasmus leaves no doubt that More had authorized the publication of his epigrams. It should be noted, however, that in his *Letter to Brixius* of 1520 More declared that the manuscript copies sent to the printer were made by others and were not corrected by More himself. In fact he claimed that earlier copies of certain poems he had issued would reveal Froben's errors. He also pointed out that it was hardly likely that the volume was completely free of printer's errors.[4] Therefore the errors of *1518*^{m} may derive not only from the faults of the compositor but also from the miscopyings of those who provided the manuscript.

In fact *1518*^{m} does contain a number of errors of a sort likely to be made by a copyist or a compositor struggling with a manuscript not easy to decipher. On three occasions the omission of headings caused two poems to be printed as one (nos. 51, 56, 81).[5] Some errors may well have been caused by a difficult manuscript: "Hei" for "Nec" (49/6), "Haec" for "Nec" (53/3), "Quin" for "Quum" (58/6), "factum" for "factu" (59/5), "detraxere" for "destruxere" (123/3), "Hunc" for "Nunc" (214/11).[6] This edition omits "E GRAECO" from two headings (103/2, 136/2), a Greek word in two Greek titles (9/1, 14/1), and one line (62/7). In his letter to Brixius (Appendix C, 626/6–30) More points out that there are many ways for errors to slip into a manuscript or printed text: a manuscript may be hard to read, a scribe or compositor may be careless, or he may retain a reading which an author has replaced by interlining a correction.

---

[1]For a complete description of *1518*^{m} and a facsimile of the title page of More's epigrams, see Gibson, no. 3. The title page border by Hans Holbein is reproduced and discussed by Arthur B. Chamberlain, *Hans Holbein the Younger,* vol. 1 (London, 1913), 191–93. Froben had first used it in 1516 for the title page of *Aeneae Platonici Christiani de immortalitate animae;* in 1518 Froben used it again for an edition of Erasmus' *Encomium matrimonii.* The lower panel portrays two scenes from the story of Lars Porsena and Mucius Scaevola.

[2]Sigs. x_4v–y1 have THOMAE MORI ET | G. LILII PROGYMNASMATA.

[3]Sig. z_1 has T. MORI EPIGRAMMATA.

[4]See below, Appendix C, 624/17–626/30, and the Commentary thereon.

[5]A similar error may well have occurred a fourth time (see below, Commentary at 193/1–28).

[6]See also the variant readings at 19/195, 63/4, 64/2, 117/4, 161/10, 198/2, 249/3, 252/10, 253/13. The block form of More's italic *N* sometimes resembles the block form of his italic *H* (see *CW 14,* 13/5 [*Non*], 227/8 [*Nam*], 541/6 [*Nam*], 541/9 [*Hec*], 567/7 [*Nam*]).

Of the approximately seventy errors in *1518*^{m} which were corrected in *1520,* all but six should probably be attributed to a copyist or compositor.[1] These errors and most of the other misprints and errors in *1518*^{m} were corrected by More in *1520*. Errors in the titles of the poems show that some of them are not due to More himself (nos. 92–94 and 261). Only about twenty titles are almost certainly More's or Erasmus'.[2]

Basel, December 1518 (*1518*^{d})

On November 13, 1518, Froben informed More that *Utopia* was being reprinted,[3] and on December 5 Lambert Hollonius, a new and not very satisfactory corrector at Froben's press, wrote to Erasmus that the printing of *Utopia* was almost finished.[4] Since the three colophons in this edition date *Utopia* November 1518 and the epigrams of More and Erasmus December 1518, Hollonius was presumably referring not merely to *Utopia* but also to one or both sets of epigrams. This edition is a page-for-page and line-for-line reprint of *1518*^{m}.[5] It corrects the errors of *1518*^{m} in only four places (8/3, 97/7, 190/28, 217/1). Of the ten new misprints it introduces into the text, only one ("AVRVM" for "AVARVM," 1/6, 2/4) is seriously misleading. The spellings *Roma, Romanus, saeculum, caelum,* and *caelestis* in *1518*^{m} are regularly changed to *Rhoma, Rhomanus, seculum, coelum,* and *coelestis* in *1518*^{d}.[6] It has a tendency to print some words capitalized in *1518*^{m} ("Medicus," "Rex," "Leo," "Epigram-

---

[1]See the variants at 19/167, 22/7–9, 135/4, 162/3, 181/6, 203/8. The errors at 75/9 and 90/14 may have been due to a copyist rather than to More.

[2]In addition to the titles of the verses on the coronation of Henry VIII (nos. 19–23), which appear in the manuscript that More caused to be prepared for Henry, More probably contributed such titles as "Versus iambici dimetri brachycatalectici" (no. 143), "e cantione Anglica" (nos. 81,82), and at least the substance of the long title of no. 148, which makes clear the satirical purpose of the verses that the unsuspecting Bernard André had taken as a compliment and proudly printed in the introduction to his own book (see the Commentary at 148/1–2). The titles of nos. 188–95, 264, and 266–69 also contain information that cannot easily be derived from the poems themselves and hence were probably supplied by More (or Erasmus).

[3]*The Correspondence of Sir Thomas More,* ed. Elizabeth F. Rogers (Princeton, 1947), p. 133; hereafter cited as "Rogers."

[4]Allen, *3*, 445.

[5]Apart from a few accidental variations, it agrees with *1518*^{m} even in signatures, page numbers, and running heads. There are a few variations in the line endings of prose passages. The last line (218/4) of sig. I_2v in *1518*^{m} has been moved to the bottom of I_2 in *1518*^{d}. For a complete description of *1518*^{d} and a facsimile of the title page of More's epigrams, see Gibson, no. 4.

[6]Cf. *CW 4,* clxxxix–cxc.

matista," "Dij") with lowercase initial letters. The border of the title page of More's epigrams is by Urs Graf.[1]

Basel, December 1520 (*1520*)

In his letter to Brixius (April 1520) More stated that Froben "himself wrote me a letter confessing that his workers were careless in printing my book and promising to reprint it more diligently."[2] In December 1520 Froben kept his promise by issuing More's epigrams for the first time in a separate volume.[3] For the most part this edition is a page-for-page and line-for-line reprint of *1518*.[4] Correspondences in spelling[5] make it clear that *1520* was set from *1518*^{d}, not from *1518*^{m}. Furthermore, when the line endings of *1518*^{m} and *1518*^{d} disagree significantly (as on sig. a_2), *1520* follows *1518*^{d}. The title page of *1520* states that it was printed from a corrected copy belonging to the author himself,[6] and the typographic evidence shows that the copy More corrected belonged to the edition of December 1518.

Although *1520* repeats thirteen errors from *1518*^{d} and introduces some forty new typographical errors,[7] its corrections and revisions of *1518* suggest the work of a careful editor—undoubtedly More himself. More than forty typographical errors from *1518* have been corrected, and, in addition to the revisions made in answer to Brixius' criticisms,[8] there are twelve places where the text has been revised to correct the prosody, improve the diction, or sharpen the sense of the poems. In no. 22, for example, More corrects the prosody of line 2 by adding "vel," then adds two lines to balance the construction with a second *vel* clause; at 90/15 he substitutes the more vivid "gerit" for "habet."[9] Three poems

---

[1]G. K. Nagler, A. Andresen, and C. Clauss, *Die Monogrammisten*, 5 vols. (Munich, 1858–79), *3*, 131, no. 30.

[2]". . . ipse literis ad me datis / a suis cessatum operis fatetur / ac pollicetur sese diligentius excusurum denuo" (Appendix C, 624/18–20). The letter from Froben seems to be lost.

[3]For a full description and a facsimile of the title page, see Gibson, no. 57. The title page border is the same as that in *1518*^{m} (see p. 5, n. 1, above).

[4]Hence sigs. a_2 and a_3 of *1520* are missigned x_2 and x_3 in accord with the signatures of *1518*. The pages do not correspond on sigs. a_2v–a_3v and sigs. k_2–l_4v of *1520* because of lines in *1518* not reprinted in *1520*.

[5]See p. 5, above.

[6]"ad emendatum exemplar ipsius autoris."

[7]The most serious error is the omission of lines 6–7 of no. 183. A cluster of errors occurs after no. 258, where the compositor was working from manuscript: see the variant readings at 260/6, 261/1, 262/20, 264/19, 264/41, 269/10.

[8]See pp. 25–32, below.

[9]See also the variants at 22/7–9, 47/7–8, 86/3, 90/14, 90/15, 93/2, 95/32, 101/4, 101/6, 137/3, 162/3, 214/13.

(nos. 51, 56, and 81) printed in *1518* as the endings of immediately preceding poems are separated and given titles. Two lines clearly intended as an alternate ending to no. 47 (lines 7–8) but printed as a separate poem in *1518* under the title "ALITER" have been dropped, and the original ending of the poem has been revised yet again. Seven titles have been improved: "E GRAECO" has been added twice (103/2, 136/2); the authorship of the Greek source has been indicated at 9/1 and 14/1; the title "Versum e Cantione Anglica" has been added to no. 82; the diction of the title of no. 91 has been improved; and the title of no. 232 has been changed from "In Ebrios" to "Sobrios Esse Difficiliores" in order to sharpen the point. Many of the spelling changes made in *1520* show a particular scrupulosity about indicating metrical length: "quattuor" for "quatuor" (149/5, 190/28, 218/4); "laevaque" for "levaque" (190/4); "illico" for "ilico" (167/16). The punctuation of *1520*, however, is especially faulty and generally inferior to that of *1518*.

More omitted from *1520* two poems that had appeared previously. One was a two-line epigram on fate (no. 270), a weak effort to translate from a definitely inferior source. The other (no. 271), on King James IV of Scotland, was evidently suppressed for political reasons. It had been written during the war with France and had stigmatized the impiety of the French cause and the treachery of Scotland. Now that England was at peace with both countries, More apparently considered that such political animosity should not be perpetuated, especially by an English court official. He alludes to this epigram briefly in a letter to Erasmus in the spring of 1520 about the Brixius controversy, pointing out that the differences between the warring nations had now been settled.[1] When More wrote the epigram in 1513 and even when he allowed it to be printed, he was a private citizen; now he was becoming a person of national importance. Another evidence of concern for his position is the suppression of a sentence (2/22) in the commendatory preface of Beatus Rhenanus. In praising More's wit the German humanist had said that just as one character in Terence remarks about another that he is every inch pure wisdom, so it would be proper to say of More that he is every inch pure jest. Evidently More did not think this exclusive emphasis on his jocularity a very fitting comment on a man who was now a member of the king's council. Besides, many of the poems are very sober and serious.

Councillor or not, in 1520 More had not lost interest in his literary work. He not only revised his earlier poems, as we have seen, but he also

---

[1]Allen, *4*, 221–22.

sent a group of eleven new epigrams to be added to the book. Four of these (nos. 259, 263–65) are personal poems, probably written after the manuscript for *1518* was sent off. Four others (nos. 266–69) are replies to Brixius' *Antimorus* (1519).[1] The remaining three (nos. 260–62) are miscellaneous and may have been written earlier. The personal poems are priceless documents of More's private character, and we may well give thanks that his justifiable pride in his own writing led him to make them public.

The Other Editions

Although the collected Latin works of More offer no new textual authority, they present certain points of interest for students of the More tradition. In 1936 Marie Delcourt pointed out in an important article[2] that the *Lucubrationes* (Basel, 1563) and the *Opera* (Louvain, 1565–66)[3] represent two different traditions, the first fostered by the disciples of Erasmus and the second by the pious English Catholic refugees, who removed all references to their hero's most famous friend. A comparison of the text of the epigrams in these two editions shows that the Basel editors used *1520*, with occasional reference to *1518*.[4] One short epigram (no. 171) was omitted, possibly because it seemed to duplicate Progymnasmata 13; and one other, "In Brixium poetam" (no. 209), was moved in order to put it next to another poem on Brixius. This edition was carefully edited and printed. The text has very few misprints and contains a number of judicious emendations. The Louvain edition, on the other hand, based as it is on *1518*^{d}, contains the three pieces omitted by More from the 1520 edition (p. 8, above), but lacks the corrections made by More for *1520* and the eleven poems added by More to that edition (nos. 259–69). Notable among these are no. 263, to Elizabeth, whom he had loved as a boy, and no. 264, to his children. Collation of the 1520 edition with that of Louvain indicates that the editors were unaware of its existence. The Louvain edition, furthermore, omits material found in *1518*. The sexually indelicate epigrams (nos. 116, 167, 235, 245, 258) and the poems in praise of Erasmus' work on the New Testament (nos. 255–57) are missing. No doubt the Louvain editors

---

[1]See Appendix B.

[2]"Recherches sur Thomas More: La tradition continentale et la tradition anglaise," *Humanisme et Renaissance, 3* (1936), 25–29.

[3]Gibson, nos. 74–76.

[4]Variants at 16/1, 22/18, 101/1, 145/4, 264/41, and especially the omission at 183/6–7 clearly show that the copy text of *1563* was *1520*. But at 10/7, 54/3, and 135/4, the editor has accepted false corrections from *1518*.

suppressed the praise of Erasmus because various works of his, including the paraphrase of the New Testament, had been condemned by ecclesiastical authorities at different times from 1527 on. Certain extant copies of editions earlier than the Louvain, such as the copy of *1518* now at Harvard, show that the praise of Erasmus has been excised or blacked out with ink.[1] Besides being based on an uncorrected edition of the epigrams this text is full of misprints.

The last edition of the *Opera*, printed at Frankfurt in 1689, announced on its title page that it was compiled from both the Basel and the Louvain editions. So far as the epigrams go, however, there is no evidence that the Louvain edition was consulted. The 1689 text follows the Basel edition faithfully and fails to introduce any of the three pieces which the Louvain edition preserved from *1518*.

Since 1520 there have been three editions of the *Epigrammata* issued separately. The first was printed at London in 1638;[2] the second appeared at the end of Arthur Cayley's *Memoirs of Sir Thomas More* (London, 1808); and the third, edited by Leicester Bradner and Charles Lynch, was published by the University of Chicago Press in 1953. The 1638 edition is a fairly careful reprint of *1520*, with one or two rearrangements in the text. It follows even the errors of *1520*. Cayley's text was derived from the *Lucubrationes* of 1563, as can be seen from the omission by both of no. 171 and by the identical relocation of no. 209. The 1953 edition was based on a collation of the 1518 and 1520 editions and was the first to contain textual notes and commentary.

From this brief review of the editions it appears that all the reprints after More's death except one, the Louvain *Opera* of 1565–66, follow the good *1520* text either directly or through the intermediation of the Basel *Lucubrationes* of 1563.

L. B. and C. A. L.

Dates of Composition

More apparently wrote all but one or two of his Latin poems over a period of about twenty years (1500–20), that is, between the ages of twenty-two and forty-two. On August 25, 1517, Erasmus wrote to Froben that More had produced epigrams when he was still growing up, most of them when he was a boy.[3] When Erasmus printed More's translation of a Greek epigram (no. 52) in the *Adagia* of 1518, he introduced it

---

[1]See the Commentary at 255/5–10.

[2]*STC*[2] 18086; Gibson, no. 58.

[3]"Epigrammata lusit adolescens admodum ac pleraque puer" (Allen, *3*, 57).

with the sentence: "Some time ago this epigram was cleverly translated by Thomas More, while he was still growing up, as follows."[1] In the account of More's life and character sent to Hutten in 1519, Erasmus says merely that More wrote epigrams in his youth.[2] On April 26, 1520, Erasmus remarked in a letter to More that most of More's epigrams had been written more than twenty years before and almost all of them more than ten years before.[3] Of More's 281 extant Latin poems, only 48 can be dated with a fair degree of certainty, only 5 can be dated before 1500, and only 6 between 1500 and 1510.[4] But Erasmus was probably thinking primarily of More's translations from the *Greek Anthology*, most of which were almost surely written before 1510.

In this connection it is important to inquire into the progress of More's Greek studies. In a letter which should probably be dated November 1501, he wrote to John Holt that he had put aside Latin and was studying Greek with William Grocyn.[5] Three years later he wrote to John Colet that Thomas Linacre, who was very proficient in Greek, was directing his studies.[6] In 1505 he was working with Erasmus on the translations of Lucian. Craig Thompson suggested that the Progymnasmata were written about 1503 or 1504.[7] In our earlier edition of More's Latin poetry (Chicago, 1953) we argued that More was not acquainted with the Greek text of no. 12 until Erasmus brought a manuscript of Arsenios' *Violetum* to England in 1509.[8] Revilo Oliver, however, has pointed out

---

[1]*Adagia* 2383, *Opera omnia*, ed. Johannes Clericus (Jean Leclerc), 10 vols. (Leiden, 1703–06), 2, 822E; hereafter cited as "*Opera omnia*." See the Commentary at 52/1–8.

[2]"Vnde et epigrammatis lusit iuuenis. . ." (Allen, *4*, 16).

[3]". . . cum pleraque tibi ante annos plus viginti scripta sint, omnia ferme ante annos decem" (Allen, *4*, 240).

[4]Georg T. Rudhart (*Thomas Morus* [Nürnberg, 1829], pp. 142–44) gave some valid evidence for dating some of the poems. The commentary on the following poems presents the available evidence for the dates given in parentheses: nos. 19–23 (late June or July 1509), 95 (late 1512 or early 1513), 101 (April 1498 or January 1515), 147 (after 1508), 148 (between 1509 and 1517), 159–61 (1497), 183–84 (September 1513), 188–95 and 209 (late 1512 or early 1513), 244 (late September 1513), 250–52 (summer 1515), 255–57 (spring 1516), 258 (1512 or 1513), 259 (1515–17), 263 (1518–19), 264 (1517–20), 265 (c. 1518), 266–69 (late 1519 or early 1520), 271 (September 1513), 272 (1495–1505), 273–74 (1496–1500), 275 (1512), 276 (September or early October 1517), 277 (October or early November 1517), 278 (1532), 279 (summer 1515), 280 (1532–35).

[5]Rogers, no. 2, lines 12–14.

[6]Rogers, no. 3, lines 65–68.

[7]*The Translations of Lucian by Erasmus and St. Thomas More* (Ithaca, N.Y., 1940), pp. 8–10. See also *CW 3/1*, xxvi–xxvii.

[8]*The Latin Epigrams of Thomas More*, ed. Leicester Bradner and Charles Lynch (Chicago, 1953), p. xii; hereafter cited as "Bradner-Lynch."

that the *Violetum* did not in fact contain the Greek of no. 12. Still, he suggests, for other reasons, that it is just as probable that the Progymnasmata were written toward the end of the decade 1500–10 as toward the beginning.[1]

L. B. and C. A. L.

Sources and Analogues

By far the most important source for More's Latin poetry is the Planudean Anthology. At least 106 poems, including 16 of the Progymnasmata, are translated from this source. Book I (*Demonstratiua et exhortatoria*) provides the source for some 50 poems; Book II (*Irrisoria et conuiualia*) for more than 40. Books III (*Sepulchralia*) and IV (*Descriptiua*) were used sparingly—ten and three times, respectively; Books VI (*Christodori descriptio*) and VII (*Amatoria*) account for only one poem each. Apart from the Planudean Anthology, the sources and analogues of More's poems are scattered and varied. We now know—thanks largely to the work of Charles Clay Doyle—that at least 7 poems are closely related to the Aesopic tradition,[2] at least 6 others to such anecdotal authors as Bebel and Poggio.[3] Nearly 10 poems turn upon philosophical problems and dilemmas drawn from an array of classical authors: Plutarch, Seneca, Cicero, Diogenes Laertius, Aristotle.[4] More's love of proverbs is displayed piecemeal throughout the epigrams, and at least 7 seem to take their epigrammatic turn from a proverb or a reversal of a proverb.[5] Only a few individual authors seem to have attracted More's attention. A poem by Martial (6.78) on a drunkard who is told that he will lose his eyesight leads More to three separate variations (nos. 199, 210, 214); another poem (no. 196) turns upon a line from Martial. Occasionally More appears to have borrowed names from Martial for his satiric characters. Lucian inspired at least two poems (nos. 139, 233), and Ausonius appears to have influenced at least two more. More's most unusual sources by far are the two English songs that he translates in nos. 63 and 64.

L. B. and C. A. L.

The Progymnasmata: Date and Sources

The Progymnasmata are eighteen short pieces of Greek text, sixteen of them epigrams from the *Greek Anthology*, each followed by Latin verse

---

[1]See p. 13, below.

[2]See nos. 42, 61, 134, 135, 180, 188, 198, 222.

[3]See nos. 63, 83, 165, 175, 203, 239.

[4]See nos. 49, 75, 77, 113, 117, 120, 131, 208, 240.

[5]See nos. 94, 107, 197, 200, 205, 218, 262.

translations by More and William Lily. The Greek texts are very nearly the easiest and least complicated that could be found. This fact has led to the supposition that the Progymnasmata were an early work, from about 1503, when More was a tyro in Greek studies; but this will not do for Lily, who was ten years older and presumably had attained considerable proficiency in Greek before he returned from Italy. It seems better to understand Progymnasmata, "preparatory exercises,"[1] in its usual application to an elementary textbook. The conspicuous example is Aphthonius' *Progymnasmata,* an elementary handbook of model rhetorical forms, that in Latin translation was among the most popular schoolbooks of the Renaissance. Within the environment of More and Lily, the title was also that of the elementary Latin grammar prepared by Thomas Linacre for St. Paul's School,[2] but rejected by Colet. Though direct evidence is lacking, it is not unreasonable to suggest that More's and Lily's Progymnasmata were also intended for use in this school, of which Lily was appointed the first high master in 1510. Since in 1512, when the school opened, Greek was apparently not yet printed in England, the book may have been used, if used at all, in manuscript copies.[3]

Whatever may have been the intentions of its authors, the Progymnasmata were in fact a stroke of pedagogical genius. Apparently it is the first of its kind, and More and Lily may be credited with the invention of the variorum translation of selected Greek epigrams that was to have a brilliant history in the schools and beyond. At least, given More's great reputation, it seems very likely that Johann Heyl (Soter) may have taken the idea from this unique work for his own variorum *Epigrammata Graeca* published at Cologne in 1525, in which the translations of More and Lily are included among many others. This was professedly a schoolbook, and one can see that the multiple translations were intended to encourage the practice of *variatio* recommended by Erasmus' *Copia.* A new edition of Heyl's selection was called for in 1528 and another in 1544, and meanwhile an enlarged edition had been published in 1529 by Janus

---

[1]See the Commentary at PROGYMNASMATA, p. 321.

[2]See the Commentary at 275/1.

[3]A similar date (c. 1510) was proposed for the Progymnasmata by Bradner and Lynch, but on insufficient grounds. Seeing that no. 12 occurs in the *Violetum* of Arsenios, they believed that a manuscript copy of this work was given to Erasmus in Venice by Girolamo Aleandro and might have been brought by him to England in 1509. But what Aleandro gave, or perhaps only lent, to Erasmus seems rather to have been the *Paroemiae* of Arsenios' father, Michael Apostolios, which does not contain this item. Erasmus' words are: "proverbiorum collectio . . . titulo Apostolii, cuius libri nobis copiam fecit Hieronymus Aleander" (*Adagia* 1001, Erasmus, *Opera omnia* 2, 405D). The *Violetum* embodies the *Paroemiae,* with copious additions by Arsenios, and it is among the latter that Progymnasmata 12 is found.

Cornarius in Basel. The same selection, but with many additions, was the basis of Henri Estienne's *Epigrammata Graeca* (1570), and on this in turn was based the *Progymnasma scholasticum* (1597) of John Stockwood. It would be pleasant to believe that the title of this large book acknowledged the modest English beginnings of its kind, but there is no hint of this, and Stockwood no doubt thought of *Progymnasma* only as properly describing a textbook designed to interest the pupils of the Tunbridge Grammar School, of which he had been headmaster. All these books are in a sense publications of More's work insofar as his translations are included in them. In 1608 in Rome, the third edition of Soter was adapted for the use of Jesuit schools.[1]

There can be no doubt that the sixteen epigrams from the Anthology in the Progymnasmata are derived from the Planudean tradition of the text and from no other source, for they have readings peculiar to this tradition. Number 13 has a mistake (duly translated by More), δὶς for εἷς, probably made by Planudes himself in his transcription,[2] while no. 11 has the correct reading, εἰκόνα . . . ἐκτὸς ἔχει, which Planudes either preserved or restored by a happy emendation where the other texts[3] are corrupt. Furthermore, no. 9 has the Planudean transposition, κεῖνον κρίνω, and no. 6 has λιμέν(α), which is in Planudes where the only other collection then available, the *Sylloge Euphemiana,* has ὁδόν.

Although it is clear that the sixteen epigrams in the Progymnasmata are derived from the *Planudea,* it does not follow that a text of that collection, manuscript or printed, was the immediate source.[4] We note, first of all, that More and Lily translated two passages of Greek, an epigram (no. 18) and a gnomic statement (no. 12), that are not in the *Planudea.* We should simply assume that they added these on their own if

---

[1]James Hutton, *The Greek Anthology in France* (Ithaca, N.Y., 1946), pp. 15–18.

[2]The emendation that removed the error is credited to Aldus Manutius; it was confirmed by the codex Palatinus when that became available in the early seventeenth century.

[3]Palatina, Crameriana, and Parisina.

[4]There is, however, some indication that the notebook or other manuscript that More and Lily had before them had been excerpted from one of the two printed editions. In the fifth line of no. 10 they have the peculiar reading ποθ' ᾅδαν, which is found in the *editio princeps* and the first Aldine, although the latter, in the ἐπιδιόρθωσις on the final pages of the volume, contains the statement ἐν ἄλλῳ, πρὸς ἅδαν, γράφεται. The "other copy" was presumably Planudes' autograph, now in the Marciana in Venice, and its reading, πρὸς Ἅιδαν, is obviously correct. If we could be certain that the error that More and Lily reproduced was peculiar to Lascaris' *editio princeps* (from which the text of the first Aldine was copied), this would be proof that their excerpts were made from one of the two printed editions.

there were no indications that the texts from the *Planudea* had been edited by a Greek scholar—possibly one who had in mind the needs of his pupils. Moreover, the most likely explanation of the peculiar reading in no. 13 is that the editor eliminated the rare and confusing spelling ἀδελφειούς by substituting the regular Attic form ἀδελφούς and then adding ὧδ' to preserve the meter.

There are, furthermore, certain errors in the Greek titles of the epigrams in the Progymnasmata which can be more readily explained as errors made in the process of selecting epigrams from Planudes. The title is normally merely a statement of authorship, and we have in the Progymnasmata some attributions that are at variance with all known traditions and seem at first sight inexplicable. The title of no. 15, an epigram describing Sappho as the tenth Muse, says that it is of uncertain authorship ('ΑΔΗΛΟΝ), although Planudes says that it is the work of Plato; but the epigram which is the next but one preceding this in Planudes also refers to Sappho as the tenth Muse and it really is ἄδηλον. Number 16, an epigram about a bronze statue of a satyr, has the title 'ΑΓΑΘΙΟΥ ΣΧΟΛΑΣΤΙΚΟΥ, although the verses are anonymous in Planudes; our title belongs to the epigram, also about a bronze statue of a satyr, that is the next but one above this in Planudes and really is the work of Agathias. Number 11 is headed 'ΑΓΑΘΙΟΥ, but in Planudes the heading is ΤΟΥ ΑΥΤΟΥ, which refers back to the same notation above the preceding epigram, which in turn refers back to its predecessor, which has a title stating that Palladas is the author. An even more curious error is found in no. 13, which has the title ΠΑΛΛΑΔΑ, although it is anonymous in Planudes. Here no juxtaposition in, or rearrangement of, the Planudean collection will explain the error. The reason, however, becomes clear when we note that our epigram concerns twins who died on the same day, and that Palladas is the author of an epigram which was understood as concerning twins who died on the same day. It seems likely, therefore, that the man who excerpted the epigrams of the Progymnasmata from the Planudean collection first put together two epigrams of almost identical subject (as he understood them) and then cancelled the less perspicuous of the two, leaving the anonymous second attributed to the author of the first.

These errors in titulature strongly suggest that More and Lily had before them a notebook, such as the humanists frequently compiled, with numerous additions and cancellations on each page. And it would follow that at the time they used that notebook, More and Lily either did not have a copy of the complete anthology or did not refer to it.

We have no means of conjecturing how extensive was the notebook we have posited as the immediate source of the texts in the Progymnasmata,[1] nor can we deduce for what purpose the collection of epigrams was made. If its purpose was use as a propaedeutic textbook for pupils, the compiler had a reason for adding the two passages that do not come from Planudes. One of these (no. 18), an epigram which, if not particularly stirring, has the merit of being particularly limpid and easy Greek, was evidently derived, probably through some intermediary, from the *Sylloge Euphemiana.*[2] The other (no. 12),[3] a maxim in prose which could be mistaken for verse, was not only very simple Greek, but served a didactic and even moral purpose in an age in which men wasted time on astrology with a credulity that almost approached the gullibility with which our own contemporaries attend to any pseudo-scientific hoax or quackery.

One other detail in the organization of the Progymnasmata remains to be noticed. The Greek texts, as we have said, are normally preceded by a title which indicates only the authorship of the epigram,[4] whereas the first of the Latin versions, whether More's or Lily's, has a Latin title which states the subject. In the Greek titles there are two exceptions. The title of no. 17, taken from Planudes, states the subject (without remarking on the authorship) and is translated to provide a title for the Latin translation. The title of no. 10, also from Planudes, in addition to informing us that the verses are of uncertain authorship, indicates the subject but is not translated above the Latin, where the title emphasizes a different aspect of the epigram.

In the Progymnasmata the Latin titles distinguish Lily's work from More's, but aside from that, all but two are such as anyone could supply from reading either the Greek text or the Latin versions. In other words, unlike the Greek titles that indicate authorship, they could have been written by anyone: by the compiler of a hypothetical collection of epigrams from the Planudean corpus, by Lily or whoever selected the pieces to be included, by Lily or More or both together when they made the Latin versions, by the persons (including a copyist and Erasmus) through

---

[1]It could, for example, have contained the Latin equivalent of no. 6, which Lily used as his translation. See the Commentary at 6/5–9.

[2]The *Sylloge Euphemiana* (a collection of eighty-two epigrams made in Constantinople c. 900 A.D.) was fairly well known; at least three manuscript copies of it made in sixteenth-century Italy are extant. The only other known collection that contains this epigram is *Sylloge* Σ^{π}, but the only known copy of this is bound in the codex Palatinus and so must be assumed to have been inaccessible in the sixteenth century. See the Commentary at 18/1–3.

[3]See the Commentary at 12/1–5.

[4]That is, either the author's name in the genitive case or one of the two standard notations, ἀδέσποτον ("anonymous") or ἄδηλον ("authorship undetermined").

whose hands the manuscript passed on its way to the publisher, or by the publisher of the *Epigrammata* in 1518.

The title of no. 13 "In duos fratres uno et natos et mortuos die," fits the correct Greek text, which says that the two brothers lie in one tomb, but not the Latin translation, derived from the Planudean corruption (δίς), which places four brothers in the tomb. The Latin title of no. 12, the prose maxim treated as verse, is even more remarkable for two reasons: it contradicts the Greek and it is fantastically wrong. The Greek title correctly states that the maxim is of unascertained authorship; the Latin is "Theophrasti apud Aulum Gellium dilemma." There is nothing to connect the anonymous and probably proverbial expression with Theophrastus.[1]

R. P. O.

[1]See the Commentary at 12/6–7.

STYLE AND PROSODY

More as a Translator

More and Lily, when they produced the Progymnasmata, had the same Greek texts before them, evidently had about the same degree of competence in both languages, and seem to have had about the same attitude toward the situations described in the original epigrams. It is only reasonable to suppose that they criticized one another's work. With the exception of two epigrams, to which we shall shortly return, they appear to have had no Latin models for their translations, and even allowing for the limitations imposed by the Latin vocabulary and metrical requirements, their versions of most of the epigrams are astonishingly alike.

Most of the translations are competent and adequate, and it would require a very nice taste to pronounce one translator superior to the other in either accuracy or elegance. Both had the same difficulty in understanding the Greek of no. 16, which says that either the satyr got into (clothed himself with) the bronze or the artist encased the satyr in bronze. Both thought, for some reason, of a more fantastic antithesis: either the satyr put on the bronze or the bronze put on the satyr. In no. 10, both distorted the Greek text, which concisely praises the Spartan woman who slew her own son when she saw that he had been a recreant in battle. When the Greek says that her speech was manly (More's *mascula verba*), it is commending her for rising above female weakness and showing masculine resolution in placing principle above sentiment. Both translators, however, felt shocked. More felt obliged to call the mother *saeva,* and Lily added a touch of the macabre, making her a *virago furens* who speaks *horrida voce.*[1] This picture of frenzy makes his the more memorable verse, but also the better illustration of the maxim *traduttore,*

---

[1]More, who probably intended "saeva" to mean "cruel" rather than "stern," drew that conclusion from the reported act, but Lily may have been influenced by *Anthologia Palatina* VII, 433, which has the mother grind her sharp teeth as she speaks, and, possibly, by *AP* VII, 531, which has her also foam at the mouth and glare at her dying son. *AP* VII, 433 is in Planudes (but, for a much improved text, see A. S. F. Gow and D. L. Page, *The Greek Anthology: Hellenistic Epigrams* [Cambridge, 1965], p. 198). Lily could have found *AP* VII, 531 in Suidas, of which the Greek text, edited by Demetrius Chalcondyles, had been printed at Milan in 1499.

William Lily. Artist unknown

traditore. In no. 13, however, Lily was much more successful than More in rendering the meaning of the Greek. In this epitaph on two brothers, More has *Lux simul una duos et parit et perimit,* and, whatever More may have intended, that means that the twins died on the day of their birth. Lily wrote *una duobus | lux et natalis, mortis et una fuit.* The brothers, being twins, were necessarily born on the same day, and it happened, by a coincidence that was particularly remarkable in centuries in which men believed in astrological determinism, that they died on the same day.

The two versions of an epigram are sometimes remarkably alike, as in no. 7. The first line of the Greek says, literally, "Onto the earth I came naked, and naked under the earth I depart." I can see no way of putting all of that into a Latin hexameter, and the following pentameter is so tight as to exclude carrying part of the meaning over into it. Both translators chose to keep *in terram* and to omit a specific reference to burial, although, of course, it would have been easy enough to stress that by writing *Nudus ut adveni, sub terram nudus abibo,* or *Vt veni nudus, sub terras rursus abibo,* or even *In terras veni nudus terram subiturus.* In the pentameter, both, I suspect, wrote *quid frustra sudo funera nuda videns?* and Lily changed *sudo* to *studeo* in his verses, that the two might not be identical. But *funera* is not quite the word for τέλος (*finis, exitus*), which, in the Greek, is naked primarily in the sense in which we speak of "the naked truth," for the writer sees the stark reality of man's inevitable end. One does not think of funerals as naked, and there is nothing to carry the metaphorical sense of *funera* as "corpses." It is noteworthy, therefore, that both translators used so awkward a rendering.

A considerable number of More's collected epigrammata are also versions of Greek epigrams, usually designated as such by the words *e Graeco,* although in a few instances that label was omitted, probably through an oversight by either More or the printer.[1] The name of the Greek author is never given. There can be no doubt about the source from which More took the Greek texts that he translated. There are seventy-nine epigrams, and they are all found in the Planudea. It seems certain, therefore, that More possessed and used a copy of either the complete Planudean Anthology or very copious extracts from it.[2] In the

[1]It was omitted with nos. 27, 35, 36, 46, 53, 55, 58, 99 (perhaps because the last distich of the Greek was not translated), 100, 130 (probably a typographical error), and 137. Two epigrams are labelled "e Graeco" but do not correspond to known Greek epigrams: nos. 50 and 72.

[2]Some have claimed that More's protégé John Clement once had the Codex Palatinus 23 (the source of the *Anthologia Palatina*) in his possession. In 1566 Henricus Stephanus wrote

Epigrammata he used that collection only, and made no translations from any Greek poet outside the anthology.

For this part of his work, unlike the Progymnasmata, we do not have before us the exact text that More was translating, and we shall therefore have to make allowances for possible errors in his Greek text. Furthermore, it is clear that More permitted himself greater liberties. The Progymnasmata could have served as models for schoolboys studying the art of verse translation; as we have seen, only one translation (no. 10) could be an intentional alteration of the meaning of the Greek original, and even there it is entirely possible that the translators did not make the change deliberately, but merely read into the Greek their own sentiments. In his own epigrams *e Graeco,* however, More did attempt to improve some by sharpening, softening, or redirecting the point of the originals.

The majority of More's translations show all the fidelity to the originals that we could reasonably expect to find when the verse of one language is translated into the verse of another. But when we come to the few that do not show such fidelity, our criticism of More's work will usually depend on our subjective estimate of the likelihood that in a given epigram More was trying to improve on the original. And we are, at that point, disconcerted by some of the faithful translations, which remind us that More's conceptions of propriety and proportion were not always our own. He chose to translate without significant change two epigrams on men of small stature. In one of these, we are told that the man was so puny that he used a strand of a spider's web to hang himself. That is grotesque enough, but it falls just within the pale of folk humor, which

---

that he had copied the anacreontic poems he published in 1555 from a manuscript in the possession of John Clement at Louvain. Because these poems now survive only in Codex Palatinus 23, Valentin Rose, in his edition of these anacreontic poems (Leipzig, 1876, pp. vi, xx–xxiv), argued that John Clement must have brought that unique codex with him to England when he returned from Italy in 1525 and taken it with him when he went to Louvain in 1550. Other scholars have argued that what Clement made available to Stephanus in 1551 was a copy of part of Codex Palatinus 23, not the codex itself or any part of it. See *Carmina Anacreontea,* ed. Karl Preisendanz (Leipzig, 1912), pp. v–x; *Anthologia Graeca,* ed. and trans. Hermann Beckby, *1,* 2d rev. ed. (Munich, 1965), 90–91; and James Hutton, *The Greek Anthology in Italy* (Ithaca, N.Y., 1935), p. 31. But (as Prof. Alan Cameron has kindly informed us) in 1926 Giovanni Mercati published a list drawn up by John Clement's son Thomas in 1573. The list of Thomas' books and manuscripts, which he had almost certainly inherited from his father, includes "Epigrammatum liber magnus duplo plura continens, quam Aldi liber impressus, et plura etiam quam liber impressus Henrici Stephani"; hence it is at least probable that John and Thomas Clement did possess Codex Palatinus 23. See Giovanni Mercati, "Sopra Giovanni Clement e i suoi manoscritti" in *Opera minori,* 5 vols. Studi e Testi 76–80 (Vatican City, 1937–1941), *4,* 307–12.

often depends, as in the tales about Paul Bunyan, on simple exaggeration; and some of us, at least, will smile. But in the second epigram we are told that Diophantus was so small that, had Epicurus seen him, the atomic theory would have been revised to state that atoms were composed of Diophanti. The disproportion is so enormous that we regard the conceit as incredibly silly; but More evidently thought it witty. That makes us wary of pronouncements about what More would or would not have wanted to change.

We can, however, identify some passages in which More's knowledge of Greek was probably inadequate (see the Commentary at 100/1–3). In no. 146 he probably misunderstood βάλλετε, and that would probably have sufficed to make him translate ἐφυβρίζουσι (of which he may not have known the exact meaning) as though it were ἐφοβήσαντο. And the most likely explanation of the mistranslation in no. 41 is that More misconstrued μάρτυς as a vocative in apposition to Ἀπολλόφανες. Those are certainly venial errors. When More's *Epigrammata* were published in 1518, the world had thirty years to wait before it would have anything that could properly be called a Greek dictionary, and complete, concise grammars lay centuries in the future.

There are also places at which it seems likely that More was misled by a corrupt text. In no. 149, of course, he had before him Planudes' error, ἀργὸς for Ἄργος.[1] We are on more uncertain ground when we come to no. 155. The Greek says that Antipatra's body is so hideous that the Parthians, if they saw her without clothes, would flee to the ends of the earth. More's translation (if we disregard the title, which may not be his) says either (a) that the woman is so ashamed of the deformity concealed by her clothes that if anyone saw her naked, she would flee to the barbarous Parthians, or (b) that she, who may well be quite beautiful, is so modest that if anyone saw her naked, she would exile herself from civilized society. A simple corruption of ἔφυγον to ἔφυγεν could have misled More; and if εἴ τις in the preceding line had been corrupted to εἷς, his translation could represent his best effort to understand the text. But it is also possible that he deliberately made a change that seemed to him an improvement.[2]

More, of course, made changes that are obviously intentional: he added a moral to no. 32, greatly improved the point of no. 47, expanded no.

---

[1]See the Commentary at 149/4.

[2]See the Commentary at 155/1–4. More also seems not to have understood the real point of no. 24, but the epigram is so obscure that its meaning seems first to have been explained by Professor Charles Lynch in "*Anthologia Palatina,* 11.46," *Classical Philology, 48* (1953), 17–19.

85, and softened no. 99 by omitting the gibe that the miser could reduce the per capita cost of his tomb by having one of his children buried with him. More's concern, after all, was to produce Latin poetry, not to provide Latin translations for the benefit of those who knew no Greek, and his notation "e Graeco" is the acknowledgement of a source, not a guarantee that his verses are a substitute for the original. When we compare his no. 130 with the Greek text, we see that More deliberately altered the next-to-last line. He remembered that he had seen elsewhere in the anthology an epigram (by the same poet, Palladas, as it happens) which makes the point that we are like a drove of swine, raised and nourished for a death that they do not foresee: πάντες τῷ θανάτῳ . . . τρεφόμεσθα. This appealed to him as a better—perhaps more vivid—figure, and he accordingly put a translation of it, *Plutoni pascimur omnes,* in the penultimate line of no. 130.[1]

Most of More's verses deal with matters that are timeless, and a considerable number of these so resemble in style and wit his translations that the reader is left with the impression that they are unacknowledged translations, and he may be tempted to search the pages of the *Anthology* for the original. These epigrams are an artistic triumph. We should remember that the humanists subjected themselves to the arduous discipline of close imitation and translation to attain a mastery of their medium. They sought so to assimilate the spirit of great literary models and so to master the technique that they could eventually produce original compositions of comparable excellence.

R. P. O.

More's Latinity and the Strictures of Brixius

Today, we should be able to write Latin that is almost perfect. We have texts based on the most minute and meticulous collation of the best extant manuscripts and on the learning accumulated by five centuries of scholarship. We have reference works of every kind, from the *Antibarbarus* of Krebs-Schmalz and the almost exhaustive grammar of Kühner-Holzweissig-Stegmann to the *Thesaurus linguae Latinae,* the most thorough lexicon that the world is likely ever to have of any language and now complete through more than half the alphabet, and the many volumes of Müller's *Handbuch* and of Pauly-Wissowa-Kroll. There are even special lexica, such as Cardinal Bacci's, for the translation into Latin of words designating modern innovations.

---

[1]See the Commentary at 130/8.

The resources that make it so easy for us to do what we have not the spirit to attempt were all wanting in More's day, when the most learned, diligent, and fastidious writers were doomed to error by corrupt texts and the lack of systematic works of reference. Our criticism of humanistic Latin must begin with a profound and solemn respect for men who accomplished what we could not have done in their circumstances, and with full awareness that it is to their achievements that we owe our ability to detect their shortcomings.

More was certainly a respectable Latinist and esteemed as such by his learned contemporaries. Today, anyone with more than a smattering of Latin can notice some shortcomings in More's prefatory letter to Henry VIII. He speaks of the king's "coronatio" (More Pref./9): of course *corona* does not mean "a crown," and in Latin the ornament placed on a king's head is *diadema* or *insigne regium.* It is obvious from the title of the first poem (19/1) that More knew that, too; he was merely using diction then currently accepted. When More wrote "praemortuum" (More Pref./22), he probably intended the somewhat unusual meaning "dead" or "quite dead," but he had some justification.[1] And although we can see why More, having begun with "tam" plus an adjective, resorted to "sui vim" (More Pref./25), the expression violates the elementary rule that the genitive of the pronoun can be used only when it is objective and the corresponding adjective would be ambiguous; the expression, therefore, is redolent of medieval barbarism.[2] In another context, *integra aetate* could, by a bold and poetic metaphor, mean what More intended, "within a whole lifetime," but when it stands immediately after a verb meaning "to grow old," the reader's mind automatically takes *integra aetate* as an adjectival phrase with its usual and normal meaning, "in the prime of life," and expects that some comparison or antithesis will be drawn. Such misdirection of the reader's mind, when no jest, satire, or oxymoron is intended, is a stylistic fault in any language.

When we notice such obvious errors, we certainly cannot be accused of hypercriticism or overnicety, but, so far as I know, none of More's con-

---

[1]The verb is frequently used to describe the effects of old age or disease, whereby some of a man's faculties, such as sight or hearing, "die" before he does, and it may be used metaphorically of the effects of vice and crime, which kill a man's moral sense while he remains alive. But there are occurrences of *praemortuus* with this meaning (e.g., Ovid, *Amores* 3.7.65; Livy 3.72.5) where a reader could not tell from the context alone that the meaning was not "completely dead." More used the verb *praemori* correctly in other epigrams (72/10, 250/6).

[2]It is proper to say, for example, *memoria tui,* meaning "memory of you," because *memoria tua* could mean "your memory (of someone else)."

temporaries animadverted upon them, and they certainly escaped the notice of More himself, first when he wrote and again when he revised. The short preface in prose and the five poems that it introduces are the only part of the epigrams for which we have manuscript evidence. As may be seen from the textual notes, the differences between the manuscript presented to Henry VIII and the first printing show that More did try to correct his Latin. In the last sentence of the preface (More Pref./29), he changed "honoratissimus . . . titulus" to "rarus . . . titulus," thus simultaneously improving the Latin and enhancing the compliment to the king. In line 68 of no. 19, he had fallen into the tyro's error of using a subjunctive after the conjunction *cum* when the reference is to past time. Of course, the subjunctive is proper when there is *some* causal relation (as there usually is) between the action of the subordinate clause and what followed it. More undoubtedly knew the rule and violated it thoughtlessly; when he revised the verses for publication, he saw how absurd it was to imply that Achilles, during one episode in his youth, was a handsome young man *because* he was disguised as a woman. He accordingly replaced the subjunctive with an indicative. It is possible that some friend had called More's attention to the error, but it is as likely that More needed no prompting to make the correction when he reread his composition.

If we wish to judge the Latinity of More's poems by the standards of his times, we may easily do so by considering Brixius' strictures on the 1518 edition of the Latin verse.[1] Germanus Brixius, a pupil of Lascaris and Musurus, friend of Erasmus, and one of the most popular Latin writers of his time,[2] was not so great a scholar as Erasmus or Longolius or Budaeus, but he was a learned man. His quarrel with More arose, as quarrels between humanists not infrequently did, from conflicting national allegiances, and it quickly became, as quarrels between humanists invariably did, a controversy over the antagonists' respective accomplishments as Latinists. More attacked Brixius for having exaggerated in a poem the valor of a French captain during the brief and fruitless war between Henry VIII and Louis XII. Brixius, following the established custom, replied in a booklet of recrimination, the *Antimorus,* with a sting in the very spelling of its title. We may feel assured that Brixius mentioned every error in More's Latin that he could detect.

---

[1]For a list and classification of Brixius' objections, see Appendix C, p. 681, Commentary at 630/10–11.

[2]In 1530 Erasmus (Allen, *9*, 32) wrote to Brixius that Froben was eager to publish anything by Brixius because "Germani Brixii nomen iam illustre est, et librum emptori per se commendat." See Appendix A, pp. 429–32.

More probably had the *Antimorus* before him when he made the revisions for the edition of 1520. The corrections which he did or did not make, which are indicated in the textual notes, give us an accurate measure of More's attitude toward classical and contemporary standards. The deviations in question fall into three distinct classes: some he corrected; some he retained; and some he tried to repair with hasty patchwork.

Certainly not all the errors in the 1518 edition were due to More. As he argued in the *Letter to Brixius,*[1] some were surely due to a copyist or a compositor. For example, at 31/4 More must have written the contracted form "coplat," which someone else erroneously changed to the more usual form "copulat."[2] But Brixius also found a few errors that it was difficult or impossible to defend. More had falsified the quantities which I here mark correctly: "herōidas," "leōninam," "mācerent."[3] More was able to correct the mistakes easily.

The errors that More did not correct may be most instructive to us. If there were only one or two instances, we could dismiss them as oversights or assume that More shirked the work of correcting them. There are enough, however, to enable us to reconstruct More's thinking, and it will be worth our while to examine some of them.

In Latin, which conforms to Greek in such matters, the word for philosophy is *phĭlŏsŏphĭa,* and a philosopher, naturally, is a *phĭlŏsŏphus;* obviously, then, the words cannot be used in heroic or elegiac verse. More, however, wrote "phīlosophīa" at 19/119, and "phīlosophus" at 261/3. I feel certain, however, that he was neither ignorant nor brashly violating language to import the words into verse. Like many of his contemporaries, More read extensively and respectfully many of the later Latin poets whose works are now read as poetry by virtually no one—and only occasionally by scholars who resolutely collect evidence of linguistic and cultural decay. Sidonius Apollinaris, Bishop of Auvergne in the late fifth century, who, despite his affectations, knew little or no Greek, habitually made the first syllable of *philosophus* long;[4] and Prudentius, a Spanish Christian of the late fourth century, made the penulti-

---

[1]See Appendix C, pp. 622–26.

[2]For other examples see the Commentary at 19/100, 19/180, 62/6, 76/10, 130/4, and 214/11. Four other errors may also be due to a scribe or typesetter (see the Commentary at 23/5, 25/5, 75/9, 90/14).

[3]19/167 181/6, 203/8.

[4]Sidonius has many such scansions in an epithalamium which is one of his more successful efforts in verse (*Carm.* 15. 43: "phīlŏsŏphōrum"; 182: "phīlŏsŏphī"; 187: "phīlŏsŏphō").

mate syllable of *sophia* long, perhaps because he misunderstood the elementary rules of Greek accentuation.[1] I feel certain that More made the errors in the first place, and later persisted in them, because he regarded such writers as sufficient authority. Similarly, he did not hesitate to use *congaudere,* a postclassical word used by late writers of prose and poetry.[2]

At 167/3 we find "ŏportunum." The correct spelling, of course, is *opportunus,* and the double consonant makes the first syllable long. The word is derived from *ob* + *portus,*[3] but with the decline in literacy in the ancient world there arose somehow the notion that it was derived from *ŏportet.* The misspelling *oportunus* appears at least as early as A.D. 261 in an inscription[4] and became the usual spelling in the Christian writers, some of whom specifically adopt the false etymology from *oportet.*[5] The error was denounced in the first work of humanistic lexicography, Niccolò Perotti's *Cornucopiae* (compiled in 1473–78, first printed in 1489, and frequently reprinted).[6] More, however, appears either to have accepted the false etymology or to have regarded the late writers as sufficient authority for the spelling; he therefore disregarded Brixius' criticism.

In all probability, More made the first syllable of *pūlĭcēs* short in both lines of no. 106 because he had seen the word so used in the pseudo-Ovidian *De pulice,* which he may have regarded as a work of late antiquity, although he surely cannot have imagined that it was Ovid's.[7] He shortened the last syllable of *impār* at 114/9 on the authority of Ausonius or Prudentius.[8] And although he undoubtedly knew that the perfect of

---

[1]Prudentius, *Contra Symmachum,* line 34. If the tonic accent in σοφία were a stress accent, the iota would be long according to the rules of accent in Latin.

[2]See the Commentary at 19/34.

[3]See Festus, *De verborum significatu,* ed. Wallace Lindsay (Leipzig, 1913), pp. 206–07; Donatus, *Commentum Terentii,* ed. Paul Weisner, 3 vols. (Leipzig, 1902–08; reprinted 1966) 2, 305 (on Terence, *Hecyra* 626). The etymology given by the ancient grammarians is correct; see A. Ernout and A. Meillet, *Dictionnaire étymologique de la langue latine,* (3rd ed., Paris, 1951), s.v. "portus."

[4]*Corpus Inscriptionum Latinarum,* ed. Theodor Mommsen et al., 16 vols. (1858–1955), *11,* 5759; hereafter cited as *CIL.*

[5]It may be worthwhile to note that Erasmus did not make this error: the correct spelling is guaranteed by the meter in his *Elegia de patientia,* 92 (*The Poems of Desiderius Erasmus,* ed. C. Reedijk [Leiden, 1956], p. 151; hereafter cited as "Reedijk"), written when he was about nineteen.

[6]*Cornucopiae* (Venice, Aldus Manutius, July 1499), sig. d_1. In the Aldine edition of 1517, the passage is in col. 97, lines 12–26.

[7]See the Commentary at 106/3–4.

[8]For example, Ausonius, *Griphus ternarii numeri,* 54; Prudentius, *Contra Symmachum,* line 168. For More's use of Ausonius see the Commentary at 54/4–5.

iŭvāre is *iūvī,* he thought that *iŭvāverit* in 143/125 was a legitimate variation.[1]

The foregoing examples suffice to show that More erred neither through ignorance nor from a determination to take with Latin the liberties that are sometimes deemed permissible in a "living language." He followed rule and precedent as scrupulously as any humanist did in practice; he differed from the stricter classicists in regarding writers, chiefly Christian, as sufficient authority, at least for some comparatively unobtrusive departures from strictly classical standards. At the moment of writing, he may not have thought of his authority for each of the locutions examined above, but I am inclined to believe that he did call some authority to mind when he decided to disregard Brixius' strictures. Had the polemic between them continued it would probably have developed into a debate *De imitatione,* comparable to the argument between Giovanni Francesco Pico della Mirandola and Bembo.[2] In the sixteenth century, the problem of imitation that had confronted the humanists from the first remained unresolved, and each writer had to choose for himself some position in the wide range of principle and practice that extended from more extreme *Ciceroniani,* who would permit nothing for which precedent could not be found in Cicero for prose and Vergil for verse, to the wildest "Beroaldistae," who delighted in extracting archaisms and strange locutions from the glossaries and in "enriching" Latin with wholesale importations from the Greek.

Besides false metrical quantities, Brixius objected to four neologisms. Although I cannot cite a use of *claudipes* by an earlier humanist, I feel certain that the word is not original with More (27/3, 28/2).[3] The objection to it is that it is tautological; a man may be *claudus,* "lame" (or *claudus altero pede,* "lame in one foot only"), or he may be *loripes* ("with weak or twisted limbs"), but it seems redundant to form a new word that means nothing more than *claudus.* The objection to More's "imbibum" (89/16), which I do not recall having seen elsewhere, is that we would not know what it meant if we did not refer to the Greek that he was translating. The word should mean, by analogy, something like "drinking in" or "not drinking." Only by referring to the Greek, in which the cup is described as "deeply hollowed," can we ascertain that More probably meant "inexhaustible," that is, a bottomless cup from which one can drink endlessly.[4]

---

[1]See the Commentary at 143/125.

[2]Edited by Giorgio Santangelo (Florence, 1954). It is noteworthy that Pico refrains from defining the range of authors whom he regards as acceptable models.

[3]See the Commentary at 27/2–28/2.

[4]See the Commentary at 89/16.

To be sure, More's word obviously has something to do with imbibing, and his choriambics trip so lightly that perhaps only a very sober pedant would stop to demand a precise definition.

At 95/12, More encountered the petty and vexatious difficulty that confronts us whenever we try to refer in Latin to current fashions in apparel—or, for that matter, to designate past modes in any language without writing a paragraph of description or providing a picture. The precise word in the vernaculars is apt to be a nonce-word, as ephemeral as the fashion it represents. For example, a statement that a man was wearing a "wide-awake" would probably convey no definite meaning to the average reader today, only a few decades after the term was in general use. In that line of his poem, More, doubtless trying to be specific, used one classical and two medieval words—and we cannot be sure precisely what he meant.[1] Brixius, who was puzzled himself, had some grounds for objecting, but More, who must have had in his own mind a clear picture of the costume he was describing, ignored the objection.

When we consider the errors that More left uncorrected, we may deplore his reliance on decadent authors or his taste in Latinity, but only in a few instances can we accuse him of having erred through ignorance or inadvertence. The fourth line of no. 206 seems to say "the grandees stood in front of their own feet." Of course, More did not mean that; here, as in the *Utopia* (*CW 4*, 579), he used the reflexive adjective loosely.[2] In 118/5, More's Latin says "he was going to die in front of his father," if it means anything at all; More, who was trying to say "before his father," confused *prae,* which, as a preposition, cannot refer to time, with *ante,* which can.

The rest of Brixius' objections deal with very minor matters. At 101/10, More has "serĭŏ," and twice he scanned "denuŏ" (5/13, 17/9): he probably thought that the correption of final *o* in Silver Latin could be extended to all adverbs;[3] both Statius and Valerius Flaccus, for example, have "verŏ," and it is entirely possible that More could have cited an example of the very word that he uses from some decadent writer. At 198/17, "omni anno" for *quotannis* or *quoque anno* would be inexcusable in prose, but it would be niggardly to deny More the license that we grant Ovid, when we permit him to write "omnis amans" ("every lover"), and "omnis calculus" ("every ballot"), and Lucan, whose "omni hora" (9.883, where it must mean "every hour") More would probably have cited in defending himself—if he did not have in mind some exact precedent.

---

[1] See the Commentary at 95/12.
[2] See the Commentary at 206/4.
[3] See the Commentary at 5/13.

At 247/19, More undoubtedly knew that "credere in daemones" or "in deum," was a solecism, but it would have been grotesque not to use the standard ecclesiastical Latin[1] when reporting a conversation in the confessional—to say nothing of the fact that the whole jest depends on that construction. The priest asks whether the man had resorted to any magic spell or incantation ("an unquam malos | ritu profano crediderit in daemonas"). The stupid penitent, misunderstanding, replies "I can scarcely believe in God" ("vix adhuc credo in deum"). Brixius knew that; he was simply being malicious—and that makes it remarkable that in this poem he did not notice "ăn" in line 6, which makes the fourth foot a pyrrhic, or "crediderat" in line 7, which was almost certainly a typographical error for "crediderit," but could have been denounced as an example of one of the worst solecisms, the use of an indicative in an indirect question.[2]

Some of the corrections that More did make in the edition of 1520, however, cannot be so easily defended. They convey an impression of haste or negligence, and, like patches that are more conspicuous than the holes they cover, make More's poetic raiment seem a little shabby. A suitable correction would have involved recasting one or more lines, but More seems to have put down the first thing that came to his mind as an expedient that would require a minimum of change. He was probably hurried and impatient. In a letter to Erasmus, written in the latter part of June 1516,[3] More, protesting a compliment that Erasmus had paid him, said,

> When you commend me on an increase in my proficiency [in Latin], I blush with shame, for I well know how much my proficiency decreases every day from what it was before. That is what necessarily happens to a man who is incessantly engaged in litigious affairs entirely foreign to every kind of learning—and it is onto that treadmill that my career has forced me. I am now so driven by this stupid business that my mind is not adequate to reflective thought, nor are my words adequate to connected discourse. If, therefore, you examine my choice of words and measure my stylistic ability—that is to say, if you count my solecisms and barbarisms—you are ordering me to keep silent.

But More was undoubtedly a prisoner of his public offices in 1516, and it is highly improbable that he was less busy four years later, when he

---

[1]See the Commentary at 247/19.

[2]But see the Commentary at 94/3.

[3]Allen 2, 259.

revised his Latin verses for a new edition. It is entirely possible that he did not have the time for careful revision.

If one is going to write an epigram about a man whose name is Nīcŏlāus, one should not try to do it in elegiacs, but More, having mistaken the quantity of the third syllable, had done so. The only real solution would have been to rewrite the whole poem in senarii, septenarii, phalaeceans, or some other verse into which a word having one short between two longs could be fitted. But More, when he came to correct no. 96, found a quick way out: he thought of the Greek variant, Νικολέως, and Latinized it (improperly). When he praised young King Henry (19/100), he meant *Mercatoribus aperit mare,* but for metrical convenience, and perhaps misled by English, he seems to have replaced the dative with *ad* and an accusative. In his attempt to patch that error, he wrote "ad mercaturas," which is not much better and must mean something like "he opened the sea for commerce."[1] In 135/4, having mistaken the quantity of "ĕdat,"[2] he obtained a long syllable by writing "indat" but made nonsense of the verse, since the verb cannot mean "to eat."[3]

How perfunctory More's revision was, may be seen most clearly from his treatment of 25/5. In the first printing, that line appeared as

> Sīc et Phĭlŏlāum quondam occīdērĕ Crētensēs

Here he combined two metrical errors (an anapaest in the second, and a cretic in the fifth foot) with a mistake in geography, for the event, as was clearly stated in More's Greek original,[4] took place at Croton, which was in the toe of the Italian boot, not in Crete. In his revision, More evidently caught at the first expedients that occurred to him, including a deformation of the philosopher's name in the way in which he had deformed Nicolaus', and so he hurriedly scribbled on his copy.

> Sīc et Phĭlŏlĕon quondam occīdērĕ Crŏtōnĕ.

He got rid of the geographical error, at the cost of leaving the verb without an expressed subject, and eliminated the cretic, but he also put a tribrach in place of the anapaest, which is certainly no improvement.[5]

---

[1]But see the Commentary at 19/100.

[2]The mistake was easily made because the common inflection of the present indicative is *ĕdo, ēs, ēst.*

[3]The chances are that More had a confused recollection of Plautus, *Casina* 247: "si ego in os meum hodie vini guttam indidi" ("[I'll be damned] if I put a drop of wine into my mouth today").

[4]οὕτω καὶ Φιλόλαον ἀνεῖλε Κρότων ποτὲ πάτρη. Note that the Greek makes it obvious that the iota in the philosopher's name is short and the alpha long.

[5]More, who made the *i* in *philosophus* long (see pp. 25–26, above), may have thought that

Nothing can be more obvious than the fact that, had he not begrudged ten more minutes of his time, More, without replacing or shifting a single word in the next line, could have constructed here a normal hexameter—indeed, since he was not hampered by overnicety in the management of elision, caesura, and diaeresis, a dozen of them. He could have easily (a) restated the subject, (b) resorted to a patronymic of the type freely coined by the humanists,[1] (c) recognized that the name of the town is not really significant, or (d) rewritten the line to emphasize one or another of the striking aspects of the situation to which he alludes. For example:

a. Sic, Philolaë, Croton te patria perdidit olim
 Sic cives Philolaum olim occidere Crotonae
b. Sic olim occidere Crotoniadae Philolaum
c. Patria sic quondam tua te, Philolaë, peremit
d. Et quondam occidit Philolaum patria magnum
 Sic Philolaum olim iugulavit turba Crotonis
 Civili sapiens errore perît Philolaus
 Sic, ingrata Croton, Philolaum sponte necasti
 Te, Philolaë, Croton insontem tradidit Orco
 Doctum sic cives mactaverunt Philolaum
 Sic Philolaum Orco misit Croto Pythagoreum

Although these examples are not exhaustive,[2] they suffice to show that More was not confronted by a problem to which his ineffectual expedient was the unique solution.

Taken as a whole, More's revisions suggest the hurried work of a man who returns to long-neglected studies in scant hours of leisure, perhaps

---

that was a permissible license that could be extended to other words beginning with *philo–*, but he cannot have imagined that that was the correct quantity; he had the Greek before him in this case, and in no. 253 he wrote *Phĭlŏmēnus* twice correctly.

[1]The city supposedly derived its name from an eponymous hero, Croton (Ovid, *Metamorphoses* 15. 55). Of course, if we permitted synaeresis, we could use *Crŏtōnjātae,* but in the following verses we shall avoid every license. (Correption of a final *o* in a nominative, as in *Crotŏ,* is Ovidian.) For example, we shall not permit elision of a long vowel before a short, although More frequently does (e.g., 59/10).

[2]It will be noted that all the verses, except the second under (a), have penthemimeral caesurae, and that all of these are masculine, except the feminine in (b). In the second under (a), the unsupported hephthemimeral caesura and the double elision (which, though common in Catullus, is disapproved by modern versifiers, who hold to strictly Ovidian standards in elegiacs) match More's practice (e.g., 222/8).

at the end of days consumed in the kind of business that few men can completely dismiss from their minds for even an hour. Offices such as those to which More had risen demand perpetual vigilance, constant ingenuity, anxious foresight, and frequent perplexity of conscience. We must not think of him, even in his hours of freedom from the demands of office and family, as a scholar serenely weighing *elegantiae* in the seclusion of his study with that peace of mind that can be known only by those who feel themselves sheltered from the furious business of the brawling world. More had long since passed the time at which he could ever be "alone with eternal things." But even if More had had all the time he wanted to revise his poems, he would probably not have removed every blemish.[1] Nor, perhaps, would most of his contemporaries have expected him to do so. What Brixius overlooked when he searched for errors gives us another view of the standards of his time. He did not notice some false quantities, such as "cucŭlus" (253/14). But what is really surprising is that he did not notice such an unidiomatic expression as "semita itur alicui"[2] or such unusual idioms as "petor aliquid" or "exigor aliquid."[3] I suspect that More may have imagined that he was using the passive of a verb rather than an adjective when he tried to make "infortunata est privigno" mean "she brings misfortune on her stepson."[4] Those are really affronts to logic, as is, on a much lesser scale, the expression "corripere aliquid in digitos," which More wrote for "grasp in the hand."[5]

The significant point is that Brixius, for all his animus, did not comment on blunders that seem glaring to us—nor did Erasmus, who presumably read his friend's verses before sending them to the printer, think it necessary to suggest changes. We may assume either that Erasmus read very hurriedly or that he regarded even such violence to syntax as permissible poetic license. There is no better proof of the uncertainty and laxity that is characteristic of all of More's contemporaries, including even those who most ostentatiously paraded their severe devotion to the strictest classical standards.

R. P. O.

---

[1]See Appendix C, p. 681, Commentary at 630/10–11.

[2]31/7. More may have been confused by the fact that one can say in Latin *itum est* ("the journey was completed") and *hac via itur Romam* ("this road leads to Rome").

[3]137/2–3, 222/8. Aulus Gellius (15.14.5) mentions that such expressions as "exigor portorium" had been adopted into Latin from Greek.

[4]241/3, where the Greek shows what More must have been trying to say.

[5]129/4.

More's Meters

If quotations from Brixius be excluded, all but thirty-five poems or parts of poems in this volume are in elegiac couplets. The other meters are:

Dactylic hexameter: nos. 26, 51, 136, 137, 146, 160, 223, 233, 235

Iambic trimeter: nos. 12 (second version), 62, 63, 66 (scazons), 85, 91, 95, 145, 245, 247

Iambic strophe: nos. 22, 111, 121, 144, 193, 277

Dactylic hexameter alternating with iambic dimeter: nos. 113, 147, 251, 266

Iambic dimeter: nos. 109, 205, 281

Hendecasyllabics: nos. 276 (second poem), 280

Second glyconic catalectic ("choriambic"): no. 89

Iambic dimeter brachycatalectic: no. 143

Of these meters, the elegiac couplet, dactylic hexameter, and iambic trimeter occur in the Greek poems which More was translating. Usually he reproduced the meters of the originals, but in nos. 91, 145, and 89 he changed to another metrical form. On the other hand, iambic strophes, iambic dimeter brachycatalectic, hendecasyllabics, and dactylic hexameter alternating with iambic dimeter occur only when More's subject matter was original.

More used dactylic hexameter only in very short pieces, as is fitting in a book of epigrams. We might have expected no. 19, written for an important public occasion, to have been written in hexameters, but perhaps More was not comfortable in this meter. In his elegiac distichs (the commonest epigram meter and doubtless the meter most practised by Renaissance schoolboys), More follows Catullus and Martial; he does not always adhere to a strict Ovidian form, which requires a disyllabic word at the end of pentameters, but admits polysyllables in that position. He is free from the medieval custom of writing a short syllable at the end of the first half of the pentameter.[1] More wrote no hendecasyllabics in his *Epigrammata,* though Catullus and Martial have many. He may have thought this form too personal and emotional, associating it with Catullus. His two hendecasyllabic poems (nos. 276 and 280) are occasional and personal. In iambic trimeter he follows Catullus, Martial, and

---

[1] In his early poetry Erasmus occasionally follows this practice (Reedijk, no. 8, line 106).

Horace (*Epode* 17). His principal models for iambic strophe were Horace (*Epodes* 1–10) and Martial (3.14). In alternating dactylic hexameters and iambic dimeters he follows Horace (*Epodes* 14, 15); Catullus and Martial do not use this metrical pattern. Iambic dimeter (the second line of an iambic strophe used alone) does not occur in any classical poet except Seneca (*Thyestes* 344 ff.). Second glyconic catalectic (or choriambic), used by More only in no. 89 as somewhat resembling the anacreontic meter of the Greek he is translating, is found in the verse of Catullus, Seneca, and Prudentius. Iambic dimeter brachycatalectic (three iambs) is not used by classical poets, but it was a recognized Latin verse form in More's time.[1]

The *Epigrammata* seem to be arranged with some care to make an impression of casualness, yet distributing topics and metrical forms so as to secure variety. There is also a harmony of tone, but this may be due to More's ethos, since the poems were written over a long period. The lyrical meters admitted are mostly those of Horace's *Epodes,* a book close in content to the epigram. There are no elevated sapphics or alcaics as in Horace's *Carmina.* Such personal emotions as appear tend to be rather objectified: his meeting with his childhood sweetheart, now in her maturity; his care for his children; a sort of epitaph for himself and his wives that is remarkable for its novel, one may say epigrammatic, ending.

L. B. and C. A. L.

Techniques of Versification

When we turn from the facts of language to the *elegantiae* of versification, we necessarily pass from the clear light of the indisputable into the brumous realm of taste and aesthetics. We *know* whether a given syllable was long or short or common and, with the exception of a few rare words found only in uncertain texts, there can be no argument; but when we try to formulate rules about the placement of caesurae, the positions in which metrical diaeresis is legitimate, permissible or obligatory coincidence of metrical ictus with normal word-accent, and the syllabic length of words that may be placed at the end of a hexameter or pentameter, we are reduced to compiling statistics about the preferences and aversions of the great poets. We know that metrical diaeresis should be avoided in the second and third feet of a hexameter, especially in the third, and we also know that this is not an arbitrary rule, for it is true that coincidence of the end of a word with the end of a foot detracts from the unity of a metrical line, and that such a coincidence at the end of the second or third foot

---

[1]See the Commentary at 143/1–2.

tends to break a hexameter into thirds or halves and is therefore particularly objectionable.

The standards of versification derived by examining the practice of great classical poets may legitimately be applied to the humanists. If their lines offend by either monotony or abnormal caesura and diaeresis, we may censure their taste and may note their failure to imitate their models in all respects, but I should be loath to go further. We surely cannot deny to the humanists the right to experiment (at their own risk) with unusual measures, such as the iambic dimeter brachycatalectic that More uses in one of his best poems or the unprecedented and complex metrical structure that Politian used to join Latin verse with the wailing music of modern stringed instruments.[1] And if they have a right thus to experiment, they are also entitled to try (at their own risk) hexameters that do not have caesurae corresponding to the statistically ascertained preferences of the great poets.

If we consider this aspect of More's verse, we find that his practice is, in general, classical, but subject to a rather conspicuous variation that does not seem to be merely a difference between early work and the presumably more expert work of later years. If we take the first 104 lines of no. 19, which was written in 1509, and arbitrarily select no. 169 to begin a sample of 104 lines from a block of epigrams, we find no very striking differences. But such differences do appear in the Progymnasmata, as will be clear from the table on the next page, in which the occurrences in More's hexameters in the Progymnasmata have been multiplied by two to make them directly comparable to the samples of 104 lines each.[2]

Noteworthy are More's greater use of the hephthemimeral line in the Progymnasmata and his relatively greater indulgence in lines in which the real break in sense is marked by diaeresis, not caesura. In his poem on the coronation, lines 32 and 76 are

> Lēgēs invălĭdae prĭŭs, | immŏ nŏcērĕ cŏactae

and

> quōquĕ mŏdō sortem fĕrăt, | et mŏdĕrētŭr ŭtramque.

The words preceding the objectionable diaeresis are pyrrhics, and words end within the foot at the points where one would expect a pen-

[1] In his lament *In Laurentium Medicen,* the last of Politian's *Odae.*

[2] The main classifications are clear, but in some details my analysis may not commend itself to everyone.

Caesurae and Diaereses in Hexameters	19/8–111	169/2–184/5	More's Progymnasmata X 2
Penthemimeral caesura	36	34	20
Bucolic diaeresis with penthemimeral caesura	1	5	2
Final diaeresis with penthemimeral caesura	3	2	2
Feminine caesura in third foot	0	3	2
Hephthemimeral caesura	7	5	14
Hephthemimeral and trithemimeral caesura	0	2	0
Trithemimeral caesura	2	0	4
Diaeresis after second foot with trithemimeral caesura	0	0	2
Diaeresis after third foot, no caesura	2	0	4
Subsidiary Diaereses			
After third foot			
Monosyllable	2	6	0
Pyrrhic word	1	1	0
After both second and third feet			
Monosyllables	0	0	3
Pyrrhic words	0	0	1

themimeral caesura. Progymnasmata 10/13 is the same kind of line:

Dēgĕnĕr Ō Spartēs gĕnŭs, | īto in Tartără tandem.

A pyrrhic word, of course, prevents coincidence of ictus and accent, so that these lines, though not perhaps admirable, will pass muster.

The really remarkable hexameters occur in no. 5, and it may be best to quote the whole quatrain.

Tamquam iam mŏrītūrus | partīs ūtĕrĕ rēbus;
tamquam vīctūrus dēnŭŏ parcĕ tŭīs.

Illĕ săpit, quī | perpēnsīs hīs rītĕ dŭōbus,
parcŭs ĕrit certō mūnĭfĭcusquĕ mŏdō.

In the second hexameter, the diaeresis is formed by a monosyllable, and there is a trithemimeral caesura which may suffice to carry the line. The first line, however, is neatly broken into two parts and the spondee, of course, makes the ictus and accent coincide—and there is not even the ghost of a true caesura. We have, in short, the situation that kindly metricians call intolerable and sterner disciplinarians abominable.[1]

I hold no brief for Thomas More, but I wonder whether what should in general be anathematized should not here be condoned. I wonder whether the Ennian crudity[2] of the verse may not be appropriate to the subject, which is not a flight of elegant fancy nor yet a rapier thrust of wit, but a maxim of practical advice about money—the kind of poetry that is not excluded from the countinghouse. The decision must be rendered by the reader.

R. P. O.

---

[1]So Basil Lanneau Gildersleeve and Gonzalez Lodge in their *Latin Grammar* (London, 1895), §784, n. 3: "The Diaeresis which is most carefully avoided is the one after the third foot, especially if that foot ends in a Spondee. . . . It is abominable when no other Caesura proper is combined with it."

[2]Cf. Ennius, *Annales* 522, *Ennianae Poesis Reliquiae,* ed. Johannes Vahlen (Leipzig, 1903), p. 94.

THE EPIGRAMS OF MORE AND ERASMUS

Two of More's poems[1] express his gratitude and admiration for a diptych commissioned by Erasmus and Peter Giles and painted by Quentyn Metsys. The joined pictures represent Peter Giles facing Erasmus, who is beginning to write his paraphrase on Paul's Epistle to the Romans. In a letter to Erasmus thanking him for the diptych, More wrote that he found a certain tickling pleasure at the thought "that distant posterity will remember me for my friendship with Erasmus, attested in letters and books and pictures and every other way."[2] When the 1518 edition of *Utopia* was still in the planning stages, Erasmus saw to it that the book included another diptych, a literary diptych of More and himself, for the last items in the volume and an integral part of it[3] were "the epigrams of the famous and learned Englishman Thomas More" and "the epigrams of Desiderius Erasmus of Rotterdam," each with its own impressive title page.

However much More and Erasmus admired fine paintings—and both wrote several epigrams designed to accompany paintings[4]—like other humanists they thought that language is a more profound image of the personality.[5] In fact, the two had produced another literary diptych some twelve years before when Erasmus was staying in More's house in London: they had collaborated and competed in translating and imitating some dialogues of Lucian, and Erasmus had seen to it that their double labors were duly published.[6] Fortunately we do not have to choose between painted and written portraits: the great portraits of Metsys, Dürer, and Holbein have survived; More's Lucianic translations have been carefully edited and studied.[7] Both parts of the poetical diptych

---

[1]The two parts of no. 276. In a modified form this essay was delivered as the inaugural birthday lecture of the Erasmus of Rotterdam Society on October 27, 1980, and was printed in the *Erasmus of Rotterdam Society Yearbook* (1981), pp. 8–29.

[2]*CWE* 5, 147.

[3]See pp. 4–5, above.

[4]More: nos. 87, 88, 92–94, 97, 98, 185, 186, 226, 227, 272. Erasmus: Reedijk, nos. 31, 68–72, 86, 106; Appendix II, no. 1.

[5]A Greek sentence prominent in Dürer's engraving of Erasmus may be translated "His writings will give you a better picture of him."

[6]*CW 3/1*, lv–lx.

[7]Not only by Craig Thompson in *CW 3/1*, but also by Alain Jolidon, "Thomas More et

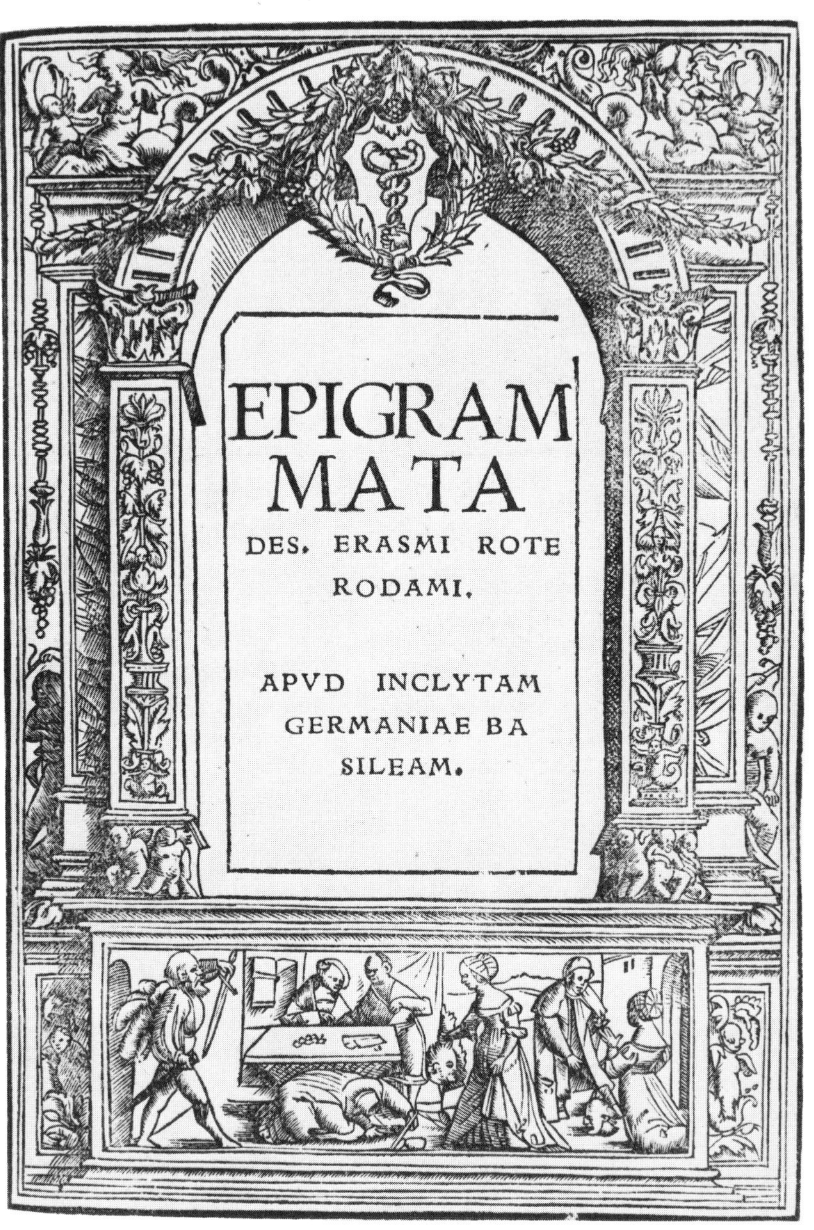

Title-page, *Epigrammata Des. Erasmi Roterodami,* Basel, March 1518 (reduced)

have also been carefully edited in 1953 and 1956. But no one has set the two collections of poetry side by side to compare them at leisure as Erasmus at least (and probably More too) clearly intended. The similarities are perhaps more striking than we would have expected. But a longer view reveals characteristic differences in temperament, talent, and outlook that confirm what we know from the other writings of the two great friends.

It was Erasmus who arranged for the publication of the *Utopia-Epigrammata* volume, which finally issued from Johann Froben's press at Basel in March 1518. Although Erasmus was in the Low Countries and in England during the two years before its publication, he apparently had considerable (if not full and final) control over its contents. As early as June 1516, Erasmus had probably proposed to More that he see to the publication of More's epigrams,[1] but not until December 1517 was Froben finally ready to issue a joint volume devoted to works of Erasmus and More. It was to have included their Lucianic translations, Erasmus' *Complaint of Peace* and *Declamation on Death,* as well as More's *Utopia* and the Latin poems of both men.[2] But, as Froben explained at the end of the December volume, it had grown too large, so that *Utopia* and the double set of epigrams were published in a separate volume in March 1518. In his preface to Erasmus' epigrams in that volume (sig. L_2), Froben claimed that, in response to the usual popular demand, he had gathered together whatever epigrams of Erasmus he could get from Beatus Rhenanus and Bruno Amerbach.

What Froben actually did was to reprint, with slight rearrangements, a number of collections of Erasmus' poems already in print, beginning with the long series from the volume originally published at Paris in 1506/07.[3] This was followed by a series written for Colet's school, originally published with Erasmus' sermon about the boy Jesus in 1511 and with Erasmus' edition of Cato's distichs, a schoolbook printed in 1514.[4] Then came four hymns to Michael, Gabriel, Raphael, and all the angels, which had been first printed years before in 1496;[5] a recent Greek poem

---

Érasme traducteurs du *Tyrannicide* (1506)," in *Thomas More 1477–1977* (Université Libre de Bruxelles: Travaux de l'Institut Interuniversitaire pour l'Etude de la Renaissance et de l'Humanisme VI, Brussels, 1980), pp. 39–69.

[1] Allen, 2, 261.

[2] Reedijk, p. 72; Allen, 2, 502.

[3] Reedijk, p. 361 (items 4 and 5).

[4] Reedijk, pp. 304–05 and 363 (items 51–52).

[5] Reedijk, p. 362 (item 39).

to the Virgin which Erasmus had offered at her shrine in Walsingham;[1] three poems in praise of Schlettstadt and its brilliant coterie of humanist scholars from volumes printed in 1514 and 1515;[2] and finally six poems never before published.[3] The epigrams of Erasmus also opened with a new poem, written in the late 1490s but never published before, a hymn in honor of Saint Ann.[4]

That the newly printed poem on Saint Ann should be given primacy of place at the head of the poems is significant, for it is really a sort of hymn for the feast of Saint Ann, an example of the liturgical poetry at which Erasmus excelled.[5] One of the new poems at the end of Erasmus' collection is a charming portrait of Andrea Ammonio, Latin secretary of Henry VIII and a dear friend of both Erasmus and More.[6] The poem shows that Ammonio shared many traits with More: humor, grace, learning, eloquence, modesty, generosity, prudent simplicity.[7] In fact Erasmus applies to Ammonio a metrical version of the proverbial phrase he had applied to More in the preface to the *Moria,* "omnium horarum homo," which had been singled out for attention in Erasmus' times and which has become famous in our time as "a man for all seasons."[8] Another poem first published in the 1518 volume ridicules the French for their cowardly flight at the Battle of the Spurs in August 1513 and was part of the poetic salvos and fusillades, including Brixius' *Chordigera,* exchanged during the wars between France and England from 1512 to

---

[1]Reedijk, no. 92.

[2]Reedijk, nos. 98, 95, 96.

[3]Reedijk, nos. 91, 101, 93, 102, 99, 103.

[4]Reedijk, no. 22. It is important to remember that Reedijk's admirable edition, which aimed at printing all extant poetry by Erasmus, includes a considerable mass of inferior early poetry which was not included in the 1518 *Epigrammata* and which was not published during Erasmus' lifetime.

[5]Another poem (Reedijk, no. 97) is displaced from its expected position to occupy the third place in the 1518 series. It is a four-line poem written extempore for Johann Witz when he had to part from Erasmus and return to Schlettstadt. Witz was to have the poem as an "absens absentis amici . . . pignus." The idea that absent friends are present to one another, however far apart, is one Erasmus had many occasions to apply to More. See, e.g., 276/11, *Moriae encomium, ASD 4/3,* 67, lines 6–7.

[6]Reedijk, no. 91.

[7]On the classical (Martial 10.47.7) and Christian (Matt. 10: 16) basis for "prudent simplicity" see Germain Marc'hadour, "Symbolisme de la colombe et du serpent," *Moreana, 1* (1963), 47–63.

[8]Erasmus attributes to Ammonius "Mores dehinc horas ad omneis commodos" (Reedijk, no. 91, line 8). For "omnium horarum homo" as applied to More by Erasmus, see *Moriae encomium, ASD 4/3,* 68, line 19 and note.

1514.[1] Erasmus included it in a letter to Ammonio written in December 1513.[2]

This letter makes it clear that Erasmus essentially agreed with More's objections to the inflated mythological style of Brixius' *Chordigera*, for he offered a critique of Ammonio's own poem on some campaigns in the French war,[3] which he praised for accuracy and restraint:

> Some would have it that a poem is not a poem unless you summon up all the gods in turn from sky, sea, and land, and cram hundreds of legendary tales into it. I myself have always liked verse that was not far removed from prose, albeit prose of the first order. . . . I take the greatest pleasure in rhetorical poems and in poetical rhetoric, such that one can sense poetry in the prose and the style of a good orator in the poetry. And whereas some other men prefer more exotic elements, my own very special approval goes to your practice of depending for your effects on the bare narrative and your concern for displaying the subject rather than your own cleverness.[4]

The kind of poetry Erasmus describes here fits very well the Latin poetry More himself wrote: rarely mythological or Ovidian, never inflated or pompous, and almost always endowed with the virtues of his prose—logical energy, muscular realism, and penetrating intelligence. Perhaps Erasmus had better reason than More to value such poetry: in his youth he had indulged in poetry which strained after the high heroic or the lavishly decorated styles,[5] and it required some years and some effort for Erasmus to "curb his magnanimity and load every rift with ore" (as Keats once advised Shelley to do). Erasmus was well aware that More's poems came closer to his own criteria of good poetry than most of his own

---

[1]Reedijk, no. 93. In this poem, and only here, Erasmus employed a technique which More also used only once (no. 242, below): he uses a quotation from Martial as a springboard for satirical wit. On the differing reactions of More and Erasmus to the French-English war of 1513 see Germain Marc'hadour, "Croisade triomphale de l'Angleterre: 1513," *Moreana, 35* (1972), 66–68.

[2]Allen, *1*, 547.

[3]This poem of Ammonio's has apparently not survived. It does not appear in *Andreae Ammonii carmina omnia*, ed. Clemente Pizzi (Florence, 1958).

[4]*CWE* 2, 270–71; Allen, *1*, 545.

[5]Some of them had been printed in 1513 without Erasmus' permission (Reedijk, nos. 23–26), but they are excluded from the 1518 collection, which does not contain many vestiges of Erasmus' florid style.

poetry did, and it is to his credit that he was willing to take his place in a literary diptych in which he knew his friend would cut a better figure.[1]

The "style of a good orator" and the virtues of More's prose are strikingly apparent in his congratulatory poem on the coronation of Henry VIII in 1509 (no. 19). About ten years earlier Erasmus had also written a laudatory poem dedicated to Prince Henry, then only a boy of eight.[2] More had taken him to visit the royal children at Eltham Palace[3] near London, and Erasmus was embarrassed because he had not brought a poetical offering (and also a little irritated with More for not having forewarned him that it would be expected). In response to a note from Prince Henry, sent to him at lunch, Erasmus quickly produced an elegant poem on the two princesses and the three princes. Both Erasmus' *Prosopopoeia Britanniae*[4] and More's coronation poem have prefaces addressed to Henry: More's witty but dignified, Erasmus' sententious and slightly patronizing (talking like a Dutch uncle to the scion of a royal house). Both poems were provided, in early manuscripts and editions, with sidenotes pointing out the major parts of the poems. Both men were about thirty years old when they wrote the poems. The two pieces fairly cry out for comparison.

Two features of More's poem set it apart from the usual gratulatory flattery that regularly sprang up overnight like mushrooms to celebrate coronations: he has something significant to say about the actual historical circumstances, and he says it by skilfully adapting the recognized oratorical pattern of the encomium. The last years of Henry VII were painful ones for the nobility and for anyone wealthy enough to fall prey to the king's fiscal and legal bureaucracy, directed with ruthless efficiency by such men as the notorious Dudley and Empson. The courts had resurrected and tortuously reapplied an ancient statute on the king's

---

[1]Allen, *1*, 4; Reedijk, p. 91.

[2]In 1504 Erasmus wrote a poem more directly comparable to More's coronation poem, an extemporaneous effusion in which a personified Burgundy welcomes Duke Philip the Handsome after an extended trip to Spain (Reedijk, no. 78). James D. Garrison, *Dryden and the Tradition of Panegyric* (Berkeley and London, 1975), finds some useful qualities in this poem (pp. 70–72, 86–87), but Erasmus was right to omit it from the 1518 volume, for it is a dismal piece to read, full of tedious truisms and trite repetitions. But we should remember that it was intended as a piece of public elocution for an actual ceremony, and on such occasions subtlety is out of place and sonority with a modicum of sense will often suffice.

[3]E. E. Reynolds, "Presidential Miscellany," *Moreana, 67–68* (1980), 15, suggests that the visit took place at Greenwich Palace, not Eltham; and he may be right.

[4]Reedijk, no. 45.

prerogative in order to increase his feudal revenues.[1] Henry VII cowed the nobility through bonds and recognizances, a system which, according to one historian, put the majority of the peerage "legally and financially in the king's power and at his mercy, so that in effect people were set under heavy penalties to guarantee the honesty and loyalty of their fellows," and which "must have created an atmosphere of chronic watchfulness, suspicion, and fear."[2] More could have ignored the real facts and feelings of the time by simply heaping panegyrical platitudes on the new king, but he chose the trickier task of praising Henry VIII primarily for banishing the injustice, fear, and oppression of his father's reign. More does not, of course, explicitly place the blame on Henry VII himself. The furthest he goes is to praise Henry VIII for rescinding some of his father's policies:

> Sic patriam, ut decuit, praetulit ille patri. (19/4)
> In this he placed, as he should, his fatherland above his father.

Brixius accused More of tactless stupidity for praising Henry VIII at the expense of Henry VII.[3] But Brixius was ignorant of the circumstances and his sort of panegyrical poetry required only a tenuous connection with reality. As More pointed out in one of his epigrams, Brixius found no difficulty in making his valorous sea-captain fight with five different weapons at one time (no. 190). More is tactful in his treatment of Henry VII, but if he was to stick to real facts and feelings he could not give a favorable view of Henry VII's last years, nor could he ignore them in praising Henry VIII.

The rhetorical plan of More's poem, which is pointed out in the sidenotes of the illuminated copy More had made for presentation to Henry, is the Aphthonian pattern for a speech of praise.[4] The scheme of Aphthonius is, according to Theodore Burgess,[5] representative. According to Aphthonius one should first give

> an exordium according to the nature of the subject matter. Then give the descent, divided into race, fatherland, forbears, and parents. Then education, which you should divide into instruction, skills, and laws. Then you should work out the most important

---

[1]See the Commentary at 19/32–33.
[2]See the Commentary at 19/26–27.
[3]See Appendix B, pp. 492–94, lines 175–239.
[4]*Progymnasmata* 8 (first printed by Aldus at Venice in 1508).
[5]"Epideictic Literature," *Studies in Classical Philology*, *3* (Chicago, 1902), pp. 120–26.

> heading of encomiums, deeds, which you should subdivide into the soul (such as fortitude and prudence), the body (such as beauty, speed, strength), and fortune (such as political power, riches, friends). After these give a comparison in order to extol what is being praised. Then an epilogue, rather like a prayer.[1]

All these headings can be found in More's poem, but his skill is revealed in his arrangement of them and his adaptation of them to the requirements of his subject matter. He gives a rather long exordium based on the joy of the crowds at the coronation: the streets, the houses, the rooftops along the route of the royal procession are thronged; some even dash ahead to get a second or third view of the king and queen.[2] More places the brief section on bodily gifts first (lines 58–67) because he intends to treat the gifts of the soul as partially revealed by Henry's appearance (lines 70–93). The two sections are separated by a two-line comparison with the beauty and valor of Achilles (68–69). Four lines on Henry's education (116–19) are inserted in the middle of the longest and most important section on his deeds (lines 94–149), which stresses the legitimacy of his claim to the throne (136–49), his just attitude toward riches and the laws (94–125), and his subjects' love for him as a safeguard against foreign or domestic disturbances (126–35). The praise of Henry concludes with the specific virtues he derives from his parents and from his paternal grandmother and his maternal grandfather (lines 150–57)—two of the four grandparents have been carefully chosen.[3] The next section (158–91) is the "laus reginae," a shorter praise of Henry's new queen which draws on the headings of ancestry but relies especially on the virtues of the soul as revealed by comparisons with classical heroines such as the Sabine women, Alcestis, Tanaquil, Cornelia, and Penelope (a judicious blend of historical and mythological figures). This part also has a touch of the Catullan epithalamium, the wish for progeny to sustain the royal house and the realm. The poem concludes (as it opened) with an apostrophe to "Anglia," including a prayer for heavenly aid to the royal couple and their descendants.

Erasmus' poem, *Prosopopoeia Britanniae,* is weak where More's is

---

[1]I have translated Aphthonius' Greek from *Aphthonii progymnasmata,* ed. Hugo Rabe (Leipzig, 1926), pp. 21–22.

[2]In *Ecclesiastes sive de ratione concionandi,* Erasmus mentions this kind of exordium, giving as an example a hymn in which Prudentius "Exordium sumit a conventu hominum solito laetiore ac frequentiore" (*Opera omnia, 5,* 868 B). Folly uses the same type in *Moriae encomium, ASD 4/3,* 72, Commentary at line 17.

[3]See the Commentary at 19/151–55.

strong—in presenting political realities—but it has its own real virtues. It is spoken by Britannia personified, who begins by speaking her own praises—a perilous tactic except for someone as shameless as Folly. Britannia need not envy, she says, the wool of India, the perfumes of Araby, the golden rivers of Spain, the Nile delta of Egypt, the vineyards of the Rhine, the fertile fields of Africa, for she can match all these. She also has a splendid climate—this was Erasmus' first visit to England and he had not been there long. She has long days, she says, conveniently forgetting that they are correspondingly short in winter. She will not boast because the Greeks and Romans called her a world unto herself, but rather because she has such a magnificent king as Henry VII, a Mars in war, a Minerva in peace, as self-sacrificing as Codrus or the Decii, as pious as Metellus or Numa, as eloquent as Nestor, as high-minded as Caesar, as generous as Maecenas, a very Jove come down from heaven to help mankind and to lead in the golden age. Alas that he cannot live forever, but may he be at least as long-lived as Nestor or Tithonus. The comparison with Tithonus is a serious mistake, if you take the time to think about it, but up to this point the poem has given no one much occasion to think. Most of the first sixty-eight lines could be applied to almost any country and almost any king.

But the rest of the poem (eighty-two lines) is a charming, detailed, and precise allegory of the five royal children as five roses on a single rosebush, cultivated by an expert gardener who may be taken to be either their earthly father or the divine gardener. Erasmus no doubt knew of the marriage of the red rose of Lancaster and the white rose of York in the persons of Henry VII and Elizabeth,[1] but he is not interested in political realities, about which he probably did not know much, surely not enough to instruct Englishmen on the subject. And so he uses the colors of the mother and father to distinguish the sexes of the children—red for the vigor of the three boys, white for the virginal innocence of the two girls. The infant Edmund is a rosebud almost entirely sheathed in its calix, a streak of red barely showing. The three-year-old Mary is a snow-white bud that has just burst its covering. The eight-year-old Henry is a red bud completely exposed but not yet open. The ten-year-old Margaret also has not yet opened her white petals, still afraid of the boisterous breezes, suffused with a faint rosy flush, either out of affinity with her brother or because of the star of her birth. The twelve-year-old Arthur has spread twelve bright red petals and promises soon to display a center of seed-bearing yellow—surely an elegant way to describe the

---

[1]Celebrated by More in no. 23.

onset of puberty. In the rest of the poem, Erasmus characterizes each, from oldest to youngest, in terms of their names. Arthur is as valiant as his knightly namesake. Margaret is as modest, smooth, and spotless as a pearl; and as a pearl sympathizes with the heavens, growing bright under clear skies, dim under the clouds, so Margaret has a special devotion to the inhabitants of heaven. Henry bears a close resemblance to the father after whom he was named. Mary promises much from her namesake, Maria, *stella maris,* the star of the sea which never sets. Edmund presented a problem, since his name was not as obviously significant and it is not easy—except for mothers and aunts, perhaps—to characterize an infant only a few months old. Erasmus solved the problem by calling on the Muses to sing lullabies and to shower the babe with sweet-smelling herbs and flowers, including garlands of red and white roses, so dear to the children's father. And he calls on the fates to tuck the infant in in his white woolen blanket and to let the spun thread of his life flow smooth and unknotted from their distaff. I have given only the main outlines of the conceit, which is expressed with lyrical suavity and delicately embroidered with some additional mythological coloring. The circumstances which called forth these two poems of More and Erasmus were obviously different, but they may nevertheless stand together as fair examples of Erasmus' lyrical gift and More's realistic and rhetorical strength.

A similar contrast emerges from the epitaphs More and Erasmus wrote for musicians. Erasmus' thirty-one-line epitaph for Jan Ockegem,[1] a Flemish composer of considerable renown then and now, is really too lyrical to be suitable for a tombstone (Erasmus knew how to write that kind when he wanted to). It also gives us little information about Ockegem, except that he wrote splendid sacred music. It does not even give his first name. But it is a beautifully musical poem in Horatian elegiambics, the sense flowing in and over the short lines. One passage (lines 16–24) may be translated:

Is that golden voice now mute,
The golden voice of Ockegem?
The voice that could move stones,
That so often resounded in the vaulted nave
With fluid and subtly modulated melodies,
Soothing the ears of the saints
and piercing the hearts of earthborn men?

---

[1]Reedijk, no. 32. See Jean-Claude Margolin, *Erasme et la musique* (Paris, 1965), pp. 81–92.

Obmutuit vox aurea,
Aurea vox Okegi,
Vel saxa flectere efficax,
Quae toties liquidis
Et arte flexilibus modis
Per sacra tecta sonans
Demulsit aures caelitum
Terrigenumque simul
Penitusque mouit pectora?

Nor is the poem without a subdued and suitable wit. The voice of Ockegem which Erasmus lingeringly repeats can refer both to his singing voice or to the polyphonic voicing of his compositions.[1] And in the conclusion the truism that death is the just and equal leveler of all is given a new twist: death is called unjust by the very fact that it is just to all men, for its province is the world of men, not the divine realm of music.

A year or two later, in 1497, More wrote an epitaph for Henry Abyngdon (no. 159), the first recipient of a bachelor of music degree at Cambridge who finally became master of the children in the Chapel Royal. His eight lines are compact, informative, dignified, "strong lines." But they are also placed in a humorous dramatic context provided by the next two poems. For Janus, who had asked More to provide the epitaph, did not like it for the very bad reason that it did not rhyme. Amused, More wrote a leonine rhyming epitaph (no. 160), a flaccid piece of "rime doggerel" as Chaucer would have called it. It was More's turn to be horrified when Janus had the doggerel carved on the tomb. Far from looking before and after like the god Janus, this wretch, More says (no. 161), is as impudent and blind as a mole and fully deserves to rest in the same tomb under the same verses.[2] This triplet of poems reveals a dominant feature of More's poems—one mostly absent from Erasmus'—a penchant for dramatic treatment and the brisk give and take of dialogue.

A set of three epitaphs Erasmus wrote for a woman named Odilia and her son also forms a dramatic group,[3] but the drama is quite different from More's—grand opera not opera buffa, Verdi not Mozart. They were apparently designed for a double tombstone surmounted by a crucifix and portraying the faces of mother and son together with two

---

[1]Reedijk, p. 223.

[2]See Susan L. Holahan, "More's Epigrams on Henry Abyngdon," *Moreana, 17* (1968), 21–26.

[3]Reedijk, nos. 29–31.

Old Testament types of Christ: Moses striking the rock to bring forth water in the desert and the brazen serpent erected to heal the Israelites.[1] In the first of Odilia's epitaphs, which is written in rather colloquial iambic trimeter, Odilia's voice startles a passerby, who pales with fear at the voice from the grave. In a sober little sermon she reassures him that her soul is indeed alive and that the bodies of the dead have been buried in the ground like seeds that will sprout up imperishable under the spring winds of the last day. She tells him she is among the souls in purgatory and begs him to pray to Christ crucified for her and the others. "If you are in a hurry," she says, "say a little prayer, asking light and peace for us, and then go on your way. Prepare yourself for your own tomb, for you will follow us before long. Farewell." The second epitaph, also Odilia's, is an elegiac aria in which she laments that death has separated her from her beloved son, who is still alive, but she takes comfort because Christ's death will heal the wound of their parting. Apart from Dante, Newman, and Thomas More himself, I know of no writers of the first rank who have attempted to portray imaginatively the feelings of the souls in purgatory. Erasmus' Ovidian lament is humanly convincing, and it is at least theologically plausible that the grief of separation from friends and loved ones should be one of the pains of purgatory. Finally, in the third epitaph, the son announces that he has joined his mother in the grave and composes a little prayer for the passerby to say for the souls in purgatory, basing it on the types of the rock and the serpent.[2] The son concludes by relating the types to their fulfillment in the blood and water which flowed from the wounds of Christ on the cross and by begging Christ to claim both him and his mother at the Last Judgment. No doubt it is easier for most modern readers to enjoy More's little comedy of epitaphs than it is to respond to Erasmus' little sepulchral opera—for much the same reasons that it is easier to enjoy Chaucer's humorous poetry[3] than to respond to *The Pearl.*

There is a melancholy, lyrical strain in Erasmus' poetry,[4] though it has

---

[1]The first epitaph at least was actually carved on Odilia's tombstone in the church of St. Gudule in Brussels, though it was destroyed during iconoclastic riots in 1577 (Reedijk, p. 219).

[2]Including the actual prayer in the epitaph is a shrewd and unusual device, for if the passerby reads the whole epitaph, he is not only asked to pray—he has already done it.

[3]A detailed examination of More's writings has begun to reveal more and more allusions to Chaucer and affinities with him. See, e.g., Alistair Fox, "Thomas More's *Dialogue* and the *Book of the Tales of Caunterbury:* 'Good Mother Wit' and Creative Imitation," in *Familiar Colloquy: Essays Presented to Arthur Edward Barker,* ed. Patricia Brückmann (Oberon Press, Ottawa, 1978), and the Index of *CW 6.*

[4]See, e.g., Reedijk, no. 40, which is the only other example in the 1518 *Epigrammata.*

perhaps been exaggerated because of his best known and perhaps best poem, *Carmen alpestre,* written in August 1506 as he crossed the Alps on his way to Italy.[1] In modern jargon it might be described as a poem of midlife crisis: he laments how the subtle thief of youth has stolen upon him almost unaware, looks back on his unsettled life of multifarious pursuits and studies, and vows from now on to focus his energies on serving Christ alone. Emotionally it is a watershed piece, like the *Folly,* which he conceived in the Alps on the return trip from Italy almost three years later. But the *Folly* bespeaks the almost manic euphoria and energy he experienced when he came back home, full of the scholarly and emotional riches of his Italian sojourn. The poem, on the other hand, is a farewell, a backward view, an infolding of the feelings. With haunting plangency, the lament wanders through the forward effort of the hexameters and the dying fall of the alternating short lines.

More's epigrams never strike such a lyrical, introspective note. In fact, in all of More's poetry and prose, there is almost nothing that could be called lyrical in the manner of Catullus, or Petrarch, or Shakespeare's sonnets, or the devotional prose of John Donne or Jeremy Taylor. When his friends or enemies praised or blamed him as a "poet," they usually referred to his talent for fictive invention and intellectual drama. More's Latin poems contain a dozen or so somber meditations on death, including his own death, but none is a cry of the heart. They gain their intensity from a pressing, paradoxical analysis of our refusal to accept the fact of death and understand its implications. It is fascinating to watch More's mind at work (and it was always working) even when he is merely playing intellectual games, such as writing seven carefully calibrated variations on a Greek epigram (nos. 27–33). His bent toward dramatic dialogue and debate is also revealed in progressively more dramatic translations of another Greek epigram.[2] But one of his original Latin poems based on dramatic debate (no. 198) is especially worthy of attention because of its affinities with *Utopia.* It is entitled "QVIS OPTIMVS REIPUBLICAE STATVS" ("What is the best form of government"), and the full title of *Utopia* (as we should remind ourselves from time to time) is "De optimo statu reipublicae deque nova insula Utopia" ("The best form of government *and* the new island of Utopia"). *And,* not *or:* the best form of government and the new island are not necessarily to be identified com-

[1]Reedijk, no. 83. D. F. S. Thomson gives a rather detailed analysis of this poem in "Erasmus as a Poet in the Context of Northern Humanism," in *Commémoration nationale d'Érasme* (Brussels, 1970), pp. 187–210.

[2]See the Commentary at 47/1–8.

pletely with one another. Number 198 is a reply to an interlocutor who has just asked which is better, a monarchy or a parliamentary form of government. More answers, arguing for a parliament, anticipating and refuting, concisely and precisely, the objections and arguments of his silent opponent.[1] But suddenly he breaks off, asking: "But why are you asking such a question? Is there a people anywhere to whom you can assign a king or a parliament just as you choose? If you can, you rule them already. But do not consider to which one you should give the power to rule. The more basic question is 'would it work?'" More turns the tables not only on his opponent but also on himself, since there was indeed a people to whom he himself could give any government he liked, but it was a "good place" which existed "no place," Utopia. The phrase "Est ne usquam populus," particularly because of the elision, suggests *Utopia,* to which More gave the name *Nusquama* in his letters to Erasmus.[2] In a letter to Erasmus written in December 1516,[3] More also playfully recounted a dream in which he saw himself as king of the Utopians, but his reverie came to an end and left him in the complex realities of a waking world. In this poem, too, after speculating about the theoretical advantages of a monarch or a parliament, he calls himself back down to the real world of expedient rather than ideal choices. The more basic "quaestio"[4] in the last line is pregnant: whether the form of government you would choose would *work* or whether the form *you* would choose would work. In other words, the main question—"an expediat"—is not which form is best but which form works in particular circumstances; or the question is whether it is expedient that you do the choosing. In the dramatic context of the poem (including its publication in the same volume with *Utopia*), the two words "an expediat" are like a struck gong reverberating in the mind.

In 1953 the editors of More's poetry, Leicester Bradner and Charles Lynch, rightly stressed the variety and engagement of More's Latin poems.[5] But when they judge Erasmus' poems to be "as dull a collection of addresses to notable persons and uninspired religious commonplaces as one could hope to find," we should temper the verdict with some qualifications and mitigating circumstances. Most of the poems about notable persons are epitaphs, not addresses, and some of these were

---

[1]Three of the opponent's arguments seem to be drawn directly from Isocrates, *Nicocles* 17–21. See the Commentary at 198/1.

[2]In September and October of 1516 (Allen, 2, 339, 346, 354, 359, 372).

[3]Allen 2, 414; *SL,* p. 85.

[4]Echoing "Quaeris" in line 1 and "Questio" in line 27.

[5]See p. 61, below.

commissioned pieces.[1] And much of the religious poetry was never intended to be "inspired," but to serve very practical purposes.[2] Five lapidary poems were requested by John Colet to be affixed to the door, the walls, and a picture of the boy Jesus at his new school, St. Paul's, and it would be hard to find a more cogent distillation of the Christian and humanistic aims of that new venture.[3] Another set of poems, written at Colet's request for the schoolboys of St. Paul's, is a verse translation of Colet's English prose code of conduct.[4] Based on the Pauline formulation "faith which works through love" (Gal. 5:6), Erasmus' lucid hexameters present what the boys should believe (the Apostles' Creed and the seven sacraments) and what they promise to do: to love God, to love themselves for God's sake, to avoid the seven deadly sins, to shun evil companions, to pray, to fast at the prescribed times, to keep their minds pure and their language clean, not to have sticky fingers, to love their parents, to honor and obey their teacher, to be loyal to their schoolfellows, to go to confession frequently, to receive communion reverently, to prepare for death by receiving the last sacraments and trusting in God's goodness. The versified Apostles' Creed seems a little stilted, but the regimen as a whole is comprehensive, well thought out, and refreshingly precise. Designed as a Christian supplement to a schoolbook of pagan wisdom, Cato's *Disticha moralia,* it was no doubt to be memorized by the very young schoolboys as an example of pure life and pure language running *pari passu.* So too, the opening poems in More's *Epigrammata,* eighteen simple Greek epigrams together with rival Latin translations by More and William Lily, the first headmaster of St. Paul's School, may also have been intended for older boys in that school.[5]

Clearly, such poems must be judged in the context of their purpose and circumstances. But some of Erasmus' best religious poetry is not intended for children: the poem to Saint Ann, first printed as the opening poem in the 1518 collection, and the suite of four poems to Michael,

---

[1]E.g., Reedijk, nos. 41–42, 64–66. We should also keep in mind Froben's remark in his preface to Erasmus' 1518 *Epigrammata:* when Erasmus was fully engaged by important works such as the *New Testament,* he was often pestered by requests for poems, and sometimes he did not know how to say no.

[2]Such as the couplets to be inscribed on a set of six new church bells dedicated to the Trinity, Mary, John the Baptist, Peter, Mary Magdalene, and all the saints (Reedijk, nos. 50–57).

[3]Reedijk, nos. 86–90, especially no. 90, a noble Horatian ode which presents a truly prophetic vision of St. Paul's School as a seedbed of a new sort of English citizen.

[4]Reedijk, no. 94.

[5]See p. 13, above.

Gabriel, Raphael, and all the angels.[1] These five poems, I suggest, are among the very best of Erasmus' poems and represent a remarkable achievement in blending classical eloquence and Christian wisdom. It was never easy for God's people to make good use of the spoils of the Egyptians,[2] and the poetical eloquence of Vergil and Horace offered special problems to their fifteenth-century admirers because Vergil's epic and Horace's patriotic odes, however complex, varied, and humanly resonant, expressed an ethos of personal and imperial aggrandizement which was often at odds with Christian humility. Martial glory could be transformed into the spiritual allegory of a psychomachia. Certain Christian episodes, like Michael's victory over Satan or Christ's harrowing of hell, might seem to lend themselves to triumphal celebration. But how can Horace help with a working-class girl whose soul was indeed magnified by the Lord but whose life had no triumphal trappings? Or with a man who worked among the lowly, the poor, the outcast? One answer was to ignore Christian themes and write about love or astronomy or gardening or syphilis or naval battles or successful princes. And this was the way chosen by many neo-Latin poets, especially in Italy. But in Northern Europe, neo-Latin poets often felt that good classical verse could and should be written on Christian themes. Erasmus himself began his poetic career (which did not extend much beyond his thirty-fifth year) with secular subjects like the torments of love, the beauties of spring, the trials and rewards of friendship. But when he was about twenty years old, he decided, together with his friend Cornelis Gerard, to devote his poetry solely to praises of the saints or to religious themes. The first fruits of this resolve were not very promising: an exclamatory lyric lucubration on the earthquake at the crucifixion, an epic excursus on the harrowing of hell, and an inflated sapphic paean to the Virgin, complete with the epic apparatus of the fall of the angels, the creation and fall of man, a council in heaven, and Gabriel's announcement in eight Horatian stanzas.[3] Clearly Apollo's steeds needed a much firmer hand on the reins.

What enabled Erasmus to achieve balance and restraint in religious

---

[1]Reedijk, nos. 22, 34–37. Erasmus apparently had a fairly high opinion of these poems, since he included them among the poems in an illuminated manuscript intended as a presentation copy to Prince Henry (Allen, *4*, Addenda, xxii). A less successful hymn to Saint Gregory (Reedijk, no. 17) might be included in this group; but it was never published during Erasmus' lifetime.

[2]Reedijk, no. 15, lines 18–19.

[3]Reedijk, nos. 19–21. It is to Erasmus' credit that he never published these poems. They survive in one known manuscript and were first printed in the Leiden *Opera omnia* of 1703–06 (Reedijk, pp. 131–33).

poetry was a practical sense of audience and purpose, the liturgical context of the hymn.[1] From personal experience of the hymns of the mass and the divine office, Erasmus knew that a hymn intended for actual liturgical use must be simple enough to be immediately intelligible to a wide audience, vivid enough to hold their attention, and rich enough to provide matter for repeated insights. Erasmus' angel poems were written for the walls of a church dedicated to Saint Michael, but their shape, tone, and language shows that they were primarily conceived as liturgical hymns.[2] In spirit and in some details they owe a good deal to medieval hymns, especially to the sapphic hymn for lauds attributed to Rabanus Maurus.[3] They are somewhat longer than most of their medieval counterparts;[4] their rhythm is less insistent; their diction, more even and judicious. Their subject matter also allows for some restrained narrative and epic touches. But there is very little of the blatant classicizing of the earlier paean to Mary. One example will suggest the difference. In the paean to Mary, Gabriel's annuciation comes in a formidable rush of Horatian eloquence that does not even allow Mary to ask her one question, "How can this be, since I know not man?" Before she can ask, Grabriel admonishes her: "Fuge suspicari," he says, "have no fear of fleshly embraces or generative conjunctions. Have no fear of the contractual duties of the alluring bed."[5] The repeated Horatian phrase "fuge

---

[1]Erasmus was a lifelong admirer and student of the hymns of Ambrose and Prudentius. In 1524 he sent a commentary on two hymns of Prudentius as a Christmas gift to Margaret Roper (*Opera omnia, 5,* 1338–48). In 1523 he wrote a mass for Our Lady of Loretto, which was well received (Reedijk, pp. 388–90; *Opera omnia, 5,* 1327–28); it has a beautiful sequence in an early medieval style.

[2]Reedijk, pp. 21, 227; Allen, *1,* 3, lines 30–36. See esp. Reedijk, no. 38, lines 65–68.

[3]*Hymni Latini medii aevi,* ed. Franz Joseph Mone, 3 vols. (Freiburg im Breisgau, 1853–55), *1,* 444, no. 311; hereafter cited as "Mone." Dr. Reedijk points out a "rather striking parallel" to Alcuin's sequence for the feast of Michael (Mone, *1,* 452–53, no. 317), but the echo seems less remarkable if we realize that both Alcuin and Erasmus are not versifying the apposite passage in *Revelation* (8: 3–4) but adapting the liturgical version of that passage in the versicles, antiphons, and responses for vespers, matins, and lauds on Michael's feast day.

[4]Mone, *1,* 438–56, nos. 306–20. In *Ciceronianus* (1528) Erasmus' spokesman Bulephoros rejects Sannazaro's *De partu Virginis* for aping ancient poets and says he prefers the single hymn of Prudentius *De natali Jesu* to all three books of Sannazaro's poem (*ASD 1/2,* 700/18–701/8; see also 702/7–11).

[5]The Latin (Reedijk, no. 19, lines 261–64) is as follows:

> Quo rogas pacto? Fuge suspicari
> Carnis amplexus geniiue nexus;
> Illecebrosi fuge suspicari
>   Foedera lecti.

suspicari" comes from a poem (*Carmina* 2.4.22) in which Horace is advising his friend Xanthias not to be ashamed of his passion for a slave girl. Having praised the girl's beauty, Horace concludes by assuring Xanthias he need not be jealous. Horace will not become his rival. "Fuge suspicari"—"have no fear of a man who has reached his fortieth year." In his poem to Michael, Erasmus borrowed a whole line and a half from Horace's hymn to Mercury (*Carmina* 1.10.17–18): "Tu pias laetis animas reponis / Sedibus. . ." ("You bring pious souls to their blissful abodes"). But here the context is compatible. Horace's hymn is dignified; Mercury, like the angels, is a messenger; and like Michael he was the *psychopompos,* the leader of souls to their final resting place.[1] Moreover, Erasmus completes the stanza quite differently from Horace by alluding to Michael's role in raising the bodies of the dead at the last day.[2]

The hymn to Saint Ann,[3] in which Erasmus gives us a distilled and Christianized version of familial *pietas,* human and divine, would repay close examination, but it is time to draw back from details and glance once more at the portraits of the two great humanists.

More's personality, as it is revealed in his Latin poetry, is remarkable for wit, humor, keen intelligence, wide-ranging interests, dramatic skill—nothing to surprise readers of his *Richard III* or the three great dialogues, *Utopia, A Dialogue Concerning Heresies,* and *A Dialogue of Comfort against Tribulation.* His interest in the paradoxes of politics, the sophistries of the law, the meaning of death, the education of his children, the responsibilities of bishops, the joys of a judicious marriage, his admiration for Erasmus' biblical scholarship, his delight in ancient coins and domestic architecture, his love of proverbs and fables and fabliaux, his dislike of affectation and hot air, his fascination with animals—it is all there. No reader can fail to be struck by the health and wholeness of his vision. But where is the holiness of Saint Thomas More? some may ask. Precisely in the wholeness and health, one might answer. But perhaps also in the humility which led him to abstain from directly doctrinal or devotional poetry. One of More's epigrams (no. 148) is a supposedly commendatory

---

[1]Louis Réau, *Iconographie de l'art chrétien,* 3 vols. (Paris, 1955–59), *2/1,* 44.

[2]According to the categories of G. W. Pigman III ("Versions of Imitation in the Renaissance," *Renaissance Quarterly, 23* [1980], 1–32), this is an example of both following and imitating a classical model, with perhaps a touch of emulation also.

[3]Reedijk, no. 22. The virtues of Erasmus' hymn become especially clear if it is compared with its medieval counterparts (Mone, *3,* 184–200, nos. 782–807) and with the inept classicizing in a group of poems to Saint Ann collected by Johannes Trithemius about 1494 (*De laudibus santissime matris Anne tractatus perquam vtiles* [Leipzig, Melchior Lotter, c. 1500], sigs. D_1–D_6).

poem on a collection of hymns by Bernard André, who wrote as if his Christian subject matter enabled him to dispense with the refinements of Latin versification. In André's volume, together with commendatory poems by Erasmus and others, More's poem looks straightforward enough.[1] But if you pay close attention, the irony emerges unmistakably from the seeming clichés. More respected ancient poetry enough to master one branch thoroughly—the Greek epigram—and apply it in Latin to his own times. Even when he did write prayers and devotional works in the Tower, he never gave free rein to personal feelings but remained within the public decorum of thoughtful exegesis or liturgical forms.

Erasmus, on the other hand, at least in his youth, never had this emotional poise—probably through no fault of his own.[2] In some of his religious poetry he gained it by learning to keep a practical, liturgical context firmly in mind. In his life, too, he seems to have gained and maintained it largely by assiduously applying his sensibility to prodigious practical tasks—the *Adagia,* the *New Testament,* the life and letters of Jerome, the editions and translations of the Fathers. Erasmus earned whatever wholeness and health he achieved—far more than some allow him—by keeping his pen to paper, executing meticulous and monumental tasks that he made sure would be of practical use to educators, scholars, theologians, and the Christian community at large. It is not for nothing that Metsys, Holbein, and Dürer all portray him actually writing. His letter writing, too, was an endless practical chore that finally produced the finest single panorama of the northern Renaissance. Only rarely, and only because of the stability he achieved by practical labors, could he rise above them to the free dramatic invention of *Julius Exclusus,* or the *Colloquia,* or the masterpiece he dedicated to his friend Thomas More, *Encomium Moriae.* If More had written nothing but his Latin poems, he would have been assured of a modest but important place in neo-Latin and vernacular literature.[3] The same cannot be said of Eras-

---

[1]See the Commentary at 148/1–22.

[2]In *Six Essays on Erasmus* (New York, 1979, pp. 68–71), John Olin makes some important qualifications of the psychoanalytic study of Erasmus' personality defects by N. H. Minnich and W. W. Meissner ("The Character of Erasmus," *American Historical Review, 83* [1978], 598–624).

[3]As is shown by the many reprintings and translations of his Latin poems (see Appendix D). In 1527 at Valladolid, in a gathering of literati which included Baldesare Castiglione, some Italians claimed that no good Latin poetry had been written north of the Alps. Peter John Olivarus refuted them, as he wrote to Erasmus, by showing them one or two epigrams of Thomas More (Allen, *6,* 475).

mus. But the double set of epigrams by the two friends is one measure of their contrasting temperaments—More's muscular equilibrium, Erasmus' achievement of sensitive poise—and one expression of their enduring friendship.

C. H. M.

SUBJECTS AND THEMES

Choice Poems

DESPITE THE OBSTACLES that More did not successfully surmount, he holds an honorable rank among modern Latin poets. He had something to say, and he said it, if not beyond criticism, yet effectively—so effectively that we gladly overlook the inevitable blemishes. Aside from the Progymnasmata, the present edition contains 263 Latin poems, ranging in length from a single line to 231 lines. If we are to estimate More's position as a Latin poet, it will be helpful to ask ourselves what poems in the present collection we would select, if we should be asked to pick out five or a dozen for an anthology.

I am more confident of our agreement on the smaller number. If we had to choose five poems that impressed themselves deeply on our memory and also represent More, showing such characteristics that if we found them mixed with selections from fifty other modern Latin poets without indication of authorship, we should be able to conjecture that they were his and no other's—if we had to do that, I think it likely that we could concur, without much debate, in choosing the epitaph for his two wives and himself (no. 258), the commemoration of his meeting with his boyhood sweetheart after twenty-five years (no. 263), his epigram on the rabbit and human heartlessness (no. 37), the discussion of the best form of government (no. 198), and the advice to Candidus on the choice of a wife (no. 143). No one of these is without errors in Latinity, but they are poems of high merit by any standard of criticism that is not exclusively grammatical.

The first three belong together because their real force lies in their disclosure of More's character—his innate nobility and his singular candor. Few men would venture to express in writing, let alone on the graven formality of a tomb, a comparison between their love for their first wife and their love for her successor; fewer would dare to utter a wish that it had been possible for them to form a *ménage à trois* while living, and a hope that they shall be together in the hereafter. It is not that such thoughts are unique; what is almost unique in More is the simple truthfulness with which he disregards the affectations of convention. In that extremely unconventional epitaph, the sincerity of his affection for his wives is as manifest as his courage in expressing it. Although a sophisticated witling of today may see in the verses only an occasion for a cynical quip, they are, if properly considered, a moving tribute to the two women and, at the same time, an attestation of the character of the man who won their devotion.

More's record of his meeting with Elizabeth, whom he had loved as a boy, has the same unmistakable and simple veracity. To be sure, it is not tactful to tell a woman that her beauty is *fanée*—certainly not when she is only thirty-nine. And it is not conventional in such circumstances to speculate about the causes of youthful ardor, and to wonder how much of it came from the desires and illusions of adolescence. But it is honest and rational.

Man's innate cruelty is often masked by an affected or vapid sentimentality. More was above both. No one knew better than the author of *Richard III* that we live in a world of blood and iron, where men, like less ambitious and cunning creatures, must suffer to live—and must often kill to live. But the hardness of heart that is needed to bear and cope with reality did not blind him to the thoughtless and wanton cruelty of those who make sport of the sufferings of even so inconsequential a being as a rabbit.

Of the five poems that we have chosen, only one exhibits what may be called wit, even in the wider sense of that word, and irony would be a better word. A reasonable and rational discussion of the relative merits of monarchy and republic is terminated by a shrewd reminder that the spinning of theories is far from reality—that the theorist has no power to give either constitution to a nation and that, even if he had that power over his fellow men, he would not willingly lay it down.

The long poem on the choice of a wife is the only one of the five that is not in elegiacs. The verse form is the most original and remarkable in the volume. Iambic dimeter brachycatalectic is a bold metrical experiment in Latin. The line is half of a normal trimeter and consists of just three iambic feet. More wrote his lines with great regularity: there is only one occurrence of an irrational spondee in the second foot.[1] The result is a tripping rhythm and a movement that carries the reader almost vertiginously along. Some might complain that More has imported into Latin too much of the regular beat of English verse or of medieval rhymed lyrics. I do not know how to answer that criticism except by saying that I do not find the rhythm objectionable and by venturing an opinion that Roman ears would not have been offended by it. The novel

[1]Line 43. It was probably to avoid a second occurrence that More ended the poem with the startling apostrophe, "te, Croese, ditior," instead of the more natural phrase, *et Croese ditior*.

meter undoubtedly has much to do with the success of the poem, which paints a picture of domestic felicity with such warmth and enthusiasm that the reader never inquires by what magic a bride who need be only *apta litteris* is transformed into a Hypatia in fifty lines. This poem, of course, wings its way above quotidian reality, but what makes it so effective is its apparent sobriety: a wife is to be chosen by rationally stated criteria, and there is no touch of Petrarchan mysticism or romantic fervor. Perhaps that is why the home that More depicts has all the charm of a scene of domestic bliss, warmed by a blazing hearth, when seen through the window by a wanderer in the frigid night.

If our hypothetical anthology were to admit a dozen poems, we might debate longer about our remaining choices. I believe, however, that we should all wish to include More's epigram (no. 260) on his escape from a tempest at sea and his return to the perils and alarms of daily life on land. That certainly echoes the proudly resigned wisdom of the man who, when most caressed by Britain's monarch, could perceive and say, without the slightest bitterness, "If my head would win him a castle in France, it should not fail to go."[1] Perhaps we could also agree on the choice of an epigram (no. 119) that is a concise and almost perfect elaboration of the convinced Christian's conception of life on earth as a many-celled prison from which he will be liberated to the life everlasting.[2] And to this we could add, as a contrasting companion piece if for no other reason, the ingenious development of the stoical perception that "nascentes morimur" (no. 75). We shall not want to omit either the neatly ironic suggestion (no. 182) that an astrologer's consistency in error may be too much for mere coincidence and so accredit him as a prophet after all, or the delightful story (no. 201) of the peasant, a true morosoph, who, when shown that potent and superior being, a king, sees only a man in fine clothes.[3] Despite the unfortunate neologism that we criticized earlier,[4] the gay anacreontic drinking song (no. 89) has much to

---

[1]William Roper, *The Lyfe of Sir Thomas Moore, Knighte,* ed. Elsie V. Hitchcock, Early English Text Society, Original Series no. 197 (Oxford, 1935), p. 21; hereafter cited as "Roper."

[2]It may be noteworthy that this is the one epigram of More's that appears in a sixteenth-century manuscript in the Biblioteca Riccardiana at Florence (2939, fol. 13ᵛ). Since it contains the variants "Carcer" for "Carceris" (line 4), "Incerto" for "In caeco" (line 7), and "Carcerem" for "Carcere" (line 8), it was probably copied from a corrupt manuscript rather than from a printed edition. It includes verses by Alciati, Buchanan, Cantalicius, Eobanus Hessus, Marcus Antonius Flaminius, Hercules Stroza, Martial, Beza, and Muretus, and concludes with the Aesopian fables of Faërnus.

[3]See the Commentary at 201/1–15.

[4]See pp. 27–28, above.

recommend it. But if we accept it, we shall, I fear, disagree about our final choice. Some will prefer, perhaps, the pithy contrast between kings' ambitions and their abilities (no. 243); others will champion the delightful satire on Fabulla (no. 245), in which the euphemistic circumlocution that may at first offend those accustomed to the more classical directness of Martial, is really contrived to add just the right touch to the affectations of the woman who has in the past secretly yielded a hundred times to each of a hundred men.

In the baker's dozen of poems we have mentioned, only four really depend on the "argutia" that Beatus Rhenanus, in his introduction, desiderated in epigrams,[1] and only two of these would support his indiscreet statement, doubtless intended as a compliment, that More "nil nisi iocus est"[2]—which surely must have been based on reports of More as a conversationalist and convivial companion, rather than on a reading of the poems. There are, to be sure, many other epigrams that do show wit, though it is more often mordant than comic. But unless the choices I have indicated are merely a reflection of my own taste and hence completely subjective, it is significant that so much of More's best work is memorable for quite other qualities.

If we knew nothing else of More, the Latin poems would suffice to show us a man of singular integrity and of the rare wisdom that can combine unflinching devotion to principle with a realistic understanding that principle will not abate for even a moment the relentless movement of the monstrous machine that is human society. We can say of him what we could not truthfully say of many poets of greater technical accomplishment: that we cannot read his best verses without wishing we could have known the man. To possess such character is to have attained a rare excellence among men; to have been able to convey it in verse is to have attained an honorable station among the poets of the world.

R. P. O.

The Humane Scope of the Poems

The first critical estimate of More's epigrams was the dedicatory letter to Pirckheimer by Beatus Rhenanus which prefaced the first edition. After praising the wit and brevity of More's poems, he pointed out how different they were in subject matter from those of Pontanus and Marullus, the two most admired Latin poets of the previous generation. Four

---

[1]See p. 72, below.

[2]See the variant reading at p. 74, Rhen. Pref./51.

hundred years later we can hardly do better than follow the path thus marked out for us, for it is the difference between More's epigrams and those of his predecessors and contemporaries which is, historically speaking, the most striking thing about them. To the Italian humanists of the fifteenth century an epigram was simply a short poem (and often not so very short at that) and was usually amatory, complimentary, or sepulchral. The early collections of epigrams are full of such poems, many of them without much pretense to wit or point. Hymns and religious poems were often interspersed. At writing short love poems, such men as Pontanus and Marullus were the best in Europe; at compact and polished flattery, Politian was a master. But love and flattery have never been the most suitable matter for epigrams. It is the pungent commentary on men and manners, on professions and classes, characteristic alike of the *Greek Anthology* and of Martial, that one misses in these men. To move from Italy to northern Europe, a case much to the point is the collection of Erasmus' epigrams published in the same volume with More's in 1518. This urbane and cosmopolitan scholar, author of the most famous satire of the sixteenth century, turned out as dull a collection of addresses to notable persons and uninspired religious commonplaces as one could hope to find.[1] More's distinction as an epigrammatist is twofold. First, he had a sharply defined sense of what he conceived an epigram to be: a short poem, normally in elegiac couplets, terse, witty, and satirical. His book contains a few poems which deviate from this rule, but 90 percent of them conform to it. Second, he banished from his writing both the licentious Ovidianism of the Italian poets and the dull religiosity of the northern humanists. In their place we find true wit and a keen eye for the ridiculous in many areas of life. It was doubtless his choice of fresher and livelier subject matter which accounts for the immediate popularity of his poems, resulting in the appearance of three editions in two years.

More's devotion to the true genius of the epigram was unquestionably fostered by his interest in the Greek Anthology. The Progymnasmata, in which More and Lily wrote rival translations, show how he put himself to school to these masters of the epigram, and the eighty-odd other translations in the volume show how extensive this training was. But if he owed a debt to Greece, he more than repaid it by popularizing Greek poetry. Hutton's register of translations and imitations of the Anthology shows again and again that More was the first to make translations of many of these epigrams.[2]

---

[1]For some qualifications of this judgment, see Reedijk, p. 112, and pp. 50–51, above.
[2]James Hutton, *The Greek Anthology in Italy* (Ithaca, N.Y., 1935), pp. 443–649.

When we turn from the poems of Pontanus or Erasmus to those of More, we feel that we are leaving the study of a scholar or a cleric and entering the world of merchants, lawyers, and courtiers. The refreshing new range of subjects may be illustrated by the following selection of his main categories. There are twenty-three epigrams on kings and government, twenty on the faults and foibles of women, thirteen on death, eleven on astrologers, eight on animals, and five on physicians. Only a half dozen are complimentary, and there are no poems of conventional piety. Although erotic poems are lacking, there is a fair amount of sexual humor of the fabliau type.

Among these topics, the most original for an epigrammatist was kingship. In fact, we know of no other sixteenth-century poet who used this theme for short poems. The ideas More developed were often commonplaces of classical and medieval political theory, but the use of them for epigrams was new. His favorite concern is for the difference between a good king and a tyrant; but it is evident from a reading of this group of epigrams that, whereas the existence of good kings is a theoretical possibility, the existence of tyrants is a present danger.[1] The attack on the policies of Henry VII, so sharply expressed in the long poem on the coronation of Henry VIII (no. 19), throws light upon the origin of some of More's thoughts about tyrants; and the opinions of Hythloday in the first book of *Utopia,* written seven years later, show that there had been no significant change in his attitude. Number 80, on death as a tyrannicide and avenger of the tyrant's suffering subjects, is expressed with such bitter and sardonic hatred as to leave no doubt that More is here giving vent to his own emotions. And finally, in a very remarkable poem on the best government for a commonwealth (no. 198), he argues at considerable length the advantages of a senate over a king. No one, he says, disagrees with a king. This goes even further than his plan for Utopia, where an elective king, who could be deposed for tyranny,[2] was provided.

The epigrams on death, though conventional in subject, are highly characteristic of More as a man. From his early experiences at the Charterhouse, where he was on the verge of withdrawing from the

---

[1]See the Commentary at 80/8–13 for a list of such epigrams. See also Wolfgang Mann's discussion of More's political thought in his *Lateinische Dichtung in England . . .* (Halle, 1939), pp. 22–78.

[2]These epigrams give considerable support to the theory of Russell Ames, in his *Citizen Thomas More and his Utopia* (Princeton, 1949), that More was a republican at heart. See also James K. McConica, "The Patrimony of Thomas More," in *History and Imagination: Essays in Honour of H. R. Trevor-Roper,* ed. H. Lloyd-Jones et al (London, 1981), pp. 67–68.

world entirely, up to the almost incredible tranquillity of his preparation for execution on the scaffold, he showed an ability to set a true value on the temporal joys of this life, without, on the other hand, despising them. More's own temperament and his characteristic piety merge here with his admiration for Greek literature. From the Anthology he selected for translation such themes as death the equalizer of rich and poor (nos. 40, 45, 46) and death the welcome end of life's evils (no. 70); and from Seneca he took the idea that life itself is only a progress towards death (no. 75).

In his original poems he emphasized the inevitability of death and the uncertainty of its time of arrival (nos. 38, 74); and he referred grimly to this world as a prison from which we are released only by death (no. 119). His whole attitude is summed up in no. 259, in which he rebukes himself for rejoicing at his escape from an easy death at sea, because a death preceded by wounds or disease might await him. Here in these epigrams is the paradox—we may say the triumph—of More's character. The greatest wit and most genial man of his age wore a hair shirt secretly and accustomed himself to looking death in the face long before he was actually called upon to meet the executioner.

This is not the place to discuss in detail the wealth of interesting material in the epigrams. Briefly we may call attention to More's sympathy with animals (nos. 37, 42, 83, 134), his attacks on unworthy churchmen (nos. 71, 176, 178, 202, 203), and the hearty gusto of his fabliaux (nos. 90, 116, 117, 133, 144, 168, 207, 222, 245, 246). Although a deeply religious man, he had an earthy Chaucerian side to his character. Ready to give up the world at a moment's notice in order to enter upon eternity, he nevertheless found the world full of interest as long as he was in it. It is this vivid interest in life in all its aspects that makes More's *Epigrammata* incomparably the best book of Latin epigrams in the sixteenth century.

L. B. and C. A. L.

A NOTE ON THE TEXTS

The Editions of 1518 and 1520

THE COPY-TEXT for this edition is the copy of the 1520 edition in the Beinecke Library at Yale University. A complete collation of copies of this edition at the University of Illinois (Urbana) and at the Folger Shakespeare Library[1] has not revealed any stop-press corrections. For the editions of March and December 1518, the collations were made from the copies in the Beinecke Library.

Normally I have reproduced the spelling, capitalization, and punctuation of the 1520 edition (or other copy texts), but where it is misleading I have corrected it and given the 1520 reading in the apparatus criticus. All exclamation marks in the text of this edition appear as question marks in the early editions, which (according to usual sixteenth-century practice) use the question mark for exclamations as well as true questions. The Latin digraphs *æ* and *œ* are reproduced here as separate letters (*ae, oe*). When *e* in the early editions represents *ae,* it appears as *ae* in this edition, but the original form is recorded in the apparatus criticus. Where the early editions print *ó* or *ô* in vocative or exclamatory expressions, this edition prints *O.* Ordinary Latin abbreviations (such as a line over a vowel to indicate a following *m* or *n,* and the *q*—abbreviations for such words as *quod, quam, quoque*) have been silently expanded. Diacritical marks to indicate a change in stress caused by an enclitic (*maiorém ne*) or to distinguish forms with the same spelling (*quàm* for the adverb, *quam* for the relative pronoun) have been omitted except when they may be useful in distinguishing such forms. Enclitic forms printed separately from the preceding word have been silently joined to them (*crimina úe* appears as *criminaue*). Turned letters have been silently corrected and differences in capitalization have not been recorded unless they influence the meaning.

In the Greek of this edition, abbreviations have been expanded and ligatures printed in accordance with modern type fonts.[2] Breathings and accents over diphthongs, which are often placed over both letters or the first letter of a diphthong in the early editions, are placed over the

[1]The Folger copy lacks sigs. X_2–X_3v.

[2]On the extraordinarily complex abbreviations and ligatures of sixteenth-century printing of Greek, see William H. Ingram, "The Ligatures of Early Printed Greek," *Greek, Roman and Byzantine Studies,* 7 (1966), 371–89.

second letter according to modern practice (unless the position in the early edition really indicates two separate letters, not a diphthong). Merely careless misprints in the breathings and accents have been silently corrected, and proper names have been regularly capitalized. We have followed the Renaissance convention of using a grave accent on the last syllable of words before a comma. In the poems added toward the end of *1520* (nos. 263, 265–68) the first line of each title is set in uppercase but the rest of the title in lowercase, probably to save space or type. We have given the whole title in uppercase in conformity with the rest of *1520*.

Two poems, here numbered 270 and 271, which appear only in *1518* (sigs. E_1v, G_2–G_2v), were omitted from *1520*. The first appeared after no. 138 (in this edition); the second, after no. 182.

The numbers assigned to the poems in this edition do not appear in the early editions:[1] Except for nos. 272–80, which do not appear in *1518* or *1520*, the following abbreviations are used in the variant readings:

- *1518*^{m} Basel, Johann Froben, March 1518, Gibson no. 3
- *1518*^{d} Basel, Johann Froben, December 1518, Gibson no. 4
- *1518* Agreement of *1518*^{m} and *1518*^{d}
- *1520* Basel, Johann Froben, 1520, Gibson no. 57
- *1563* Basel, Episcopius, *Lucubrationes,* 1563, Gibson no. 74
- *1565* Louvain, Johann Bogard, *Omnia . . . opera,* 1565, Gibson no. 75a.

Poems Not in the Editions of 1518 and 1520

No. 272 first appeared in More's *The Workes . . . in the Englysh tonge* ([London, William Rastell, 1557], *STC*[2] 18076; cited in the variants as "*1557*"), sig. ¶$_4$, on which my text is based.

Nos. 273 and 274 first appeared as complimentary poems at the beginning and end of John Holt's *Lac puerorum. Anglice Mylke for chyldren,* a Latin grammar dedicated to John Cardinal Morton, Archbishop of Canterbury, and designed for the use of his pageboys at Lambeth Palace, where Holt was schoolmaster. It must have been written before Morton's death in 1500, but it survives only in four later editions:[2]

1. Antwerp, Adrian van Berghen [c. 1506–10] (Nijhoff-Kronenberg 3179, *STC* 13606), cited as *V*. This edition survives only in fragments at the British Library and at libraries in Oxford and Cambridge.[3]

---

[1]My numbers differ from those in Bradner-Lynch because I do not begin a new series after the Progymnasmata (see Appendix E).

[2]I am grateful to Katharine Pantzer for providing information about the following editions from her forthcoming revision of *STC*.

[3]R. I. Page has informed me that the fragments at Corpus Christi College, Cambridge,

2. London, Wynkyn de Worde [c. 1508] (*STC* 13604), sigs. A_1v–A_2 and H_4, cited as *W*. I have used a photograph of the copy in the British Library.[1]

3. London, Richard Pynson [1510?] (*STC* 13605), sigs. A_1v–A_2 and E_6v, cited as *P*. I have used a microfilm of the copy in the British Library.

4. Antwerp, Govaert Bac [c. 1511] (Nijhoff-Kronenberg 4440[2]), cited as *B*. I have used a facsimile of sigs. a_1v and g_3v in the unique copy at the University of Illinois in Urbana, printed by Harris Fletcher in *Studies in Honor of T. W. Baldwin,* ed. D. C. Allen (Urbana, 1958), pp. 57–58.[3]

I have taken *W,* the earliest complete edition, as my copy text, but I have modernized the punctuation and capitalization, which can be seen in their original form in the illustrations following p. 295, below, and in William Nelson's diplomatic transcription of *W* (with variants from *V* and *P*).[4]

No. 275 first appeared on sig. A_1v of *Linacri progymnasmata grammatices vulgaria* (London, John Rastell, [1512]; *STC*[2] 15635), prepared by Thomas Linacre for St. Paul's School. I have based my text on a microfilm of the copy in the British Library (cited in the variants as *R*).

No. 276, consisting of two poems on Quentin Metsys' diptych of Erasmus and Peter Giles, was sent to Peter Giles by More in a letter written at Calais on October 7, 1517.[5] I have based my text on the three earliest sources: the Deventer manuscript, fols. 207–08 (*D*);[6] *Auctarium selectarum aliquot epistolarum* (Basel, Johann Froben, August 1518; Gibson, no. 145), sigs. s_4–s_4v, the first printed version (*A*); and *Epistolae D. Erasmi Roterodami ad diuersos* (Basel, Johann Froben, August 31, 1521; Gibson, no. 146), sigs. m_6–m_6v, the second printed version (*E*).[7] I have taken the Deventer manuscript as my copy text, but I have modernized the capital-

do not contain either of the two epigrams by More. Of the fragments of three copies of *Lac puerorum* in the Cambridge University Library, one (Syn. 6.50.1–3, University Microfilm No. 1315) contains More's Epigram 274, appearing on sig. H_4v, but the leaf has been cropped so that one or more words at the end of each line are missing and the last three lines are entirely lacking.

[1]The library of Lambeth Palace has a fragment of one leaf (E_5) of another edition by Wynkyn de Worde (c. 1508), but the fragment does not contain More's epigrams.

[2]Part 3, sec. 3, p. 11.

[3]Parts of Holt's *Lac* seem to have been included in a Latin grammar printed in Antwerp about 1507 by Jan van Doesborch (Nijhoff-Kronenberg 4282), fragments of which are in Cambridge University Library; but the fragments do not contain More's epigrams.

[4]"Thomas More, Grammarian and Orator," *PMLA, 58* (1943), 342–43.

[5]Allen, *3,* 106–07. This letter has also been edited by Rogers, pp. 98–100.

[6]Corrections added to the Deventer manuscript are cited as D^c.

[7]I have used a photograph of the Deventer manuscript, a microfilm of the *Auctarium,*

Thomas Linacre. Artist unknown

ization and punctuation, which may be seen in their original form in the illustrations following p. 299.

No. 277 was sent to Erasmus by More in a letter written at Calais on November 5, 1517.[1] I have based my text on the same sources as for no. 276,[2] except for the Deventer manuscript, which does not contain the letter. The copy text is the *Auctarium.*

No. 278 was first printed in *Doctissima D. Thomae Mori . . . Epistola, in qua . . . respondet Literis Ioannis Pomerani* (Louvain, John Fowler, 1568; Gibson no. 61) on the verso of the title page; this edition is my copy text (*F*).[3] The six lines also appear in British Library MS. Royal 17.D.xiv, fols. 453–453^{v} (*L*). The first four lines appear in Nicholas Harpsfield's *Life of More,* ed. Elsie Hitchcock and R. W. Chambers, EETS Original Series no. 186 (Oxford, 1932), p. 181 (*H*). All six lines appear as the first two poems written on the flyleaf at the end of a copy of Vives' edition of Augustine's *De civitate Dei* (Basel, Johann Froben, 1522)[4] in the sacristy library of the Catholic church in Lower Brailes, Warwickshire (*Br*).[5] They are followed by no. 280 and two English poems, "Lewys the lost lover" and "Dauy the dycer" (*EW,* sigs. XX_8v–YY_1).[6] Each of the five poems is attributed to "Thomae Mori" in the left margin.[7]

---

and the copy of *Epistolae . . . ad diuersos* in the Beinecke Rare Book Library at Yale University.

[1]Allen, *3,* 133.

[2]*Auctarium,* sig. t_2, and sig. n_1 in *Epistolae . . . ad diuersos.*

[3]I have used a xerox of the copy in the Princeton University Library and a photograph of the copy in the Huntington Library.

[4]The volume is misdated 1512 in the colophon.

[5]It is no. 47 in the library. I am grateful to Mrs. Margaret Suffolk and to the late Neil Ker for bringing this leaf to my attention.

[6]The couplet 278/9–10 (without heading) is followed by 278/3–6 (headed "Aliud"). The Latin poems are written in an italic hand; the English poems, in a secretary hand. The handwriting, as Neil Ker has kindly informed me, probably belongs to the third quarter of the sixteenth century. A Latin note in the same italic hand in the upper righthand corner of the leaf refers to the second book of Augustine's *Retractationes* and to the eighteenth chapter of some book of *De civitate Dei.* The binding is ornamented with roll AN. g (1) and ornament B (3) in J. Basil Oldham's *English Blind-stamped Bindings* (Cambridge, 1952), pp. 43, 59, which were used in London between 1514 and 1534. According to Neil Ker, owners' names in the book are: "J. Ball" (whose name appears in many other books in the library at Lower Brailes), "Brudenell," "Thomas Brudenell est possessor," and "George Brudenell." According to David Rogers, Thomas is probably the first Earl of Cardigan (1578–1663) and George is probably the third Earl of Cardigan (1685–1732). Both were bibliophiles who added to the library at Deene Park; see Joan Wake, *The Brudenells of Deene* (London, 1953; 2nd rev. ed., 1954), pp. 165, 239, 473. The great-grandfather of the first earl was John Brudenell (1461–1531), chief justice of the common pleas during the last ten years of his life.

[7]For the couplet 278/9–10 the identification has been changed from "Thomas Morus" to "Thomae Mori" by altering the final letters.

No. 279 was written in a flyleaf of a codex containing the works of Jerome Busleyden.[1] My copy text is the facsimile and transcription in Henry de Vocht's *Jerome de Busleyden, Founder of the Louvain Collegium Trilingue: His Life and Writings, Humanistica Lovaniensia 9* (Turnhout, 1950), 155, 257 (*Bu*). Although Professor de Vocht confidently asserted that these lines were in More's own hand, he gave no convincing evidence; they are almost certainly not autograph.[2]

No. 280 follows the two parts of no. 278 on the flyleaf of the volume at Lower Brailes mentioned above as a source for no. 278. Like the four other poems on the flyleaf, all of which there is sufficient evidence to assign to More, it is ascribed to "Thomae Mori" in the left margin. Though it occurs nowhere else, as far as I know, its position among four genuine poems in an early manuscript gives us at least an initial presumption that it is also genuine. The abbreviations in the copy text have been silently expanded, and punctuation, which is completely lacking in the copy text, has been added.

No. 281 was first printed in Cuthbert's Tunstall's *De arte supputandi libri quattuor* (London, R. Pynson, 14 October 1522, *STC*[2] 24319, sig. s_4), which is my copy text. Tunstall's treatise on arithmetic, which was dedicated to More,[3] was reprinted in Paris (Robert Estienne, 1529 and 1538) and Strassburg (1544 and 1551).

More may well have written the two poems in the prefatory matter of *Utopia* (*CW 4*, 18, 20) and the three poems against Luther at the end of his *Responsio* (*CW 5*, 694–99, 982). A Latin epitaph given by John Weever in his *Ancient Funerall Monuments* (1631) was almost certainly written to commemorate More's mother Agnes (d. 1499) and his uncle Abel (d. 1486), but there is no evidence that More wrote it.[4] For two distinct Latin couplets assigned to More without any good authority, see James Granger, *A Supplement Consisting of Corrections and Large Additions to a Biographical History of England . . .* (London, 1774), p. 30, and Peter Beal, *Index of English Literary Manuscripts* (London and New York, 1980–), *1/2*, 348. Horace Walpole mentions (but does not present) verses More was said to have written on two Holbein drawings (Riches and Poverty); see *Anecdotes of Painting in England,* in *The Works of Horace Walpole,* 5 vols. (London, 1798), *3*, 74–75.

---

[1]Royal Library, Brussels, MS. 15676–77, p. 62.

[2]Even allowing for the rapid cursive of the Valencia autograph (*CW 14/1*) and the bookish formality of the lines in the Busleyden manuscript, there are no characteristic similarities and there are some striking differences: the curved ascenders of *b* and *l,* the descender of *g,* and the absence of More's characteristic final descending stroke in *n.*

[3]The dedicatory letter is Rogers, no. 111, pp. 265–67.

[4]It is reprinted, translated, and discussed by Germain Marc'hadour, "The Death-year of Thomas More's Mother," *Moreana, 63/2* (1979), 13–16.

TEXT AND TRANSLATIONS

EPIGRAMMATA

Clarissimi Disertissimique Viri
THOMAE MORI Britanni
ad emendatum exemplar
ipsius autoris
excusa

THE EPIGRAMS

Of the Very Famous & Learned
Englishman THOMAS MORE
printed to agree
with the author's own
corrected copy

BEATVS RHENANVS BILIBALDO PIRCHEIMERO, MAXIMILIANI CAESARIS A CONSILIO, ET SENATORI NVRENBERGENSI S.D.

BELLE prorsus conuenire mihi uisum fuit, clarissime Bilibalde, si THOMAE MORI illius Britanniae decoris Epigrammata, quae nuper ERASMVS noster Roterodamus, ad me misit, tibi nominatim inscriberem. Siquidem multis adeo rebus similes inter uos estis. Vterque iuris peritus, uterque cum Rhomane tum Graece doctus, uterque non in publicis modo suae ciuitatis functionibus uersans, sed et ob singularem negociorum explicandorum dexteritatem, et in dandis consilijs prudentiam, suo quisque principi charissimus, ille potentissimo Britannorum regi Henrico, tu sacratissimo Caesari MAXIMILIANO. Nam quid de fortunis attinet commemorare, quas utrique possidetis amplissimas, ut uel hoc quicquid est ornamenti, quod ex diuitijs accedere putatur, neutri desit, quin potius aedendis uirtutum maxime liberalitatis exemplis abunde supersit materia. Sed et utrique pater obtigit non minus literis, quam senatoria familia clarus. Itaque cum amicitiae similitudo sit autor et aequalitas, hanc [a_2] MORI foeturam tibi nuncupare congruentissimum duxi, ut quem multis alioqui nominibus amore prosequeris, de his etiam Epigrammatis impensius complectaris, ames, magnifacias. Huc adde, quod nemini rectius mitti poterant hi lepidissimi lusus, quam ei, qui in hanc, quod aiunt, harenam aliquando sit descendere solitus. Nam is demum nouerit, quam sit egregia res doctum epigramma, quisquis ipse fuerit, suum non nunquam ingenium in hoc exercitationis genere periclitatus. Sed enim, id quod te non latet, argutiam habeat epigramma cum

---

9 Rhomane] Romane, *1518*[m], Rhomane, *1518*[d], Rhomanae, *1520* 10 uterque] Vterque *1518 1520* 20 *Signatures* a_2 *and* a_3 *are mismarked* x_2 *and* x_3 *in 1520, because reprint was made from 1518.*

BEATUS RHENANUS GREETS WILLIBALD PIRCKHEIMER, COUNCILLOR TO THE EMPEROR MAXIMILIAN AND MEMBER OF THE NUREMBERG SENATE

It has seemed to me, most renowned Willibald, exquisitely fitting to inscribe to you in particular this book that our friend Erasmus of Rotterdam recently sent to me, the *Epigrams* of Thomas More, that ornament of Britain, since you and More resemble each other in so many respects. You are both skilled in the law, both learned in Greek as well as Latin. Not only are you both occupied in the public duties of your respective states, but, because of your unusual skill in resolving problems and your wisdom in council, you are both very dear to your rulers, the one to the very powerful King Henry of England, the other to the most holy Emperor Maximilian. Why mention wealth, which you both have in great plenty, so that neither of you lacks whatever distinction is thought to accrue from riches, or rather so that you both have the means in plentiful abundance for setting examples of good deeds, particularly deeds of generosity. Both of you had fathers noted no less for their learning than for their distinguished birth. And so, since likeness and equality are the source of friendship, I have decided that it is very appropriate to dedicate this work of More's to you so that, although for many other reasons you already honor the author with your affection, you may as a result of these *Epigrams* embrace, love, and esteem him even more. And furthermore, there is no one to whom these most delightful diversions can be sent more fittingly than to one who has himself been wont from time to time to descend, as they say, into the same arena. That is to say, if anyone has himself at one time or another tried out his ingenuity at this kind of composition, he is the very man who will know how remarkable a thing is a learned epigram. Truly an epigram, as you know, must have wit combined with brevity; it must be lighthearted, and then

BEATVS RENANVS SELEZES TADIENSIS.
Plurima ſcripta Notis preclara, Beate, beaſti,
Eſtque beata tuo Teutonis ora ſtylo:
Quapropter varijs felix celebrabere terris;
Dumq; beas alios te ſimul ipſe beas.
35

Beatus Rhenanus, in P. Galle, In *Virorum doctorum . . . effigies* XLIII, Antwerp, 1572

Willibald Pirckheimer, by Albrecht Dürer

breuitate coniunctam, sit festiuum, et acclamatiunculis, quae ἐπιφωνήματα Graeci uocant, subinde claudatur. Quas sane dotes omneis cumulatissime licet in his Moricis Epigrammatibus reperire, praesertim in his quae ipse genuit: nam in caeteris, quae e Graecis uersa sunt, inuentionis laus priscis tribuitur. Quanquam hic quoque non minus magni fieri meretur commode reddens ex aliena lingua, quam scribens: labor certe uertentis saepe maior. Siquidem qui scribit, liber est, et inuentioni libere uacat: at qui transfert, ad aliud subinde respicere cogitur, nimirum ad id quod uertendum desumpsit: quod quoties fit, multo plus sudat ingenium, quam cum suum aliquid progignit. Vtrobique sane mirus est THOMAS MORVS: nam elegantissime componit, et felicissime uertit. Quam fluunt suauiter huius carmina! Quam est hic nihil coactum! Quam sunt omnia facilia! Nihil hic du[a_2v]rum, nihil scabrum, nihil tenebricosum. Candidus est, argutus, Latinus. Porro gratissima quadam festiuitate sic omnia temperat, ut nihil unquam uiderim lepidius. Crediderim ego Musas quicquid usquam est iocorum, leporis, salium, in hunc contulisse. Quam lusit eleganter ad Sabinum alienos pro suis tollentem liberos! Quam salse Lalum ridet, qui uideri Gallus tam ambitiose cupiebat! Sunt autem huius sales nequaquam mordaces, sed candidi, melliti, blandi, et quiduis potius quam amarulenti. Iocatur enim, sed ubique citra dentem: ridet, sed citra contumeliam. Iam inter epigrammatographos Pontanum et Marullum in primis hodie miratur Italia: at dispeream, si non tantundem in hoc est naturae, utilitatis uero plus. Nisi si quis inde magnopere se credit iuuari, dum suam Neaeram celebrat Marullus, et in multis αἰνίττεται, Heraclitum quendam agens, aut dum Io. Pontanus ueterum nobis epigrammatistarum nequitias refert, quibus nihil sit frigidius, et boni uiri lectione magis indignum, ne dicam Christiani. Scilicet usque adeo uetustatem istis aemulari, cordi fuit. Quam ne contaminarent, sic a sacris abstinuerunt, ut a Graecis olim Pomponius Laetus, ne Rhomanae linguae castimoniam uiolaret, homo superstitiose Rho-

51 contumeliam.] contumeliam. Proinde quemadmodum Syrus Therentianus Demeam belle praedicans, Tu quantus quantus, inquit, nil nisi sapientia es, ita de MORO dicere licebit, Quantus quantus est, nil nisi iocus est. *1518*   54 Nisi] nisi *1518 1520*   55 αἰνίττεται] αἰνίπτεται *1518*[d] *1520*   59 Quam] quam *1518 1520*   61 Rhomanae] Romanae *1518*[m] *1520*   74/61–76/1 Rhomanus] Romanus *1518*[m]

it must end promptly with a witty point which the Greeks call ἐπιφώνημα. Surely one may find all these properties in these *Epigrams* of More, especially in those which he himself composed; in the others, which are translated from the Greek, the credit for originality belongs to the ancients. Still, here too, More deserves to be rated as high for translating well from a foreign tongue as for his own work. Undoubtedly the labor of a translator is often greater. This is so because the author is unfettered and freely at liberty to use whatever occurs to him, but the translator is required to keep something else continually in sight; that is, of course, what he has chosen to translate. Whenever this is the case, his skill is much more severely taxed than when he produces something of his own.

In both these fields Thomas More is very remarkable, for he composes most tastefully and translates most happily. How pleasantly his poetry flows! How utterly unforced is his work! How adroit it all is! Here is nothing harsh, nothing rough, nothing obscure. He is bright, sharp, a master of Latin. Furthermore, he seasons all his work with a certain very delightful humor so that I have never seen anything more charming. I could believe that the Muses conferred upon him all there is anywhere of mirth, charm, and wit. How gracefully he pokes fun at Sabinus for bringing up another's children as his own. How wittily he ridicules Lalus, who went to such lengths in his desire to seem French. And yet his witticisms are by no means ill-natured, but rather are honest, sweet, mild, anything but bitter. He provokes laughter, but in every case without pain; he ridicules, but without abuse.

At present Italy admires Pontanus and Marullus more than most epigrammatists, but I would wager my life that there is just as much inherent skill in this author of ours and more profit, unless it is possible that someone think it very profitable when Marullus celebrates his Neaera and in many places speaks in riddles, acting like another Heraclitus, or when Johannes Pontanus revives for us the lewdness of the ancient epigrammatists; and nothing could be more uninteresting or less worth reading for a man of principles, not to mention a man of Christian principles. Of course, they longed to imitate antiquity. To preserve the appearance of antiquity untainted, they avoided what was Christian just as Pomponius Laetus, a man excessively Roman, avoided what was Greek, lest he destroy the purity of the Latin language.

manus. Caeterum quemadmodum hi lusus MORI ingenium ostendunt et insignem eruditionem, sic iudicium nimirum acre, quod de rebus habet, ex VTOPIA cumu[a_3]latissime eluxerit. De qua paucis obiter meminero, quod hanc accuratissimus in literis BVDAEVS, incomparabilis ille melioris eruditionis antistes, et ingens, atque adeo unicum Galliarum decus, ita ut decebat, luculenta praefatione laudauit. Habet ea hoc genus decreta, qualia nec apud Platonem, nec apud Aristotelem, aut etiam Iustiniani uestri Pandectas sit reperire. Et docet minus forsan philosophice, quam illi, sed magis Christiane. Quanquam (audi per Musas bellam historiam) cum hic nuper in quodam grauium aliquot uirorum consessu, Vtopiae mentio orta fuisset, et illam ego laudibus ueherem, negabat quidam pinguis plus habendum MORO gratiae, quam actuario cuipiam scribae, qui in curia aliorum sententias duntaxat enotet, doriphorematis ritu (quod aiunt) interim assidendo, nihil ipse censens, quod diceret ea omnia ex Hythlodaei ore excepta, et a MORO tantum in literas missa. Proinde MORVM nullo laudandum alioqui nomine, nisi quod haec commode retulisset. Et non deerant, qui hominis iudicio uelut rectissime sentientis album adijcerent calculum. ἆρα οὐ σὺ τουτονὶ τοῦ Μώρου χαριεντισμὸν δέχῃ, τοιούτους ἄνδρας οὐ τοὺς τυχόντας ἀλλὰ τοὺς δοκίμους παρὰ τοῖς πολλοῖς, καὶ ταῦτα θεολόγους πλανήσαντος; Postremo si hoc quoque scire cupis, Guil. Lilius, MORI sodalis, cum quo uertendis Graecis epigrammatibus iam olim collusit, quae Progymnasmatum titulo sunt inscri[a_3v]pta, Britannus est, uir omnifariam doctus, non modo Graecos autores, sed et eius nationis mores uernaculos domestice notos habens, ut qui in insula Rhodo fuerit aliquot annos commoratus. Is nunc ludum literarium, quem Londini Coletus instituit, magna cum laude exercet. Quod superest, cum tibi per occupationes licebit, quibus in obeundis legationibus administrandaque Republica, laboriosissime distraheris, hoc libelli in manum cape, lege, et MORO, cuius os, ut puto, nondum uidisti, sed ex scriptis iam pridem cognitum habes, faue. Bene Vale clarissime uir. Basileae .VII. Cal. Martias. Anno M.D. XVIII. [a_4]

---

77 censens,] censens. *1518 1520* 81 χαριεντισμὸν] χακριεντισμὸν *1518*[d] 89 commoratus. Is] commoratus. is *1518* commoratus, is *1520* 94 puto,] *1518*, puto *1520*

Well, just as these amusing trifles of More's demonstrate his natural gifts and his unusual learning, so the very keen judgment he has in politics will be quite apparent from his *Utopia*. Of that I shall make only brief mention in passing because it was praised in a magnificent preface, as well it might be, by a most exacting scholar, Budé, that supreme master of the nobler learning, that great and even unmatched glory of France. The *Utopia* contains such principles as cannot be found in Plato, in Aristotle, or even in the *Pandects* of your Justinian. Its lessons are less philosophical, perhaps, than theirs but more Christian. And yet (listen, by the Muses, to a good story) when the *Utopia* was mentioned here recently at a certain gathering of a few responsible men and when I praised it, a certain dolt insisted that no more thanks were due to More than to any secretary who merely records the opinions of others at a council, sitting in after the fashion of an "extra," as they say, and without expressing any opinions of his own, because all More said was taken from the mouth of Hythloday and merely written down by More. Therefore, he said, More deserved praise only because he had recorded these matters well. And there were some present who approved the fellow's opinion as that of a man of very sound perception. Do you not, then, welcome this elegant wit of More, who can impose upon such men as these, no ordinary men, but widely respected and theologians at that?

Finally, in case you would like to know this too, William Lily, More's companion with whom he contended in the translation from the Greek of the epigrams included in this volume under the title *Progymnasmata*, is an Englishman, learned in every way, intimately familiar not only with the Greek authors, but also with the customs native to that people, in that he spent some years on the island of Rhodes. He now conducts with great success a grammar school founded by Colet in London.

I have only this left to say: when you have the opportunity, amid the duties which keep you so very busy conferring with embassies and administering the state, pick up this book, read it, and become an admirer of More, whose face, I think, you have not yet seen; but you have known him a long time from his writings. Farewell, most illustrious sir.

Basel
February 23, 1518

PROGYMNASMATA
THOMAE MORI ET GVILIELMI LILII SODALIVM

1

ΛΟΥΚΙΛΛΙΟΥ

Μῦν ᾽Ασκληπιάδης ὁ φιλάργυρος εἶδεν ἐν οἴκῳ,
Καὶ τί ποιεῖς, φησιν, φίλτατε μῦ παρ᾽ ἐμοί;
῾Ηδὺ δ᾽ ὁ μῦς γελάσας, μηδὲν φίλε, φησὶ, φοβηθῄς,
Οὐχὶ τροφῆς παρὰ σοὶ χρῄζομεν, ἀλλὰ μονῆς.

T. MORI. IN AVARVM

Murem Asclepiades ut apud se uidit auarus,
Mus quid in aede facis, dixit, amice mea?
Mus blande arridens, tolle, inquit, amice timorem,
Hic ego non uictum quaero, sed hospitium.

G. LILII.

Murem Asclepiades in tecto uidit auarus,
Et quid apud me O mus, inquit, amice facis?
Mus ridens, inquit, nihil O uerearis amice,
Non abs te uictum, sed mihi quaero domum.

2

ΠΑΛΛΑΔΑ.

Πλοῦτον μὲν πλουτοῦντος ἔχεις, ψυχὴν δὲ πένητος.
῏Ω τοῖς κληρονόμοις πλούσιε, σοὶ δὲ πένης.

G. LILII IN AVARVM.

Diuitias locupletis habes, animam sed egeni.
Haeredi O diues, sed tibi solus egens. [a$_4$v]

1/4 δ᾽ ὁ] *1518*, δ᾽ *1520*, δὲ *1520* (*errata*) 6 AVARVM] AVRVM *1518*^{d} **2**/4 AVARVM] AVRVM *1518*^{d}

PROGYMNASMATA
EXERCISES BY THE FRIENDLY RIVALS THOMAS MORE AND WILLIAM LILY

1

THOMAS MORE'S, ON A MISER

When Asclepiades the miser saw a mouse in his house, he said, "Friend mouse, what are you doing in my home?" The mouse, with a pleasant smile, replied, "Lay aside your fear, my friend; it is not board but lodging I want here."

WILLIAM LILY'S

Asclepiades the miser saw a mouse in his house and said, "Friend mouse, what are you doing in here with me?" The mouse smiled and said, "Have no fear, friend; what I want of you is not board but room."

2

WILLIAM LILY'S, ON A MISER

You have the wealth of a rich man, but a pauper's spirit—you who are wealthy in your heir's behalf, but poor for yourself alone.

T. MORI

Diuitias locupletis habes, inopis tibi mens est.
O miser haeredi diues, inopsque tibi.

3

ΛΟΥΚΙΑΝΟΥ.

Ἀγρὸς Ἀχαιμενίδου γενόμην ποτέ, νῦν δὲ Μενίππου,
Καὶ πάλιν ἐξ ἑτέρου, βήσομαι εἰς ἕτερον.
Καὶ γὰρ ἐκεῖνος ἔχειν μέ ποτ᾽ ᾤετο. καὶ πάλιν οὗτος
Οἴεται. εἰμὶ δ᾽ ὅλως οὐδενὸς, ἀλλὰ τύχης.

G. LILII DE POSSESSIONIBVS INCERTIS.

Nuper Achaemenidae, sed nunc sumus arua Menippi,
Et nunc hunc rursus, nunc alium petimus.
Ille etenim nuper, nunc et nos alter habere
Se putat: at nobis nil nisi casus inest.

T. MORI.

Nuper Achaemenidae fueram, nunc ecce Menippi,
Adque alium rursus deueniam ex alio.
Me proprium nunc iste putat, proprium ille putabat.
Ast ego nullius sum, nisi sortis ager.

4

ἌΔΗΛΟΝ.

Σώματα πολλὰ τρέφειν, καὶ δώματα πολλ᾽ ἀνεγείρειν,
Ἄτραπος εἰς πενίην ἐστὶν ἑτοιμοτάτη.

T. MORI DE LVXV IMMODICO.

Multas aedificare domos, et pascere multos,
Est ad pauperiem semita recta quidem.

G. LILII.

Corpora multa alere, et complures ponere sedes, [b$_1$]
Ipsa est ad summam semita pauperiem.

2/9 tibi.] *1518*, tibi, *1520*   4/2 πολλ᾽] πολλὰ *1518*

THOMAS MORE'S

You have the wealth of a rich man, but yours is a poor man's mind, unhappy man, rich for your heir and poor for yourself.

3

WILLIAM LILY'S, ON THE UNCERTAINTY OF PROPERTY

We fields recently belonged to Achaemenides, but now Menippus owns us. And we fall now to this one and then again to another, for not long ago that fellow thought he owned us, and now another thinks he does. We are composed of nothing but Chance.

THOMAS MORE'S

Not long ago I belonged to Achaemenides; now, presto, I belong to Menippus. And I shall pass again from one to another. This one thinks he owns me, that one thought he did. But really I am only Luck's field.

4

THOMAS MORE'S, ON EXTRAVAGANCE

To build many residences and to feed many people is surely the direct road to poverty.

WILLIAM LILY'S

To support many perons and to establish numerous residences—that is the road to extreme poverty.

5

ΛΟΥΚΙΑΝΟΥ.

‘Ὡς τεθνηξόμενος τῶν σῶν ἀγαθῶν ἀπόλαυε,
‘Ὡς δὲ βιωσόμενος, φείδεο σῶν κτεάνων.
Ἔστι δ’ ἀνὴρ σοφὸς οὗτος, ὃς ἄμφω ταῦτα νοήσας,
Φειδοῖ, καὶ δαπάνῃ μέτρον ἐφηρμόσατο.

G. LILII DE MODERATO SVMPTV

Diuitijs utare tuis, tanquam moriturus.
Tanquam uicturus, parcito diuitijs.
Vir sapiens est ille quidem, qui haec ambo uolutans
Parcit, quique modum sumptibus applicuit.

T. MORI.

Tanquam iam moriturus partis utere rebus,
Tanquam uicturus denuo parce tuis.
Ille sapit, qui perpensis hijs rite duobus,
Parcus erit certo munificusque modo.

6

ἌΔΗΛΟΝ.

’Ελπὶς καὶ σὺ τύχη, μέγα χαίρετε. τὸν λιμέν’ εὗρον.
Οὐδὲν ἐμοὶ, χ’ ὑμῖν. παίζετε τοὺς μετ’ ἐμέ.

T. MORI DE CONTEMPTV FORTVNAE.

Iam portum inueni, Spes et Fortuna ualete.
Nil mihi uobiscum est, ludite nunc alios.

G. LILII.

Inueni portum, Spes et Fortuna ualete.
Nil mihi uobiscum, ludite nunc alios. [b$_1$v]

7

ΠΑΛΛΑΔΑ.

Γῆς ἐπέβην γυμνός, γυμνὸς θ’ ὑπὸ γαῖαν ἄπειμι,
Καὶ τί μάτην μοχθῶ, γυμνὸν ὁρῶν τὸ τέλος;

5/2 ἀπόλαυε] ἀπόλαβε *1518* 4 οὗτος,] *1518*, οὗτος. *1520* 7/1 ΠΑΛΛΑΔΑ] *1518*, ΠΑΛΛΑ *1520*

5

WILLIAM LILY'S, ON REASON-
ABLE EXPENDITURE

May you make use of your wealth as if you were marked for death, and conserve your wealth as if you were destined to live. Truly, he is the wise man who, by pondering both these attitudes, conserves his wealth and sets a limit to his spending.

THOMAS MORE'S

As though death were at hand, enjoy the wealth you have acquired. And again, spare your wealth as if you were certain to live. The wise man is he who, by a proper consideration of these alternatives, is both frugal and generous in due measure.

6

THOMAS MORE'S, ON SCORNING LUCK

Now I have reached port; Hope and Luck, farewell. You have nothing to do with me. Now make sport of others.

WILLIAM LILY'S

I have reached port; Hope and Luck, farewell. You have nothing to do with me. Now make sport of others.

7

G. LILII DE MORTE

Ingredior nudus terram, egredior quoque nudus,
Quid frustra studeo, funera nuda uidens?

T. MORI

Nudus ut in terram ueni, sic nudus abibo.
Quid frustra sudo, funera nuda uidens?

8

ἌΔΗΛΟΝ.

Οἶνος, καὶ τὰ λοετρὰ, καὶ ἡ περὶ Κύπριν ἐρωὴ,
Ὀξυτέρην πέμπει τὴν ὁδὸν εἰς ἀΐδην.

T. MORI DE LVXV ET LIBIDINE.

Si quis ad infernos properet descendere manes,
Huc iter accelerant, balnea, uina, Venus.

G. LILII.

Nos caligantis rapiunt ad tecta tyranni,
Praecipiti cursu, balnea, uina, Venus.

9

ΠΑΛΛΑΔΑ.

Οὐχ οὕτω βλάπτει μισεῖν ὁ λέγων ἀναφανδὸν,
Ὥσπερ ὁ τὴν καθαρὰν ψευδόμενος φιλίαν.
Τὸν μὲν γὰρ μισοῦντα προειδότες, ἐκτρεπόμεσθα,
Τὸν δὲ λέγοντα φιλεῖν, οὐ προφυλασσόμεθα.
Ἐχθρὸν ἐγὼ κεῖνον κρίνω βαρὺν, ὅς ποτε λάθρῃ
Τὴν ἀπὸ τῆς φιλίης πίστιν ἔχων, ἀδικεῖ. [b$_2$]

T. MORI, DE FICTO AMICO.

Non aeque nocet hic, qui sese odisse fatetur,
Atque hic qui puram fingit amicitiam.
Osorem monitus fugio: fugisse sed illum
Quomodo qui se me fingit amare, queo?

7/6 studeo,] *1518*, studeo. *1520* **8**/3 ἀΐδην] ἀήδιν *1518*^{m} **9**/1 ΠΑΛΛΑΔΑ.] *om.* *1518* 5 Τὸν δὲ] τὸνδε *1518*^{m}, τόνδε *1518*^{d}, Τόνδε *1520*

WILLIAM LILY'S, ON DEATH

Naked I arrive on earth, naked, too, I leave. Why do I strive in vain, knowing as I do that death is naked?

THOMAS MORE'S

Just as surely as I came on earth naked, so surely naked shall I quit it. Why do I struggle in vain, knowing as I do that death is naked?

8

THOMAS MORE'S, ON SELF-INDULGENCE AND LUST

If anyone is in haste to join the shades of the dead below, then baths and wine and the pleasures of love shorten the journey thither.

WILLIAM LILY'S

It is baths and wine and the pleasures of love which drag us in headlong haste to the domain of the prince of darkness.

9

THOMAS MORE'S, ON A FALSE FRIEND

The man who admits his hatred does less harm than he who pretends unqualified affection. When I am warned, I avoid the man who hates me, but how can I avoid one who pretends to be

Pessimus hic certe est inimicus, quisquis amicus
  Creditus, occulta subdolus arte nocet.

G. LILII.

Non is tam laedit, liquide qui dixerit, odi,
  Quam qui synceram fingit amicitiam.
Vitabis certe quem noueris esse nocentem,
  Ast illum nunquam qui tibi dixit, amo.
Ille mihi grauis est hostis, qui clam nocuisse
  Gaudet, quique fidem fert in amicitia.

10

ʼΕΊΣ ΛΆΚΑΙΝΑΝ ῎ΑΔΗΛΟΝ

Γυμνὸν ἰδοῦσα Λάκαινα παλίντροπον ἐκ πολέμοιο
  Παῖδ' ἑὸν εἰς πάτραν ὠκὺν ἱέντα πόδα,
'Αντίη ἀΐξασα, δι' ἥπατος ἤλασε λόγχην,
  Ἄρρενα ῥηξαμένη φθόγγον ἐπὶ κταμένῳ,
'Αλλότριον Σπάρτας εἶπεν γένος, ἔρρε ποθ' ᾅδαν,
  Ἔρρ' ἐπεὶ ἐψεύσω πατρίδα, καὶ γενέταν.

T. MORI. DE MILITE SPARTANO.

In patriam amissis celeri pede dum redit armis,
  Conspiciens gnatum saeua Lacaena suum,
Obuia sublata corpus transuerberat hasta,
  Haec super occisum mascula uerba loquens. [b_2v]
Degener O Spartes genus, ito in Tartara tandem.
  Ito degeneras, et patria, et genere.

GVIL. LILII.

Quum nudum e bello gnatum remeare Lacaena
  Vidit, et in patrios accelerare lares,
Insultans contra, pectus traiecerat hasta.
  Horrida in extinctum uoce uirago furens,
Spartanam quando es patriam mentitus, auosque,
  Ad manes tandem degener, inquit, abi.

9/18 nocentem,] *1518,* nocentem. *1520* **10**/3 εἰς] ἐς *1518*[m] 7 γενέταν.] γενέταν, *1520,* γενέτας. *1518 1563* 17 lares,] lares. *1518 1520* 19 in extinctum] *1518,* inextinctum *1520;* furens,] furens. *1518 1520* 20 auosque,] *1518,* auosque. *1520*

my friend? Undoubtedly, one's worst enemy is he who in the guise of friend deceitfully works mischief by unsuspected guile.

WILLIAM LILY'S

The man who frankly says, "I hate you," does less damage than the man who pretends innocent friendship. Obviously, you will avoid the one you know is dangerous, but not the one who says, "I am your friend." I say that he is a deadly enemy who delights to do secret injury and still enjoys the confidence of friendship.

10

THOMAS MORE'S, ON A SPARTAN SOLDIER

A cruel Spartan mother saw her son as he was hurrying home after losing his weapons. She snatched up a spear, confronted him, and thrust him through. Then over her murdered son she spoke these unwomanly words: "Unnatural son of Sparta, go now at last to the abode of the dead. Go, you are a disgrace to Sparta and to your family."

WILLIAM LILY'S

When a Spartan mother saw her son, stripped of his arms in battle, returning in haste to his father's house, she leaped upon him and pierced his breast with a spear. Then in a hair-raising speech the maddened creature, more like a man than a woman, addressed the corpse: "Since you have belied your native land of Sparta and your forebears, unnatural son, depart at last to join the dead."

11

᾿ΑΓΑΘΙΟΥ

Χωλὸν ἔχεις τὸν νοῦν ὡς τὸν πόδα, καὶ γὰρ ἀληθῶς
Εἰκόνα τῶν ἐντὸς σὴ φύσις ἐκτὸς ἔχει.

T. MORI. IN CLAVDVM ET STVPIDVM.

Clauda tibi mens est, ut pes: natura notasque
Exterior certas interioris habet.

G. LILII.

Tardus es ingenio, ut pedibus: natura etenim dat
Exterius specimen, quod latet interius.

12

῎ΑΔΗΛΟΝ.

Εἰ μὲν ἦν μαθεῖν ἃ δεῖ παθεῖν,
Καὶ μὴ παθεῖν, καλὸν ἦν τὸ μαθεῖν.
Εἰ δὲ δεῖ παθεῖν ἃ δεῖ μαθεῖν,
Τί δεῖ μαθεῖν; παθεῖν γὰρ χρῆ.

T. MORI THEOPHRASTI APVD AVLVM GELLIVM DILEMMA.

Si uitare queas, quae sunt patienda, sciendo, [b3]
Scire quidem pulchrum, quae paterere, foret.
Sin quae praescieris uitandi est nulla potestas,
Quid praescire iuuat, quae patiere tamen?

G. LILII.

Si posset casus quisquam praescire futuros,
Et uitare simul, scire suaue foret.
Sin patienda tibi prorsus quae scire requiris,
Quid praescisse iuuat? namque necesse pati.

T. MORI, CARMINE IAMBICO TRIMETRO

Praescire si queas, quae oporteat pati,
Queasque non pati, bonum est ut praescias.
At si te oporteat, licet scias, pati,
Praescire quid iuuat? necesse enim est pati.

11

THOMAS MORE'S, ON A MAN BOTH LAME AND STUPID

Your mind is as lame as your leg, and your external condition gives sure signs of your inner state.

WILLIAM LILY'S

You are as slow in your wits as you are afoot, for your outward appearance gives a sample of what lies hidden within.

12

THOMAS MORE'S, THE DILEMMA OF THEOPHRASTUS, FROM AULUS GELLIUS

If by merely knowing your appointed troubles you could avoid them, then surely it would be a fine thing to know what troubles you would encounter. But if you do not have the power to avoid the troubles which you know are coming, what help is it to learn in advance of the suffering you must endure in any case?

WILLIAM LILY'S

If it were possible for you to see misfortunes approaching and, with your foresight, to avoid them, then it would be pleasant to know them. But if you must inevitably suffer the misfortunes you seek to discover, what good is foresight, for you must endure them in any case.

A POEM IN IAMBIC TRIMETER BY THOMAS MORE

If you could discover in advance what suffering you must endure, and if you could avoid it, then it would be good for you to know. But if, despite your knowledge, suffer you must, what advantage is there in knowing, for the suffering is inevitable.

13

ΠΑΛΛΑΔΑ.

Δὶς δύ' ἀδελφοὺς ὦδ' ἐπέχει τάφος. ἓν γάρ ἐπέσχον,
῏Ημαρ καὶ γενεῆς οἱ δύο, καὶ θανάτου.

T. MORI, IN DVOS FRATRES, VNO
ET NATOS ET MORTVOS DIE.

Quatuor hic tumulus fratres complectitur: ex his
Lux simul una duos et parit, et perimit.

G. LILII.

Quatuor hic tumulus fratres habet, una duobus
Lux et natalis, mortis et una fuit.

14

᾿ΑΔΈΣΠΟΤΟΝ.

Ζεὺς, κύκνος, ταῦρος, σάτυρος, χρυσὸς δι' ἔρωτα
Λήδης, Εὐρώπης, 'Αντιόπης, Δανάης. [b$_3$v]

T. MORI. DE IOVE MVTATO.

Taurus, olor, satyrusque ob amorem et Iuppiter aurum est
Europes, Ledes, Antiopes, Danaes.

GVIL. LILII.

Taurus, olor, satyrus, per amorem Iuppiter aurum
Europae, Ledes, Antiopae, Danaes.

15

῎ΑΔΗΛΟΝ.

'Εννέα τὰς Μούσας φασίν τινες: ὥς όλιγώρως·
'Ηνίδε καὶ Σαπφὼ Λεσβόθεν ἡ δεκάτη.

T. MORI IN SAPPHO.

Musas esse nouem referunt, sed prorsus aberrant.
Lesbica iam Sappho Pieris est decima.

13/6 tumulus] *1518 1520* (*errata*), tumultus *1520;* complectitur:] complectitur. *1518 1520* 9 habet] *1518 1520* (*errata*), habebit *1520* **14**/1 'ΑΔΈΣΠΟΤΟΝ.] *om. 1518* 2 ταῦρος,] *1518,* ταῦρος *1520* **15**/2 ὀλιγώρως·] ὀλιγώρως *1518 1520* 3 'Ηνίδε] ἠνί δε *1518*[m], ἠνὶ δὲ *1518*[d], Ηνὶ δὲ *1520* 4 SAPPHO.] *1518,* SAPPHO, *1520*

13

THOMAS MORE'S, ON TWO BROTHERS WHO WERE BORN AND DIED ON THE SAME DAY

This tomb contains four brothers. Two of them a single day brought to birth and to death.

WILLIAM LILY'S

This tomb contains four brothers. Two of them were born on the same day and on the same day died.

14

THOMAS MORE'S, ON JUPITER TRANSFORMED

Jupiter was a bull, a swan, a satyr, and gold, for love of Europa, Leda, Antiope, Danae.

WILLIAM LILY'S

Jupiter became a bull, a swan, a satyr, gold, for love of Europa, Leda, Antiope, Danae.

15

THOMAS MORE'S, ON SAPPHO

They say there are nine Muses. Clearly they are mistaken. Now Sappho of Lesbos is the tenth daughter of Pierus.

G. LILII.

Quam temere dixere nouem quidam esse sorores.
Musarum, en Sappho Lesbis adest decima.

16

ʼΑΓΑΘΙΟΥ ΣΧΟΛΑΣΤΙΚΟΥ.

Ἢ σάτυρος τὸν χαλκὸν ὑπέδραμεν, ἢ διὰ τέχνης
Χαλκὸς ἀναγκασθεὶς, ἀμφεχύθη σατύρῳ.

G. LILII. IN AEREAM SATYRI STATVAM.

Aut Satyrus fusus circum aes, aut arte coactum
Illud idem circum fusum erat aes Satyro.

T. MORI.

Prorsum admiranda dum circumflectitur arte,
Aut Satyrum hoc tegit aes, aut Satyro aes tegitur.

EIVSDEM.

Aut isti Satyrus iam circumflectitur aeri, [b_4]
Aut isto Satyrus iam circumflectitur aere.

17

ʼΕΙΣ ʼΑΓΑΛΜΑ ΝΙΟΒΗΣ.

Ἐκ ζωῆς με θεοὶ τεῦξαν λίθον· ἐκ δὲ λίθοιο
ζωὴν Πραξιτέλης ἔμπαλιν εἰργάσατο.

G. LILII. IN STATVAM NIOBES

Ex uita saxum Dij me fecere: sed ipse
Ex saxo uitam denuo Praxiteles.

T. MORI.

Dij ex uiua lapidem fecere: at quum lapis essem,
Me uiuam fecit denuo Praxiteles.

15/8 sorores.] sorores *1518, 1520* **16**/1 ΣΚΟΛΑΣΤΙΚΟΥ.] *1518,* ΣΚΟΛΑΤΙΚΟΥ *1520 1563* 8 arte,] *1518,* arte. *1520* 12 Aut . . . aere.] *Not indented 1518*
17/9 fecit] *1518 1520* (*errata*), secit *1520*

WILLIAM LILY'S

How rashly some have said that the sisters are nine! Lo, here is Lesbian Sappho the tenth of the Muses.

16

WILLIAM LILY'S, ON A BRONZE IMAGE OF A SATYR

Either a satyr was applied to the bronze or, induced by artistry, that same bronze was applied to a satyr.

THOMAS MORE'S

This bronze, while it was being worked with thoroughly admirable skill, either coated a satyr or was inclosed by a satyr.

ANOTHER VERSION BY MORE

Either a satyr is fitted to that bronze statue, or a satyr is fitted with that bronze statue.

17

WILLIAM LILY'S, ON A STATUE OF NIOBE

The gods deprived me of life and turned me to stone. But it was Praxiteles who from stone restored me to life.

THOMAS MORE'S

The gods changed me from a living creature to stone; but when I was stone, Praxiteles made me live again.

18

ΣΊΜΩΝΊΔΟΥ.

Δῆμος ’Αθηναίων σὲ Νεοπτόλεμ’ εἰκόνι τῆδε
Τίμησ’ εὐνοίης εὐσεβίης θ’ ἕνεκα.

T. MORI, IN STATVAM NEOPTOLEMI.

Cecropis urbs te tota Neoptoleme hac statua ornat.
Vt faciat, faciunt hinc amor, hinc pietas.

G. LILII.

Hoc te donarat propter pietatem et amorem,
Signo Cecropidum turba Neoptoleme.

FINIS PROGYMNASMATON THOMAE MORI,
ET GVILIELMI LILII SODALIVM. [b$_4$v]

18/5 ornat.] *1518*, ornat, *1520*

18

THOMAS MORE'S, ON A STATUE OF NEOPTOLEMUS

The entire city of Cecrops honors you, Neoptolemus, with this statue. It is in part your devotion and in part your loyalty which cause the city to do you this honor.

WILLIAM LILY'S

The people of Athens, Neoptolemus, have honored you with this statue because of your devotion and loyalty.

END OF THE PREPARATORY EXERCISES
WRITTEN IN FRIENDLY COLLABORATION
BY THOMAS MORE AND WILLIAM LILY

EPIGRAMMATA
CLARISSIMI DISERTISSIMIQVE VIRI THOMAE MORI BRITANNI, PLERAQVE E GRAECIS VERSA.

VEREOR, illustrissime princeps, dum more uirginum, quae satis formae suae non fidunt, picturae lenocinio gratiam illepidis uersiculis comparare studeo, ne eos qua maxime dote placere potuissent, id est ipsius rei nouitate, fraudarim. Nam quum illico in praesentem coronationem tuam conscriptos eos pictori exornandos dedissem, effecit certe podagra, qua protinus quam opus inchoauit, incommodissime tentatus est, ut eos nunc tandem, serius aliquanto quam res postulare uidebatur, exhibeam. Itaque (si tecum pro insita humanitate tua liberius agi sinis) haud scio, maioremne gratiam uersiculis nostris pictoris manus adiecerint, an pedes ademerint. Quippe quibus effectum est, ut mihi uerendum sit, ne non minus sera, ac proinde intempestiua uideri tibi possit haec nostra gratulatio, quam [c_1] olim Tiberio principi uisa est, Iliensium illa consolatio, qua eum de morte filij, iamdiu defuncti, consolabantur, quam ille faceta dicacitate delusit, respondens se eorum quoque uicem dolere, quod bonum militem amisissent Hectorem: uerum eorum officium, ad luctum non senescentem modo, sed plane praemortuum, non potuit esse non ridiculum: meum uero ab hoc uitio uendicat immensa illa de celebri coronatione tua laetitia: quae quum pectoribus omnium tam efficacem sui uim ac praesentiam impresserit, ut senescere uel integra aetate non possit, effecit nimirum, ut hoc meum officium non sero re

---

1–4 EPIGRAMMATA . . . VERSA.] *1518 1520,* Thomas Morus Potentissimo Britanniae Galliaeque Regi Henrico VIII° foelicissimo. S. D. *L* 8 illico] ilico *1518*^{m} 9 praesentem] presentem *L* 9–10 conscriptos eos . . . dedissem] eos conscriptos pictori exornandos tradidissem *L* 10 protinus] *L 1518,* proinus *1520* 13–14 maioremne] *L 1518,* maiorem̃ ne *1520* 17 haec] hec *L* principi] Caesari *L* 22 praemortuum] premortuum *L* 24 laetitia] letitia *L* 25 ac] atque *L;* praesentiam] presentiam *L*

EPIGRAMS
OF THE VERY FAMOUS AND LEARNED ENGLISHMAN THOMAS MORE IN LARGE PART TRANSLATED FROM THE GREEK

I FEAR, most glorious prince, that while I was trying to win favor for my awkward verses by the addition of color (like maidens who have insufficient confidence in their beauty), I may have robbed them of that characteristic by which they could have given you the greatest pleasure—I mean timeliness. For when I had finished writing them at the time of your coronation and had handed them over to an illuminator for decoration, an attack of the gout, no less, by which the illuminator was most inopportunely afflicted immediately upon undertaking the task, has caused me to present my verses to you only now, considerably later than the circumstances seemed to require. And so (if, in accord with your inherent kindness, you give me leave to deal informally with the matter) I do not know whether greater charm was given to my verses by the illuminator's hands or taken from them by his feet. In any case it is because of his feet that I am constrained to fear that my expression of joy may seem to you no less late, no less untimely, than, in antiquity, the famous expression of sorrow by the citizens of Troy seemed to the Emperor Tiberius. The Trojans commiserated with the Emperor on the loss of a son who had been dead for a long time. The Emperor with ready wit made fun of their condolences by saying that he too sympathized with them in their loss of that noble warrior Hector. But their effort, directed at a grief that was not merely fading but had wholly passed away, could not be anything but ridiculous. Mine, however, is preserved from this defect by the immeasurable rejoicing occasioned by your thronged coronation; for since that joy has filled the hearts of all with an emotion so strong and lasting that it cannot fade even in a whole lifetime, the result is that this offering of mine seems to have arrived, not late and when the event was past and

peracta atque euanida, sed praesens in rem praesentem peruenisse uideatur. Vale princeps illustrissime, et (qui nouus ac rarus regum titulus est) amatissime.

27 praesens] presens *L*; praesentem] presentem *L* 28–29 Vale . . . amatissime] Vale Princeps optime Maximeque et (qui nouus idemque Honoratissimus Regum titulus est) Amatissime *L*

forgotten, but in time and while the event is still with us. Farewell, most glorious and (although this title is strange and rare for kings) most beloved prince.

19

IN SVSCEPTI DIADEMATIS DIEM HENRICI OCTAVI, ILLVSTRISSIMI AC FAVSTISSIMI BRITANNIARVM REGIS, AC CATHERINAE REGINAE EIVS FELICISSIMAE, THOMAE MORI LONDONIENSIS CARMEN GRATVLATORIVM.

SI qua dies unquam, si quod fuit Anglia tempus,
  Gratia quo superis esset agenda tibi,[c_1v]
Haec est illa dies niueo signanda lapillo,
  Laeta dies fastis annumeranda tuis.
Meta haec seruitij est, haec libertatis origo,
  Tristitiae finis, laetitiaeque caput.
Nam iuuenem secli decus O memorabile nostri
  Vngit, et in regem praeficit ista tuum.
Regem qui populi non unius usque, sed orbis
  Imperio dignus totius unus erat.
Regem qui cunctis lachrymas detergat ocellis,
  Gaudia pro longo substituat gemitu.
Omnia discussis arrident pectora curis,
  Vt solet excussa nube nitere dies.
Iam populus uultu liber praecurrit amoeno,
  Iam uix laetitiam concipit ipse suam.
Gaudet, ouat, gestit, tali sibi rege triumphat,
  Nec quicquam nisi rex quolibet ore sonat.
Nobilitas, uulgi iamdudum obnoxia faeci,
  Nobilitas, nimium nomen inane diu,
Nunc caput attollit, nunc tali rege triumphat,
  Et merito causas unde triumphet, habet.

19/1–7 IN SVSCEPTI . . . GRATVLATORIVM] in suscepti Diadematis diem Henrici Octaui Britanniarum Galliarumque Regis augustissimi faustissimi. Ac Catherinae Reginae eius foelicissimae Carmen gratulatorium Thomae Mori Londinensis *L* 8 tempus,] *1518*[m], tempus. *L 1518*[d] *1520* 9 agenda] habenda *L;* tibi,] tibi: *L,* tibi. *1518 1520* 10 Haec] Hec *L* 11 Laeta] Leta *L* 12 haec . . . haec] hec . . . hec *L* 13 Tristitiae] Tristitie *L;* laetitiaeque] letitiaeque *L* 14 secli] saecli *1518*[m]; nostri] nosti *L* 15 praeficit] preficit *L* 22 praecurrit] procurrit *L;* amoeno] ameno *L* 23 laetitiam] leticiam *L* 24 rege triumphat] principe plaudit *L* 26 faeci] *L,* feci *1518 1520 1563 1565*

19
ON THE CORONATION DAY OF HENRY VIII, MOST GLORIOUS AND BLESSED KING OF THE BRITISH ISLES, AND OF CATHERINE HIS MOST HAPPY QUEEN, A POETICAL EXPRESSION OF GOOD WISHES BY THOMAS MORE OF LONDON

IF EVER there was a day, England, if ever there was a time for you to give thanks to those above, this is that happy day, one to be marked with a pure white stone and put in your calendar. This day is the limit of our slavery, the beginning of our freedom, the end of sadness, the source of joy, for this day consecrates a young man who is the everlasting glory of our time and makes him your king—a king who is worthy not merely to govern a single people but singly to rule the whole world—such a king as will wipe the tears from every eye and put joy in the place of our long distress. Every heart smiles to see its cares dispelled, as the day shines bright when clouds are scattered. Now the people, freed, run before their king with bright faces. Their joy is almost beyond their own comprehension. They rejoice, they exult, they leap for joy and celebrate their having such a king. "The King" is all that any mouth can say.

The nobility, long since at the mercy of the dregs of the population, the nobility, whose title has too long been without meaning, now lifts its head, now rejoices in such a king, and has proper

Mercator uarijs deterritus ante tributis,
Nunc maris insuetas puppe resulcat aquas.
Leges inualidae prius, imo nocere coactae,
Nunc uires gaudent obtinuisse suas.
Congaudent omnes pariter pariterque rependunt
Omnes uenturo damna priora bono. [c2]
Iam quas abdiderat caecis timor ante latebris,
Promere quisque suas gaudet et audet opes.
Iam iuuat O, potuit tot furum si qua tot uncas
Tam circumspectas fallere praeda manus.
Non iam diuitias ullum est (magnum esse solebat)
Quaesitas nullo crimen habere dolo.
Non metus occultos insibilat aure susurros,
Nemo quod taceat, quodue susurret, habet.
Iam delatores uolupe est contemnere, nemo
Deferri, nisi qui detulit ante, timet.
Conueniunt igitur simul aetas, sexus, et ordo,
Causaque non ullum continet ulla domi,
Quo minus intersint, dum sacris rite peractis,
Rex init auspicijs regna Britanna bonis.
Quacunque ingreditur, studio conferta uidendi
Vix sinit angustam turba patere uiam.
Opplenturque domus, et pondere tecta laborant.
Tollitur affectu clamor ubique nouo,
Nec semel est uidisse satis, loca plurima mutant,
Si qua rursus eum parte uidere queant.
Ter spectare iuuat: quid ni hunc spectare iuuaret,
Quo natura nihil finxit amabilius?
Mille inter comites excelsior omnibus extat,
Et dignum augusto corpore robur habet.
Nec minus ille manu est agilis, quam pectore fortis,
Seu res districto debeat ense geri, [c2v]
Seu quum protentis auide concurritur hastis,
Seu petat oppositum missa sagitta locum.

19/32 imo] immo *L* 33 obtinuisse] optinuisse *L* 36 caecis] cecis *L* 39 praeda] preda *L* 41 Quaesitas] Quesitas *L* 43 quodue] quodque *L* 47 domi,] domi: *L*, domi. *1518 1520* 52 laborant.] *L*, laborant, *1518 1520* 56–58 *L has in margin* LAVS A CORPORIS DOTIBVS *This and the other marginal annotations to this poem may be in a later hand.* 61 geri,] geri. *L 1518 1520* 62 quum protentis] cum pretentis *L*

reason for rejoicing. The merchant, heretofore deterred by numerous taxes, now once again plows seas grown unfamiliar. Laws, heretofore powerless—yes, even laws put to unjust ends—now happily have regained their proper authority. All are equally happy. All weigh their earlier losses against the advantages to come. Now each man happily does not hesitate to show the possessions which in the past his fear kept hidden in dark seclusion. Now there is enjoyment in any profit which managed to escape the many sly clutching hands of the many thieves. No longer is it a criminal offense to own property which was honestly acquired (formerly it was a serious offense). No longer does fear hiss whispered secrets in one's ear, for no one has secrets either to keep or to whisper. Now it is a delight to ignore informers. Only ex-informers fear informers now.

The people gather together, every age, both sexes, and all ranks. There is no reason why they should lurk in their homes and not take part while the king, after completion of the proper ceremonies, undertakes, amid happy auspices, the rule of Britain. Wherever he goes, the dense crowd in their desire to look upon him leaves hardly a narrow lane for his passage. The houses are filled to overflowing, the rooftops strain to support the weight of spectators. On all sides there arises a shout of new good will. Nor are the people satisfied to see the king just once; they change their vantage points time and time again in the hope that, from one place or another, they may see him again. Three times they delight to see him—and why not? This king, than whom Nature has created nothing more deserving of love.

Among a thousand noble companions he stands out taller than any. And he has strength worthy of his regal person. His hand, too, is as skilled as his heart is brave, whether there is an issue to be settled by the naked sword, or an eager charge with leveled lances, or an arrow aimed to strike a target. There is fiery power in his

Ignea uis oculis, Venus insidet ore, genisque
  Est color, in geminis qui solet esse rosis.
Illa quidem facies alacri ueneranda uigore
  Esse potest tenerae uirginis, esse uiri.
Talis erat, Nympham quum se simulauit Achilles.
  Talis, ubi Aemonijs Hectora traxit equis.
O si animi praestans una cum corpore uirtus
  Cerni, natura non prohibente, queat.
Imo etiam uultu uirtus pellucet ab ipso,
  Est facies animi nuncia aperta boni,
Quam matura graui sedeat prudentia mente,
  Quam non solliciti pectoris alta quies,
Quoque modo sortem ferat, et moderetur utranque,
  Quanta uerecundae cura pudicitiae.
Quam tranquilla fouet placidum clementia pectus,
  Quam procul ex illo fastus abest animo,
Principis egregius nostri (quas fingere non est)
  Prae se fert certas uultus et ipse notas.
At qua iustitia est, regnandi quas habet artes,
  Prosequitur populum qua pietate suum,
Haec facile ex uultu fiunt illustria nostro,
  Haec sunt ex nostris conspicienda bonis.
Quod sic afficimur, quod libertate potimur,
  Quodque abiere timor, damna, pericla, dolor, [c3]
Quod rediere simul, pax, commoda, gaudia, risus,
  Eximij uirtus principis inde patet.
Eneruare bonas immensa licentia mentes
  Idque etiam in magnis assolet ingenijs.
At quamuis erat ante pius, mores tamen illi
  Imperium dignos attulit imperio.
Nam bona quae pauci sera fecere senecta,
  Protinus in primo praestitit ille die.

19/68 simulauit] simularet *L* 70 praestans] prestans *L* 70–73 *L has in margin* LAVS AB ANIMI VIRTVTIBVS 72 Imo] Immo *L* 73 boni,] boni *L*, boni. *1518 1520* 77 pudicitiae.] pudicitie: *L*, pudicitiae, *1518 1520* 80 egregius] aegregius *L* 81 Prae] Pre *L* 85 Haec] Hec *L* 87 pericla,] *L 1518*, pericla *1520* 90 mentes] mentes. *L*, mentes, *1518 1520* 94 senecta,] *1518*, senecta: *L*, senecta. *1520* 94–98 *L has in margin* LAVS A REBVS GESTIS 95 praestitit] prestitit *L*; die.] *L 1518*, die, *1520*

eyes, beauty in his face, and such color in his cheeks as is typical of twin roses. In fact, that face, admirable for its animated strength, could belong to either a young girl or a man. Thus Achilles looked when he pretended to be a maiden, thus he looked when he dragged Hector behind his Thessalian steeds.

Ah, if only nature would permit that, like his body, the outstanding excellence of his mind be visible to the eye. Nay but in fact his virtue does shine forth from his very face; his countenance bears the open message of a good heart, revealing how ripe the wisdom that dwells in his judicious mind, how profound the calm of his untroubled breast, how he bears his lot and manages it whether it be good or bad, how great his care for modest chastity. How serene the clemency that warms his gentle heart, how far removed from arrogance his mind, of these the noble countenance of our prince itself displays the indubitable signs, signs that admit no counterfeit. But his justice, the skill he has in the art of ruling, his sense of responsibility in the treatment of his people—these can easily be discerned from our faces, these must be perceived from the prosperity we enjoy. In that we are treated thus and are gaining our liberty, in that fear, harm, danger, grief have vanished, while peace, ease, joy, and laughter have returned—therein is revealed the excellence of our distinguished prince.

Unlimited power has a tendency to weaken good minds, and that even in the case of very gifted men. But howsoever dutiful he was before, his crown has brought our prince a character which deserves to rule, for he has provided promptly on his first day such advantages as few rulers have granted in extreme old age.

Illico correptos inclusit carcere, quisquis
  Consilio regnum laeserat ante malo.
Qui delator erat, uinclis constringitur arctis,
  Vt mala quae multis fecerat, ipse ferat.
Ad mercaturas aperit mare: si quod ab illis
  Durius exactum est ante, remisit onus.
Despectusque diu magnatum nobilis ordo,
  Obtinuit primo pristina iura die.
Ille magistratus et munera publica, uendi
  Quae sueuere malis, donat habenda bonis.
Et uersis rerum uicibus feliciter, ante
  Quae tulit indoctus praemia, doctus habet.
Legibus antiquam (nam uersae euertere regnum
  Debuerant) subito uimque decusque dedit.
Omnis cumque prius prorsus descisceret ordo,
  Protinus est omnis redditus ordo sibi.
Quid quod in his etiam uoluit rescindere quaedam,
  Vt populo possit commodus esse suo, [c3v]
Quae tamen ante suo nouit placuisse parenti?
  Sic patriam, ut decuit, praetulit ille patri.
Nec miror: quid enim non principe fiat ab illo,
  Cui cultum ingenuis artibus ingenium est,
Castalio quem fonte nouem lauere sorores,
  Imbuit et monitis Philosophia suis?
Nominibus populus multis obnoxius omnis
  Regi erat: hoc unum pertimuitque malum.
At rex, hinc metui quum posset, posset et inde
  Congerere immensas, si uoluisset, opes,
Omnibus ignouit: securos reddidit omnes,
  Sollicitique malum substulit omne metus.
Ergo alios populi reges timuere, sed istum,
  Per quem nunc nihil est quod timeatur, amant.

19/100 mercaturas] mercatores *L 1518*   103 obtinuit] optinuit *L*   106 feliciter] foeliciter *L*   107 Quae] Que *L*   111 sibi.] *L 1518*, sibi, *1520*   112 his] ijs *L*   113 suo,] suo? *L*, suo. *1518 1520*   115 praetulit] pretulit *L*   116–118 *L has in margin* LAVS A LITTERIS   117 est,] est? *L 1518 1520*   119 suis?] *L*, suis. *1518 1520*   120–124 *L has in margin* RES GESTAS PERSEQVITVR   123 opes,] opes: *L*, opes. *1518 1520*   124 omnes,] omnes. *L 1518 1520*

He has instantly arrested and imprisoned anyone who by plots had harmed the realm. Whoever was an informer is closely fettered and confined, so that he himself suffers the woes which he imposed on many. Our prince opened the sea for trade. If any overharsh duties were required of the merchants, he lightened their load. And the long-scorned nobility recovered on our prince's first day the ancient rights of nobles. He now gives to good men the honors and public offices which used to be sold to evil men. By a happy reversal of circumstances, learned men now have the prerogatives which ignoramuses carried off in the past. Our prince without delay has restored to the laws their ancient force and dignity (for they had been perverted so as to subvert the realm). And although formerly each rank in the state was changing character completely, now at once every rank is restored. What if, in the hope of being kind to his people, he decided to retract certain provisions of the law which he knew his father had approved? In this he placed, as he should, his country before his father. This preference does not surprise me; what could lie beyond the powers of a prince whose natural gifts have been enhanced by a liberal education, a prince bathed by the nine sisters in the Castalian fount and steeped in philosophy's own precepts? The whole people used to be, on many counts, in debt to the king, and this in particular was the evil they feared. But our king, though he could have inspired fear in this way and could have gathered from this source immense riches, if he had wished to do so, has forgiven the debts of all, and rendered all secure, removing all the evil of distressing fear. Hence it is that, while other kings have been feared by their subjects, this king is loved, since now through his action they have no cause for fear.

LAUS A LITTERIS

Hec miror: quid enim non principe fiat ab illo
Cuj cultum ingenuis artibus ingenium est?
Castalio quem fonte nouem lauere sorores.
Imbuit et monitis philosophia suis.

RES GESTAS PERSEQUUTUR

Nobilibus populus multis obnoxius omnis
Regi erat. hoc unum pertimuitq: malum.
At rex, hunc metuj, quum posset, posset et inde,
Congerere immensas si voluisset opes:
Omnibus ignouit. securos reddidit omnes.
Sollicitiq: malum sustulit omne metus.
Ergo alios populi reges timuere, sed istum
Per quem nunc nihil est: quod timeatur: amat.
Hostibus o princeps multum metuende superbis.

From the presentation manuscript of nos. 19–23 made for Henry VIII

Spectet, sine omen, non potuit melius.
Principibus nostris uberrima tempora spōdet:
& Phoebus radiis & Iouis uxor aquis.

The Tudor Rose, in the presentation manuscript made for Henry VIII

Hostibus O princeps multum metuende superbis.
O populo princeps non metuende tuo.
Illi te metuunt: nos te ueneramur, amamus.
Illis, noster erit, cur metuaris, amor.
Sic te securum, demptoque satellite tutum,
Vndique praestabunt, hinc amor, inde timor.
Extera bella quidem, coeat si Gallia Scotis,
Sit tantum concors Anglia, nemo timet.
At procul intestina aberunt certamina: nam quae
Semina, quas causas unde oriantur, habent?
Primum equidem de iure tuae tituloque coronae
Quaestio iam non est ulla, nec esse potest. [c4]
Quae certare solet iam tu pars utraque solus,
Nobilis hanc litem soluit uterque parens.
Ast magis abs te etiam est populi procul ira, tumultus
Impia ciuilis quae solet esse caput.
Ciuibus ipse tuis tam charus es omnibus unus,
Vt nemo possit charior esse sibi.
Quod si forte duces committeret ira potentes,
Soluetur nutu protinus illa tuo.
Tanta tibi est maiestatis reuerentia sacrae,
Virtutes merito quam peperere tuae.
Quae tibi sunt, fuerant patrum quaecunque tuorum.
Secula prisca quibus nil habuere prius.
Est tibi namque tui princeps prudentia patris.
Estque tibi matris dextra benigna tuae.
Est tibi mens auiae, mens relligiosa paternae.
Est tibi materni nobile pectus aui.
Quid mirum ergo, nouo si gaudeat Anglia more,
Cum qualis nunquam rexerat ante, regat?
Quid quod laeticia haec, quae uisa est non potuisse
Crescere, coniugio creuit adaucta tuo?
Coniugio, superi quod decreuere benigni,
Quo tibi, quoque tuis consuluere bene.

19/132 tutum,] *1518*, tutum. *L 1520* 133 praestabunt] prestabunt *L* 136 nam quae] Namquae *L*, namque *1518* 139 Quaestio] Questio *L* 140 Quae] Que *L* 142 Ast] At *L* 150 Quae] Que *L*; quaecunque] quecunque *L* 152 namque] *1518*, nāq: *L*, nanque *1520* 154 relligiosa] religiosa *1518*; paternae.] paterna; *1565* 157 Cum] Quum *L* 158 laeticia haec,] *1518*, letitia hec *L*, laeticia haec *1520* 158–61 *L has in margin* LAVS REGINAE

O prince, terror to your proud enemies but not to your own people, it is your enemies who fear you; we revere and love you. Our love for you will prove the reason for their fear. And thus it is that, in the absence of sycophants, your subjects' love and your enemies' fear will hedge you round in peace and safety. As for wars beyond the borders—if the French, for instance, join with the Scots—no one is afraid, provided that England is not divided. And internal strife there will not be, for what cause, what reason, is there to provoke it? Most important, concerning your right and title to the crown, there is no opposition, nor can there be. You, all by yourself, represent both sides of the quarrel which usually arises; the fact that both your parents were high-born disposes of this problem. And anyway the anger of the people, a wicked thing, common source of civil disturbance, is even more remote from you. To all your subjects you are so dear that no man could be dearer to himself. But if perchance wrath were to bring powerful chieftains to war, your nod will promptly put an end to that wrath, such reverence for your sacred majesty have your virtues justly created. And whatever virtues your ancestors had, these are yours too, not excelled in ages past. For you, sire, have your father's wisdom, you have your mother's kindly strength, the devout intelligence of your paternal grandmother, the noble heart of your mother's father. What wonder, then, if England rejoices in a fashion heretofore unknown, since she has such a king as she never had before?

And then there is the fact that this joy, apparently as great as it could be, was increased by your marriage—a marriage which the kindly powers above arranged and in which they planned well for

Illa tibi coniunx, laetus communia tecum
Quam uidit populus sceptra tenere tuus,
Cuius habent tantam coelestia numina curam,
Vt thalamis ornent, nobilitentque tuis. [c_4v]
Illa est, quae priscas uincat pietate Sabinas,
Maiestate sacras uicerit hemitheas.
Illa uel Alcestes castos aequarit amores,
Vel prompto superet consilio Tanaquil.
Illo ore, hoc uultu, forma est spectabilis illa,
Quae talem ac tantam sola decere potest.
Eloquio facunda cui Cornelia cedat,
Inque maritali Penelopeia fide.
Illa tibi princeps multos deuota per annos,
Sola tui longa mansit amore mora.
Non illam germana soror, nec patria flexit,
Non potuit mater, non reuocare pater.
Vnum te matri, te praetulit illa sorori.
Te patriae, et charo praetulit illa patri.
Illa tibi felix populos, hinc inde potentes
Non dissoluenda iunxit amicitia.
Regibus orta quidem magnis, nihiloque minorum est
Regum, quam quibus est orta, futura parens.
Hactenus una tui nauem tenet ancora regni,
Vna, sat illa quidem firma, sed una tamen.
At regina tibi sexu foecunda uirili
Vndique firmatam perpetuamque dabit.
Proueniunt illi magna ex te commoda, rursus
Ex illa ueniunt commoda magna tibi.
Non alia ulla fuit certe te digna marito.
Illa non alius coniuge dignus erat. [d_1]
Anglia thura feras, sacrumque potentius omni
Thure, bonas mentes innocuasque manus,

19/162 laetus] letus *L;* communia] comunia *L* 164 coelestia] caelestia *1518*^{m} 166 quae] que *L;* pietate] grauitate *L;* Sabinas,] Sabinas. *L 1518 1520* 167 hemitheas.] Heroidas. *L,* heroidas. *1518,* hemitheas *1520* 168 Alcestes] Alcestae *L,* Acestes *1518 1520;* aequarit] equarit *L* 172 facunda] *L,* foecunda *1518 1520 1563,* faecunda *1565* 176 nec] non *L* 179 praetulit] pretulit *L* 180 felix] foelix *L;* hinc inde] hinc et inde *1518* 186 tibi] breuj *L* 190 certe] certae *L* 193 manus,] manus. *L 1518 1520*

you and yours. In her you have as wife one whom your people have been happy to see sharing your power, one for whom the powers above care so much that they distinguish her and honor her by marriage with you. She it is who could vanquish the ancient Sabine women in devotion, and in dignity the holy, half-divine heroines of Greece. She could equal the unselfish love of Alcestis or, in her unfailing judgment, outdo Tanaquil. In her expression, in her countenance, there is a remarkable beauty uniquely appropriate for one so great and good. The well-spoken Cornelia would yield to her in eloquence; she is like Penelope in loyalty to a husband. This lady, prince, vowed to you for many years, through a long time of waiting remained alone for love of you. Neither her own sister nor her native land could win her from her way; neither her mother nor her father could dissuade her. It was you, none other, whom she preferred to her mother, sister, native land, and beloved father. This blessed lady has joined in lasting alliance two nations, each of them powerful. She is descended from great kings, to be sure; and she will be the mother of kings as great as her ancestors. Until now one anchor has protected your ship of state—a strong one, yet only one. But your queen, fruitful in male offspring, will render it on all sides stable and everlasting. Great advantage is yours because of her, and similarly is hers because of you. There has been no other woman, surely, worthy to have you as husband, nor any other man worthy to have her as wife.

England! bring incense, and an offering more potent than all incense—loyal hearts and innocent hands, that heaven, as it has

Connubium ut superi hoc, sicut fecere, secundent,
Vt data coelesti sceptra regantur ope,
Vtque ipsis gestata diu haec diademata, tandem
Et natus nati gestet, et inde nepos.

20

EIVSDEM, IN SVBITVM IMBREM, QVI IN POMPA REGIS AC REGINAE LARGE OBORTVS, NEC SOLEM ABSTVLIT, NEC DVRAVIT.

Dum peterent sacras rex et regina coronas,
Pompa qua nunquam pulchrior ulla fuit,
Aureus explicuit late se Phoebus, eratque
Leta dies populi consona pectoribus.
Ast ubi iam mediam celebris peruenit in urbem,
Tota statim aethereis pompa rigatur aquis.
Nulla tamen Phoebi subduxit lumina nubes,
Et minima nimbus perstetit ille mora.
Res bene contra aestus cecidit, rem siue quis ipsam
Spectet, siue omen, non potuit melius.
Principibus nostris uberrima tempora spondent,
Et Phoebus radijs, et Iouis uxor aquis.

21

EIVSDEM AD REGEM.

Cuncta Plato cecinit tempus quae proferat ullum
Saepe fuisse olim, saepe aliquando fore. [d_1v]
Ver fugit ut celeri, celerique reuertitur anno,
Bruma pari ut spacio quae fuit ante, redit,

19/194 sicut] *L,* sicuti *1518 1520* 195 Vt] *L 1518,* Et *1520;* coelesti] caelesti *1518*^{m}; ope,] ope. *L 1518 1520* 196 haec] hec *L* 197 natus nati] gnatus gnati *L* **20**/1 IMBREM,] *1518,* IMBREM. 1520 2 LARGE] largiter *L* 5 coronas,] *1518,* coronas: *L,* coronas. *1520* 6 fuit,] fuit: *L,* fuit. *1518 1520* 8 Leta] Laeta *1518* 9 Ast] *L 1520* (*errata*), At *1518 1520* 11 Phoebi] *L 1518,* phoebi *1520* 12 perstetit] perstitit *1563* 13 aestus] estus *L* 15 spondent,] *1518,* spondent: *L,* spondent. *1520* **21**/1 EIVSDEM AD REGEM] Eiusdem ad Regem De aureo seclo per eum redeunte Epigramma *L* 2 quae] que *L;* ullum] ullum: *L,* ullum. *1518 1520* 5 spacio] spatio *L;* quae] que *L;* redit,] redit: *L,* redit. *1518 1520*

made this marriage, may bless it, that the scepter may be swayed with the help of heaven that gave it, and that these crowns may long be worn by these two, and may at length be worn by their son's son and their descendants thereafter.

20

ON A SUDDEN RAIN-STORM WHICH FORMED DURING THE ROYAL PROCESSION BUT NEITHER OBSCURED THE SUN NOR LASTED LONG BY THOMAS MORE

While the king and queen, in as beautiful a procession as there ever was, made their way to receive their sacred crowns, a golden sun shone all around, and the day, like the hearts of the people, was cheerful. But as soon as the great procession reached midtown, the whole procession was drenched with rain. No cloud, however, obscured the sun's light, and the storm itself lingered only a very short time. It was a lucky relief from the heat; whether one regards the phenomenon itself, or the omen, it could not have been better. To our rulers, days of abundance are promised by Phoebus with his sunshine and by Jove's wife with her rains.

21

TO THE KING, BY THOMAS MORE

Plato foretold that everything which any particular time can produce had often existed and would often exist again sometime in the future. "As spring is banished and returns with the swift passage of the year, as winter at regular intervals returns as it was

Sic inquit rapidi post longa uolumina coeli
  Cuncta per innumeras sunt reditura uices.
Aurea prima sata est aetas, argentea post hanc.
  Aerea post illam, ferrea nuper erat.
Aurea te princeps redierunt principe secla.
  O possit uates hactenus esse Plato.

22

EIVSDEM AD REGEM DE SPECTACVLIS EQVESTRIBVS PER EVM EDITIS EPODON IAMBICVM.

Quaecunque reges ediderunt hactenus
  Equestrium spectacula,
Lugubris illa semper aliqua reddidit
  Vel calamitas insignia,
Vel casus aliquis prospero parum Ioue
  Admixtus inter ludicra,
Aut tabido transuerberati militis
  Madens harena sanguine,
Aut lanceis icta ungulisue sonipedum
  Obtrita plebs ferocium,
Turbamue comprimens simul miserrimam
  Lapsae ruina machinae.
Verum tua haec spectacula O rex omnium
  Quae uidimus pulcherrima,
Non ulla clades, sed tua digna indole [d$_2$]
  Insignit innocentia.

21/6 rapidi] *L 1518,* rapidi, *1520;* coeli] celi *L,* caeli *1518*^{m} 9 Aerea] Aenea *L* 10 secla] saecla *1518* 11 Plato.] *L 1518,* Plato *1520* **22**/1 REGEM] *L 1518,* REGFM *1520* 2 EDITIS] *L,* AEDITIS *1518,* AFDITIS *1520* 3 EPODON IAMBICVM] Epigramma Iambico Carmine *L* 4 ediderunt] *L,* aediderunt *1518 1520;* hactenus] *L 1518,* hactenus. *1520* 7 Vel] *om. L 1518;* insignia,] insignia. *L 1518 1520* 8–9 Vel casus . . . inter ludicra] *om. L 1518* 9 ludicra,] ludicra. *1520* 10 tabido] *L 1518,* rabido *1520* 11 sanguine,] sanguine. *L 1518 1520* 13 ferocium,] *1518,* ferocium. *L 1520* 14 comprimens] collidens *L;* miserrimam] *L 1518,* miserrimam. *1520* 16 haec] hec *L;* spectacula O rex] Princeps spectacula *L* 17 Quae] *L 1518,* Qnae *1520* 18 Non ulla] *L 1518,* Nonnulla *1520 1563;* indole] *1518,* indole: *L,* indole. *1520*

before, just so," he said, "after many revolutions of the speeding sky all things in countless alternations will be again." The golden age came first, then the silver; after that the bronze, and recently the iron age. In your reign, sire, the golden age has returned. Ah, that Plato should be able to foresee as far as this!

22

TO THE KING ON THE TOURNAMENT HELD BY HIM, AN IAMBIC EPODE BY THOMAS MORE

All the tournaments kings have held until now have been marked by some sad mishap or by disaster thrust among the festivities by ill luck. Sometimes the ground has been drenched with the life-blood of a stricken knight; sometimes commoners have been struck by lances or have been trampled by the pounding hoofs of the maddened steeds; sometimes a scaffolding has collapsed and crushed the wretched spectators. But this tournament of yours, sire, the most beautiful we have ever seen, is disfigured by no misfortune; rather it is conspicuous for such freedom from trouble as is appropriate to your character.

23

EIVSDEM DE VTRAQVE ROSA IN VNVM COALITA

Purpureae uicina fuit rosa candida, utranque
  Vtraque dum certant, sit prior utra, premit.
Vtraque sed florem rosa iam coalescit in unum,
  Quoque potest uno lis cadit illa modo.
Nunc rosa consurgit, nunc pullulat una, sed omneis
  Vna habet haec dotes, quas habuere duae.
Scilicet huic uni species, decor, atque uenustas,
  Et color, et uirtus, est utriusque rosae.
Alterutram ergo rosam uel solam quisquis amauit,
  Hanc in qua nunc est, quicquid amauit amet.
At qui tam ferus est, ut non amet, ille timebit.
  Nempe etiam spinas flos habet iste suas.

24

IN RHETOREM INDOCTVM. E GRAECO.

Quinque Soloecismis donaui Rhetora Flaccum,
  Quinque statim decies reddidit ille mihi.
Nunc numero hos, inquit, paucos contentus habeto.
  Mensura accipies quando redibo Cypro.

25

IN SVSPITIONEM E GRAECO.

Magnam habet in rebus uim ac pondus, opinio. Non uis
  Laedere: uelle tamen si uideare, peris.
Sic et Philoleon quondam occidere Crotone
  Quem falso credunt uelle tyrannum agere. [d$_2$v]

23/1–2 EIVSDEM . . . COALITA] Eiusdem De Rosa utraque in unum florem coalita Epigramma *L* 5 coalescit] coaleuit *L 1518* 7 consurgit, nunc pullulat] se pandit/nunc se explicat *L* 8 haec] hec *L* 9 species] speties *L;* decor, atque uenustas] odor, atque uoluptas *L* 11 amauit,] amauit: *L,* amauit. *1518 1520* 12 amet.] *1518,* amet/ *L,* amet *1520* 14 *after this poem* Τελος *appears in L* **24**/3 Flaccum] Flacchum *1518* **25**/3 Non] non *1518 1520;* uis] *1518,* uis, *1520* 4 Laedere:] Laedere, *1518 1520* 5 Philoleon] Philolaum *1518;* Crotone] Cretenses, *1518,* Crotone. *1520*

23

ON TWO ROSES WHICH BECAME ONE

BY THOMAS MORE

A white rose grew near a red one, and in their struggle to demonstrate superiority each crowded the other. But both roses are combined to become one flower, and the contest ends the only way it can. Now only one rosebush grows and buds, but this one has all the qualities of both. In other words, this one rose has the beauty, grace, loveliness, color, and strength which used to belong to both. Therefore, if anyone loved either one of these roses, let him love this one in which is found whatever he loved. But if anyone is so fierce that he will not love this rose, then he will fear it, for this flower has its own thorns, too.

24

ON AN IGNORANT RHETORICIAN

FROM THE GREEK

I presented the rhetorician Flaccus with five solecisms; promptly he repaid me with fifty. Said he, "Be content now to have these few, reckoned by number; you will receive them by the bushel when I get back from Cyprus."

25

ON SUSPICION

FROM THE GREEK

The impression one creates has great influence, great weight, in the affairs of men. You have no desire to do any harm; but, if you seem to have, you are done for. Thus in Crotona they killed Philolaus long ago in the mistaken belief that he wanted to play the tyrant.

26

IN RHETOREM INFANTEM SCITE PICTVM E GRAECO.

Ipse tacet Sextus, Sexti meditatur imago.
Ipsa est rhetor imago, ab imagine rhetor imago est.

27

IN CAECVM ET CLAVDVM MENDICOS.

Claudipedem gestat caecis uicinus ocellis,
Conducitque oculos arte, locatque pedes.

28

ALITER.

Caecus claudipedem gestat, prudenter uterque
Rem gerit, atque oculos hic locat, ille pedes.

29

ALITER.

Caecus fert claudum, atque opera conducit eadem,
Istius ille oculos, illius iste pedes.

30

ALITER

Claudum caecus onus graue, sed tamen utile uectat.
Prospicit atque oculis huic regit ille pedes.

31

IDEM FVSIVS.

Tristis erat nimium miseris fortuna duobus,
Huic oculos, illi dempsit iniqua pedes.
Sors illos coplat similis, claudum uehit alter.
Sic sua communi damna leuant opera.
Hic pedibus quouis alienis ambulat, itur
Huic recta alterius semita luminibus.

30/3 oculis] oculis, *1518 1520* **31**/2 fortuna] Fortuna *1518* 4 coplat] copulat *1518* 7 luminibus.] *1518*, luminibus, *1520*

26

ON A SKILFULLY MADE PICTURE OF A SPEECHLESS RHETORICIAN FROM THE GREEK

Sextus himself is silent; the picture of Sextus exercises his art. The picture itself is the rhetorician; by means of the picture the rhetorician has become a picture.

27

ON TWO BEGGARS, ONE LAME, ONE BLIND

A blind neighbor carries a lame man about; by a skilful combination he borrows eyes and lends feet.

28

ANOTHER VERSION

A blind man carries a lame man around. They manage the situation with skill; the latter lends his eyes, the former his feet.

29

ANOTHER VERSION

A blind man carries a lame man; and so, by a combined effort, one borrows eyes, the other feet.

30

ANOTHER VERSION

A blind man carries a lame man, a heavy but a useful load: he looks ahead and with his eyes he guides the other's feet.

31

THE SAME TOPIC AT GREATER LENGTH

Very sad misfortune overtook two unhappy men and cruelly deprived the one of his eyes, the other of his feet. Their common misery united them. The lame man rides upon the other. Thus by cooperation they mitigate each other's handicaps. The lame man goes anywhere with the help of the other's feet, the blind man travels a path determined by the other's eyes.

32

IDEM ALITER.

Vtilius nihil esse potest, quam fidus amicus,
  Qui tua damna suo leniat officio. [d3]
Foedera contraxere simul mendicus uterque
  Cum claudo solidae caecus amicitiae.
Claudo caecus ait, collo gestabere nostro.
  Retulit hic, oculis caece regere meis.
Alta superborum fugitat penetralia regum,
  Inque casa concors paupere regnat amor.

33

ALITER

Cum claudo caecus sic lege paciscitur aequa, ut
  Hic ferat illum humeris, hunc regat ille oculis.

34

PINVS NAVTICA LOQVITVR VENTO SVBVERSA E GRAECO.

Pinus ego uentis facile superabilis arbor,
  Stulte, quid undiuagam me facis ergo ratem?
An non augurium metuis? quum persequitur me
  In terra, Boreạm qui fugiam in pelago?

35

IDEM ALITER.

Ventis pinus humo sternor, quid mittor in undas?
  Iam nunc passa prius quam nato naufragium.

36

IN NAVIM EXVSTAM.

Iam ratis aequoreas oneraria fugerat undas.
  Matris at in terrae deperijt sinibus.

32/7 Retulit] Rettulit *1518*ᵐ; regere] regēre *1518*, regêre *1520* **33**/2 paciscitur] *1518 1520* (*errata*), pascitur *1520* **34**/5 Stulte,] Stulte *1518 1520* **35**/3 prius quam] prius quàm *1518*, prius, quàm *1520* **36**/3 Matris] *1518*, Matris, *1520*

32
ANOTHER VERSION OF THE SAME TOPIC

There can be nothing more helpful than a loyal friend, who by his own efforts assuages your hurts. Two beggars formed an alliance of firm friendship—a blind man and a lame one. The blind man said to the lame one, "You must ride upon my shoulders." The latter answered, "You, blind friend, must find your way by means of my eyes." The love which unites shuns the castles of proud kings and prevails in the humble hut.

33
ANOTHER VERSION

A blind man made with a lame man a mutually helpful arrangement by which the one carried his partner on his shoulders and the other by his own eyes directed his partner's feet.

34
A PINE TREE BLOWN DOWN BY THE WIND AND DESTINED FOR SERVICE AT SEA SPEAKS, FROM THE GREEK

I am a pine tree, easy victim of the winds. And so why, stupid man, are you making me into a ship to roam the seas? Aren't you afraid of the omen? If Boreas hunts me down on land, how will I escape him at sea?

35
ANOTHER VERSION OF THE SAME TOPIC

Why am I, a pine tree laid low by the winds, being sent to sea? I was shipwrecked before I was afloat.

36
ON A SHIP WHICH BURNED UP

A cargo ship had escaped the waves of the sea, but perished on the bosom of her mother, the land. She caught fire, and, as she

Corripitur flammis, atque ardens auxiliares
  Quas maris hostiles fugerat, optat aquas. [d3v]

37

CVNICVLA LOQVITVR QVAE ELAPSA MVSTELAE INCIDIT IN DISPOSITA VENATORVM RETIA.

Mustelam obliquo dilapsa foramine fugi.
  Sed feror humanos heu misera in laqueos.
Hic ego non uitam celerem, non impetro mortem.
  Seruor ut heu rapidis obijciar canibus.
Qui mea dum laniant scelerato uiscera morsu,
  Spectat, et effuso sanguine ridet homo.
O durum genus, atque fera truculentius omni,
  Nex cui crudelem praebet acerba iocum.

38

INNOCENTIAM OBNOXIAM ESSE INIVRIAE E GRAECO.

Ausus erit mordere malum uel mus, uetus hoc est
  Verbum, sed longe res habet ipsa secus.
Innocuos audet uel mus mordere, nocentem
  Tangere non audet territus ipse draco.

39

IN EFFLATVM VENTRIS E GRAECO.

Te crepitus perdit, nimium si uentre retentes.
  Te propere emissus seruat item crepitus.
Si crepitus seruare potest et perdere, nunquid
  Terrificis crepitus regibus aequa potest?

37/8 morsu,] *1518,* morsu. *1520* 10 omni,] *1518,* omni. *1520* **38**/5 nocentem] *1518,* nocentem, *1520* **39**/5 perdere, nunquid] *1518,* perdere. nunquid. *1520*

burned, she wished for help from that which she had escaped—the hostile waters of the sea.

37
COMMENTS OF A RABBIT WHICH, AFTER ELUDING A WEASEL, FELL INTO NETS SPREAD BY HUNTERS

The weasel I did escape by darting through an opening off to one side, but—alas for me, miserable creature—then I rushed into the hunting nets of men. Now I cannot save my life or win quick death. They are saving me, alas, only to throw me to the ravening hounds. Now, while the hounds tear my flesh to pieces with their wicked teeth, a man looks on and smiles at the bloodshed. Insensate breed, more savage than any beast, to find cruel amusement in bitter slaughter!

38
INNOCENCE INVITES INJURY
FROM THE GREEK

"Even a mouse will dare to bite an evil man," the old proverb says, but the fact of the matter is utterly different. It is the harmless folk whom even the mouse dares to bite. To touch a criminal even a serpent is afraid.

39
ON BREAKING WIND
FROM THE GREEK

A fart, if you keep it too long in your belly, kills you; on the other hand, it can save your life if it is promptly let out. If a fart can save or destroy you, then is it not as powerful as dreaded kings?

40
DE MORTIS AEQVALITATE
E GRAECO.

Victor ad Herculeas penetres, licet usque columnas,
  Te terrae cum alijs pars manet aequa tamen. [d_4]
Iro par moriere, obolo non ditior uno,
  Et tua te (sed non iam tua) soluet humus.

41
IN SORDIDVM
E GRAECO.

Te ditem appellant omnes, ego plane inopem te.
  Nam facit usus opes, testis Apollophanes.
Si tu utare tuis, tua fiunt. Sin tua serues,
  Haeredi, tua iam nunc aliena facis.

42
VENATVS ARANEAE.

Insidiata uagam comprehendit aranea muscam,
  Et lentis trepidam cassibus implicuit.
Iamque hiat in morsum, sed saepe os inter et offam,
  Vt uerbum uetus est, multa uenire solent.
Sors muscae miseretur, et aduersatur Arachnae,
  Inque malam e misera transtulit exitium.
En stimulante fame properans inuadis utranque,
  Sturne, ruunt casses, haec fugit, illa perit.
Sic misero spes est plerunque secure sub ipsa,
  Inter et armatos mille malo metus est.

43
IN CYNICVM STVLTE ABSTINENTEM
E GRAECO.

Barbati Cynici, baculoque uagantis egeni,
  In coena magnam conspicimus sophiam.

40/2 GRAECO] *1518*, GRACO *1520* **41**/5 Sin] sin *1518 1520* **42**/1 ARANEAE.] *1518*, ARANEAE, *1520* 2 comprehendit] comprhendit *1518* 4 offam,] *1518*, offam. *1520* 8 utranque,] utramque *1518*, utranque *1520* **43**/4 sophiam] *1518*, Sophiam *1520*

40
ON EQUALITY IN DEATH
FROM THE GREEK

Though you conquer the world even to the pillars of Hercules, still the amount of earth which ultimately will be yours is the same as any man's. You will die as Irus' equal, not a penny richer; and your land (yours no longer) will consume you.

41
ON A MEAN MAN
FROM THE GREEK

Everyone calls you rich; I say you are downright poor, for use makes wealth, Apollophanes, witness as you are. If you use what you have, it is yours; but if you save it for your heir, then you are even now giving it away.

42
THE HUNTING OF A SPIDER

A lurking spider caught a stray fly and entangled it, to its terror, in a sticky web. The spider's mouth was open for a bite; but, as the old proverb says, much can happen between the mouth and the morsel. Fate, taking pity on the fly and opposing the spider, allotted destruction not to the victim but to the aggressor. Now you, starling, in hungry haste attack both creatures. The web collapses, the fly escapes, the spider perishes. Thus for the wretch under the very blade of the axe there is often some hope, and for the evildoer, even among a thousand armed guards, there is reason to fear.

43
ON A CYNIC WHO PRACTICED RESTRAINT IN FOOLISH FASHION
FROM THE GREEK

At a dinner we observed the great wisdom of an unshaven Cynic who wandered about with his poor man's staff. Now this

Scilicet hic raphanis Cynicus primum atque lupino,
Ne uirtus uentri seruiat, abstinuit.
At niueum postquam bulbum conspexit ocellis
Iam rigidum et sapiens excutit ingenium [d_4v]
Flagitat atque auide spem praeter deuorat omnem.
Virtuti bulbus, nil ait officiet.

44

EPITAPHIVM MEDICI E GRAECO.

Thessalus Hippocrates, Cous genere, hac iacet urna
Phoebi immortalis semine progenitus.
Crebra trophaea tulit morborum armis medicinae,
Laus cui magna, nec id sorte, sed arte fuit.

45

IN SERVVM MORTVVM E GRAECO.

Hic seruus dum uixit, erat, nunc mortuus idem
Non quam tu Dari magne minora potest.

46

IN ANCILLAM MORTVAM.

Ante fuit solo Sosime corpore serua,
Nunc fato pars est haec quoque missa manu.

47

IN PISCATOREM ADAMATVM E GRAECO.

Pisces dum captat piscator, diuitis illum
Nata uidet, uisi flagrat amore uiri.
Deinde uiro nubit, sic illi ex paupere uita,
Magna superbarum copia uenit opum.
Muneris hoc nostri est Venus inquit. Verba retorquens
Fortuna haec nostri est muneris, inquit hera.

47/4 uiri.] *1518,* uiri *1520* 7–8 Muneris . . . hera.] Adstetit et ridens Fortuna ait, heu Venus haud iam | Mars erat iste tuus, Mars erat iste meus. | ALITER | Mars erat iste meus, Venus, inquit, uerba retorquens, | Illico Sors eadem, Mars erat iste meus. *1518* 7 inquit. Verba] inquit, uerba *1520*

Cynic began by refusing radishes and pulse, lest—he said—his virtue become his belly's slave. But when he had glimpsed a snow-white onion, he shed his character of unyielding wisdom, asked for it, and with unexpected relish gobbled it all up. "Onions," he said, "do virtue no harm."

44

PHYSICIAN'S EPITAPH

FROM THE GREEK

Hippocrates, of Coan descent, who lived in Thessaly and belonged to immortal Phoebus' line, reposes in this urn. Often he routed disease by the force of his healing art. Great glory was his, not because of his luck, but because of his skill.

45

ON A DEAD SLAVE

FROM THE GREEK

While he lived, this man was a slave. But now, in death, he wields no less power than you, mighty Darius.

46

ON A DEAD SERVING-WOMAN

Before Sosima was a slave only in body. Now even that part of her has been freed by death.

47

ON A BELOVED FISHERMAN

FROM THE GREEK

While a fisherman was catching fish, the daughter of a rich man saw him and fell violently in love with him. Then she was married to the man. Thus in place of a life of poverty he acquired great store of proud wealth. Venus said, "This is my doing." Mistress Fortune, throwing back these words, replied, "It is my doing."

48

IN REPENTE FELICEM E MISERO
E GRAECO.

Non tibi quod faueat, sic te fortuna leuauit.
Vel de te liqueat uult, sibi quid liceat. [e_1]

49

IN MEDIOCRITATEM
E GRAECO.

Inuidia est peior miseratio, Pindarus inquit.
Felici inuidiam splendida uita facit.
At nimium miseros miseramur. Dent superi ut sim,
Nec nimium felix, nec miserandus ego.
Scilicet extremis longe mediocria praestant.
Infima calcantur, summa repente ruunt.

50

NIHIL PRODESSE TORQVERI METV MALI VENTVRI
E GRAECO.

Cur patimur stulti, nanque haec uecordia nostra,
Vrat ut indomitus pectora nostra metus?
Seu mala non uenient, iam nos metus urit inanis.
Sin uenient, aliud fit metus ipse malum.

51

MONOSTICHVM E GRAECO IN LAVDEM
POEMATIS HOMERICI.

Ipse quidem cecini, scripsit diuinus Homerus.

52

IN RIDICVLVM IVDICIVM
E GRAECO.

Lis agitur, surdusque reus, surdus fuit actor.
Ipse tamen iudex surdus utroque magis.

48/3 fortuna] Fortuna *1518* 4 liqueat uult, sibi] liqueat, uult sibi, *1518 1520* **49**/5 miseramur . . . sim,] miseramur, Pindarus inquit. *1518*, miseramur, dent superi ut sim, *1520* 6 Nec nimium] Hei nimium *1518* **50**/3 stulti,] *1518*, stulti. *1520;* nanque] namque *1518*[d]; uecordia] uaecordia *1518* 4 Vrat] *1518*, Vrat, *1520;* metus?] metus. *1518 1520* **51**/1–2 MONOSTICHVM . . . HOMERICI] *om. 1518, which prints the monostich as line 7 of no. 50* 2 HOMERICI.] *1520*, homerici. e Graeco. *1563*

48

ON A MAN WHOSE FORTUNE CHANGED SUDDENLY FROM BAD TO GOOD

FROM THE GREEK

It is not because Fortune loves you that she has raised you so high. She merely wishes to demonstrate even in your case how great is her power.

49

ON AVOIDING EXTREMES

FROM THE GREEK

Pity is worse than envy, Pindar says. The successful man's luxurious life causes envy, but we pity those who are exceedingly unfortunate. May the powers above grant that I be neither too successful nor an object of pity. Obviously, the life that lies between is far preferable to either of the extremes. What is at the bottom is trodden upon; what is at the top, falls suddenly.

50

THAT THERE IS NO POINT IN WORRYING ABOUT FUTURE TROUBLES

FROM THE GREEK

Fools that we are, why do we permit—our folly lies in permitting—fear unmastered to sear our hearts? Either the trouble is not going to come, in which case we suffer now from needless fear, or if it is going to come, we are making fear itself a further trouble.

51

ONE LINE IN PRAISE OF HOMER'S POEM

FROM THE GREEK

It was I who composed the poem, but divine Homer wrote it out.

52

ON A COMICAL TRIAL

FROM THE GREEK

A case was being tried. The defendant was deaf, the plaintiff was deaf, and the judge himself was deafer than either. The

Pro aedibus hic petit aes, quinto iam mense peracto.
Ille refert, tota nocte mihi acta mola est.
Aspicit hos iudex, et quid contenditis, inquit.
An non utrique est mater? utrique alite.

53
AD LVCERNAM NOCTVRNAM.

Lychne, reuersuram ter te iurauit amica.
Nec redit, O poenas det tibi, si deus es. [e_1v]
Ludenti cum nocte places extinguere, et aufer
Tam sacra tam sacris lumina luminibus.

54
LAIS ANVS AD SPECVLVM E GRAECO.

Nequiter arrisi tibi, quae modo, Graecia, amantum
Turbam in uestibulis Lais habens iuuenum,
Hoc Veneri speculum dico, nam me cernere talem
Qualis sum nolo, qualis eram nequeo.

55
IN MORTIS DIEM OMNIBVS INCERTVM.

Non ego quos rapuit mors, defleo. Defleo uiuos,
Quos urunt longo fata futura metu.

56
ALIVD.

Fleres, si scires unum tua tempora mensem.
Rides, quum non sit forsitan una dies.

57
IN APVM INDVSTRIAM E GRAECO.

Mellis apes fluuios ipsae sibi in aethere fingunt.
Ipsae quos habitant aedificant thalamos.

52/8 mater? . . . alite.] *1518,* mater, . . . alite? *1520* **53**/2 Lychne,] Lychne *1518 1520* 3 Nec] Haec *1518* **54**/3 modo, Graecia, amantum] modo gratia, amantum *1518,* modo Graecia amantum, *1520,* modo gratia? amantum *1563* **55**/1 INCERTVM.] *1518,* INCERTVM, *1520* 2 Defleo] defleo *1518 1520;* uiuos,] *1518,* uiuos. *1520* **56**/1 ALIVD] *om. 1518, which prints nos. 55 and 56 as one* **57**/3 ipsae] *1518;* ipse *1520*

plaintiff demanded five months' rent for a house. The defendant replied, "My mill was running all night." The judge looked up at them and said, "What is your quarrel? She is the mother of both of you, isn't she? Both of you, support her."

53
TO A LAMP BURNING AT NIGHT

Thrice my mistress swore by you, lamp, that she would return. She has not come. Mete out your punishment, if you are a god. Some night when she finds you pleasant for her dalliance, go out and deprive her cursed eyes of your blessed light.

54
LAIS, AS AN OLD WOMAN, AT HER MIRROR
FROM THE GREEK

I am Lais, who not long ago laughed wantonly at you, Greece, when I had at my doors a throng of youthful lovers. But now I dedicate to Venus this mirror, for the woman I am I do not wish to see, the woman I was I cannot.

55
ON THE DAY OF DEATH, UNKNOWN TO ALL MEN

The dead I do not mourn; I mourn the living, vexed by the lasting fear of death still to come.

56
ANOTHER VERSION

You would be weeping if you knew you had one month to live; you laugh, although you may not have a day.

57
ON THE DILIGENCE OF BEES
FROM THE GREEK

The bees themselves make their own streams of honey in the air, make the chambers where they dwell. The bee is generous to

Grata apis humanae frugesque facillima uitae est.
  Non bouis aut curuae falcis egebit ope.
Tantum opus hic situla est, ubi dulcia pocula mellis
  Vbertim paruo fundat ab alueolo.
Congaudete sacrae, uarios et pascite flores,
  Aetherei uolucres nectaris artifices.

58

IN ANVM FVCIS FRVSTRA VTENTEM.

Saepe caput tinguis, nunquam tinctura senectam,
  Aut tensura genis quae tibi ruga tuis.
Desine iam faciem stibio perfundere totam, [e$_2$]
  Ne persona tibi haec sit modo, non facies.
Quum nihil assequeris fuco stibioque, quid amens
  Vis tibi? nunquam Hecuben haec facient, Helenen.

59

IN HOMINIS NATIVITATEM E GRAECO.

Heus homo si memor es, quid te dum gigneret, egit
  Tum pater, ex anino iam tumor ille cadet,
At Plato te fastu dum somniat inflat inani,
  Aeternumque uocat semen et aethereum.
Factus es ecce luto, quid suspicis alta? sed istud
  Plasmate qui te ornat nobiliore feret.
Quin si uera uoles, audire, libidine foeda
  Natus es e coitu, guttula et e misera.

60

DE ASTROLOGO RIDICVLO.

Non Cumaea sacro uates correpta furore,
  Certius afflata mente futura uidet,
Quam meus astrologus diuina clarus in arte
  Praeuidet inspecto sydere praeterita.

57/5 humanae] *1518*, humanae, *1520* 6 bouis] *1518*, bouis, *1520* **58**/3 genis] *1518*, genis, *1520* 6 Quum] *1518*, Quin *1520* 7 Helenen.] *1518*, Helenen, *1520* **59**/5 fastu] factum *1518;* somniat] somniat, *1518 1520* 6 aethereum.] *1518*, aethereum *1520* 8 Plasmate qui te ornat] Plasmate, qui te ornat, *1518 1520* **60**/3 uidet,] uidet. *1518 1520*

men, and its fruit is most accessible to the life of men. There is no need for the help of ox or hooked reaping knife. All that is needed here is a jar into which it pours generously sweet cups of honey from its little vessel. Holy creatures, go your way happily; feed upon the variegated flowers, you winged makers of ethereal nectar.

58
ON AN OLD WOMAN WHO USES DYE IN VAIN

You keep dyeing your hair, but you will never dye old age or smooth the wrinkles of your cheeks. Now stop sprinkling your whole face with powder, lest you end up with a mask, not a face. Since you will get nowhere with paint and powder, madwoman, what are you about? These devices will never make a Helen of a Hecuba.

59
ON THE BIRTH OF MEN FROM THE GREEK

Look here, mortal, if you recall what your father did in engendering you, then pride will vanish from your spirit. Plato, on the other hand, in his dream, puffs you up with vain pride and says your seed is everlasting and celestial. Observe, you are fashioned of mire. What reason have you for high aspirations? But that is what one will say who decks you out in a lofty fiction. Rather, if you want to hear the truth, you were born of coition amid shameful lust and of a pitiful droplet.

60
ON A FOOLISH ASTROLOGER

The prophetess of Cumae in the grip of her sacred frenzy does not with her inspired vision see more clearly the events to come than my astrologer, famous in the art of soothsaying, foresees, after a look at the stars, the events of the past.

61

ALIVD IN ASTROLOGVM VXORIS IMPVDICAE MARITVM.

Astra tibi aethereo pandunt sese omnia uati,
  Omnibus et quae sint fata futura, monent.
Omnibus ast uxor quod se tua publicat, id te
  Astra, licet uideant omnia, nulla monent.

62

IN EVNDEM IAMBICVM.

O chare nobis syderum coelestium
Inspector astris, ipse nunc Phoebus tibi
Optem libenter indicare clanculum [e$_2$v]
Quiddam, quod ad te pertinens quam maxime,
Dum cuncta lustro, deprehendi pridie
Quam tu redires nuper ex Aula domum.
Sed territat Venus, minatur et mihi
Secundum amorem, qui nihilo secundior
Mihi sit futurus, quam fuit Daphnes prior,
Quicquam cuiuis garrulus si deferam
De se marito, quale detuli prius.
Nescibis ergo hoc, caeteras rerum uices
Docebo te. Nuptae sed in rebus tuae
Si quid tua non cedat ex sententia,
Hoc omnibus prius patebit, quam tibi.

63

ALIVD IN EVNDEM.

Quid inter alta stulte quaeris sydera
In humo manentis coniugis mores tuae?
Quid alta spectas? infra id est cui tu times.
Dum iam tu, agat quid illa, quaeris in polo,
Haec quae libebat, interim egit in solo.

61/4 Omnibus] *1518,* Omnibus, *1520* **62**/2 coelestium] caelestium *1518*^{m} 4 clanculum] *1518,* clanculum. *1520* 6 pridie] pridie. *1518 1520* 7 Quam . . . domum.] *om. 1518* 14 Nuptae] nuptae *1518;* nuptae, *1520;* tuae] *1518,* tuae. *1520* **63**/4 spectas?] *1518,* spectas *1520;* infra] infiet, *1518,* infra, *1520;* times.] times? *1518 1520*

61

ANOTHER ON AN ASTROLOGER WHOSE WIFE WAS LEWD

All the stars explain themselves to you, the prophet of the skies, and inform you of the destiny of everyone. But the fact that your wife gives herself to everyone—of that fact the stars, though they see everything, have not informed you.

62

IAMBICS ON THE SAME MAN

Observer of the stars above, beloved of us heavenly bodies, I myself, Phoebus, would be very glad now to tell you a little secret, most emphatically your concern, which I learned as I passed over the world the day before you came home recently from court. But Venus frightens me off and threatens me with a new love affair that will be no more successful than my earlier one with Daphne if I report to anyone at all such information as I once reported to her husband about her. Therefore, this fact you will not learn. Of all other changes in fortune I shall keep you informed, but as concerns your wife, if anything turns up contrary to your wishes, the whole world will know it before you do.

63

ANOTHER VERSION ON THE SAME MAN

Foolish fellow, why do you search the stars for the character of your wife? Your wife is on the ground. Why do you peer on high? What you are fearful about is down here. While you are asking the heavens what she is doing, she meanwhile managed to do what she liked upon the ground.

64

ALIVD IN ASTROLOGVM EVNDEM.

Sydera uestigas inter coelestia demens,
  Cur dubia semper mente quid uxor agat?
Si nescis qualis tibi sit, crede esse pudicam,
  Quod tibi persuades si bene, iam bene habes.
Quid cognoscere uis, quae non nisi cognita laedunt?
  Quid fieri studio uis miser ipse tuo?
Hic furor haud dubie est, quum iam desistere possis, [e3]
  Quaerere sollicite quod reperire times.

65

ALIVD IN ASTROLOGVM.

Saturnus procul est, iamque olim caecus, ut aiunt,
  Nec prope discernens a puero lapidem.
Luna uerecundis formosa incedit ocellis,
  Nec nisi uirgineum uirgo uidere potest.
Iuppiter Europen, Martem Venus, et Venerem Mars,
  Daphnen Sol, Hyrcen Mercurius recolit.
Hinc factum astrologe est, tua quum capit uxor amantes,
  Sydera significent ut nihil inde tibi.

66

DE FORMA DILEMMA IAMBIS TRIMETRIS SCAZONTIBVS.

Quid forma confert, Hercules nihil cerno.
Si ferueas, deformis ecce formosa est.
Sin frigeas, formosa iam sit informis.
Quid forma confert, Hercules nihil cerno.

67

DE ASTROLOGO DE QVO SVPRA.

Saepe suam inspectis uxorem Candidus astris,
  Praedicat en uates omnibus esse bonam.

64/2 uestigas] uestigans *1518;* coelestia] caelestia *1518*^{m} 6 uis,] *1518,* uis. *1520* 8 possis,] *1518,* possis. *1520* **65**/2 caecus] caesus *1518;* aiunt,] *1518,* aiunt. *1520* 5 potest.] potes. *1518,* potest *1520* 8 est,] *1518,* est. *1520* 9 significent] *1518,* significent, *1520* **67**/3 Praedicat] *1518,* Praedicat. *1520*

64

ANOTHER VERSION ON THE SAME ASTROLOGER

Why, madman, are you always searching among the stars, with suspicious mind, to discover what your wife is up to? If you do not know what kind of wife you have, believe that she is chaste. If you persuade yourself thoroughly that she is, you are well off. Why do you seek to learn what does not hurt you until you learn it? Why do you seek to make yourself miserable by your own persistence? This is madness, and no doubt of it, since you can stop right now anxiously seeking what you fear to find.

65

ANOTHER VERSION ON THE ASTROLOGER

Saturn is far away and long since blind, they say; unable he is to distinguish at close range between a boy and a stone. The lovely moon, as she journeys, is too shy to look and, maiden that she is, can see only the chaste. Jupiter is busy with Europa, Venus with Mars, Mars with Venus, the Sun with Daphne, and Mercury with Hyrce. That is why, astrologer, when your wife takes lovers, the stars give you no hint of the matter.

66

THE DILEMMA OF BEAUTY, IN SCAZONS

I do not know, by Hercules, what beauty contributes. If you are passionately in love, then presto! the ugly woman is beautiful; if you are unmoved, then even the beautiful woman may be repulsive. I do not know, by Hercules, what beauty contributes.

67

ON THE ASTROLOGER MENTIONED ABOVE

Candidus—what a prophet he is—after examining the stars, proclaimed his wife's goodness to everyone. When his wife left

Inspectis iterum, postquam uxor adultera fugit,
  Praedicit uates omnibus esse malam.

68

PARAENESIS AD VIRTVTEM VERAM.

Heu miseris quicquid misero blanditur in orbe,
  Illico marcescens, ut rosa uerna cadit.
Nec quenquam usque adeo placidis complectitur ulnis
  Sors, ut non aliqua parte molesta premat. [e3v]
Imbibe uirtutes, et inania gaudia sperne.
  Sunt animi comites gaudia uera boni.

69

AD CONTEMPTVM HVIVS VITAE.

Nos uelut instabiles uentus quatit omnis aristas,
  Quolibet impellunt spes, dolor, ira, metus.
Nil habet in rebus pondus mortalibus ullum.
  Momento pudor est, si moueare leui.

70

MORTEM NON ESSE METVENDAM CVM SIT FINIS MALORVM E GRAECO.

Non stultum est mortem matrem timuisse quietis?
  Quam fugiunt morbi, moestaque pauperies?
Sola semel miseris sese mortalibus offert,
  Nec quisquam est ad quem mors iterum redijt.
At reliqui morbi uarij, multique uicissim
  Nunc hunc, nunc illum, terque quaterque premunt.

71

IN EPISCOPVM QVENDAM SORDIDVM AC PERPARCVM.

Vita Sibyllinos mea si duraret in annos,
  Non bonitas unquam praesulis excideret.
Iugera multa soli locat, amplas possidet urbes,
  Centum stipatus progreditur famulis.

68/4 ulnis] *1518,* ulnis, *1520*   7 boni.] *1518,* boni, *1520*   **69**/4 habet] hahet *1518*[d]

him for a lover, the prophet took another look at the stars and predicted her badness to everyone.

68

EXHORTATION TO TRUE VIRTUE

Alas, whatever in this miserable world attracts miserable man withers at once and dies like the spring rose. Fortune has never yet taken anyone into her comforting arms without squeezing him uncomfortably somewhere. Drink in the virtues; abstain from vain joys. True joys are the companions of the noble spirit.

69

ON SCORNING THIS LIFE

As every wind strikes and bends ears of grain, so hope and grief and wrath and fear drive us where they will. In the affairs of mortals nothing has real weight. You should be ashamed if you are moved by a light touch.

70

THAT ONE OUGHT NOT TO FEAR DEATH SINCE IT IS THE END OF SUFFERING FROM THE GREEK

Is it not stupid to fear death, which is the mother of peace? which banishes disease and dismal poverty? Death alone visits miserable mortals only once; there is none to whom death has come a second time. But other afflictions, many and varied, take their turns, attacking now this victim and now that, time and time again.

71

ON A CERTAIN MEAN AND STINGY BISHOP

If I were to live as long as the Sibyl, I should never forget the kindness of the bishop. He is proprietor of many acres of rented land, possesses large cities, and travels with a retinue of a hundred

Me tamen exigui census, quum nuper adirem,
Excipit, et uere comiter alloquitur.
Quin abiens nigri gustarem ut pocula uini,
E loculo clauem liberat ipse suo. [e4]

72
DE VICISSITVDINE FORTVNAE E GRAECO.

Lubrica non seruat certum fortuna tenorem,
Sed rotat instabilem caeca subinde rotam.
Sternere summa libet, libet infima tollere, rerum
Inque uicem nulla uertere lege uices.
Maxima quum bona sunt, iam sunt mala proxima, rursus
Maxima quum mala sunt, proxima iam bona sunt.
Forti animo mala fer, nec bis miser esto dolore,
Ne cito uenturis praemoriare bonis.

73
VITA BREVIS.

Non tibi uiuacem furor est spondere senectam?
Quum non sit uitae certa uel hora tuae.
Finge age Nestoreum sis peruenturus in aeuum,
Longa tument multis tempora foeta malis.
Omnia ut effugias uiridis quibus angitur aetas,
Taedia longa tibi curua senecta feret.
Tu tamen ad seros (nulli quod contigit) annos
Vt uenias, nullo percitus ante malo,
Hoc tamen exiguum est. Vbi nunc tot Nestoris anni?
Ex tanto superest tempore nulla dies.

74
PATIENTIA.

Tristia qui pateris perfer, Sors tristia soluet.
Quod si non faciat Sors, tibi mors faciet.

72/3 fortuna] Fortuna *1518* 8 sunt.] *1518,* sunt, *1520* 10 Ne] *1518,* Nec *1520*
73/4 Nestoreum] *1518,* Nestoreum, *1520* 6 uiridis] *1518,* uiridis, *1520* 9 malo,] malo. *1518 1520* 10 est. Vbi] est. ubi *1518,* est, ubi *1520* 11 dies.] *1518,* dies, *1520*

attendants. And yet, when recently I approached him, although I am a man of very small property, still he received me and addressed me in really agreeable fashion. As a matter of fact, in order that I might taste a cup of his port before leaving, he himself extracted his key from his own purse.

72
ON FICKLE FORTUNE
FROM THE GREEK

Slippery Fortune observes no definite method but continually, unseeing, turns her restless wheel. She delights to strike down the highest, to raise the lowest, and, without principle, to produce alternations of man's lot. When your prosperity is greatest, then trouble is closest at hand; contrariwise, when your troubles are at their height, prosperity is nearest. Endure your troubles with brave heart; do not by grieving be twice unhappy lest you hurry yourself into the grave just before prosperity comes.

73
LIFE IS SHORT

Is it not madness for you to count upon an active old age?—since not even an hour of life is guaranteed. Come, imagine you will live to be as old as Nestor—then your long life will teem with numerous woes. Though you outlive all the troubles of your vigorous years, bent old age will bring you lasting wearisome burdens. And even so, though you live untroubled (as never happens) to a ripe old age, this too is a trifle. Where are Nestor's many years now? Of a life so long there remains not a single day.

74
ENDURANCE

Sufferer, endure; Chance will end your sorrow. And what Chance does not do for you Death will do.

75

VITA IPSA CVRSVS AD MORTEM EST.

Nugamur, mortemque procul, procul esse putamus.
At medijs latet haec abdita uisceribus. [e4v]
Scilicet ex illa, qua primum nascimur hora,
Prorepunt iuncto uitaque morsque pede.
Partem aliquam furtim qua se metitur, et ipsam
Surripit e uita quaelibet hora tua.
Paulatim morimur, momento extinguimur uno,
Sic oleo lampas deficiente perit.
Vt nihil interimat, tamen ipso in tempore mors est.
Quin nunc, interea dum loquimur, morimur.

76

DIVES AVARVS PAVPER EST SIBI E GRAECO.

Diuitias animi solas ego iudico ueras,
Qui rebus pluris se facit ipse suis.
Hunc adeo ditem, hunc opulentum rite uocamus,
Magnarum quis sit qui uidet usus opum.
Calculus at si quem misere numerandus adurit,
Qui misere semper diuitias cumulet,
Hic ut apes paruo crebroque foramine fosso,
Sudat in alueolo, mella alij comedunt.

77

DILEMMA EPICVRI.

Deijciat miseram tibi nulla molestia mentem.
Si longa est, leuis est; si grauis est, breuis est.

78

CONTRA

Deijcit heu miseram, prosternit et utraque mentem.
Longa nec ulla leuis, nec grauis ulla breuis.

75/9 Sic oleo lampas] Vt lampas oleo *1518* **76**/3 ueras,] ueras. *1518,* ueras., *1520* 4 suis.] *1520,* suis, *1518* 8 cumulet,] cumulet. *1518 1520* 10 mella] mel *1518* **77**/3 est;] est. *1518 1520* **78**/3 Longa] *1518,* Longa, *1520;* leuis,] *1518,* leuis. *1520*

75

LIFE ITSELF IS A JOURNEY TOWARD DEATH

We waste our time and think that death is far, far away. But it lies hidden deep in our entrails. In fact, from the very hour of our birth, life and death steal forward together, step by step. An hour, in the process of measuring itself out, secretly steals that very measure from your life. Little by little we die, but in a single instant we cease to exist; thus a lamp goes out when its oil is gone. Even when it does not kill, death is present in time itself. Why, even now, while we are talking, we are dying.

76

THE GREEDY RICH MAN IS POOR FOR HIMSELF FROM THE GREEK

The only true riches, in my judgment, are those of the mind which values itself above its possessions. The man we rightly call rich, the man we rightly call wealthy is one who sees how to use his great wealth. But if anyone is always wretchedly heaping up riches, wretchedly consumed by the need to count money, this man toils like the bee in its little many-celled hive. Others eat the honey.

77

THE DILEMMA OF EPICURUS

Let no trouble drive you to misery. If the trouble is lasting, it is easy to bear; if it is hard to bear, it does not last long.

78

THE OPPOSITE OPINION

Alas, both kinds of sorrow drive us to misery and break our hearts: a long sorrow is never light and a heavy sorrow is never brief.

79

DE MORTE.

Somniat, hic ditem qui se putat esse, uidetque
Morte experrectus illico quam sit inops. [f_1]

80

SOLA MORS TYRANNICIDA EST.

Duriter es quicunque uiris oppressus iniquis,
Spem cape, spes luctus leniat alma tuos.
Versilis in melius uel te Fortuna reponet,
Vt solet excussa nube nitere dies.
Aut libertatis uindex frendente tyranno,
Eruet iniecta mors miserata manu.
Auferet haec (quo plus tibi gratificetur) et illum,
Afferet atque tuos protinus ante pedes.
Ille opibus tantis, fastuque elatus inani,
Ille ferox crebris ante satellitibus,
Hic neque toruus erit, uultu nec ut ante superbo,
Sed miser abiectus, solus, inermis, inops.
O quid uita tibi dedit unquam tale? uicissim
Iam ridendus erit, qui metuendus erat.

81

CARMEN VERSVM
E CANTIONE ANGLICA.

O Cor triste malis misere immersumque profundis
Rumpere: sit poenae terminus iste tuae.
Sanguinolenta tuae dominae tua uulnera pande,
Illa breui est, quae nos diuidet una duos.
Quam miser ergo diu sic heu lachrymabo, querarque:
Mors ades, et tantis horrida solue malis.

79/2 uidetque] *1518,* uidetque, *1520* **80**/1 TYRANNICIDA] *1518,* TYANNICIDA *1520* 3 cape,] cape. *1518 1520* **81**/1–2 CARMEN . . . ANGLICA] *om. 1518, which prints nos. 80 and 81 as one*

79
ON DEATH

He is dreaming who thinks that in this life he is rich; and when death wakes him up, he sees at once how poor he is.

80
DEATH UNASSISTED KILLS TYRANTS

You who have been cruelly persecuted at the hands of unjust men, no matter who you are, take hope. Let kindly hope alleviate your sufferings. A turn of fortune will improve your state—like the sun shining through scattered clouds—or the defender of liberty. Death, touched by pity, will put forth her hand, while the tyrant rages, and rescue you. Death will snatch him away too (the more to please you) and will lay him right before your feet. He who was so carried away by his great wealth and his empty pride, he who once upon a time amid his thronging courtiers was so bold, O, he will not be fierce, will not wear an expression of pride. He will be an object of pity, cast down from his high place, abandoned, helpless, penniless. What gift has life ever given you to compare with this gift? The tables are turned: the man once so fearsome deserves only a laugh.

81
A POEM TRANSLATED FROM AN ENGLISH SONG

Break, sad heart, pitiably engulfed in deepest woe. Let this be the end of your punishment. Show your mistress your bloody wounds. It is she only who will presently part us two. Alas, how long shall I in my misery thus weep and complain? Come, dreaded death, and release me from such monstrous woes.

82

IN AMICAM FOEDIFRAGAM IOCOSVM, VERSVM E CANTIONE ANGLICA.

Dij melius, uenere mihi hac quae somnia nocte!
  Tota semel mundi machina uersa ruit. [f_1v]
Nec sua lux Phoebo constabat, nec sua Phoebae
  Iamque tumens omnem strauerat aequor humum.
Maius adhuc mirum, uox en mihi dicere uisa est,
  Heus tua iam pactam fregit amica fidem.

83

DE CVNICVLO BIS CAPTO.

E rete extrahor, e digitis in rete relabor.
  Heu semel heu fugi, bis miser ut caperer.

84

IN VIRGINEM MORIBVS HAVD VIRGINEIS.

Blanda, salax, petulans, audax, uaga, garrula uirgo,
  Si uirgo est, uirgo est bis quoque quae peperit.

85

IN VXORES.

Hoc quisque dicit, rebus in mortalibus
Quod tristius sit, ac magis uiros grauet,
Natura nil produxit his uxoribus.
Hoc quisque dicit, dicit, at ducit tamen.
Quin sex sepultis, septimam ducit tamen.

86

IN EASDEM.

Res uxor grauis est, poterit tamen utilis esse,
  Si propere moriens det sua cuncta tibi.

82/2 VERSVM . . . ANGLICA] *om. 1518*   5 Phoebae] Phoebe *1518 1520*   **84/4** est bis] *1518,* est, bis *1520*   **86/3** Si . . . tibi.] Si sua det propere se moriente tibi. *1518*

82

A JESTING POEM TO A FAITHLESS MISTRESS, TRANSLATED FROM AN ENGLISH SONG

May the gods preserve us! What dreams I had last night! The whole universe was overturned and fell to ruin. The sun's light did not survive, nor the moon's; and the swollen deep overwhelmed the land. Even more remarkable—you hear?—a voice seemed to say, "Just look, your mistress has broken the promise she made."

83

ON A RABBIT TWICE CAUGHT

They were lifting me out of the net; out of their hands I slipped—back into the net again. Alas, alas, poor me! Escaping once only means captured twice.

84

ON A MAID WITH UNMAIDENLY HABITS

If this maid, who is a seductive, wanton, saucy, footloose, talkative flirt, is a maiden, then so is a woman who has twice borne children.

85

ON WIVES

This is what every man says: "Nature has not produced anything in this life more troublesome, more burdensome, to man than these wives of ours." That is what he says; but still he marries. Yes, when his sixth wife dies, he marries a seventh.

86

ON THE SAME

A wife is a burden, but she could be useful—if she dies betimes and leaves you all she owns.

87

IN IMAGINEM DISSIMILEM. E GRAECO.

Haec tua quam nuper pinxit Diodorus imago,
Cuiusuis magis est, quam tua Menodote.

88

IN EANDEM.

Sic se totum isthac expressit imagine pictor,
Vt nulli tam sit, quam tibi dissimilis.

89

CHORIAMBICVM DE VITA SVAVI. E GRAECO.

Non est cura mihi Gygis, [f$_2$]
Qui rex Sardibus imperat.
Aurum non ego persequor,
Reges non miser aemulor.
Curae est, barba suauibus
Vnguentis mihi perfluat.
Curae est, ut redolentibus
Cingam tempora floribus.
Curae sunt hodierna mi,
Nam quis Crastina nouerit?
Tornato bene Mulciber
Argento mihi poculum
Iam nunc effice concauum,
Et quantum potes imbibum.
Et fac illud ut ambiant
Non currus, neque sydera,
Orion neque flebilis.
Vites fac uirides mihi,
Botri fac mihi rideant
Pulchro cum Dionysio.

89/3 Gygis,] *1518*, Gygis. *1520* 12 Crastina] crastina *1518* 14 poculum] poculum. *1518*^{m}, poculum, *1518*^{d} *1520* 20 mihi,] mihi. *1518* *1520*

87

ON A POOR PORTRAIT
FROM THE GREEK

This painting of you which Diodorus recently painted, Menodotus, is anyone's portrait rather than yours.

88

ON THE SAME PORTRAIT

In that portrait of you it is himself the painter has revealed, and so thoroughly that it resembles nobody as little as it resembles you.

89

CHORIAMBICS ON THE PLEASANT LIFE
FROM THE GREEK

I care nothing about Gyges, king of Sardis. My search is not for gold; I do not make myself miserable by competing with kings. My ambition is to have my beard well anointed with agreeable perfumes, my brow wreathed with fragrant blossoms. I am concerned with today, for who can know tomorrow? Now, Vulcan, make me a well-rounded silver cup, make it deep and as inexhaustible as you can. And have it decorated round about, not with chariots, constellations, or doleful Orion—instead make green vines and grapes to charm me, and add a handsome figure of Dionysus.

90

IN MEDICVM IMPOSTOREM, QVI GVTTVLAM FICTI BALSAMI MAGNO VENDIDIT.

Febre laboranti medicus, feret O tibi certe
  Aut nihil, aut tantum balsamus, inquit, opem.
Sed nemo me praeter habet, perpaululum et ipse.
  Gutta emitur libris non minus una decem. [f_2v]
Nunc mihi quinque dabis, reliquas mihi quinque daturus
  Sanus, ut has nunquam te moriente, petam.
Nunquam rem facies, tanto in discrimine qui uis
  Tam charae guttae ponere dimidium.
Pacta placent, minimoque e uitro et sindone tecto,
  Iacta petit gladij cuspide gutta merum.
Abluat ut uino mucronem, aeger rogat: absit,
  Inquit, adhuc libras bis gerit ille decem.
Gutta, ait, una sat est, et erat satis: unica tantum
  Gutta potest: unam uix bibit, et moritur.
O nimis aduerso contractum sydere pactum.
  Hinc guttae, hinc uitae dimidium perijt.

91

IN FVCATAM E GRAECO

Tinguis capillos foemina: at qui scis, rogas?
Nigri fuere quum referres e foro.

92

IN IMAGINEM MALE REDDITAM.

Effigie studuit tua in hac ostendere pictor,
  Expressisse queat quam tibi dissimilem.

90/5 balsamus] bulsamus *1518*[d] 6 ipse.] ipse, *1518 1520* 7 decem.] decem, *1518 1520* 10 qui uis] *1518,* quiuis *1520* 14 rogat] obsecrat *1518* 15 gerit] habet *1518* **91**/4 *Indented in 1518 and 1520.* **92**/1 REDDITAM] PICTAM *1518*

90

ON A DISHONEST PHYSICIAN WHO SOLD A MERE DROP OF PRETENDED MEDICINE FOR A HIGH PRICE

A physician said to a patient who was suffering from a fever, "If anything will help you, balm will. But only I have it, and I have very little. The price is not less than ten pounds a drop. You give me five now, and the other five when you are well, with the understanding that if you die I shall never try to collect the second five. You will win no advantage in this great crisis if you try to settle for half of the very expensive drop." They agreed, and a drop from a tiny linen-wrapped vial was dropped from a dagger-point into wine. The patient asked the physician to rinse off the point in the wine. But he said, "By no means; the point still holds twice the value of your ten pounds. One drop is enough." And it was enough. Just one drop did it. The patient had hardly drunk the single drop when he died. O, what a very unlucky arrangement! One participant lost half his drop, the other half his life.

91

ON A WOMAN ARTIFICIALLY BEAUTIFIED FROM THE GREEK

Madam, you dye your hair; but you ask, "How do you know?" Well, your hair was black when you brought it home from the marketplace.

92

ON A FAULTY PORTRAIT

In this portrait of yours the artist tried to show how unlike you he could make it.

93

IN IMAGINEM BENE REDDITAM.

Hac tua tam uere facies expressa tabella,
  Vt iam non tabula haec sit tibi, sed speculum.

94

IN EANDEM.

Quam mihi monstrasti demiror Posthume pictor,
  Effigiem quanta finxerat arte tuam.
Inspicit hanc quisquis, si te conspexerit unquam,
  Si non artificis tangitur inuidia, [f_3]
Tam simile hic ouo non esse fatebitur ouum,
  Effigies haec est quam tibi dissimilis.

95

IN ANGLVM GALLICAE LINGVAE AFFECTATOREM.

Amicus et sodalis est Lalus mihi,
Britanniaque natus, altusque insula.
At cum Britannos Galliae cultoribus
Oceanus ingens, lingua, mores dirimant,
Spernit tamen Lalus Britannica omnia.
Miratur, expetitque cuncta Gallica.
Toga superbit ambulans in Gallica,
Amatque multum Gallicas lacernulas.
Zona, locello, atque ense gaudet Gallico,
Filtro, bireto, pileoque Gallico,
Et calceis, et subligare Gallico,
Totoque denique apparatu Gallico.
Nam et unum habet ministrum, eumque Gallicum,
Sed quem (licet uelit) nec ipsa Gallia
Tractare quiret plus (opinor) Gallice,
Stipendij nihil dat, atque id Gallice.
Vestitque tritis pannulis, et Gallice hoc.

93/1 IN . . . REDDITAM] IN EANDEM *1518* 2 uere facies] uere est facies *1518* **94**/1 IN EANDEM] *See Commentary.* 4 unquam] *1518,* unqnam *1520* 6 simile] *1563,* similem *1518 1520 1565* **95**/7 omnia.] *1518,* omnia, *1520* 15 Gallicum,] Gallicum. *1518 1520*

93
ON AN ACCURATE PORTRAIT

Your likeness is so truly portrayed in this picture that it is not your picture, but your mirror.

94
ON THE SAME PORTRAIT

I marvel at the great skill with which the artist painted the portrait of you which you showed me, Posthumus. If anyone who has ever seen you looks at this picture, unless he is prejudiced by envy of the artist, he will confess that the similarity between one egg and another is not so great as the discrepancy between you and your portrait.

95
ON AN ENGLISHMAN WHO AFFECTED TO SPEAK FRENCH

My friend and companion, Lalus, was born in Britain and brought up on our island. Nevertheless, although a mighty sea, their languages, and their customs separate Englishmen and the inhabitants of France, Lalus still is scornful of all things English. All things French he admires and wants. He struts about in French dress; he is very fond of little French capes. He is happy with his belt, his purse, his sword—if they are French; with his hat, his beret, his cap—if they are French. He delights in French shoes, French underclothes, and, to put it briefly, in an outfit French from head to toe. Why, he even has one servant, and he is a Frenchman. But France herself, I think, could not, if she tried, treat him in more French a fashion: he pays the servant nothing, like a Frenchman; he clothes him in wornout rags, in the French

Alit cibo paruo, et malo, idque Gallice.
Labore multo exercet, atque hoc Gallice.
Pugnisque crebro pulsat, idque Gallice.
In coetu et in uia, et foro, et frequentia
Rixatur, obiurgatque semper Gallice. [f3v]
Quid? Gallice illud? imo semigallice.
Sermonem enim (ni fallor) ille Gallicum
Tam callet omnem, quam Latinum Psytacus.
Crescit tamen, sibique nimirum placet,
Verbis tribus, si quid loquatur Gallicis.
Aut Gallicis si quid nequit uocabulis,
Conatur id, uerbis licet non Gallicis,
Canore saltem personare Gallico,
Palato hiante acutulo quodam sono,
Et foeminae instar garrientis molliter,
Sed ore pleno, tanquam id impleant fabae,
Balbutiens uidelicet suauiter
Pressis quibusdam literis, Galli quibus
Ineptientes abstinent, nihil secus,
Quam uulpe gallus, rupibusque nauita.
Sic ergo linguam ille et Latinam Gallice,
Et Gallice linguam sonat Britannicam.
Et Gallice linguam refert Lombardicam.
Et Gallice linguam refert Hispanicam.
Et Gallice linguam sonat Germanicam.
Et Gallice omnem, praeter unam Gallicam.
Nam Gallicam solam sonat Britannice.
At quisquis insula satus Britannica,
Sic patriam insolens fastidiet suam,
Vt more simiae laboret fingere,
Et aemulari Gallicas ineptias, [f4]
Ex amne Gallo ego hunc opinor ebrium.
Ergo ex Britanno ut Gallus esse nititur,
Sic dij iubete, fiat ex gallo capus.

95/24 Gallice.] *1518,* Gallice, *1520*   32 Canore] Sonoque *1518*   35 fabae,] *1518,* fabae *1520*   50 ineptias,] *1518,* ineptias. *1520*

manner; he feeds him little and that little poor, as the French do; he works him hard, like the French; he strikes him often, like a Frenchman; at social gatherings, and on the street, and in the market-place, and in public he quarrels with him and abuses him always in the French fashion. What! Have I said that he does this in French fashion? I should say rather in half-French fashion. For, unless I am mistaken, he is as familiar with the French language in general as a parrot is with Latin. Still he swells with pride and is, naturally, pleased with himself if he gets off three words in French. If there is anything he cannot say in French, then he tries to say it—granted the words are not French—at least with a French accent, with open palate, a shrill sort of sound, effeminate, like women's chatter, but lisping prettily you may be sure, as though his mouth were full of beans, and pronouncing with emphasis the letters which the foolish French avoid as the cock avoids the fox or the sailor the cliffs. And so it is with this kind of French accent that he speaks Latin, English, Italian, Spanish, German, and every language except only French; for French is the one language he speaks with an English accent. But if any native of Britain in this haughty way scorns his native land in an apelike effort to feign and counterfeit the follies of the French, I think that such a man is intoxicated from drinking of the River Gallus. Therefore, since he is trying to change from Englishman to Frenchman, order him, ye gods, to change from cock to capon.

96

IN NICOLAVM MALVM MEDICVM.

Nunc uideo haud rerum tantum, sed et ipsa uirorum
Nomina, non temere, sed ratione dari.
Nicoleus nomen medici est: qui conuenit? inquis,
Hoc potius nomen debuit esse ducis:
Dux populos armis uincit: sed et iste uenenis
Et populum, et forteis sternit ubique duces.
Saepe ducem bello repetunt, bis nemo rebellat
Huic medico: uero est nomine Nicoleus.

97

IN IMAGINEM ELEGANTEM, SED DEFORMISSIMI.

Ipsam iudice me Venerem superabat Apellis,
Haec tua quae uisa est nuper imago mihi.
Pictor in hanc omnes unam consumpserat artes,
Spectari hac una quid ualuit, uoluit.
Qualis in ore decor, qui nasus, qualia labra,
O quales oculi, qualis ubique color.
Tam fuit ex omni longe pulcherrima parte,
Quam fuit a nulla parte tibi similis.

98

IN IMAGINEM DISSIMILEM.

Nuper ut ingredior pictoris forte tabernam,
Effigies oculis est tua uisa meis. [f_4v]
Ex te dum pictor sic exprimat omnia, uultum
Immotum credo te tenuisse diu.
Sic te totum inspecta refert: intelligo cuia est
Protinus ut pictor rettulit esse tuam.

96/4 Nicoleus] Nicolaus *1518* 9 medico:] medico, *1518 1520;* Nicoleus] Nicolaus *1518* **97**/7 Qualis in ore] Qualia in re *1518*[m]

96
ON NICOLAUS, A WICKED PHYSICIAN

Now I understand that names not only of things but also of people are acquired in no haphazard way but with some reason. There is a physician named Nicolaus. You say, "In what way is that appropriate? It would make a better name for a general." Well, it is by arms that a general conquers nations, but by his poisonous potions this physician lays low the nation and brave generals on every hand. A general's enemies often fight a second battle with him, but no one encounters this physician twice. He is truly named, is Nicolaus.

97
ON THE HANDSOME PORTRAIT OF A VERY UGLY MAN

That picture of you which I saw recently was, in my opinion, superior to the Venus of Apelles. The painter used up all his skill in that one picture; he wanted to show in that one picture what he could do. What beauty of face! that nose! such lips! what eyes! such color everywhere! Just as surely as the picture was in every respect by far the most beautiful of portraits, so surely did it fail to look like you in any respect.

98
ON AN UNSUCCESSFUL PORTRAIT

When I happened recently to enter an artist's studio, your portrait met my eyes. While the painter thus reproduced all your characteristics, you, I am sure, kept your expression unchanged for a long time. A look at the portrait brought you so completely before me that I knew whose portrait it was the instant the artist told me it was yours.

99

IN PARCVM MORIENTEM.

Chrysalus heu moritur diues, dolet, ingemit, unquam
Nemo magis tristi pectore fata tulit.
Non quoniam ipse perit, cui nil se uilius ipso est,
Sed nummi pereunt quattuor in tumulum.

100

IN GRAMMATICVM PVTIDVM.

Quum mihi grammaticus mentem subit Heliodorus,
Nostra Soloecismos illico lingua timet.

101

IN PROGNOSTEN RIDICVLVM.

Hoc anno in regno rex nobilis ille quiescet
Gallorum, celeber scripserat astrologus.
Rex uix incepto uita defungitur anno,
Iam nil se uates quo tueatur, habet.
Rem quidam risu coepit defendere, uerum est
Augurium, rex iam nonne quieuit? ait.
Latius hoc uerbum prorepit, et undique ridens
Id populus, rex iam nonne quieuit? ait.
Audit ut in populo hoc uates, iam serio uerum est
Augurium, rex iam nonne quieuit? ait.

102

IN VEHEMENTER NASVTVM.
E GRAECO.

Nunquam Procle manu nares emungere possis.
Nam tua nare manus, magna licet, minor est. [g_1]
Quando Iouem inclamas sternutans? quippe nec audis
Tam procul ab nasus prominet aure tuus.

99/1 MORIENTEM] *1518,* MORIENTVM *1520* **100**/1 GRAMMATICVM] *1518,* GRAMMTICVM *1520* **101**/1 PROGNOSTEN] *1518,* PROGNOSTEVM *1520 1563* 4 Rex uix incepto] *1520* (*errata*), Rex ubi uix coepto *1518,* Rex uix coepto *1520* 6 risu] prorsum *1518* **102**/5 sternutans?] sternutans, *1518 1520*

99

ON A DYING MISER

Alas, rich Chrysalus is dying. He mourns; he groans; no one ever died more reluctantly. He is mourning not because he is parting with his life—there is nothing he holds cheaper than himself—but because he is parting with four coins for a grave.

100

ON A ROTTEN GRAMMARIAN

When I think of the grammarian Heliodorus, my tongue immediately begins to dread solecisms.

101

ON A SILLY SEER

A renowned astrologer predicted, "That noble ruler, the king of the French, this year will be at peace in his realm." The year had hardly begun when the king died. The seer was defenseless. Someone undertook jokingly to explain the matter by saying, "The prophecy is true; is not the king at peace?" The story spread and spread; and the people on every hand laughingly said, "Is not the king at peace?" When the seer heard this comment from the people, then he said in earnest, "The prophecy is true; is not the king at peace?"

102

ON A MAN WITH A HUGE NOSE

FROM THE GREEK

Proclus, you could never wipe your nose by hand, for your hand, large as it is, is smaller than your nose. When do you cry "Jupiter" upon sneezing? For obviously you do not hear anything, since your nose extends out so very far away from your ears.

103

IN POETAM FVRIOSVM
E GRAECO.

Sunt etiam in Musis furiae, quibus ipse poeta
  Fis, per quas temere carmina multa facis.
Ergo age plurima scribe precor, tibi nempe furorem
  Non ego maiorem quem precer inuenio.

104

IN PERPVSILLVM
E GRAECO.

Grus ne te rapiat Pygmaeo sanguine gaudens,
  Si sapias, media tutus in urbe mane.

105

NEGLIGENDI VVLGI RVMORES
E GRAECO.

Tu teipsum oblectes, et uulgi uerba loquacis
  Sperne: bene hic de te dicet, et ille male.

106

IN FATVVM
E GRAECO.

Quem mordent pulices extinguit Morio lychnon.
Non me, inquit, cernent amplius hi pulices.

107

DE SOMNO
E GRAECO
SENTENTIA ARISTOTELIS.

Ferme dimidium uitae, dormitur: in illo
  Aequales spacio diues, inopsque iacent.
Ergo Croese tibi regum ditissime, uitae
  Ferme dimidio par erat Irus egens.

103/2 E GRAECO.] *om.* *1518* 5 furorem] *1518,* furorem, *1520* **105**/1 NEGLIGENDI] NEGLIGENDOS *1518*^{m}, NEGLIGENDVS *1518*^{d} 3 teipsum] teip sum *1520* 4 Sperne:] Sperne. *1518,* Sperne, *1520* **106**/4 hi] hij *1518*^{m}; pulices.] *1518,* pulices, *1520* **107**/4 dormitur:] dormitur. *1518,* dormitur, *1520* 5 Aequales] *1518,* Aeqnales *1520*

103
ON A MAD POET
FROM THE GREEK

Even among the Muses there are Furies, and it is they who make you the poet you are and inspire you to write many poems without thought. Come now, I entreat you, write ever so many poems, for I find no greater fury to entreat for you than that.

104
ON A TINY MAN
FROM THE GREEK

To be safe, stay well within the city if you are wise, so that no crane—they love the blood of pygmies—may grab you.

105
COMMON GOSSIP OUGHT TO BE IGNORED
FROM THE GREEK

Just please yourself and scorn the comments of the chattering mob. One among them will praise, another defame you.

106
ON A FOOL
FROM THE GREEK

When the fleas bite Morio, he puts out his light and says, "These fleas will not see me now."

107
ON SLEEP
FROM THE GREEK
AN ARISTOTELIAN PROVERB

Almost half of life is sleep. During that period the rich and the poor lie equal. And so, Croesus, wealthiest of kings, for almost half a lifetime Irus the beggar was your equal.

108

ALIVD.

Non es, dum in somno es, dum nec te uiuere sentis,
Felix, at somnus ni ueniat, miser es. [g_1v]
Qui felix igitur sorte indulgente superbit,
Inflatusque leui prosperitate tumet,
Nox quoties uenit, aut toties iam desinit esse
Felix, aut toties incipit esse miser.

109

QVID INTER TYRANNVM ET PRINCIPEM.

Legitimus immanissimis
Rex hoc tyrannis interest.
Seruos tyrannus quos regit,
Rex liberos putat suos.

110

SOLLICITAM ESSE TYRANNI VITAM

Magna diem magnis exhaurit cura tyrannis,
Nocte uenit requies, si tamen ulla uenit.
Nec tamen hi pluma requiescunt mollius ulla
In dura pauper quam requiescit humo.
Ergo tyranne tibi haec pars felicissima uitae est,
In qua mendico par tamen esse uelis.

111

BONVM PRINCIPEM ESSE PATREM
NON DOMINVM
IAMBICVM.

Princeps pius nunquam carebit liberis.
Totius est regni pater.
Princeps abundat ergo felicissimus,
Tot liberis, quot ciuibus.

108/5 tumet,] tumet. *1518 1520* **109**/3 tyrannis] *1518,* tyranis *1520* 4 regit,] *1518,* regit. *1520*

108
ANOTHER VERSION

While you are sleeping and do not perceive that you are alive, you are not happy; but if sleep does not come, you are miserable. And so any happy man, proud of his good luck, haughty, and swollen by fleeting prosperity, must, every night, either cease to be happy or begin to be miserable.

109
THE DIFFERENCE BETWEEN A TYRANT AND A KING

A king who respects the law differs from cruel tyrants thus: a tyrant rules his subjects as slaves; a king thinks of his as his own children.

110
THAT THE TYRANT'S LIFE IS TROUBLED

Great anxiety wears away the waking hours of the mighty tyrant; peace comes at night if it comes at all. But the tyrant does not rest more comfortably on any soft bed than the poor man does on the hard ground. Therefore, tyrant, the happiest part of your life is that in which you willingly become no better than a beggar.

111
THAT THE GOOD KING IS A FATHER NOT A MASTER
IAMBICS

A devoted king will never lack children; he is father to the whole kingdom. And so it is that a true king is abundantly blessed in having as many children as he has subjects.

112

DE BONO REGE ET POPVLO.

Totum est unus homo regnum, idque cohaeret amore.
Rex caput est, populus caetera membra facit. [g_2]
Rex quot habet ciues (dolet ergo perdere quenquam)
Tot numerat parteis corporis ipse sui.
Exponit populus sese pro rege putatque
Quilibet hunc proprij corporis esse caput.

113

BONA NON COGNOSCI NISI DVM AMITTVNTVR.

Perdendo bona nostra fere cognoscimus omnes.
Dum possidemus, spernimus.
Sic populo quoque saepe malus, sed sero benignum
Commendat haeres principem.

114

TYRANNVM IN SOMNO NIHIL DIFFERRE A PLEBEIO.

Erigit ergo tuas insane superbia cristas,
Quod flexo curuat se tibi turba genu,
Quod populus nudo surgat tibi uertice, quod sit
Multorum in manibus uitaque, morsque tuis.
At somnus quoties artus adstringit inertes,
Haec tua iam toties gloria dic ubi sit?
Tunc ignaue iaces trunco non impar inani,
Aut paulo functis ante cadaueribus.
Quod nisi conclusus timide intra tecta lateres,
In cuiusque foret iam tua uita manu.

115

DE PRINCIPE BONO ET MALO.

Quid bonus est princeps? Canis est custos gregis inde
Qui fugat ore lupos. Quid malus? ipse lupus. [g_2v]

112/3 est,] *1518,* est. *1520* 6 putatque] *1518,* putatque. *1520* **114**/3 cristas,] *1518,* cristas. *1520* 4 genu,] genu. *1518 1520* 5 uertice,] *1518,* uertice. *1520* 7 inertes,] *1518,* inertes. *1520* 10 cadaueribus.] *1518,* cadaueribus *1520* **115**/2 princeps? Canis] princeps, canis *1518 1520;* gregis] *1518,* gregis, *1520* 3 lupos. Quid] lupos. quid *1518,* lupos, quid *1520*

112
ON THE GOOD KING AND HIS PEOPLE

A kingdom in all its parts is like a man; it is held together by natural affection. The king is the head; the people form the other parts. Every citizen the king has he considers a part of his own body (that is why he grieves at the loss of a single one). The people risk themselves to save the king and everyone thinks of him as the head of his own body.

113
THAT OUR ADVANTAGES ARE RECOGNIZED ONLY WHEN THEY VANISH

Almost all of us recognize our advantages by losing them. While we have them, we ignore them. In this way, also, an evil successor frequently, but too late, enhances the people's memory of a good ruler.

114
THAT THE TYRANT WHILE HE SLEEPS IS NO DIFFERENT FROM THE COMMONER

Well then, you madman, it is pride which makes you carry your head so high—because the throng bows to you on bended knee, because the people rise and uncover for you, because you have in your power the life and death of many. But whenever sleep secures your body in inactivity, then, tell me, where is this glory of yours? Then you lie, useless creature, like a lifeless log or like a recent corpse. But if you were not lying protected, like a coward, unseen indoors, your own life would be at the disposal of any man.

115
ON KINGS, GOOD AND BAD

What is a good king? He is a watchdog, guardian of the flock, who by barking keeps the wolves from the sheep. What is the bad king? He is the wolf.

116

IN RAPTOREM ET PATRONVM.

Raptam se queritur uirgo, crimenque negari
Non potuit. Raptor iam periturus erat.
Callidus at subito patronus protrahit ipse
Membrum deducta ueste uirile rei,
Hoccine uirgo tua membrum fuit, inquit, in aluo?
Illa uerecundo mota pudore negat.
Vicimus O iudex, clamat patronus. Ea ipsa est.
Id negat en sine quo se negat ipsa rapi.

117

IN FVREM ET PATRONVM.

Dum furti metuit damnari Clepticus, amplo
Non sine consuluit munere causidicum.
Hic ubi saepe diuque immensa uolumina uoluit,
Spero, ait, effugies Cleptice, si fugias.

118

IN ASTROLOGVM QVI FACTVM PRAEDIXIT E GRAECO.

Saepe patri frater quod debuit esse superstes,
Hoc uelut uno omnes astrologi ore canunt.
Ast Hermoclides obiturum prae patre solus
Dixit, sed dixit postquam obijsse uidet.

119

IN HVIVS VITAE VANITATEM.

Damnati ac morituri in terrae claudimur omnes
Carcere, in hoc mortem carcere nemo fugit.
Carceris in multas describitur area partes,
Inque alijs alij partibus aedificant. [g3]

116/1–9 IN RAPTOREM . . . rapi] *om. 1565* 3 Raptor] raptor *1518 1520* 4 Callidus] *1518,* Callidus, *1520* 8 iudex,] iudex *1518 1520;* patronus. Ea] patronus. ea *1518,* patronus, ea *1520;* est.] *1518,* est *1520* **117**/3 causidicum.] causidicum *1518*^{m}, causidicum, *1518*^{d} *1520* 4 Hic] Sic *1518* **118**/5 solus] *1518,* solus. *1520* 6 uidet.] *1518*^{d}, uidet, *1518*^{m} *1520* **119**/3 fugit.] fugit, *1518 1520*

116

ON A RAPIST AND HIS LAWYER

A girl charged that she had been raped. There was no denying the accusation. The rapist was doomed. But his clever lawyer suddenly opened the defendant's clothing and took out his male organ. Said the lawyer, "My girl, is this the organ that was in your belly?" The girl was so ashamed that she said, "No." The lawyer cried, "Your honor, we have won this case. She is the one, she herself denies the very thing in the absence of which she also denies she was raped."

117

ON A THIEF AND HIS LAWYER

While Snatch was afraid that he would be convicted of theft, he consulted a lawyer—at a considerable price. When the lawyer had pondered, frequently and long, his mighty tomes, he said, "Snatch, you will get off, I hope, if you take off."

118

ON AN ASTROLOGER WHO PROPHESIED AFTER THE EVENT

FROM THE GREEK

Astrologers frequently and unanimously told father that his brother was bound to survive him. Now, only Hermoclides said the brother would die first, but he said it after seeing that he was dead.

119

ON THE VANITY OF THIS LIFE

We are all shut up in the prison of this world under sentence of death. In this prison none escapes death. The land within the prison is divided into many sections, and men build their dwell-

Non aliter quam de regno de carcere certant.
  In caeco cupidus carcere condit opes,
Carcere obambulat hic uagus, hic uincitur in antro.
  Hic seruit, regit hic, hic canit, ille gemit.
Iam quoque dum carcer non tanquam carcer amatur,
  Hinc alijs alij mortibus extrahimur.

120

REGEM NON SATELLITIVM SED VIRTVS REDDIT TVTVM

Non timor inuisus, non alta palatia regem,
  Non compilata plebe tuentur opes,
Non rigidus uili mercabilis aere satelles
  Qui sic alterius fiet ut huius erat.
Tutus erit, populum qui sic regit, utiliorem
  Vt populus nullum censeat esse sibi.

121

POPVLVS CONSENTIENS REGNVM DAT ET AVFERT.

Quicunque multis uir uiris unus praeest,
  Hoc debet his quibus praeest.
Praeesse debet neutiquam diutius
  Hi quam uolent quibus praeest.
Quid impotentes principes superbiunt?
  Quod imperant precario?

122

IN PERPVSILLVM E GRAECO.

Ex atomis Epicurus totum fabricat orbem,
  Alchime, dum nihil his credidit esse minus. [g3v]
Ex te fecisset, si tum Diophante fuisses,
  Nempe atomis multo es tu Diophante minor.
Aut forte ex atomis iam caetera scriberet esse,
  Ast ipsas ex te scriberet esse atomos.

120/3 regem,] *1518,* regem. *1520* **122**/3 orbem,] orbem. *1518 1520* 4 minus.] minus, *1518 1520*

ings in different sections. As if the prison were a kingdom, the inmates struggle for position. The avaricious man hoards up wealth within the dark prison. One man wanders freely in the prison, another lies shackled in his cave; this man serves, that one rules; this one sings, that one groans. And then, while we are still in love with the prison as if it were no prison, we are escorted out of it, one way or another, by death.

120
A KING IS PROTECTED, NOT BY A CORPS OF GUARDS, BUT BY HIS OWN GOOD QUALITIES

Not fear (accompanied by hatred), not towering palaces, not wealth wrung from a plundered people protects a king. The stern bodyguard, hired for a pittance, offers no protection, for the guard will serve a new master as he served the old. He will be safe who so rules his people that they judge none other would promote their interests better.

121
THE CONSENT OF THE PEOPLE BOTH BESTOWS AND WITHDRAWS SOVEREIGNTY

Any one man who has command of many men owes his authority to those whom he commands; he ought to have command not one instant longer than his subjects wish. Why are impotent kings so proud? Because they rule merely on sufferance?

122
ON A TINY MAN
FROM THE GREEK

Epicurus constructed the whole world out of atoms, Alchimus, since he believed that there was nothing smaller than atoms. If you, Diophantus, had been alive at that time, he would have made the world out of you, for surely you, Diophantus, are much smaller than an atom. Or perhaps in that case he would have taught that everything else is made of atoms, but that the atoms themselves are made out of you.

123

IN AMOREM CASTVM ET INCESTVM E GRAECO.

Hi duo destruxere duos incestus, et almus,
Dum contra occurrunt, hinc amor, inde pudor.
Phaedram amor Hippolyti consumpserat igneus, ipsum
Interimitque sacer proh pudor Hippolytum.

124

IN VRBEM RHOMAM E GRAECO.

Gradiui genus Hector aue, si quid sub humo audis,
Respira, et patriae nomine cresce tuae.
Ilios urbs colitur, nunc inclyta gens colit illam,
Quam tu Marte minor, Martis amica tamen.
Myrmidones periere, ades et dic Hector Achilli,
Esse sub Aeneadis undique Thessaliam.

125

DE MEDIOCRITATE E GRAECO.

Ingratum est quicquid nimium est: sic semper amarum est,
Vt uerbum uetus est, mel quoque si nimium est.

126

IN VEHEMENTER INFELICEM E GRAECO.

Nunquam uixisti O pauper nunquam morieris.
Nempe miser uisus uiuere mortuus es.
At quibus immensa est fortuna, pecunia multa,
His uitae finem mors aliquando facit. [g$_4$]

123/3 destruxere] detraxere *1518;* almus,] *1518,* almus. *1520* 5 Phaedram] Phedram *1518* **124**/1 RHOMAM] ROMAM *1518*^{m} 7 Myrmidones] Mirmydones *1518;* Achilli,] *1518,* Achilli. *1520* **125**/3 est: sic] est. sic *1518 1520;* est,] *1518,* est. *1520*

123

ON LOVE, CHASTE AND UNCHASTE

FROM THE GREEK

These two conflicting emotions, one sinful and one ennobling, lust on one side and modesty on the other, brought death to two people. A consuming passion for Hippolytus destroyed Phaedra; and as for Hippolytus, alas, his holy chastity killed him.

124

ON THE CITY OF ROME

FROM THE GREEK

Hail, Hector, descendant of Mars; if you can hear at all beneath the earth, breathe again and take pride in the name of your native land. A city of Ilium lives, inhabited now by a glorious race—a race less powerful in battle than you, but still beloved of Mars. The Myrmidons have perished. Come, Hector, and tell Achilles that all Thessaly is subject to the descendants of Aeneas.

125

ON AVOIDING EXTREMES

FROM THE GREEK

Too much of anything is unpleasant. Thus even honey, as the old adage says, is always bitter if there is too much of it.

126

ON AN EXTREMELY UNHAPPY MAN

FROM THE GREEK

You have never lived, poor man, and you will never die, for, although you seem alive, in your misery you are dead. But death at last does make an end of life for those who have untold success and great wealth.

127

IN PYTHAGORAE ECHEMYTHIAM E GRAECO.

Rebus in humanis magna est doctrina tacere,
Testis erit sapiens hic mihi Pythagoras.
Nempe loqui doctus, reliquos docet ille tacere,
Magnum hoc ad requiem pharmacon inueniens.

128

RIDICVLVM IN GELLIAM.

Quid modo seclorum miremur monstra priorum,
Quod loquitur taurus, quod cadit imbre lapis?
Monstra antiqua nouum superat: surrexerat ecce
Ante tenebrosum Gellia uesper heri.
Plus dicturus eram, nisi me ridere putares,
Surrexit mediam, sed tamen ante diem.
Mira licet saepe illa tamen uidere priores,
Saepe potest forsan cernere posteritas,
Istud at hesternam nemo unquam uiderat ante,
Et post hanc poterit nemo uidere diem.

129

IN PALLADEM VENEREMQVE E GRAECO.

Cur ita me laedis Venerem Tritonia uirgo,
Corripis in digitos cur mea dona tuos?
Scilicet Idaeis memor esto in rupibus olim
Me non te pulchram censuit esse Paris.
Hasta tua est, ensisque tuus, mihi uendico malum.
Mars modo sit malo pristinus ille satis. [g$_4$v]

130

VITAM HOMINIS ESSE NIHIL.

Nos tenuem strictis spirantes aëra fibris,
Viuimus et Phoebi lampada conspicimus.

127/5 tacere,] tacere. *1518 1520* **128**/2 seclorum] saeclorum *1518*^{m} 3 cadit] *1518*, cadet *1520*, lapis?] lapis. *1518 1520* 4 superat:] superat. *1518*, superat, *1520*; ecce] *1518*^{d}, ecce, *1518*^{m}, ecce. *1520* 5 heri.] heri, *1518 1520* 8 saepe] *1518*, saepe, *1520* **129**/3 Tritonia] tritonia *1518* **130**/1 NIHIL.] *1518*, NIHIL, *1520*

127
ON PYTHAGORAS' TACITURNITY
FROM THE GREEK

In human affairs silence is great wisdom. On this point the wiseman Pythagoras will be my witness: himself a learned speaker, he taught others to keep quiet, since he found this was a potent drug to promote tranquillity.

128
A JOKE ON GELLIA

Why should we marvel only at the wonders of ages past—that a bull spoke or a stone fell in a rainstorm? There is a new wonder greater than the old. Just look, Gellia rose from her bed yesterday before the shadowy dusk. I was going to tell you more, but you would think I was joking. Well, just the same, she did get up before midday. Although ages past often saw those old marvels, though future ages will perhaps be able to see them as often, still, until yesterday no one had ever seen the miracle I describe, and after today no one will be able to see it ever again.

129
ON PALLAS AND VENUS
FROM THE GREEK

O Tritonian virgin, why do you wrong me, Venus, so? Why do you clutch my prize in your fingers? Remember that on the rocky side of Ida, if I may remind you, it was I, not you, whom Paris judged beautiful. The spear is yours, and the sword; but I claim the apple. Let the ancient contest suffice for the apple.

130
THAT HUMAN LIFE IS NOTHING

Breathing the unsubstantial air through narrow openings in our bodies, we live and look upon Phoebus' light. We are, every

Quotquot uiuimus hic sumus omnes organa, sed quae
Viuificis animat flatibus aura leuis.
Quod tua si tenuem restringat palma uaporem
Eripiens animam miseris usque Stygem.
Sic sumus ergo nihil, Plutoni pascimur omnes,
E flatu minimo nos leuis aura fouet.

131

IN PVGIONEM EBETEM EBETIS E GRAECO.

Plumbeus hic mucro tuus est obtusus, ebesque,
Mucro aciem ingenij fert tuus iste tui.

132

DE GLORIA ET POPVLI IVDICIO.

Maxima pars hominum fama sibi plaudit inani,
Atque leuis uento fertur in astra leui.
Quid populi tibi uoce places? saepe optima caecus
Dat uicio, et temere deteriora probat.
Sollicitus pendes alieno semper ab ore,
Ne laudem cerdo quam dedit, eripiat.
Fors tamen irridet quo tu laudante superbis.
Ex animo laudet, laus tamen illa fugit.
Quid tibi fama facit? toto lauderis ab orbe,
Articulus doleat, quid tibi fama facit? [h_1]

133

RIDICVLVM IN MINISTRVM.

Muscas e cratere tulit conuiua priusquam
Ipse bibit, reddit rursus, ut ipse bibit.
Addidit et causam, muscas ego non amo, dixit,
Sed tamen e uobis nescio num quis amet.

130/4 sed quae] quae *1518,* quaeque *1565* 5 leuis.] leuis, *1518 1520* 6 Quod] Quot *1518* 7 Stygem] stygem *1518 1520* **131**/4 tui.] *1518,* tui *1520* **132**/2 inani,] *1518,* inani. *1520* 4 caecus] caecus, *1518 1520* 5 probat.] *1518,* probat, *1520* 6 ore,] ore. *1518 1520* 8 Fors] *1518,* ors *1520* **133**/2 priusquam] *1518,* prius, quam *1520*

man alive, mere instruments—but such instruments as drafts of thin air endow with the breath of life. But if your hand should interrupt the delicate process of breathing, then you will tear out a living soul and send it to the underworld. This, then, is why we are nothing. We are all fattened up for Death; and what nourishes us is little breaths of thin air.

131
ON A DULLARD'S DULL DAGGER
FROM THE GREEK

This leaden point of yours is blunt and dull. The point is as sharp as your wits.

132
ON FAME AND POPULAR OPINION

Most men congratulate themselves if they attain to fame, empty though it is; and, because they are light-minded, they are lifted to the stars by the fickle wind of opinion. Why do you derive satisfaction from the comments of the populace? In their blindness they often interpret what is best as a failing and thoughlessly approve what is very reprehensible. You hang everlastingly upon a stranger's opinion for fear that some cobbler will retract the praise he has conferred. Perhaps the man whose praise makes you proud is mocking you. Though he praise you from his heart, that praise is ephemeral. What does fame do for you? You may be praised by the whole world, but if you have an aching joint, what does fame do for you?

133
JOKE ABOUT A WAITER

A certain guest at a banquet removed some flies from the mixing-bowl before he drank. When he had had his drink he put the flies back. He explained, "I do not like flies; but then, I do not know—some of you may like them."

134
DE CANE VENANTE.

Os canis implet anas, alium capturus hiabat,
  Non capit: at quam iam ceperat ore fugit.
Sic miser interea dum rem captas alienam,
  Saepius et merito perdis auare tuam.

135
CANIS IN PRAESEPI.
AVARVS HOMO.

In praesepe canis foeno nec uescitur ipse,
  Nec sinit ut foenum qui cupit indat equus.
Seruat auarus opes, opibus non utitur ipse,
  Atque alios uti qui cupiunt, prohibet.

136
IN ORESTEM PARANTEM OCCIDERE MATREM.
E GRAECO.

Qua gladium intrudes per uentremne, an ne papillas?
Te peperit uenter, te lactauere papillae.

137
QVOD PAVCIS ORANDVS DEVS.

Da bona siue rogere deus, seu nulla rogere,
Et mala siue rogere nega, seu nulla rogere. [h_1v]

138
IN DIGAMOS.
E GRAECO.

Qui capit uxorem defuncta uxore secundam,
  Naufragus in tumido bis natat ille freto.

134/2 anas,] anas *1518 1520* **135**/4 indat] edat *1518 1563* **136**/2 E GRAECO.] *om. 1518* 4 peperit uenter,] *1518,* peperit, inter *1520,* peperit, uenter *1520* (*errata*) **137**/1 QVOD] QVID *1518* 3 Et . . . rogere.] Et procul a nobis mala quaeque petentibus aufer, | Et mala siue petare nega, seu nulla petare. *1518;* rogere.] rogere *1520* **138**/4 *After this poem in 1518 comes the poem* IN FATVM E GRAECO, *which is omitted in 1520 (see no. 270).*

134
ON A HUNTING DOG

One duck was in the dog's mouth when he opened it to catch another. He missed it, and the one he had already caught escaped from his mouth. In this way, miser, while you wretchedly strive to ensnare the property of another, you more often than not lose your own; and it serves you right.

135
THE MISER IS A DOG IN THE MANGER

The dog in the manger does not himself eat the hay, nor does he let the horse, who wants hay, take any. The miser guards his wealth, does not use it himself. And those who want to put it to some use he keeps at a distance.

136
TO ORESTES, ABOUT TO KILL HIS MOTHER
FROM THE GREEK

Where will you thrust the sword, through the womb or through the breast? The womb bore you, the breasts gave you suck.

137
WHAT WE SHOULD ASK FROM GOD, IN FEW WORDS

Give us, God, what is good, whether you are asked or not; and, asked or not, withhold what is evil.

138
ON MEN TWICE MARRIED
FROM THE GREEK

The widower who marries again is a shipwrecked sailor who a second time sails the stormy sea.

139

DE SOMNO AEQVANTE PAVPEREM CVM DIVITE.

Somne quies uitae, spes et solamen egenis,
Diuitibus noctu, quos facis esse pares,
Tristia demulces lethaeo pectora rore,
Excutis et sensum totius inde mali.
Laeta benignus opes inopi per somnia mittis.
Quid falsas rides diues opes inopis?
Diuitibus uerae curas, tormenta, dolores,
Pauperibus falsae gaudia uera ferunt.

140

IN DEFORMEM ET IMPROBVM, E GRAECO.

Pingere difficile est animum, depingere corpus,
Hoc facile est. In te sunt tamen ambo secus.
Nam prauos animi mores natura reuelans,
Fecit ut emineant undique perspicui.
Sed formae portenta tuae deformia membra
Quis pingat? quando haec cernere nemo uelit?

141

IN CAPPADOCEM VIRVLENTVM E GRAECO.

Vipera Cappadocem mordens mala protinus hausto
Tabifico perijt sanguine Cappadocis. [h_2]

142

IN STATVAM FERREAM, E GRAECO.

Effigiem statuere tibi rex perditor orbis
Ex ferro, ut longe uilius aere foret.
Hoc fecere fames, caedes, furor, acris egestas,
Haec tua quis omnes perdit auaritia.

139/3 uitae,] uitae *1518 1520* 4 pares,] pares. *1518 1520* **139**/9 uerae] uere *1518 1520* (*see Commentary*) 10 falsae] false *1518* **140**/4 In] in *1518 1520* **141**/3 hausto] hausto, *1518 1520* **142**/5 furor, acris] furor aeris, *1518 1520* (*see Commentary*) 6 tua] tua, *1518 1520*

139
ON SLEEP, WHICH MAKES THE POOR MAN THE RICH MAN'S EQUAL

O sleep, peaceful part of life, hope and comfort of the poor, whom by night you make equal to the rich, you soothe sad hearts with the gentle dew of forgetfulness and drive away all awareness of woe. Generously in happy dreams you confer wealth upon the poor man. Why do you, rich man, scorn the poor man's fancied wealth? Real wealth brings to the rich worry, pain, and grief; imagined wealth brings the poor real joy.

140
ON AN UGLY, WICKED MAN
FROM THE GREEK

It is difficult to represent a soul, easy to portray a body. In your case the opposite is true, for your appearance so reveals your vicious habits that they are easily discernible all over you. But who would paint your ugly bodily parts, the omens of your inner form, since no one would willingly look at them?

141
ON A POISONOUS CAPPADOCIAN
FROM THE GREEK

A deadly viper bit a Cappadocian: having imbibed the corrosive blood of the Cappadocian, it died at once.

142
ON AN IRON STATUE
FROM THE GREEK

To you, the king who ravaged the world, they set up a statue of iron—as far cheaper than bronze. This economy was the result of starvation, slaughter, wrath, and cruel poverty. These are the instruments by which your greed has ravaged all.

143

VERSVS IAMBICI DIMETRI BRACHY-CATALECTICI AD CANDIDVM, QVALIS VXOR DELIGENDA.

Iam tempus id petit
Monetque Candide,
Vagis amoribus
Tandem renuncies,
Tandemque desinas
Incerta Cypridis
Sequi cubilia.
Quaerasque uirginem,
Quam rite iam tibi
Concorde uincias
Amore coniugem,
Quae iam genus tuum,
Quo nil beatius,
Foecunda dulcibus
Natis adaugeat.
Pater tibi tuus
Hoc ante praestitit.
Quod a prioribus
Prius receperis
Non absque foenore
Repende posteris.
Non sit tibi tamen
Haec cura maxima
Spectare Candide
Quid dotis afferat,
Quam situe candida.
Infirmus est amor,
Quem stultus impetus
Decore concitus
Parit, uel improbus
Ardor pecuniae.

143/8 desinas] sinas *1565* 18 adaugeat.] adaugeat, *1518 1520* 20 praestitit.] praestitit, *1518 1520*

143

TO CANDIDUS: HOW TO CHOOSE A WIFE
A POEM IN IAMBIC DIMETER BRACHYCATALECTIC

Your time of life, Candidus, is now reaching a point where it suggests that at last you reject temporary attachments, that you cease at last to pursue haphazard love affairs, and that you find a girl to take as wife formally and in mutual devotion. Let her be fruitful and add sweet children to your most splendid line. Your father did as much for you. Hand on with increase to your descendants what you have already received from your ancestors.

Still, do not let your primary concern be how much dowry she brings or how beautiful she is. Weakness marks any love which arises either from a blind impulse roused by mere beauty or from a base love of money.

Quicunque amauerit
Propter pecuniam
Amatur huic nihil [h_2v]
Praeter pecuniam.
Capta pecunia
Vanescit ilico
Item fugax amor,
Fereque iam prius
Perit quam nascitur.
At nec pecunia,
Quam auarus antea
Miser cupiuerat,
Iuuare postea
Quicquam potest, ubi
Quam non amauerit
Inuitus attamen
Omnino cogitur
Tenere coniugem.
Quid forma? numquid haec
Vel febre decidit?
Annisue deperit?
Vt sole flosculus:
Tum defluentibus
Genae coloribus,
Amor ligauerant
Quem haec sola uincula,
Solutus aufugit.
At uerus est amor
Quem mente perspicax,
Ratione consule
Prudens iniuerit;
Et quem bono omine
Virtutis inclytae,
(Quae certa permanens

143/40 ilico] ilico, *1518 1520* 50 Inuitus] Inuitus. *1518,* Inuitus, *1520* 56 flosculus:] *1520,* flosculus *1518* 58 coloribus,] coloribus. *1518 1520* 59 Amor] Amor, *1518 1520* 65 iniuerit;] iniuerit. *1518 1520*

The man who loves for money's sake loves only money. As soon as he acquires the money, his fleeting love is gone and dies almost before it is born. And the money, which in his miserable selfishness he had coveted earlier, cannot help him in the least later on when he is required, however unwilling, to keep the wife he does not love.

What is beauty? Does it not fail in sickness, perish with time? Like a flower in the sun. Then, when the bloom leaves her cheek, a love secured only by such ties as these breaks free and is gone forever. Only a man of intelligence and foresight, with reason for his guide, can enter upon true love. True love is inspired, with happy promise, by respect for a woman's glorious virtue, a noble

Non febre decidit,
Annisue deperit)
Respectus efficit.
Primum ergo quam uoles
Amice, ducere,
Quibus parentibus
Sit orta perspice:
Vt mater optimis
Sit culta moribus,
Cuius tenellula
Mores puellula
Insugat, exprimat.
Tum qua sit indole,
Quam dulcis, hoc uide,
Vt ore uirginis
Insit serenitas,
Ab ore uirginis
Absitque toruitas;
At rursus ut tamen
Sit in genis pudor,
Nec ore uirginis [h_3]
Insit procacitas.
Et sit quieta, nec
Cingat salacibus
Viros lacertulis.
Vultu modesta sit,
Nec spectet undique
Vagis ocellulis.
Proculque stulta sit
Paruis labellulis
Semper loquacitas,
Proculque rusticum
Semper silentium.
Sit illa uel modo

143/70 deperit)] deperit, *1518* deperit,) *1520* 73 Amice, ducere,] Amice ducere. *1518 1520* 75 perspice:] perspice. *1518 1520* 86 toruitas;] toruitas. *1518 1520* 90 procacitas.] procacitas, *1518 1520* 93 lacertulis.] lacertulis, *1518 1520* 99 loquacitas,] loquacitas. *1518 1520*

gift which endures, does not fail in sickness, does not perish with the years.

And so, my friend, if you desire to marry, first observe what kind of parents the lady has. See to it that her mother is revered for the excellence of her character which is sucked in and expressed by her tender and impressionable little girl.

Next see to this: what sort of personality she has; how agreeable she is. Let her maidenly countenance be calm and without severity. But let her modesty bring blushes to her cheeks; let her glance not be provocative. Let her be mild-mannered, not throwing her slender arms wantonly around men's necks. Let her glances be restrained; let her have no roving eye. Let her pretty lips always be free of pointless garrulity and also of boorish taciturnity. Let

Instructa literis,
Vel talis ut modo
Sit apta literis,
Felix, quibus bene
Priscis ab optimis
Possit libellulis
Vitam beantia
Haurire dogmata.
Armata, cum quibus
Nec illa prosperis
Superba turgeat,
Nec illa turbidis
Misella lugeat
Prostrata casibus.
Iucunda sic erit
Semper, nec unquam erit
Grauis, molestaue
Vitae comes tuae.
Quae docta paruulos,
Docebit et tuos
Cum lacte literas
Olim nepotulos.
Iam te iuuauerit
Viros relinquere,
Doctaeque coniugis
Sinu quiescere,
Dum grata te fouet,
Manuque mobili
Dum plectra personant
Et uoce (qua nec est
Progne sororculae
Tuae suauior)
Amoena cantilat,
Apollo quae uelit

143/105 literis,] literis. *1518 1520* 116 casibus.] casibus *1518 1520* 128 quiescere,] quiescere. *1518 1520* 130 mobili] mobili. *1518 1520* 131 personant] personat. *1518*, personant. *1520* 134 suauior] suauior. *1518 1520* 135 cantilat,] *1518*, cantilat. *1520*

her be either just finishing her education or ready to begin it immediately. Happy is the woman whose education permits her to derive from the best of ancient works the principles which confer a blessing on life. Armed with this learning, she would not yield to pride in prosperity, nor to grief in distress—even though misfortune strike her down. For this reason your lifetime companion will be ever agreeable, never a trouble or a burden. If she is well instructed herself, then some day she will teach your little grandsons, at an early age, to read.

You will be glad to leave the company of men and to seek repose in the bosom of your accomplished wife, the while she attends to your comfort, and while under her dexterous touch the plucked strings resound, while in a sweet voice (as sweet, Procne, as your sister's) she sings delightful songs such as Apollo would be

Audire carmina.
Iam te iuuauerit
Sermone blandulo
Docto tamen, dies
Noctesque ducere, [h3v]
Notare uerbula
Mellita maximis
Non absque gratijs
Ab ore melleo
Semper fluentia,
Quibus coherceat
Si quando te leuet
Inane gaudium,
Quibus leuauerit,
Siquando deprimat
Te moeror anxius,
Certabit in quibus
Summa eloquentia
Iam cum omnium graui
Rerum scientia.
Talem olim ego putem,
Et uatis Orphei
Fuisse coniugem
Nec unquam ab inferis
Curasset improbo
Labore foeminam
Referre rusticam.
Talemque credimus
Nasonis inclytam,
Quae uel patrem queat
Aequare carmine,
Fuisse filiam.
Talemque suspicor
(Qua nulla charior
Vnquam fuit patri,

143/141 ducere,] ducere. *1518 1520* 147 coherceat] cohaerceat. *1518 1520* 152 anxius,] anxius *1518 1520* 153 Certabit] Certabit, *1518 1520*

glad to hear. Then you will be glad to spend days and nights in pleasant and intelligent conversation, listening to the sweet words which ever most charmingly flow from her honeyed mouth. By her comments she would restrain you if ever vain success should exalt you and would comfort you if grievous sorrow should cast you down. When she speaks, it will be difficult to choose between her perfect power of expression and her thoughtful understanding of all kinds of affairs.

I should think that the wife of the bard Orpheus long ago was such a woman; he would never have devoted such enormous effort to recovering from the underworld an uncultivated woman.

Such a woman, I believe, was Ovid's famous daughter, who could rival in poetical composition even her own father.

Such a woman, I suspect, was Tullia—never was daughter more

Quo nemo doctior)
Fuisse Tulliam.
Talisque, quae tulit
Gracchos duos, fuit,
Quae quos tulit, bonis
Instruxit artibus.
Nec profuit minus
Magistra quam parens.
Quid prisca secula
Tandem reuoluimus?
Vtcunque rusticum,
Vnam tamen tenet
Nostrumque uirginem,
Tenet, sed unicam,
At sic ut unicam
Plerisque praeferat,
Cuique conferat
Ex hijs, fuisse, quae
Narrantur omnibus
Tot retro seculis,
Quae nunc et ultimam
Monet Britanniam [h_4]
Perlata pennulis
Famae uolucribus,
Laus atque gloria
Orbis puellula
Totius unica,
Ac non modo suae
Cassandra patriae.
Dic ergo Candide,
Si talis et tibi
Puella nuberet,
Quales ego tibi

143/180 Quid] *1518*, Qutd *1520;* secula] saecula, *1518*[m], secula, *1518*[d] *1520* 184 uirginem,] uirginem *1518 1520* 187 praeferat,] praeferat. *1518 1520* 191 seculis] *1518*[d] *1520*, saeculis *1518*[m] 194 pennulis] penulis *1518* 195 Famae] Fame *1518 1520;* uolucribus,] uolucribus. *1518 1520* 201 Candide] *1518*[m], candide *1518*[d] *1520*

beloved by a father, himself in learning second to none.

Such a woman was the mother of the two Gracchi. She taught her sons right principles; she accomplished no less as their teacher than she did as their mother.

Why do I continue to contemplate ancient times? After all, our age, however rude it may be, does have one maiden, though it has only one, whom it may set above almost all others and compare with any of those women whose stories come down to us from ages past. Borne high upon the soaring wings of fame, she now gives warning even to remotest Britain, the one and only boast and glory of the whole world, not merely the Cassandra of her own country.

Say Candidus, if you were to marry a woman such as those I

Supra recensui,
Desit licet queas
Formam requirere,
Dotisue quod parum
Lucrere conqueri?
Hic sermo uerus est,
Quaecunque sit, satis
Est bella quae placet,
Nec quisquam habet magis
Quam qui sibi satis
Quodcunque habet, putat.
Sic nunc me amet mea,
Vt nil ego tibi,
Amice, mentiar.
Cuicunque gratiam
Formae negauerit
Natura uirgini,
Certe licet siet
Carbone nigrior,
Foret tamen mihi hac
Virtutis indole
Olore pulchrior.
Cuicunque lubrica
Dotem negauerit
Fortuna uirgini,
Certe siet licet
Vel Iro egentior,
Foret tamen mihi hac
Virtutis indole
Te Croese ditior.

144

RIDICVLVM IN MINACEM.

Thrasonis uxorem bubulcus rusticus
Absente eo uitiauerat.

143/205 recensui,] recensui. *1518 1520* 207 requirere,] requirere. *1518 1520* 209 conqueri?] conqueri, *1518 1520* 214 sibi satis] *1518,* tibi satis. *1520* 215 putat.] *1518,* putat, *1520* 217 tibi,] tibi *1518 1520* 218 Amice,] Amice *1518 1520* **144**/2 bubulcus] *1518*[d] *1520,* Bubulcus *1518*[m]

have mentioned above, could you, even if she were not beautiful, find her wanting or complain that you gain too little by her dowry? This is the truth of the matter: whatever her looks, she is beautiful enough if her looks give pleasure; and no man possesses more than he who is content with what he has.

May my own wife cease to love me if I am not telling you the truth, my friend. If Nature has denied the gift of beauty to a girl, yes, though she be blacker than coal, still, if she has this virtuous disposition, she would be in my eyes fairer than the swan. If fickle Fortune has denied her a dowry, yes, though she be poorer than Irus, still, if she has this virtuous disposition, she would be in my eyes richer, Croesus, than you.

144

A FUNNY STORY ABOUT A SWAGGERER

While Thraso the soldier was away, a rough herdsman seduced

Domum reuersus miles ut rem comperit,
Armatus et ferus insilit. [h_4v]
Tandem assecutus solum in agris rusticum,
Heus clamat heus heus furcifer.
Restat bubulcus, saxaque in sinum legit.
Ille ense stricto clamitat,
Tu coniugem meam attigisti carnifex?
Respondit imperterritus,
Feci: fateris? inquit. At ego omnes deos,
Deasque testor, O scelus,
In pectus hunc ensem tibi capulo tenus,
Ni fassus esses, abderem.

145
DE MEDIOCRITATE
E GRAECO.

Agros ego haud porrectiores appeto.
Non auream aut Gygis beatitudinem.
Quae sit satis sibi, uita sat eadem est mihi.
Illud nihil nimis, nimis mihi placet.

146
HECTOR MORIENS.
E GRAECO.

Proijcitote meum, Danai, post fata cadauer,
Nam metuunt lepores occisi membra leonis.

147
IN STVLTVM POETAM.

Scripserat Aeneam nulli pietate secundum,
Vates secundus nemini.
Quidam igitur regem dum uult laudare, Maronem
Pulchre aemulatus scilicet,
Hic hic est, inquit, princeps cui nemo secundus.
Hac laude rex indignus est, [i_1]

144/6 rusticum,] *1518,* rusticum. *1520* 12 fateris? inquit.] fateris, inquit? *1518 1520* 13 testor,] testor *1518 1520* **145**/4 beatitudinem] *1518,* beatudinem *1520 1563* 5 mihi.] mihi, *1518 1520* 6 nihil] nil *1565;* mihi] *om.* 1565 **146**/3 meum, Danai,] meum Danai *1518 1520*

his wife. When the soldier came home and heard the story, he picked up his sword and rushed in savage pursuit. When at length he found the rustic alone in a field, he shouted, "You, say, you there, you rascal." The herdsman stopped and picked up an armful of stones. The soldier, with drawn sword, shouted, "Did you lay hand on my wife, you scoundrel?" The herdsman calmly answered, "I did." "You confess it," said the soldier. "By all the gods and goddesses, you villain, I swear that I would plunge this sword hilt-deep into your heart if you had not confessed."

145

ON AVOIDING EXTREMES

FROM THE GREEK

I have no desire for more spacious fields; I do not want the golden bliss of Gyges. Living enough to sustain life is living enough for me. That saying "Avoid excess" suits me excessively.

146

HECTOR DYING

FROM THE GREEK

Get rid of my body when I am dead, you Greeks, for hares fear the carcass of a lion.

147

ON A STUPID POET

The poet who is second to none wrote long ago that in piety Aeneas was second to none. And so a certain fellow who wanted to praise the king said—in elegant imitation of Vergil, of course—"Here is a king to whom no one is second." The king does not

Ipse sed est uates dignissimus. Ergo age demus
Vtrique laudem debitam.
Hic hic est igitur uates, cui nemo secundus,
Rex qui secundus nemini.

148

IN QVENDAM QVI SCRIPSERAT HYMNOS DE DIVIS PARVM DOCTE, TESTATVS IN PRAEFATIONE SE EX TEMPORE SCRIPSISSE NEC SERVASSE LEGES CARMINVM, ET ARGVMENTVM NON RECIPERE ELOQVENTIAM.

Hic sacer Andreae cunctos ex ordine fastos
Perstringit mira cum breuitate liber.
Ipsos quos cecinit superos, dum scriberet omneis,
Credibile est uati consuluisse suo.
Nam subito scripsit, sed sic ut scribere posset
Quantumuis longo tempore non melius.
Et pia materia est, priscisque intactus ab ipsis
Seruatus fato est huic operi iste stilus,
Seque quod ad numeros non anxius obligat omnes,
Hoc quoque non uitio sed ratione facit.
Maiestas operis metro esse obnoxia non uult,
Nempe ibi libertas est, ubi spiritus est. [i_1v]
Ipsa operis pietas indocto sufficit, at tu
Castalio quisquis fonte bibisse soles,
Singula si trutines, erit hinc tibi tanta uoluptas,
Quanta tibi ex alio non fuit ante libro.

149

IN STRATOPHONTA PVGILEM IGNAVVM E GRAECO.

Dux Ithacus, patria bis denos abfuit annos.
Quum redijt, celeri cognitus usque cani est.

147/8 Ipse] *1518,* Ipse, *1520;* dignissimus. Ergo] dignissimus. ergo *1518,* dignissimus, ergo *1520* 11 nemini.] *1518*[m] *1520,* memini, *1518*[d] **148**/11 posset] *1518,* posset. *1520* 15 omnes,] *1518,* omnes. *1520* 18 est.] est, *1518 1520* **149**/3 annos.] *1518,* annos, *1520*

deserve such praise as this; but the poet himself richly deserves it. So let us give each the praise which is his due: here is a poet, then, to whom no one is second; here is a king who is second to none.

148

ON A CERTAIN AUTHOR WHO IN UNLEARNED STYLE WROTE HYMNS IN HONOR OF THE SAINTS, EXPLAINING IN HIS PREFACE THAT HE WROTE THEM IN AN OFFHAND WAY WITHOUT OBSERVING THE RULES OF METER AND THAT HIS SUBJECT MATTER REQUIRED NO ELOQUENCE

This sacred book of André's contains within marvelously small compass all the feast days of the year in chronological order. It is credible that all the saints celebrated here took counsel for their poet when he wrote; for he wrote in haste, but even so with all the time in the world he could not have written better. His subject matter is religious, and his style was untouched by the ancients and kept in reserve by fate for the present work. If he does not anxiously restrict himself to all the usual quantities, this too is not done by mistake but for a reason. The majesty of the work refuses to be subjected to metrical rule. Assuredly, where the Spirit is, there also is liberty. For the unlearned reader the piety of the book alone suffices; but you who are one accustomed to drink from the Castalian spring will receive such pleasure from this book, if you examine it closely, as you have never had before from any other.

149

ON STRATOPHON, A WORTHLESS PRIZEFIGHTER FROM THE GREEK

Ulysses, warrior-king of Ithaca, was away from home for twenty years; when he returned, he was still recognized by his swift dog.

Te pugil O Stratophon, certantem quattuor horas,
Et canis et populus dedidicere simul.
Quin etiam speculum de te si consulis ipse,
Iuratus Stratophon te Stratophonta neges.

150

IN PVGILEM IGNAVVM

E GRAECO.

Nesimus ecce pugil uatem consultat Olympum,
An uentura sibi sera senecta foret.
Fors rude donatus uiues, ait ille, minatur
Certanti gelidus sed tibi falce deus.

151

IN PARASITVM

E GRAECO.

Stare putes stadio Eutychides quum curreret, at quum
Curreret ad coenam, nempe uolare putes.

152

IN BIBONEM

E GRAECO.

Serta, unguenta, meo ne gratificare sepulchro.
Vina, focus, lapidi sumptus inanis erit.
Haec mihi da uiuo. Cineres miscere falerno,
Nempe lutum facere est, non dare uina mihi. [i_2]

153

IN BIBONEM

E GRAECO.

E terra genitus, sub terram morte recondar.
Ergo lagena mihi terrea plena ueni.

149/5 quattuor] quatuor *1518* 7 te] *1518,* te, *1520* 8 neges.] *1518,* neges *1520* **150**/4 foret.] *1518,* foret, *1520* 6 gelidus] *1518,* gelidus, *1520* **151**/3 Eutychides] *1518,* Eutichydes *1520* **152**/3 sepulchro.] *1518,* sepulchro, *1520* 5 uiuo. Cineres] uiuo, cineres *1518 1520* **153**/3 recondar.] recondar, *1518 1520* 4 ueni.] *1518,* ueni, *1520*

Well, prizefighter Stratophon, now that you have fought for four hours, your dog and your fellow citizens alike could no longer recognize you. As a matter of fact, Stratophon, if you looked at yourself in a mirror, you would yourself under oath deny that you are Stratophon.

150
ON A WORTHLESS PRIZEFIGHTER
FROM THE GREEK

Here is Nesimus, a prizefighter, who asks the prophet Olympus if advanced old age is to be his lot. The prophet answers, "Perhaps you will live if you retire; but, as long as you continue fighting, the god who brings the chill of death threatens you with his scythe."

151
ON A PARASITE
FROM THE GREEK

When Eutychides runs a race in the stadium, you would think he was standing still; but when he runs to dinner, you would think he was flying.

152
ON A DRINKER
FROM THE GREEK

Do not offer wreaths and unguents at my tomb. To buy wine and warmth for a stone will be a useless expense. Give me these things while I am alive, for throwing good wine on my ashes gives me no wine; it just makes mud.

153
ON A DRINKER
FROM THE GREEK

I was born of earth; when I die, I shall be restored to earth. Therefore, come to me full, earthen bottle.

154

IN MVLIEREM FOEDAM
E GRAECO.

Te speculum fallit, speculum nam Gellia uerum,
  Si semel inspiceres, nunquam iterum inspiceres.

155

IN FOEDAM
E GRAECO.

Fugerit ad Parthos, uel ad Herculis usque columnas,
  Visa semel, positis uestibus, Antipatra.

156

IN FOEDAM
E GRAECO.

Qui miser uxorem deformem duxit, habebit
  Vespere, iam accenso lumine, adhuc tenebras.

157

IN BARBA TANTVM PHILOSOPHVM.
E GRAECO.

Si promissa facit sapientem barba, quid obstat
  Barbatus possit quin caper esse Plato?

158

DE LICENTIA.

Vltra concessos indulta licentia fines
  Prouehitur celeri, non reuocanda gradu.
Si patiare pedem calcet tibi uespere coniunx,
  Calcabit surgens haec tibi mane caput.

159

EPITAPHIVM ABYNGDONII CANTORIS.

Attrahat huc oculos, aures attraxerat olim
  Nobilis Henricus cantor Abyngdonius. [i_2v]

157/4 caper] caper, *1518 1520*   **158**/5 mane] mane, *1518 1520*

154

ON AN UGLY WOMAN

FROM THE GREEK

Your looking glass deceives you, Gellia, for, if you once looked into a true looking glass, you would never look again.

155

ON AN UGLY WOMAN

FROM THE GREEK

Antipatra would run to Parthia or to the pillars of Hercules if anyone caught a glimpse of her naked.

156

ON AN UGLY WOMAN

FROM THE GREEK

The unhappy man who has an ugly wife will still have darkness when the lamps are lighted in the evening.

157

ON A MAN WHO WAS A PHILOSOPHER ONLY BY REASON OF HIS BEARD

FROM THE GREEK

If an untrimmed beard makes a philosopher, why could not a bearded goat be a Plato?

158

ON GRANTING LIBERTIES

Freedom, if unrestrained, exceeds quickly and irrevocably its proper bounds. If you let your wife stamp on your foot tonight, tomorrow upon rising she will stamp on your head.

159

EPITAPH OF ABYNGDON, THE SINGER

Let the famed singer, Henry Abyngdon, draw your eyes hither; there was a time when he drew your ears with his music. Not long

Vnus erat, nuper mira qui uoce sonaret.
  Organa qui scite tangeret, unus erat.
Vellensis primo templi decus, inde sacellum
  Rex illo uoluit nobilitare suum.
Nunc illum Regi rapuit deus, intulit astris,
  Ipsis ut noua sit gloria caelitibus.

160

ALTERVM DE EODEM.

Hic iacet Henricus, semper pietatis amicus.
Nomen Abyngdon erat, si quis sua nomina quaerat.
Vuellis hic ecclesia fuerat succentor in alma,
Regis et in bella cantor fuit ipse capella.
Millibus in mille cantor fuit optimus ille.
Praeter et haec ista, fuit optimus orgaquenista.
Nunc igitur Christe quoniam tibi seruijt iste
  Semper in orbe soli, da sibi regna poli.

161

IN IANVM HAEREDEM ABYNGDONII.

Scripsi elegum carmen, Iano me haerede rogante,
  Quod tumulum Henrici signet Abyngdonij.
Displicet, et doctis bene displicuisset, at illi
  Displicet hoc tantum, si quid inest melius.
Non resonant isti uersus, ait; illico sensi
  Qualeis lactucas, talia labra petant.
Ridendos ergo ridens effutio uersus.
  Hos uorat applaudens Ianus utraque manu.
Hos tumulo inscalpsit, sub eundem protinus obdi
  Atque ijsdem dignus uersibus ipse legi. [i3]
Ante retroque bifrons Ianus deus omnia uidit.
  Talpa, effrons uidet hic Ianus utrinque nihil.

160/7 orgaquenista.] *1518,* orgaq́ȝ nista, *1520* 8 iste] *1518,* iste, *1520*
161/3 Abyngdonij.] Abyngdonij, *1520* 4 displicuisset,] displicuisset. *1518 1520* 6 ait;] ait, *1518 1520;* sensi] *1518,* sensi. *1520* 10 inscalpsit] insculpsit *1518;* obdi] obdi, *1518,* obdi. *1520* 11 uersibus] *1518,* uersibus, *1520* 13 uidet] *1518,* uidet, *1520*

ago he sang in a voice marvelous beyond compare and played the organ with incomparable skill. At first he was the pride of the church at Wells; then the king decided that he should lend his fame to the Chapel Royal. Now God has taken him away from the king and installed him among the stars to add glory to the very inhabitants of heaven.

160

ANOTHER EPITAPH ON THE SAME MAN

Here lies Henry, the constant friend of piety. Abyngdon was his family name, if anyone should want his full name. He was once succentor of the kindly church at Wells; and later he became chanter in the beautiful Chapel Royal. He was the best singer among a million. And besides this he was the best of organists. And so now, Christ, since he served you always on earth, admit him to the Kingdom of Heaven.

161

ON JANUS, ABYNGDON'S HEIR

I wrote a poem in elegiac couplets to mark the tomb of Henry Abyngdon at the request of his heir, Janus. Janus did not like it—and it might well have failed to please learned men. But Janus disliked only its better parts. "These verses of yours do not rhyme," he said. I realized at once what kind of inferior food such lips as his like. With a laugh I blurted out some laughable verses. He clapped his hands with delight and gobbled them up. These are the verses he had inscribed on the tomb. He deserves to be thrust forthwith into the same tomb and to be distinguished by the same epitaph. The two-faced god, Janus, sees everything in front of him and behind him. This barefaced Janus, like a faceless mole, sees nothing before or behind.

162

AD AVLICVM.

Saepe mihi iactas faciles te ad principis aures
  Libere et arbitrio ludere saepe tuo.
Sic inter domitos sine noxa saepe leones
  Luditur, ac noxae non sine saepe metu.
Infremit incerta crebra indignatio caussa
  Et subito mors est, qui modo ludus erat.
Tuta tibi non est, ut sit secura uoluptas.
  Magna tibi est, mihi sit dummodo certa minor.

163

IN TYNDALVM DEBITOREM.

Ante meos quam credideram tibi Tyndale nummos
  Quum libuit, licuit te mihi saepe frui.
At nunc si tibi me fors angulus offerat ullus,
  Haud secus ac uiso qui pauet angue, fugis.
Non fuit unquam animus mihi crede reposcere nummos.
  Non fuit, at ne te perdere cogar, erit.
Perdere te saluo nummos uolo, perdere utrunque
  Nolo, sat alterutrum sit perijsse mihi.
Ergo tibi nummis, aut te mihi redde, retentis.
  Aut tu cum nummis te mihi redde meis.
Quod tibi si neutrum placeat, nummi mihi saltem
  Fac redeant, at tu non rediture, Vale. [i3v]

164

IN MENDICVM GERENTEM SE PRO MEDICO.

Tu te fers medicum, nos te plus esse fatemur,
  Vna tibi plus est litera, quam medico.

162/2 aures] *1518,* aures. *1520*   3 Libere . . . tuo] Liber, et arbitrio ludis ut ipse tuo *1518*   4 leones] leones, *1518 1520*   5 metu.] *1518,* metu, *1520*   8 uoluptas.] uoluptas *1518 1520*   **163**/5 uiso] uiso, *1518 1520*   7 fuit,] *1518,* fuit. *1520;* erit.] *1518,* erit *1520*   8 utrunque] *1518,* utrunque, *1520*

162
TO A COURTIER

You often boast to me that you have the king's ear and often have fun with him, freely and according to your own whims. This is like having fun with tamed lions—often it is harmless, but just as often there is the fear of harm. Often he roars in rage for no known reason, and suddenly the fun becomes fatal. The pleasure you get is not safe enough to relieve you of anxiety. For you it is a great pleasure. As for me, let my pleasure be less great—and safe.

163
TO TYNDAL, HIS DEBTOR

Before I lent you the money, Tyndal, I had the pleasure of your company as often as I liked. But now, if you happen to see me around some corner, you run from me in terror like a man who has just seen a snake. I had no intention of asking for my money back. I had none, but rather than be forced to lose you, I shall. To keep you I am willing to lose the money; but I am not willing to lose both—one or the other is loss enough for me. Therefore, either keep the money and give me back your friendship, or give me back your friendship and the money too. But if neither way pleases you, then at least see that I do not lose my money. And you, lost friend, farewell.

164
ON A BEGGAR WHO PRETENDS HE IS A PHYSICIAN

You pass yourself off as a physician; we grant you that and more. You are one letter more (*mendicus*) than physician (*medicus*).

165

IN VXOREM IMPVDICAM.

Est foecunda mei, foecunda est uxor Arati,
Nempe suo genuit ter sine foeta uiro.

166

IN PERPVSILLVM E GRAECO.

Vt fugeret miserae Diophantus taedia uitae,
Vsus Arachneo est stamine, pro laqueo.

167

DE PVELLA QVAE RAPTVM FINXIT.

Conspiceret solam iuuenis cum forte puellam,
Et sibi oportunum crederet esse locum,
Improbus inuitam cupidis amplectitur ulnis,
Basiaque et plusquam basia ferre parat.
Illa reluctata est, legemque irata minatur,
Qua miser, effuso sanguine, raptor obit.
Instetit ille tamen iuuenili ardore proteruus,
Nunc precibus satagit, nunc superare metu.
Non precibus, non illa metu superata reclamat.
Calce petit, mordet dente, manuque ferit.
Ira subit iuuenem iam pene libidine maior,
Et ferus, O demens siccine pergis, ait.
Per tibi ego hunc ensem iuro, simul extulit ensem,
Commoda ni iaceas, ac taceas, abeo. [i4]
Illico succubuit tam tristi territa uerbo,
Atque age, sed quod agis, ui tamen, inquit, agis.

168

IN CHRYSALVM.

Chrysalus in syluis loculos quum conderet, haesit,
Certa loci possent, quae sibi signa capi.
At super ut summa raucum uidet arbore coruum,

167/1–17 DE PVELLA . . . agis.] *om.* 1565 3 locum,] *1518,* locum. *1520* 4 ulnis,] *1518,* ulnis. *1520* 16 Illico] Ilico *1518;* succubuit] *1518 1520* (*errata*), succubit *1520*

165

ON AN UNFAITHFUL WIFE

Fruitful, how very fruitful is the wife of my friend Aratus. Yes, three times she has conceived and borne fruit with no help from her husband.

166

ON A TINY MAN

FROM THE GREEK

To escape the dull grind of his miserable life, Diophantus used a spider's thread, used it for a noose.

167

ON A GIRL WHO FEIGNED RAPE

When a young man saw a girl all by herself and thought that this was his chance, the rascal put his eager arms around her—unwilling as she was—and was prepared to give her kisses, and more than kisses too. She struggled against him and angrily cited the law which condemns wretched rapists to have their heads cut off. But still, with a young man's eagerness, the shameless fellow did his best to win her over either by coaxing or threatening. She resisted both coaxing and threats; she screamed. She kicked him, bit him, struck him. The young man's anger grew almost as great as his lust. Savagely he said, "You wildcat, so that's the way it is. I swear to you by this sword"—and he drew his weapon—" if you do not lie down nice and easy, and shut up, I'll go away." Terrified by so dire a threat she lay down at once and said, "Go ahead and do it, but what you do you do by force."

168

ON CHRYSALUS

When Chrysalus was burying his treasure chest in the forest, he stopped to think what sure marks he could find to locate the spot. And when he saw a noisy crow in the top of a tree he said, "Here

Hic mihi conspicua est, inquit, abitque, nota.
Capti sola scopi redeuntem copia lusit,
Nam sua iam in quauis arbore signa uidet.

169

IN ASTROLOGVM.

Dum tua quos noster celebrat pro uatibus error
Fata cient positu syderis astrologi,
Haec dum stella fauet, dumque haec tibi stella minatur,
Pendula mens inter spemque, metumque tua est.
Prospera seu uenient, uenient reticentibus illis,
Assolet et subitum laetius esse bonum.
Seu uenient aduersa diu nescire iuuabit,
Vsura et medij temporis usque frui.
Quin iubeo fatis etiam prohibentibus ipsis,
Fac tibi mens hilares transigat aequa dies.

170

IN CRVCE DIGNVM
E GRAECO

Mastaurωn elementa tibi duo subtrahe prima,
Nemo te reliquis dignior esse potest.

171

EPITAPHIVM
E GRAECO.

Quatuor hic tumulus fratres complectitur; ex his
Proh dolor una duos lux parit, ac perimit. [i_4v]

172

E GRAECO.

Fortis erat bello Timocritus, hic iacet ergo.
Fortibus haud parcis Mars fere, sed timidis.

168/5 nota.] nota *1518*, nota, *1520* **169**/2 error] error, *1518 1520* 3 astrologi,] Astrologi, *1518*, astrologi. *1520* 8 iuuabit,] iuuabit. *1518 1520* 9 Vsura] *1518*, Vsura, *1520* **171**/1–4 EPITAPHIVM . . . perimit.] *om. 1563* 3 complectitur;] complectitur, *1518 1520* **172**/3 fere,] *1518*, ferè. *1520*, fere *1520* (*errata*)

is an outstanding landmark," and went away. When he came back, the mere supersufficiency of the sighting he had taken baffled him, for he saw his marks in every tree.

169
ON AN ASTROLOGER

While astrologers (who, through our own mistake, are honored as prophets) are producing your destiny in accordance with the position of a star, while this star is promising and that one threatening, your mind swings back and forth between hope and fear. If good fortune is to come, it will come, though the astrologers keep silent; and unexpected good luck usually gives more pleasure. If, on the other hand, bad luck is to come, then it is better to know nothing of it as long as possible and to enjoy the time until it arrives. In fact, this is what I advise, in the very teeth of the fates themselves: keep your equanimity and spend your days in good spirits.

170
ON A MAN WHO OUGHT TO BE CRUCIFIED
FROM THE GREEK

Take away the first two letters of your "Mastauron"; no one can more richly deserve what is left than you do.

171
AN EPITAPH
FROM THE GREEK

This tomb contains four brothers. To two of them, alas, a single day brought life and death.

172
FROM THE GREEK

Timocritus was brave in battle. That is why he lies here. It is not the brave, but the cowardly whom you spare, brutal Mars.

173
E GRAECO.

Ista Neoclidae gnatos habet urna gemellos,
Seruitio hic patriam liberat, hic uitio.

174
AD QVENDAM CVI VXOR MALA DOMI.

Vxor amice tibi est semper mala: quum male tractas,
Fit peior, sed fit pessima quando bene.
Sed bona si moriatur erit, melior tamen id si
Te faciat uiuo, ast optima si propere.

175
DE NAVTIS EIICIENTIBVS MONACHVM IN TEMPESTATE, CVI FVERANT CONFESSI.

Cum tumida horrisonis insurgeret unda procellis,
Et maris in lassam ferueret ira ratem,
Relligio timidis illabitur anxia nautis.
Heu parat, exclamant hoc mala uita malum.
Vectores inter Monachus fuit; huius in aurem
Se properant uitijs exonerare suis,
Ast ubi senserunt nihilo sibi mitius aequor,
Sed rapido puppim uix superesse freto,
Quid miri est ait unus, aqua si uix ratis extat?
Nostrorum scelerum pondere adhuc premitur. $[k_1]$
Quin monachum hunc, in quem culpas exhausimus omneis,
Eijcite, et secum hinc crimina nostra ferat.
Dicta probant, rapiuntque uirum, simul in mare torquent,
Et lintrem leuius quam prius isse ferunt.
Hinc hinc quam grauis est peccati sarcina, disce,
Cuius non potuit pondera ferre ratis.

175/5 ratem,] *1518,* ratem. *1520* 6 timidis] tumidis *1518;* nautis.] nautis, *1518 1520* 8 fuit;] fuit, *1518,* fuit *1520;* aurem] *1518,* aurem, *1520* 11 freto,] freto. *1518 1520* 12 extat?] extat, *1518 1520*

173
FROM THE GREEK

That urn you see there contains a pair—both sons of Neoclides; one freed his fatherland from slavery, the other from vice.

174
ON A MAN
WHO HAS A SHREWISH WIFE AT HOME

My friend, your wife is always bad. When you treat her badly, she gets worse, but when you treat her well, she becomes worst of all. But if she dies, she will be a good wife; better if she dies while you are alive; and best of all if she dies soon.

175
ON SOME SAILORS WHO MADE THEIR CONFESSIONS TO A MONK DURING A STORM AND THEN THREW HIM OVERBOARD

When the heaving sea in a roaring storm was rising high and the anger of the waves was raging against the struggling ship, the frightened sailors were overcome by religious scruples. They cried, "Our ill-spent lives have brought on these ills." There was a monk among the passengers. Into his ear they hastily unloaded their sins. But when they observed that the sea had not in the least calmed down, that, rather, the ship was just barely afloat on the rushing waters, one of them cried out, "No wonder our ship is barely afloat! All this time it has been weighed down by our cargo of sin. Why not throw overboard this monk on whom we emptied out all our guilt, and let him take our sins away with him?" The sailors approve of what he said; they lay hold of the man; they heave him into the sea. And—so they say—the ship sailed lighter than before. Now the moral of this story: learn from it how heavy is a load of sin, since a ship cannot sustain its weight.

176

AD CANDIDVM, PAROCHVM VITAE IMPROBAE.

Factus es O populi pastor mi Candide magni,
Ter tibi, terque tuo gratulor ergo gregi.
Aut mihi iudicium minuit fauor, aut tuus usquam
Non potuit talem grex habuisse patrem.
Non tibi uanarum est fastosa scientia rerum,
Quippe nec in populum est utilis illa tuum.
At rarae tibi sunt uirtutes, sic tibi raros
Patribus ex priscis credo fuisse pares.
Quid faciant, fugiantue tui, quo cernere possint
Vita potest claro pro speculo esse tua.
Tantum opus admonitu est, ut te intueantur, et ut tu
Quae facis, haec fugiant: quae fugis, haec faciant.

177

E GRAECO.

Naufragus hac situs est, iacet illa rusticus urna.
Ad Styga siue solo par uia, siue salo.

178

IN POSTHVMVM EPISCOPVM.

Praesul es, et merito praefectus Posthume sacris,
Quo magis in toto non erat orbe sacer. [k_1v]
Gaudeo tam magnum, tam sanctum gaudeo munus,
Tandem non temere nunc, uelut ante dari.
Nempe errare solet temerarius impetus, at te
Delectum magna sedulitate patet,
Namque ubi de multis tantummodo sumitur unus,
Saepe malus casu, pessimus arte uenit.
At te, de multis legitur si millibus unus,
Stultior haud possit, deteriorue legi.

176/2 IMPROBAE] PROBAE *1565* 11 possint] possint. *1518 1520* **177**/3 Styga] styga *1518 1520*

176

TO CANDIDUS, A PASTOR WHO LED AN EVIL LIFE

My dear Candidus, you have been made pastor of a large congregation. Therefore, I heartily congratulate you and your flock. Either partiality has damaged my judgment, or it is not possible that your flock ever before had such a priest. You do not have knowledge of vain disciplines to make you proud; clearly, such knowledge is of no use to your congregation. Moreover, yours are rare virtues; just as rare, I believe, were men like you among the ancient fathers. Your life can function as a conspicuous model by which your people can decide what to do and what to avoid. All that is needed is to advise them to observe you closely, avoid what you do, and do what you avoid.

177

FROM THE GREEK

In this urn reposes a sailor, in that a farmer. By land or by sea the journey is the same; it ends at the Styx.

178

ON BISHOP POSTHUMUS

You are now a bishop, Posthumus, and it is only proper that you have this extraordinary authority, for in the whole world there never was a more extraordinary man than you. I rejoice that, at last, so important and inviolable an office is no longer conferred at random, as it used to be. I say this because a random impulse is likely to be wrong; but, as for you, it is plain that you were selected with great care. Actually, when just one man is taken from among many, he often turns out, by chance, to be bad or, by deliberate choice, to be the very worst. But in your case, if one is to be taken from many thousands, he could hardly match you in stupidity and wickedness.

179

DE BOLLANO.

Vrticis lectum Bollano urentibus omnem
Insternunt socij, quum cubiturus erat.
Se tamen urticis ustum negat, haud negat illas
In tenebris nudum se reperisse tamen.
Vnguibus aut igitur uitata carne necesse est,
Aut nudis tantum dentibus inciderint.
Cum tamen in tenebris illaesus repperit herbas,
Vrticas quanam repperit esse nota?

180

DE VVLPE AEGROTA ET LEONE APOLOGVS

Dum iacet angusta uulpes aegrota cauerna,
Ante fores blando constitit ore leo.
Ecquid amica uales? cito me lambente ualebis,
Nescis in lingua uis mihi quanta mea.
Lingua tibi medica est, uulpes ait: at nocet illud
Vicinos quod habet tam bona lingua malos. [k_2]

181

DE LEONE ET LYSIMACHO.

Dum domitus placido leo lamberet ore magistrum,
Prouocat exemplo quemlibet ipse suo.
Cumque diu ex tanta prodiret nemo corona,
Prosilijt forti pectore Lysimachus.
Ipse, ait, audebo linguam tetigisse leonis
Sed tam uicinis dentibus haud faciam.

182

IN FABIANVM ASTROLOGVM.

Vno multa die de rebus fata futuris,
Credula quum de te turba frequenter emat,

179/9 quanam] qua nam *1518 1520;* nota?] nota, *1518 1520* **180**/8 malos.] *1518*^{m}, malos, *1518*^{d} *1520* **181**/2 leo] 1518^{d} *1520,* Leo *1518*^{m} 4 corona,] *1518,* corona. *1520* 6 linguam tetigisse leonis] leoninam tangere linguam, *1518* **182**/2 futuris,] *1518 1520* (*errata*), faturis, *1520*

179
ON BOLLANUS

Just before Bollanus lay down, his companions strewed his whole bed with stinging nettles. Yet he said he had not been stung; even so, he did not deny that he did find them when he was undressed and in the dark. Therefore it must be that they avoided his flesh and came in contact only with his nails or his bared teeth. And yet, since he encountered the leaves in the dark without being stung, how did he discover that they were nettles?

180
FABLE OF THE SICK FOX AND THE LION

While a fox lay sick in his narrow den, a smooth-tongued lion took his stand at the entrance. Said he, "Tell me, my friend, don't you feel well? You will soon get well if you let me lick you. You just do not know the power of my tongue." "Your tongue," said the fox, "has healing powers; but the trouble is that such a good tongue has bad neighbors."

181
ON A LION AND LYSIMACHUS

While a tamed lion harmlessly licked his trainer, the trainer invited one and all to put themselves in his place. After a long time, when no one among the large crowd of spectators had come forward, brave-hearted Lysimachus leaped up. Said he, "I am brave enough to endure the touch of the lion's tongue, but his teeth are so close to his tongue that I shall not do it."

182
ON FABIAN, THE ASTROLOGER

Now that credulous people, in great numbers, every day, are buying from you great quantities of predictions, if among the

Inter multa unum si fors mendacia uerum est,
Illico uis uatem te Fabiane putem.
At tu de rebus semper mentire futuris.
Si potes hoc, uatem te Fabiane putem.

183

IN REGEM SCOTIAE, QVI ARCEM NORHAMAM PRODITAM SIBI TAMEN OPPUGNAVIT DISSIMVLANS PRODITAM ESSE.

Scote quid oppugnas Norhamam uiribus arcem
Ante tibi falsa proditione datam?
An fraudis pudet? at tam multis, et tot apertis
In uitijs non est illa pudenda tuis.
Artibus ergo malis capta fuit arce uoluptas
Magna tibi forsan, sed breuis illa fuit.
Teque, tuisque mala (merita sed) morte peremptis,
Arx intra est paucos capta, recepta dies.
Proditor inque tuo peteret cum praemia regno,
Mors sceleri est merces reddita digna suo. [k$_2$v]
Proditor ut pereat, pereat cui proditur hostis,
Inuicta in fatis arx habet ista suis.

184

EPITAPHIVM IACOBI REGIS SCOTORVM.

Scotorum Iacobus princeps, regno hostis amico
Fortis et infelix hac ego condor humo.
Quanta animi fuerat, fidei uis tanta fuisset.
Caetera contigerant non inhonesta mihi.
Sed pudet heu iactare, queri piget, ergo tacebo,
Garrulaque O utinam fama tacere uelis.
Vos tamen, O reges moneo, rex nuper et ipse,
Ne sit (ut esse solet) nomen inane fides.

182/7 hoc,] *1518*^{m}, hoc. *1518*^{d}, hoc: 1520; putem.] *1518*, putem, *1520* *After this poem in 1518 comes the poem* IN IACOBVM REGEM SCOTORVM, *which is omitted in 1520 (see no. 271).* **183**/4 oppugnas] *1518*, oppugnans *1520;* arcem] arcem? *1518 1520* 5 datam?] datam. *1518 1520* 6–7 An fraudis . . . tuis.] *1518, om. 1520 1563* 8 arce] arce, *1518 1520* 10 peremptis,] *1520*, peremptis. *1518* 14 pereat cui] *1518*^{m}, pereat, cui *1518*^{d} *1520;* hostis,] hostis. *1518 1520* **184**/8 tamen,] tamen *1518 1520*

many lies you tell there is, by chance, a single truth, then, Fabian, right off, you want me to think you a prophet. But make your predictions invariably wrong. If you can keep this up, Fabian, I might think you a prophet.

183

ON THE KING OF SCOTLAND, WHO ATTACKED NORHAM CASTLE WHICH HAD ALREADY BEEN BETRAYED TO HIM, PRETENDING THAT IT HAD NOT

Scot, why do you launch an armed attack on Norham Castle, which had already been treacherously betrayed into your hands? Are you ashamed of your deceitfulness? Your vices are so many and so notorious that this one should cause you no shame. Your pleasure in taking the castle by artful deception may have been great, but it was short. Within a few days, after the wretched but richly deserved destruction of you and yours, the captured castle was recaptured. And when the betrayer asked for his reward in your realm, he received the wages worthy of his crime, death. It is the destiny of that invincible castle that not only the man who betrays it should perish but also the man to whom he betrays it.

184

AN EPITAPH FOR JAMES KING OF THE SCOTS

It is I, James, King of the Scots, brave and ill-starred enemy of a friendly kingdom, who am interred beneath this sod. Would that my loyalty had been equal to my courage. The sequel with its shame for me would not have happened. But, alas, it is shameful to boast and repugnant to complain—therefore, I shall say no more. And I hope, O chattering Infamy, that you may be willing to keep silent. You kings (I was once a king myself) I warn you not to let loyalty become, as it often does, a meaningless word.

185

IN MALVM PICTOREM.

Exprimit egregia pictor mirabilis arte,
Dira canis pauitans ut fugit ora lepus.
Intima naturae scrutatus uiscera fingit
In cursu leporem retro metu aspicere.
Tam bene qui leporem fugientem expresserit, opto
Sit lepus, et fugiens ipse retro aspiciat.

186

IN EVNDEM.

Cum cane sic pictus lepus est, ut dicere nemo
Esset uterue canis posset, uterue lepus.
Pictor ubi hoc didicit, quod inerti defuit arti,
Suppleuit miro callidus ingenio.
Res ut aperta foret, longeque facesseret error,
Subscripsit tantum, est hic canis, iste lepus. [k3]

187

DE TYNDARO.

Non minimo insignem naso dum forte puellam
Basiat, en uoluit Tyndarus esse dicax.
Frustra ait ergo tuis mea profero labra labellis,
Nostra procul nasus distinet ora tuus.
Protinus erubuit, tacitaque incanduit ira,
Nempe parum salso tacta puella sale.
Nasus ab ore meus tua si tenet oscula, dixit,
Qua nasus non est hac dare parte potes.

188

IN BRIXIVM GERMANVM FALSA SCRIBENTEM DE CHORDIGERA NAVE GALLORVM ET HERVEO EIVS DVCE.

Heruea dum celebras Brixi, tua carmina damnas.
Nam tibi scripta mala est res bene gesta, fide.

185/4 fingit] fingit, *1518 1520* **187**/7 salso] *1518 1520* (*errata*), falso *1520*
188/1 BRIXIVM GERMANVM] GERMANVM BRIXIVM *1563*

185
ON A BAD PAINTER

A painter admired for his extraordinary skill showed in a picture how a frightened hare flees a dog's cruel jaws. After pondering the innermost secrets of nature, he represented the hare as looking backward in terror during its flight. I hope that the painter who succeeded thus in showing a fleeing hare may himself become a hare and, during his effort to escape, look back.

186
ON THE SAME PAINTER

A hare and a dog were painted in such fashion that no one could determine which was the dog and which the hare. When the artist learned that this was so, with marvelous ingenuity he supplied what his insufficient skill had left out. To make the matter plain and banish ambiguity, he merely wrote at the bottom, "This is the dog; that, the hare."

187
ON TYNDARUS

While Tyndarus happened to be kissing a girl whose outstanding characteristic was not the smallness of her nose, he felt a sudden impulse to be witty about it. Said he, "I cannot make my lips reach yours, for your nose keeps my mouth at a distance." The girl immediately blushed and burned with repressed anger, stung by his not very witty witticism. "If my nose keeps your kisses from my mouth," she said, "then you can kiss me here, where I have no nose."

188
ON GERMAN BRIXIUS, WHO WRITES FALSEHOODS ABOUT THE FRENCH SHIP *CORDELIÈRE* AND HER CAPTAIN, HERVÉ

Brixius, while you try to win fame for Hervé, you defeat the purpose of your poetry, for with bad faith you have recorded his

Historiam spondes illa Germane poesi
Quae modo quum non sit uera, nec historia est.
Aut odio incipiant, aut indulgere fauori,
Et quisnam historijs qui modo credat, erit?
Iamque nec ipse tuus per te laudem Herueus ullam
Sublata rerum possit habere fide.

189

IN EVNDEM DE EODEM HERVEO ET EADEM NAVE. QVAE IN PVGNA NAVALI CONFLAGRAVIT.

Brixius immerita quod sustulit Heruea laude,
Quod merito aduersum fraudat honore ducem, [k3v]
Quod de chordigera mendacia mille carina
Contra quam sese res habuere, canat,
Non equidem miror, neque prauo falsa fauore
Quod uoluit prudens scribere, credo tamen.
Sed de chordigera, uatem qui uera doceret,
Quiuit adhuc reducem nemo referre pedem.
Ipse tamen (sciret quo certius omnia) dignus,
Qui media praesens naue fuisset, erat.

190

VERSVS EXCERPTI E CHORDIGERA BRIXII, AD QVOS ALLVDVNT QVAEDAM EPIGRAMMATA SEQVENTIA.

Circumeunt unum dextra laeuaque Britanni
Heruea, tela uolant brumali grandine plura
In caput unius Heruei, quae fortiter heros
Excutiens clypeo, contraria in agmina uertit.

190 (cont)

POSTEA DE EADEM CHORDIGERA.

Ipse suos Herueus comites hortatur, et instat,
Atque inter primos audax magno impete in hostes

188/9 credat] credit *1518* **189**/5 ducem,] ducem. *1518 1520* 6 chordigera] *1518*[d] *1520,* Chordigera *1518*[m] 6 carina] carina, *1518* 7 canat,] canat. *1518 1520* 8 fauore] fauore, *1518 1520* 10 chordigera] Chordigera *1518*[m] 13 erat.] erat *1520* **190**/4 dextra] dextra, *1518 1520;* laeuaque] leuaque *1518* 9 instat,] *1518,* instat. *1520*

good deeds. In the poem, Germanus, you promise us a history, but since it is not at all true, it is not history either. Let historians begin to show either prejudice or favoritism, and who will there be to lend any credence at all to histories? Now this very Hervé of yours has lost his praise because of you, for what praise can he have without belief in the facts?

189

ON THE SAME AUTHOR DEALING WITH THE SAME HERVÉ AND THE SAME SHIP (WHICH WAS BURNED UP IN A NAVAL BATTLE)

I am not at all surprised that Brixius has conferred upon Hervé praise which he did not earn, and has deprived the opposing captain of his due honor, and has celebrated, in his poem on the ship *Cordelière,* a thousand lies which are the very opposite of the facts. Still I don't believe he deliberately set out to write falsehoods because of a perverse prejudice. Rather, it was simply that no survivor has yet been able to come back to tell the bard the truth about the *Cordelière.* But for him to learn the whole truth, the right thing would have been for him to be aboard himself—amidships.

190

VERSES TAKEN FROM BRIXIUS' *CHORDIGERA* BECAUSE SOME OF THE FOLLOWING EPIGRAMS MAKE FUN OF THEM

Left and right the Britons surround Hervé as he stands alone. Shaft upon shaft flies in a wintry hailstorm toward the head of Hervé alone, but the hero boldly shakes them off with his shield and turns them back against the other side.

A LATER INCIDENT FROM THE SAME POEM *CHORDIGERA*

Hervé spurs his comrades on and himself presses forward. In the front ranks of a mighty attack, he drives boldly into the en-

Inuehitur, ferit hos misso per tempora telo.
Transigit huic gladio costas, huic ilia nudat.
Decutit his caput, impacta per colla bipenni.
His latus, his humeros hasta perstringit acuta.

190 (cont)

EPIGRAMMA MORI ALLVDENS AD VERSVS SVPERIORES.

Quod ferit hos Herueus misso per tempora telo,
  Iliaque et costas transigit huic gladio, [k_4]
Decutit his caput impacta per colla bipenni,
  His humeros hasta perforat, atque latus,
Tum clypeo aduersa quod tela uolantia parte
  Fortiter excutiens unde uolant, regerit,
Effugit hoc sensum, tot telis pugnet ut unus,
  Isque cui clypeo est altera onusta manus.
Fortis huic pugnae rerum natura repugnat.
  Praeteritum quiddam est hac puto parte tibi.
Namque ubi magnanimum produxeris Heruea, telis
  Pugnantem pariter quattuor, et clypeo,
Forte tibi exciderat, sed debuit ante moneri
  Lector, tunc Herueo quinque fuisse manus.

191

ALIVD DE EODEM.

Miraris clypeum, gladium, hastam, tela, bipennem,
  Herueus quoque gerat belligeretque modo.
Dextera crudeli manus est armata bipenni,
  Instructa est gladio saeua sinistra suo.
Iam telum, telique uicem quae praebeat, hastam
  Fortiter (impressis dentibus) ore tenet.
At quia tela caput brumali grandine plura
  Inuolitant, clypeum collocat in capite.
Duritia capitis draco cesserit, ungue Celaeno,
  Sic elephas illi dentibus impar erat.

190/14 perstringit] *1518*, prestringit *1520* 17 ferit] *1518*, ferit, *1520* 18 gladio,] gladio. *1518 1520* 19 bipenni,] bipenni. *1518 1520* 20 latus,] latus. *1518 1520* 22 regerit,] regerit. *1518 1520* 25 repugnat.] repugnat, *1518 1520* 28 quattuor] quatuor *1518;* et] det *1518*[m] **191**/10 Celaeno] Celeno *1518*

emy. Some he strikes down with a javelin through the temples; through another's ribs he thrusts his sword; he lays open the guts of another; with ax-blows to the neck he cuts off the heads of some, or wounds a flank or shoulder with his sharp spear.

MORE'S EPIGRAM MOCKING THE VERSES ABOVE

As for the statements that Hervé struck some enemies down with javelins through their temples, thrust his sword through the guts or ribs of others, severed the heads of some with ax-blows to the neck, pierced the shoulders and flanks of others, and as for his bravely fending off with his shield the hurtled missiles of the enemy and returning them to their source—all this is beyond the reach of understanding, how one man could fight with so many weapons, and that while one arm was burdened with a shield. Unyielding nature herself contradicts this battle. I think that in this passage you omitted something. For when you represented heroic Hervé fighting with four weapons and a shield all at the same time, perhaps the fact slipped your mind, but your reader ought to have been informed in advance that Hervé had five hands.

191

ANOTHER ON THE SAME SUBJECT

You wonder how Hervé could carry shield, sword, spear, javelins, and ax and fight with them, too. Well, his right hand is armed with the merciless battle-ax, his dire left is equipped with a sword all its own. At the same time he boldly holds (with clenched teeth) in his mouth the javelin, and the spear to take the javelin's place. And because missiles thicker than wintry hail fly toward his head, on his head he wears his shield. A dragon would not have so hard a head, nor Celaeno such claws; thus the elephant with his

Ergo nouum aduersos monstrum procurrit in hostes,
Terribilis rictu, terribilisque manu. [k_4v]

192

HIC PRIMVS VERSVS BRIXII EST, QVO HERVEA IAM MORITVRVM DE SE FACIT VATICINANTEM.

Inter Phoebeos non aspernandus alumnos
Heruei magna canit Brixius acta ducis.
Inter Phoebeos non aspernandus alumnos,
Herueum, hostes, socios, concremat atque rates.
Inter Phoebeos non aspernandus alumnos,
Vnde igitur uates, quae cecinit, didicit?
Inter Phoebeos non aspernandus alumnos,
Phoebeo reliquum est audiat ex tripode.

193

IN EVNDEM VERSVS POETARVM SVFFVRANTEM.

Priscos poetas nemo te colit magis,
Legitue diligentius.
Nam nemo priscis e poetis omnibus
Est, cuius ipse ex uersibus,
Non hinc et inde flosculos et gemmulas
Manu capaci legeris,
Vatem redonans tanto honore protinus,
Scriptis tuis ut inseras.
Beasque uatem: nempe quae tu congeris,
Suos parentes indicant,
Magisque resplendent tua inter carmina,
Quam nocte lucent sydera.

Tantum decus uati inuidere nemini
Soles, amicus omnium, [l_1]
Ne quis, decus prioris olim seculi,
Neglectus abs te defleat.

193/7 flosculos] flosculos, *1518 1520* 8 legeris,] legeris. *1518 1520*

tusks could not equal him. And so, as he rushed against the enemy, he was a strange monster, inspiring terror with both his arm and his grin.

192
THE FIRST LINE IN THIS POEM IS BY BRIXIUS WHO PRESENTS A PROPHECY ABOUT HIMSELF MADE BY HERVÉ, WHO WAS SOON TO DIE

One not to be despised among the disciples of Phoebus, the poet Brixius celebrated the mighty deeds of Captain Hervé.

One not to be despised among the disciples of Phoebus burned up Hervé, his enemies, his companions, and the ships.

How, then, did this poet not to be despised among the disciples of Phoebus—how did he learn what his poem tells?

The only conclusion is that one not to be despised among the disciples of Phoebus heard it from the tripod of Phoebus.

193
ON THE SAME WRITER'S THEFT OF LINES FROM THE POETS

No one cultivates the ancient poets more than you or culls from them more diligently, for there is not one among the ancient poets from whose lines, here and there, you have not culled little blossoms and buds by the handful; and you immediately repay the poet by the great honor of being slipped in with what you write. And you do bestow a blessing on the bard, for what you gather proclaims its origin and shines out among your lines more brightly than the stars gleaming in the night sky.

So great an honor you never begrudge to any bard, a friend to them all, so that no one of them, once the glory of an age that is past, now needs to weep at your neglect. Therefore, lest the hal-

Ergo sacrati ne poetarum modi
Longo situ obsolescerent,
Iniuria tu uindicatos temporis
Nouo nitore percolis.
Hoc est uetustis arte nouitatem dare,
Qua re nihil felicius.
Ars O beata, quisquis arte isthac tamen
Vetusta nouitati dabit,
Is arte nulla (quamlibet sudet diu)
Nouis uetustatem dabit.

194

ALLVSIO AD CENOTAPHIVM HERVEI.

Heruea cum Decijs unum conferre duobus,
Aetas te Brixi iudice nostra potest.
Sed tamen hoc distant, illi quod sponte peribant,
Hic perijt, quoniam non potuit fugere.

195

PHOEBVS BRIXIVM ALLOQVITVR.

Vis de grandisono quid sentio scire libello,
Qui arma, necemque Heruei bellipotentis habet?
Ergo sacer Phoebo sacra haec oracula uates
Accipe, Phoebaeo reddita de tripode.
Vna opere in toto deest syllaba, mille supersunt.
Plenum opus est, nam quid posset abesse minus? [l_1v]
Vna uno haec legitur, sed non legitur tibi, mense,
Mens Et plus quam medium syllaba mensis habet.

196

AD SABINVM, CVI VXOR ABSENTI CONCEPIT.

Subsidium uitae, serae spes una senectae,
Nata tibi est soboles, curre Sabine domum.

193/20 obsolescerent,] obsolescerent. *1518 1520* 26 dabit] dadit *1518*[d] **195**/5 Phoebaeo] Phoebeo *1518* 8 tibi,] tibi *1518 1520* 9 habet.] *In 1563 no. 209 follows this poem.*

lowed measures of the poets perish of long disuse, you save them from the injuries of time and adorn them with new luster. This is by art to give new life to what is old—there is no happier gift than this. O blessed art!—and yet whoever, employing your artistic method, shall insert his antique borrowings in a new context, will by no effort of art, however long he sweats about it, succeed in imparting their antiquity to his own new verses.

194

A MOCKING COMMENT ON THE CENOTAPH OF HERVÉ

According to your judgment, Brixius, our age can match the two Decii in the single person of Hervé. And yet there is this difference: the Decii died of their own free will; Hervé, because he could not run away.

195

PHOEBUS ADDRESSES BRIXIUS

Do you want to know what I think of that grandiloquent little book which recounts the derring-do and the death of Hervé, mighty in battle? Well, then, poet sacred to Phoebus, hear these sacred oracles delivered by Phoebus' tripod. In the whole work one syllable is missing; there are a thousand to spare. The work is full up, for what could be less than what you omitted? The syllable I mean can be picked out of only one month (though it has not been picked out for you) and it contains more than half of *mensis* (month). *mens* (intelligence)

196

TO SABINUS, WHOSE WIFE BECAME PREGNANT IN HIS ABSENCE

Sabinus, hurry home; to you is born a child, the support of your existence, the only hope of your extreme old age. Hurry; you

Curre, salutanda est uxor foecunda, uidenda est
Chara tibi soboles, curre Sabine domum.
Curre, inquam, ac propera, nimiumque uidebere lentus,
Quantumuis properes, curre Sabine domum.
Iam queritur coniunx de te tua, iam tua de te
Conqueritur soboles, curre Sabine domum.
Nunquam ingratus ades, neque cum soboles tibi nata est,
Sed neque cum genita est, curre Sabine domum.
Curre, ut adesse, puer sacro dum fonte lauatur,
Nunc saltem possis, curre Sabine domum.

197

AD CANDIDVM LAVDANTEM SANCTOS VIROS, CVM IPSE ESSET MALVS.

Saepe bonos laudas, imitaris Candide nunquam.
Laudo, inquis, posita Candidus inuidia.
Nam quicunque bonos imitatur, et aemulus idem est.
O lacte, O niuibus Candide candidior.

198

QVIS OPTIMVS REIPVB. STATVS.

Quaeris uter melius, Rex ne imperet an ne Senatus.
Neuter (quod saepe est) si sit uterque malus. [l_2]
Sin sit uterque bonus, numero praestare Senatum,
Inque bonis multis plus reor esse boni.
Difficile est numerum forsan reperire bonorum,
Sic facile est unum saepius esse malum,
Et fuerit medius saepe inter utrunque Senatus,
Sed tibi uix unquam Rex mediocris erit.
Consilioque malus regitur meliore Senator,
Rex consultores sed regit ipse suos.
Alter ut eligitur populo, sic nascitur alter.
Sors hic caeca regit, certum ibi consilium.
Illeque se factum populo, populum sibi factum
Scilicet hic ut sint quos regat ipse putat.

196/5 uidenda est] uidenda est. *1518 1520* **198**/2 an ne] an ue *1518* 14 factum] *1518*[m], factum, *1518*[d] *1520*

must greet your fruitful wife, see the beloved offspring—hurry home, Sabinus. Hurry, I say, and waste no time about it; and, hurry as you may, you will seem too slow. Hurry home, Sabinus. Now your wife is complaining about you, the baby is crying for you; Sabinus, hurry home. Because you are an ungrateful fellow, you are never there, not at the birth, not even at the conception; hurry home, Sabinus. Hurry to be in time at least for the boy's baptism. Sabinus, hurry home.

197

TO CANDIDUS, WHO PRAISED HOLY MEN ALTHOUGH HE HIMSELF WAS EVIL

You often praise good men; you never, Candidus, imitate them. You say, "I, Candidus, praise them without envy, for whoever imitates good men also envies them." O Candidus, ingenuous innocent, whiter than milk or snow.

198

WHAT IS THE BEST FORM OF GOVERNMENT

You ask which governs better, a king or a senate. Neither, if (as is frequently the case) both are bad. But if both are good, then I think that the senate, because of its numbers, is the better and that the greater good lies in numerous good men. Perhaps it is difficult to find a group of good men; even more frequently it is easy for a monarch to be bad. A senate would occupy a position between good and bad; but hardly ever will you have a king who is not either good or bad. An evil senator is influenced by advice from better men than he; but a king is himself the ruler of his advisers. A senator is elected by the people to rule; a king attains this end by being born. In the one case blind chance is supreme; in the other, a reasonable agreement. The one feels that he was made senator by the people; the other feels that the people were created for him so that, of course, he may have subjects to rule.

Rex est in primo semper blandissimus anno,
Omni anno consul rex erit ergo nouus.
Rex cupidus longo populum corroserit aeuo.
Si consul malus est, spes melioris adest.
Nec me nota mouet quae pastam fabula muscam
Ferre iubet, subeat ne male pransa locum.
Fallitur, expleri regem qui credit auarum,
Nunquam haec non uacuam mittet hirudo cutem.
At patrum consulta grauis dissensio turbat,
Regi dissentit nemo, malum hoc grauius.
Nam quum de magnis uaria est sententia rebus,
Quaestio sed tamen haec nascitur unde tibi?
Est ne usquam populus, cui regem siue Senatum
Praeficere arbitrio tu potes ipse tuo? [l_2v]
Si potes hoc, regnas: nec iam cui, consule, tradas
Imperium: prior est quaestio, an expediat.

199

DE FVSCO POTORE.

Potando medicus perituros dixit ocellos
Fusco, qui cum se consuluisset, ait:
Perdere dulcius est potando, quam ut mea seruem
Erodenda pigris lumina uermiculis.

200

AD AMICVM.

Litera nostra tuis quantum mihi colligo scriptis,
Sera tibi ueniet, nec tibi sera tamen.
Nec bello ueniunt intempestiua peracto,
Quae bello poterant tela iuuare nihil.

201

DE REGE ET RVSTICO.

Rusticus in syluis nutritus uenit in urbem,
Rusticior Fauno, rusticior Satyro.

199/3 ait:] ait, *1518*, ait. *1520*   **200**/3 tibi ueniet] tib ueniet *1518*[d]

A king in his first year is always very mild indeed, and so every year the consul will be like a new king. Over a long time a greedy king will gnaw away at his people. If a consul is evil, there is hope of improvement. I am not swayed by the well-known fable which recommends that one endure the well-fed fly lest a hungry one take its place. It is a mistake to believe that a greedy king can be satisfied; such a leech never leaves flesh until it is drained.

But, you say, a serious disagreement impedes a senate's decisions, while no one disagrees with a king. But that is the worse evil of the two, for when there is a difference of opinion about important matters—but say, what started you on this inquiry anyway? Is there anywhere a people upon whom you yourself, by your own decision, can impose either a king or a senate? If this does lie within your power, you are king. Stop considering to whom you may give power. The more basic question is whether it would do any good if you could.

199

ON FUSCUS, THE DRINKER

His physician told Fuscus that drinking would destroy his eyes. When Fuscus had considered the matter, he said, "I would rather destroy my eyes by drinking than preserve them to be gnawed out by crawling worms."

200

TO A FRIEND

I gather from what you write that my letter will come too late. But it won't be too late for you—no more than weapons which arrive after the war is over can be said to arrive too late, if those weapons would have been of no use anyway.

201

ON THE KING AND THE PEASANT

A forest-bred peasant, more naive than Faunus or a satyr, came

En populus plena stetit hinc, stetit inde platea,
Vnaque uox tota, Rex uenit, urbe fuit.
Rusticus insolita uocis nouitate mouetur,
Quidnam ita respectet turba, uidere cupit.
Rex subito inuehitur, celebri praeeunte caterua,
Aureus excelso conspiciendus equo.
Tum uero ingeminant, uiuat rex: undique regem
Attonito populus suspicit ore suum.
Rusticus, O ubi rex? ubi rex est? clamat: at unus,
Ille, ait, est illo qui sedet altus equo. [l3]
Hiccine rex? puto me derides, rusticus inquit.
Ille mihi picta ueste uidetur homo.

202

IN EPISCOPVM ILLITERATVM, DE QVO ANTE EPIGRAMMA EST SVB NOMINE POSTHVMI.

Magne pater clamas, occidit littera, in ore
Hoc unum, occidit littera semper habes,
Cauisti bene tu, ne te ulla occidere possit
Littera, non ulla est littera nota tibi.
Nec frustra metuis ne occidat littera, scis non
Viuificet qui te spiritus esse tibi.

203

DE SACERDOTE RIDICVLE ADMONENTE POPVLVM DE IEIVNIO, CVM DIES IAM PRAETERISSET.

Admonuit populum noster cum forte sacerdos,
Proxima quos fastos afferat hebdomada,
Martyris Andreae magnum et memorabile festum est.
Scitis, ait, charus quam fuit ille deo.
Squalida lasciuam tenuent ieiunia carnem,
Hoc suetum est, sancti hoc instituere patres.
Praemoneo ergo omneis, in martyris huius honorem,
Quod ieiunari debuit, inquit, heri.

201/12 rex?] *1518*, rex *1520* **203**/6 est.] est, *1518 1520* 8 tenuent] macerent *1518*

to town. See there! the inhabitants have taken places on either side to fill the avenue, and throughout the city all one could hear was the cry, "The king is coming." The peasant was roused by the strange news and longed to see what the crowd was watching for so eagerly. Suddenly the king rode by, in full view, resplendent with gold, escorted by a large company, and astride a tall horse. Then the crowd really did roar: "Long live the king"; and with rapt expressions they gazed up at the king. The peasant cried out, "Where is the king? Where is the king?" And one of the bystanders replied, "There he is, the one mounted high on that horse over there." The peasant said, "Is that the king? I think you are making fun of me. To me he looks like a man in fancy dress."

202

ON THE ILLITERATE BISHOP TO WHOM AN EARLIER EPIGRAM REFERRED UNDER THE NAME OF POSTHUMUS

You, mighty father, exclaim, "The letter kills." This single phrase "The letter kills" you have always in your mouth. You have taken good care that no letter may kill you; you do not know any letter. And not idle is your fear that the letter may kill; you know that you do not have the spirit which will give you life.

203

ON THE PRIEST WHO FOOLISHLY WARNED HIS PARISHIONERS OF A FAST DAY WHEN THE DAY HAD ALREADY PASSED

When our priest, as it happened, was advising his parishioners of the saints' calendar for the coming week, he said, "The feast of Saint Andrew the Martyr is a great and memorable feast; you know how dear to God Andrew was. Let austere fasting mortify the wayward flesh; this is the custom, established by the holy fathers. Therefore I forewarn you all that in honor of this martyr you ought to have fasted yesterday."

204
DE QVODAM MALE CANTANTE ET BENE LEGENTE.

Tam male cantasti, possis ut episcopus esse.
Tam bene legisti, ut non tamen esse queas. [l_3v]
Non satis esse putet, siquis uitabit utrumuis,
Sed fieri si uis praesul, utrunque caue.

205
AD SABINVM.

Quos ante coniunx quattuor
Natos Sabine protulit,
Multum ecce dissimiles tibi,
Tuos nec ipse deputas.
Sed quem tibi puellulum
Enixa iam nuperrime est,
Solum tibi simillimum
Pro quattuor complecteris.
Adulterinos quattuor
Vocas, repellis, abdicas.
Hunc unicum ceu γνήσιον,
Qui sit tibi haeres, destinas.
Hunc ergo in ulnis gestiens,
Exosculandum ab omnibus,
Vt filium fert simia,
Totam per urbem baiulas.
Atqui graues tradunt Sophi,
Quibus laborque, studiumque id est,
Secreta quicquid efficit
Natura perscrutarier,
Ergo graues tradunt Sophi,
Quodcunque matres interim
Imaginantur fortiter, [l_4]
Dum liberis datur opera,
Eius latenter et notas,
Certas et indelebileis,

204/5 putet] puto *1518* **205**/21 perscrutarier,] perscrutarier. *1518 1520*

204
ON A MAN WHO SANG BADLY AND READ WELL

You sang so badly that you could be a bishop, but you read so well that you could not. Let no one imagine that it is enough to avoid success in the one or the other. No, if you want to become a bishop be careful on both counts.

205
TO SABINUS

Look here, Sabinus, the four children whom your wife has borne up to now do not in the least resemble you; you yourself do not consider them yours. But, in preference to the four, you take to your heart the little fellow she has most recently borne, the only one who is very like you. You call the four illegitimate, you keep them at a distance, you disown them. You have appointed this youngest one, as the only legitimate son, to be your heir; and, like an ape carrying her young, you carry him in your arms all over town for everyone to kiss and coddle. And yet weighty scholars who direct all their efforts at uncovering the secret effects of nature—weighty scholars, I say, tell us that whatever image dominates the mother's mind when the child is begotten, secretly in some mysterious way imposes accurate and indelible traces of

Modoque inexplicabili
In semen ipsum congeri,
Quibus receptis intime,
Simulque concrescentibus
A mente matris insitam
Natus refert imaginem.
Quum tot abesses millibus,
Dum gignit uxor quattuor,
Quod esset admodum tui
Secura, dissimiles parit.
Sed unus omnium hic puer
Tui refert imaginem,
Quod mater, hunc dum concipit,
Sollicita de te plurimum,
Te tota cogitauerat,
Dum pertimescit anxia,
Ne tu Sabine incommodus
Velutque Lupus in fabulam
Superuenires interim.

206

DE PRINCIPE ET RVSTICO SELANDO RIDICVLVM.

Quum spectaret aquas princeps, in ponte resedit,
  Primoresque suos ante stetere pedes. [l_4v]
Rusticus adsedit, modico tamen interuallo,
  Ciuilemque dato se putat esse loco.
Suscitat hunc quidam et, cum principe, dixit, eodem
  Ponte sedere audes, rustice? non ne pudet?
Ille refert, scelus est in eodem ponte sedere?
  Quid si pons longus millia dena foret?

207

DE AVLICO RIDICVLVM.

Quum descendit equo, de circumstantibus uni
  Aulicus, hunc teneas quisquis es, inquit, equum.

205/35 quattuor] quatuor *1518* **206**/4 pedes.] pedes, *1518 1520* 7 quidam et,] quidam, et *1518 1520* 8 audes,] audes *1518 1520* **207**/3 Aulicus,] Aulicus *1518 1520*

itself upon the seed; these marks penetrate deeply and grow with the embryo, and thus the child reflects the image inbred in it from the mother's mind. When your wife conceived the four children she was quite unconcerned about you because you were so many miles away. That is why she bore children who do not resemble you. But this son, of all your children, looks like you because at his conception his mother was very much concerned about you and had you completely on her mind; she was worried for fear you, Sabinus, might inconveniently arrive on the scene, as we say "speak of the devil."

206

A FUNNY STORY ABOUT A PRINCE AND A PEASANT FROM ZEELAND

A prince, as he gazed at the water, sat down on a bridge, and his nobles stood respectfully about. A peasant sat down, too, but not near by, and thought himself polite because of the distance he kept. A certain courtier got him up and said, "Peasant, do you dare to sit on the same bridge with the prince? Aren't you ashamed?" The peasant answered, "Is it wrong to sit on the same bridge? What if the bridge were ten miles long?"

207

A FUNNY STORY ABOUT A COURTIER

A courtier, dismounting from his horse, said to one of the bystanders, "You—whoever you are—hold this horse." The by-

Ille, ut erat pauidus, dixit, domine ergo ferocem
  Hunc rogo qui teneat, sufficit unus, equum?
Vnus ait potis est retinere. Subintulit ille,
  Si potis est unus, tu potes ipse tuum.

208

IN MILITEM FVGACEM, ET ANVLATVM.

Aureus iste manus, miles, cur annulus ornat
  Iure tuos ornet qui meliore pedes?
Vtilior nuper, meliorque in Marte feroci
  Planta tibi palmis una duabus erat.

209

IN BRIXIVM POETAM.

Brixi tale tuo natum est aenigma libello
  A Sphinge opponi possit ut Oedipodi.
Chordigera est tibi tota frequens, tibi non tamen usquam est
Cor   Cordigerae in toto syllaba prima libro.

210

IN TVSCVM POTOREM.

Perdis, ait Tusco medicus, tua lumina uino.
  Consultat secum quid uelit ergo sequi. [m_1]
Sydera, terra, fretumque solent quaecunque uideri,
  Omnia sunt, inquit, uisa reuisa mihi.
Multa mihi sed uina tamen gustanda supersunt,
  Multa refert annus quum noua musta nouus.
Iam certus, firmusque, ualebitis inquit ocelli,
  Nempe satis uidi, non satis usque bibi.

211

IN ARNVM PERIVRVM

Iurasti satis Arne diu, tandem obtinuisti,
  Iurare ut posthac iam tibi non sit opus.

207/6 retinere. Subintulit] retinere, subintulit *1518 1520;* ille,] ille. *1518 1520* **208**/2 manus, miles,] manus miles *1518 1520* **209**/1–5 IN BRIXIVM . . . libro.] *In 1565 this poem follows no. 195.* 4 Chordigera] Cordigera *1518* **210**/2 Perdis,] Perdis *1518 1520;* medicus,] medicus *1518 1520* 6 mihi] *1518,* mihi, *1520* 7 annus] *1518,* annus, *1520* **211**/3 Iurare] *1518,* Iurare, *1520;* posthac] *1518,* post hac *1520*

stander, because he was frightened, said, "My lord, I ask you, is one man enough then to hold this savage horse?" The courtier said, "One man can hold him." The bystander rejoined, "If one man can, then you can hold your horse yourself."

208

TO A SOLDIER WHO RAN AWAY AND WHO WAS WEARING A RING

Soldier, why does that golden ring of yours decorate your hands? It would more properly decorate your feet. In that recent fierce battle either one of your feet was more helpful and more successful than both your hands.

209

TO THE POET BRIXIUS

Brixius, such an enigma arises in your book as might be proposed by the Sphinx to Oedipus: you have the whole word *Chordigera* time and time again, but nowhere in your whole book do you have the first syllable of *Cordigera*.

cor (heart)

210

ON TUSCUS THE DRINKER

"You are ruining your eyes with wine," said the physician to Tuscus. Therefore, Tuscus took thought what course to follow. He observed, "Sky, land, sea, whatever people usually see, I have seen again and again. And yet many a wine remains to be tasted when the new year brings its many new vintages." Then he made his decision and said with firm resolve, "Farewell, eyes, for I have seen enough, but to date enough I have not drunk."

211

TO ARNUS, A PERJURER

Arnus, you have been swearing oaths long enough; you have finally reached such a point that hereafter you need not swear. By

Coepit ubique tuo uir iuratissime uerbo
Quam iuramento non minor esse fides.

212

IN EVNDEM.

Et semper iuras, et cunctis Arne minaris.
Vis scire utilitas quae uenit inde tibi?
Sic iuras, ut nemo tibi iam denique credat.
Sic minitaris, ut has nemo minas metuat.

213

IN EVNDEM.

Arno nemo magis pedibus ualet usque, sed olim
Frigore contractas perdidit ille manus.
Optat bella tamen. Cui pes citus, utraque manca est
Cui manus, in bello scis puto, quid faciet.
At cui lingua procax, manus est ignaua, procax est
Huic non ignaua lingua secanda manu.

214

DE MARVLLO.

Admonuit medicus lippum Theodore Marullum,
Ne uinum (caecus ni uelit esse) bibat. [m_1v]
Pareat ut medico (quanquam aegre) abstemius esse
Ecce duos totos sustinet usque dies.
Post sitit assueti reuocatus imagine uini,
Iamque foras medico uera minante ruit.
Ventum erat ad uinum, quum sic sua lumina moestus
Affatur, posito iam peritura mero.
Huc iter est, huc me fidi duxistis ocelli,
Nunc bibite, et dulces ambo ualete duces.
Gustus odorque manent, miratur abire colorem,
In nigras abeunt lumina dum tenebras.

211/4 uerbo] *1518*, uerbo, *1520* **212**/2 Et] Te *1518;* minaris.] minaris, *1518 1520* **213**/4 tamen. Cui] tamen, cui *1518 1520;* est] *1518*, est, *1520* 6 procax est] *1518*, procax est, *1520* **214**/2 lippum] *1518*, Lippum *1520* 4 esse] *1518*, esse, *1520* 8 moestus] *1518*, moestus, *1520* 11 Nunc] Hunc *1518* 12 colorem,] *1518*, colorem. *1520* 13 abeunt] subeunt *1518*

this time, you outstanding oathtaker, there is no place where your word is not as good as your oath.

212
TO THE SAME PERJURER

You are always swearing oaths, Arnus, and threatening everyone. Do you want to know what advantage you win by such conduct? The result of your swearing is that now in the end no one believes you; the result of your threats, that they frighten no one.

213
ON THE SAME ARNUS

All this time no one has been better equipped with feet than Arnus, but some time ago he lost the use of his hands as the result of frostbite. Still he wants to fight. I suppose you know what a man will accomplish in a fight if his feet are swift and both his hands disabled. But if a man's tongue is shameless and his hand inactive, then this man's shameless tongue ought to be cut out by an active hand.

214
ON MARULLUS

His physician warned blear-eyed Marullus, Theodore, not to drink any wine unless he was willing to be blind. To obey his doctor (though reluctantly), for two whole days, mark you, he endured to go without. Thereafter, he grew thirsty at the memory of his accustomed wine and then rushed out of doors despite the truth of the physician's warning. He had made his way to the wine when he gloomily addressed his eyes (destined to perish now that his wine was before him). "Here my journey ends; here you, my faithful eyes, have led me. Now drink, and, sweet guides, farewell." The taste and the bouquet remained; he stared at the vanishing color as his sight vanished in utter darkness. He miti-

Hoc tamen aduersum lenit solamine casum,
Dote meri minima quod cariturus erat.

215

IN RISCVM EQVITEM IMBELLEM.

Riscus eques prudens longoque peritus ab usu,
Dissimiles, causa non sine, pascit equos.
Nanque alit ille duos: uolucrem praeuerterit alter,
Alter sed pigro pigrior est asino.
Hic ergo non festinantem ad praelia defert,
Ille prius tuba quam clanxerit, inde refert.

216

IN GELLIAM.

Mentitur qui te dicit mea Gellia fuscam,
Iudice me non es Gellia fusca, nigra es.

217

IN EANDEM.

Candida sum, dicis. Fateor, sed candida quum sis,
Cur tibi candorem hunc obtegit atra cutis? [m_2]

218

IN EVPARIPHVM VESTE OPPIGNERATO FVNDO EMPTA.

Non miror sudare tuae te pondere uestis,
Quattuor haec terrae iugera uestis habet.
Quantum uiuenti tibi terrae ingesseris usquam
Tam magnum tumulum, nec tumulatus habet.

215/1 IMBELLEM.] *1518* IMBELLEM, *1520* 2 prudens] *1518,* prudens, *1520* 4 Nanque] Namque *1518*[d]; duos:] duos, *1518 1520* 5 pigro] pigro, *1518 1520* **217**/1 IN] IA *1518*[m] 2 sum, dicis.] sum dicis, *1518 1520;* Fateor,] fateor, *1518,* fateor. *1520* **218**/1 EVPARIPHVM] EVPARYPHVM *1518* 4 Quattuor] Quatuor *1518* 5 usquam] *1518,* usquam. *1520*

gated his misfortune with the comforting thought that it was the least of the wine's benefits which he must forgo.

215

ON RISCUS, AN UNWARLIKE KNIGHT

Riscus, a prudent knight, skilled by long experience, keeps horses of different kinds, and not without reason. For he keeps two, one swifter than a bird, the other slower than a plodding ass. And so the latter mount delivers him, in no haste, to battle; the former, before the trumpet sounds, brings him back.

216

TO GELLIA

Gellia, my dear, he lies who says you are dark; in my estimation, Gellia, you are not dark, you are black.

217

TO THE SAME GELLIA

"I am fair," you say. I agree. But since you are fair, why does a dark skin conceal this fairness of yours?

218

TO EUPARIPHUS, WHO MORTGAGED HIS FARM TO BUY CLOTHING

I do not wonder that you sweat under the weight of your clothing; this costume of yours contains four acres of land. Not even a man in his grave has so great a mound of earth over him as you will have laid upon yourself, wherever you may be, while still alive.

219

IN GAREMANVM VENDITIS AGRIS PAVPEREM.

En patrios nuper Garemanus uendidit agros,
Nunc subito fama uiuere fertur inops.
Non illi ingenium, non illi industria defit,
Verum inimica uiro fata nocere puto.
Nam putres fuluo glebas mutauerat auro
Callidus, et nunquam rem tamen ille facit.

220

AD SABINVM.

Interiere duae, coniunx tibi tertia nupsit,
Nec tibi fida tamen de tribus ulla fuit.
Non tantum ergo tuas, sed damnas improbe totum
Foemineum irata mente Sabine genus.
Si tamen hanc aequa rem uis expendere lance,
Fies erga ipsas mitior ipse tuas.
Nam tres quum fuerint ijsdem tibi moribus omnes,
Astra haec nascenti fata dedere tibi.
Si genesis tua te semper iubet esse cucullum,
Scilicet expectas uxor ut astra regat? [m$_2$v]
Casta futura alij fuerat. Quod adultera tecum est,
Hoc merito fatis imputat illa tuis.

221

IN NAVFRAGVM MORSVM A VIPERA IN LITTORE E GRAECO.

Aequoris insanas euasit naufragus undas,
Tristius Afra salo praebet harena solum.
Dum iacet ecce graui pressus prope littora somno
Nudus, et infesto fessus abusque freto,
Vipera trux perimit. Frustra fugis aequora frustra,
Heu miser, in terris debita fata tibi.

219/2 PAVPEREM.] *1518,* PAVPEREM, *1520* 7 auro] *1518,* auro, *1520* 8 facit.] *1518,* facit *1520* **220**/12 fuerat.] *1518,* fuerat, *1520;* Quod] quod *1518 1520* **221**/1 VIPERA] VIPERA. *1520* 6 freto,] *1518,* freto. *1520* 7 perimit. Frustra] perimit, frustra *1518 1520*

219

ON GAREMANUS, WHO WAS POOR AFTER SELLING HIS LANDS

Recently Garemanus sold his ancestral estate; now, all of a sudden, rumor says he is living in poverty. It is not that he lacks skill or effort; rather I think that a hostile fate is doing him a bad turn, for he cleverly exchanged his moldy earth for yellow gold, and even so he never makes a profit.

220

TO SABINUS

Two wives are dead; a third wife now is yours. And yet not one of the three has been faithful to you. Hence, Sabinus, in your angry heart you wickedly condemn not only your own wives but the whole female sex. But if you are willing to weigh this problem on the scales of justice, you will be less severe even on your own wives. For, since all three of your wives treated you the same way, it must be that the stars at your birth imposed this fate upon you. If your destiny requires that you be forever a cuckold, can it be that you expect your wife to control the stars? She would have been faithful to some other man. That with you she is an adultress she rightly attributes to your fate.

221

ON A SHIPWRECKED SAILOR BITTEN BY A SNAKE WHEN HE REACHED SHORE FROM THE GREEK

A shipwrecked sailor escaped the raging waters of the sea; the sands of Africa provided him with ground more cruel than the sea. While he lay there on the shore, sound asleep, naked, worn out, far from the hostile sea, a deadly snake killed him. In vain poor fellow, in vain did you escape the deep; your allotted fate awaited you on land.

222

DE CHIRVRGO ET ANV.

Vnxit anus aegros uelans Chirurgus ocellos,
  Vtile persuadens hoc fore quinque dies.
Interea mappas, pelues, mortaria, discos,
  Quicquid onus tutum non facit, inde rapit.
Quum sanata oculos circumtulit illa reuinctos,
  Instrumenta suae sentit abesse domus.
Mercedem ergo exacta, tua contingeret, inquit,
  Vberior pactum est, ut mihi uisus ope.
At uideo nunc quam ante minus, quorum usus in aede est.
  Vidi multa prius, nunc uideo inde nihil.

223

AD QVENDAM.

Quam tibi mens leuis est, tibi si pes tam leuis esset,
In medio leporem posses praeuertere campo.

224

DE HERODE ET HERODIADE. [m3]

Coram Herode Herodiadis dum filia saltat,
  Dum quo debuerat displicuisse placet
Ebrius affectu rex coniugis, ebrius illo
  Fortunae luxu, praetereaque mero,
Opta ait O uirgo, dabitur, iurauimus, huius
  Dimidium regni poscere si libeat.
Impia suggestu sceleratae filia matris,
  Inquit, Baptistae da precor ergo caput.
Dona petis uirgo (si saltatricula uirgo est)
  Quae uix sustineas cernere dona petis.
O funesta parens, O natae dira nouerca,
  Saltare, atque homines quam iugulare doces.
Rex dolet, et tristis concedit, nempe coactus
  Iurisiurandi relligione sui.

222/10 est.] est, *1518 1520* **223**/1 QVENDAM] QVENDAM LEVEM *1563* 3 *Indented in 1520.* **224**/5 mero,] mero. *1518 1520* 9 Baptistae] *1518,* Bapistae *1520* 10 saltatricula] *1518,* saltat tricola *1520* 14 coactus] *1518,* coactus, *1520*

222

A PHYSICIAN AND AN OLD WOMAN

A physician applied ointment to an old woman's ailing eyes, bandaged them, and assured her that five days of such treatment would be effective. Meanwhile, he stole her napkins, bowls, basins, dishes, and whatever was not protected by its own weight. When she was cured and looked about without the bandage, she perceived that the furnishings of her home were missing. Therefore, when she was asked to pay her bill, she said, "The agreement between us requires that my sight be improved by your efforts. Actually, I see less than before, at least of the utensils in my house. I saw many of them before; now I see none."

223

TO AN UNIDENTIFIED PERSON

If you were as light on your feet as you are in the head, you could outrun a hare on level ground.

224

ON HEROD AND HERODIAS

While the daughter of Herodias was dancing for Herod and pleasing him in a way which ought to have displeased him, King Herod, inebriated with love for his wife, inebriated by his excess of good fortune, and drunk besides with wine, said, "State your wish, maiden; it shall be yours, by my oath, even if it is your pleasure to ask for half this realm." The wicked girl, at the prompting of her evil mother, replied, "In that case give me, please, the head of John the Baptist."

The favor you ask, maiden (if such dancing girls as you are maidens)—the favor you ask is such a favor as you can hardly bear to look upon. O deadly parent, O cruel stepmother to your own daughter, for you teach her to be a dancer and to cut the throats of men.

The king regrets his promise; reluctantly he yields, forced no

O regem fidum, sed tunc tantummodo fidum,
Maius perfidia est quum scelus, ipsa fides.

225

AD QVENDAM EBRIOSVM.

Tecum in colloquium quod non properantius iui,
Segniciem incusas, conquererisque meam.
Confiteor uere, tibi non in tempore ueni,
Serior, aut citior debuit hora legi.
Aut utinam eiusdem uenissem mane diei,
Aut tibi uenissem mane sequente die.
Nunc res luce nimis tractari coepit adulta,
Quando tua factum est ebrietate nihil. [m3v]

226

IN PICTVRAM HERODIANAE MENSAE.

Sanguine funesta est Herodis mensa uirili,
Sanguine funesta est mensaque Flaminij.
Tam similes caedes, similes fecere puellae,
Illam saltatrix obtinet, hanc meretrix.
Id tamen intererat, meretrici uita nocentis,
At saltatrici penditur innocui.

227

IN EANDEM PICTVRAM.

Ora uiri foedo sancti fluitantia tabo,
Decussumque gerit regia mensa caput.
Corpora sic regi rex Atreus ambo Thyesti
Natorum apposuit frater edenda patri.
Sic regi Odrysio natum regina peremptum
Fida soror, genitrix perfida ponit Ityn.
Talia regales ornant bellaria mensas,
Crede mihi, non est pauperis iste cibus.

224/17 quum] *1518 1520 1565*, quàm *1520* (*errata*) **225**/2 colloquium] *1518*, colloquium, *1520* **226**/3 est] est, *1518 1520;* Flaminij] Flamminij *1518* **227**/4 Thyesti] *1518*, Thyesti, *1520* 5 patri.] *1518*, patri, *1520* 7 soror,] *1518*, soror. *1520*

doubt by a scrupulous regard for his oath. Here is a king true to his word, but true to it only when to be true is a worse crime than to be false to it.

225

TO AN UNNAMED DRUNKARD

Because I did not make greater haste to arrive for my conversation with you, you rebuke my tardiness and complain. Truly, I confess, I did not meet you at the proper time. I ought to have chosen an hour either later or earlier. Would that I had arrived either early the same day or early on the next. Now we have started to do business when the day is too far advanced, and because you are drunk it has come to nothing.

226

ON A PICTURE OF HEROD'S TABLE

By the blood of man Herod's table was polluted; polluted, too, the table of Flaminius. These two murders, so much alike, were brought about by two young women of similar characters. A dancing girl accomplished the one, a prostitute the other. But there was this difference: the prostitute's pay was the life of a criminal; that of the dancer, the life of an innocent man.

227

ON THE SAME PICTURE

The king's table bears a severed head and a saint's countenance dripping with hideous gore. So too King Atreus, King Thyestes' brother, served as food to Thyestes the bodies of his two sons. Similarly, to the Thracian king his queen, a loyal sister but a treacherous mother, served their murdered son, Itys. Such delicacies as these mark the tables of kings; I assure you this is not a poor man's fare.

228

IN VEHEMENTER NASVTVM
E GRAECO.

Si tuus ad solem statuatur nasus hiante
Ore, bene ostendas dentibus, hora quota est.

229

IN FVCATVM
E GRAECO.

Quur emitur fucus, coma, dens, mel, ceraque, posset
Quum persona tibi tota minoris emi?

230

IN HISTRIONEM
E GRAECO.

Caetera ad historiam, quiddam tamen, id quoque magnum,
Iam tibi saltatum contra erat historiam. [m_4]
Dum Nioben ageres, stabas tanquam lapis esses,
Quum fieres Capaneus, ecce repente cadis.
At Canacem gladio referens, quum uiuus abisti,
Hoc tibi saltatum contra erat historiam.

231

IN HISTRIONEM
E GRAECO.

Saltauit Nioben, saltauit Daphnida Memphis,
Ligneus ut Daphnen, saxeus ut Nioben.

232

SOBRIOS ESSE DIFFICILIORES
E GRAECO.

Vespere quum bibimus homines sumus, atque benigni,
Mane homini siccus trux fera surgit homo.

228/3 nasus] nasus, *1518 1520* **230**/6 Capaneus] Canapeus *1518 1520*, Ganapeus *1565* (*see Commentary*) **232**/1 SOBRIOS ESSE DIFFICILIORES] *1563*, IN EBRIOS *1518*, SOARIOS ESSE DIFFICILIORES *1520*

228

TO A MAN WITH AN EXTREMELY LONG NOSE

FROM THE GREEK

If your nose should be pointed up toward the sun and your mouth kept open, you could show the time of day on your teeth.

229

TO A MAN COSMETICALLY BEAUTIFIED

FROM THE GREEK

Why do you buy rouge, hair, teeth, honey, and wax when at less expense you could buy a complete mask?

230

TO AN ACTOR

FROM THE GREEK

Your dancing in all respects but one was in harmony with the stories, but in one way—and that an important one—it was contrary to the story. While you played the part of Niobe, you stood as though made of stone; when you were Capaneus, you fell suddenly; but when you played Canace with the sword and came away alive, that was dancing contrary to the story.

231

ON AN ACTOR

FROM THE GREEK

Memphis danced the parts of Niobe and of Daphne. Daphne he played as though he were made of wood, Niobe as though made of stone.

232

THAT SOBER MEN ARE VERY SURLY

FROM THE GREEK

In the evening, when we are drinking, we are human beings, and kind ones; but in the morning a man who gets up with a thirst is a savage beast to his fellow man.

233

IN ANDREAM IN MARE VOMENTEM.

Gratus es Andrea, dignusque cui bene fiat.
Nam pisces toties qui te pauere, repascis.

234

DE EODEM.

Aequoris edisti pisces, irascitur aequor.
  Eque tuo foetus exigit ore suos.

235

IN PVELLAM DIVARICATIS TIBIIS EQVITANTEM.

Ergo puella uiri quis te negat esse capacem,
Quum tua tam magnum circumdant crura caballum?

236

AD GALLVM SVBLEGENTEM VETERVM CARMINA.

Vatibus idem animusque, et uere spiritus idem,
  Qui fuit antiquis, est modo Galle tibi.
Carmina nanque eadem, uersusque frequenter eosdem,
  Quos fecere illi, tu quoque Galle facis. [m_4v]

237

IN SCVRRAM PAVPEREM.

Scurra ubi iam fures totam sibi nocte uideret
  Scrutanteis magna sedulitate domum,
Risit, et O media quid uos hic nocte uidetis
  Miror, ait, media nil ego cerno die.

235/1–4 IN PVELLAM . . . caballum?] *om. 1565*   **236**/2 CARMINA.] *1518,* CARMINA, *1520*   5 nanque] namque *1518*[d]   **237**/1 IN SCVRRAM] *See Commentary.*   2 uideret] *1518,* uideret, *1520*   3 domum,] *1518,* domum. *1520*   4 uidetis] *1518,* uidetis. *1520*

233
TO ANDREW AS HE VOMITED INTO THE SEA

You are a grateful and well-deserving person, Andrew, for you pay back the fish, which have so often fed you, by feeding them.

234
ON THE SAME ANDREW

You have eaten the fish which belong to the sea; the sea is angry and demands from your mouth her progeny.

235
TO A GIRL WHO RODE HER HORSE ASTRIDE

Well, my girl, no one could deny that you can take a man, since your legs can straddle so large a horse.

236
TO A FRENCHMAN WHO APPROPRIATED THE POETRY OF THE ANCIENTS

Frenchman, the same insight and even the very same inspiration the ancient poets had now belongs to you. For the poems they wrote, and often the lines too, are the same as what you write.

237
ON A POVERTY-STRICKEN JOKESTER

When a jokester saw burglars searching his whole house with great care in the dark of night, he laughed and said, "I wonder what you see here in the middle of the night: I can see nothing in the middle of the day."

238

DE SOLLICITA POTENTVM VITA.

Semper habet miseras immensa potentia curas,
  Anxia perpetuis sollicitudinibus.
Non prodit, multis nisi circumseptus ab armis,
  Non nisi gustato uescitur ante cibo.
Tutamenta quidem sunt haec, tamen haec male tutum
  Illum, aliter tutus qui nequit esse, docent.
Nempe satellitium, metuendos admonet enses,
  Toxica praegustans esse timenda docet.
Ergo timore locus quisnam uacat hic? ubi gignunt
  Haec eadem, pellunt quae metuenda, metum.

239

IN PRIVIGNVM COLLAPSA NOVERCAE STATVA OPPRESSVM E GRAECO.

Flore nouercalem cingis priuigne columnam,
  Morte ratus mores interijsse malos.
Te tamen illa premit subito inclinata; nouercae,
  Si priuigne sapis, ipsa sepulchra fuge.

240

AD QVENDAM POETAM EXTEMPORALEM.

Hos quid te scripisse mones ex tempore uersus?
  Nam liber hoc loquitur, te reticente, tuus. [n_1]

241

IN NOVERCAS E GRAECO.

Priuigno uel amans infortunata nouerca est,
  Hippolyto grauis, hoc Phaedra docere potest.

238/4 prodit, multis] *1518*, prodit multis, *1520* 6 tutum] *1518*, tutum, *1520* 10 gignunt] gignunt, *1518 1520* 11 eadem, pellunt] eadem pellunt, *1518 1520*; metum.] *1518*, metum *1520* **239**/1 NOVERCAE] *1518*, NOVERCAE. *1520* 6 inclinata;] inclinata, *1518 1520* **240**/4 tuus.] *1518*, tuus *1520*

238
ON THE ANXIOUS LIFE OF RULERS

Immense power always brings miserable worries, tormented as it is by ever-present fears. Such a person does not venture out unless surrounded by a large armed guard, does not eat food which has not been tasted in advance. Certainly these precautions are aids to safety; yet they show that a man is not safe if he cannot be safe without them. Thus a bodyguard reveals fear of an assassin's sword. A food-taster manifests fear of poison. And so what place is without fear in such a life?—where even the very means of repelling what is to be feared themselves engender fear.

239
TO A STEPSON, CRUSHED BY THE FALL OF HIS STEPMOTHER'S STATUE
FROM THE GREEK

Putting wreaths of flowers on your stepmother's monument, you think that her death has put an end to her malicious behavior. But suddenly the column topples and crushes you. Stepson, if you are wise, flee even the tomb of your stepmother.

240
TO A CERTAIN POET WHO WROTE EXTEMPORE

Why do you inform us that you wrote these verses extempore? Your book, you see, apart from any explanation from you, tells us as much.

241
ON STEPMOTHERS
FROM THE GREEK

Even a loving stepmother is a misfortune to her stepson. Phaedra, so grievous to Hippolytus, proves the point.

242

IN QVENDAM QVI DICEBAT CARMINIBVS SVIS NON DEFVTVRVM GENIVM.

Hoc habet Hispani festiuum epigramma poetae,
  Victurus Genium debet habere liber.
Dum legis hunc uersum, iam tu quoque scribere uersus
  Tota mente paras, sed sine mente tamen.
Quaeue canas, qualiue modo contemnis; ea est spes
  Victura haec Genio qualiacunque suo.
Nanque tuis Genium uir tam geniose Camoenis,
  Non dubitas aliquem mox alicunde fore.
Tu tamen (et cariturus erit) tuus hic liber, opta
  Vt careat Genio, qui caret ingenio.
Cui Genius uitam producat si quis, erit quis
  Ex Genijs, adsunt qui tibi mille, malis.
Sed neque sic uiuet, uati si credis eidem,
  Nam non uiuere, sed uita ualere bene est.
Quod si uita libri est iugi languescere probro,
  Detur et aeterna uiuere morte tibi.

243

DE CVPIDITATE REGNANDI.

Regibus e multis regnum cui sufficit unum,
  Vix Rex unus erit, si tamen unus erit. [n_1v]
Regibus e multis regnum bene qui regat unum,
  Vix tamen unus erit, si tamen unus erit.

244

DE DEDITIONE NERVIAE HENRICO VIII. ANGLIAE REGI.

Belliger inuictam domuit te Neruia Caesar,
  Non tamen extremis absque utriusque malis.
Te capit Henricus, capit et sine sanguine, princeps
  Magno tam maior Caesare quam melior.

242/5 uersus] *1518,* uersus, *1520* 7 contemnis;] contemnis, *1518 1520* 8 Genio] *1518,* genio *1520* 9 Nanque] Namque *1518* **243**/5 erit, si] *1518,* erit. si *1520*

242

TO ONE WHO SAID THAT HIS POEMS WOULD NOT LACK GENIUS

A witty epigram of the Spanish poet contains this thought: "To live, a book must have genius." Having read this verse, you set your whole mind on writing poetry yourself, but it turns out to be mindless. The subject and style of your song are matters beneath your notice, such is your confidence that whatever you sing is sure to live by its own genius. For you have no doubt, O man of genius, that presently some sort of genius from somewhere or other will settle on your Muse. Instead you ought to hope (this hope will be fulfilled) that this book of yours may have no genius, since it has no genuine talent. Any genius which might prolong the life of this book will be one of those evil geniuses which you have about you by the thousand. But, even so, your book will not live—if you can take the word of the same poet—for life does not mean merely living; it means living with health and strength. Still, if, for a book, to live is to languish in unending infamy, then may yours also live in eternal death.

243

ON LUST FOR POWER

Among many kings there will be scarcely one, if there is really one, who is satisfied to have one kingdom. And yet among many kings there will be scarcely one, if there is really one, who rules a single kingdom well.

244

ON THE SURRENDER OF TOURNAI TO HENRY VIII, KING OF ENGLAND

Warlike Caesar vanquished you, Tournai, till then unconquered, but not without disaster to both sides. Henry, a king both mightier and better than Caesar, has taken you without blood-

Sensit honorificum sibi rex cepisse, tibique
Vtile sensisti non minus ipsa capi.

245

DE FABVLLA ET ATTALO.

Fabulla nuper nescio quid Attalo
Irata, et illum commouere gestiens,
Ostendereque quam prorsus hunc nihili putet,
Iurauit illi, si sibi centum forent
Membra, mulier quibus fit, e centum tamen
Praestare dignaretur haud unum Attalo.
Non? inquit ille. Quae, malum, est isthaec noua
Frugalitas tibi? quaeue parsimonia?
Certe solebas esse liberalior.
Vnum ne de centum grauareris modo
Auara commodare? at aliquando unicum
Tantum quum haberes, unicum tamen, uiris
Centum solebas dare benigna centies.
Hei metuo ne quid ista portendat tibi
Monstrosa tandem parcitas, magni mali. [n_2]

246

DE FEBRICITANTE ET MEDICO BIBACI.

Febre laboraret mihi quum puer Hemitritaeo,
Forte ibi Sauromatae posco medentis opem.
Sensit ut admoto salientem pollice uenam,
Fortis, ait, calor est, sed calor ille cadet.
Flagitat ergo cyphum, fundumque exhaurit ad imum,
Quantum nec Bitias ebibiturus erat,
Haurit, ad aequaleis aegrotum prouocat haustus,
Et facere hoc temere ne uideatur, ait,
Aestuat hic ualde, ualde bibat ergo necesse est,
Non paruo obruitur magna liquore pyra.

244/7 cepisse] coepisse *1518* **245**/1–16 DE FABVLLA . . . mali.] *om. 1565* 7 Attalo.] *1518,* Attalo, *1520* 8 Non? inquit ille. Quae] Non inquit ille? quae *1518 1520* **246**/4 Sensit] *1518,* Sensit, *1520;* uenam,] *1518,* uenam *1520* 9 ait,] *1518,* ait. *1520*

shed. The king felt that he had gained honor by taking you, and you yourself felt it no less advantageous to be taken.

245
ON FABULLA AND ATTALUS

Recently when Fabulla was angry for some reason with Attalus and wanted to upset him and show how completely she scorned him, she swore to him that if she had a hundred of the parts which are exclusively a woman's she would not condescend to offer so much as one to Attalus. "Wouldn't you?" said he. "What the devil is this new restraint, this new stinginess of yours? Surely you used to be more generous. You couldn't bring yourself, you stingy broad, to put at my disposal a single one from among a hundred? But once upon a time when you had only one, it was your kindly habit to offer that one to a hundred men a hundred times each. What a pity! I fear this unnatural frugality of yours, after so long a time, may mean you have very bad times ahead of you."

246
ON THE FEVERISH PATIENT AND THE DRINKING PHYSICIAN

When a servant boy of mine was suffering from a semi-tertian fever, I chanced on that occasion to call upon the services of a Sarmatian physician. When he had applied his thumb and felt the boy's leaping pulse, he said, "His temperature is high, but it will go down." And so he asked for a cup and drained it to the last drop, as not even Bitias could have done. After his drink he urged the patient to a similar dose, and, in an effort to lend some reason to his conduct, he said, "This man's fever is unusually high; his drinks therefore must be unusually large. A large fire cannot be put out by a little liquid."

247

DE HESPERO CONFITENTE.

Ex more sacro dum sacerdoti Hesperus
Commissa fassus expiaret crimina,
Explorat huius ille conscientiam,
Et cautus omne examinat scelerum genus,
Interque multa quaerit, an unquam malos
Ritu prophano crediderat in daemonas.
Vah egone credam in daemones, inquit, pater?
Multo labore uix adhuc credo in deum.

248

DE OCCASIONE DEO.
E GRAECO.

Vnde erat hic plastes? Sicyonius. At quis erat, dic.
  Lysippus. Tu quis? tempus ego omne domans.
Cur summis instas digitis? roto semper. At alas
  Cur pedibus gestas? ut leuis aura feror. [n_2v]
At dextram cur armat acuta nouacula? signum est,
  Quod conferri acies non potis ulla mihi est.
Cur coma fronte iacet? quod qui me prendere captat,
  Praeueniat. Caluum est cur tibi retro caput?
Quod postquam leuibus praeceps effugero pennis,
  Nil aget a tergo qui reuocare uolet.
Vnde igitur posses documentum sumere, talem
  Artificis posuit me tibi docta manus.

249

DE PHYLLIDE ET PRISCO
IMPARITER AMANTIBVS.

Tam Phyllis cupido bene nubet candida Prisco,
  Quam bene spumanti uitrea lympha mero.

247/7 daemonas.] *1518,* daemonas, *1520* 8 daemones, inquit,] *1518,* daemones. inquit *1520* **248**/3 Sicyonius. At] Sicyonius. at *1518,* Sicyonius, at *1520;* dic.] *1518,* dic *1520* 4 Lysippus. Tu] Lycippus. tu *1518,* Lysippus, tu *1520* 5 semper. At] semper. at *1518,* semper, at *1520* 10 Praeueniat. Caluum] Praeueniat. caluum *1518,* Praeueniat, caluum *1520* **249**/3 Tam] Clam *1518*

247

ON HESPERUS AT CONFESSION

When Hesperus was purging himself of his sins by confessing them to a priest in accordance with sacred usage, the priest, probing Hesperus' conscience, carefully sought for every kind of sin and, among many questions, asked if Hesperus had ever in pagan fashion believed in evil spirits. "What! I believe in evil spirits, Father?" said he; "I still have all I can do to believe in God."

248

ON THE GOD OPPORTUNITY

FROM THE GREEK

From what place did this sculptor come?
Sicyon.
Well, who was he, tell me.
Lysippus.
Who are you?
I am Opportunity, master of all things
Why are you standing on tiptoe?
I am always turning about.
But why do you have wings on your feet?
I move like a fleeting breeze.
Well, why is your right hand armed with a sharp razor?
It is symbolic of the fact that no fine edge can be compared with me.
Why does a lock of hair lie upon your brow?
Because if anyone tries to catch me, he must get ahead of me.
Why is the back of your head bald?
Because once I get away in headlong flight on my swift wings, anyone behind me who wants to bring me back will have no success whatever.
Thus the talented hand of the sculptor, as you may see, has displayed me in such form as to permit you to learn a lesson.

249

ON PHYLLIS AND PRISCUS, WHO LOVED WITH UNEQUAL FERVOR

The wedding of beautiful Phyllis and impatient Priscus is as happy as the mixing of foaming wine and crystal-clear water.

Phyllida Priscus amat calido feruentius igne,
　Frigidius gelida Priscus amatur aqua.
Iungetur tuto, nam si simul ardeat illa,
　Sustineat flammas quae domus una duas?

250

DE NVMMIS ANTIQVIS APVD HIERONYMVM BVSLIDIANVM SERVATIS.

Rhoma suis olim ducibus quam debuit, illi
　Tam debent omnes Buslidiane tibi.
Rhoma suis ducibus seruata est, ipse reseruas
　Rhomanos Rhoma praemoriente duces.
Nam quae Caesareos antiqua nomismata uultus,
　Aut referunt claros tumue priusue uiros, [n3]
Haec tu seclorum studio quaesita priorum
　Congeris, et solas has tibi ducis opes.
Cunque triumphaleis densus cinis occulat arcus,
　Ipse triumphantum nomen, et ora tenes.
Nec iam Pyramides procerum monumenta suorum
　Tam sunt, quam pyxis Buslidiane tua.

251

AD EVNDEM.

Ecquid adhuc placidam mi Buslidiane Camoenam
　Tua coerces capsula?
In tenebras abdis cur dignam luce? Quid illi,
　Quid inuides mortalibus?
Musae fama tuae toto debetur ab orbe,
　Quid huic repellis gloriam?
Gratus ab hac fructus toti debetur et orbi,
　Quid unus obstas omnibus?

250/3 Rhoma] Roma *1518*^{m}; illi] *1518,* illi, *1520*　5 Rhoma] Roma *1518*^{m}　6 Rhomanos Rhoma] *1518*^{d} *1520,* Romanos Roma *1518*^{m}　7 Caesareos] *1518,* caesareos *1520*　8 uiros,] *1518,* uiros. *1520*　9 priorum] *1518,* priorum, *1520*　13 suorum] *1518,* suorum. *1520*　**251**/2 Camoenam] *1518,* Camoenam. *1520*　4 luce? Quid illi,] luce, quid illi? *1518 1520*

Priscus' love for Phyllis is hotter than searing fire, Phyllis' for Priscus colder than ice water. Their union will be safe, for, if she should blaze along with him, what home could withstand two such flames at once?

250
ON ANCIENT COINS PRESERVED IN THE HOME OF JEROME BUSLEYDEN

What Rome once upon a time owed to her leaders, all those leaders, Busleyden, owe to you. Rome was saved by her leaders; you preserve Rome's leaders, now that Rome is dead, for with devotion to antiquity you seek out and collect the old coins which present the features of the emperors or of men famous in imperial times or earlier; and these coins you reckon your only form of wealth. Now when thick dust conceals their triumphal arches, you keep the names and features of the triumphant heroes. The pyramids are not such memorials to their noble dead as your coin-box, Busleyden, has now become.

251
ANOTHER TO BUSLEYDEN

Why, my dear Busleyden, do you still keep your gentle Muse within the confines of your own writing box? Why do you keep her in the dark when she deserves the light? Why do you deny this favor to her? Why deny it to humanity? Your Muse ought to be known all over the world. Why do you refuse her this glory? And the whole world ought to enjoy your charming Muse. You alone

The courtyard of Jerome Busleyden's home, by J. B. De Noter

62. Thome Mori tetrasthicon.

Seu numeris astricta probas, seu libera uerba,
Si pia scripta tibi, si tibi docta placent:
Hec lege, quae musis, que plenus Apolline scripsit,
Buslidius patrij gloria rara soli.

No. 279 on the flyleaf of a codex of Jerome Busleyden's poems, Brussels

An tibi casta procul coetu cohibenda uirili
Cohors uidetur uirginum?
Sunt haec uirginibus fateor metuenda, sed illis
Deuirginari quae queunt.
Ede tuam intrepidus, pudor est inflexilis illi.
Nec ille rudis, aut rusticus.
Vt tua non ipsi cessura est uirgo Dianae
Pudore grata lacteo,
Sic tua non ipsi cessura est uirgo Mineruae
Sensu, lepore, gratia. [n3v]

252

AD BVSLIDIANVM DE AEDIBVS MAGNIFICIS MECHLINIAE.

Culta modo fixis dum contemplabar ocellis
Ornamenta tuae Buslidiane domus,
Obstupui: quonam exoratis carmine fatis
Tot rursus ueteres nactus es artifices?
Nam reor illustres uafris ambagibus aedes,
Non nisi Daedaleas aedificasse manus.
Quod pictum est illic, pinxisse uidetur Apelles,
Quod scalptum credas esse Myronis opus.
Plastica quum uideo, Lysippi suspicor artem,
Quum statuas, doctum cogito Praxitelem.
Disticha quodque notant opus, at quae disticha uellet,
Si non composuit, composuisse Maro.
Organa tam uarias modulis imitantia uoces,
Sola tamen ueteres uel potuisse negem.
Ergo domus tota est, uel secli nobile prisci,
Aut quod prisca nouum secula uincat opus.
At domus haec noua nunc, tarde seroque senescat,
Tunc uideat dominum, nec tamen usque senem.

251/10 uirili] *1518,* uirili, *1520* 14 Ede] Aede *1518 1520* 16 Dianae] *1518,* Dianae. *1520* 18 Mineruae] *1518,* Mineruae. *1520* **252**/3 fixis] *1518,* fixis, *1520;* ocellis] ocellis, *1518,* ocellis. *1520* 4 domus,] *1518,* domus. *1520* 5 Obstupui:] Obstupui *1518,* Obstupui, *1520* 7 illustres] illustreis *1518* 10 scalptum] sculptum *1518* 13 Disticha] Disticha, *1518 1520* 16 ueteres] *1518,* ueteres, *1520* 17 secli] saecli *1518*[m] 18 secula] saecula *1518*[m]; opus.] *1518,* opus, *1520* 19 tarde] tarde, *1518 1520*

thwart all men; why? Does it seem to you that the chaste band of maidens ought to be kept far from the society of men? This, I grant you, is for maidens a source of anxiety, but only for such as can be deprived of their virginity. Have no fear; publish your Muse—she has an unyielding chastity which is neither awkward nor ignorant. Just as surely as your charming Muse will not be inferior to Diana herself in spotless chastity, so surely will she be not inferior to Minerva herself in taste, in wit, and in beauty.

252
TO BUSLEYDEN ON HIS SPLENDID HOUSE AT MECHLIN

While recently I gazed with fascinated eyes at the tasteful decorations in your house, Busleyden, I was amazed: by what incantation have you charmed the fates so as to bring back so many ancient masters? For I think that only the hands of Daedalus could have built that famous house of yours with its artfully winding passages. The pictures here Apelles seems to have painted. The sculptures one might believe to be the work of Myron. When I looked upon the works modelled in clay I thought them the product of Lysippus' art. The statues made me think of the master Praxiteles. Couplets identify every work of art, but couplets such as Vergil, if he did not write them, might wish that he had. Only the organ which imitates such a range of voices with its pipes is, I think, beyond the powers even of the ancients. And so your whole house is either a noble work of antiquity or a modern work such as to surpass antiquity. But may this house, which is now new, be long and slow to grow old, and even then may it see its master not yet grown old.

253

DE PHILOMENO ET AGNA CONIVGATIS MALA FIDE.

En redeunt nostro Veneris miracula seclo
  Qualia nec prisco tempore facta reor.
Flos iuuenes inter Philomenus, et Agna puellas,
  Iunguntur Paphiae rite fauore Deae. [n4]
Ille sed heu nimium laudata uoce superbit,
  Illa tumet placidi laudibus ingenij.
Ergo coniugium uotis tam saepe petitum
  Non Veneri acceptum, sed retulere sibi.
Ingratis adimit formam Dea, neue coirent
  Mutati, dispar indit utrique genus.
Mox Philomenus auem quauis aestate canentem,
  In cuculum, inque auidam uertitur Agna lupam.

254

MEDICINAE AD TOLLENDOS FOETORES ANHELITVS PROVENIENTES A CIBIS QVIBVSDAM.

Sectile ne tetros porrum tibi spiret odores,
  Protinus a porro fac mihi cepe uores.
Denuo foetorem si uis depellere cepae,
  Hoc facile efficient allia mansa tibi.
Spiritus at si post etiam grauis allia restat,
  Aut nihil, aut tantum tollere merda potest.

255

AD LECTOREM DE NOVO TESTAMENTO, VERSO AB ERASMO ROTERODAMO.

Sanctum opus, et docti labor immortalis ERASMI
  Prodit, et O populis commoda quanta uehit!
Lex noua, nam ueteri primum est interprete laesa,
  Scribentum uaria post uitiata manu.

253/3 seclo] saeclo *1518*[m] 4 reor.] *1518*, reor, *1520* 5 Agna] *1518*, agna *1520* 7 Ille] *1518*, Ille, *1520* 9 petitum] *1518*, petitum. *1520* 13 aucm] enim *1518* 14 Agna] agna *1518 1520* **254**/1–9 MEDICINAE . . . potest.] *This is the last poem in 1565.* 6 cepae] cepe *1518 1520* 9 potest.] *1518*, potest, *1520* **255**/6 manu.] *1518*, manu, *1520*

253
ON THE FAITHLESS MARRIAGE OF PHILOMENUS AND AGNA

Behold in our time such miracles of Venus as I think were not brought to pass even in the days of old. Philomenus, flower of the young men, and Agna, flower of the girls, were formally joined by the kindness of the Paphian goddess. But he, unfortunately, was vain of his overrated voice, and she was proud of the praise her gentle disposition had won. Their marriage, for which they had prayed so often, they attributed not to Venus but to themselves. Because of their ingratitude, the goddess changed their shapes, and, lest they come together after the change, she made them into incompatible species. Soon Philomenus was changed to the bird which sings each summer, the cuckoo; and Agna became an insatiable she-wolf.

254
REMEDIES FOR ENDING THE FOUL BREATH WHICH RESULTS FROM CERTAIN FOODS

So that your chopped leeks may not waft their loathsome odors, take my advice and eat an onion right after the leeks. Then again if you want to get rid of the foul smell of the onion, the chewing of garlic will easily accomplish that for you. But if your breath remains offensive even after the garlic, then either it is incurable or nothing but shit will remove it.

255
TO THE READER, ON THE TRANSLATION OF THE NEW TESTAMENT BY ERASMUS OF ROTTERDAM

A holy work, an immortal achievement of the learned Erasmus is coming out; and how great are the advantages it brings to men! for the new law was first marred by the ancient translator and then further damaged by the inaccurate copying of scribes.

Sustulerat forsan mendas Hieronymus olim,
  Sed periere pigro tam bona scripta situ. [n_4v]
Tota igitur demptis uersa est iam denuo mendis,
  Atque noua CHRISTI lex noua luce nitet.
Nec tamen ambitiose singula uerba notauit,
  Sanctum habuit quicquid uel mediocre fuit.
Quo fit ut haec celeri si quis praeteruolet ala,
  Huic nihil hic magni forte putetur agi.
Idem si presso relegat uestigia gressu,
  Censebit maius commodiusue nihil.

256

AD REVERENDISSIMVM .&C. THOMAM CARDINALEM ET ARCHIEPISCOPVM EBORACENSEM IN LIBRVM NOVI TESTAMENTI EI AB ERASMO DATVM.

Vnice doctorum pater ac patrone uirorum,
  Pieridum pendet, cuius ab ore chorus,
Cui populus quantum defert et cedit honore,
  Virtutes infra est tantum honor ipse tuas,
Ab liber iste tuo longe tibi uenit ERASMO.
  Hunc precor hoc animo quo dedit ipse, cape.
Nec dubito, capies, operi nam iure fauorem
  Autor, et autori conciliabit opus.
Ille tui cultor semper fuit, est opus ipsum
  Lex CHRISTI, studium quae fuit usque tuum.
Illa paratur ab hac prudens tibi lege facultas,
  Qua Momo coram reddere iura potes. [o_1]
Namque ita perplexas populo mirante querelas
  Discutis, ut uictus non queat ipse queri.
Non humana tibi facit hoc sollertia, sed lex
  Christi, iudicijs unica norma tuis.
Ergo opus hoc placido Praesul dignissime uultu
  Excipe, et autori (quod facis) usque faue.

255/10 noua luce] noua, luce *1518 1520* 13 fit] *1518,* fit, *1520* **256**/5 DATVM.] *1518,* DATVM, *1520* 6 pater] pater, *1518 1520* 7 chorus,] *1518,* chorus. *1520* 9 tuas,] tuas. *1518 1520* 10 ERASMO.] *1518,* ERASMO, *1520* 12 fauorem] *1518,* fauorem, *1520* 18 Namque] Nanque *1520 catchword*

Jerome long ago may have removed errors, but his readings, excellent as they were, have been lost by long neglect. That is why the whole work has been corrected and translated anew. And Christ's new law shines with new splendor. Erasmus has not ostentatiously disputed the text word by word; he has considered inviolable whatever is at least passable. And so it is that, if anyone skims over this version in rapid flight, he would perhaps think that nothing of importance is afoot, but, if he retraces his steps closely, he will decide that nothing could be finer or more helpful.

256

TO THE MOST REVEREND, ETC., THOMAS, CARDINAL AND ARCHBISHOP OF YORK, ON THE NEW TESTAMENT PRESENTED TO HIM BY ERASMUS

Incomparable father and patron of learned men, you to whose words the Pierian band listens with admiration, you whose honors, despite the respect and esteem of the people, fall far short of your worth—this book of yours has come a long way, from your friend Erasmus. I beg that you receive it in the same spirit which prompted him to send it. Nor have I any doubt that you will do so, for the author will quite rightly win favor for his work, and the work for its author. Erasmus has always been among your admirers; the work itself is the law of Christ, which has ever been your preoccupation. That law provides you with the prudence and the authority which enable you to administer justice even in the face of carping critics. For when disputants engage in intricate quarrels, to the amazement of ordinary people, you sort everything out so well that even the loser cannot complain. It is no mere human adroitness which enables you to do this, but the law of Christ, the sole criterion on which your judgments rest. Therefore, most worthy prelate, accept this book with serenity and favor and continue in the future to cherish the author as you do now.

257

AD REVERENDISSIMVM &C. ARCHIEPISCOPVM CANTVARIENSEM.

Quod bene sunt collata tuo pie praesul ERASMO
Tanta tua toties munera prompta manu,
Quam non ducat iners, quae tu facis ocia, monstrant
Multa, sed in primis indicat istud opus.
Aediderit quamuis numerosa uolumina, fructu
Non sine, uincit opus cuncta priora nouum.
Cunctorum utilitas, sed honor te est inter, et illum.
Praestitit ille operam, tu bone praesul opem.
At partem ille suam toto tibi pectore cedit.
Quicquid agit, meritis imputat omne tuis.
Hunc petit ille sui fructum pater alme laboris,
Charus ut hoc tu sis omnibus, ille tibi.

258

EPITAPHIVM IN SEPVLCHRO IOHANNAE OLIM VXORIS MORI, DESTINANTIS IDEM SEPVLCHRVM ET SIBI ET ALICIAE POSTERIORI VXORI.

Chara Thomae iacet hic Iohanna uxorcula Mori,
Qui tumulum Aliciae hunc destino, quique mihi. [o_1v]
Vna mihi dedit hoc coniuncta uirentibus annis,
Me uocet ut puer et trina puella patrem.
Altera priuignis (quae gloria rara nouercae est)
Tam pia, quam gnatis uix fuit ulla suis.
Altera sic mecum uixit, sic altera uiuit,
Charior incertum est, haec sit, an haec fuerit.
O simul O iuncti poteramus uiuere nos tres
Quam bene, si fatum relligioque sinant.

257/11 cedit.] cedit, *1518 1520* **258**/1–4 EPITAPHIVM . . . VXORI.] *om. Er 1557 Ba T (See Commentary).* 5 Thomae] Thoma *Ba;* hic] *Er 1557 Ba T,* hoc *1518 1520;* Iohanna] Ioanna *Er 1557 Ba T;* uxorcula] Vxorcula *T* 6 Aliciae] Alicie *1557,* Aliciciae *T* 7 annis,] annis *T* 8 puer] *Er 1557 Ba T,* puer, *1518 1520* 9 quae] que *1557;* nouercae] nouercoe *1557,* Novercae *T* 10 suis.] svis, *T* 11 uixit, sic] vixit sic *T* 12 incertum] insertum *T;* sit] sic *1557;* haec fuerit] illa fuit *T* 13 tres] tres, *1557* 14 fatum] factum *1557;* relligioque] religioque *Er 1557 Ba,* religioq *T*

257

TO THE MOST REVEREND, ETC., ARCHBISHOP OF CANTERBURY

That you were right, devout prelate, in bestowing such numerous and generous gifts on your protégé Erasmus, how far he is from wasting the leisure you provide for him, is shown by many things, but above all by this work. Though he has published many books, and they have exercised a wholesome influence, this new one surpasses all that have preceded it. The advantages which this book brings belong to all, but the honor it confers is shared by you and him. He provided the labor; you, kind bishop, provided the support. Yet wholeheartedly he yields his share of the credit to you; whatever he does, he imputes it to your merits. The fruit that he seeks from his labor, kind father, is this: that by this book you win the love of all men, and that he win yours.

258

EPITAPH ON THE TOMB OF JANE, DECEASED WIFE OF MORE, WHO INTENDS THE SAME TOMB FOR HIMSELF AND ALICE, HIS SECOND WIFE

Here lies Jane, the beloved wife of Thomas More, who intend that this same tomb shall be Alice's and mine, too. One of them, my wife in the years of our vigorous youth, has made me father of a son and three daughters; the other has been as devoted to her stepchildren (a rare and splendid attainment in a stepmother) as very few mothers are to their own children. The one lived out her life with me, and the other still lives with me on such terms that I cannot decide whether I did love the one or do love the other more. O, how happily we could have lived all three together if fate

At societ tumulus, societ nos obsecro coelum.
  Sic mors, non potuit quod dare uita, dabit.

259

AD SE GESTIENTEM LAETICIA QVOD EVASERAT TEMPESTATEM.

QVid iuuat insanas maris euasisse procellas?
  Laeticia est, ut non sit tibi uana, breuis.
Talis febre quies aegris intermicat, illa
  Dum per acerba statas itque reditque uices.
Quam te plura manent optata tristia terra,
  In rapido fuerant quam subeunda freto?
Aut ferrum aut uarij praecedent funera morbi,
  Quorum uno est quouis mors minus ipsa grauis.
Quin eadem tumidas frustra uitata per undas
  Te premet in plumis insidiosa tamen.

260

IN PINGVEM QVENDAM PATREM CVI FREQVENS ERAT IN ORE SCIENTIA INFLAT.

Quemlibet inflat, ais, uel teste scientia Paulo,
  Hanc fugis: unde igitur tu, pater ample, tumes?
Vix gestas crasso turgentem abdomine uentrem [o_2]
  Inflaturque leui mens tibi stulticia.

261

IN CHELONVM.

Cur adeo inuisum est pigri tibi nomen aselli?
  Olim erat hoc magnus, Chelone, philosophus.

258/15 coelum] caelum *1518*^{m} *Ba* 16 mors,] Mors *T After this poem, the last in 1518, appeared the following words, not printed anywhere in 1520:* EPIGRAMMATVM CLARISSIMI DISERTISSIMIQVE VIRI THOMAE MORI, CIVIS ET VICECOMITIS LONDINENSIS, FINIS. **259**/3 QVid] *Block letter for* Q *1520;* procellas?] procellas *1520* 9 funera] fuuera *1520* **260**/4 inflat, ais,] inflat ais *1520* 5 fugis:] fugis, *1520;* igitur] igitut *1520;* tu,] tu *1520;* ample,] ample *1520* **261**/1 CHELONVM] *1563*, CELONIVM *1520. (See Commentary).* 2 inuisum] iniuisum *1520;* aselli?] aselli *1520* 3 magnus, Chelone,] magnus Chelone *1520*

and religion permitted. But the grave will unite us, and I pray that heaven will unite us too. Thus death will give what life could not.

259

TO HIMSELF AS HE REJOICED AT HAVING ESCAPED FROM A STORM

What good is it to have escaped the raging tempests of the sea? Your joy must be either brief or groundless. It is like the relief which suddenly flashes upon men sick with fever, as the painful fits go away and return in their fixed cycles. How many more troubles await you on the land you yearned for than you would have had to endure on the rushing turmoil of the sea. Your death will be ushered in by the scalpel or various diseases, any one of which is more grievous to bear than death itself. Yes, that same death which you escaped to no purpose on the swelling sea will overwhelm you on your pillow, only more treacherously.

260

TO A CERTAIN FAT PRIEST WHOSE HABIT IT WAS TO SAY "LEARNING PUFFS UP"

According to you, though others are puffed up with learning, as Paul teaches, you avoid it. How is it then, O substantial father, that you are so swollen? You can hardly manage your bloated belly with its flabby paunch, and your mind is puffed up with empty folly.

261

TO CHELONUS

Why is the name of stolid ass so hateful to you? Once upon a time a philosopher was great on this account, Chelonus. Still, lest

Ne tamen ipse nihil diferre puteris ab illo
Aureus ille fuit, plumbeus ipse magis.
Illi mens hominis asinino in corpore mansit
At tibi in humano est corpore mens asini.

262

DE FELE ET MVRE.

Muscipula exemptum feli dum porrigo murem
Haud auido praedam protinus ore uorat.
Sed trepidum in media captiuum exponere terra
Sustinet, et miris ludere laeta modis.
Adnutat cauda, tremulis inspectat ocellis,
Et lasciua caput iactat in omne latus.
Molliter attonitum pede suscitat, ire parantem
Corripit, inque uicem datque negatque uiam.
Mox pede sublimem iaculatur, et excipit ore,
Deinde abit, et falsae spem facit usque fugae.
Excubat, et saltu fugientem laeta reprendit
Protinus inque locum quo fuga coepta redit.
Digrediturque iterum mirandoque improba sensu
Quae misero mens est experimenta capit.
Hoc dum saepe facit, securaque longius exit,
Mus rimam subito repperit et subijt.
Illa cito reuocata gradu frustra obsidet antrum.
Hic latebra tectus tutus ab hoste fuit.
Muscipula occiderat, nisi quod tutela salusque [o$_2$v]
Feles, interitus quae solet esse, fuit.

263

GRATVLATVR QVOD EAM REPPERIT INCOLVMEM QVAM OLIM FERME PVER AMAVERAT.

VIuis adhuc primis O me mihi charior annis,
Redderis atque oculis Elisabetha meis.

261/5 magis.] magis *1520* **262**/6 cauda,] cauda *1520* 8 suscitat,] suscitat *1520;* parantem] parantem, *1520* 11 fugae.] fugae *1520* 16 exit,] exit *1520* 20 Muscipula] *1563*, Manscipula *1520* 21 Feles,] Feles *1520;* esse,] esse *1520* **263**/4 annis,] annis *1520* 5 meis.] meis *1520*

you be thought not to differ from him at all, he was golden, you are more leaden. He had the mind of a man in the body of an ass; you have, in the body of a man, the mind of an ass.

262
ON A CAT AND A MOUSE

When I held out to the cat the mouse I had taken from a trap she did not immediately and ravenously eat her prize. With great restraint she placed her trembling prey on open ground and happily toyed with it in extraordinary fashion. She twitched her tail, watched the mouse with shifty eyes, and playfully turned her head from side to side. Gently, with a paw, she provoked the terrified mouse into moving, and when it started to move she stopped it; and alternately she let it go and caught it again. Soon with her paw she tossed it up high and caught it in her mouth. Then she walked away from it and gave it the false hope of still being able to escape. She lay down to watch at a distance, and, as the mouse made off, she joyfully leaped upon it and immediately returned to the spot from which it had fled. Again she left it, and, with amazing perception, the wicked creature made tests of the poor mouse's intentions. While she was repeating this performance and confidently going farther away, the mouse suddenly found a crack and was gone. The cat rushed to the hole and sat on guard—in vain. The mouse, protected in its hiding place, was safe from its enemy. It would have died in the trap if what ordinarily destroys it had not protected and saved it—a cat.

263
HE EXPRESSES HIS JOY AT FINDING SAFE AND SOUND HER WHOM HE HAD ONCE LOVED AS A MERE BOY

You are really still alive, Elizabeth, dearer to me in my early years than I was myself, and once again my eyes behold you. What

Quae mala distinuit mihi te fortuna tot annos?
Pene puer uidi, pene reuiso senex.
Annos uita quater mihi quattuor egerat, inde
Aut duo defuerant aut duo pene tibi,
Quum tuus innocuo rapuit me uultus amore,
Vultus, qui quò nunc fugit ab ore tuo?
Cum quondam dilecta mihi succurrit imago,
Hei facies quam nil illius ista refert.
Tempora quae, tenerae nunquam non inuida formae,
Te rapuere tibi, non rapuere mihi.
Ille decor nostros toties remoratus ocellos
Nunc tenet a uultu pectora nostra tuo.
Languidus admoto solet ignis crescere flatu,
Frigidus obruerat quem suus ante cinis.
Tuque facis quamuis longe diuersa priori
Vt micet admonitu flamma uetusta nouo.
Iam subit illa dies quae ludentem obtulit olim
Inter uirgineos te mihi prima choros,
Lactea cum flaui decuerunt colla capilli,
Cum gena par niuibus uisa, labella rosis,
Cum tua perstringunt oculos duo sydera nostros
Perque oculos intrant in mea corda meos, [o3]
Cum uelut attactu stupefactus fulminis haesi,
Pendulus a uultu tempora longa tuo,
Cum socijs risum exhibuit nostrisque tuisque
Tam rudis et simplex et male tectus amor.
Sic tua me cepit species: seu maxima uere
Seu maior uisa est quam fuit, esse mihi.
Seu fuit in causa primae lanugo iuuentae
Cumque noua suetus pube uenire calor.
Sydera seu quaedam nostro communia natu,
Viribus afflarant utraque corda suis.
Namque tui consors arcani conscia pectus
Garrula prodiderat concaluisse tuum.

263/6 annos?] annos *1520* 7 uidi,] uidi *1520* 9 tibi,] tibi. *1520* 18 flatu,] flatu *1520* 23 choros,] choros. *1520* 25 rosis,] rosis. *1520* 27 meos,] meos. *1520* 29 tuo,] tuo. *1520* 38 pectus] pectus, *1520*

bad luck has kept you from me all these many years! When I was just a boy, I saw you first; now when I am almost an old man, I see you again. Sixteen years I had lived—you were about two years younger—when your face inspired me with innocent devotion. That face is now no part of your appearance; where has it gone? When the vision I once loved comes before me, I see, alas, how utterly your actual appearance fails to resemble it. The years, always envious of young beauty, have robbed you of yourself but have not robbed me of you. That beauty of countenance to which my eyes so often clung now occupies my heart. It is natural for a dying fire, though buried in its own cold ashes, to flare up when a gust of air blows on it. And however much you are changed from what you were, you make the old flame glow by giving me this new reminder. There comes now to my mind that distant day which first revealed you to me as you enjoyed yourself amid a band of dancing maidens. Your yellow hair enhanced the pure white of your neck; your cheeks looked like snow, your lips like roses; your eyes, like two stars, dazed our eyes and through my eyes made their way into my heart: I was helpless, as though stunned by a lightning-stroke, when I gazed and continued to gaze upon your face. Then, too, our comrades and yours laughed at our love, so awkward, so frank and so obvious. Thus did your beauty take me captive. Either yours was perfect beauty, or I lent it more perfection than it had; perhaps the stirrings of adolescence and the ardor which accompanies the approach of manhood were the reason, or perhaps certain stars we shared at birth had influenced both our hearts. For a gossipy companion of yours who was in on the secret revealed that your heart, too, was moved.

Hinc datus est custos ipsique potentior astris
Ianua quos uellent illa coire uetat.
Ergo ita disiunctos diuersaque fata secutos,
Tot nunc post hyemes reddidit ista dies.
Ista dies qua rara meo mihi laetior aeuo,
Contigit occursu sospitis alma tui.
Tu praedata meos olim sine crimine sensus,
Nunc quoque non ullo crimine chara manes.
Castus amor fuerat; ne nunc incestior esset,
Si minus hoc probitas, ipsa dies faceret.
At superos qui lustra boni post quinque ualentem
Te retulere mihi, me retulere tibi,
Comprecor ut lustris iterum post quinque peractis
Incolumis rursus contuar incolumem. [o3v]

264

T. MORVS MARGARETAE ELISABETHAE CECILIAE AC IOANNI DVLCISSIMIS LIBERIS S. P.

QVattuor una meos inuisat epistola natos
Seruet et incolumes a patre missa salus.
Dum peragratur iter, pluuioque madescimus imbre
Dumque luto implicitus saepius haeret equus,
Hoc tamen interea uobis excogito carmen
Quod gratum (quanquam sit rude) spero fore.
Collegisse animi licet hinc documenta paterni,
Quanto plus oculis uos amet ipse suis.
Quem non putre solum, quem non male turbidus aer,
Exiguusque altas trans equus actus aquas
A uobis poterant diuellere, quo minus omni
Se memorem uestri comprobet esse loco.
Nam crebro dum nutat equus casumque minatur
Condere non uersus desinit ille tamen.
Carmina quae multis uacuo uix pectore manant
Sollicito patrius rite ministrat amor.

263/41 Ianua] Ianua, *1520* 48 fuerat;] fuerat, *1520* 51 tibi,] tibi. *1520*
264/7 equus,] equus: *1520* 13 aquas] aquas. *1520* 19 patrius] *1563*, patruus *1520*

On this account a chaperon was imposed upon us, and a door strong enough to thwart our very destiny kept apart a pair whom the stars wished to bring together. And then that notable day after so many years brought us together, far separated though we were in the pursuit of our different destinies, that day propitious in my finding you alive and well—seldom in my life have I met a happier day. Once upon a time you innocently stole my heart; now too, and innocently still, you are dear to me. Our love was blameless; if duty could not keep it so, that day itself would be enough to keep love blameless still. Well, I beg the saints above, who, after twenty-five years, have kindly brought us together in good health, that I may be preserved to see you safe and sound again at the end of twenty-five years more.

264

THOMAS MORE SENDS BEST WISHES TO HIS BELOVED CHILDREN, MARGARET, ELIZABETH CECILIA, AND JOHN

I hope that a single letter to all four of you may find my children in good health and that your father's good wishes may keep you so. In the meantime, while I am making a journey, drenched by a soaking rain, and while my mount, too frequently, is bogged down in the mud, I compose these verses for you in the hope that, although unpolished, they may give you pleasure. From these verses you may gather an indication of your father's feelings for you—how much more than his own eyes he loves you; for the mud, the miserably stormy weather, and having to urge a small horse through deep waters have not been able to distract his thoughts from you or to prevent his proving that, wherever he is, he thinks of you. For instance, when—and it is often—his horse stumbles and threatens to fall, your father is not interrupted in the composition of his verses. Many people can hardly write poetry even when their hearts are at ease, but a father's love duly provides verses even when he is in distress. It is not so strange that

Non adeo mirum si uos ego pectore toto
  Complector, nam non est genuisse nihil.
Prouida coniunxit soboli natura parentem,
  Atque animos nodo colligat Herculeo.
Inde mihi tenerae est illa indulgentia mentis,
  Vos tam saepe meo sueta fouere sinu.
Inde est uos ego quod soleo pauisse placenta,
  Mitia cum pulchris et dare mala piris.
Inde quod et Serum textis ornare solebam, [o4]
  Quod nunquam potui uos ego flere pati.
Scitis enim quam crebra dedi oscula, uerbera rara.
  Flagrum pauonis non nisi cauda fuit.
Hanc tamen admoui timideque et molliter ipsam,
  Ne uibex teneras signet amara nates.
Ah ferus est dicique pater non ille meretur,
  Qui lachrymas nati non fleat ipse sui.
Nescio quid faciant alij, sed uos bene scitis
  Ingenium quam sit molle piumque mihi.
Semper enim quos progenui uehementer amaui
  Et facilis (debet quod pater esse) fui.
At nunc tanta meo moles accreuit amori
  Vt mihi iam uidear, uos nec amasse prius.
Hoc faciunt mores puerili aetate seniles,
  Artibus hoc faciunt pectora culta bonis.
Hoc facit eloquio formatae gratia linguae
  Pensaque tam certo singula uerba modo.
Haec mea tam miro pertentant pectora motu
  Astringuntque meis nunc ita pignoribus,
Vt iam quod genui, quae patribus unica multis
  Causa est adfectus, sit prope nulla mei.
Ergo natorum charissima turba meorum
  Pergite uos uestro conciliare patri.

264/23 Herculeo.] Herculeo *1520* 26 placenta,] placenta: *1520* 28 Serum] *1563*, serum *1520;* solebam,] solebam *1520* 30 rara.] rara, *1520* 37 mihi.] mihi *1520* 41 uidear] *1563*, uideor *1520*. *(See Commentary)* 42 seniles,] seniles *1520* 47 pignoribus,] pignoribus: *1520* 49 est] est, *1520*

I love you with my whole heart, for being a father is not a tie which can be ignored. Nature in her wisdom has attached the parent to the child and bound their minds together with a Herculean knot. Thence comes that tenderness of a loving heart that accustoms me to take you so often into my arms. That is why I regularly fed you cake and gave you ripe apples and fancy pears. That is why I used to dress you in silken garments and why I never could endure to hear you cry. You know, for example, how often I kissed you, how seldom I whipped you. My whip was never anything but a peacock's tail. Even this I wielded hesitantly and gently so as not to mark your tender backsides with painful welts. Ah, brutal and unworthy to be called father is he who does not himself weep at the tears of his child. How other fathers act I do not know, but you know well how soft and kind I am by temperament, for I have always intensely loved the children I begot, and I have always been (as a father should be) easy to win over. But now my love has grown so much that it seems to me I did not love you at all before. This is because you combine the wise behavior of old age with the years of childhood, because your hearts have been informed with genuine learning, because you have learned to speak with grace and eloquence, weighing each word carefully. These accomplishments tug at my heart so wonderfully, they bind me to my children so closely, that what, for many fathers, is the only reason for their affection—I mean the fact that they begot their children—has almost nothing to do with my love for you. Therefore, my dear little troop of children, continue to endear yourselves to your father and, by those same

Et quibus effectum est uobis uirtutibus istud
Vt mihi iam uidear uos nec amasse prius,
Efficitote (potestis enim) uirtutibus ijsdem,
Vt posthac uidear uos nec amare modo. [o4v]

265

EXCVSAT QVOD DVM LOQVERETVR CVM EXIMIO QVODAM PATRE, NOBILEM QVANDAM MATRONAM INGRESSAM THALAMVM, ATQVE ALIQVANDIV COLLOQVENTIBVS ILLIS ADSTANTEM NON ANIMADVERTERAT.

QVum tua dignata est bonitas me uisere nuper,
Atque humilem praesul magne subire casam:
Interea dum uerba seris tam dulcia mecum
Penderem ut uultu totus ab ipse tuo,
Ecce, quod ah mihi sero mei retulere ministri,
Nempe (ubi tot res est acta diebus) heri,
Matrona ingreditur, cultu spectanda superbo
Sed quem forma tamen uicit, et hanc probitas.
Venit in usque thorum, stetit et mihi tempore longo
Proxima, contingens et cubito cubitum.
Inspicit antiquae selecta numismata formae,
Claraque tam claris gaudet imaginibus.
Sumere dignatur tenuis bellaria mensae,
Venit et a dulci dulcior ore sapor.
Nostra nec in tantum uertuntur lumina lumen
O mihi plus ipso nate stupore stupor.
Nunc ignosco mei quod non monuere ministri,
Tam stupidum certe nemo putauit herum.
Oh oculos, longe qui prospexisse solebant,
Si qua refudisset tale puella iubar.
An senui? torpentque meo mihi corpore sensus?
Surgenti an genius mane sinister erat? [o5]

264/53 prius,] prius. *1520* 55 uos] uos, *1520* **265**/8 QVum] *Block letter for* Q *1520* 12 Ecce, quod] Ecce (quod *1520;* ministri,] ministri *1520* 13 heri,] heri *1520* 18 formae,] formae. *1520*

accomplishments which make me think that I had not loved you before, make me think hereafter (for you can do it) that I do not love you now.

265

HE APOLOGIZES BECAUSE WHILE CONVERSING WITH A PROMINENT CLERIC HE HAD FAILED TO NOTICE A CERTAIN NOBLE LADY WHO ENTERED THE ROOM AND STOOD BESIDE THEM FOR SOME TIME AS THEY TALKED

Mighty prelate, on that recent occasion when Your Excellency saw fit to pay me a call and to enter my humble house, while you were conversing with me so pleasantly that my attention was entirely focused on your countenance, observe! a lady entered—as my servants informed me too late, yesterday in fact, when the matter was many days past. Her splendid attire was eye-catching, but it was outshone by her beauty, which is in turn surpassed by her virtue. She came right up to our couch and stood very near me for a long time, right at my elbow. She selected and examined some ancient coins, and famous herself, found pleasure in the famous portraits on them. She deigned to take some sweets from my scanty table, and their taste grew sweeter in her own sweet mouth. And yet our eyes failed to observe even so brilliant a beauty as hers. Alas, for my inborn dullness, duller than dull! Now I forgive my servants for not warning me. Surely no one of them thought his master so dull. O eyes, which used to be able to perceive from a distance such splendor radiating from any girl! Have I grown old? And is perception dulled in this body of mine? Or did an evil spirit attend my rising that morning? Or did you

An tu, ne nisi te quicquam sentire ualerem,
Surpueras lepido me mihi colloquio?
Arte lyraque feras in se conuerterat Orpheus,
In te mellifluis uertor et ipse sonis.
Sed tuus intentat magnum lepor iste periclum,
Neglectam sese ne putet illa mihi,
Hospita ne limis quum tam prope staret ocellis
Vidisse, et uisam dissimulasse ferar.
At uel hiulca prius mihi terra dehisceret optem,
Quam sit in hoc animo tam fera barbaries,
Vt si quando, leues ueluti mihi missa per auras
In thalamum penetret candida nympha meum,
Non saltem aspiciam (si plura licere negetur)
Quaque licet memet candidus insinuem.
Vt miserum est non posse loqui! nam cuncta fatetur,
Qui sermonis inops nulla negare potest.
Nunc mihi sermonis quia non est copia Galli
Quae sola est dominae patria lingua meae,
Omnibus absoluar, non excusabimur uni
Iudice qua, causa statque caditque mea.
Vulnus ab Aemonia qui quondam pertulit hasta,
Rursus ab Aemonia est cuspide nactus opem.
Dedecus hoc lepidae quoniam peperere fabellae
(Quum dominae et mihi me surripuere) tuae,
Dedecus hoc lepidae debent purgare fabellae
Meque meae dominae conciliare tuae. [o5v]

266

VERSVS SVMPTI EX ANTIMORO BRIXII AD QVOS ALLVDIT EPIGRAMMA QVOD SVBIVNGITVR.

Haec mihi dictanti adstabant dirae auribus omnes,
Et furiae infernis concita turba uadis:

265/35 mihi,] mihi. *1520* 36 ocellis] ocellis, *1520* 40 auras] auras, *1520* 46 Galli] galli *1520* 47 meae,] meae. *1520* 48 absoluar,] absoluar *1520* 51 opem.] opem, *1520* 54 fabellae] fabellae, *1520* **266**/6 uadis:] uadis. *1520*

beguile me with your charming conversation so that I was unable to be aware of anything but you? Orpheus, by his skill with the lyre, entranced wild beasts; I too was cast into a trance by your mellifluous speech. But that charm of yours imposed the great risk that the lady think I had neglected her, a risk that I be reported to have seen her, standing so near to me, out of the corner of my eye and then pretended not to have seen her. But I would that the earth split open and swallow me rather than that there be found in my heart a rudeness so brutal that when a fair nymph, wafted so to speak by some breath of air, enters my room, I fail to look at her at least (if the occasion allows no more) and, if it is permitted, fairly win her favor. How miserable it is not to be able to speak! For whoever cannot deny anything because he does not speak the language, tactily admits everything. Now, because I have little command of French (my lady speaks only her native French), I shall be innocent in the eyes of all, but not forgiven by the one lady in whose court my plea must stand or fall. He who was wounded long ago by the Haemonian spear, from that same spear won help. Since your gift of charming speech (which made me forget myself and ignore the lady) was the cause of this disgraceful deed, your gift of charming speech ought to wipe away this disgrace and restore me to my lady's good graces.

266

VERSES QUOTED FROM BRIXIUS' *ANTI–MORUS* BECAUSE THEY ARE THE SUBJECT OF THE EPIGRAM BELOW

About my ears as I said these things there hovered all the goddesses of vengeance and the Furies, a troop roused from the

Alecto, et sacris caput irretita colubris,
   Tisiphone, et terrens ore Megaera truci.

MORVS.

Brixius audiuit postquam id reprehendere multos,
   Quod falsa tantum scriberet,
Corrigere ut possit uicium hoc, aliquid modo uisum est
   Verum quod esset aedere,
Quod foret indubium, quod uerum nemo negaret,
   Authore quanquam Brixio.
Vix reperit quicquam cui non tamen ipsius omnem
   Fidem eleuaret uanitas.
Ast ubi dispexit mentemque per omnia torsit
   Deliberabundus diu,
Vnum tandem, omnes una quod uoce fatentur,
   Omni esse uero uerius,
Inuenit et scribit lepidum lepidissimus omnes
   Cingere caput sibi furias.

267

IN CHORDIGERAM NAVEM ET ANTIMORVM SYLVAM GERMANI BRIXII GALLI:

Brixius en Germanus habet syluamque ratemque
   Diues opum terra, diues opum pelago.
Vtraque uis illi quid praestat scire? uehuntur
   In rate stulticiae, syluam habitant furiae.

268

IN HVNC HENDECASYLLABVM IMO TREDECIM SYLLABARVM VERSVM GERMANI BRIXII GALLI EX ANTIMORO SVMPTVM.

Excussisse hominumque in ora protulisse. [o_6]

266/10 multos,] multos: *1520*   11 scriberet,] scriberet. *1520*   13 esset aedere,] esset, aedere. *1520*   16 omnem] omnem, *1520*   19 diu,] diu. *1520*   21 uerius,] uerius. *1520*   **267**/5 terra,] terra *1520*

nethermost depths: Alecto and Tisiphone, her head surrounded by loathsome snakes, and frightful Megaera, with her savage face.

MORE

After Brixius heard that many readers had complained that he wrote only lies, in order to correct this defect he then decided to publish something which would be true, which would be unquestioned, which no one would contradict, even though Brixius was the author. It was difficult for him to find anything which his own lack of truth had not robbed of credibility. But when he had looked about, pondered long, and forced his mind to consider everything, then at last he did find one thing which all mankind unanimously agrees is truer than any truth; and, most charming fellow that he is, he wrote that all the Furies surrounded his charming head.

267

ON THE SHIP *CORDELIÈRE* AND THE *ANTIMORUS*, A COLLECTION OF POEMS BY THE FRENCHMAN GERMANUS BRIXIUS

Behold, Germanus Brixius, rich in resources on both land and sea, has a forest (*sylua*) and a raft. Do you want to know what advantage each affords him? His follies ride his raft, the Furies inhabit his forest.

268

ON THE FOLLOWING HENDECASYLLABIC, OR RATHER THIRTEEN-SYLLABLE, VERSE FROM THE *ANTIMORUS* OF THE FRENCHMAN GERMANUS BRIXIUS

To discover and to offer to the gaze of men.

MORVS.

Quod uersus adeo faceres enormiter amplos
Quam nemo antiquus nemo poeta nouus,
Saepe diu mecum miratus quaerere coepi
Accidit hoc Brixi qua ratione tibi?
At tandem didici metiri te tua suetum
Non numero aut pedibus carmina, sed cubitis.

269

IN IDEM.

Carmina Germani quod in hendecasyllaba, lector,
Syllaba coniecta est terna super decimam,
Da ueniam: haud didicit tantum numerare, ut ab uno,
Ordine perueniat rectus ad undecimum.
Nolo mihi numeret stellas aut aequoris undas,
Criminaue (hoc plus est) carminis ipse sui.
Pergama si numeret quot sunt obsessa per annos,
Si poterit Musas dinumerare nouem,
Octo pedes Cancri, septena uel ostia Nili,
Fastorumue libros qui tibi, Naso, manent,
Si numeret coeli plagas, Phoebiue caballos,
Tres numeret furias, ter tribus ipse furens,
Ipse suos (sed ne certem sine pignore, dura
Si uincar uinci conditione uolo)
Ipse suos oculos (quum sint duo) si numerarit,
Vnum ego tunc patiar perterebretis ei.

FINIS.

268/8 nouus,] nouus: *1520* **269**/2 hendecasyllaba, lector,] hendecasyllaba lector *1520* 3 decimam,] decimam. *1520* 9 Musas] musas *1520;* nouem,] nouem. *1520* 10 Cancri] cancri *1520;* ostia] hostia *1520 1563* 11 tibi, Naso, manent,] tibi Naso manent. *1520* 15 uolo] uolo. *1520* 17 ei.] *The word* FINIS *follows on the same line in 1520, after which comes the list of errata.*

MORE

After being puzzled on frequent occasions over a long period at your writing verses so immoderately long—such verses as no poet, ancient or modern, ever wrote—I set about to discover, Brixius, how this had happened to you. And, finally, I found that it is your custom to measure your verses not by meter or by feet but by the yard.

269

ON THE SAME TOPIC

Reader, forgive Germain for putting thirteen syllables into a poem in hendecasyllabics. He has hardly learned to count well enough to go in order correctly from one to eleven. Let him not count for me the stars or the waves of the sea or—this is a more difficult task—the errors in his own poetry. If he can count the years of the siege of Troy or the nine Muses or the eight legs of Cancer or the seven mouths of the Nile or, Ovid, the immortal books of your *Fasti;* if he can count the regions of the sky or the horses of Phoebus or the three Furies (although he is three times as mad as three Furies could make him); if he can count his own—but I won't gamble without stakes, if I lose I want it to be a big loss—if he can count, I say, his own eyes (though he has just two), then I'll let you gouge out one of his.

THE END

POEMS IN THE 1518 EDITION BUT NOT IN THE 1520 EDITION

270

IN FATVM.

E GRAECO.

Si ferris ferre et fer; sin irasceris, et te
Laeseris, et quod fert te feret, immo trahet.

271

IN IACOBVM REGEM SCOTORVM.

Dum pius Henricus uictricibus asserit armis
Rhomano te iterum, Gallia, pontifici,
Scotorum Iacobus regnum rex ecce Britannum
Occupat, infestis impius agminibus.
Foedera non illum toties iurata morantur,
Coniugis in fratrem quin ferat arma suae,
Quin Gallo fidei comitem se adiungeret hosti,
Quin cuperet Petri mergere nauiculam.
Nec mirum est, scelera haec si uir conceperit: infans
Caede patris teneras imbuit ante manus.
Ergo uolente Deo, perijt cum strage suorum.
Exitus et scelerum qui solet esse fuit.

270/3 fer;] fer. *1518* **271**/3 Rhomano] Romano *1518*[m]; iterum, Gallia,] iterum Gallia *1518* 7 suae,] suae. *1518* 10 conceperit:] conceperit, *1518* 13 esse] esse, *1518*

270
ON FATE
FROM THE GREEK

If you are being borne along, then be borne along and bear with it. But if you become angry, then not only will you do yourself harm but also whatever bears you will continue to do so—yes, will even drag you.

271
ON JAMES, KING OF THE SCOTS

While loyal Henry with victorious armies was reclaiming you, France, for the Roman Pontiff, behold! James, King of the Scots, was disloyally trying to take by armed force the kingdom of the Britons. The treaties he had so often sworn to did not deter him from bearing arms against his own wife's brother, or from joining the French enemy as a faithful ally, or from his desire to sink the ship of Peter. It is no wonder that as a man he committed these crimes; before this as a boy he dyed his young hands in his father's blood. Therefore, in accordance with the will of God, he has perished amid the slaughter of his men. And the result of wrongdoing was just what it usually is.

272

[VERSES FROM THE LAST OF A SERIES OF NINE PAGEANTS PAINTED ON CLOTH]

In the nynth pageant was painted a Poet sitting in a chayre. And ouer this pageant were there writen these verses in latin folowyng.

The Poet.

Has fictas quemcunque iuuat spectare figuras,
  Sed mira veros quas putat arte homines,
Ille potest veris animum sic pascere rebus,
  Vt pictis oculos pascit imaginibus.
Namque videbit vti fragilis bona lubrica mundi
  Tam cito non veniunt, quam cito pretereunt.
Gaudia laus et honor celeri pede omnia cedunt,
  Qui manet excepto semper amore dei.
Ergo homines, leuibus iamiam diffidite rebus,
  Nulla recessuro spes adhibenda bono.
Qui dabit eternam nobis pro munere vitam,
  In permansuro ponite vota deo.

272/8 homines,] homines. *1557* 9 veris] veris, *1557* 10 pascit] poscit *1557* 11 mundi] mundi, *1557* 12 pretereunt.] pretereunt, *1557* 13 honor] honor, *1557* 16 bono.] bono, *1557*

272

[VERSES FROM THE LAST OF A SERIES OF NINE PAGEANTS PAINTED ON CLOTH]

THE POET

If anyone delights in looking at these imaginary figures, but (because of the painter's marvelous skill) thinks them to be real men, he can feast his mind on the realities themselves, just as he feasts his eyes upon the painted images. For he will see that the elusive goods of this perishable world do not come so readily as they pass away. Pleasures, praise, homage, all things quickly disappear—except the love of God, which endures forever. Therefore, mortals, put no confidence hereafter in trivialities, no hope in transitory advantage; offer your prayers to the everlasting God, who will grant us the gift of eternal life.

273

Thomae Morae, diserti adolescentuli in lucubraciunculas Holtiadae. Epigramma.

Quem legis Holtiadae tenerum pia furta libellum,
  Seu vir seu puer es, lac puerile voca.
Dulce sed et meritum liber hic me iudice nomen,
  Lactea qui pueris dogmata prestat, habet.
Vos Angli legite haec iuuenes, in maxima quorum
  Exiguum quamuis commoda surgit opus.
Quae vos in minimum legitis digesta libellum
  Precepta in paucos pauca legenda dies,
Holtiades eadem vigili quesita labore
  Legit ab innumeris pauca voluminibus.
Sedulus ille vagus sese circumtulit agris.
  Mellifice officio quam bene functus apis.
Quicquid ibi in dulces sapidi congessit aceruos
  Mellis in hunc paruum rettulit alueolum.
Hoc opus Anglorum cupienti intrare iuuentae
  Prima sit in reliquam ianua grammaticam.
Hanc tamen ante forem docti struxere, sed horum
  Quisque suos Latio fecerat ore modos.
Quid bene fulta penus prodest tibi, quando retentat
  Ianua magnificos irreseranda cibos?
Angle puer, Latio quid ages sermone? sapisse
  Non potes in primo verba Latina die.
Te decet altricis tenerum recubare sub alis
  Discereque ex verbis non tua verba tuis.
Structa sed et verbis iam pridem ianua nostris
  Grammatice, verum si fateamur, erat.
Illa tamen vetus et tunsu lacerata frequenti
  Quae vix assiduo pulsa labore crepat.

273/1 Thomae Morae] Thome more *W P B* 2 Holtiadae] Holtiade *W P B;* Epigramma] *W P,* Epygramma *B* 3 Holtiadae] Holtiade *W P,* holtiade *B* 7 haec] hec *W P B* 9 Quae] Que *W P B* 13 Sedulus] *B,* Sedulis *W P;* vagus] vagis *W P B;* circumtulit] circuntulit *PB* 16 rettulit] *B,* retulit *W P* 17 cupienti] *W B,* cupicte *P;* iuuentae] *iuuente W P B* 18 grammaticam] *W P,* grammaticem *B* 20 Latio] latio *W,* lacio *B,* latino, *P* 22 magnificos] *W P,* magnificas *B* 23 Latio] latio *W P,* lacio *B* 28 Grammatice,] Grammatice / *W P,* Grammatice *B;* fateamur,] fateamur *W P B;* erat.] *B,* erat / *W P* 29 tunsu] *W P,* tunsi *B* 30 Quae] Que *W P B;* vix] *P B,* xix *W*

273

ON THE SCHOLARLY LABORS OF HOLT AN EPIGRAM BY THE LEARNED YOUTH THOMAS MORE

This gentle book of Holt's which you are reading, these kindly pilferings, whether you are man or boy, you are to call by the name "Milk for Children." In my judgment this book which gives to boys lessons like milk has a pleasant name and an appropriate one, too. Read these lessons, you young men of England; it is for your very great advantage that the book, small though it be, appears. The few rules arranged in a tiny book which you read in a few days Holt with sleepless effort has sought out and chosen from countless volumes. He wandered diligently all over the fields. How well he has performed the task of the honey-gathering bee! In his travels whatever tasty honey he gathered into sweet stores he has brought to this little hive. Let this work be the introduction, the door to the rest of grammar, for the English youth who wish to enter. To be sure, learned men built doors before this one, but each of them imposed his limits because he used the Latin language. What good to you is a strong larder if a door which you cannot open keeps you from the sumptuous food? English boy, how will you manage in Latin? You cannot, on the first day, understand Latin words. It is only proper that while you are young you lie under a protector's wings and that you learn the foreign language by means of your native speech. A door to grammar in English had been built long before, if we confess the truth. But that door was old, marked by frequent knocking, such a door as barely squeaks open to perpetual pound-

Prima pars

¶ Ad reuerendissimū dñm suum dñm Johannem morton Cantuarieñ. archipresulem/totiusq; Anglie primatem et titulo sancte Anastasie cardinalem Johannes holt Epigramma.

Hoc operis quodcunq; pater dignissime cernis
Holtiades domino dedicat omne suo
Autor vt instituit tantillum opus edere primum
Et tibi non tactas dedere primitias
Incussit validos tanti censura timores
Patris: ab incepto me tua pena trahens
Sed tamen in miseros pietas quam suggeris om̄es
Et michi presentem plus pius ipse facis
Abscidit a pauido vanos michi corde timores
Quod michi mentis erat/perfice/perge/iubens
Ergo faue lingue censor venerande latine
Tam cito vix natum ne moriatur opus
Quicquid erit placido supplex precor excipe vultu
Ingenium arbitrio dasq; rapisq; tuo
Hec equidem in varium breuiter collecta moretum
Ex multis rapui furta pudica locis
Unde tui causam pater alma dedere nepotes
In sibi perpetuas vtilitatis opes
Edideram celebri Lamithe pie presul in aula
Digna volens pueris commoda ferre tuis.

¶ Thome more/diserti adolescentuli in lucubraciūnculas Holtiade. Epigramma.

John Holt, *Lac puerorum,* London, c. 1508 (*STC* 13604), with no. 273

Opusculi

Quem legis Holtiade tenerum pia furta libellum
Seu vir seu puer es/lac puerile voca
Dulce/sed et meritum liber hic me iudice nomen
Lactea qui pueris dogmata prestat/habet
Vos angli legite hec iuuenes/in maxima quorum
Exiguum q̄uis commoda surgit opus
Que vos in minimũ legitis digesta libellum
Precepta in paucos pauca legenda dies
Holtiades eadem vigili quesita labore
Legit ab innumeris pauca voluminibus
Sedulis ille vagis sese circũtulit agris.
Mellifice officio q̄ bene functus apis
Quicquid ibi in dulces sapidi congessit aceruos
Mellis in hunc paruum retulit alueolum
Hoc opus anglorum cupienti intrare iuuente
Prima sit in reliquam ianua grammaticam
Hanc tamen ante forem docti struxere/sed horum
Quisq; suos latio/fecerat ore modos
Quid bene fulta penus prodest tibi/quãdo retentat.
Janua magnificos irreseranda cibos
Angle puer latio quid ages sermone/sapisse
Non potes in primo verba latina die
Te decet altricis tenerum recubare sub alis
Discereq; ex verbisnon tua verba tuis
Structa/sed et verbis iam pridem ianua nostris
Grammatice/verum si fateamur erat/
Illa tamen vetus et tunsu lacerata frequenti;
Que rix assiduo pulsa labore crepat
Janua nostra noua est/tenereq; facillima turbe
Ad digiti minimũ q̄cito aperta sonum

A.ii.

John Holt, *Lac puerorum*, London, c. 1508 (*STC* 13604), with no. 273

¶ Thome more epygramma

Macte puer gaude lepido quicūq3 libello
  Deliciis tuis pastus es holtiade
Nec tibi dat carnes nec acer bos arbuta fructus
  Dat tibi que dulci pocula lacte fluunt
Carnis in inualida massa grauis incubat aluo
  Arbuta non sapide sunt leuis humor aque.
At lac ꝙ infantē sine pondere nutrit alumnū.
  Lactis ꝙ infanti dulcis in ore sapor.
Pastus es hoc igitur/visum est decuisse nequibat
  Grandia tam tenerum pondera ferre iecur
Nunc vbi desieris lactare/alimenta monemus
  Non mellita nimis fortia sume magis.
Ergo aut Sulpitii placida lepidissime mensa
  Utilibus Phoce vel satur esto cibis.
Aut Sepontini bibito noua musta Perotti
  Aut diomedeis condita mulsa cadis
Aut alium quēcūq3 velis imitarier opta/
  Dulcia qui caute misceat vtilibus
Precipue sed Sulpicii documēta capessēs
  Holti consiliis vse vel vse meis.
Discenda holtiades heteroclita liquit ab illo
  Et quodcunq3 tenent nomina queq3 genus.
Recta leges illic que sit constructio/sed post
  Preterita ꝙ verbis iuncta supina suis.
Sedulus ꝙ tandem longe pulcherrima disces
  Carmina limitibus continuisse suis.
Ergo musarum choreas ingressa iuuentus
  Quum per Sulpitiū plectra lyramq3 geres.
Dic mode/ferre lyrā quū dextra nequiuerat/holtius.
  Ad monuit labris vbera chara meis.

John Holt, *Lac puerorum,* London, c. 1508 (*STC* 13604), with no. 274

Ianua nostra noua est teneraeque facillima turbae,
Ad digiti minimum quam cito aperta sonum.

274
Thomae Morae epygramma

Macte puer, gaude lepido quicumque libello
Delicijsque tuis pastus es Holtiadae.
Nec tibi dat carnes nec acerbos arbuta fructus,
Dat tibi quae dulci pocula lacte fluunt.
Carnis in inualida massa grauis incubat aluo,
Arbuta non sapidae sunt leuis humor aquae.
At lac et infantem sine pondere nutrit alumnum,
Lactis et infanti dulcis in ore sapor.
Pastus es hoc igitur. Visum est decuisse, nequibat
Grandia tam tenerum pondera ferre iecur.
Nunc vbi desieris lactare, alimenta monemus
Non mellita nimis, fortia sume magis.
Ergo aut Sulpitii placida lepidissime mensa
Vtilibus Phocae vel satur esto cibis.
Aut Sepontini bibito noua musta Perotti
Aut Diomedeis condita mulsa cadis
Aut alium quemcumque velis imitarier opta,
Dulcia qui caute misceat vtilibus.
Precipue sed Sulpicii documenta capesses,
Holti consiliis vse vel vse meis.
Discenda Holtiades heteroclita liquit ab illo
Et quodcunque tenent nomina quaeque genus.
Recta leges illic quae sit constructio, sed post
Preterita et verbis iuncta supina suis.

273/31 teneraeque] tenereque *W P B;* turbae] turbe *W P B* **274**/1 Thomae Morae] Thome more *V W P B* 2 quicumque] quicunque *B* 3 Delicijsque] *B,* Delicijs *V,* Delicus *W P;* tuis] *W P,* tui *B;* Holtiadae] holtiade *W P B,* holt[iade] *V* 5 quae] que *W P B,* qu[e] *V* 7 sapidae] sapide *V W P B;* aquae] aque *W P B* 12 Nunc] unc *B;* lactare] *W P,* lactere *B;* monemus] monemu *B* 13 nimis] *W P,* minus *B* 14 Sulpitii] *W,* Sulpicij *V,* Sulpitij *P,* sulpitij *B* 15 Phocae] Phoce *V W P B;* cibis] *W B,* cibus *P* 17 Diomedeis] diomedeis *W P,* dyomedeis *V B* 18 quemcumque] quemcunque *B;* imitarier opta] *W P,* imitari exopta *B* 20 Sulpicii] *W,* Sulpicij *P V,* Sulpitij *B;* capesses] *W B,* capisses *P* 22 heteroclita] *W P,* heteroclyta *B* 23 quaeque] queque *W P B* 24 quae] que *V W P B;* constructio, sed post] *W P,* constructio post hoc *B*

ing. Our door is new and very easy for the young crowd. How promptly it opens at the slightest tapping of a finger!

274
AN EPIGRAM BY THOMAS MORE

Good boy! Rejoice whoever you are if you have been nourished, to your delight, by Holt's elegant book. He does not offer you meat or the bitter berries of the arbutus tree. He gives you cups aflow with sweet milk. Lumps of meat lie heavy on a tender stomach, and arbutus berries are mere moisture, such as belongs to tasteless water. But milk nourishes without distress even a child, and the taste of milk is sweet in the mouth of the young. That is why you have been fed on this. It was clear that this was the proper way: your constitution, so undeveloped, could not bear great burdens. Now that you have been weaned, we suggest a diet not too bland; take something stouter. That is, dine most elegantly at the untroubled board of Sulpicius or eat your fill of the helpful nourishment of Phocas; or drink the new wine of Perotti of Siponto or the potions aged in the casks of Diomedes. Or choose any other you may wish to follow, provided that he knows how to combine what is pleasant with what is useful. But you who take Holt's advice and you who take mine will be eager for the teachings of Sulpicius above all. Holt has left heteroclites and the gender of the various nouns to be learned from Sulpicius. There you will read what is the right construction, but only after you have studied the past tenses and the supines which belong to each verb.

Sedulus et tandem longe pulcherrima disces
  Carmina limitibus continuisse suis.
Ergo musarum choreas ingressa iuuentus,
  Quum per Sulpitium plectra lyramque geres,
Dic modo, ferre lyram quum dextra nequiuerat, Holtus
  Admouit labris vbera chara meis.

275

Thomae Mori in progymnasmata Linacri

Qui leget haec sensim docti precepta Linacri
  Dicere (si teneat quae legit inde) volet:
Post tot grammatices immensa volumina paruus
  Non tamen incassum prodiit iste liber.
Exiguus liber est. Sed gemmae more nitentis
  Exiguo magnum corpore fert precium.

276

Versus in tabulam duplicem, in qua Erasmus ac Petrus Aegidius simul erant expressi per egregium artificem Quintinum, sic ut apud Erasmum exordientem Paraphrasin in epistolam ad Rhomanos, picti libri titulos praeferrent suos, et Petrus epistolam teneret, Mori manu inscriptam ipsi, quam et ipsam pictor effinxerat.

TABELLA LOQVITVR.

Quanti olim fuerant Pollux et Castor amici,
  Erasmum tantos Aegidiumque fero.
Morus ab his dolet esse loco, coniunctus amore
  Tam prope quam quisquam vix queat esse sibi.
Sic desyderio est consultum absentis, ut horum
  Reddat amans animum littera, corpus ego.

274/26 longe] *W P B*, longa *V* 28 choreas] *W P V*, chorum *B* 29 Sulpitium] *W P*, Sulpicium *B* 30 modo] *B*, mode *W P*; Holtus] *W*, holtus *B*, hultus *P* 31 admouit] *B*, admonuit *W P* **275**/1 Thomae] Thome *R;* Mori] mori *R;* Linacri] linacri *R* 2 haec] hec *R;* Linacri] linacri *R* 3 quae] que *R;* volet:] volet *R* 5 liber.] liber *R* 6 gemmae] *gemme R* **276**/1–5 Versus . . . effinxerat.] *A E, om. D* 3–4 Rhomanos] Romanos *E* 5 ipsam] *A*, ipse *E* 8 Aegidiumque] *A E*, Egidiumque *D* 11 desyderio] D^{c} *A*, desiderio *D E* 12 littera] *D*, litera *A E*

And if you are industrious, you will learn finally that by far the most beautiful poems are those which have kept within their boundaries. Therefore, you young men, when you have entered the company of the Muses, when, thanks to Sulpicius, you carry your plectrum and lyre, then say, "When my right hand could not hold the lyre, it was Holt who offered a pap welcome to my lips."

275

THOMAS MORE ON LINACRE'S PROGYMNASMATA

Whoever reads with care these rules by the learned Linacre will, if he retains what he reads here, want to say, "After so many huge volumes on grammar, this book, small as it is, has not come out in vain. The book is very small, but, like a sparkling jewel, with its diminutive size it has high value."

276

Verses on a two-part picture, in which Erasmus and Peter Giles are portrayed together by the outstanding artist Quentin in such a way that near Erasmus, as he begins his *Paraphrase of the Epistle to the Romans,* the books in the picture reveal their titles, and Peter holds a letter written to him in More's hand—even this the painter has put in the picture.

THE PICTURE SPEAKS

I show Erasmus and Giles, friends as dear to each other as were Castor and Pollux of old. More grieves to be absent from them in space, since in affection he is united with them so closely that a man could scarcely be closer to himself. They arranged to satisfy their absent friend's longing for them: a loving letter represents their minds, I their bodies.

187

deum! mors Busleidii, hominis cum non vulgariter eruditi, tum animi & amoris
in nos atque in omnes candidi. Mihi adeo hic desidendum est in principium septem-
bris, ut vix duos dies impetrare licuerit, quibus ad oppidum Audomari transcur-
rerem, praecipue ut Abbatem viderem saltem Sancti Bertini, quem tu mihi olim
descripseras; repperi plane talem invitatus atque exceptus largiter ab illo in convivio;
Homo prolixe quosuis, me vero valde offusus. Senex iucundissimus ad memoriam
tui rejuvenescens. Vale, charissime Erasme. Tunstallus in Angliam rediit.
Iterum vale. Caleto ~~vij die~~ Octobris, Anno 1517.

Po

Edit. Basil. p. 125.

Mi charissime Petre salue, misere cupio ecquid tu convalescas intelligere.
vid. col. 287. c. quae res non minori mihi curae est, quam quiduis mei. Itaque & inquiro diligenter,
& omnes omnium voces excipio sollicitus, aliquot mihi meliores de te spes
renunciarunt, seu quod opto compertas siue ut desideriis meis inseruiant.
Scripsi litteras Erasmo nostro, eas tibi apertas mitto. signabis ipse, nihil opus est
quod illi scribitur clanculum ad te venire, Versiculos quos in tabellam tam
insignite fieri quam illa scite depicta est ad te perscripsi. Tu si digna videbuntur
Erasmo imparti, alioqui vulcano dedas. Vale vij octobris

Tabella Loquitur.

Quanti olim fuerant Pollux & Castor amici,
Erasmum tantos Egidiumque fero.

Aeij

202

The Deventer manuscript of no. 276

Morus ab his dolet esse loco, coniunctus amore
Iam prope q quisq vix queat esse sibi
Sic desiderio est consultum absentis, ut horum
Reddat amans animum littera, corpus ego.

Ipse Loquor

Tu quos aspicis, agnitos opinor
Ex vultu tibi, si prius vel unq
Visos, sin minus indicabit alterum
Ipsi littera scripta, Nomen alter.
Ne sis nescius, certe scribit ipse
Qq is qui fiet, ut taceret ipse
Inscripti poterant docere libri
Toto qui celebres legũtur orbe
Quintine o veteris novator artis
Magno non minor artifex Apelle
Mire composito potens colore
Vitam adfingere mortuis figuris
Hei cur effigies labore tanto
Factas tam bene, talium virorum
Quales prisca tulere secla raros
Quales tempora nostra rariores

The Deventer manuscript of no. 276

188

Quales haud scio post futura an ullos
Se iuuit fragili indidisse ligno
Donadas materie fideliori
Quę seruare datas queat perhennes
O si sic poteras tueque formę, et
Votis consuluisse posterorum
Nam si secula quę sequentur ulli
Seruabunt studium artium bonorum
Nec mars horridus obteret Mineruam
Quanti hanc posteritas emat tabellam!

Mi Petre cum omnia mirifice Quintinus noster expresserit, quam mirifice in primis falsarium videtur prestare posse, nam ita inscriptionem litterarum ad te mearum imitatus est, ut ne ipse idem iterum possem itidem. quare nisi aut ille in suum aliquem usum, aut tu in tuum eam seruas epistolam. Remitte rogo ad me, duplicabit miraculum apposita cum tabella. Sin autem perierit aut vobis usui erit, ego experior meę manus imitatorem ipse rursus imitari. Vale cum lepidissima coniuge.

Cuthbertus Tunstal Erasmo S. P. D.

Ep. CCLXXII. N. E. Vix tandem hispaniarum rex in regnum nauigauit, & ego ex Selandia cum meis vix saluus redeo, usque adeo tetro & plane pestilenti caeli illius infestatus odore, ut multorum dierum inedia nondum

Aiiij

208

The Deventer manuscript of no. 276

Erasmus, by Quentin Metsys

Peter Giles, by Quentin Metsys

IPSE LOQVOR MORVS.

Tu quos aspicis, agnitos opinor
Ex vultu tibi, si prius vel vnquam
Visos, sin minus, indicabit altrum
Ipsi littera scripta, nomen alter,
Ne sis nescius, ecce scribit ipse,
Quanquam is qui siet, ut taceret ipse,
Inscripti poterant docere libri,
Toto qui celebres leguntur orbe.
Quintine O veteris nouator artis,
Magno non minor artifex Apelle,
Mire composito potens colore
Vitam adfingere mortuis figuris,
Hei cur effigies labore tanto
Factas tam bene, talium virorum
Quales prisca tulere secla raros,
Quales tempora nostra rariores,
Quales haud scio post futura an vllos,
Te iuuit fragili indidisse ligno,
Dandas materiae fideliori,
Quae seruare datas queat perennes?
O si sic poteras tuaeque famae, et
Votis consuluisse posterorum!
Nam si secula quae sequentur ullum
Seruabunt studium artium bonarum
Nec Mars horridus obteret Mineruam,
Quanti hanc posteritas emat tabellam!

277

[ON A FRIAR WHO OBJECTED TO COMPARING FRIENDS WITH BROTHERS]

Duos amicos uersibus paucis modo
  Magnos uolens ostendere,

276/13 IPSE LOQVOR MORVS] *E,* Ipse loquor *D,* IPSE LOQVOR. *A* 17 littera] *D,* litera *A E* 19 siet] *A E,* fiet *D* 28 raros] *D*[c] *A E,* roros *D* 31 ligno] *A E,* lingno *D* 32 materiae] *A E,* materie *D* 33 perennes] *A E,* perhennes *D* **277**/3 modo] modo, *A E*

MORE HIMSELF SPEAKS

I think you recognize from their faces those whom you see here if you have ever seen them before. If not, then the letter written to the one will identify him; and notice, so that you should know the name of the other, he is writing it himself. To be sure, the books which bear his name—so well known and widely read all over the world—could tell you who he is, even if he himself were not doing so. Quentin, reviver of an ancient art, not less an artist than great Apelles, marvelously gifted to lend life by a mixture of colors to lifeless shapes, alas, why were you satisfied to paint on perishable wood portraits so painstakingly, so beautifully, done—portraits of such men as antiquity produced but seldom, such men as our own day produces less frequently still, such men as the future, I suspect, may not produce at all. These portraits you have done ought to have been entrusted to a more enduring medium which could preserve through the years what it had received. O, if you could only have looked out for your own fame and the desires of posterity; for if future ages preserve any love of the fine arts and if savage warfare does not obliterate the arts, then what a price posterity would pay for this picture!

277

[ON A FRIAR WHO OBJECTED TO COMPARING FRIENDS WITH BROTHERS]

To show that two men were great friends, I recently said in a

Tantos amicos dixeram, quanti olim erant
  Castorque Polluxque inuicem.
Fratres amicis, ait, inepte comparas,
  Ineptiens fraterculus.
Quid ni? inquam. An alteri esse quisquam amicior
  Quam frater est fratri potest?
Irrisit ille inscitiam tantam meam,
  Qui rem tam apertam nesciam.
Est ampla nobis, inquit, ac frequens domus,
  Plus quam ducentis fratribus,
Sed ex ducentis, pereo, si reperis duos
  Fratres amicos inuicem.

278

D. Thomae Mori Tetrastichon ab ipso conscriptum, triennio antequam mortem oppeteret.

Moraris, si sit spes hic tibi longa morandi:
  Hoc te vel morus, More, monere potest.
Desine morari, et caelo meditare morari:
  Hoc te vel morus, More, monere potest.

Aliud eiusdem Distichon eodem conscriptum tempore.

Qui memor es Mori, longae tibi tempora vitae
  Sint, et ad aeternam peruia porta, mori.

279

Thomae Mori Tetrasthicon

Seu numeris astricta probas, seu libera uerba,
  Si pia scripta tibi, si tibi docta placent,
Haec lege, quae musis, quae plenus Apolline scripsit,
  Buslidius patrij gloria rara soli.

277/7 comparas,] *E*, comparas. *A* 9 ni? inquam. An] ni inquam? an *A E;* amicior] amici-or, *A E* 10 est] est, *A E* 13 nobis,] *E*, nobis *A* **278**/1–2 D. Thomae . . . oppeteret.] *F, om. L H Br* 4 morus] *F*, Morus *L H Br;* More] *F H L*, morus *Br* 5 caelo] *H Br*, coelo *F L;* meditare] *F H Br*, metitare *L* 6 morus . . . potest] *F*, Morus. More, monere potest. *H*, Morus etc. *L*, Morus, more, monere potest. *Br* 7–8 Aliud . . . tempore.] *F, om. L* 9 es] *F*, est *L* **279**/1 Thomae] Thome *Bu* 4 Haec] Hec *Bu;* quae plenus] que plenus *Bu*

few lines of verse that they were as great friends as Castor and Pollux were of old. A foolish friar said, "It is foolish to compare friends to brothers." "Why not?" I answered. "Do you think that any man can be a better friend to another than brother is to brother?" He laughed at my extraordinary ignorance—that I should be unaware of so obvious a fact. He said, "We have a large and crowded monastery with more than two hundred brothers, but from among the two hundred I'd wager my life you won't find two brothers who are friends."

278

A QUATRAIN OF SIR THOMAS MORE WRITTEN THREE YEARS BEFORE HE DIED

You are playing the fool if you expect to stay long here below. Even a fool, More, can tell you that much. Stop playing the fool and contemplate staying in heaven. Even a fool, More, can tell you that much.

ANOTHER DISTYCH BY THE SAME AUTHOR WRITTEN AT THE SAME TIME

You who remember More, may your lifetime be long and your death an open gate to eternal life.

279

A QUATRAIN BY THOMAS MORE

If your taste is for poetry or for prose, if piety or learning delights you, then read these works by Busleyden, who is inspired by Apollo and the Muses, and who is the precious glory of his native land.

Rear flyleaf, Augustine, *De civitate Dei,* Basel, 1512 [1522] containing nos. 278 and 280 (reduced)

280

Misisti mihi quae legenda legi;
Legi sed pariter libens dolensque,
Valde atrocia non videre laetus.
Istis congruit autor ipse scriptis:
Vir nunquam bonus, optimusque semper,
Vir vere malus, optimus malorum.

281

[A MATHEMATICAL MNEMONIC]

A plure deme plusculum.
Minus minori subtrahe.
Pluri minus coniungito.
Atque ad minus plus adijce.

280/1 legenda] *followed by cancelled* misi

280

The things you sent me to read I have read, but I read them with both pleasure and pain, happy to see nothing utterly horrible. The author himself corresponds to these writings of his: a man never good, and always the best, a man truly bad, the best of the bad.

281

[A MATHEMATICAL MNEMONIC]

Subtract more from more. Subtract less from less. Add less to more. Add more to less.

COMMENTARY

COMMENTARY

THE FOLLOWING bibliography and list of abbreviations includes the titles of all works cited frequently in the Commentary and Introduction. The titles of works referred to only once or occurring in a brief cluster of references are given in full as they occur. Biblical citations and quotations are from the Clementine Vulgate. Except for the Greek Anthology, citations and quotations of Latin and Greek authors (unless otherwise noted) are from the readily available texts of the Loeb editions, which are cited here with the permission of the Harvard University Press. Quotations of the Greek Anthology are from Aldus' edition (Venice, 1503). Greek passages are identified by their location in the Palatine Anthology (e.g., *AP* IX, 61), which was not available to More, because modern readers can find them there more easily. But we have also given locations in the Planudean Anthology upon which More drew. Thus "*Pl.* I, 5 (εἰς ἀνδρείους), 1 (εἰς Λάκαιναν), sig. A_4v" means that the poem is in Book I of the Planudean Anthology, in the fifth section (title in parentheses), the first poem (title, if any, in parentheses) in that section, on sig. A_4v of the Aldine edition of 1503. Modern editions generally give the Planudean numbering from Planudes' autograph (Codex Marcianus 481, completed in September 1301), but the arrangement of the poems in the autograph was considerably altered in the manuscript and printed tradition available to More. For the handling of abbreviations, breathings, accents, and capitalization in these quotations, see above, pp. 64–65.

The numbers introducing notes in the Commentary (e.g., 31/6–7) refer not to page and line numbers (as in the other volumes of this edition), but rather to poem and line numbers. The prefatory epistles of Rhenanus and More are designated "Rhen. Pref." and "More Pref.," followed by continuous line numbers.

BIBLIOGRAPHY AND SHORT TITLES

Adams, R. P. *The Better Part of Valor: More, Erasmus, Colet and Vives on Humanism, War, and Peace,* Seattle, 1962. Cited as "Adams."

Allen, P. S., and H. M. Allen. *See* Erasmus.

Anthologia Latina, ed. Alexander Riese, Leipzig, 1869–70. Cited as "*Anthologia Latina.*"

Anthologie Grecque: Première partie, Anthologie Palatine, ed. Pierre Waltz, 10 vols., Paris, 1928–74. Cited as "Waltz."

AP. Anthologia Palatina. See Paton, W. R.

ASD. See Erasmus.

BB. Bibliotheca Belgica: Bibliographie générale des Pays Bas, ed. F. van der Haeghen, 2nd Series, Ghent, 1898–1923; reissued by Marie-Thérèse Lenger, 6 vols. (Brussels, 1964–70).

Bebel, *Facetiae. Heinrich Bebels Facetien,* ed. Gustav Bebermeyer, Bibliothek des Literarischen Vereins in Stuttgart 276, Leipzig, 1931. Cited as "Bebel, *Facetiae.*"

Bradner-Lynch. *See* More.

Briefwechsel des Beatus Rhenanus, ed. Adalbert Horawitz and Karl Hartfelder, Leipzig, 1886.

Campbell, Lorne, Margaret Mann Phillips, Hubertus Schulte Herbrüggen, and Joseph B. Trapp, "Quentin Matsys, Desiderius Erasmus, Pieter Gillis and Thomas More," *Burlington Magazine, 120* (November 1978), 716–25.

CCSL. Corpus Christianorum: Series Latina, Turnhout, 1953–. Vols. numbered to 176, of which 92 had been published by 1980.

Chrimes, S. B. *Henry VII,* London, 1972. Cited as "Chrimes."

CIL. Corpus Inscriptionum Latinarum, ed. Theodor Mommsen et al., 16 vols., Berlin, 1858–1955.

Corpus iuris civilis. See Mommsen and Krueger.

CW. See More.

CWE. See Erasmus.

De la Garanderie, Marie-Madeleine. "Un Erasmien français: Germain de Brie," *Colloquia Erasmiana Turonensia,* Paris, 1972, *1,* 359–79.

De Vocht, Henry. *Jerome de Busleyden, Founder of the Louvain Collegium Trilingue: His Life and Writings, Humanistica Lovaniensia 9,* Turnhout, 1950. Cited as "De Vocht, *Busleyden.*"

Dickinson, Francis H., ed. *Missale ad usum insignis et praeclarae ecclesiae Sarum,* Oxford and London, 1861–83. Cited as "Dickinson."

DNB. Dictionary of National Biography, 63 vols., London, 1885–1900.

Doyle, Charles Clay. "On the Neglected Sources of Some Epigrams by Thomas More," *Moreana, 46* (1975), 5–11. Cited as "Doyle, 'Neglected Sources.'"

———. "The Background of More's Epigrams," *Moreana, 55–56* (1977), 61–64. Cited as "Doyle, 'Background.'"

Du Cange, Charles du Fresne. *Glossarium mediae et infimae Latinitatis,* Paris, 1883–87; reprint, Graz, 1954. Cited as "Du Cange."

Dübner, Friedrich, and Edme Cougny, eds. *Epigrammatum Anthologia Palatina,* 3 vols., Paris, 1864–90. Cited as "Dübner-Cougny."

Eckert, Willehad, and Christoph von Imhoff. *Willibald Pirckheimer,* Cologne, 1971.

EETS. Early English Text Society.

Emden, A. B. *A Biographical Register of the University of Oxford to A.D. 1500 [and] A.D. 1501 to 1540,* 4 vols., Oxford, 1957–74. Cited as "Emden."

Erasmi opuscula, ed. W. K. Ferguson, The Hague, 1933. Cited as "*Erasmi opuscula.*"

Erasmus, Desiderius. *The Adages,* comp. and trans. Margaret Mann Phillips, Cambridge, 1964.

———. *The Collected Works of Erasmus,* trans. R. A. B. Mynors and D. F. S. Thomson and ann. Wallace K. Ferguson, James K. McConica, and Peter G. Bietenholz, 5 vols., Toronto, 1974–. Cited as *CWE.*

———. *Opera omnia,* ed. Johannes Clericus (Jean Leclerc), 10 vols., Leiden, 1703–06. Cited as "*Opera omnia.*"

———. *Opera omnia Desiderii Erasmi Roterodami,* ed. J. H. Waszink et al., 8 vols., Amsterdam, 1969–. Cited as *ASD.*

———. *Opus epistolarum Des. Erasmi Roterodami,* ed. P. S. Allen, H. M. Allen, et al., 12 vols., Oxford, 1906–58. Cited as "Allen."

———. *The Poems of Desiderius Erasmus,* ed. C. Reedijk, Leiden, 1956. Cited as "Reedijk."

Essential Articles. See Sylvester, Richard S., and Germain Marc'hadour.

EW. See More.

Garin, E., ed. *Prosatori latini del Quattrocento,* Milan, 1952. Cited as "Garin."

Garrison, James D. *Dryden and the Tradition of Panegyric,* Berkeley, Los Angeles, and London, 1975. Cited as "Garrison."

Garrod, H. W. Review of *The Latin Epigrams of Thomas More* (Bradner-Lynch), *Review of English Studies,* New Series, 5 (1954), 181–85. Cited as "Garrod."

German Baroque Literature: A Descriptive Catalogue of the Collection of Harold Jantz, and a Guide to the Collection on Microfilm, 2 vols., New Haven, 1974. Cited as "Jantz."

Gibson, R. W., and J. Max Patrick. *St. Thomas More: A Preliminary Bibliography of His Works and of Moreana to the Year 1750,* New Haven, 1961. Cited as "Gibson."

Graesse, Theodor, F. Benedict, and H. Plechl, eds. *Orbis Latinus: Lexikon lateinischer geographischer Namen des Mittelalters und der Neuzeit,* 3 vols., Braunschweig, 1972. Cited as "*Orbis Latinus.*"

Hall, Edward. *Chronicle,* ed. Sir Henry Ellis, London, 1809. Cited as "Hall."

Harpsfield, Nicholas. *The Life and Death of Sr Thomas Moore,* ed. Elsie V. Hitchcock, EETS Original Series no. 186, London, 1932. Cited as "Harpsfield."

Henkel, Arthur, and Albrecht Schöne. *Emblemata: Handbuch zur Sinnbildkunst des XVI. und XVII. Jahrhunderts,* Stuttgart, 1967. Cited as "Henkel-Schöne."

Hervieux, Leopold. *Les Fabulistes latins,* 5 vols., Paris, 1893–99; reprint, New York, Burt Franklin, [1967]. Cited as "Hervieux."

Hudson, Hoyt Hopewell. *The Epigram in the English Renaissance,* Princeton, 1947. Cited as "Hudson."

Hughes, Paul L., and James F. Larkin. *Tudor Royal Proclamations:* Vol. 1, *The Early Tudors (1485–1553),* New Haven, 1964. Cited as "Hughes-Larkin."

Hutton, James. *The Greek Anthology in France and in the Latin Writers of the Netherlands to the Year 1800,* Ithaca, N.Y., 1946. Cited as "Hutton, *Anthology in France.*"

———. *The Greek Anthology in Italy to the Year 1800,* Ithaca, N.Y., 1935. Cited as "Hutton, *Anthology in Italy.*"

Inventaire chronologique. See Moreau, Brigitte.

Jantz. See *German Baroque Literature.*

Keil, Heinrich, ed. *Grammatici Latini,* 7 vols., Leipzig, 1857–80. Cited as "Keil."

Kühner, Raphael, and Carl Stegmann. *Ausführliche Grammatik der lateinischen Sprache,* Hannover, 1912–14. Cited as "Kühner-Stegmann."

Lander, J. R. "Bonds, Coercion, and Fear: Henry VII and the Peerage," in J. G. Rowe and W. H. Stockdale, eds., *Florilegium Historiale: Essays Presented to Wallace K. Ferguson,* Toronto, 1971, pp. 327–67. Cited as "Lander."

Latham, R. E. *Revised Medieval Latin Word-List from British and Irish Sources,* London, 1965. Cited as "Latham."

Lausberg, Heinrich. *Handbuch der literarischen Rhetorik,* Munich, 1960. Cited as "Lausberg."

Lebeuf, Jean. *Mémoires concernant l'histoire d'Auxerre,* Paris, 1743. Cited as "Lebeuf."

Leutsch, E. L., and F. G. Schneidewin, eds. *Corpus paroemiographorum graecorum,* 2 vols., Göttingen, 1839–51. Cited as "Leutsch-Schneidewin."

Lewis, Charlton T., and Charles Short. *A Latin Dictionary,* Oxford, 1879; reprint, Oxford, 1958. Cited as "Lewis-Short."

Liddell, H. G., and Robert Scott. *A Greek-English Lexicon,* 8th ed., New York, 1897. Cited as "Liddell-Scott."

LP. Letters and Papers, Foreign and Domestic, of the Reign of Henry VIII, ed. J. S. Brewer, James Gairdner, and R. H. Brodie, 21 vols., London, 1862–1932.

Mackie, R. L. *King James IV of Scotland,* Edinburgh and London, 1958.

Mann, Wolfgang. *Lateinische Dichtung in England vom Ausgang des Frühhumanismus bis zum Regierungsantritt Elisabeths,* Halle/Saale, 1939.

Marc'hadour, Germain. "A Name for All Seasons," in Richard S. Sylvester and Germain Marc'hadour, eds., *Essential Articles for the Study of Thomas More,* Hamden, Conn., 1977, pp. 539–62.

Marsden, John. *Philomorus,* London, 1878.

Mommsen, Theodor, and Paul Krueger, eds. *Corpus iuris civilis,* 3 vols., Berlin, 1912–28. Cited as "Mommsen-Krueger."

Mone, Franz Joseph, ed. *Hymni Latini medii aevi,* 3 vols., Freiburg im Breisgau, 1853–55. Cited as "Mone."

More, Thomas. *The Yale Edition of the Complete Works of St. Thomas More:* Vol. 2, *The History of King Richard III,* ed. R. S. Sylvester; Vol. 3, Part I, *Translations of Lucian,* ed. C. R. Thompson; Vol. 4, *Utopia,* ed. Edward Surtz, S. J., and J. H. Hexter; Vol. 5, *Responsio ad Lutherum,* ed. J. M. Headley, trans. Sister Scholastica Mandeville; Vol. 6, *Dialogue Concerning Heresies,* ed. T. M. C. Lawler, R. Marius, and G. Marc'hadour; Vol. 8, *The Confutation of Tyndale's Answer,* ed. L. A. Schuster, R. C. Marius, J. P. Lusardi, and R. J. Schoeck; Vol. 9, *The Apology,* ed. J. B. Trapp; Vol. 12, *A Dialogue of Comfort,* ed. L. L. Martz and F. Manley; Vol. 13, *Treatise on the Passion, etc.,* ed. G. Haupt; Vol. 14, *De Tristitia Christi,* ed. C. H. Miller; New Haven and London, 1963–. Cited as *CW 2, CW 3/1, CW 4, CW 5, CW 6, CW 8, CW 9, CW 12, CW 13,* and *CW 14.*

_____. *The Correspondence of Sir Thomas More,* ed. Elizabeth F. Rogers, Princeton, 1947. Cited as "Rogers."

_____. *The English Works of Sir Thomas More,* ed. W. E. Campbell, R. W. Chambers, and A. W. Reed, 2 vols., London, 1931.

_____. *The Latin Epigrams of Thomas More,* ed. Leicester Bradner and Charles A. Lynch, Chicago, 1953. Cited as "Bradner-Lynch."

______. *Selected Letters,* ed. Elizabeth F. Rogers, trans. Marcus Haworth, S. J., New Haven and London, 1961. Cited as *SL.*

______. *The Workes . . . in the Englysh tonge,* London, 1557. Cited as *EW.*

Moreau, Brigitte. *Inventaire chronologique des éditions parisiennes du* XVIe *siècle:* Vol. 1, *1500–1510;* Vol. 2, *1511–1520,* Paris, 1972–77. Cited as "*Inventaire chronologique.*"

Nelson, William. *John Skelton, Laureate,* New York, 1939. Cited as "Nelson, *John Skelton.*"

______. "Thomas More, Grammarian and Orator," *PMLA, 58* (1943), 337–52; reprinted in *Essential Articles,* pp. 150–60.

Nijhoff, Wouter, and M. E. Kronenberg. *Nederlandsche Bibliographie van 1500 tot 1540,* 3 vols., 's-Gravenhage, 1923–71. Cited as "Nijhoff-Kronenberg."

OED. Oxford English Dictionary, 13 vols., Oxford, 1933.

Orbis Latinus. See Graesse.

Orme, Nicholas. *English Schools in the Middle Ages,* London, 1973.

Otto, August. *Die Sprichwörter und sprichwörtlichen Redensarten der Römer,* Leipzig, 1890. Cited as "Otto."

Paton, W. R., ed. and trans. *The Greek Anthology,* 5 vols., Loeb Classical Library, Cambridge, Mass., 1917–39.

Perry, Ben E. *Aesopica,* Urbana, Ill., 1952. Cited as "Perry, *Aesopica.*"

PG. Patrologiae Cursus Completus: Series Graeca, ed. J.–P. Migne, 161 vols., Paris, 1857–66.

Pico, G. "De Imitatione," in G. Santangelo, ed., *Le epistole "De Imitatione" di Gianfrancesco Pico della Mirandola e di Pietro Bembo,* Florence, 1954.

Pl. Planudean Anthology, Venice, Aldus Manutius, 1503.

PL. Patrologiae Cursus Completus: Series Latina, ed. J.–P. Migne, 221 vols., Paris, 1844–1903.

Poggio Bracciolini. *Facetiae,* 2 vols., Paris, 1879. Cited as "Poggio, *Facetiae.*"

Proctor, Robert, and Frank Isaac. *An Index to the Early Printed Books in the British Museum,* London, 1898–1938. Cited as "Proctor and Isaac."

Quicherat, Louis. *Thesaurus poeticus linguae Latinae,* rev. Émile Chatelain, Paris, 1922; reprint, Hildesheim, 1967. Cited as "Quicherat."

Réau, Louis. *Iconographie de l'art chrétien,* 3 vols., Paris, 1955–59. Cited as "Réau."

Reedijk. *See* Erasmus.

Reicke, Emil, ed. *Willibald Pirckheimers Briefwechsel,* 2 vols., Munich, 1940, 1956.

Reynolds, E. E. *The Field is Won: The Life and Death of Saint Thomas More,* London, 1968. Cited as "Reynolds."

Rhenanus, Beatus. *See Briefwechsel des Beatus Rhenanus.*

Robbins, Rossell H., ed. *Secular Lyrics of the* XIV*th and* XV*th Centuries,* Oxford, 1952. Cited as "Robbins."

Rogers. *See* More.

Roper, William. *The Lyfe of Sir Thomas Moore, knighte,* ed. Elsie V. Hitchcock, EETS Original Series no. 197, London, 1935. Cited as "Roper."

Rudhart, Georg T. *Thomas Morus,* Nürnberg, 1829.

Scarisbrick, J. J. *Henry VIII,* Berkeley and Los Angeles, 1968. Cited as 'Scarisbrick."

SL. See More.

Spitz, Lewis W. *The Religious Renaissance of the German Humanists,* Cambridge, Mass., 1963.

Spont, Alfred. *Letters and Papers Relating to the War with France 1512–1513,* London 1897. Cited as "Spont."

STC. A Short-Title Catalogue of Books Printed in England, Scotland, and Ireland . . . 1475–1640, ed. A. W. Pollard and G. R. Redgrave, London, 1926.

*STC*². Revised ed. of *STC,* ed. W. A. Jackson and K. Pantzer; vol. 2, London, 1976; vol. 1, in press.

Stone, Donald, Jr. "The *Herveus* of Germanus Brixius," *Humanistica Lovaniensia, 29* (1980), 177–93.

Sylvester, Richard S., ed. *St. Thomas More: Action and Contemplation,* New Haven and London, 1972.

Sylvester, Richard S., and Germain Marc'hadour, eds. *Essential Articles for the Study of Thomas More,* Hamden, Conn., 1977. Cited as "*Essential Articles.*"

Thomason. See p. 708, footnote 2, below.

Tilley, Morris P. *A Dictionary of the Proverbs in England in the Sixteenth and Seventeenth Centuries,* Ann Arbor, 1950. Cited as "Tilley."

TLL. Thesaurus Linguae Latinae. 18 vols., Leipzig, 1900–.

Tracy, James. *The Politics of Erasmus,* Toronto, Buffalo, and London, 1978.

Vergil, Polydore. *Anglica historia,* ed. Denys Hay, London, 1950. Cited as "Polydore Vergil."

Walther, Hans, ed. *Proverbia sententiaeque Latinitatis medii aevi,* 6 vols., Göttingen, 1963–. Cited as "Walther."

Waltz. *See Anthologie Grecque.*

Whiting, Bartlett Jere. *Proverbs, Sentences, and Proverbial Phrases from English Writings Mainly before 1500,* Cambridge, Mass., 1968. Cited as "Whiting."

Wing, Donald. *Short-Title Catalogue of Books Printed in England, Scotland,*

Ireland, Wales, and British America and of English Books Printed in other Countries 1641–1700, 3 vols., New York, 1945–51. Cited as "Wing."

———. Second edition, 3 vols., of which two have appeared, New York, 1972–. Cited as "Wing^2."

Rhen. Pref./1–4 **BEATUS . . . S. D.** In a letter of August 25, 1517 (Allen, *3*, 57), Erasmus mentions a preface by Beatus Rhenanus intended to precede both the *Utopia* and the *Epigrammata*. It has been suggested (*CW 4*, cxcii) that the prefatory letter printed here (dated February 23, 1518, and printed in March 1518) is the one mentioned by Erasmus, which was wrongly made to serve as a preface only to the *Epigrammata*. If this is the earlier preface, Rhenanus must have revised it for its present function: it stresses the poems, mentioning the *Utopia* only briefly ("obiter," line 65) at the end, and would not have been suitable for a position before the *Utopia*. Beatus Rhenanus (Beat Bild, 1485–1547), educated at Schlettstadt and the University of Paris, was a learned editorial assistant at the presses of Henri Estienne in Paris, Lazare and Matthias Schürer in Strassburg, and (after 1515) Johann Froben in Basel (*Neue deutsche Biographie, 1* [Berlin, 1953], 682–83). He was especially important as an editor of Seneca, Tertullian, Tacitus, and Livy (for a bibliography of his works see *Briefwechsel des Beatus Rhenanus*, ed. Adalbert Horawitz and Karl Hartfelder [Leipzig, 1886], pp. 592–618). Between 1508 and 1518 Rhenanus wrote at least twenty-six dedicatory epistles for various works, including a collection of epigrams by Marullus (Strassburg, 1509) and another by Janus Pannonius (Basel, July 1518); see *Briefwechsel*, pp. 26–27, 116–17. Willibald Pirckheimer (1470–1530), a humanist from a wealthy, patrician family, was active as a city councillor in Nürnberg (1496–1501 and 1506–23) and was named an imperial councillor by Emperor Maximilian in 1499. See Niklas Holzberg, *Willibald Pirckheimer* (Munich, 1981), and Lewis Spitz, in *The Religious Renaissance of the German Humanists* (Cambridge, Mass., 1963), pp. 155–96. His friend Beatus Rhenanus was instrumental in beginning his epistolary friendship with Erasmus in 1515 (Allen, 2, 40–41, 46–47, 174–75).

Rhen. Pref./7 **ERASMVS . . . misit.** In May 1517 Erasmus sent them to Rhenanus at Basel (Allen, 2, 576; *3*, 1, 6).

Rhen. Pref./8 **similes . . . estis.** To the similarities he mentions Rhenanus might have added that both More and Pirckheimer were interested in ancient coins (see nos. 250 and 265 and Pirckheimer's *Priscorum numismatum ad Nurembergensis monetae valorem facta aestimatio*, Tübingen, 1533), that both were translators of Lucian (see *CW 3/1* and, for Pirckheimer's six Lucianic translations, Willehad Eckert and Christoph von Imhoff, *Willibald Pirckheimer* [Cologne, 1971], p. 371, and Holzberg, pp. 155–58, 221–26, 248–58, 298–301), that both were known for the learning of their womenfolk (Erasmus, *Colloquium Abbatis et Eruditae, ASD 1/3*, 407), and that both delighted in the paradoxical encomium (More defended Erasmus' *Moria*, dedicated to him, and

Pirckheimer wrote its most notable successor, *Podagrae laus* [Nürnberg, 1522]).

Rhen. Pref./9 **iuris . . . doctus.** Pirckheimer studied both law and Greek in Padua and Pavia from 1488 to 1495.

Rhen. Pref./10 **publicis . . . uersans.** By August 1517 More was a member of the royal council (Geoffrey Elton, "Thomas More, Councillor," in Richard S. Sylvester, ed., *St. Thomas More: Action and Contemplation* [New Haven and London, 1972], p. 89).

Rhen. Pref./14–15 **de fortunis . . . amplissimas.** Pirckheimer, who was descended from generations of traders and bankers (Eckert and von Imhoff, pp. 19–22), was wealthier than More.

Rhen. Pref./18–19 **pater . . . clarus.** In his epitaph More said he was born of a family "non celebri sed honesta" and that his father was a knight and a judge of the King's Bench (Allen, *10*, 260–61; see also *10*, 136). Sir John (1453–1530) assumed the prestigious rank of sergeant at law in 1503 (Margaret Hastings, "The Ancestry of Sir Thomas More," in *Essential Articles*, p. 99). Willibald's father, John, received a doctorate of both laws at Padua in 1465 (Spitz, p. 157). Described as "patricius Noribergensis," he was a legal counselor in the service of Emperor Frederick III, the Prince-bishop of Eichstätt, the duke of Bavaria, and the archduke of Tyrol (Eckert and von Imhoff, p. 9, and Emil Reicke ed., *Willibald Pirckheimers Briefwechsel*, 2 vols. [Munich, 1940, 1956], Humanistenbriefe IV and V, *1*, 3–8).

Rhen. Pref./19–20 **amicitiae . . . aequalitas.** Erasmus, *Adagia* 120–21 (*Opera omnia*, 2 78–79.

Rhen. Pref./24–25 **ei . . . solitus.** For some of Pirckheimer's Latin epigrams, including two translated from the *Greek Anthology* (IX, 359–60), see Reicke, *Pirckheimers Briefwechsel*, *1*, 32–60.

Rhen. Pref./29–30 **acclamatiunculis . . . ἐπιφωνήματα.** Quintilian 8.5.11: "Est enim epiphonema rei narratae vel probatae summa acclamatio." See Erasmus, *De Copia, Opera omnia*, *1*, 97C–E.

Rhen. Pref./33 **inuentionis.** Invention, the first of the five traditional parts of rhetoric, meant finding or discovering what to say. Of the four remaining parts (disposition, eloquence, memory, pronunciation) the translator is almost completely limited to eloquence, choosing his words and figures.

Rhen. Pref./39 **Vtrobique sane mirus.** On More as a translator see the Introduction, pp. 18–22.

Rhen. Pref./47–48 **Sabinum . . . Gallus.** See nos. 95, 196, 205, 220.

Rhen. Pref./51 **contumeliam.** The passage omitted after this word in *1520* may be translated: "Hence, just as Syrus in the play by Terence neatly praises Demea by saying 'You are every inch pure wisdom,' so it will be proper to say of More 'He is every inch pure jest.'" Perhaps the allusion to Terence (*Adelphoe* 394) was omitted as inappropriate because Demea is actually foolish and Syrus is an insincere flatterer.

Rhen. Pref./52 **Pontanum et Marullum.** In his dedicatory epistle to *Michaelis Tarchaniotae Marulli Constantinopolitani Epigrammata et Hymni* (Strassburg, Matthias Schürer, July 1509), Rhenanus denies that Marullus (who came in 1453 to Italy, where he died in 1500) and Johannes Jovianus Pontanus (1426–1503) are the equals of the ancients and the best models for modern poets. In particular he criticizes Marullus for following the ancients so closely as to neglect Christianity (*Briefwechsel*, pp. 26–27). In Erasmus' *Ciceronianus* Nosoponus remarks "Marulli pauca legi, tolerabilia si minus haberent paganitatis" and Bulephorus says of Pontanus "In epigrammatibus plus tulisset laudis, si vitasset obscoenitatem. . . ." (*ASD 1/2*, 666, 700). See the Introduction, p. 52. For the northern humanists' ambivalence about pagan themes in the late fifteenth century, see Jozef IJsewijn, "La Poesia latina all'epoca di Giano Pannonio," *Acta Litteraria Academiae Scientiarum Hungaricae, 14* (1972), 336–37.

Rhen. Pref./55 **Heraclitum.** Like those of other pre-Socratics, his fragmentary sayings are often enigmatic.

Rhen. Pref./60 **Pomponius Laetus.** The illegitimate son of Giovanni Sanseverino, the count of Marsico, Giulio Pomponio Leto (1428–97) was the pupil of Pietro Montopolita and Lorenzo Valla, whom he succeeded as the leader of the Roman Academy. Though Leto was devoted to Roman antiquities and literature, the belief that he deliberately avoided learning Greek is false. It originated in a letter by his pupil Sabellicus and was later repeated by Vives. See Vladimiro Zabughin, *Giulio Pomponio Leto,* 2 vols. (Rome, 1909–10), *1,* 28, 282; *2,* 46. Erasmus seems to accept the legend in *Ciceronianus, ASD 1/2,* 666.

Rhen. Pref./66–68 **BVDAEVS . . . laudauit.** *CW 4,* 4–15.

Rhen. Pref./69 **Iustiniani uestri.** "Your" Justinian because Pirckheimer was a student of civil law.

Rhen. Pref./74–78 **negabat . . . missa.** This stupid critic had apparently taken More's joke seriously (*CW 4,* 38/5–8). *Doriphorema* is a Greek word that normally means "bodyguard," but Lucian (*Quomodo historia conscribenda sit*) uses it, as Rhenanus does here, to mean "mute actors in a stageplay." Cf. *CW 4*, 98/10–23.

Rhen. Pref./80–81 **album . . . calculum.** Erasmus, *Adagia* 453 (*Opera omnia*, 2, 202B).

Rhen. Pref./84–91 **Guil. Lilius . . . exercet.** William Lily (1468–1522), first headmaster of Colet's grammar school at St. Paul's and principal contributor to its famous grammar, made a Mediterranean tour between 1488 and 1492, studying Greek at Rhodes and Latin in Rome and Venice under Giovanni Sulpicio and Pomponio Leto (see note to Rhen. Pref./60, above). See Emden, p. 1147.

Rhen. Pref./94–95 **cuius os . . . habes.** Pirckheimer could have seen More's translations of Lucian (Paris, 1506, 1514; Venice, 1516; Basel, 1517) and *Utopia* (Louvain, 1516; Paris, 1517). On October 16, 1515, Erasmus wrote Pirckheimer that More had shown him a translation by Pirckheimer (Allen, 2, 151).

PROGYMNASMATA. Προγυμνάσματα (Latin *praeexercitationes*) meant literally "warm-up" exercises for athletic or military training, but it was also regularly used to designate preliminary rhetorical exercises designed to prepare the beginning student for full-fledged rhetorical training. For a detailed and documented summary see Lausberg, pp. 532–46. The principal ancient examples, extending from the first to the sixth century after Christ, are by Ailios Theon, Hermogenes, Nicolaus Sophista, Priscian, and (above all) Aphthonius. The principal subdivisions of progymnasmata were: *fabula, narratio, chria, sententia, refutatio, locus communis, laus, vituperatio, comparatio, sermocinatio, descriptio, thesis,* and *legis latio.* A number of More's and Lily's translations belong to these categories: *fabula* (no. 1), *comparatio* (nos. 2, 9), *sermocinatio* (no. 3), *sententia* (nos. 4, 5, 7, 8), *vituperatio* (no. 11), *laus* (nos. 15–18). And no. 10 would be a perfect *chria* if the Spartan woman were identified as a well-known historical figure. More important, the title shows that More conceived of his own epigrams as embodying the skill of a full-fledged rhetorician: the best preparation for imitating ancient epigrams and writing original ones is translating epigrams from the *Greek Anthology.*

1/1–5 ΛΟΥΚΙΛΛΙΟΥ . . . μονῆς. *AP* XI, 391. *Pl.* II, 50 (εἰς φειδωλούς), 22, sig. O_3.

2/1–3 ΠΑΛΛΑΔΑ . . . πένης. *AP* XI, 294. *Pl.* II, 50 (εἰς φειδωλούς), 12, sig. O_2.

3/1–5 ΛΟΥΚΙΑΝΟΥ . . . τύχης. *AP* IX, 74. *Pl.* I, 79 (εἰς τύχην), 2, sig. H_8v. Cf. Lucian, *Nigrinus* 26, and St. Basil, *Homilia in Psalmum 61* (*PG 29*, 481). See also *CW 12*, 208/3–10 and Commentary.

3/7–14 **Nuper . . . nunc.** In their use of *nuper* and *nunc* More and Lily were probably influenced by Horace's expression of the idea (*Sermones* 2.2.133–35):

> nunc ager Umbreni sub nomine, nuper Ofelli
> dictus, erit nulli proprius, sed cedet in usum
> nunc mihi, nunc alii.

4/1–3 ἌΔΗΛΟΝ . . . ἑτοιμοτάτη. *AP* X, 119. *Pl.* I, 12 (εἰς αὐτάρκειαν) (ζῆσον λογισμῷ καὶ μένεις ἀνενδέης), sig. B_2. By writing "Multas . . . multos" More (unlike Lily) tried to approximate the echoing sounds of Σώματα . . . δώματα.

5/1–5 ΛΟΥΚΙΑΝΟΥ . . . ἐφηρμόσατο. *AP* X, 26. *Pl.* I, 12 (εἰς αὐτάρκειαν), 6, sig. B_2.

5/13 **denuo.** Brixius rightly objected to More's scansion "dēnŭŏ" instead of "dēnŭō" (Appendix B, 518/13–16). But a similar adverbial formation, *modo,* is usually scanned *mŏdŏ* (though Plautus, Lucretius, and Cicero also scan it *mŏdō*). See Quicherat, pp. 685–86. More gives the same scansion of "dēnŭŏ" at 17/9.

6/1–3 ἌΔΗΛΟΝ . . . ἐμέ. *AP* IX, 49. *Pl.* I, 79 (εἰς τύχην), 1, sig. H_8v.

6/4–6 **T. MORI . . . alios.** Cf. More's verses on flattering Fortune, written in the Tower (Roper, p. 82).

6/5–9 **Iam . . . alios.** Latin forms of this epigram were widespread in ancient inscriptions (*CIL, 8,* no. 27904; *9,* no. 4756, lines 11–12; *11,* no. 6435, lines 15–16; *Inscriptiones christianae urbis Romae septimo saeculo antiquiores,* ed. Giovanni Battista de Rossi, 2 vols. [Rome, 1857–88], 2, 267, no. 20). One of these, an inscription on a sarcophagus now in the Lateran Museum, is close to the wording of More and Lily (*CIL, 6,* no. 11743):

> Euasi effugi. Spes et Fortuna ualete,
> Nil mihi uobiscum est; ludificate alios.

A version identical to Lily's was inscribed on the tomb of Francesco Pucci, who was buried at Rome in 1512 (anonymous articles in *Notes and Queries,* 9th Series, 2, [1898], 229, and 10th Series, *9* (1908), 324). The same wording was also printed among the poems of Janus Pannonius (1434–72) edited by Joannes Sambucus (*Iani Pannonii Episcopi Quinque-eccles: illius Antiquis vatibus comparandi, recentioribus certe anteponendi, quae vspiam reperiri adhuc potuerunt, omnia* [Vienna, 1569; reprint, Budapest, 1972], sig. T_2v). Sambucus included it in a group of poems he claimed were never before printed, and in fact it does not appear in any earlier edition of Pannonius' poems, including Sambucus' own earlier edition (Padua, 1559); see *Notes and Queries,* 10th Series, *9* (1908), 324. Pannonius' eighteenth-century editors, Sámuel Teleki and Sándor Kovásznay, accepted it as Pannonius' in their two-volume edition (Utrecht, 1784, *1,* 531) because they found it in a manuscript taken by Lambecius from the Royal Corvinian Library at Buda to Vienna in 1666 (*1,* v, xiv; *2,* 388); they gave the title "In Spem et Fortunam" (instead of Sambucus' "In Fortunam") and identified it as translated "E Graeco. Anthol. L. I. cap. 80." The latest edition of Pannonius (*Jani Pannonii Opera Latine et Hungarice* [Budapest, 1972]) omits it. Without more evidence it is hard to say who borrowed from whom. Hudson concludes his discussion of the couplet in England with the remark: "How much Lily and More had to do with putting this epigram into currency, we do not know. We can say, however, that the version which became most popular appears in no printed book earlier than More's *Epigrammata;* and there it is attributed to William Lily" (Hudson, p. 41). The couplet, in Latin and vernacular forms, was very popular from the sixteenth to the eighteenth century in Italy, France, England, Spain, and even Sweden. See Hutton, *Anthology in Italy,* pp. 27, 522, and *Anthology in France,* pp. 514–18, 670–71; H.-M. Féret and Marcel Bataillon, "A propos d'une épitaphe d'André de Laguna," *Humanisme et Renaissance,* 7 (1940), 122–27; Hudson, pp. 38–41; and Johan Bergman, "Ett antikt epigrams vandring genom skilda sekler och länder," *Eranos, 40* (1942), 9–15, and especially the thorough discussion in Otto Weinreich, *So nah ist die Antike* (Munich, 1970), pp. 97–180.

7/1–3 ΠΑΛΛΑΔΑ . . . τέλος; *AP* X, 58. *Pl.* I, 13 (εἰς τὸν ἀνθρώπινον βίον), 6, sig. B_3.

7/5–9 **Ingredior . . . uidens?** Cf. Job 1:21, Eccles. 5:14, Propertius 3.5.14, and More's verses for the *Boke of Fortune:* "Remember nature sent the hyther bare . . ." (*EW,* sig. C_8).

8/1–3 ἌΔΗΛΟΝ . . . ἀΐδην. *AP* X, 112. *Pl.* I, 36 (εἰς θάνατον καὶ θανόντας), 24, sig. D_8. Cf. Plutarch, *De sanitate tuenda, Moralia* 128CD.

8/6,9 **balnea . . . Venus.** More and Lily borrowed this phrase, directly or indirectly, from ancient inscriptions; for example, *CIL, 6,* no. 15258:

> Balnea, vina, Venus corrumpunt corpora nostra,
> Sed vitam faciunt balnea, vina, Venus.

Cf. also *CIL, 3,* no. 12274c; *5,* no. 390*; *6,* part 5, no. 1649*; *14,* no. 914; and Einar Engström, *Carmina Latina Epigraphica* (Göteborg, 1911), no. 148.

9/1–7 ΠΑΛΛΑΔΑ . . . ἀδικεῖ. *AP* X, 121. *Pl.* I, 41 (εἰς κόλακας), 5, sig. E_4v.

10/1–7 'ΕἸΣ . . . γενέταν. *AP* IX, 61. *Pl.* I, 5 (εἰς ανδρέιους), 1 (εἰς Λάκαιναν), sig. A_4v. Cf. *AP* VII, 230, 433, and 531. See the Introduction, p. 18.

11/1–3 'ΑΓΑΘΙΟΥ . . . ἔχει. *AP* XI, 273. *Pl.* II, 53 (εἰς χωλούς), 1, sig. O_4v. The attribution to Agathios is apparently found only here.

12/1–5 "ΑΔΗΛΟΝ . . . χρῆ. The precise source of this Greek text, which is not verse but prose, cannot readily be determined. It occurs in the *Violetum* of Arsenius (Leutsch-Schneidewin, 2, 381); in a collection of sayings published by J. Fr. Boissonade (*Anecdota Graeca e Codicibus Regiis,* 5 vols. [Paris, 1829–33], *1,* 117); in an early Byzantine collection assembled by Maximus (*PG 91,* col. 924), which Konrad Gesner conflated with another by Antonius in 1546 (see Reinhold Dressler, "Quaestiones criticae ad Maximi et Antonii gnomologias spectantes," *Jahrbücher für classische Philologie,* Supplementband *5* [1864–72], 307–50). And it may occur in various known but still unpublished collections, some of them preserved in manuscripts now in England. On all these collections of quasi-philosophical *dicta,* the fullest information is given by Marcel Richard in the *Dictionnaire de spiritualité ascétique et mystique* (Paris, 1937–), *5* (1962), 475–512 (see especially 488–94). In Arsenius, Boissonade, and Maximus, the saying is not anonymous (as More's and Lily's text is said to be) but is attributed to Democritus (see F. W. A. Mullach, *Fragmenta Philosophorum Graecorum,* 3 vols. [Paris, 1881–83], *1,* 379). The saying has also been attributed to Sotades (Hermann Diels, *Die Fragmente der Vorsokratiker,* 3 vols. [Berlin, 1910–12; reprint, Zürich, 1966], 2, 222).

12/6–7 **THEOPHRASTI . . . DILEMMA.** The Greek is nowhere else attributed to Theophrastus, nor does it occur in Gellius, though a somewhat similar argument is attributed to Favorinus by Gellius (*Noctes Atticae* 14.1.36). Since the Greek is plainly labeled as of uncertain authorship, it is highly unlikely that More or Lily is responsible for the false title. Perhaps a marginal note by More, Lily, or someone else, pointing out the similarity to the passage in Gellius but falsely attributing it to Theophrastus, was wrongly made into a title. This could easily have happened if some or all of the titles in the printer's manuscript were written in the margins.

12/17–21 **T. MORI . . . pati.** More's second version, in iambic trimeter, was perhaps an attempt to approximate what he regarded as the meter of the original. Though the Greek maxim is prose, ringing the changes on the two infinitives produces a jingling effect and a suggestion of iambic verse. In fact, if we admit anacrusis in the first and third lines of the Greek and allow a cyclic anapest and an irrational spondee in the last two lines, we have a quatrain of iambic dimeters.

13/1–3 ΠΑΛΛΑΔΑ . . . θανάτου. *AP* VII, 323. *Pl.* III, 3 (εἰς ἀδελφούς), 2, sig. P_1. This is also, so far as we know, the only attribution to Palladas.

13/2 Δὶς . . . ὧδ'. The reading ἀδελφοὺς ὧδ' (for ἀδελφειοὺς) appears only here (see the Introduction, p. 15). The error Δὶς (for Εἶς) appears also in the manuscripts and printed editions current before 1518 and was first corrected in the Aldine edition of 1531.

13/4–7 **T. MORI . . . perimit.** For More's second version of this epigram see no. 171.

14/1–3 'ΑΔΈΣΠΟΤΟΝ . . . Δανάης. *AP* IX, 48. *Pl.* I, 37 (εἰς θεούς), 2, sig. D_8. The idea had been used for satirical purposes (Lucian, *Dialogues of the Gods, Eros and Zeus*) and for religious exhortation (Gregory Nazianzen, *Precepts for Virgins,* lines 499–501, *PG 37,* 617–18.

15/1–3 "ΑΔΗΛΟΝ . . . δεκάτη. *AP* IX, 506. *Pl.* I, 66 (εἰς ποιητάς), 13 (εἰς Σάπφω), 2, sigs. G_6–G_6v. For many ancient analogs see Waltz, *8,* 68.

15/7–8 **sorores. Musarum.** Lily may have written "sorores Musas," as Garrod asserts in his review of Bradner-Lynch (p. 184), but placing a period after "sorores" makes the verses satisfactory as printed. Cf. Martial 2.22.1: "Quid mihi vobiscum est, o Phoebe novemque sorores?"

16/1–3 'ΑΓΑΘΙΟΥ . . . σατύρῳ. *AP* XVI, 246. *Pl.* IV, 12 (εἰς ἀγάλματα θεῶν καὶ θεαινῶν), 97 (εἰς ἕτερον σάτυρον), sig. BB_3. See the Introduction, p. 18.

17/1–3 'ΕΙΣ . . . εἰργάσατο. *AP* XVI, 129. *Pl.* IV, 9 (εἰς ἡρωΐδας), 1 (εἰς ἄγαλμα Νιόβης), sig. Z_6. A statue of Niobe's children, carved by either Praxiteles or Scopas, is mentioned by Pliny (*Historia naturalis* 36.4.28).

17/5–6 **uita . . . uitam.** Garrod (p. 184) says that these are misprints for *uiua* and *uiuam*; but it seems more likely that Lily was keeping rather slavishly to the Greek.

18/1–3 ΣΊΜΩΝΊΔΟΥ . . . ἕνεκα. We do not know where More or Lily acquired this Greek distich. It is preserved in only two manuscripts. One of these—MS. 1773 in the Bibliothèque Nationale in Paris—was written by Bartolomeo Comparini de Prato in 1493 and passed through the hands of Cardinal Niccolò Ridolfi (d. 1550), his nephew Pietro Strozzi, and Catherine de' Medici into the Royal Library at Paris in about 1590 (Henri Omont, *Inventaire sommaire des manuscrits grecs de la Bibliothèque nationale,* 4 vols. [Paris, 1886–98; reprint, 1898], *1,* vi–vii, xxx; *2,* 140). The other source is eight leaves added to the front of MS. Palatinus 23 (Marcus Boas, *De epigrammatis Simonideis pars prior: commentatio critica de epigrammatum traditione* [Groningen, 1905], pp. 171, 191, and Waltz, pp. lv–lvi). The attribution to Simonides is incorrect (*Poetae Lyrici Graeci,* ed. Theodor Bergk, 3 vols., 3rd ed. [Leipzig, 1866–67], *3,* 1187).

More Pref./5–29 This prefatory epistle is not a dedication of all the epigrams to Henry VIII but only of the five coronation poems which follow immediately, as is shown by its appearance with only these poems in British Museum MS. Cotton Titus D IV, More's presentation copy to the king (designated *L* in the variants). See below, Appendix B, 494/240–495/257, and Appendix C, 650/12–20.

More Pref./9–10 **pictori . . . dedissem.** There was a professional group of "limners" or illuminators in London in the late fifteenth and early sixteenth centuries, some of them employed to illuminate official documents such as the Rolls of Pleas in the Court of King's Bench (Erna Auerbach, *Tudor Artists: A Study of Painters in the Royal Service and of Portraiture on Illuminated Documents from the Accession of Henry VIII to the Death of Elizabeth I* [London, 1954], pp. 17–35). John Roper, protonotary of the King's Bench, and his son William, chief clerk, commissioned a limner to illuminate the Trinity Roll of 1518 with their names and joint coats of arms. The illuminations More commissioned for the presentation copy of his coronation poems seems to follow the style in the Rolls of Pleas in the later years of Henry VII: "A square or oblong . . . is filled completely with a design of floral patterns intermingled with scrolls and grotesques. . . . Often the Tudor rose appears beautifully drawn and shaded or the crowned arms of France and England. . . . (Auerbach, pp. 24–25, 31–32).

More Pref./17–21 **Tiberio . . . Hectorem.** Suetonius, *Tiberius* 52,2.

More Pref./23 **praemortuum.** See the Introduction, p. 23.

19/1 **IN . . . DIEM.** Henry VIII and his queen Catherine were crowned at Westminster Abbey on Sunday, June 24, 1509.

19/3 **BRITANNIARVM REGIS.** The omission of Henry's claim to the throne of France, which occurs in the presentation copy both here and in the salutation of the prefatory epistle, is probably to be explained by the negotiations for peace between England and France which were initiated early in 1518 and culminated in the Treaty of London on October 2, 1518 (Scarisbrick, pp. 70–72).

19/6–7 **CARMEN GRATVLATORIVM.** For More's place in the tradition of royal panegyric see Garrison: a comparison with Claudian's *Panegyricus de quarto consulatu Honorii Augusti* (pp. 72–75); More's balancing of opposites in Henry (pp. 78–79); and More's use of the topos of the coronation procession (pp. 85–86). Henry Peacham, in *The Complete Gentleman* (1622; ed. Virgil B. Heltzel [Ithaca, N.Y., 1962], p. 104), expressed his admiration for this and other Latin poems by More.

19/10 **dies . . . lapillo.** The idea of associating white and black stones with happy and unhappy days derives from a Thracian custom of marking the days of the year by placing black or white stones in an urn (Pliny, *Historia naturalis* 7.40.131). Cf. Pliny the Younger, *Epistolae* 6.11.3; Persius 2.1; Erasmus, *Adagia* 454 (*Opera omnia,* 2, 202F–203C).

19/11 **dies . . . tuis.** June 24 was already both a secular holiday (Midsummer Day) and a religious feast (Nativity of John the Baptist); the coronation gives yet another reason to celebrate it.

19/14 **iuuenem.** Henry's eighteenth birthday was June 28, 1509.

19/18 **qui . . . ocellis.** Cf. Rev. 21:4 and Isa. 25:8.

19/25 **Nec . . . sonat.** During the coronation it was "demaunded of the people, whether they would receiue, obey, and take the same moste noble Prince, for their kyng, who with greate reuerence, loue, and desire, saied and cried, ye ye" (Hall, p. 509).

19/26–27 **Nobilitas . . . diu.** One method employed by Henry VII to cow the nobility was attainder, but a "second method of discipline and control (if so it may be called) lay in bonds and recognizances: a terrifying system of suspended penalties. . . . Out of sixty-two peerage families in existence between 1485 and 1509, a total of forty-six or forty-seven were for some part of Henry's reign at the king's mercy. Seven were under attainder, thirty-six, of whom five were also heavily fined, gave bonds and recognizances, another was probably also fined, and three more were at some time under subpoenas which carried financial penalties. . . . The mere numbers of families, great as they were, give only an inadequate idea of the complications and dangers which this intensified system brought with it. . . . There thus developed in the later years of Henry VII's reign an immensely tangled, complicated series of relationships in which a majority of the peerage were legally and financially in the king's power and at his mercy, so that in effect people were set under heavy penalties to guarantee the honesty and loyalty of their fellows. The system was so extensive that it must have created an atmosphere of chronic watchfulness, suspicion, and fear" (Lander, pp. 335, 347). Such exactions placed the nobility at the mercy of the *uulgi faeces* because they were administered by royal officials of low birth, such as Dudley and Empson.

19/28–29 **Nunc . . . habet.** Henry VIII "cancelled at least forty-five recognizances during the first year of his reign and one hundred and thirty more over the next five years. In fifty-one cases the recognizances were stated to have been unjustly extorted" (Lander, p. 352). Erasmus' former patron, William Blount, Lord Mountjoy, who had himself been burdened with recognizances during the reign of Henry VII (Lander, pp. 340–41), wrote Erasmus on May 27, 1509: "Heaven smiles, earth rejoices; all is milk and honey and nectar. Tight-fistedness is well and truly banished. Generosity scatters wealth with unstinting hand" (*CWE* 2, 147–48).

19/30–31 **Mercator . . . aquas.** The guild of Merchant Adventurers certainly suffered severely between the summer of 1493 and February 1496; for political reasons Henry forbade all trade with the Netherlands. Nor was Henry able to make many inroads into the commercial preserves of the powerful Hansa merchants (Chrimes, pp. 31–36). There was, in fact, to be no increase in foreign trade during the reign of Henry VIII: "Maritime expansion was to be checked again by the taxation for Henry VIII's wars, by the diversion of capital to land speculation during the Reformation, above all by the irresistible attraction of Antwerp in its golden age" (R. B. Wernham, *Before the Armada: The Growth of English Foreign Policy 1485–1588* [London, 1966], p. 76).

19/32–33 **Leges . . . suas.** A thirteenth-century delcaration of common law, the *Statuta de praerogativa regis,* was exploited by Henry VII to increase his feudal revenues. It "had become obsolete and misunderstood by the fifteenth century, but it provided a solid text which could be reinterpreted, glossed, and made to cover possibilities that were not originally envisaged in the different economic and social circumstances of the thirteenth century." In 1495, for the first time, the *Statuta* became the subject of readings at Lincoln's Inn and the Inner Temple (Chrimes, p. 210).

19/34 **Congaudent.** Brixius wrongly claimed that *congaudere* was not acceptable in good prose or poetry unless one was willing to accept Lyra or

Scotus as good writers (Appendix B, 528/7–16). It is used by Fortunatus and appears frequently in patristic prose (e.g., Augustine, Ambrose). See *TLL* 4, 272. See 1 Cor. 12:26, 13:6. Brixius also objected to its use at 57/9.

19/36–41 **Iam . . . dolo.** No doubt many did try to conceal their resources from the tax collectors of Henry VII. But that would do no good against the principle of the "fork," attributed to Henry VII's chancellor Cardinal Morton and applied in the collection of "benevolent" loans: whoever spends little must have much saved and whoever spends much must have the means to do so. See Chrimes, p. 203.

19/44 **delatores.** This word is especially frequent in the writings of Tacitus and Suetonius because of the atmosphere of poisonous intrigue at the courts of the early Roman emperors. By comparison Henry VII's policies seem wholesome enough. Statutes of 1495 and 1504 did reward informers against those who illegally maintained "retainers," but most cases initiated by informers were against the avoidance of customs; and most of the informers were Crown officials. See Chrimes, pp. 170, 190, 192.

19/50 **Quacunque ingreditur.** This phrase suggests that the following lines refer not only to the procession from Westminster Abbey to Westminster Hall after the coronation itself, but also to Henry's progress from Richmond to the Tower on June 21 and the even more splendid procession of Henry and Catherine from the Tower to Westminster Palace on June 23 (Hall, pp. 507–09).

19/56–58 Sidenote: **LAVS A CORPORIS DOTIBVS.** Though More may not be responsible for them, this sidenote and the others in *L* (lines 70–73, 94–98, 116–18, 120–24, 158–61) indicate that he is following recognized topics of epideictic oratory. See the Introduction, pp. 43–44.

19/58 **Mille . . . extat.** When Saul was chosen king, he stood "in medio populi, et altior fuit universo populo ab humero et sursum" (1 Kings 10:23). Cf. *Aeneid* 4.141–42.

19/61–63 **ense . . . locum.** Henry's prowess with sword and bow were celebrated, but he was an especially avid participant in jousts and tourneys: "Through the summer of 1508 the prince of Wales, still only just seventeen, had hurled his keen, tireless body into the fury of the tournament and excelled all his opponents, and his accession to the throne would inaugurate a festival of apparently endless jousting and tilting, at which the king ever carried away the prizes" (Scarisbrick, p. 14).

19/65 **geminis . . . rosis.** Probably not two red roses, one for each cheek, but a white rose and a red one for the rosy cheeks against the white complexion. Cf. no. 23. In More's presentation copy both the illumination following this poem and another following the next epigram contain "twin" or double roses: in each the five petals of a red rose enclose the five smaller petals of a white one.

19/67 **tenerae uirginis.** In 1515 an Italian visitor also found Henry's "round face so very beautiful that it would become a pretty woman" (*LP*, 2, 116–17, no. 395).

19/68–69 **Talis . . . equis.** According to a post-Homeric legend one of Achilles' parents, who knew he would die at Troy, disguised him as a girl and hid him among the daughters of King Lycomodes at Scyros (see, e.g., Statius, *Achilleis* 1.335–37; Ovid, *Metamorphoses* 13.162–70). Achilles' treatment of Hector's body was well known from the *Iliad* (22.395–404).

19/70–73 Sidenote: **LAVS AB ANIMI VIRTVTIBVS.** See the note to 19/56–58.

19/72–73 **uultu . . . aperta.** Cf. no. 11.

19/94–95 **Nam . . . die.** A variation on the topos "puer-senex" (Ernst Curtius, *European Literature and the Latin Middle Ages* [New York, 1953], pp. 98–101).

19/94–98 Sidenote: **LAVS A REBVS GESTIS.** See the note to 19/56–58.

19/96–99 **Illico . . . ferat.** More accepts, at least for the purposes of panegyric, the current opinion of Henry VII's councillors, Richard Empson, Edmund Dudley, and their agents: "These outlaries, olde recognisances of the peace and good abering, escapes, ryottes and innumerable statutes penal, were put in execucion and called vpon by Empson and Dudley, so that euery man, both of the spiritualtie and temporaltie, hauing either lande or substaunce, was called to this pluckyng bancket. . . . For these two rauenynge wolues had suche a garde of false periured persons apperteignynge to them, which were by their commaundement empanyeled on euery quest, that the king was sure to wynne whosoeuer lost. Learned men in the lawe, when they were requyred of their aduise, would saye to agree is the best counsayll that I can geue you. By this vndewe meanes, these couetous persones filled the kynges cofers, and enryched themselues. And at this vnreasonable and extorte doynge, noble men grudged, meane men kycked, poore men lamented, preachers openly at Paules crosse and other places exclamed, rebuked and detested . . ." (Hall, pp. 502–03). On April 23, 1509, Henry VIII had them imprisoned in the Tower, where they remained until they were executed the following year (Scarisbrick, p. 12). Some of their assistants were arrested and punished on the pillory (Hall, p. 506). See Appendix C, pp. 638–42.

19/100–01 **Ad mercaturas . . . onus.** Brixius rightly objected to "ad mercatores" in *1518* (Appendix B, 526/3–8). But, even though this error is found in the presentation copy prepared for Henry VIII (*L*), the error may well have been that of a copyist. I find no evidence that Henry VIII opened the seas to commercial ships, but his confirmation of his father's pardon (proclaimed on April 25, 1509) did assert that he wished to protect "merchants, denizen and stranger, clothiers, artificers, and folks of all manner of mysteries and occupations" from "any fear of forfeiture by reason of any light and untrue informations or wrong surmises of customers, comptrollers, or searchers, or of any persons calling themself promoters or by reason of any statutes or ordinances made of long time past, given, put in ure, use, or execution, till now of late time. And his grace shall provide for the reformation of the great extremity and rigor wherewith his said subjects have been grievously vexed and troubled in time past, so that they shall now freely, quietly, and surely, without fear of any such wrongs, hereafter occupy their feats of merchandise, clothmaking, and all other mysteries and occupations" (Hughes-Larkin, pp. 80–81).

19/102–03 **Despectusque . . . die.** See note to 19/26–27, above. ". . . Henry VIII cancelled at least forty-five recognizances during the first year of his reign and one hundred and thirty more over the next five years. In fifty-one cases the recognizances were stated to have been unjustly extorted. . . . Henry reduced the use of the system *in terrorem* over peers to minute proportions, though he did not discard it completely. . . . [He] cancelled bonds and recognizances affecting ten other peers [besides Lord Burgavenny and the Earl of Northumberland] during the first year of his reign. In two cases the recognizances were stated to have been unjustly taken. Even some of the land which Empson and Dudley had questionably wrung from peers for the crown was restored" (Lander, p. 352). The nobility also received considerable benefits from Henry VIII's Accession Pardon of April 25, 1509 (Hughes-Larkin, pp. 81–83).

19/112–14 **Quid quod . . . parenti?** Henry VIII did indeed repudiate some of his father's measures (see preceding note). But Henry VII had himself granted a pardon in his last days, and Henry VIII's Accession Pardon, like any such pardon, was bound, in the nature of the case, to make void some judgments issued under his father.

19/115 **Sic . . . patri.** Cf. Erasmus' *Panegyricus ad Philippum* (1504): "Verum a tali quoque patre diuelli sustinens te patriae votis reddere festinabas, cui secundum deum primas pietatis partes deberi magnus authorum consensus est" (*ASD 4/1*, 46, lines 653–55).

19/116–18 Sidenote: **LAVS A LITTERIS.** See note to 19/56–58.

19/116–19 **Nec miror . . . suis?** We have very little information about the substance of Henry's education, but it was probably not unlike that of his elder brother, Arthur, whose tutor, Bernard André, said his royal pupil had mastered "in grammar: Guarinus, Perottus, Pomponius, Sulpitius, Aulus Gellius, and Valla; in poetry: Homer, Vergil, Lucan, Ovid, Silius, Plautus, and Terence; in oratory: the *Offices, Letters,* and *Paradoxes* of Cicero, and Quintilian; in history: Thucydides, Livy, the *Commentaries* of Caesar, Suetonius, Cornelius Tacitus, Pliny, Valerius Maximus, Sallust, and Eusebius" (Nelson, *John Skelton,* p. 15). John Skelton, who was Henry's tutor from about 1495 to 1502 and who wrote for him *Speculum principis* (1501), says of his pupil:

> I yaue hym drynke of the sugryd welle
> Of Eliconys waters crystallyne,
> Aqueintyng hym with the Musys nyne. (Nelson, *John Skelton,* p. 48)

In *Prosopopoeia Britanniae,* written in the autumn of 1499 and dedicated to Prince Henry, Erasmus wrote:

> Iam puer Henricus genitoris nomine laetus,
> Monstrante fonteis vate Skeltono sacros
> Palladias teneris meditatur ab vnguibus artes.

See Reedijk, pp. 252–53. In 1504–05 Henry had a new tutor, William Hoone (Nelson, *John Skelton,* p. 75).

19/119 **Philosophia.** Brixius claimed, with justification, that *phĭlŏsŏphĭă* is the correct scansion, not More's "phīlŏsŏphīă" (Appendix B, 514/3–8). But Sidonius does scan *philosophus* with the first syllable long, and Prudentius and Fortunatus give the scansion *sophīa.* See Quicherat, pp. 829, 1056, and the Introduction, pp. 25–26.

19/120–24 Sidenote: **RES GESTAS PERSEQVITVR.** See note to 19/56–58.

19/124 **Omnibus ignouit.** Henry did cancel many recognizances, both for peers and commoners (Lander, pp. 351–52); but he specifically excluded "debts and accounts" from his confirmation of his father's pardon (Hughes-Larkin, p. 79).

19/132–33 **Sic te . . . timor.** Cf. nos. 114 and 120.

19/134 **coeat . . . Scotis.** France often recruited Scotland as an ally against England, for example in 1491 and 1496 (Chrimes, pp. 86–89). In such a venture, Scotland suffered a notable defeat at Flodden in 1513 (see note to 183/5).

19/138–39 **Primum . . . potest.** Substantially, but not entirely true, or else Henry would not have had Edmund de la Pole (son of the sister of Edward IV) executed in 1513.

19/141 **Nobilis . . . parens.** Henry VIII united the red and white roses because his mother Elizabeth was Yorkist (daughter of Edward IV) and his father Henry was Lancastrian (grandson of the widow of Henry V). See no. 23.

19/152 **prudentia patris.** "Prudence" and "policy" as basic qualities of Henry VII are not only fixed in our minds by Bacon's life of him but are also applied to him by knowledgeable contemporaries like Polydore Vergil and John Fisher (Chrimes, pp. 298–300). See Appendix C, 642/ 1–2.

19/153 **matris . . . tuae.** "Queen Elizabeth was described by contemporaries as a very handsome woman and of great ability, as beloved, as a woman of the greatest charity and humanity" (Chrimes, p. 302). More wrote "A Rueful Lamentation" in verse on her death in 1503 (*CW* 2, 119–22).

19/154–55 **Est tibi . . . aui.** The mother of Henry VII was Margaret Beaufort, Countess of Richmond and Derby, patron of John Fisher; she founded divinity professorships at Oxford and Cambridge and the colleges of Corpus Christi and St. John's at Cambridge. The father of Henry VIII's mother was Edward IV; in *The History of Richard the Third* More twice calls him "noble" (*CW* 2, 3/18 and 5/22). Of the omitted grandparents, Edmund Tudor (Henry VII's father) died in his midtwenties and Elizabeth Woodville (Edward IV's queen), although she is an eloquent heroine in More's *Richard the Third,* was deprived of her lands in 1487 and died in retirement.

19/158–61 Sidenote: **LAVS REGINAE.** See note to 19/56–58.

19/166 **priscas . . . Sabinas.** The intervention of the Sabine women ended a war between the Sabines and the Romans: "not only did they agree on peace, but they made one people out of the two" (Livy 1.13.4). Cf. 19/180–81.

19/167 **hemitheas.** Brixius (Appendix B, 514/10–26) rightly objected to the scansion *herŏidas* in *1518.*

19/168 **Alcestes.** Best known from the *Alcestis* of Euripides, she willingly died in the place of her husband Admetus.

19/169 **Tanaquil.** Wife of Tarquinius Priscus, king of Rome (616–579 B.C.), Tanaquil, through shrewd advice and force of character, obtained the kingship for her husband and later for her son-in-law (Livy 1.57; also 1.34, 39, and 41).

19/172 **facunda.** The reading of *1518* and *1520,* "foecunda," is probably a copyist's or printer's error. Cornelia, mother of the two Gracchi, had twelve children, but only three survived to adulthood. Her letters were admired by Cicero, who said that "her sons were nursed not less by their mother's speech than at her breast" (*Brutus* 58.211).

19/173 **Penelopeia fide.** Cf. Ovid, *Tristia* 5.14.35–36:

> aspicis ut longo teneat laudabilis aevo
> nomen inextinctum Penelopea fides?

19/174–75 **Illa . . . mora.** Catherine did remain in England from April 1502, when her first husband, Arthur, Henry's elder brother, died, until her marriage to Henry on June 11, 1509, not out of love for Prince Henry, with whom she probably had little contact, but because of the political aims of her parents. Henry VII treated her rather shabbily and even Prince Henry, on June 27, 1505, repudiated the marriage contract to which he had agreed some two years previously (probably at the behest of his father, who had political reasons for keeping Spain dangling). See Scarisbrick, pp. 8–9.

19/176–79 **Non illam . . . patri.** An echo of Catullus 64.116–20, about Ariadne leaving home out of love for Theseus:

> Sed quid ego a primo digressus carmine plura
> commemorem, ut linquens genitoris filia vultum,
> ut consanguineae complexum, ut denique matris,
> quae misera in gnata deperdita leta [*sic MSS., lege* laetabatur]
> omnibus his Thesei dulcem praeoptarit amorem. . . .

Cf. also Vergil, *Georgics* 2.496, 3.262. Catherine's parents, Ferdinand and Isabella, did not wish her to return to Spain; they were eager for her to promote an alliance between England and Spain by marrying Henry. It might seem inappropriate here even to allude indirectly to Adriadne, who was cruelly abandoned by Thesus on Naxos, but there is a dark background for many of the shining ladies More has mentioned: the rape of the Sabine women, the intrigue and assassination of Tarquinius Priscus, the revolt of Cornelia's sons, the slaughter of Penelope's suitors and the maidservants.

19/180 **hinc inde.** Brixius objected to the hypermetrical "hinc et inde" of

1518 (Appendix B, 514/27–29), which More corrected for *1520*. But the error was probably introduced by a compositor or copyist (see the Introduction, pp. 5–6).

20/1–4 **IMBREM . . . DVRAVIT.** The rainstorm occurred on June 23, 1509, the day before the coronation, as Henry and Catherine proceeded with a splendid entourage from the Tower to Westminster Palace. According to Grafton's chronicle, "when y[e] compaignie was thus w[t] all honoure passed, ymediatly ensued a goodly compaignie of gentlemen & well apointed, and after theim came the quene sittyng in a horsse litter alone, clothed in a riche mantell of tissue, in her heare, w[t] a circulet of silke, golde, and perle, aboute her head. But when her grace was a litle passed the signe of the cardinalles hat in Cornehill, suche a sodein showre there came, & fell w[t] suche force & thicknesse, y[t] the canapy borne ouer her was not sufficient to defend her from wetyng of her mantell & furre of powderd ermines w[t]in y[e] same, but y[t] she was fain to be conueighed vnder the houell of the drapers stalles till y[e] shower were ouer passed, whiche was not long, and then she passed on her waie. . . ." (*The Chronicle of Iohn Hardyng . . . together with the Continuation by Richard Grafton . . .*, ed. Henry Ellis [London, 1812], p. 591). The same passage occurs in *The Great Chronicle of London,* ed. A. H. Thomas and I. D. Thornley (London, 1938), p. 340.

20/12 **perstetit.** The usual form (whether from *persto* or *persisto*) is *perstitit.* But see the note to 167/8, below.

21/2–7 **Cuncta . . . uices.** With a certain poetic license, More attributes to Plato a strict doctrine of eternal recurrence which has more in common with the *palingenesia* of the Stoics than with any explicit pronouncement of Plato (see *Stoicorum veterum fragmenta,* ed. Hans F. A. von Arnim [Leipzig, 1903–24], 2, 625–26). Plato does expound political cycles and the four ages of gold, silver, bronze, and iron in his *Republic* (8.3, 546a–547c), a passage Marsilio Ficino associated with Vergil's fourth eclogue (*Commentarius in locum Platonis ex octavo libro de republica de mutatione reipublicae per numerum fatalem,* in *Opera omnia* [Basel, 1576], 2, 1425): "Plato denique quasi vaticinatus videatur, in his saeculis et temporibus quae ad numerum perfectum veniunt vel referunt, divinos quosdam homines exoriri, in quos fines saeculorum pervenerunt. Huc tendit forsitan illud:

> Ultima Cumei iam venit carminis aetas.
> Magnus ab integro seclorum nascitur ordo
> [Iam redit et Virgo, redeunt Saturnia regna,]
> Iam nova progenies coelo dimittitur alto . . . [*Eclogues* 4. 4–7]

Vergil's lines had been interpreted by Servius [*Eclogues* 4.4] as an expression of *palingenesia:* [Ea Sibylla] "dixit etiam, finitis omnibus saeculis rursus eadem renovari; quam rem etiam philosophi hac disputatione colligunt, dicentes completo magno anno, omnia sydera in ortus suos redire, et referri rursus eodem motu. Quod si est idem syderum motus, necesse est omnia quae fuerunt habeant iterationem. Universa enim ex astrorum motu pendere manifestum est. Hoc secutus Virgilius dicit reverti aurea saecula et iterari omnia quae fuerunt." In *Theologia Platonica de immortalitate animorum,* XV, iii (*Opera omnia, 1,* 391), Ficino also associated Plato's *Politicus* (269b–269d) with *palingenesia,* giving the revolutions of the seasons as an example.

21/4–5 **Ver. . . redit.** Cf. Horace, *Carmina* 4.7.9–12.

21/8 **Aurea . . . aetas.** Quoted from Ovid, *Metamorphoses* 1.89.

22/1–2 **SPECTACVLIS EQVESTRIBVS.** The two-day tournament following the coronation was a very elaborate combat between the knights of Pallas and the knights of Diana (Hall, pp. 510–12).

22/7–9 **Vel calamitas . . . ludicra.** Revising for *1520,* More corrected the meter by adding "Vel" before "calamitas" and then balanced "Vel . . . insignia" by adding the new correlative phrase "Vel . . . ludicra."

22/10–11 **tabido . . . sanguine.** On January 12, 1510 Henry VIII and William Compton fought incognito in a tournament at Richmond. Compton was badly wounded and almost died (Hall, p. 513). Though warned not to risk his life in the lists (Hall, p. 521), Henry was almost killed in March 1524, when he charged his opponent without putting down his visor (Hall, p. 674).

22/12 **Aut lanceis . . . sonipedum.** Because of the meter, Garrod (p. 183) says that "lanceis icta" is a printer's error for "icta lanceis." But if one scans *lāncĕīs* (that is, without the synizesis that would make it *lāncēīs*), the meter is perfectly acceptable as it stands.

22/14 **comprimens.** The "collidens" in *L* is metrically acceptable, but it suggests repeated pounding, not continuous crushing.

22/15 **machinae.** This probably refers to the scaffolds (or "stages") built around the lists for spectators, but the tournaments also featured other large and precarious structures, particularly the huge, movable pageant cars made to look like castles or mountains complete with forests and towers, large enough to conceal several mounted knights within them and escorted by scores of attendants. See Hall, pp. 511–12, 520, 533–34, 689, and *The Great Chronicle of London,* ed. A. H. Thomas and I. D. Thornley (London, 1938), pp. 341–43, 368–71.

22/16 **spectacula O rex.** This revision, which first appeared in *1518*, improved the meter by changing a trochee in the fourth foot to an iamb.

22/18–19 **Non ulla . . . innocentia.** That no one was injured or killed during the coronation tournament was perhaps due to Henry's prudence. On the second day of the tournament, when the knights of Diana presented to the queen the terms of a challenge to their opponents, the queen consulted Henry, who "conceiuyng, that there was some grudge, and displeasure betwene theim, thynkyng if suche request wer to theim graunted, some inconuenience might ensue, would not there vnto agre, so that for the appeasyng thereof, it was awarded that bothe parties, should tourney togethers, geuyng but a certain strokes" (Hall, p. 512). Even so, Henry had to intervene to separate the combatants (Thomas and Thornley, *Great Chronicle*, p. 343).

23/1–2 **ROSA . . . COALITA.** See notes to 19/65 and 19/141.

23/5 **coalescit.** Brixius rightly objected to the form *coaleuit* in *1518* instead of *coaluit* (Appendix B, 526/9–13). Although *coaleuit* is not unprecedented (*TLL 3*, 1381, line 30), More may well have written "coalescit," the erroneous change being due to a copyist or a compositor.

24/1–6 **IN RHETOREM . . . Cypro.** Translated from *AP* XI, 146. *Pl.* II, 46 (εἰς ῥήτορας), 5, sig. N_2.

> Ἑπτὰ σολοικισμοὺς Φλάκκῳ τῷ ῥήτορι δῶρον
>   πέμψας, ἀντέλαβον πεντάκι διακοσίους.
> καὶ νῦν μέν φησιν τούτους ἀριθμῷ σοι ἔπεμψα.
>   τοῦ λοιποῦ δὲ μέτρῳ, πρὸς Κύπρον ἐρχόμενος.

For a different interpretation of the Greek and some comments on More's modifications in his translation see Lynch, "*Anthologia Palatina* 11.146," *Classical Philology*, *48* (1953), 17–19. Flaccus may be guilty of the solecism of believing that the word *solecism* derives from the city of Soloi in Cyprus, whereas it actually derives from Soloi in Cilicia (Diogenes Laertius 1.51).

25/1–6 **IN SVSPITIONEM . . . agere.** Translated from *AP* VII, 126. *Pl.* III, 32 (εἰς φιλοσόφους), 31 (εἰς Φιλόλαον), sig. X_7v.

> Τὴν ὑπόνοιαν πᾶσι μάλιστα λέγω θεραπεύειν.
>   εἰ γὰρ καὶ μὴ δρᾷς, ἀλλὰ δοκεῖς, ἀτυχεῖς.
> οὕτω καὶ Φιλόλαον ἀνεῖλε Κρότων ποτὲ πάτρη,
>   ὥς μιν ἔδοξε θέλειν δῶμα τύραννον ἔχειν.

According to Diogenes Laertius, who quotes this epigram (8.84), Philolaus of Croton was a Pythagorean philosopher, a contemporary of Plato.

25/5 **Philoleon . . . Crotone.** Brixius rightly objected to "Phīlŏlāŭm" in *1518* (Appendix B, 516/20–29). More's change to "Philoleon" relies on λεώς (an alternative form of λαός), but there is little justification for the long *i* in *Phīloleon.* See the note on 19/119. Brixius also ridiculed More for translating "Cretenses" (see Appendix B, 496/263–65, 516/11–29), but unless More's Greek manuscript had the metrically indefensible Κρήτη for Κρότων, it is unlikely that More wrote "Cretenses." The error is probably due to a copyist who felt the need to provide *occidere* with a subject (see Appendix C, 626/23–30).

26/1–4 **IN RHETOREM . . . est.** Translated from *AP* XI, 145. *Pl.* II, 46 (εἰς ῥήτορας), 4, sig. N_2.

> Εἰκὼν ἡ Σέξτου μελετᾷ, Σέξτος δὲ σιωπᾷ.
> ῥήτωρ ἦν εἰκών· ὁ δὲ ῥήτωρ, εἰκόνος εἰκών.

This epigram was apparently aimed at a rhetorician who was incapable of speaking in public; hence his statue, which at least seemed to speak, was superior to the original (Waltz, *10,* 256).

27/1–29/3 **IN CAECVM . . . pedes.** Number 27 is a translation of *AP* IX, 13a. *Pl.* I, 4 (εἰς ἀναπήρους), 3, sig. A_4.

> Ἀνέρα τις λιπόγυιον ὑπὲρ νώτοιο λιπαυγὴς
> ἦγε, πόδας χρήσας, ὄμματα χρησάμενος.

Numbers 28 and 29 are variations made possible by the fact that the ideas of borrowing and lending, expressed by one verb in Greek, are divided between two words in Latin (*conducere* and *locare*). Speaking of the Christian charity which even the poor can extend to one another, Augustine says: "Iste non potest ambulare; qui potest ambulare, pedes suos accommodat claudo; qui uidet, oculos suos accommodat caeco. . . ." (*Enarratio in Ps. CXXV,* 12, *CCSL 40,* 1854). Two poems on the same theme were wrongly attributed to Ausonius and printed with his works in Venice (1496, 1501, 1507, 1517) and Parma (1499); see *Decimi Magni Ausonii Burdigalensis Opuscula,* ed. Rudolf Peiper (Leipzig, 1886), pp. 419, 422.

27/2–28/2 **Claudipedem . . . claudipedem.** Brixius objected to this neologism, asserting that *loripedem* would have done quite as well (Appendix B, 526/31–528/6). But *loripes* might mean "limber-footed" as well as "crook-footed," and More's coinage allows him to get "lame," "foot," "blind," and "eye" into one line. Forcellini (*4,* 640) gives forty-eight adjectives formed with the suffix *–pes,* such as *curvipes, alipes, duripes* (Egidio Forcellini, *Totius Latinitatis Lexicon,* 6 vols., rev. Giuseppe Furlanetto and Vincentio de Vit, [Prato, 1858–75]).

30/1–3 **ALITER . . . pedes.** The new principle of this variation is to divide the actions of the two men equally between the two lines: the blind man carries (line 1), the lame man guides (line 2).

31/1–7 **IDEM . . . luminibus.** Adapted from *AP* IX, 11. *Pl.* I, 4 (εἰς ἀναπήρους), 1, sig. A_3v.

> Πηρὸς ὁ μὲν, γυίοις, ὁ δ' ἄρ' ὄμμασιν· ἀμφότεροι δὲ,
>   εἰς αὑτοὺς τὸ τύχης ἐνδεὲς ἠράνισαν.
> τυφλὸς γὰρ λιπόγυιον ἐπωμάδιον βάρος αἴρων,
>   ταῖς κείνου φωναῖς ἀτραπὸν ὠρθοβάτει.
> πάντα δὲ ταῦτ' ἐδίδαξε πικρὴ πάντολμος ἀνάγκη,
>   ἀλλήλοις μερίσαι τοὐλλιπὲς εἰς ἔλεον.

AP IX, 12 and 13b are similar but not as close to More's version. All three Greek epigrams have an ontological emphasis: two imperfect beings fit with each other so as to form one whole being. More tends to stress the moral value of mutual assistance (line 5).

31/4 **coplat.** Brixius rightly objected to the scansion "cŏpŭlāt" (Appendix B, 518/17–21). But More almost surely wrote "coplat," which was erroneously changed by a copyist or a compositor.

32/1–9 **IDEM . . . amor.** This "imitation" has no close equivalent in Greek and is, in effect, an original composition. More's contributions are moral (a firm agreement of friendship), dramatic (direct address), and political (the contrast with proud kings).

33/1–3 **ALITER . . . oculis.** A return to the simple variations of nos. 27–30. The new principle here is to place both actions, carrying and guiding, in the second line; the first line now expresses the idea of a fair bargain or agreement introduced in no. 32.

34/1–7 **PINVS . . . pelago?** Translated from *AP* IX, 376. *Pl.* I, 56 (εἰς νῆας), 8, sig. F_6v.

> Τίπτε με τὴν ἀνέμοισιν ἁλώσιμον ἤλεε τέκτων,
>   τήνδε πίτυν τεύχεις νῆα θαλασσοπόρον;
> οὐδ' οἰωνὸν ἔδεισας, ὅτι βορέης μ' ἐδίωξεν
>   ἐν χθονί; πῶς ἀνέμους φεύξομαι ἐν πελάγει;

But More translates as if there were a question mark after ἔδεισας and a comma after χθονί.

34/4 **facile.** Garrod (p. 183) points out that More wrongly makes the last syllable of this word long.

35/1–3 **IDEM . . . naufragium.** Translated from *AP* IX, 30. *Pl.* I, 56 (εἰς νῆας), 1, sig. F_6.

> Ἐκλάσθην ἐπὶ γῆς ἀνέμῳ πίτυς. ἐς τί με πόντῳ
> στέλλετε ναυηγὸν κλῶνα πρὸ ναυτιλίης;

36/1–5 **IN NAVIM . . . aquas.** Translated from *AP* IX, 398. *Pl.* I, 56 (εἰς νῆας), 12, sig. F_7.

> Ὁλκὰς ὕδωρ προφυγοῦσα πολυφλοίσβοιο θαλάσσης,
> ἐν χθονὸς ἀγκοίναις ὤλετο μητερίαις,
> ἱσταμένην γὰρ πυρσὸς ἐπέφλεγε· καιομένη δὲ,
> δυσμενέων ὑδάτων συμμαχίην ἐκάλει.

37/1–11 **CVNICVLA . . . iocum.** Reminiscent of *AP* IX, 14, 17, 18, 94, 371 (*Pl.* I, 40, 2; I, 33, 7–8; I, 40, 4; I, 33, 9), where, however, there is no mention of the cruelty of man. The most famous example of a hare tormented by the cruelty of dogs and hunters is Shakespeare's "poor Wat" in *Venus and Adonis* (lines 679–708), but the theme had been presented in English before More's time. In a middle-English poem of nineteen quatrains a hare complains (Robbins, p. 109):

> There is no best in þe word, I wene,
> hert, hynd, buke ne dowe,
> That suffuris halfe so myche tene
> As doth þe sylly wat—go where he go.
>
> ȝeyfe a genttylmane wyl have any game,
> And fynd me in forme where I syte,
> ffor dred of lossynge of his name
> I wot wele he wyle not me hyte.
>
> ffor an acuris bred he wyll me leue,
> Or he wyll let his hondes rene;
> Of all þe men þat beth a-lyue
> I am most be-hold to genttyl-men!
>
> As sone as I can ren to þe laye,
> A-non þe grey-hondys wyl me have;
> My bowels beth I-þrowe a-waye,
> And I ame bore home on a stavfe.

Cf. no. 83 and *CW 4*, 170, 457–58.

37/6 **celerem.** The punctuation of *1518* and *1520* takes "celerem" with "uitam," but it would seem more natural to take it with "mortem." Actually it can go with both: the rabbit leads a life of speed and has just tried to save its life by speedy flight; now it does not get a speedy death.

38/1–6 **INNOCENTIAM . . . draco.** Translated from *AP* IX, 379. *Pl.* I, 70 (εἰς πονηρούς), 1, sig. H_4.

Φασὶ παροιμιακῶς κἂν μῦς δάκοι ἄνδρα πονηρόν.
  ἀλλὰ τόδ' οὐχ οὕτω φημὶ προσῆκε λέγειν,
ἀλλὰ δάκοι κἂν μῦς ἀγαθοὺς, καὶ ἀπράγμονας ἄ[ν]δρας.
  τὸν δὲ κακὸν δεδιὼς, δήξεται οὐδὲ δράκων.

In lines 1 and 3 More translated μῦς, which agrees with the edition of 1494 and with the text of 1503; but the reading ὗς, from the Planudean autograph (Marcianus 481), is cited by Aldus in the corrigenda of 1503. The correct reading may well be αἶξ or οἶς (see Waltz, *8*, 14–15, and Leutsch-Schneidewin, *1*, 268 and *2*, 229, 471). But Erasmus, who knew the proverb "Even a goat bites a bad man," quotes and translates the first line of this Greek epigram in the same form that More followed, noting that the unknown author "invertit proverbium, dicens bonos viros vel a mure morderi, malis ne draconem quidem audere dentes admoliri, h. e. insontibus passim noceri, propterea quod ii impune laedi posse videantur, utpote non relaturi injuriam" (*Adagia* 896–97, *Opera omnia, 2*, 332–33).

39/1–6 **IN EFFLATVM . . . potest?** Translated from *AP* XI, 395. *Pl.* II, 44 (εἰς πορδήν), 1, sigs. N_1–N_1v.

Πορδὴ ἀποκτείνει πολλοὺς ἀδιέξοδος οὖσα.
  πορδὴ καὶ σώζει τραυλὸν ἱεῖσα μέλος.
οὐκοῦν εἰ σώζει, καὶ ἀποκτείνει πάλι πορδὴ,
  τοῖς βασιλεῦσιν ἴσην πορδὴ ἔχει δύναμιν.

Cf. Suetonius, *Claudius* 32.

40/1–6 **DE MORTIS . . . humus.** Translated from *AP* XI, 209. *Pl.* II, 45 (εἰς παροριστάς), 1, sig. N_1v.

Κἂν μέχρις Ἡρακλέους στηλῶν ἔλθῃς παρορίζων,
  γῆς μέρος ἀνθρώποις πᾶσιν ἴσον σε μένει·
κείσῃ δ' Ἴρῳ ὁμοῖος, ἔχων ὀβολοῦ πλέον οὐδὲν,
  εἰς τὴν οὐκ ἔτι σὴν γῆν ἀναλυόμενος.

40/5 **Iro . . . uno.** Irus is the beggar in book 18 of the *Odyssey* (see 107/7 and 143/231). The obol refers to the coin placed in the mouth of a dead man to pay the underworld ferryman Charon for passage across the Styx.

41/1–6 **IN SORDIDVM . . . facis.** Translated from *AP* XI, 166. *Pl.* II, 50 (εἰς φειδωλούς), 2, sig. O_1.

Πλουτεῖν φασί σε πάντες. ἐγὼ δέ σέ φημι πένεσθαι.
χρῆσις γὰρ πλούτου, μάρτυς Ἀπολλόφανες.
ἂν μετέχῃς αὐτῶν σὺ, σὰ γίγνεται, ἂν δὲ φυλάττῃς
κληρονόμοις, ἀπὸ νῦν γίγνεται ἀλλότρια.

41/4 **Nam . . . Apollophanes.** The false punctuation in his text apparently led More astray: the comma should come after μάρτυς, not before it, and the sense of the Greek is "For use, O Apollophanes, is what gives testimony to riches." The difficulty was noticed by the editors of *Epigrammatum Graecorum annotationibus Joannis Brodaei Turonensis, nec non Vincentii Obsopoei & Graecis in pleraque epigrammata scholiis illustratorum libri VII. Accesserunt Henrici Stephani in quosdam Anthologiae epigrammatum locos annotationes* (Frankfurt, 1600): "In aliis editionibus interpungitur hic versus, Χρῆσις γὰρ πλούτου, μάρτυς Απολλόφανες, quam interpunctionem falsam esse non animaduertens Morus, ita vertit

Te ditem appellant omnes, ego plane inopem te.
Nam facit usus opes: testis Apollophanes.

Tanti est bene interpungere. Quanquam & hoc debuit animaduertisse Morus, non esse Απολλοφανής, sed Απολλόφανες: nisi forte secundam verbi substantiui personam subaudiendam censuit, & aduerbium ὦ" (p. 267, sig. d_7). It is possible that More intended his Latin to mean "[of that you are] a witness, [O] Apollophanes" or that his text had the readings πλούτος and Απολλοφανής (which do not, however, appear in the editions of 1494 and 1503).

42/1–11 **VENATVS . . . metus est.** An extension and reversal of the Aesopic fable of the spider that traps a wasp in its net and devours it (Perry, *Aesopica,* p. 630).

42/2 **comprehendit.** The meter requires, and More probably wrote, "comprendit."

42/4–5 **saepe . . . solent.** See Aulus Gellius 13.18.1–3 and Erasmus' *Adagia* 402 (*Opera omnia,* 2, 182).

43/1–10 **IN CYNICVM . . . officiet.** Translated from *AP* XI, 410. *Pl.* II, 52 (εἰς φιλοσόφους), 11, Sig. O_4v.

Τοῦ πωγωνοφόρου κυνικοῦ τοῦ βακτροπροσαίτου,
εἴδομεν ἐν δείπνῳ τὴν μεγάλην σοφίην.
θέρμων μὲν γὰρ πρῶτον ἀπέσχετο, καὶ ῥαφανίδων,

μὴ δεῖν δουλεύειν γαστρὶ λέγων ἀρετήν.
εὖτε δ' ἐν ὀφθαλμοῖσιν ἴδεν χιονώδεα βολβὸν
στρυφνὴν, πινυτὸν ἤδη ἔκλεπτε νόον,
ᾔτησεν παρὰ προσδοκίαν, καὶ ἔτρωγεν ἀληθῶς,
κοὐδὲν ἔφη βολβὸν τὴν ἀρετὴν ἀδικεῖν.

43/3 **Cynici.** The cynics were known for eccentric and shameless acts in public (see *CW 14*, Commentary at 573/2). See Appendix C, 652/2–5.

43/7–10 **bulbum . . . bulbus.** More's text had βολβὸν instead of the correct reading given in *AP:* βόλβαν (Latin *vulva*), a rare word meaning "a sow's womb," considered to be a culinary delicacy. The Greek βολβός (Latin *bulbus*) referred to various bulbous roots, medicinal and edible, including the onion; but since none of them were considered any more appetizing than radishes or pulse, the force of the epigram is lost. See *TLL 2*, 2238–39 and *Thesaurus graecae linguae*, ed. Henri Estienne, rev. C. B. Hase, W. Dindorf, and L. Dindorf, 8 vols. in 9 (Paris 1831–65), 2, 315. More also omitted στρυφνὴν, which refers to a sour sauce served with sow's womb but has no relevance to onions.

44/1–6 **EPITAPHIVM . . . fuit.** Translated from *AP* VII, 135. *Pl.* III, 15 (εἰς ἰατρούς), 2, sig. S_1.

Θεσσαλὸς Ἱπποκράτης, Κῷος γένος, ἐνθάδε κεῖται,
Φοίβου ἀπὸ ῥίζης ἀθανάτου γεγαὼς,
πλεῖστα τρόπαια νόσων στήσας ὅπλοις ὑγιείης,
δόξαν ἑλὼν πολλὴν οὐ τύχῃ ἀλλὰ τέχνῃ.

44/6 **sorte . . . arte.** More matches the echoing sounds of τύχῃ . . . τέχνῃ.

45/1–4 **IN SERVVM . . . potest.** Translated from *AP* VII, 538. *Pl.* III, 13 (εἰς δούλους), 6, sig. R_7.

Μάνης οὗτος ἀνὴρ ἦν ζῶν ποτέ. νῦν δὲ τεθνηκὼς,
ἶσον Δαρείῳ τῷ μεγάλῳ δύναται.

46/1–3 **IN ANCILLAM . . . manu.** Translated from *AP* VII, 553. *Pl.* III, 13 (εἰς δούλους), 3, sig. R_6v.

Ζωσίμη, ἡ πρὶν ἐοῦσα μόνῳ τῷ σώματι δούλη,
καὶ τῷ σώματι νῦν εὗρεν ἐλευθερίην.

Garrod (p. 183) points out that More makes the middle syllable of "Sosime" long instead of short.

47/1–8 **IN PISCATOREM . . . hera.** Translated from *AP* IX, 442. *Pl.* I, 79 (εἰς τύχην), 9, sig. I_1.

> Γριπεύς τις μογέεσκεν ἐπ' ἰχθύσι· τόνδ' ἐσιδοῦσα
> εὐκτέανος κούρη, θυμὸν ἔκαμνε πόθῳ.
> καί μιν θῆκε σύνευνον. ὁ δ' ἐκ βιότοιο πενιχροῦ
> δέξατο παντοίης ὄγκον ἀγηνορίης·
> ἡ δὲ Τύχη γελόωσα, παρίστατο. καὶ ποτὶ Κύπριν
> οὐ τεὸς οὗτος ἀγὼν, ἀλλ' ἐμός ἐστιν ἔφη.

The last two lines of the Greek can be translated: "Fortune stood nearby smiling and said to Venus, 'This not your doing, but mine.'" The point is to undermine, gently, the sentimental idea that true love brings marriage, wealth, and happiness ever after. In his first version More adds a little sting to Fortune's smiling gibe by referring to the fisherman as "Mars" in the sense "victor" or "victory." For Mars was the lover, but not the husband, of Venus; they had, in fact, been trapped in bed and exposed to ridicule by Venus' surly husband, Vulcan (Homer, *Odyssey* 8.266–366). The alternative version in *1518* heightens the drama by making Venus speak first, only to be undercut by having her own words turned against her; but it suffers from having Venus herself introduce the embarrassing parallel with Mars. The final version retains the dramatic exchange and gains some force from the emphatic position of "hera," but the tone of smiling raillery is gone.

48/1–4 **IN REPENTE . . . liceat.** Translated from *AP* IX, 530. *Pl.* I, 79 (εἰς τύχην), 10, sig. I_1.

> Οὐκ ἐθέλουσα Τύχη σε προήγαγεν, ἀλλ' ἵνα δείξῃ
> ὡς ὅτι καὶ μέχρι σοῦ πάντα ποιεῖν δύναται.

49/1–8 **IN MEDIOCRITATEM . . . ruunt.** Translated from *AP* X, 51. *Pl.* I, 82 (εἰς φθόνον), 1, sig. I_3.

> Ὁ φθόνος οἰκτιρμοῦ κατὰ Πίνδαρόν ἐστιν ἀμείνων.
> οἱ βασκαινόμενοι, λαμπρὸν ἔχουσι βίον.
> τοὺς δὲ λίαν ἀτυχεῖς, οἰκτείρομεν. ἀλλά τις εἴην
> μήτ' ἄγαν εὐδαίμων, μήτ' ἐλεεινὸς ἐγώ.
> ἡ μεσότης γὰρ ἄριστον. ἐπεὶ τὰ μὲν ἄκρα πέφυκε
> κινδύνους ἐπάγειν, ἔσχατα δ' ὕβριν ἔχει.

Cf. Erasmus' more diffuse translation in *Adagia* 3387 (*Opera omnia, 2,* 1044).

49/3 **Pindarus inquit.** *Pythian* 1.85.

50/1–6 **NIHIL . . . malum.** The Greek source of this epigram is uncertain. More's Latin bears a certain resemblance to no. 12, but there the subject is knowledge rather than fear of impending evil. More's argument also resembles Epicurus' dilemma: οὐθὲν γάρ ἐστιν ἐν τῷ ζῆν δεινὸν τῷ κατειληφότι γνησίως τὸ μηθὲν ὑπάρχειν ἐν τῷ μὴ ζῆν δεινόν. ὥστε ματαῖος ὁ λέγων δεδιέναι τὸν θάνατον οὐχ ὅτι λυπήσει παρῶν, ἀλλ' ὅτι λυπεῖ μέλλων. ὃ γὰρ παρὸν οὐκ ἐνοχλεῖ, προσδοκώμενον κενῶς λυπεῖ. τὸ φρικωδέστατον οὖν τῶν κακῶν ὁ θάνατος οὐθὲν πρὸς ἡμᾶς, ἐπειδή περ ὅταν μὲν ἡμεῖς ὦμεν, ὁ θάνατος οὐ πάρεστιν· ὅταν δ' ὁ θάνατος παρῇ, τόθ' ἡμεῖς οὐκ ἐσμέν (For there is nothing to fear in living for the man who genuinely apprehends that there is nothing to fear in not living. Foolish therefore is the one who says that he fears death not because it will bring grief when it is at hand but because it brings grief when it is impending. For that which brings no annoyance when it is at hand brings grief groundlessly when it is anticipated. Thus the most terrifying of evils, death, is nothing to us, since whenever we are, death is not at hand, while whenever death is at hand, we then are not); Diogenes Laertius 10. 125. Erasmus attributes the dilemma to Diogenes the Cynic in *Apophthegmata* 3.197 (*Opera omnia, 4,* 189 EF). Cf. Lucretius 3.931–37 and 3.1049; and see *CW 4,* 443–53. But More's argument concerns fears of all sorts, not only fear of death, and it requires no disbelief in immortality. In his second couplet More seems to rely on a stoic notion: "Quaedam ergo nos magis torquent quam debent; quaedam ante torquent quam debent; quaedam torquent, cum omnino non debent. Aut augemus dolorem aut fingimus aut praecipimus" (Seneca, *Epistulae morales* 13.5; cf. also 24.1). Cf. Cicero, *De natura deorum* 3.6.14. In *De conscribendis epistolis* (*ASD 1/2,* 371) Erasmus gives the following example of an argument he calls *complexio* (equivalent to "dilemma"): "De futuris euentis angi metu non debemus: etenim si bona sint, frustra metuimus; sin aduersa, infelicitatem duplicamus." Cf. no. 169, below.

51/1–3 **MONOSTICHVM . . . Homerus.** Translated from *AP* IX, 455. *Pl.* I, 66 (εἰς ποιητάς), (τίνας εἴποι [ἂν] λόγους Ἀπόλλων περὶ Ὁμήρου), sig. G_5v.

Ἤειδον μὲν ἐγὼν, ἐχάρασσε δὲ θεῖος Ὅμηρος.

The Planudean tradition, including the Aldine edition of 1503, gave a heading which identified the speaker as Apollo: "What Apollo would say about Homer." If More supplied a title identifying the speaker—as he probably did, since otherwise the line does not make much sense—it was omitted in *1518,* which printed this monostich as the last line of no. 50. Whoever supplied the title for *1520* apparently recognized that the line is a separate epigram in praise of Homer but did not know who the imagined speaker is.

52/1–8 **IN RIDICVLVM . . . alite.** Translated from *AP* XI, 251. *Pl.* II, 30 (εἰς κωφούς), 1, sig. M_1v.

Δυσκώφῳ δύσκωφος ἐκρίνετο. καὶ πολὺ μᾶλλον
ἦν ὁ κριτὴς τούτων τῶν δύο κωφότερος·
ὧν ὁ μὲν, ἀντέλεγεν τὸ ἐνοίκιον αὐτὸν ὀφείλειν
μηνῶν πένθ'. ὁ δ' ἔφη νυκτὸς ἀληλεκέναι.
ἐμβλέψας δ' αὐτοῖς ὁ κριτὴς, λέγει, εἰς τί μάχεσθε;
μήτηρ ἔσθ' ὑμῖν; ἀμφότεροι τρέφετε.

More's translation was printed as III. iv. 83 in Erasmus' expanded *Adagia* of 1518 (Johann Froben, Basel), preceded by the comment "Id Thomas Morus olim adolescens scite vertit hunc in modum" (p. 533, sig. Y_3). This edition, dated 1518 on its title page, concludes with a letter to the reader by Froben dated November 27, 1517 and a colophon dated September 1517, so that it may contain the earliest printing of More's translation (E94 in F. van der Haeghen's *Bibliotheca Belgica,* 2nd Series [Ghent and The Hague, 1891–1923], vol. 6). It has "autor" for "actor" in line 3. More's translation was reprinted in the *Adagia* of 1520 (Aldus, Venice, E95 and Froben, Basel, E96) with the same variant; "actor" appears in the reprintings of 1523 (Froben, Basel, E97), 1526 (Froben, Basel, E98), 1551 (Jerome Froben and Nicolaus Episcopius, E110), and the Leiden *Opera omnia* of 1703–06 (2, 822). The editions of 1508 (Aldus, Venice, E89) and 1515 (Froben, Basel, E93) contain the adage but not More's translation.

53/1–5 **AD LVCERNAM . . . luminibus.** Translated from *AP* V, 7. *Pl.* VII (ἑταιρικὰ ἀποφθέγματα), 113, sig. LL_3.

Λύχνε, σὲ γὰρ παρεοῦσα τρὶς ὤμοσεν Ἡράκλεια
ἥξειν· κοὐχ ἥκει· λύχνε, σὺ δ' εἰ θεὸς εἶ,
τὴν δολίην ἐπάμυνον. ὅταν φίλον ἔνδον ἔχουσα
παίζῃ, ἀποσβεσθεὶς, μηκέτι φῶς πάρεχε.

On lovers attributing divinity to lamps, see Plutarch, *Moralia* 513F. The wordplay "sacra . . . sacris lumina luminibus" is not present in the Greek. More plays on a double meaning ("sacred," "accursed") especially well known because of Vergil's "auri sacra fames" (*Aeneid* 3.57). Cf. 178/3 and 195/4. Erasmus makes the same pun at *ASD 1/3,* 653/13–16.

54/1–6 **LAIS . . . nequeo.** Translated from *AP* VI, 1. *Pl.* VI, 8 (ἀπὸ γυναικῶν), 1, sig. GG_6v.

Ἡ σοβαρὸν γελάσασα καθ' Ἑλλάδος, ἡ τῶν ἐρώντων
ἑσμὸν ἐνὶ προθύροις Λαῒς ἔχουσα νέων,
τῇ Παφίῃ τὸ κάτοπτρον· ἐπεὶ τοίη μὲν ὁρᾶσθαι
οὐκ ἐθέλω· οἵη δ' ἦν πάρος, οὐ δύναμαι.

"AD SPECVLVM" in the title does not mean "[speaking] to her mirror," but rather "[sitting or standing] at her mirror." The phrase was frequently used in this sense (Seneca, *Naturales quaestiones* 1.16.9, 1.17.2–5; Pliny, *Historia naturalis* 35.40.147; Martial 6.64.4; Suetonius, *Caligula* 50.1) and is not an error caused by the misprint "gratia" in *1518*. The editor of *1563* found "Graecia" in his copytext, but changed it to "gratia" from *1518*, trying to make sense of it by adding a question mark.

54/5–6 **Hoc . . . nequeo.** More draws upon Ausonius' version of this epigram (*Epigrammata* 65):

De Laide Dicante Veneri Speculum Suum
Lais anus Veneri speculum dico: dignum habeat se
aeterna aeternum forma ministerium.
at mihi nullus in hoc usus, quia cernere talem,
qualis sum, nolo, qualis eram, nequeo.

55/1–3 **IN MORTIS . . . metu.** Translated from *AP* XI, 282. *Pl.* I, 38 (εἰς ἰατρούς), 7 (εἰς ἀεὶ νοσοῦντας), sig. E_2v.

Τοὺς καταλείψαντας γλυκερὸν φάος οὐκ ἔτι θρηνῶ,
τοὺς δ' ἐπὶ προσδοκίῃ ζῶντας ἀεὶ θανάτου.

55/3 **urunt . . . metu.** More's phrasing seems to have been influenced by 50/4–5. Cf. also the passage from Diogenes Laertius in the note to 50/1–6.

56/1–3 **ALIVD . . . dies.** In *1518* "ALIVD" was omitted and this alternative version (or rather, variation) was wrongly attached to the preceding epigram, no. 55.

57/1–10 **IN APVM . . . artifices.** Translated from *AP* IX, 404, *Pl.* I, 59 (εἰς ὄρνις), 6, sig. G_1v.

Ἀ καλὸν αὐτοπόνητον ἐν αἰθέρι ῥεῦμα μελισσῶν,
αἱ πλασταὶ χειρῶν αὐτοπαγεῖς θαλάμαι,
προίκιος ἀνθρώπων βιότῳ χάρις, οὐχὶ μακέλλας,
οὐ βοός, οὐ γαμψῶν δευομένα δρεπάνων,
γαυλοῦ δὲ σμικροῖο, τόθι γλυκὺ νᾶμα μέλισσα
πηγάζει σκήνευς δαψιλὲς ἐξ ὀλίγου,
χαίροισθ' εὐαγέες, καὶ ἐν ἄνθεσι ποιμαίνοισθε
αἰθερίου πτηναὶ νέκταρος ἐργάτιδες.

57/5 **frugesque.** This nominative singular form is attested, though not as common as *frux* or *frugis* (*TLL 6/1*, 1448, lines 21–24).

57/8 **alueolo.** Although elsewhere (76/10) More uses this word in the rare sense "beehive" (*TLL 1*, 1789, lines 5–6), it normally designates concave or hollow vessels of various kinds. It is a diminutive of *alveus,* which can mean "beehive" (*TLL 1,* 1789, lines 62–70) but which normally refers to concave vessels. Both are derived from *alvus,* which can also mean "beehive," but usually means "belly" or "womb" (*TLL 1,* 1800–04). The Greek σκῆνος can mean "hut" or "tent," but here it clearly means "body" (viewed as a sort of tabernacle or container). Though "situla" suggests More meant "alueolo" to mean "beehive," he may have used it here in the feasible but unprecedented sense of "little belly" or "tiny womb."

57/9 **Congaudete.** See note to 19/34.

58/1–7 **IN ANVM . . . Helenen.** Translated from *AP* XI, 408. *Pl.* II, 9 (εἰς γραίας), 9, sig. K_6v.

> Τὴν κεφαλὴν βάπτεις, τὸ δὲ γῆρας οὔποτε βάψεις,
> οὐδὲ παρειάων ῥυτίδας ἐκτανύσεις.
> μὴ τοίνυν τὸ πρόσωπον ἅπαν ψιμύθῳ κατάπλαττε,
> ὥστε προσωπεῖον, κοὐχὶ πρόσωπον ἔχειν.
> οὐδὲν γὰρ πλέον ἐστί· τί μαίνεαι; οὔποτε φῦκος,
> καὶ ψίμυθος, τεύξει τὴν Ἑκάβην Ἑλένην.

58/2–3 **tinctura . . . tensura.** The echoing sounds here were perhaps intended as some compensation for the loss of the word-play προσωπεῖον . . . πρόσωπον (borrowed by Gregory Nazianzen in *Poemata moralia* 29.4, *PG 37,* 884).

59/1–10 **IN HOMINIS . . . misera.** Translated from *AP* X, 45. *Pl.* I, 80 (εἰς ὑπεροψίαν), 2, sig. I_2v.

> Ἂν μνήμης ἄνθρωπε λάβῃς ὁ πατήρ σε τί ποιῶν
> ἔσπειρεν, παύσῃ τῆς μεγαλοφροσύνης.
> ἀλλ' ὁ Πλάτων σοι τῦφον ὀνειρώσσων ἐνέφυσεν,
> ἀθάνατόν σε λέγων, καὶ φυτὸν οὐράνιον.
> ἐκ πηλοῦ γέγονας. τί φρονεῖς μέγα; τοῦτο μὲν οὕτως
> εἶπ' ἄν τις κοσμῶν πλάσματι σεμνοτέρῳ.
> εἰ δὲ λόγον ζητεῖς τὸν ἀληθινὸν, ἐξ ἀκολάστου
> λαγνείας γέγονας, καὶ μιαρᾶς ῥανίδος.

59/5–6 **Plato . . . aethereum.** See Plato, *Timaeus* 90A.

59/10 **Natus . . . misera.** Cf. Sap. 7:1–5 and *CW 6,* 79/21–22.

60/1–5 **DE ASTROLOGO . . . praeterita.** Number 118 (from the Greek) has a similar theme. More wrote eleven epigrams satirizing astrologers (nos. 60–65, 67, 101, 118, 169, 182), six of them on an astrologer to whom the stars did not reveal that his wife was unfaithful. During the years 1498–1503 an Italian astrologer with the Anglicized name William Parron courted the favor of Henry VII, to whom he dedicated four annual prognostications and a treatise *De astrorum vi fatali* (1499). In the treatise he attempts to refute a book against astrology by an author More admired, Giovanni Pico della Mirandola's *Disputationes adversus astrologiam divinatricem* (printed at Bologna in 1495 or 1496). Parron also claimed that he had predicted in the late 1480s that one Edward Frank would come to a bad end, and indeed Frank was executed for treason in 1490. But since the claim was made nine years after the event, this might seem to be an example of "foreseeing the past." In a treatise dedicated to Henry, Prince of Wales, during Christmastide in 1502 Parron rashly predicted that Henry's mother, Elizabeth of York, would live to be over eighty. She died on February 11, 1503. In his elegy on her death More makes her complain of "false astrolagy and deuynatrice" (*EW*, sig. C_4v). See C. A. J. Armstrong, "An Italian Astrologer at the Court of Henry VII," in *Italian Renaissance Studies*, ed. E. F. Jacob (London, 1960), pp. 433–54.

61/3–6 **Astra . . . monent.** These lines, combined with 65/2–9 to form one epigram, were quoted and praised by Cornelius Agrippa in *De incertitudine & vanitate scientiarum et artium* (Antwerp, 1530). They were translated into Italian by Lodovico Domenichi in his translation (Venice, 1547) of Agrippa's *De incertitudine.* Domenichi also included his translation of these lines in *La Nobiltà delle donne* (Venice, 1549), an adaptation of a similar work by Agrippa. The lines appeared in English (1569), French (1582), Dutch (1651), and German (1713) when *De incertitudine* was translated into these languages. See Marianne S. Meijer, "Thomas More, Lodovico Domenichi et 'L'honneur du sexe feminin,'" *Moreana, 38* (1973), 37–41; and her "Les aventures de deux epigrammes de Thomas More," *Moreana, 50* (1976), 5–9. The Aesopic analogue of this anecdote (Doyle, "Neglected Sources," pp. 8–9) tells of a prophet whose house was robbed rather than of a cuckolded astrologer. Mr. Doyle has also pointed out that in the Persian *Golestān* (or *Rose Garden*) of Saádí (c. 1213–92), the cuckoldry form survives: "An astrologer entered his house and finding a stranger in company with his wife abused him, and called him such opprobrious names that a quarrel and strife ensued. A shrewd man, being informed of this, said to the astrologer: 'What do you know of the heavenly bodies, when you cannot tell what goes on in your own house?'" (W. A. Clouston, *Flowers from a Persian Garden, and Other Papers* [London, 1890], pp. 36–37).

62/6 **pridie.** Since the line following this word had been omitted in *1518* (almost surely through the error of a copyist or a compositor), Brixius was right to point out that "pridie" was not correctly used here. He refers to Valla's *Elegantiae,* where we are told that *pridie* should not be used with reference to today but only to some past or future day (Laurentius Valla, *Opera omnia* [Basel, 1540; reprint, Turin, 1962], *1*, 66).

62/7 **ex Aula.** The astrologer William Parron (see note to 60/1–5) had contacts with the court of Henry VII.

63/1–6 **ALIVD . . . solo.** Cf. the similar poem in Heinrich Bebel's *Facetiae* (first printed at Strassburg in 1508; reprinted there in 1509, 1512, and 1514, and at Paris in 1516):

> *Faceta illusio cuiusdam senis amatoris zelotypi*
>
> Zelotypus noster caelestia sidera noscit:
> Quicquid et in caelo volvitur, ipse videt.
> Visus acutus enim nimis, at mirabile magnum
> In terram veluti talpa videre solet.
> Nam rivalis iter tritum non viderat unquam
> Inque domo propria sub proprioque toro.

See Bebel, *Facetiae,* p. 100.

63/2 **stulte.** This word could be either vocative or adverbial.

65/2–3 **Saturnus . . . lapidem.** "Caecus" refers not to literal blindness (which Hesiod specifically denies in *Theogony* 465) but to the negligence which caused Saturn (Kronos) to swallow a stone instead of his son Zeus (*Theogony* 485–91). In Ptolemaean astronomy Saturn was the most distant planet.

65/6–7 **Iuppiter . . . recolit.** The amours of these planetary gods were well known from Ovid's *Metamorphoses* 1.452–567, 2.708–51, 2.846–75, 4.171–89.

66/1–6 **DE FORMA . . . cerno.** "Hercules" in lines 3 and 6 may well be an exclamation, though *mehercules, hercule,* and *mehercule* are more common than *hercules.* But if the moral exhortation against feminine beauty is addressed to Hercules, More may have had in mind the tradition of Hercules at the crossroads, addressed by feminine personifications of Virtue and Pleasure. More's lines would be suitable on the lips of Virtue, though nothing very close to them occurs in the many versions of the fable listed and discussed by Erwin Panofsky in *Hercules am Scheidewege und andere antike Bildstoffe in der neueren Kunst,* Studien der Bibliothek Warburg Herausgegeben von Fritz Saxl XVIII (Leipzig and Berlin, 1930), pp. 42–55.

67/1 **SVPRA.** See nos. 61–65.

67/2 **Candidus.** Martial applies this name to a cuckold (3.26, 12.38).

68/1 **PARAENESIS . . . VERAM.** Perhaps More uses *paraenesis* (common in Greek but very rare in Latin) instead of *exhortatio* because the Greek word has specifically rhetorical overtones; Aphthonius (*Progymnasmata* 1) applies it to the moral exhortation attached to a fable. Seneca translates *paraeneticen* [sc. philosophiam] as "praeceptivam" (*Epistulae morales* 95.1). At first "veram" seems superfluous, but some philosophies, especially Stoicism, considered a definition of virtue that attached any importance whatever to the goods of this world or of fortune (as the Epicureans and Peripatetics did) to be radically false.

68/3 **Illico . . . cadit.** On the topos of the withering rose as a symbol of worldly pleasure, see Don Cameron Allen. *Image and Meaning: Metaphoric Traditions in Renaissance Poetry* (Baltimore, 1960), pp. 67–79.

68/4 **complectitur ulnis.** In his poem for the *Boke of Fortune* More says that Fortune will "Embrace the in her arms . . ." (*EW,* sig. C_7v).

69/2–3 **Nos uelut . . . metus.** Perhaps suggested by lines 3–4 of *AP* X, 74. *Pl.* I, 8 (εἰς ἀρετήν), 5, sig. A_8.

Μήτε βαθυκτεάνοιο τύχης κουφίζεο ῥοίζῳ,
  μήτε σέο γνάμψῃ φροντὶς ἐλευθερίην.
πᾶς γὰρ ὑπ' ἀσταθέεσσι βίος πολεμίζεται αὔραις,
  τῇ, καὶ τῇ θαμινῶς ἀντιμεθελκόμενος.
ἡ δ' ἀρετὴ, σταθερόν τι, καὶ ἄτροπον· ἧς ἔπι μούνης,
  κύματα θαρσαλέως ποντοπόρει βιότου.

70/1–9 **MORTEM . . . premunt.** Translated from *AP* X, 69. *Pl.* I, 36 (εἰς θάνατον καὶ θανόντας), 1, sig. D_5v–D_6.

Τὸν θάνατον τί φοβεῖσθε, τὸν ἡσυχίης γενετῆρα;
  τὸν παύοντα νόσους, καὶ πενίης ὀδύνας;
μοῦνος ἅπαξ θνητοῖς παραγίγνεται. οὐδέ ποτ' αὐτὸν
  εἶδέν τις θνητῶν δεύτερον ἐρχόμενον.
αἱ δὲ νόσοι, πολλαὶ, καὶ ποικίλαι, ἄλλοτ' ἐπ' ἄλλον
  ἐρχόμεναι θνητῶν, καὶ μεταβαλλόμεναι.

71/3 **Vita . . . annos.** See Erasmus, *Adagia* 3050 (*Opera omnia,* 2, 981B).

71/5–6 **Iugera . . . famulis.** This may suggest Cardinal Wolsey (see, e.g., George Cavendish, *The Life and Death of Cardinal Wolsey,* ed. Richard S. Sylvester, EETS Original Series no. 243 [Oxford, 1959], pp. 19–25). But Wolsey was not especially stingy or petty, and there were other wealthy bishops in England.

71/7 **exigui census.** Cf. Horace, *Epistolae* 1.1.43.

72/1–10 **DE VICISSITVDINE . . . bonis.** More translated directly four poems (nos. 3, 6, 47, 48) from the Planudean group "On Fortune," all four of which appear on facing pages (sigs. H_8v and I_1) in the Aldine edition of 1503. This poem, which is essentially original, seems to be "e Graeco" in the sense that it was suggested by four other poems from the Planudean group on fortune (*Pl.* I, 79, nos. 13, 15, 16, 19; *AP* X, 62, 66, 80, and 96), which also appear on the next pair of facing pages (sigs. I_1v and I_2) in the 1503 edition. Blind Fortune and her wheel were proverbial (Otto, p. 142) and More did not need recourse to *Pl.* I, 79, nos. 16 and 19 for the idea that Fortune swiftly exalts or throws down her victims. Even the epithet "Lubrica," which matches ὀλισθηρῆς . . . τύχης in *Pl.* I, 79, 15, line 4, is not uncommon elsewhere (*TLL* 7, 1689, lines 63–65). But More's "nulla lege" (line 6) is close to the opening of *Pl.* I, 79, 13: Οὐ λόγον, οὐ νόμον οἶδε τύχη. But cf. Οὐδὲν κατὰ λόγον γίγνεθ' ὧν ποιεῖ τύχη (*Menandri Sententiae,* ed. Siegfried Jaekel [Leipzig, 1964], p. 125, and Stobaeus, *Anthologium* 1.7.5, ed. C. Wachsmuth and O. Hense, 5 vols. [Berlin, 1884–1912], *1,* 91).

73/1–11 **VITA . . . dies.** Perhaps suggested by lines 1–2 of *AP* X, 100. *Pl.* II, 47 (Συμποτικὰ ἀστεῖσματα), 32, sig. N_7.

> Ἀνθρώποις ὀλίγος μὲν ὁ πᾶς χρόνος, ὅν ποτε δειλοὶ
> ζῶμεν· κἢν πολιὸν γῆρας ἅπασι μένῃ,
> τῆς δ' ἀκμῆς καὶ μᾶλλον. ὅτ' οὖν χρόνος ὅριος [sic] ἡμῖν,
> πάντα χύδην ἔστω, ψαλμὸς, ἔρως, προπόσεις.
> χειμὼν τοὐντεῦθεν γήρως βάρος. οὐδὲ δέκα μνῶν
> στήσεις. τοιαύτη σ' ἐκδέχετ' ὀρχιπέδη.

But More does not draw the hedonistic conclusion of the Greek epigram.

73/7 **curua senecta.** Cf. Ovid, *Ars amatoria* 2.670: "Iam veniet tacito curva senecta pede."

75/4–9 **Scilicet . . . perit.** More seems to paraphrase a passage from Seneca (*Epistulae morales* 24.20): "Memini te illum locum aliquando tractasse, non repente nos in mortem incidere, sed minutatim procedere; cotidie morimur. Cotidie enim demitur aliqua pars vitae, et tunc quoque, cum crescimus, vita decrescit. Infantiam amisimus, deinde pueritiam, deinde adulescentiam. Usque ad hesternum, quicquid transît temporis, perît; hunc ipsum, quem agimus, diem cum morte dividimus. Quemadmodum clepsydram non extremum stillicidium exhaurit, sed quicquid ante defluxit, sic ultima hora, qua esse desinimus, non sola mortem facit, sed sola consummat; tunc ad illam pervenimus, sed diu venimus." Cf. also Sap. 5:13 and the saying of Theophrastus (Diogenes Laertius 5.41): ἡμεῖς γὰρ ὁπότ' ἀρχόμεθα ζῆν, τότ' ἀποθνήσκομεν.

75/9 **Sic oleo lampas.** Brixius rightly objected to the scansion of "V̄t lāmpās ŏlĕō," since "lāmpăs" is the only correct scansion (Appendix B, 518/22–26). But the error may well have been due to a compositor or copyist who wrote "lampas oleo" for More's "oleo lampas."

75/11 **dum loquimur, morimur.** Cf. Horace, *Carmina* 1.11.7–8: dum loquimur, fugerit invida aetas.

76/1–10 **DIVES . . . comedunt.** Translated from *AP* X, 41. *Pl.* I, 65 (εἰς πλουτοῦντας), 3, sig. G_4v.

> Πλοῦτος ὁ τῆς ψυχῆς, πλοῦτος μόνος ἐστὶν ἀληθής.
> τἆλλα δ' ἔχει αὐτὴν πλείονα τῶν κτεάνων.
> τόνδε πολυκτέανον, καὶ πλούσιόν ἐστι δίκαιον
> κλῄζειν, ὃς χρῆσθαι τοῖς ἀγαθοῖς δύναται.
> εἰ δέ τις ἐν ψήφοις κατατήκεται, ἄλλον ἐπ' ἄλλῳ
> σωρεύειν ἀεὶ πλοῦτον ἐπειγόμενος,
> οὗτος ὁποῖα μέλισσα πολυτρήτοις ἐνὶ σύμβλοις
> μοχθήσει, ἑτέρων δρεψομένων τὸ μέλι.

76/10 **mella alij.** Brixius objected to the scansion *mel* in *1518* (Appendix B, 516/30–33). But the elision shows that this was probably a copyist's or compositor's error, not More's. See the Introduction, pp. 5–6.

77/1–3 **DILEMMA . . . est.** *Epicurea,* ed. Hermann Usener (Leipzig, 1887; reprint, Rome, 1963), pp. 72, 292; Diogenes Laertius 10.133 and 140; *Epicuro,* trans. Ettore Bignone (Bari, 1920; reprint, Rome, 1964), pp. 57, 149. Marcus Aurelius (7.33) and Tertullian (*Apologeticus* 45.6) cite this Epicurean doctrine, and Plutarch (*Moralia* 36B) calls it a "much admired statement originating with Epicurus." But More's immediate source is probably Cicero (*De finibus* 2.7.22): "Iam doloris medicamenta illa Epicurea tamquam de narthecio proment: 'Si gravis, brevis: si longus, levis.'"

78/1–3 **CONTRA . . . breuis.** It is not surprising that More should have turned the Epicurean dilemma on its head, since both Cicero (*Tusculanae disputationes* 2.19.44, 3.17.38) and Plutarch (*Moralia* 1087E–1088A) attacked it, primarily on the ground that some severe pains are also long-lasting.

79/1–3 **DE MORTE . . . inops.** Cf. Ps. 75:6 and Luke 12:19–20. See note to 139/1–10 and *CW 13,* 64/33–65/4.

80/8–13 **Auferet . . . inops.** Cf. the parable of Dives and Lazarus (Luke 16:19–26). On tyranny see also nos. 110, 114, 120, 121, 142, 162, 198, 201, 227, 238, 243.

81/1–8 **CARMEN . . . malis.** The English song from which this epigram was translated has not yet been discovered. The sentiment is very common in songs of More's time; see, e.g., Robbins, nos. 165, 167–69. Six lines beginning "My whofull herte plonged yn heuynesse" in MS. Ff. 1.6 of the Cambridge University Library are fairly close to More's Latin; they are reprinted by Rossell H. Robbins in "The Findern Anthology," *PMLA, 69* (1954), 638.

82/1–8 **IN AMICAM . . . fidem.** A. J. Sabol located the source of this epigram in the Fairfax manuscript (British Library Add. MS. 5654, ff. 13v–15), dating from about 1500 (*Modern Language Notes, 63* [1948], 542):

> Benedicite what dremyd I this nyȝt
> me thought the worlde was turnyd vp so downe,
> the son, the moone had lost ther force and lyȝt;
> the see also drownyd both towre and towne
> yett more mervell how that I hard the sownde
> of onys voice sayyng, 'bere In thy mynd
> thi lady hath forgoten to be kynd.'

In *Music and Poetry in the Early Tudor Court* (London, 1961), John Stevens published the contents of this songbook, including this song (p. 357). For modern editions of the music of the English song see Nan C. Carpenter, "Note on Two Epigrams of More," *Moreana, 50* (1976), 11, and the same author's "St. Thomas More and Music: The Epigrams," *Renaissance Quarterly, 30* (1977), 24–25.

82/4 **mundi . . . ruit.** Cf. Lucretius 5.96.

83/1–3 **DE CVNICVLO . . . caperer.** See note to 37/1–11.

84/1–4 **IN VIRGINEM . . . peperit.** See Poggio, *Facetiae* no. 154, 2, 51–52: "De montano qui filiam desponsare volebat. Cupiebat ex oppido Pergula montanus desponsare uni ex vicinis juvenem filiam. Quam ille conspicatus, ut cum nimium teneram et adolescentiorem respueret, insulsus pater: 'Maturior est,' inquit, 'quam opineris; tres enim jam filios peperit ex clerico Sacerdotis nostri.' "

85/1–6 **IN VXORES . . . tamen.** Expanded from *AP* X, 116. *Pl.* I, 15 (εἰς γάμον), 7, sig. B_4v.

> Οὐκ ἔστι γήμας, ὅστις οὐ χειμάζεται.
> λέγουσι πάντες, καὶ γαμοῦσιν εἰδότες.

86/1–3 **IN EASDEM . . . tibi.** Cf. no. 174.

87/1–3 **IN IMAGINEM . . . Menodote.** Translated from *AP* XI, 213. *Pl.* II, 19 (εἰς ζωγράφους), 1, sig. L_4v.

Εἰκόνα Μηνοδότου γράψας Διόδωρος, ἔθηκε.
  πλὴν τοῦ Μηνοδότου πᾶσιν ὁμοιοτάτην.

89/1–22 **CHORIAMBICVM . . . Dionysio.** Translated from *AP* XI, 47–48. *Pl.* II, 47 (συμποτικὰ ἀστεΐσματα), 17, sigs. N_4v–N_5.

Οὔ μοι μέλει Γύγαο
τοῦ Σαρδίων ἄνακτος,
οὔθ' αἱρέει με χρυσὸς,
οὐδὲ φθονῶ τυράννοις,
ἐμοὶ μέλει μύροισι
καταβρέχειν ὑπήνην,
ἐμοὶ μέλει ῥόδοισι
καταστέφειν κάρηνα.
τὸ σήμερον μέλει μοι,
τὸ δ' αὔριον τίς οἶδε.
τὸν ἄργυρον τορεύσας
Ἥφαιστέ μοι ποίησον,
ποτήριον δὲ κοῖλον
ὅσον δύνῃ, βάθυνον.
ποίει δέ μοι κατ' αὐτοῦ,
μήδ' ἄστρα, μήδ' ἁμάξας,
μὴ στυγνὸν 'Ωρίωνα,
ἀλλ' ἀμπέλους χλοώσας,
καὶ βότρυας γελῶντας
σὺν τῷ καλῷ Λυαίῳ.

In all printed editions of the Planudean Anthology before 1549, these two Greek epigrams are combined into one, as they are in most manuscripts of Anacreon (Waltz, *10*, 89). In *AP* and Planudes' autograph (Codex Marcianus 481) they are given as two, the first ending at line 10. Gellius (19.9.6) also quotes the second one alone (in a slightly different form). Like More, the two printed editions available to him (Florence, 1494, and Venice, 1503) omit the line πανοπλίαν μὲν οὐχί after line 12 of the Greek given here. More's translation was reprinted (probably from *1518*[d]) at the end of *De imitatione eruditorum quorundam libelli* . . . (Strassburg, Ioannes Albertus, March, 1535, sig. h_3v). The book contains treatises on imitation by Celio Calcagnini, Giovanni Battista Giraldi, Giovanni Francesco Pico della Mirandola, Pietro Bembo, Angelo Poliziano, Paulus Cortesius, Melanchthon, and Quintilian. See Bob de Graaf, "More's *Choriambicum de vita suavi* as a fill-up in a 16th-century

Strasburg Schoolbook," *Moreana, 23* (1969), 53–55. More's poem is a Latin translation but it is clear that for him translation was one stage in the larger process of imitation.

89/3 **Gygis.** Garrod (p. 183) correctly points out that here and at 145/3 More wrongly takes the first syllable of *Gygis* as short. But here at least there is some reason for More's mistake, since the Greek text is corrupt. The Ionian genetive Γύγαο would have to be scanned ˘ ˉ ˘ to fit the meter. Editors have emended the text in various ways (Waltz, *10,* 88–89).

89/13–19 **Tornato . . . flebilis.** A mock-heroic allusion to the shield of Achilles made by Hephaestus (Homer, *Iliad* 18.480–89).

89/16 **imbibum.** Brixius rightly pointed out that "imbibus" does not appear in any Latin writer whatsoever (Appendix B, 528/22–530/9). It still does not appear in any of the classical or medieval dictionaries. Following the analogy of *immensus* for *immensurabilis* or *immotus* for *immobilis,* More apparently coined it to mean "not capable of being drunk up completely, inexhaustible" (it translates βάθυνον, "deep").

89/17 **fac.** Garrod (p. 183) points out that More wrongly makes "fac" long.

89/22 **Dionysio.** Garrod (p. 183) says that "sense and metre require *Dionyso.*" Indeed it might be argued that glyconic lines sometimes conclude with a pherecratic, as in Catullus 34 and 61, but these poems consist of strophes in which only three or four glyconics are concluded with a pherecratic, whereas More's poem has nineteen glyconics before the concluding line. The only precedent for a long series of glyconics followed by a pherecratic is Seneca's *Hercules Oetaeus* 1031–60, but the pherecratic occurs in the middle of a long chorus (1031–1130) which is otherwise uniformly glyconic. There are no pherecratics in Seneca's other glyconic passages (*Oedipus* 882–914, *Hercules furens* 875–95, *Thyestes* 336–403, *Medea* 75–92) nor in the longer glyconic passages of Boethius (*Consolatio philosophiae* 1.6, 2.8, 3.12, 4.3, 5.4) or Prudentius (*Peristephanon liber* 7). The form *Dionysius* had been used for the god Bacchus by other authors before More, including Fulgentius and Ausonius (*TLL, Onomasticon 3,* 174, lines 62–64, and 178, lines 69–71). Moreover, though Henricus Stephanus gives the correct Greek form Διόνυσος (*Thesaurus graecae linguae* [Paris, 1572], *5,* 762, sig. $\iota\iota_2$r), the following Latin dictionaries of the fifteenth and sixteenth centuries give *only* the form Dionysius as the name of Bacchus:

Giovanni Balbi, *Catholicon* (Venice, Hermannus Liechtenstein, 1487), sig. r_4v; a reprint (Venice, 1490), sig. p_7v.

Ambrogio Calepino, *Dictionarium* (Venice, Peter Liechtensteyn, 1506), sigs. e_7v and m_7v; a reprint (Strassburg, Matthias Schürer, December 1516), sigs. f_6 and o_6.

Carolus Stephanus, *Dictionarium historicum, geographicum, poeticum* (Lyons, 1595), sigs. Aa_2v–Aa_3.

Thomas Cooper, *Thesaurus linguae Romanae et Britannicae . . . Accessit Dictionarium historicum et poeticum* . . . (London, 1578). sigs. $Ffffff_3$ and $Iiiiii_1$v.

90/5 **balsamus.** The usual form is *balsamum* but there is some precedent for *balsamus* (*TLL* 2, 1710, lines 1–2, and Latham) and βάλσαμος (Stephanus 2, 97D). The resin of the balsam tree was used not only for perfumes and unguents but also for healing purposes (Celsus 5.3–6; 5.20.6; 6.6.34). The word had probably not yet taken on its alchemical meaning: "a healthful preservative essence, of oily and softly penetrative nature, conceived by Paracelsus to exist in all organic bodies" (*OED*, s.v. *balsam* 4 and *balsamum* 3).

90/14 **Abluat . . . Absit.** Brixius objected to the *1518* reading "obsecrat" for "rogat" (Appendix B, 516/34–518/4). But if More originally wrote the metrically acceptable line "Abluat ut uino aeger mucronem obsecrat. Absit," the error might well be due to a copyist or compositor, not to More.

91/1–4 **IN FVCATAM . . . foro.** Adapted from *AP* XI, 68. *Pl.* II, 9 (εἰς γραίας), 2, sig. K_6.

> Τὰς τρίχας ὦ Νίκυλλα, τινὲς βάπτειν σε λέγουσιν,
> ἅς σὺ μελαινοτάτας ἐξ ἀγορᾶς ἐπρίω.

The Greek epigram is sarcastic: "Some say, Nicylla, that you dye your hair, but you bought it as black as coal in the market" (cf. Waltz, *10*, 242). More adds a dramatic interchange ("at qui scis, rogas?") and a further twist: the woman bought a black wig at the market and has now dyed it another color (cf. Hutton, *Anthology in France*, p. 230). Cf. Martial 6.12:

> Iurat capillos esse, quos emit, suos
> Fabulla: numquid ergo, Paule, peierat?

Though the Greek is an elegiac distich, More (like Martial) writes a couplet in iambic trimeter.

92/1–3 **IN IMAGINEM . . . dissimilem.** Cf. *AP* XI, 213 (*Pl.* II, 19 [εἰς ζωγράφους], 1, sig. L_4v).

94/1 **IN EANDEM.** In *1518* no. 93 was incorrectly headed "IN EANDEM," so that the titles of both nos. 93 and 94 referred back to the bad portrait of no. 92 (incorrectly for no. 93 but correctly for no. 94). Whoever corrected the title of 93 in *1520* forgot to change the title of 94.

94/3 **finxerat.** Garrod (p. 184) says that this is a misprint for *finxerit,* but the correction is not necessary. In classical Latin we would expect the subjunctive in such an indirect question, but the indicative is common in early and colloquial Latin, especially Plautus (Kühner-Stegmann, 2/2, 491–92). See *CW 14,* 189/10–11.

94/6 **ouo . . . ouum.** A proverb (Otto 1318; Erasmus, *Adagia* 1707, *Opera omnia,* 2 641B). We are lulled by the proverb until it is suddenly reversed in the last word of the poem.

95/1–53 **IN ANGLVM . . . capus.** In a letter of 1520 (Allen *4,* 221, no. 1087, lines 181–82) More told Erasmus that he wrote this epigram about an Englishman who foolishly affected French speech and manners while England was at war with France (January 1512 to August 1514). In his *Letter to Brixius* (see below, Appendix C, 604/18–30) More says he wrote it "eodem tempore" that Brixius' *Chordigera* came into his hands (adding "haud scio an etiam tum excusum typis"). Brixius had finished the *Chordigera* by October 23, 1512, and the first printed edition was issued by Badius in Paris on January 15, 1513. Hence it seems likely that More wrote this epigram late in 1512 or early in 1513. Cf. Lucilius' lines on Albucius (quoted by Cicero, *De finibus* 1.3.9) and (for the mocking repetition) Martial 2.7. Julius Caesar Scaliger admired this epigram: "Extat viri omni tyrannide maioris Thomae Mori adeo festiuum epigramma, ut cum eo quid comparem vix habeam. Ibi sodalem suum peregrina Britannice, Britannica peregrinis moribus affectantem taxat adeo, ut ostendat eum, qui sese ad Gallicum modum per omnia componere cuperet, Gallica omnia nihil minus, quam Gallice assequi. Quare quod seuere & composite descripsit Cicero [his definition of *ineptus* in *De oratore* 2.4], Anglicus ille Socrates & argumento & numeris explicauit" ("Epistola ad Arnoldum Feronum Atticum de Verbo Inepti" in *Epistolae et orationes* [Leiden, 1600], p. 423, sig. Dd_4).

95/3 **Amicus et sodalis.** This need not mean that the fop was about More's age (thirty-five), for in the title of the Progymnasmata (p. 78, above) More and Lily are called "sodales," though Lily was about ten years older than More.

95/3 **Lalus.** Probably suggested by λάλος, "talkative, babbling."

95/6 **dirimant.** Garrod (p. 183) points out that More wrongly makes the first syllable of this word long. The error probably stems from the fact that there are many Latin verbs formed with the prefix *dī–*.

95/12 **Filtro, bireto, pileoque.** Apparently intended to designate hats of various kinds. *Filtrum* and *bir(r)etum* are medieval words: the first meant "felt" or various objects made of felt, including hats (J. H. Baxter and Charles Johnson, *Medieval Latin Word-List from British and Irish Sources* [London, 1934; reprint, London, 1947]; Albert Blaise, *Dictionnaire latin-français des auteurs chrétiens* [Turnhout, 1954]; J. F. Niermeyer, *Mediae Latinitatis Lexicon Minus* [Leiden, 1954–63]; Du Cange, Latham); the second meant "cap" or "beret" (Latham, Niermeyer). Brixius objected to the medieval *filtrum,* by which he thought More might have meant *chlamys,* "cloak" (see Appendix B, 530/10–21), but there is only very slight precedent for that meaning in Latin, and the English *felt* (*OED* s.v. *felt sb.*[1], 2b) and the French *feutre* (*feltre*) were used before and during the sixteenth century to mean "a felt hat" but never to mean "a cloak" (Adolf Tobler and Erhard Lommatzsch, *Altfranzösisches Wörterbuch,* 10 vols. [Wiesbaden, 1925–76], *3,* 1796, and *Grand Larousse de la langue française,* 6 vols. [Paris, 1971–78], *3,* 1932). The classical word *pil(l)eus* was used in the sixteenth century as a general term including various kinds of head-gear. Niccolò Perotti (*Cornucopiae* [Paris, 1514], sig. m_6v) defines it as "tegmen capitis." Ambrogio Calepino (*Dictionarium undecim linguarum* . . . [Basel, 1598], sig. Zz_2v) gives the following definitions and translations: "Tegmen capitis . . . Gal. Vn chappeau ou bonnet à couurir la teste. Ital. Cappello, baretta. Germ. Ein Hut/ Baret/ Kappen . . . Hisp. Sombrero . . . Ang. A cap or bonet." Thomas Cooper (*Thesaurus linguae Romanae et Britannicae* [London, 1565], sig. $AAAaa_5$v) translates "a cappe or bonet."

95/27 **callet . . . Psytacus.** Ben Jonson (*New Inn,* I, iii, 4): "He prates Latine And 'twere a parrat, or a play-boy." Cf. Tilley, P60; Walther, 25008; and Chaucer, Prologue to *The Canterbury Tales,* lines 637–43.

95/29 **Verbis tribus.** Otto 1870: "tria verba non potest iungere."

95/39 **uulpe . . . navita.** Cf. Chaucer's "Nun's Priest's Tale," VII, lines 3273–81 and "Franklin's Tale," lines 859–80.

95/42 **Lombardicam.** On Lombardy in the sense "Italy" see *CW 6,* Commentary at 233/32–234/4.

95/49 **more simiae.** Cf. Erasmus, *Adagia* 611 (*Opera omnia, 2,* 265AB): "Simia simia est, etiamsi aurea gestet insignia."

95/51–53 **amne Gallo . . . capus.** Those who drank of the river Gallus in Phrygia were said to go mad. From this river the Galli, emasculated and hysterical priests of the Phrygian goddess Cybele, took their name (Ovid, *Fasti* 4.361–65). Cf. Walther, 8258a:

> Ex gallo capo fierent si sepe capones
> Galli, non esset Gallica in orbe lues.

96/2–3 **Nunc . . . dari.** For the opposing positions of Plato and Aristotle on this point see *CW 5*, Commentary at 584/11 and 584/17–19.

96/5 **nomen . . . ducis.** The etymology from νίκη and λαός was not esoteric because it was the first one given in the life of St. Nicolaus in the *Legenda aurea* of Jacobus de Voragine (ed. Th. Graesse [Dresden and Leipzig, 1846], p. 22). William Caxton (London, May 20, 1493) translated as follows: "Nycholas is said of Nichos / whiche is to saye victory & of laos peple / Soo nicholas is asmoche to say / as victorie of people that is victorie of synne / whiche ben fowle people" (sig. f_4). See *CW 5*, Commentary at 584/17–19.

96/4 **Nicoleus.** Here and in line 9 Brixius objected to the scansion "Nīcŏlăūs" (Appendix B, 518/6–9). *Nicoleus* is metrically acceptable (see note to 25/5) but very unusual.

96/6 **uenenis.** In a legal context *venenum* could mean "a potion, whether harmful or beneficial" (*Digesta* 50.16.236, Mommsen-Krueger *1*, 919), but here the neutral sense is overwhelmed by the predominant meaning, "poison."

97/3 **Venerem . . . Apellis.** In antiquity Apelles' Aphrodite rising from the sea was the most famous painting by the most famous painter. See *AP* XVI, 178–82, and Johannes A. Overbeck, *Die antiken Schriftquellen zur Geschichte der bildenden Künste bei den Griechen* (Leipzig, 1868), pp. 344–51. Cf. 252/9, 276/3.

97/6–8 **Spectari . . . color.** The anecdote about combining the most beautiful features of several persons into a single portrait is most closely associated with Zeuxis (Cicero, *De inventione* 2.1.1–3; Erasmus, *Ciceronianus, ASD 1/2*, 616–17, 620).

97/10 **a nulla . . . similis.** Apart from the unfortunate clue in the title ("SED DEFORMISSIMI"), the trap is not sprung until the last word, where we expect "dissimilis."

99/1–5 **IN PARCVM . . . tumulum.** Adapted from *AP* XI, 170. *Pl.* II, 50 (εἰς φειδωλούς), 6, sig. O_1v.

> Δακρύει Φείδων ὁ φιλάργυρος οὐχ ὅτι θνήσκει,
> ἀλλ' ὅτι πέντε μνῶν τὴν σορὸν ἐπρίατο.
> ταῦτ' αὐτῷ χαρίσασθε. καὶ ὡς τόπος ἐστὶν ἐν αὐτῇ,
> τῶν πολλῶν τεκνίων ἕν τι προσεμβάλετε.

More expanded the first couplet of the Greek and omitted the second, perhaps because of the brutal suggestion that a small child of the miser be tossed into the sarcophagus as "une économie finale" (Waltz, *10*, 259).

99/2 **Chrysalus.** More changes the miser's name from Φείδων (φειδός means "thrifty," which appears in the Latin title as "PARCVM"). He took the name from a thieving servant in Plautus' *Bacchidae* who puns on the meaning of his own name (χρυσός, gold): "Ceterum quantum lubet me poscitote aurum: ego dabo. Quid mihi refert Chrysalo esse nomen, nisi factis probo?" (lines 703–04). The name also suggests χρυσαλλίς, a chrysalis, the gold-colored sheath from which a butterfly emerges. In Christian art the emergence of the butterfly from its chrysalis was a symbol of resurrection (*Lexikon der christlichen Ikonographie,* ed. Engelbert Kirschbaum et al., 8 vols. [Rome, 1968–76], *4,* 96; cf. Basil, *Hexaemeron* 8.8, *PG 29,* 184D). A late sixteenth-century emblem shows a butterfly emerging from its chrysalis, with the verses:

> Coeca voluptatum, o juvenes, abrumpite vincla,
> Libera erunt vestra his pectora vindiciis.

See Henkel-Schöne, col. 912.

100/1–3 **IN GRAMMATICVM . . . timet.** Translated from *AP* XI, 138. *Pl.* II, 10 (εἰς γραμματικούς), 1, sig. K_7.

> Ἂν τοῦ γραμματικοῦ μνησθῶ μόνον Ἡλιοδώρου,
> εὐθὺ σολοικίζον τὸ στόμα μου δέδεται.

More's Latin says that the tongue dreads solecisms; the Greek says that the mouth is bound (perhaps by enchantment) to solecize (see Waltz, *10,* 123, and Dübner-Cougny, *2,* 373; cf. *AP* XI, 148). In either case the thought of Heliodorus is enough to corrupt the speech of others. More may have confused δέω (to bind) with δείδω (to fear), since both are irregular, semideponent verbs which have the perfect stem δεδ–. The change from "mihi" to "Nostra," both referring to a singular first person, is a bit awkward ("Mea" would not fit the meter); perhaps More wished to suggest that not merely "my tongue" but "our language" fears solecisms at the thought of Heliodorus.

101/1–11 **IN PROGNOSTEN . . . ait.** This could refer to two French kings: Charles VIII (died April 7 or 8, 1498) or Louis XII (died January 1, 1515). See note to 60/1–5.

101/10 **Audit ut.** *Ut* in a temporal sense (when, as soon as) with the historical present is a rare construction (Kühner-Stegmann, *2/2,* 361–62). Brixius rightly objected to More's scansion "sērĭŏ" instead of "sērĭō" (Appendix B, 518/10–13). But see note to 5/13.

102/1–6 **IN VEHEMENTER . . . tuus.** Translated from *AP* XI, 268. *Pl.* II, 13 (εἰς δυσειδεῖς), 11, sig. L_1v.

Οὐ δύναται τῇ χειρὶ Πρόκλος τὴν ῥῖν' ἀπομύσσειν,
τῆς ῥινὸς γὰρ ἔχει τὴν χέρα μικροτέρην.
οὐδὲ λέγει Ζεῦ σῶσον ἐὰν πταρῇ. οὐ γὰρ ἀκούει
τῆς ῥινός. πολὺ γὰρ τῆς ἀκοῆς ἀπέχει.

103/1–6 **IN POETAM . . . inuenio.** Translated from *AP* XI, 127. *Pl.* II, 40 (εἰς ποιητάς), 1, sig. M_6.

Εἰσὶ καὶ ἐν Μούσησιν 'Εριννύες, αἵ σε ποιοῦσι
ποιητὴν, ἀνθ' ὧν πολλὰ γράφεις ἀκρίτως.
τοίνυν σου δέομαι γράφε πλείονα. μείζονα γάρ σοι
εὔξασθαι ταύτης οὐ δύναμαι μανίην.

104/1–4 **IN PERPVSILLVM . . . mane.** Translated from *AP* XI, 369. *Pl.* II, 7 (εἰς βραχεῖς), 2, sig. K_5v.

'Ασφαλέως οἴκησον ἐν ἄστεϊ, μή σε κολάψῃ
αἵματι πυγμαίων ἡδομένη γέρανος.

Cf. Ovid, *Fasti* 6.176: "quae Pygmaeo sanguine gaudet, avem." See also Homer, *Iliad* 3.2–7; Aristotle, *History of Animals* 8.12 (596b), *Histoire des animaux,* ed. Pierre Louis, 3 vols. (Paris, 1969), *3,* 28; and Aelian, *Characteristics of Animals* 15.29

105/1–4 **NEGLIGENDI . . . male.** Translated from *AP* IX, 50. *Pl.* I, 87 (εἰς φροντίδας), I, sig. I_6.

Τὴν σαυτοῦ φρένα τέρπε. δυσηλεγέων δὲ πολιτῶν
ἄλλος τις σε κακῶς, ἄλλος ἄμεινον ἐρεῖ.

106/1–4 **IN FATVVM . . . pulices.** Translated from *AP* XI, 432. *Pl.* II, 3 (εἰς ἀνοήτους), 2, sig. K_3.

Ἔσβεσε τὸν λύχνον μῶρος, ψυλλῶν ὑπὸ πολλῶν
δακνόμενος, λέξας οὐκ ἔτι με βλέπετε.

106/3–4 **pulices . . . pulices.** Brixius rightly points out that the correct scansion is "pūlĭcēs," not More's "pŭlĭcēs" (Appendix B, 518/27–520/7). The scansion *pŭlēx* is found only in the pseudo-Ovidian *De pulice* of Ofilius Sergianus (*Poetae latini minores,* ed. Nicolas E. Lemaire, 7 vols. [Paris, 1824–26], 7, 275).

106/3 **Morio.** More preserves the sound of the Greek μῶρος and the suggestion of a pun on his own name. See no. 278 and Germain Marc'hadour, "A Name for All Seasons," *Essential Articles,* pp. 539–62.

107/1–7 **DE SOMNO . . . egens.** Erasmus, *Adagia* 1009 (*Opera omnia,* 2, 409D–F): "Dimidio vitae nihil differunt felices ab infelicibus." Erasmus quoted and translated Aristotle's *Nicomachean Ethics* 1.13.12 (1102b): "but when they are asleep you cannot tell a good man from a bad one (whence the saying that for half their lives there is no difference between the happy and the miserable)." He also refers to Aristotle's use of the saying in his *Eudemian Ethics* 2.1.15 (1219b). Cf. *CW 4*, 40/7.

107/7 **Irus.** See note to 40/5, above, and 143/231, below.

108/1–7 **ALIVD . . . miser.** Unlike the preceding epigram, which shows the basic equality of the rich and the poor, this variation concentrates on the rich man alone and argues by constructing a dilemma, one of More's favorite procedures (cf. nos. 12, 23, 50, 66, 72, 77–78).

109/5 **Rex . . . suos.** Cf. no. 111 and *CW 6*, 490–91. In his note on *Utopia* 194/2 (*CW 4*, 488), Fr. Surtz traces the long tradition of the king as the father of his people. More plays on two senses of *liberi:* "children" and "freemen." In Erasmus' colloquy *Virgo* μισόγαμος, for example, Eubulus remarks: "Vnde et liberi vocantur filii familias, quod absint a conditione seruorum" (*ASD 1/3*, 294, lines 192–93). Cf. Terence, *Adelphoe* 74–78.

110/1–7 **SOLLICITAM . . . uelis.** A variation of no. 107, which provides the second proposition of the syllogism (in three distichs):

> A tyrant finds happiness only in sleep.
> But in sleep he is equal to a poor man.
> Therefore a tyrant is happy only when he is equal to a poor man.

The last word "uelis" gives a surprising new twist not provided for in the syllogism itself.

111/1–7 **BONVM . . . ciuibus.** Cf. no. 109.

112/2–3 **Totum . . . facit.** The conception of the state as "corpus reipublicae mysticum" made up of the king (the head) and his people (the members) had a long and important legal development in the three centuries preceding More's time (Ernst H. Kantorowicz, *The King's Two Bodies: A Study in Mediaeval Political Theology* [Princeton, 1957; reprint 1966], pp. 207–32). In More's time "the old organological concept distinguishing between head and limbs still prevailed, and the king was merely the head in which the mystical or political body of the realm culminated. In that sense, Henry VIII, in 1542, addressed his council: 'We be informed by our judges that we at no time stand so highly in our estate royal as in the time of Parliament, wherein we as head and you as members are conjoined and knit together in one body politic'" (Kantorowicz, p. 228).

112/6 **Exponit . . . rege.** Cf. Jean Gerson: "Secundum quod per naturalem instinctum omnia membra in uno solo corpore sese exponunt pro capitis salute, pariformiter esse debent in corpore mystico verorum subditorum ad suum dominum" (quoted by Kantorowicz, pp. 218–19).

113/1–6 **BONA . . . principem.** The verse form (dactylic hexameters alternating with iambic dimeters) is that of Horace's *Epodes* 14 and 15. Charles Clay Doyle has pointed out that Valerius Maximus (*Facta dictaque memorabilia* 6.2, Externa 2) tells of an old woman who prays for the tyrant Dionysius' life, having prayed for the death of his predecessors and seen each replaced by a worse. The story also appears in *Gesta Romanorum,* cap. 53 (ed. Hermann Oesterley [Berlin, 1872], p. 349) and in the *Facezie* of Lodovico Carbone (1435–82), ed. Abd-el-kader Salza (Livorno, 1900), no. 62, pp. 43–44. Cf. Erasmus, *ASD 4/1,* 138/67–68.

114/1–12 **TYRANNVM . . . manu.** Another variation on no. 107. Here sleep causes the tyrant to lose not only his supposed happiness but also his personal power.

114/9 **trunco . . . inani.** Cf. Juvenal's "truncoque similimus Hermae" (8.53), which More quotes in his *Letter to Dorp* (Rogers, no. 15, p. 55, line 951). Here and at 191/4 Brixius claims that the second syllable of "impar" ought to be long (Appendix B, 520/8–25). But Prudentius and Sidonius scan it short (Quicherat, p. 519). See the Introduction, p. 26.

115/1–3 **DE PRINCIPE . . . lupus.** In his note on *Utopia* 94/15 (*CW 4,* 367), Fr. Surtz traces the long tradition of the king as shepherd of his people. Charles Clay Doyle has pointed out that, apart from the boldness of calling a king a dog, this epigram varies the analogy between king and shepherd in a significant way: sheep enrich the shepherd but the sheepdog gains nothing from them. Cf. John 10:12.

117/2 **Clepticus.** This name (here translated "Snatch") is derived from κλεπτικός, "thievish."

117/5 **effugies . . . fugias.** Charles Clay Doyle has pointed out that Plutarch (*Moralia* 186E) tells the following anecdote about Alcibiades: "Summoned from Sicily by the Athenians to be tried for his life, he went into hiding, saying that it is silly for a man under indictment to seek a way to get off when he can get away." The Greek antithesis ἀποφυγεῖν . . . φυγεῖν parallels More's "effugies . . . fugias." Aelian (*Varia historia* 13.38.10) includes the same antithesis in his account of the incident.

118/1–6 **IN ASTROLOGVM . . . uidet.** Translated from *AP* XI, 159. *Pl.* II, 6 (εἰς ἀστρολόγους), 1, sig. K_4.

Τῷ πατρί μου τὸν ἀδελφὸν οἱ ἀστρολόγοι μακρόγηρων
  πάντες ἐμαντεύσανθ' ὡς ἀφ' ἑνὸς στόματος.
ἀλλ' Ἑρμοκλείδης, αὐτὸν μόνος εἶπε πρόμοιρον.
  εἶπε δ' ὅτ' αὐτὸν ἔσω νεκρὸν ἐκοπτόμεθα.

118/5 **prae.** Brixius (Appendix B, 530/22–532/4) rightly objected to More's use of *prae* as a preposition meaning "before (in time)," though it frequently has that sense as a prefix (as in "PRAEDIXIT" in the title of this poem). Perhaps More was led astray by πρόμοιρον, since πρό as a preposition frequently means "before (in time)." "Prae patre" might be strained to mean "in front of his father" (cf. Tacitus, *Annales* 14.35.1).

119/1–11 **IN HVIVS . . . extrahimur.** More expanded this parallel between the world and a prison in his *Four last thynges* (1522, *EW*, sig. fg_2v) and his *Dialogue of Comfort against Tribulation* (*CW 12*, 258–80, 428).

120/1–8 **REGEM . . . sibi.** Charles Clay Doyle has pointed out a parallel in Seneca's *De clementia* (1.19.6): "Non opus est instruere in altum editas arces . . . Salvum regem clementia in aperto praestabit. Unum est inexpugnabile munimentum amor civium." Cf. also Plutarch, *Moralia* 208B and Erasmus, *Institutio principis christiani* (*ASD 4/1*, 154–55, lines 584–89).

121/1–2 **POPVLVS . . . AVFERT.** In his notes on *CW 4*, 96/3 and 194/3, Fr. Surtz traced the idea that a true king rules over free and consenting subjects from Aristotle and Xenophon to Aquinas and Erasmus. For Erasmus' "notion that *consensus* was the true foundation of royal government" see James Tracy, *The Politics of Erasmus* (Toronto, Buffalo, and London, 1978), p. 35.

121/8 **precario?** Cf. Mommsen-Krueger, *1*, 750: "Precarium est, quod precibus petenti utendum conceditur tamdiu, quamdiu is qui concessit patitur. Quod genus liberalitatis ex iure gentium descendit. Et distat a donatione eo, quod qui donat, sic dat, ne recipiat, at qui precario concedit, sic dat quasi tunc recepturus, cum sibi libuerit precarium solvere."

122/1–8 **IN PERPVSILLVM . . . atomos.** Translated from *AP* XI, 103. *Pl.* II, 32 (εἰς λεπτούς), 8, sig. M_3.

Ἐξ ἀτόμων Ἐπίκουρος ὅλον τὸν κόσμον ἔγραψεν,
  εἶναι τοῦτο δοκῶν Ἄλκιμε λεπτότατον.
εἰ δὲ τότ' ἦν Διόφαντος, ἔγραψεν ἂν ἐκ Διοφάντου,
  τοῦ καὶ τῶν ἀτόμων πουλύ τι λεπτοτέρου.
ἢ τὰ μὲν ἄλλ' ἔγραψε συνεστάναι ἐξ ἀτόμων ἄν,
  ἐκ τούτου δ' αὐτὰς Ἄλκιμε τὰς ἀτόμους.

More departs from the Greek by changing the direct address, in midstream, from Alchimus to Diophantus.

123/1–6 **IN AMOREM . . . Hippolytum.** Translated from *AP* IX, 132. *Pl.* I, 77 (εἰς σωφροσύνην), 2, sig. H_7v.

Σωφροσύνη, καὶ ἔρως, κατ' ἐναντίον ἀλλήλοισιν
ἐλθόντες, ψυχὰς ὤλεσαν ἀμφότεροι.
Φαίδρην μὲν κτεῖνεν πυρόεις πόθος Ἱππολύτοιο,
Ἱππόλυτον δ' ἁγνὴ πέφνε σαοφροσύνη.

124/1–8 **IN VRBEM . . . Thessaliam.** Translated from *AP* IX, 387. *Pl.* I, 69 (εἰς πόλεις), 4, sig. H_1v.

Ἕκτορ, ἀρήϊον αἷμα, κατὰ χθονὸς εἴ που ἀκούεις,
χαῖρε, καὶ ἄμπνευσον βαιὸν ὑπὲρ πατρίδος.
Ἴλιον οἰκεῖται, κλεινὴ πόλις, ἄνδρας ἔχουσα
σοῦ μὲν ἀφαυροτέρους, ἀλλ' ἔτ' ἀρηϊφίλους.
Μυρμιδόνες δ' ἀπόλοντο. παρίστασο, καὶ λέγ' Ἀχιλλεῖ,
θεσσαλίην κεῖσθαι παισὶν ὑπ' Αἰνεάδαις.

One line of a translation by Germanicus Caesar (*Anthologia Latina,* no. 708) is very close to More's version: "Te Marte inferior, Martis amica tamen." But this resemblance is probably fortuitous, for Germanicus' translation seems to have survived in only one manuscript and was not printed until 1579 (*Poetae latini minores,* ed. Aemilius Baehrens, 6 vols. [Leipzig, 1879–86], *4,* 13). The title "IN VRBEM RHOMAM" rests on a misunderstanding of the Greek, which refers not to Rome as a new Ilium but to the city of Ilium itself, which was rebuilt by the Romans.

125/1–4 **DE MEDIOCRITATE . . . est.** Translated from *AP* XVI, 16. *PL.* I, 47 (εἰς μετριότητα), 2, sig. F_1v.

Πᾶν τὸ περιττὸν, ἄκαιρον, ἐπεὶ λόγος ἐστὶ παλαιὸς,
ὥς καὶ τοῦ μέλιτος τὸ πλέον ἐστὶ χολή.

125/3 **Ingratum . . . nimium est.** Cf. the proverb "nil nimis" (Otto, no. 1229; Walther, 16078), but More's phrasing is closer to Seneca (*De tranquillitate animi* 9.6): "Vitiosum est ubique, quod nimium est."

125/3–4 **amarum . . . nimium est.** Otto, no. 1083.

126/1–6 **IN VEHEMENTER . . . facit.** Translated from *AP* X, 63. *Pl.* I, 73 (εἰς πτωχούς), 2, sig. H_6.

Μηδέποτε ζήσας ὁ πένης βροτὸς, οὐδ' ἀποθνήσκει.
καὶ ζῆν γὰρ δοκέων, ὡς νέκυς ἦν ὁ τάλας.
οἱ δὲ τύχας μεγάλας, καὶ χρήματα πολλὰ λαχόντες,
οὗτοι τὸν θάνατον πτῶσιν ἔχουσι βίου.

127/1–6 **IN PYTHAGORAE . . . inueniens.** Translated from *AP* X, 46. *Pl.* I, 74 (εἰς σιωπήν), 1, sig. H_6v.

Ἡ μεγάλη παίδευσις ἐν ἀ[ν]θρώποισι, σιωπή.
  μάρτυρα Πυθαγόραν τὸν σοφὸν αὐτὸν ἔχω.
ὃς λαλέειν εἰδὼς, ἑτέρους ἐδίδασκε σιωπᾶν,
  φάρμακον ἡσυχίης ἐγκρατὲς εὑράμενος.

See Diogenes Laertius 8.10. The title transliterates ἐχεμυθία, a word used specifically to designate the Pythagorean precept of silence (Plutarch, *Life of Numa* 8.6 and *Table-talk* 8.1 [*Moralia* 728D]; Athenaeus 7.308D).

128/3 **loquitur taurus.** More may be thinking of the brazen bull of Phalaris (which changed human sounds into the lowings of a bull, Cicero, *De republica* 3.30.42) or of the Egyptian bulls which embodied Apis (which were oracular, Pliny, *Historia naturalis* 8.71.185), though, strictly speaking, neither spoke. Livy mentions a speaking ox (24.10.10).

128/3 **cadit imbre lapis.** There were frequent reports of stones falling like rain (probably meteor showers). See Cicero, *De divinatione* 1.43.98 and *De natura deorum* 2.5.14; Pomponius Mela, *De chorographia* 2.78; Livy 21.62.5, 23.31.15.

128/5 **uesper.** The neuter accusative *vesper* is extremely rare (Varro, *De lingua latina* 7.50 and 9.73). It may be a copyist's error, since the usual form *vesperum* would be metrically possible by elision with "heri."

129/1–8 **IN PALLADEM . . . satis.** Translated from *AP* IX, 576. *Pl.* I, 37 (εἰς θεούς), 8, sigs. D_8v–E_1.

Παρθένε Τριτογένεια, τί τὴν Κύπριν ἄρτι με λυπεῖς;
  ἁρπάξασα δ' ἐμὸν δῶρον, ἔχεις παλάμῃ;
μέμνησαι τὸ πάροιθεν ἐν Ἰδαίοις σκοπέλοισιν,
  ὡς Πάρις οὐ σὲ καλὴν, ἀλλ' ἔμ' ἐδογμάτισε;
σὸν· δόρυ, καὶ σάκος ἐστίν. ἐμὸν δὲ τὸ μῆλον ὑπάρχει.
  ἀρκεῖ τῷ μήλῳ κεῖνος ὁ πρὶν πόλεμος.

Aphrodite speaks to Pallas Athene, who holds an apple in her hand.

129/3 **Tritonia uirgo?** Cf. Vergil, *Aeneid* 11.483.

129/8 **Mars . . . malo.** The Greek means "Let that war of long ago [at Troy] be enough to claim the apple"—that is, do not start a new war over an apple. Perhaps More puns on "mālo" (apple) and "mălo" (evil). Plautus had made the same pun (*Amphitryon* 723–24).

130/1–9 **VITAM . . . fouet.** Translated from *AP* X, 75. *Pl.* I, 80 (εἰς ὑπεροψίαν), 3, sig. I_3.

> Ἠέρα λεπταλέον μυκτηρόθεν ἀμπνείοντες,
> ζώομεν, ἠελίου λαμπάδα δερκόμενοι,
> πάντες, ὅσοι ζῶμεν κατὰ τὸν βίον. ὄργανα δ' ἐσμὲν,
> αὔραις ζωογόνοις πνεύματα δεχνύμενοι.
> εἰ δέ τις οὖν ὀλίγην παλάμῃ σφίγξειεν ἀϋτμὴν,
> ψυχὴν συλήσας, εἰς ἀΐδην κατάγει.
> οὕτως οὐδὲν ἐόντες, ἀγηνορίῃ τρεφόμεσθα,
> πνοιῆς ἐξ ὀλίγης ἠέρα βοσκόμενοι.

130/4 **sed quae.** Brixius objected to "quae" alone in *1518* (Appendix B, 514/30–516/10), but the Greek (δ') shows that the omission was due to a copyist or a compositor.

130/8 **Plutoni . . . omnes.** *AP* X, 75 has here ἀγηνορίῃ τρεφόμεσθα, "we are nourished by pride." More substituted a phrase from *AP* X, 85 (*Pl.* I, 36 [εἰς θάνατον], 2, sig. D_6):

> πάντες τῷ θανάτῳ τηρούμεθα καὶ τρεφόμεσθα
> ὡς ἀγέλη χοίρων σφαζομένων ἀλόγως.

"We are all kept and fed for death, like a herd of swine to be slain without reason." "Plutoni" was perhaps suggested by ἀΐδην, which originally meant Hades, god of the underworld, but later came to mean simply "underworld, grave."

131/1–4 **PVGIONEM . . . mucro.** Cicero answers a weak argument with the exclamation "O plumbeum pugionem!" (*De finibus* 4.18.48).

131/2 **E GRAECO.** Charles Clay Doyle has pointed out a parallel in a saying of the philosopher Diogenes reported by Diogenes Laertius (6.65): "Noticing a handsome youth chattering in unseemly fashion, 'Are you not ashamed,' he said, 'to draw a dagger of lead from an ivory scabbard?'" In *Adagia* 625 (*Opera omnia,* 2, 272C) Erasmus quoted and translated the Greek.

132/5 **deteriora probat.** Cf. Ovid, *Metamorphoses* 7.20–21.

132/11 **Articulus . . . facit?** In *1518* this poem is followed by no. 270, which does not appear in *1520*.

133/1–2 **MINISTRVM . . . conuiua.** Unless we take the "ministrum" of the title in the general sense "steward, official," it seems to conflict with "conuiua" in the poem.

134/1–5 **DE CANE . . . tuam.** More may have found hints in the fable of the dog who loses a piece of meat when he goes after its shadow in the water. See Perry, *Aesopica,* no. 133, p. 372, and Hervieux, *2,* 765, no. 73. Cf. also the fable of the fox who loses a rooster when he opens his mouth to taunt his pursuers (Hervieux, *2,* 772, no. 258) and *CW 6,* 369/20–22 and Commentary.

134/4 **captas.** This word has strong overtones of legacy-hunting (as in Jonson's *Volpone*). See *Digesta* 29.6.1 (Mommsen-Krueger, *1,* 453).

135/1–6 **CANIS . . . prohibet.** Cf. Perry, *Aesopica,* p. 276; *Fabulae Aesopicae Collectae,* ed. Karl Halm (Leipzig, 1889), no. 228, p. 111; Hervieux *2,* 290, no. 66; Whiting H565; Tilley, D513; Erasmus, *Adagia* 913 (*Opera omnia,* 2, 371F). For other examples see Doyle, "Background," p. 62.

135/4 **indat.** Brixius rightly objected to More's scansion "ēdăt" instead of "ĕdăt" in *1518* (Appendix B, 520/26–522/13). "Indat" corrects the meter but hardly improves the sense. In using "indo" in this way More may have had in mind Plautus, *Casina* 247.

136/1–4 **IN ORESTEM . . . papillae.** Translated from *AP* IX, 126. *Pl.* I, 29 (εἰς εὐχαρίστους καὶ ἀχαρίστους), 5 (τίνας ἂν εἴποι λόγους Κλυταιμνήστρα, μέλλοντος αὐτὴν σφάξειν 'Ορέστου), sig. C_7v:

> Πῇ ξίφος ἰθύνεις; κατὰ γαστέρος, ἢ κατὰ μαζῶν;
> γαστὴρ, ἥ σ' ἐλόχευσεν· ἀνεθρέψοντα δὲ μαζοί.

The epigram is imagined as spoken by Clytemnestra to Orestes as he is about to stab her.

137/1–3 **QVOD . . . rogere.** Translated from *AP* X, 108. *Pl.* I, 30 (εἰς εὐχήν), 4, sig. C_8.

> Ζεῦ βασιλεῦ, τὰ μὲν ἐσθλὰ καὶ εὐχομένοις, καὶ ἀνεύκτοις
> ἄμμι δίδου. τὰ δὲ λυγρὰ, καὶ εὐχομένων ἀπερύκοις.

For the revision cf. the note to no. 47. The first two lines of *1518* are closest to the Greek. The third line of *1518* was apparently intended as a substitute for the second. In *1520* More changed "petare" to "rogere." But the passive of either word, followed by an accusative ("nulla") seems to be almost unprecedented (Kühner-Stegmann, *2/1,* 301). But see the Introduction, p. 32.

138/1–4 **IN DIGAMOS . . . freto.** *AP* IX, 133. *Pl.* I, 15 (εἰς γάμον), 1, sig. B_4.

> Εἴ τις ἅπαξ γήμας, πάλι δεύτερα λέκτρα διώκει,
> ναυηγὸς πλώει δὶς βυθὸν ἀργαλέον.

Brixius objected to "capit uxorem" for the more usual "ducit uxorem" (Appendix B, 532/5–15), but *capere* is frequently used in the sense "choose" (*TLL*, s.v. III A 1 b) and Plautus (*Trinummus* 64) uses "ignotam [uxorem] capere" to mean "take an unknown wife." For More's second marriage in 1511, within a month of the death of his first wife, see Allen, *4*, 19.

139/1–10 **DE SOMNO . . . ferunt.** Cf. Lucian, *The Dream or the Cock*, which presents the miseries of the rich and a poor man's happy dream of wealth. Erasmus' translation of this dialogue, together with More's translations of Lucian, was published at Paris in 1506 and 1514 (*Opera omnia, ASD 1/1*, 472–87). Cf. nos. 107, 108, 110.

139/9 **uerae.** *1563* gives this more correct reading. *1520* changed "false" to "falsae" in line 10, but neglected to change "uere" to "uerae." The diphthong *ae* was frequently printed *e* or *ę* in the early sixteenth century, but not in *1518* or *1520*.

140/1–8 **IN DEFORMEM . . . uelit?** Translated from *AP* XI, 412. *Pl.* II, 43 (εἰς πονηρούς), 13, sig. N_1.

> Ψυχὴν μὲν γράψαι, χαλεπόν. μορφὴν δὲ χαράξαι,
> ῥᾴδιον. ἀλλ' ἐπὶ σοὶ τοὔμπαλιν ἀμφότερα.
> τῆς μὲν γὰρ ψυχῆς τὸ διάστροφον ἔξω ἄγουσα
> ἐν τοῖς φαινομένοις ἡ φύσις εἰργάσατο.
> τὸν δ' ἐπὶ τῆς μορφῆς θόρυβον, καὶ σώματος ὕβριν,
> πῶς ἄν τις γράψῃ, μήδ' ἐσιδεῖν ἐθέλων;

140/7 **formae . . . membra.** The Greek uses μορφή consistently in the simple sense of "outward appearance" but achieves witty dissonance in σώματος ὕβριν, since ὕβρις is not a bodily but a moral quality. More substitutes "corpus" for μορφὴν in line 1 (where he could easily have written "formam") but in line 7 he puns on "formae . . . deformia." "Deformia" clearly refers to bodily ugliness, but "forma," in the Aristotelian hylomorphism dominant in the schools, designated the invisible active principle of an essence, and man's "form" was regularly identified with his soul. *Forma* also regularly meant "corporal beauty" (as in no. 143/53) so that it pinpoints the contrast between inner and outer qualities.

141/1–4 **IN CAPPADOCEM . . . Cappadocis.** Translated from *AP* XI, 237. *Pl.* II, 43 (εἰς πονηρούς), 9, sig. M_8v.

Καππαδόκην πότ' ἔχιδνα κακὴ δάκεν, ἀλλὰ καὶ αὐτὴ
κάτθανε, γευσαμένη αἵματος ἰοβόλου.

In both the Palatine and Planudean anthologies the next epigram begins: "The Cappadocians are always bad." See also Martial 6.85.3; Lucan 3.244.

142/1–6 **IN STATVAM . . . auaritia.** Translated from *AP* XI, 270. *Pl.* II, 50 (εἰς φειδωλούς), 19 (εἰς εἰκόνα 'Αναστασίου βασιλέως ἐν τῷ 'Ευρίπῳ), sig. O_2v.

Εἰκόνα σοι βασιλεῦ κοσμοφθόρε τήνδε σιδήρου
ἄνθεσαν, ὡς χαλκοῦ πολλὸν ἀτιμοτέρην,
ἀντὶ φόνου, πενίης τ' ὀλοῆς, λιμοῦ τε, καὶ ὀργῆς.
οἷς πάντας φθείρεις ἐκ φιλοχρημοσύνης.

142/5 **acris.** As Garrod (p. 184) suggests, "furor aeris, egestas" in *1518* and *1520* is almost surely a misprint for "furor, acris egestas," which matches the Greek perfectly. Cf. Lucretius 3.65: "acris egestas." But More may have intended an ironical contrast between the "fury of bronze" (weapons or money used in war) and the bronze lacking in the tyrant's statue (line 4).

142/6 **quis.** The meter (quīs) shows that this is an archaic form of *quibus.*

143/1–234 **VERSVS . . . ditior.** This poem appeared on sigs. M_2–M_3 of *De generibus ebriosorum et ebrietate vitanda, jocus quodlibeti erphurdien. lepidissimus* [by Jacob Hartlieb] . . . *item de meretricum in suos amatores, et concubinarum in sacerdotes fide* [auctore Paulo Oleario], printed by Gregorius Comiander at Worms (Gibson, no. 338, and J. G. Theodor Graesse, *Trésor de livres rares et précieux,* 7 vols. [Dresden, 1859–69], 2, 343–44). In the Bodleian copy of this edition the date 1515 appears at the end of the preface (the edition is otherwise undated). But the Bodleian copy of another edition of *De generibus ebriosorum* (which does not contain More's poem), printed at Nürnberg and dated 1516, retains the date 1515 at the end of the preface. According to Nicolas Barker, the three copies of this work in the British Library, none of which contains More's poem, belong to two editions (Erfurt, Matthaeus Maler, n.d. [September–October 1515] and Mainz, Johann Schoeffer, 1516; Proctor and Isaac, nos. 11241 and 9860); on typographic grounds it is clear that the Mainz edition is derived from the Erfurt edition. In the Worms edition the text of More's poem is identical with that in *1518,* even to the spelling and the technical description of the meter in the title; it may well have been reprinted from *1518.* More's poem was reprinted in the pamphlet *Rythmus Codri* [Antonii

Urcei] *festiuissimus. Carmen Mori urbanissimum. I* [sic] *Lusus Camicziani uerissimus* (Leipzig, Melchior Lotter, 1519, sigs. A_3v–B_1v), and part of it appeared in Addison and Steele's *The Guardian,* no. 163, September 16, 1713 (Gibson, no. 160).

More's poem bears some resemblance to a *declamatio suasoria,* a kind of rhetorical exercise practiced in the schools (Lausberg, *1,* 548–49). More's answer to Lucian's *Tyrannicide* is an example of another sort of *declamatio,* the *controversia* (see *CW 3/1,* xxxii–xxxiv, 152–54). The *suasoria* was a speech giving advice on some point, often in historical circumstances or in the imaginary language of a historical character. In *De conscribendis epistolis,* Erasmus gave an example of an *epistola suasoria* persuading a young man to marry which uses some of the same arguments and examples as More (*ASD 1/2,* 411, line 12; 412, line 1; 421, lines 17–23; 423, lines 20–21). More follows Quintilian's opinion (3.8.6, 3.8.59) that in a *suasoria* a formal exordium is unnecessary (Erasmus gives similar advice in *De conscribendis epistolis, ASD 1/2,* 323). His *narratio* is a simple statement of the occasion (it is time for Candidus to marry—a duty for one of his high station in life). The proposition follows: one should not choose a wife for the sake of beauty or money. The confirmation describes the qualities and advantages of a good wife and concludes with a series of examples. The peroration recapitulates the point that one should not marry for beauty or money. What is quite uncharacteristic of the usual *suasoria,* however, is the elegance and ease of More's poem, emphasized by the flow of syntax under the ripple of the meter. Quintilian had found it necessary to decry the excessive vehemence of the ordinary *suasoria* and to advise moderation (3.8.59–60).

A nine-line poem entitled "De electione coniugii" in *Anthologia Latina* (no. 224) advises that a wife be chosen for beauty and character, not for money.

143/1–2 **IAMBICI DIMETRI BRACHYCATALECTICI.** The line consists of an iambic dimeter (four iambs) minus the last two syllables—what in English prosody would be called iambic trimeter. The verse form was not used by ancient poets. But it is mentioned by Servius, *De centum metris* (Keil, *4,* 458): "[Metrum] euripidium constat dimetro [iambico] brachycatalecto, ut est hoc, 'Aiax furit dolens.'" Niccolò Perotti (*Grammatica . . . cum additionibus regularum et metrice artis* [Deventer, Richard Pafraet, April 11, 1504], sig. R_8) and Giovanni Sulpizio (*. . . de versuum scansione . . . De pedibus & diuersis generibus carminum precepta* [Venice, Ioannes Tacuinus de Tridino, September 24, 1516], sig. E_3) both quote Servius, but give a different example: "deae decus meum" (see notes to

274/12, 274/16, 274/26–31, below). More's meter here bears some resemblance, in its use of rhyming short lines, to current Latin modes (rhyming prose, the liturgical sequence) and English verse forms (court song, Skeltonics); see Nelson, *John Skelton,* pp. 87–101. But More's verse is basically quantitative, not accentual, and his use of rhyme and *similiter cadentes* is less insistent and more subtle than in those Latin and English forms.

143/4–14 **Iam . . . coniugem.** Cf. Terence, *Andria* 444–47.

143/29 **candida.** "Beautiful," but playing on the name Candidus ("upright, frank") in line 27.

143/76–80 **Vt mater . . . exprimat.** Cf. Alexander Barclay, *The Ship of Fools* (1509), ed. T. H. Jamieson, 2 vols. (Edinburgh, 1874), *1,* 236:

> An olde prouerbe hath longe agone be sayde
> That oft the sone in maners lyke wyll be
> Vnto the Father, and in lyke wyse the mayde
> Or doughter, vnto the mother wyll agre

143/80 **Insugat.** *Insugere* does not appear in the classical or medieval dictionaries, but it seems to be such a natural formation that Brixius and others have not noticed it.

143/100–101 **Proculque . . . silentium.** More described Jane Shore as "neque silentio rustico, neque immodica dicacitate notabilis" (*CW* 2, 56/5).

143/105 **apta literis.** Erasmus says that More provided for the education of his first wife, Jane Colt: "Hanc et literis instituendam curauit et omni musices genere doctam reddidit" (Allen, *4,* 18).

143/125 **iuuauerit.** Brixius objected to this form (instead of the usual "iuuerit") here and in line 138 (Appendix B, 526/13–26). But Forcellini still gives the perfect form *iuvavi,* though he admits he cannot find certain examples of it. More could have reasonably surmised that *iuvavi* was used in ancient times from the survival of the future participle *iuvaturus* in Sallust, *Jugurtha* 47.2 and Pliny, *Epistolae* 4.15.3. *Adiuvavi* also appears in *Corpus iuris civilis,* Digesta 34.9.5, 40.2.15 (Mommsen-Krueger, *1,* 178, 426).

143/131 **plectra personant.** Brixius objected to "plectra personat" in *1518* (Appendix B, 526/27–30). This would be an acceptable though postclassical construction (Lewis-Short, s.v. *persono,* IIC), but More probably wrote "personant" ("personāt"), which became changed in transmission. *Plectra personant* in the sense "the pluck resounds" is barely acceptable (Lewis-Short, s.v. *persono,* I A).

143/161–62 **improbo Labore.** Cf. Vergil, *Georgics* 1.145–46: "labor omnia vicit/improbus. . . ."

143/165–68 **Nasonis . . . filiam.** The gifted Perilla, to whom Ovid addressed *Tristia* 3.7, was probably his stepdaughter. Cf. *Tristia* 3.7.12: "doctaque non patrio carmina more canis?"

143/173 **Tulliam.** Tullia (c. 78–45 B.C.) was the beloved daughter of Cicero.

143/174–79 **quae tulit . . . parens.** See note to 19/172.

143/183–200 **Vnam . . . patriae.** This unmarried lady, presumably of high birth, who apparently resides in Britain but is renowned throughout the world, has not been identified. Wolfgang Mann, in *Lateinische Dichtung in England vom Ausgang des Frühhumanismus bis zum Regierungsantritt Elisabeths* (Halle/Saale, 1939), p. 59, suggests that "Cassandra" stands for Princess Margaret, Henry VIII's sister, and uses this assumption to date the poem before 1502, the year of her marriage. But she could just as easily stand for Henry's other sister, Mary, who was married in 1514. James Hutton has suggested Catherine of Aragon, who was married to Prince Arthur on November 14, 1501 ("A Speculation on Two Passages in the Latin Poems of Thomas More" in *Essays on Renaissance Poetry,* ed. Rita Guerlac [Ithaca, N.Y., and London, 1980], pp. 230–38). In no. 19/165–73 Catherine is praised in a comparison with famous ladies of ancient times, some of whom, like Cassandra, have ominous overtones (see note to 19/176–79). But "perlata pennulis Famae" (lines 194–95) does not necessarily mean "brought *hither*" to outlying Britain on the wings of fame; it may simply mean "carried far and wide." "Monet" (line 193) does not necessarily mean "gives warning" to remotest Britain (we know of no such warning from Catherine), but may mean simply "instructs."

143/192–93 **ultimam . . . Britanniam.** Cf. Catullus 11.11–12 ("ultimosque Britannos") and 29.4 ("ultima Britannia").

143/194–195 **pennulis . . . uolucribus.** Cf. Vergil, *Aeneid* 4.180: "[famae] pernicibus alis."

143/216 **mea.** If this is understood to mean "my [wife]," it could refer to More's first wife Jane (whom he married in late 1504 or early 1505) or to his second wife Alice (see above, note to 138/1–4). But it may refer to a sweetheart or fiancée.

143/223 **Carbone nigrior.** A proverbial expression (Otto, no. 349; Whiting, C324; Tilley, C458). Cf. Appendix C, 658/13–14.

143/226 **Olore pulchrior.** A proverbial simile for feminine beauty (Otto, no. 495; Whiting, S929–30).

143/231–34 **Iro . . . ditior.** Cf. Ovid, *Tristia* 3.7.42: "Irus et est subito, qui modo Croesus erat." See notes to 40/5 and 143/165–68.

144/2 **Thrasonis.** Thraso is the name of a braggart soldier in Terence's *Eunuch.*

144/14–15 **In pectus . . . abderem.** Cf. *Aeneid* 2.553: "lateri capulo tenus abdidit ensem."

145/1–6 **DE MEDIOCRITATE . . . placet.** Translated from *AP* IX, 110. *Pl.* I, 12 (εἰς αὐτάρκειαν), 2, sig. B_1v.

> Οὐ στέργω βαθυληΐους ἀρούρας,
> οὐκ ὄλβον πολύχρυσον οἷα Γύγης.
> αὐτάρκους ἔραμαι βίου Μακρῖνε.
> τὸ μηθὲν γὰρ ἄγαν, ἄγαν με τέρπει.

The Greek meter is phaleucian (hendecasyllabic); More writes iambic trimeters.

145/4 **Gygis.** More wrongly takes the first syllable of this word as short. See the note to 89/3.

145/6 **nihil nimis.** Otto, no. 1229; Walther, 16078. See note to 125/3, above.

146/1–4 **HECTOR . . . leonis.** Translated from *AP* XVI, 4. *Pl.* I, 5 (εἰς ἀνδρειαν καὶ ἀνδρείους), 14 (τίνας [ἂν εἴποι] λόγους ὁ αὐτὸς [sc. Ἕκτωρ] τιτρωσκόμενος ὑπὸ Ἑλλήνων), sig. A_6.

> Βάλλετε νῦν μετὰ πότμον ἐμὸν δέμας, ὄττι καὶ αὐτοὶ
> νεκροῦ σῶμα λέοντος ἐφυβρίζουσι λαγωοί.

146/3 **Proijcitote.** More seems to have misunderstood Βάλλετε, which here means "hurl [weapons] at, strike," for he translates as if it meant "throw out, dispose of." But βάλλω can be applied to persons in the sense "throw" (Liddell-Scott, s.v. II 2 b).

147/1 **STVLTVM POETAM.** The poet satirized is Pietro Carmeliano, Latin secretary to Henry VII. His unfortunate phrase occurred in a poem written in 1508 to celebrate the betrothal of Princess Mary to Charles of Castile (. . . *honorifica gesta solemnes cerimonie & triumphi* . . . ,

London, R. Pynson [1508], *STC* 4659). See Nelson, *John Skelton,* p. 36, where the line is quoted: "Henricus frater / princeps cui nemo secundus."

147/2–3 **Scripserat . . . nemini.** Carmeliano paraphrased Vergil, *Aeneid* 1.544–45:

rex erat Aeneas nobis, quo iustior alter
nec pietate fuit, nec bello maior et armis.

148/1–22 **IN QVENDAM . . . libro.** This poem was first published at Paris on July 7, 1517 by Badius Ascensius as a commendatory poem in the front (sig. A_2) of a book of hymns for the liturgical year by Bernard André: *Hymni Christiani Bernardi Andreae poetae Regii, multiiugo metrorum genere compositi per totius anni circulum: In quos sunt plurimorum illustrium virorum carmina commendatiua in fronte & post calcem ponenda* (*Inventaire chronologique,* 2, no. 1511). (I have consulted a microfilm of the copy in the British Library.) The text presents no substantive variants from *1518* and *1520* but the heading is "In Hymnos Bernardi Andreae Tolosatis poetae regii, Thomae mori Hexadecastichon." The dedication to Henry VII in André's volume (sig. A_3) does not say what the heading of *1518* and *1520* reports but rather that André, being over fifty-six years old, after Christmas 1509, in the second regnal year of Henry VIII (which, however, began on April 25, 1510), wrote these poems as a sort of penance for the sins of his youth. He resembles Prudentius, he says, in age but not in wit or elegance, but he calls his work "castigatum" and points out that he imitates the meters of Boethius and Horace's odes. At the end of his poems, in a brief plea for Henry's indulgence, André does say that he wrote his poems "fere ex tempore." More may not have written the heading in *1518* and *1520,* which could have been derived from More's poem itself; on the other hand, More may have seen André's poems in manuscript, with a different preface. More's poem follows a commendatory poem by Faustus Andrelinus and is followed by the laudatory verses of William Lily, Erasmus, and Guilielmus Gualterus; all of them praise André's poetry in a straightforward way, stressing his superiority to pagan poets because of his subject matter. William Nelson (*John Skelton,* pp. 35–36) suggests quite rightly that More's "'eulogy' savors strongly of double meanings," but it is written with such delicate ambiguity that in its original setting the irony is not immediately apparent. In his poem "Ad lectorem" (sig. A_3v) André is so smug about the superiority of his subject matter that he confidently consigns a long list of Greek and Latin heroes and poets to hell fire and damnation. The volume concludes with two commendatory poems by Andreas Ammonius and Ioannes Boerius Genuensis (sigs. L_2v–L_3), André's reply to Boerius, and two poems addressed by André to More (sig. L_3):

Ad Morum de eodem carmen trimetrum
Trochaicum, acatalecticum.

Nunc iambeis trochaicum metiar
Damno chori parumper obsequere
More sub tua tamen lima recinens
Finies paucis quod optarunt proceres.

Ad eundem trochaicum tetrametrum Acatalecticum.

More quod iubes trochaeo lusitauimus probe
Quo Boerio Ioanni gratias rependimus:
Hymnulos qui non disertos laudat & probat meos
Quicquid autem laudis ille buccinat velut Maro
Ecce soli Christe tibi reddimus perenniter.

Both these poems are catalectic, not acatalectic. The scansion and the meaning of the first (especially the first two lines) is far from certain but it may mean: "Now I will measure out a trochaic poem to add to the iambics. Indulge a while the loss suffered by the [heavenly] choir. More, if you sing it again under your polishing file, you will complete in a few [verses] what the courtiers desired." He seems to be writing about his own verses in reply to Boerius, but they are metrically so chaotic that it is hard to say whether they are iambic or trochaic. The second poem may be translated: "I have quite fulfilled the exercise you set me by offering my thanks to Boerius in a trochaic poem. He praises my unlearned little hymns and approves of them. Whatever praise he trumpets forth like another Vergil, behold, we render it always, Christ, to you alone." Cf. no. 240. On André see Emden, *1*, 33, and Gilbert Tournoy, "Two Poems Written by Erasmus for Bernard André," *Humanistica Lovaniensia,* 27 (1978), 45–51.

148/8 **mira cum breuitate.** Brixius was wrong when he asserted that "cum" ought to have been omitted from this phrase (Appendix B, 532/16–25). When an adjective accompanies an ablative of manner, *cum* is often omitted but it is also often included, and by many good writers such as Cicero (Kühner-Stegmann, 2/*1*, 410–11).

148/18 **ibi libertas . . . est.** 2 Cor. 3:17: "Dominus autem Spiritus est: Ubi autem Spiritus Domini, ibi libertas."

149/1–8 **IN STRATOPHONTA . . . neges.** Translated from *AP* XI, 77. *Pl.* II, 1 (εἰς ἀγωνιστάς) 2, sig. K_1v.

Εἰκοσέτους σωθέντος Ὀδυσσέος εἰς τὰ πατρῷα,
ἔγνω τὴν μορφὴν ἀργὸς ἰδὼν ὁ κύων.

ἀλλὰ σὺ πυκτεύσας Στρατοφῶν ἐπὶ τέσσαρας ὥρας,
  οὐ κυσὶν ἄγνωστος, τῇ δὲ πόλει γέγονας.
ἢν ἐθέλῃς δὲ πρόσωπον ἰδεῖν ἐς ἔσοπτρα σεαυτοῦ,
  οὐκ εἰμὶ Στρατοφῶν αὐτὸς ἐρεῖς ὀμόσας.

149/4 **celeri.** More's Greek, like the editions of Lascaris (1494) and Aldus (1503), probably had ἀργὸς, the adjective, not Ἄργος, the name of Odysseus' dog (*Odyssey* 17.292). But he knew that the dog's name was derived from the adjective and he may have intended "celeri" as a name (just as in English we might translate "Speedy" or "Swift-foot," not "Argos").

150/1–6 **IN PVGILEM . . . deus.** Translated from *AP* XI, 161. *Pl.* II, 6 (εἰς ἀστρολόγους), 4, sig. K_4v.

Πρὸς τὸν μάντιν Ὄλυμπον Ὀνήσιμος ἦλθεν ὁ πύκτης,
  εἰ μέλλει γηρᾶν βουλόμενος προμαθεῖν.
κἀκεῖνος ναί φησιν, ἐὰν ἤδη καταλύσῃς.
  ἂν δέ γε πυκτεύῃς, ὡροθετεῖ σε Κρόνος.

150/3 **Nesimus.** Perhaps More dropped the first syllable of the Greek name not only for metrical reasons but also because the Greek word means "useful, profitable."

150/6 **gelidus . . . deus.** More's vivid periphrasis for Κρόνος derives from the medieval tradition which changed the cold, malevolent, planetary Saturn into the figure of Father Time with his scythe. See Erwin Panofsky, *Studies in Iconology: Humanistic Themes in the Art of the Renaissance* (New York, Evanston, and London, 1939; reprint, 1962), pp. 69–93. "Tyme" appeared in the seventh "pageant" picture for which More wrote verses (see no. 272), apparently without his sickle or scythe but "with horyloge in hande" (*EW*, sig. ¶$_3$v).

151/1–4 **IN PARASITVM . . . putes.** Translated from *AP* XI, 208. *Pl.* II, 31 (εἰς λαιμάργους), 4, sig. M_2.

Ἦν βραδὺς Εὐτιχίδης σταδιοδρόμος, ἀλλ' ἐπὶ δεῖπνον
  ἔτρεχεν, ὥστε λέγειν, Εὐτυχίδης πέταται.

151/4 **nempe.** This word is very awkward here—perhaps a clumsy reminiscence of Horace, *Sermones* 1.10.1.

152/1–6 **IN BIBONEM . . . mihi.** Translated from *AP* XI, 8. *Pl.* II, 47 (συμποτικὰ ἀστεῖσματα), 3, sigs. N_3–N_3v.

Μὴ μύρα, μὴ στεφάνους λιθίναις στήλαισι χαρίζου,
  μὴ δὲ τὸ πῦρ φλέξῃς. εἰς κενὸν ἡ δαπάνη.

ζῶντί μοι εἴ τι θέλεις, χάρισαι, τέφρην δὲ μεθύσκων,
πηλὸν ποιήσεις, κοὐχ ὁ θανὼν τίεται.

The Greek verses actually appear on a tombstone (*CIL, 6,* 14672), but in the Planudean collection this epigram and no. 153 appear under the heading "witticisms suitable to a drinking party," so that the heading "In Bibonem" is not inappropriate.

152/6 **non . . . mihi.** More substituted this phrase for the last four Greek words, which provide a rather flat conclusion ("a dead man is not honored"). The Palatine Anthology has the more forceful reading πίεται ("will not drink").

153/1–4 **IN BIBONEM . . . ueni.** Translated from *AP* XI, 43. *Pl.* II, 47 (συμποτικὰ ἀστεῖσματα), 41, sig. N_8.

Δός μοι τοὐκ γαίης πεπονημένον ἁδὺ κύπελλον,
ἆς γενόμην, καὶ ὑφ' ᾇ κείσομ' ἀποφθίμενος.

See note to 152/1–6.

153/3 **E terra . . . recondar.** Cf. Gen. 3:19: "In sudore vultus tui vesceris pane, donec revertaris in terram de qua sumptus es: quia pulvis es et in pulverem reverteris." The passage was especially well known because of the formula used in the Sarum rite when applying the ashes on Ash Wednesday: "Memento homo quia cinis es; et in cinerem reverteris" (Dickinson, col. 134). The Roman missal had "pulvis" and "pulverem" (*Missale Romanum Mediolani, 1474,* ed. Robert Lippe, 2 vols., Henry Bradshaw Society 17 and 33 [London, 1899 and 1907], *1,* 48 and *2,* 33).

154/1–4 **IN MVLIEREM . . . iterum inspiceres.** Translated from *AP* XI, 266. *Pl.* II, 13 (εἰς δυσειδεῖς), 9, sig. L_1v.

Ψευδὲς ἔσοπτρον ἔχει Δημοσθενίς. εἰ γὰρ ἀληθὲς
ἔβλεπεν, οὐκ ἂν ὅλως ἤθελεν αὐτὸ βλέπειν.

155/1–4 **IN FOEDAM . . . Antipatra.** Translated from *AP* XI, 201. *Pl.* II, 13 (εἰς δυσειδεῖς), 8, sig. L_1v.

'Αντιπάτραν γυμνὴν εἴ τις Πάρθοισιν ἔδειξεν,
ἔκτοθεν ἂν στηλῶν Ἡρακλέους ἔφυγον.

More's Latin does not express the meaning of the Greek, which may be translated: "If anyone had shown Antipatra naked to the Parthians, they would have fled outside the Pillars of Heracles." The name Antipatra, which means "over against the fatherland," may have suggested that she fled from her native country Parthia on the extreme east of the civilized world to Gibraltar on the extreme west. More's Greek text may also have had the error ἔφυγεν for ἔφυγον. Perhaps More intended to intensify the meaning by saying she was so ugly that if anyone saw her naked she would flee from civilized society to the barbarous Parthians or the uninhabited Atlantic. Since the Planudean heading is "ugly persons," it seems unlikely that the title "In foedam" was erroneously supplied by some editor and that More intended to praise Antipatra's modesty. Garrod (p. 184) suggests that More wrote "a Parthis."

156/1–4 **IN FOEDAM . . . tenebras.** Translated from *AP* XI, 287. *Pl.* II, 13 (εἰς δυσειδεῖς), 12, sig. L_1v.

> Ὁ τὴν γυναῖκα τὴν ἄμορφον δυστυχῶν,
> λύχνους ἀνάψας ἑσπέρας, σκότος βλέπει.

The Greek lines are in iambic trimeter, but More translated them into an elegiac distich.

157/1–4 **IN BARBA . . . Plato?** Translated from *AP* XI, 430. *Pl.* II, 52 (εἰς φιλοσόφους), 8, sig. O_4.

> Εἰ τὸ τρέφειν πώγωνα δοκεῖ σοφίαν περιποιεῖν,
> καὶ τράγος εὐπώγων, εὔστολός ἐστι Πλάτων.

The quip about the beards of philosophers and goats was proverbial. See Erasmus, *Adagia* 195 (*Opera omnia,* 2, 104DE) and his *Moriae encomium, ASD 4/3,* 80, line 152; Bebel, *Facetiae,* p. 17.

158/4–5 **Si patiare . . . caput.** As Charles Clay Doyle has pointed out, in *The dictes or sayengis of the philosophhres* (trans. Anthony Woodville [London, W. Caxton, 1477], *STC* 6826), Diogenes says: "If thou yeue power to thy wyff onely to trede upon thy fote on the morowe she wold trede upon thy hede" (fol. 24[r]). For other fifteenth-century translations before Woodville's, see *Dicts or Sayings of the Philosophers,* ed. Curt F. Bühler, Early English Text Society, Original Series no. 211 (London, 1941).

159/1–9 **EPITAPHIVM . . . caelitibus.** Henry Abyngdon (c. 1418–c. September 1497), singer, organist, and composer, was the first recipient of a Bachelor of Music degree at Cambridge (1463). He became succentor (deputy to the precentor) at Wells Cathedral on November 24, 1447. He was master of the boys in the Chapel Royal from 1455 to 1478 and master of St. Catherine's Hospital in Bristol after 1478. See *Grove's Dictionary of Music and Musicians,* 5th ed., 10 vols., ed. Eric Blom (London, 1954–61), *1,* 19; and W. H. Grattan Flood, "Henry Abyngdon, Mus. Bac., Choirmaster of the King's Chapel in 1455," *Musical Times,* June 1,

1911, pp. 377–78. For a literary analysis, thematic and stylistic, of this poem and the next two, considered as a single unit, see Susan L. Holahan, "More's Epigrams on Henry Abyngdon," *Moreana, 17* (1968), 21–26.

160/1–9 **ALTERVM . . . poli.** This "poem" is written in leonine verse: quantitative hexameters (sometimes combined with pentameters, as in line 9) in which the word preceding the caesura rhymes with the last word in each line. Erasmus wrote a mocking leonine couplet (Reedijk, Appendix I, no. 5, p. 387). The form was practiced from the ninth to the fifteenth century; F. J. E. Raby called it "one of the most unhappy devices that poets have ever made use of" (*A History of Secular Latin Poetry in the Middle Ages,* 2 vols., 2nd ed. [Oxford, 1957], 2, 1 and 348). More included here some obviously false quantities: "hic" (line 4), "mille" (line 6), "ista" (line 7). Brixius admitted that More wrote this poem as a jest, but he claimed More was fit only for such clownish poetry (Appendix B, 508/500–510/519 and 546/7–12).

160/7 **orgaquenista.** Such a division (called tmesis) was a recognized figure in classical poetry (Quintilian, *Institutio oratoria* 8.6.66; Servius on *Aeneid* 1.412), but it was rare (Vergil, *Georgics* 3.381; Ennius, *Annales* 609–10) and not applied to enclitics. More was probably mocking the first verse of chapter 2 ("De figuris barbarismi et soloecismi") in *Graecismus,* a medieval grammar by Ebrardus Bethuniensis (ed. Johannes Wrobel, Breslau, 1887, p. 10): "Est *soloecismus* uitium ceu *barba*que *rismus.*" Erasmus criticized this well-known grammar (*Antibarbari, ASD 1/1,* 61). Possibly More is thinking of the startling tmesis in the first line of a famous and widespread sequence for the feast of Mary's nativity: "Alle caeleste necnon et perenne luia" (*Analecta Hymnica Medii Aevi, 53* [Leipzig, 1911], no. 197; Dickinson, col. 896). The tmesis was ridiculed by purists in the eighteenth century (see Jean Evenou, "De la prose au cantique," *La Maison-Dieu, 145* [1981], 80). But the division of "Alleluia" was probably related to the manner of choral performance. The typography of *1520* (orgaq́ȝ nista) highlights the oddity of inserting the enclitic *–que* within "organista."

160/9 **orbe soli.** The combination of circular and flat is part of the parody. The form "sibi" instead of "ei" is a medievalism.

161/7 **lactucas . . . labra.** A proverbial expression ("like lips, like lettuce") used when stupidity finds matching stupidity. See Erasmus, *Adagia* 971, *Opera omnia, 2,* 386D; Otto, no. 896; Whiting, L372; Tilley, L326.

161/13 **Talpa.** Erasmus, *Adagia* 255: "Talpa caecior" (*Opera omnia, 2,* 133F). Otto, no. 1739.

162/6–7 **indignatio . . . mors est.** Cf. Prov. 16:14: "Indignatio regis nuntii mortis." See also Roper, p. 71; Henkel-Schöne, col. 378; Erasmus, *Adagia* 1411 (*Opera omnia,* 2, 557D).

163/1 **TYNDALVM.** John H. Marsden, in *Philomorus* (London, 1878), p. 236, says that the Tyndal of this epigram was William Tyndale, the biblical translator. Marsden bases his argument on the similarity between this epigram and an anecdote in one of Hugh Latimer's sermons (his seventh sermon on the Lord's Prayer, in *Sermons* [New York and London, 1906], pp. 374–75) about a rich London merchant who was avoided on the streets by a poor man who owed him money. Marsden gives no evidence for his claim that the anecdote refers to Humphrey Monmouth, a London merchant who supported William Tyndale for about six months. But even if we accept the identification, Monmouth became acquainted with Tyndale for the first time in 1523, five years after this epigram was first printed (see *CW 8,* 1158–59, 1174–75). Nor is Latimer's anecdote very close to the epigram, for the merchant is avoided because of his heretical opinions, not because of money owed him.

163/5 **uiso . . . angue.** Cf. Otto, no. 108.

164/1–4 **IN MENDICVM . . . medico.** Plautus plays on *medicus-mendicus* (*Rudens,* 1304–06). Charles Clay Doyle ("John Owen and Thomas More: An Analog," *Moreana, 67–68* [1980], 40–41) pointed out that John Owen (1564–1627/28) imitated the word-play *mendicus-medicus* in Book I, no. 21 of his *Epigrammata* (ed. John R. C. Martyn [Leiden, 1976]). See Appendix D, p. 703, below.

165/1–3 **IN VXOREM . . . uiro.** There is an analogue in Bebel's *Facetiae* (p. 24): "In eadem militia meruit ad aliquot annos mihi notissimus; qui cum ad duos annos ab uxore abfuisset, ipsa nihilominus puerum peperit. Quod ubique narrare solebat: se habere fetuosam et fructiferam mulierem, quae se etiam absente pueros gigneret."

166/1–4 **IN PERPVSILLVM . . . laqueo.** Translated from *AP* XI, 111. *Pl.* II, 32 (εἰς λεπτούς), 14, sig. M_3v.

> Βουλόμενός ποθ' ὁ λεπτὸς ἀπάγξασθαι Διόφαντος,
> νῆμα λαβὼν ἀράχνης, αὑτὸν ἀπηγχόνισεν.

166/3 **taedia vitae.** Aulus Gellius 6.18.11; Walther, 30970a.

166/4 **Arachneo.** As the meter shows, this word stands for "Arachnaeo" (*TLL* 2, 392, lines 17–23).

167/3 **oportunum.** Brixius (Appendix B, 522/14–23) objected to More's taking the first syllable of "oportunum" as short. The usual spelling and scansion is *ŏpportunus*, but the alternate spelling *oportunus* is not uncommon in postclassical writers, and the quantity of the first syllable of this form is uncertain (*Oxford Latin Dictionary*, ed. P. G. W. Glare [Oxford, 1982], s.v.).

167/8 **Instetit.** Normally "institit," but there are a few epigraphical precedents for "insteti" (*TLL* 7, 1999, line 5). See note to 20/12.

167/14 **ensem.** An indelicate pun. In *Priapeia* 9.5 and 20.2 Priapus compares his weapon to the weapons of the other gods, including the *ensis* of Mars.

168/2 **Chrysalus.** See note to 99/2.

169/1–11 **IN ASTROLOGVM . . . dies.** Cf. nos. 12 and 50.

170/1–4 **IN CRVCE . . . potest.** Translated from *AP* XI, 230. *Pl.* II, 43 (εἰς πονηρούς), 5, sig. M_8v.

> Μασταύρων ἀφελὼν δύο γράμματα Μάρκε τὰ πρῶτα,
> ἄξιος εἶ πολλῶν τῶν ὑπολειπομένων.

Μασταύρων indicates that Marcus was born in the city of Mastaura. The point of the epigram is that taking away the first two letters leaves the Greek word for "crosses" (in the grammatically required genitive plural).

171/1–4 **EPITAPHIVM . . . perimit.** For the Greek and More's other translation, see no. 13. The Greek could mean that the twins died before they were a day old or that they died later (by a coincidence worthy of an epigram) within the space of one day. Unlike no. 13 (where More chose the first alternative), his translation here is as ambiguous as the Greek. See the Introduction, p. 19.

172/1–3 **E GRAECO . . . timidis.** Translated from *AP* VII, 160. *Pl.* III, 5 (εἰς ἀνδρείους), 1, sig. P_1v.

> Καρτερὸς ἐν πολέμοις Τιμόκριτος, οὗ τόδε σᾶμα.
> Ἄρης δ' οὐκ ἀγαθῶν φείδεται, ἀλλὰ κακῶν.

172/3 **fere.** More added this ironical epithet.

173/1–3 **E GRAECO . . . uitio.** Translated from *AP* VII, 72. *Pl.* III, 5 (εἰς ἀνδρείους), 4, sig. P_1v.

> Χαῖρε Νεοκλείδα, δίδυμον γένος. ὧν ὁ μὲν ὑμῶν,
> πατρίδα δουλοσύνας ῥύσαθ', ὁ δ' ἀφροσύνας.

The Palatine lemma says that these lines refer to Themistocles and Epicurus, both of whose fathers were named Neocles. Since More had no way of knowing who the two heroes addressed in the Greek were, he must have assumed that the words were addressed to two heroes buried in the same tomb.

173/2 **Neoclidae.** Unlike the Greek, this means "of the son of Neocles."

173/3 **Seruitio . . . uitio.** More preserved the echoing sounds of the Greek. The use of the present tense in "liberat" instead of the past (as in the Greek) may have been a deliberate and significant change: the valor of the one (by his past deeds) still keeps his country free and the wisdom of the other (in his writings and pupils) still keeps his country upright.

174/1–5 **AD QVENDAM . . . propere.** Cf. no. 86; *AP* XI, 381.

175/1–19 **DE NAVTIS . . . ratis.** Charles Clay Doyle has pointed out that More's basic pun on "grauis" (a literal versus a moral sense) was anticipated in a well-known anecdote recounted in Bebel's *Facetiae* (p. 19): "Alius, cum coorta tempestate universi res ponderosiores in mare proiicere iuberentur, uxorem suam in mare primam proiecit: nullam se graviorem rem habere testatus." For several medieval analogues of Bebel's story see Albert Wesselski, ed., *Heinrich Bebels Schwänke zum ersten Male in vollständiger Übertragung,* 2 vols. (Leipzig and Munich, 1907), *1,* 134–35. A translation of More's epigram by Sir Nicholas Bacon in a sixteenth-century manuscript was first printed by the Daniel Press in 1919 (Gibson, no. 178).

176/1–2 **AD CANDIDVM . . . IMPROBAE.** Cf. no. 197.

176/7 **uanarum . . . rerum.** Cf. 1 Cor. 8:1: "Scientia inflat."

176/9 **rarae . . . raros.** An ironical ambiguity: "outstanding" versus "very few."

177/1–3 **E GRAECO . . . salo.** Translated from *AP* VII, 265. *Pl.* III, 22 (εἰς ναυαγήσαντας), 3, sig. S_4.

> Ναυηγοῦ τάφος εἰμί. ὁ δ' ἀντίον ἐστὶ γεωργοῦ,
> ὡς ἁλὶ, καὶ γαίῃ ξυνὸς ὕπεστ' Ἀΐδης.

178/1–11 **IN POSTHVMVM . . . legi.** Cf. no. 202. John H. Marsden (*Philomorus* [London, 1878], pp. 135–39) thought this epigram was directed against James Stanley, who became bishop of Ely in 1506; but his argument is not convincing (see Allen, *1,* 159, n. 6).

178/3 **sacer.** The ambiguity of this word ("sacred, holy" versus "accursed, wicked") is not resolved until the last line. See note to 53/1–5.

180/1–8 **DE VVLPE . . . malos.** For an Aesopic analogue see Doyle, "Neglected Sources," p. 9.

180/4 **blando . . . ore.** Cf. Ovid, *Metamorphoses* 13.555.

180/8 **Vicinos . . . malos.** Cf. Walther, 33291f: "Vicinum habet prauum, ipse qui se iactitat." See also Erasmus, *Moriae encomium, ASD 4/3,* 74, Commentary at lines 43–44.

181/1–7 **DE LEONE . . . faciam.** In Justinus' abridgment of Trogus Pompeius' *Historiae Philippicae* (15.3.4–6) Lysimachus, the valorous general of Alexander the Great, kills a fierce lion by ripping out its tongue.

181/6 **linguam . . . leonis.** Brixius rightly objected to More's scansion "leŏninam" in *1518,* since the single occurrence of *leoninus* in classical verse (Plautus, *Menaechmi* 159) makes the second syllable long.

183/1 **ARCEM NORHAMAM.** Norham Castle, near the town of Norham, had been for centuries an important English border fortress. In 1498 a Scottish force had attacked it unsuccessfully. See James D. Mackenzie, *The Castles of England: Their Story and Structure,* 2 vols. (New York, 1896), 2, 408–11.

183/4 **oppugnas . . . arcem.** On August 22, 1513, while Henry VIII was fighting in France, James IV invaded England. He besieged Norham Castle from August 22 to August 28, when the castle surrendered. See R. L. Mackie, *King James IV of Scotland* (Edinburgh and London, 1958), pp. 248–49.

183/5–13 **falsa proditione . . . digna suo.** "The Battle of Flodden Field," a poem dating from the middle of the sixteenth century, perpetuated the rumor (apparently unfounded) that the castle was betrayed by one of its defenders and that after the surrender the traitor claimed his reward from James IV, who had him hanged. The ballad, of which there is a manuscript dated 1636, was printed in 1664 and 1774. See *The Battle of Floddon Field: A Poem of the Sixteenth Century,* ed. Henry Weber (Edinburgh, 1808), pp. ix–xvi, 31–35. The Scottish troops partially destroyed the castle. When James and most of his army were slaughtered at Flodden Field on September 9, 1513, the castle was recovered by the English (*LP, 1,* 672, no. 4457; 688–89, no. 4523). See also Hubert E. H. Jerningham, *Norham Castle* (Edinburgh, 1883), pp. 20–38.

183/6–7 **An fraudis . . . tuis.** These lines, which were printed in *1518,* were erroneously omitted by the compositor of *1520.*

183/13 **Mors . . . suo.** Cf. Rom. 6:23 ("Stipendia enim peccati, mors") and Heb. 2:2.

184/2 **Iacobus . . . amico.** More wrongly scans "Ĭăcŏbus" instead of "Ĭăcōbus," but Venantius Fortunatus (5.2.20; 8.3.144) had done the same. One reason why England and Scotland ought to have been friendly was that James IV had married Margaret, Henry VIII's sister, in 1503.

184/3 **hac . . . humo.** Another abusive mock epitaph for James IV written by Pietro Carmeliano (see note to 147/1) was published by Pynson near the end of November 1513; see *LP, 1/2,* no. 2246, p. 1008; Allen, *1,* 540, lines 43–44; and Nelson, *John Skelton,* p. 36. At this time James had not yet been buried, and indeed it appears that he never received Christian burial. He had twice bound himself to uphold his peace treaties with England under pain of excommunication (*LP, 1/2,* no. 2469, p. 1088); when James invaded England in 1513, England's temporal ally Pope Julius II had no qualms about actually excommunicating him. James' stripped corpse was identified "by its privie tokens" the day after the Battle of Flodden, whereupon the victorious English commander transferred it to Berwick, had it carefully embalmed and enveloped in lead, and then shipped it away to the south, to the monastery at Sheen or Richmond, a suburb of London, to await new developments (Hall, p. 564; cf. *LP, 1/2,* no. 2651, p. 1157). Meanwhile (October 12, 1513) Henry had petitioned the new Pope, Leo X, to repeal Julius II's excommunication of James and permit him to be given a state burial in St. Paul's in London; although Leo responded by giving his formal permission in a letter of November 29, it appears that new reasons of state convinced Henry that he ought not in fact to give James a respectable burial (*LP, 1/2,* no. 2355, pp. 1047–48; no. 2469, pp. 1088–89). The first draft of Polydore Vergil's *Anglica historia,* concluded not later than the spring of 1514, states that James' corpse has been "kept for a long time unburied" at the Carthusian monastery at Sheen, because James died excommunicate, but ends on a note of explicit uncertainty as to whether the corpse is indeed to be buried in the imminent future (*Anglica historia,* ed. Denys Hay [London, 1950], pp. 220–21; for the dating, see p. xiv). In a thorough recasting of this text, not released till well after the dissolution of the monasteries, Vergil studiously avoids any hint that James had not deserved Christian burial since he died excommunicate but still places his corpse at the "Bethlehem convent of the Carthusian order at London"—that is, Sheen or Richmond again. John Stow's 1603 *Survey of London* (Oxford, 1908), *1,* 298, reports further indignities suffered at Sheen by the Scottish king's restless remains. All of this, in conjunction with More's own remark in the *Letter to Brixius* (Appendix C, 618/23–30) that James' corpse had been kept without burial for so many *years,* makes it highly likely that More composed his mock epitaph for James shortly after the Battle of Flodden, at about the same time that Carmeliano composed his, in the mistaken belief that Henry would at length make a public display of his own magnanimity by burying his enemy.

184/4 **fidei.** A war between England and Scotland (1495–98) came to an end when James IV and Henry VII ratified a treaty (1499) calling for a truce during the lifetimes of the two monarchs. In 1502, as part of the preparations for the marriage of Margaret and James IV, the two kings agreed to a treaty of perpetual peace, which was confirmed by James IV and Henry VIII in 1509. After negotiating with France in 1512, however, James IV sent a herald on July 26, 1513, to declare war on England. See Mackie, *James IV,* pp. 78–102, 200–01, 213–19, 223–45. On the unreliability of treaties in European power politics, see *Utopia, CW 4,* 87–89, 197–99, 352–53, 356–57.

185/5 **retro . . . aspicere.** The painter chose the unnatural pose to heighten the pathos. But a hare's eyes are so placed that it can see behind without turning its head; and even if this were not so, no hare with ordinary common sense would endanger its life to satisfy its curiosity. More kept pet rabbits in his garden (see Erasmus' colloquy "Amicitia," *ASD 1/3,* 706–07).

186/1–7 **IN EVNDEM . . . lepus.** In a letter to Erasmus (March or April 1520) on Brixius' *Antimorus,* More compares Brixius to this inept painter: "Denique quam lepidis ironiis eludet [lector aequuus] ironias Brixii! quippe tam illepidas, vt lectorem admoneant pictoris cuiusdam, omnino talis qualis Brixius est poeta; qui cum leporem atque canem depinxisset ita similes vt internosci non possent, tandem vter canis esset, vter lepus, subscriptione solers indicauit" (Allen, *4,* 223). More's play here on "lepidis," "illepidas," "leporem," "lepus" suggests that in this epigram and in no. 185 he may have intended a play on *lepos* (grace, charm) and *lepus* (hare).

187/1–9 **DE TYNDARO . . . potes.** The British Library Sloane MS. 2117 (fol. 243v), a medical commonplace book written probably in the first half of the seventeenth century, contains the following translation:

Sir Thomas Moors Epigrams:

A louely lass that had a Roman nose:
meeting with Tyndarus: he would haue kist her:
but when he should haue mett her at the close:
I would quoth he: but cannot kiss you sister:
for had not your Egregious long nose bin:
I would haue kist your lipps: & not your chin:
the poore wench blusht: & burnt with secrett ire:
which sett her changing colour all on flame:
And saith to him: to furnish your desire:
since that you faine would kiss: & craue the same:

> because my nose no more: shall let your will:
> kiss where is none: there freely take your fill:

(I have omitted the colons at the beginning of each line.)
This translation was printed in Thomas Heywood's Γυναικεῖον: *or nine bookes of various history, concerning women* (London, 1624), *STC* 13326 (sigs. Z_6v–Aa_1). For other translations and analogues see Charles Clay Doyle, "Where I Have No Nose," *Folklore Women's Communication, 15* (Spring 1978), 21–23.

187/3 **dicax.** See *CW 14,* 1030, Commentary at 289/6.

188/1 **BRIXIVM GERMANVM.** For More's quarrel with Brixius see below, Appendices A, B, and C. The elements of the name (Germanus Brixius, Germain de Brie) are deliberately reversed here to make a pun on *Germanus* in the sense "Germanic, barbaric." More also punned on Brixius' name "Germanus" in his letter to Brixius (see Appendix C, 632/12 and Commentary.). Misled by this pun, two later writers thought that Brixius was from Germany: Lilius Gregorius Gyraldus, *De poetis nostrorum temporum* (1551), ed. Karl Wotke, Lateinische Literaturdenkmäler des XV. und XVI. Jahrhunderts no. 10 (Berlin, 1894), p. 65; Henry Peacham, *Compleat Gentleman* (1634), ed. Vergil B. Heltzel (Ithaca, N.Y., 1962), p. 104.

188/6–7 **Historiam . . . est.** Cf. Erasmus, *Ciceronianus* (*ASD 1/2,* 645, lines 3–4): "Historia, si fidem detrahas, ne nomen quidem historiae meretur."

189/1–13 **IN EVNDEM . . . erat.** In a letter to Erasmus (March–April 1520, Allen, *4* 220), More denied Brixius' accusation that More's epigrams against him could rightly be called "dirae" or "execrationes." Even the epigram in which Martial (11.93) wishes that the poetaster Theodorus had burned up with his house—a grimmer wish than More's in this epigram—is not strong enough to be classified so. More goes on to say:

> Ego vero, etiamsi dignum duxi Brixium qui, quo vitare tam impudenter mentiendi necessitatem posset, in media fuisset Chordigera: non optaui tamen istud ei, nec ignem imprecatus sum, quem effugerunt etiam multi qui fuerunt in naue. Neque enim quisque statim imprecatur ea cuilibet, quibus illum censet ac pronunciat dignum. Nam et Brixius, opinor, fures dignos ducit suspendio, dignos ducit adulteros, dignos hauddubie periuros; a quibus haud ita multis absunt parasangis mendaces: nec tamen, reor, vsqueadeo immitis est vt iis omnibus, tantae nimirum parti mortalium, semel imprecetur interitum. Quod voti genus vt inclementissimum fuerit, ita nec ipsi fortasse Brixio satis tutum.

190/4–14 **Circumeunt . . . acuta.** See Appendix A, 450/59–62, 452/109–14.

191/10 **Celaeno.** One of the harpies, noted for grasping claws (Vergil, *Aeneid* 3.211–17).

191/11 **impar.** See note to 114/9.

192/11 **audiat.** Sense and grammar seem to require "audiuerit."

193/1–28 **IN EVNDEM . . . dabit.** I have added extra space after line 14 to suggest (what is almost certainly true) that More wrote these lines not as one epigram, but two, as Daniel Kinney has argued in *Moreana, 70* (1981), 37–44. In a letter to Erasmus written in the spring of 1520, More reckons up all the epigrams against Brixius by name in *1518* and gives their subject matter. He mentions ten, two of which are directed against Brixius' pilferings from classical poets (Allen, *4,* 220). If these lines are taken as one epigram, then *1518* contains only nine poems against Brixius and only one against his plagiarism. If it is counted as two epigrams, *1518* matches More's reckoning perfectly. Lines 3–14 treat poetical phrases as flowers to be cultivated and plucked, culminating in the surprising new twist of stars against the night sky. Lines 15–28 develop the motif of combining the old with the new. On the other hand, it is possible that More intended to include no. 236 among his poems against Brixius; it is against plagiarizing from ancient poets but is addressed not to Brixius but merely "ad Gallum."

193/13–14 **Magisque . . . sydera.** Cf. Quintilian, *Institutio oratoria* 2.12.7, an attack on the extravagant style of undisciplined sententious speakers. Quintilian is playing on Cicero, *De oratore* 3.26.101.

193/25–28 **Ars . . . dabit.** Cf. Pliny, *Historia naturalis* pref. 15: "Res ardua uetustis nouitatem dare, nouis auctoritatem. . . ."

194/1–3 **ALLVSIO . . . potest.** For Brixius' lines on the cenotaph of Hervé, see Appendix A, 464/354–64.

194/2 **Decijs.** Publius Decius Mus in 340 B.C. and his son in 295 B.C. deliberately chose death at the hands of the enemy in the belief that such deaths would win victory for Roman arms (Livy 8.6.8–13, 8.9.1–2, 10.28.13–18).

195/2 **Vis . . . libello.** More may be mocking Jerome Aleander's *ex cathedra* endorsement of Brixius' *Chordigera,* which opens with a similar statement (see Appendix A, 440/16–17).

195/4 **sacer . . . sacra.** See note to 53/1–5.

195/7 **Plenum opus.** In his letter prefixed to the *Chordigera,* Brixius fears lest he seem to restrict to the narrow space of a letter the virtues of

Queen Anne, "quas diffusior pleni operis campus vix capiat" (see Appendix A, 446/17–19).

195/8–9 **Vna . . . (habet).** The only Latin month in which the letters of *mens* appear is *Novembris*. Brixius' preface to his *Chordigera* is dated "decimo Kal. Nouemb. M. D. XII." (October 23, 1512). See Appendix A, 446/33. In the first edition of *Poeticarum institutionum libri tres* (Amsterdam: Elzevir, 1647), Gerardus Iohannes Vossius attributes a similar remark to Erasmus: "de cuius [sc. Fausti Andrelini] poemat[i]is scite aiebat Erasmus unicam in iis syllabam desiderari. Ea erat νοῦς sive mens" (sig. A_1v). In Vossius this remark follows a similar one from Theocritus, quoted in Greek. The general target is poets who care more for fine words than for sense. Vossius himself gives no source for Erasmus. Erasmus reports the *bon mot* of Theocritus (*Opera omnia, 4,* 312A), but does not apply it to Andrelini.

196/1–14 **AD SABINVM . . . domum.** The repetition is reminiscent of Martial (e.g., 1.77, 1.109, 2.33). For Sabinus' troubles with his wives see also nos. 205 and 220.

197/1–6 **AD CANDIDVM . . . candidior.** More plays on the meanings of Candidus' name: "white" and "ingenuous."

197/6 **lacte . . . candidior.** Both comparisons (milk and snow) are proverbial (and especially Ovidian); see Otto, 898 and 1231. But they are also scriptural: the teeth of Juda, the ancestor of Christ, are "lacte candidiores" (Gen. 49:12), and the garments of Christ at the transfiguration are "candida nimis velut nix" (Mark 9:2; see also Ps. 50:9, Dan. 7:9, and Rev. 1:14). Particularly close is Jeremiah's description of the Nazarenes in Jerusalem before the fall of the city: "candidiores Nazaraei ejus nive, nitidiores lacte" (Lam. 4:7). Gregory (*Moralia* 32.22; *PL 76,* col. 663) applies Jeremiah's description to men who seem not only to imitate but even to surpass holy men of ancient times: "Quid ergo per nivem nisi candor vitae coelestis, quid per lac nisi temporalis dispensationis administratio demonstratur? Et quia plerumque continentes viri in Ecclesia tam mira opera faciunt, ut ab eis multi qui coelestem vitam tenuerunt, multi qui terrena bene dispensaverunt, superari videantur, et candidiores nive, et nitidiores lacte referuntur." Such virtue, Gregory goes on to say, may be spurious if it is vitiated by pride, but the men he describes, after they have fallen into sin and learned true humility, repent and recover. More's Candidus, however, displays a cynical pride which expresses itself in a spurious humility.

198/1 **QVIS . . . STATVS.** The question of the best form of government—usually considered under the divisions of rule by one, a few, or many—had been discussed from the time of Herodotus (3.81–82), Plato (*Republic* 8.2–19, 544E–569C; *Politicus* 302A–303B), and Aristotle (*Politics* 3.12.2–4.7.6, 1288B–1294B). In defending monarchy as the best form of government, Isocrates (*Nicocles* 17–21) advances three arguments that More specifically rejects: (1) a king makes better use of his counselors; (2) a king performs better than those who have only an annual term of office; (3) monarchy avoids the dissension prevalent in governmental assemblies. Girolamo Aleandro's edition of the Greek of *Nicocles* was printed in Paris, perhaps in 1509; this text is bound together with a copy of More's *Utopia* (Louvain, 1516) in the Beinecke Library at Yale. Erasmus' translation of *Nicocles* was first printed together with his *Institutio principis christiani* in 1516. The advantages of monarchy or a republican form of government were much debated by Italian (especially Florentine) humanists in the fifteenth century (Hans Baron, *The Crisis of the Early Italian Renaissance,* rev. ed. [Princeton, 1966], pp. 404–30). The phrase "OPTIMVS REIPVB. STATVS" suggests the bearing of this poem on *Utopia,* with which it was published in the March and December editions of 1518, for the full title of the prose work is "De optimo reipublicae statu deque noua insula Vtopia."

198/2 **uter . . . Senatus.** *Utopia* hardly gives a clear answer to this question since it seems that the island as Hythloday knew it had no one king, but a "princeps" and a "senatus" in each of the fifty-four city-states (*CW 4,* 112/15–20, 122/9–124/17), though the original conqueror, Utopus, ruled the whole island (*CW 4,* 112/1–15). Matters of interest to the whole island are discussed annually at the capital, Amaurotum, by a national senate consisting of three members from each city (*CW 4,* 112/22–25, 116/25–28).

198/17 **Omni anno.** Brixius called this phrase a solecism (see Appendix B, 532/26–534/7), and he singled out as a similar solecism in More's Latin prose, "omni die" in *Utopia* (*CW 4,* 122/28 and Commentary thereon). But Juvenal wrote "semper et omni nocte dieque" (3.104–05). See Introduction, p. 28.

198/20–21 **nota . . . locum.** The Aesopic fable of the hedgehog who offers to brush away the flies tormenting a fox derives from Aristotle's *Rhetoric* (2.20.6–7, 1393B); see Perry, *Aesopica* no. 427, p. 490, and Plutarch, *Moralia* 790D. Flavius Josephus (*Jewish Antiquities* 18.5.172–76) reports a story told by the emperor Tiberius about a man who refused to brush flies from his wounds. Tiberius applies the tale to his policy of appointing governors to long terms: "If . . . those appointed kept their posts longer, they would be gorged with their robberies and would by the very bulk of them be more sluggish in pursuit of further gain." Erasmus

(*De duplici copia, Opera omnia, 1,* 98E) and Listrius in his commentary on Erasmus' *Moria* attribute the fable to Themistocles (*ASD 4/3,* 100). Charles Clay Doyle has pointed out that the fable may be related to the proverb "A hungry fly bites sore" (Whiting, F337; Tilley, F402).

198/27–31 **Quaestio . . . expediat.** More seems to address himself here with humorous self-deprecation since there was indeed a people to whom he could give whatever government he liked, but it was a "good place" which existed "noplace." See the Introduction, p. 50.

199/1–5 **DE FVSCO . . . uermiculis.** This epigram, no. 210, and no. 214 are progressively elaborate and dramatic imitations of Martial 6.78:

> Potor nobilis, Aule, lumine uno
> luscus Phryx erat alteroque lippus.
> huic Heras medicus "Bibas caveto:
> vinum si biberis, nihil videbis."
> ridens Phryx oculo "Valebis" inquit.
> misceri sibi protinus deunces
> sed crebros iubet. exitum requiris?
> vinum Phryx, oculus bibit venenum.

200/4–5 **Nec bello . . . nihil.** A new twist on the proverb "Machinas post bellum adferre" (Erasmus, *Adagia* 2017, *Opera omnia, 2,* 721B; cf. *Adagia* 2517, *Opera omnia, 2,* 853A).

201/1–15 **DE REGE . . . homo.** This epigram was translated into English in *Tales, and quicke answeres, very mery, and pleasant to rede,* printed by Thomas Berthelet about 1532 (*STC*[2] 23665, ed. P. M. Zall, in *A Hundred Merry Tales and Other English Jestbooks of the Fifteenth and Sixteenth Centuries* [Lincoln, Nebraska, 1963], no. 41, p. 274). The translation adds the following moral at the end: "By this tale ye may perceive (as Lycurgus proved by experience [Plutarch, *Moralia* 3AB]) that nourishing, good bringing up and exercise been more apt to lead folk to humanity and the doing of honest things than Nature herself. They for the most part are noble, free and virtuous which in their youth been well nourished up and virtuously endoctrined." Our first tendency is to interpret the story quite differently, more like the incident of the Anemolian ambassadors in *Utopia* (*CW 4,* 152/26–156/9): the naive peasant, unspoiled by the conventions of conspicuous consumption, fails to see why the crowd is so amazed by a mere man in rich clothing. But in More's time regal magnificence was taken as a proper expression of the dignity and duty of royal office (*CW 4,* 244/19–21 and the Commentary thereon; Erasmus, *Moria, ASD 4/3,* 169). On the difficulties of determining precisely More's attitude toward splendor and magnificence in *Utopia,* see Ward S. Allen, "The Tone of More's Farewell to *Utopia:* A Reply to J. H. Hexter," *Moreana, 51* (1976), 108–18.

202/1–2 **DE QVO . . . EPIGRAMMA.** See no. 178.

202/4–9 **occidit . . . spiritus.** 2 Cor. 3:6: "[Deus] idoneos nos fecit ministros novi testamenti: non littera, sed Spiritu: littera enim occidit, Spiritus autem vivificat." Cf. no. 260.

202/9 **spiritus.** We might expect the accusative with *esse,* but the nominative appears because the word has been "attracted" into the relative clause (Kühner-Stegmann, 2/2, 309–11).

203/1–11 **DE SACERDOTE . . . heri.** Cf. Poggio, *Facetiae,* no. 11, *1,* 31–33. Jokes based on sermons are frequent in Bebel's *Facetiae* (e.g., pp. 31, 33, 40, 73, 74, 89, 124, 129, 130, 134, 135, 149, 161).

203/8 **tenuent.** Brixius objected to More's "mǎcerent" on metrical grounds (Appendix B, 522/29–524/9). The usual scansion is "mācero," but Juvencus and Priscian Caesariensis have "mǎcero" (Quicherat, p. 639).

203/8–11 **ieiunia . . . heri.** In the West it was customary to fast on the vigils of major feasts such as Saint Andrew's day (November 30). The mass for the vigil of Saint Andrew in the Sarum rite mentions that Christians observe the vigil "jejuniis et devotis officiis" (Dickinson, col. 659). Since the fasting ought to have occurred yesterday, the priest is preaching on the feast day itself.

204/3–4 **male cantasti . . . legisti.** As Charles Clay Doyle has pointed out, Quintilian (1.8.2) quotes a remark of Gaius Caesar condemning an effeminately melodious way of reading poetry: "Si cantas, male cantas; si legis, cantas." Erasmus said that More had a good speaking voice but "ad musicam vocalem a natura non videtur esse compositus, etiamsi delectatur omni musices genere" (Allen, *4,* 15).

204/5–6 **utrumuis . . . utrunque.** The verbal play is elegant: "one or the other" versus "one and the other."

205/1–46 **AD SABINVM . . . interim.** Cf. nos. 196 and 220. The following Dutch adaptation of this poem by the son of a man named Van Duybilt is written in a seventeenth-century hand on ff. 114–114[v] of Sloane Manuscript 2764 in the British Library:

Hier op heeft den hoog-geleerden Thomas Morus een aardig spitsdichtken op gemaekt, 't welk ik al met de saeke overeenkomende geraeden hebbe [eenig son v Duybilt] alhier bij te stellen.

Ik hoor, Sabine, dat dijn wijf
U heeft geschonken sonen vijf:
En dat gij van dees d'eerste vier,
Om dat s'u lijken niet een zier,
Verworpt, als niet het maexel dijn.
Maer dijnen kent alleen te zijn
Den vijfden; en dat voor gewis,
Om dat hij heel dijn nogni is.
Maer zegt mij eens, ô lieve knecht,
Hebt gij ook dese saek' heel recht.
Gij'n weet der wijsen kerel niet,
Die hier van geven dit bediedt,
Dat 's wijfs inbeelding is soo sterk
Als sij is doende met dat werk,
Dat sij in 't saed 't welk sij als dan
Ontfangt, gedaent indrucken kan,
Niet naer hems mans oft hem gestalt,
Maer naer dat hem gedachte valt.
Als wierden d'eerste vier gemaekt,
Doen waerd gij buyten's huis geraekt
Soo verre, dat dijn wijf gerust,
Terwijl hem boel hem heeft gekust,
In 't minst op u niet eens en docht,
En t'elven eenen soon voord brocht,
In wien dijn aensicht niet en blijkt,
Maer d'een' oft d'andre pel gelijkt.
Doen wird geklutst het vijfde kind,
Waert gij soo wijd niet in de wind,
Oft gijn soud als onwaerde gast
Hem hebben lichtelijk verrast.
Dies sij gestaedig docht op u,
End' hadde voor dijne komst' een gru.
Soo dat te voorschijn quam hier naer
Een waere beeld van valsche vaer.
Daerom laet vrij, naer mijn vermaen,
Den vijfden bij sijn broerkens gaen.
Soo sult gij doen, Sabine, wel
Naer het verhefschen van dit spel:
Ik segge van dijne krachten flouw,
En van den aert van dijne vrouw.

205/16 **Vt filium fert simia.** In the *Apology* More alluded to Aesop's fable about the ape who was ridiculed for entering her ugly offspring in a beauty contest sponsored by Jupiter for the animals: "Nor I vse not to folowe the condycion of Isopes ape, y[t] thought her own babes so beuteouse, & so farre passyng in all goodly feature and favour" (*CW 9,* 3/8–10 and the Commentary thereon). See Perry, *Aesopica,* no. 364, p. 472 and Avianus, no. 14; Hervieux, *3,* 272; *Fables,* ed. Françoise Gaide [Paris, 1980], p. 92). Cf. *CW 4,* 56/32–33 and the Commentary thereon; Erasmus, *Adagia* 2489, *Opera omnia, 2,* 848D; Whiting, A138; Tilley, A270.

205/18–33 **Atqui . . . imaginem.** Among the causes of resemblance between parents and offspring, Pliny mentions "haustae . . . imagines sub ipso conceptu" (*Historia naturalis* 7.12.52). According to Michael Scot (died c. 1235) in his *Liber phisionomiae,* "uerum est quod si mulier sit iuuenis: cum in coitu sit memor sui uel uiri uel alterius: et proprie cum semen diffundit generatiuum genitum erit omnino similis. et iam probatum est milies et in animalibus" (Venice, 1477, sigs. A_8–A_8v). This work, which was sometimes entitled *De secretis naturae* (cf. More's "Secreta quicquid efficit Natura," lines 20–21) was printed at least 20 times in the late fifteenth century (Lynn Thorndike, *Michael Scot* [London and Edinburgh, 1965], p. 87). The "incipit" of the Venice edition of 1477 suggests the esoteric obscurantism which More mocks by repetition and ponderous diction: "Incipit Liber Phisionomiae: quem compilauit magister Michael Scotus ad preces D. Federici romanorum imperatoris. Scientia cuius est multum tenenda in secreto: eo quod est magnae efficaciae: Continens secreta artis naturae: quae sufficiunt omni astrologo" (sig. A_4). Albertus Magnus discusses the same phenomenon, citing Galen and Avicenna (*De animalibus,* lib. 22, tract. 1, cap. 3, ed. Hermann Stadler, 2 vols. [Münster, 1916–20], *2,* 1352; *Quaestiones super De animalibus,* lib. 7, q. 3, and lib. 18, q. 3, ed. Ephrem Filthaut [Münster, 1955], pp. 172, 298). The physician Livin Lemmens (1505–68) made the same point, quoting More's epigram (except for lines 12–16 and 19–22), in *De occultis naturae miraculis* (1559 and 1567); see Emile V. Telle, "De la Ressemblance des enfants aux pères: Thomas More et l'embryologie," *Moreana, 18* (1968), 21–22. For a more positive view of investigating the secrets of nature see *CW 4,* 182/12–13 and the Commentary thereon.

205/19 **laborque.** The "–que" of *1518* and *1520* makes the line hypermetrical and was omitted in *1565*.

205/45 **Lupus in fabulam.** The proverbial "lupus in fabula" ("the wolf in the midst of a conversation") applies to the sudden silence which falls on a conversation when the person under discussion unexpectedly arrives on the scene (Otto, no. 988; Erasmus, *Adagia* 3450, *Opera omnia, 2,* 1065B–F). The accusative "fabulam" is correct because of "superuenires."

206/2 **SELANDO.** "Selandus" is an adjective formed from *Selandia*, Zeeland in the Low Countries (*Orbis Latinus: Lexikon lateinischer geographischer Namen des Mittelalters und der Neuzeit*, ed. Th. Graesse, F. Benedict, H. Plechl, 3 vols. [Braunschweig, 1972], *3*, 359). In his colloquy "Naufragium" Erasmus associates a Zeelander with the Batavians as well known for "crassum ingenium" (*ASD 1/3*, 104–05). Zeelanders were thought to be similar to Dutchmen, as Gerardus (Geldenhouwer) Noviomagus remarked in a letter printed in Martin van Dorp's *Dialogus* . . . (Louvain, Dirk Martens, 1514, sigs. G_3–G_3v): "Zelandis ferme ii mores, is cultus, qui est Hollandus. Zelandus lingua nonnihil citatiore quam Hollandus est." The Dutch were proverbial for their dullness (see Erasmus, *Moriae encomium, ASD 4/3*, 84, lines 254–55 and n.; *Adagia* 3535, *Opera omnia, 2*, 1083F–1084E).

206/4 **suos.** The use of "suos" is quite awkward here, but Brixius' objection that grammar requires "eius" (Appendix B, 534/8–30) fails to take into account the considerable freedom with which good classical writers used *suus* where we would normally expect *eius* (Kühner-Stegmann, *2/1*, 604). Brixius claims to find the same error in three places in *Utopia* (*CW 4*, 80/26, 136/17, 136/30).

208/1–5 **IN MILITEM . . . erat.** Charles Clay Doyle has pointed out an analogue in Plutarch's *Life of Cato* (9.4): "he had no use for a soldier who plied his hands on the march, and his feet in battle," Cf. Whiting, H325 (To fight with one's heels) and Tilley, P34 (One pair of heels [legs, feet] is worth two pair of hands).

209/5 **Cor.** More refers to the heart as the seat, not of feelings (which are hardly lacking in *Chordigera*), but of intelligence or wisdom (*TLL 4*, 937).

210/1–9 **IN TVSCVM . . . bibi.** See note to 199/1–5.

211/1–5 **IN ARNVM . . . fides.** William Patten, in *The expedicion into Scotlande of Edward, duke of Soomerset* (1548, *STC*[2] 19476.5) refers to this epigram: "But these Skottes (as men that ar neuer so iuste, and in nothing so true as in breache of promys and vsyng vntruth) neither cam, nor by like ment to cum: And yet sure take I this no fetch of no fine deuise, onles thei mean hereby to wyn, that thei shal nede neuer after to promys; vsyng the feate of Arnus, who with his all weys swearyng and his euer liyng, at last obteined that his bare woorde was as much in credyt as his solemn oth, but his solemn oth indeede no more then an impudent lye" (sigs. O_3–O_3v). Cf. Whiting, W609; Tilley, M458.

212/4–5 **Sic . . . metuat.** One of the jests in *Mensa philosophica*, frequently printed between 1475 and 1517, lists the first two of the four kinds of fools: a person who threatens until he is no longer feared and one who swears until he is no longer believed (Thomas F. Dunn, *The Facetiae of the Mensa Philosophica,* Washington University Studies, New Series, Language and Literature no. 5 [St. Louis, 1934], pp. 9–11, 34). Cf. Plutarch, *Moralia* 801B.

214/1–15 **DE MARVLLO . . . erat.** See note to 199/1–5.

214/11 **Nunc.** Brixius objected to "Hunc" in *1518,* claiming it should be "hoc" (Appendix B, 540/13–21). He ironically denies the mistake could be due to a misprint, but it obviously was (see the Introduction, p. 5).

215/1–7 **IN RISCVM . . . refert.** Charles Clay Doyle has pointed out the remark of the Emperor Probus about a swift horse: "Fugitivo militi potius quam forti hic equus convenit" (Flavius Vopiscus' life of Probus [8.3] in *Scriptores historiae Augustae*).

218/1 **EVPARIPHVM.** From εὐπάρυφος, "a person wearing a splendid garment with a purple border" (Latin *praetextatus*). In his Latin version of Lucian's *De mercede conductis* (9), written while he was with More in 1505–06, Erasmus translated the word as "opulentus" (*ASD 1/1,* 557, line 31).

218/4 **Quattuor . . . habet.** Cf. Tilley, L452: "He wears a whole lordship on his back" (the earliest example cited is from 1596). William Camden tells the following anecdote in his *Remains Concerning Britain* (1605): "There was a Noble man merrily conceited, and riotously given, that having lately sold a Mannor of an hundred tenements, came ruffling into the Court, in a new suit, saying, 'Am not I a mighty man, that bear an hundred houses on my back?' Which Cardinal Woolsey hearing, said, 'You might have better imployed it in paying your debts.' 'Indeed, my Lord,' quoth he, 'you say well; for my Lord my father owed my master your father, three half-pence for a Calf's head; hold, here is two pence for it'" (*Remains* . . . [East Ardsley, England, 1974], p. 298). See Appendix D, pp. 701–02, below.

220/1–13 **AD SABINVM . . . tuis.** Cf. nos. 196 and 205.

220/10 **cucullum.** The usual form is *cuculus,* but the spelling *cucullus* sometimes occurs in manuscripts (*TLL,* s.v. *cuculus*) and is given for the year 1517 with the meaning "cuckold" in J. H. Baxter and Charles Johnson, *Medieval Latin Word-List from British and Irish Sources* (London, 1934; reprint, 1947). See note to 253/14.

221/1–8 **IN NAVFRAGVM . . . tibi.** Translated from *AP,* VII, 290. *Pl.* III, 22 (εἰς ναυαγήσαντας), 17, sig. S_5.

Στατυλλίου φλάκκου.

Λαίλαπα, καὶ μανίην, ὀλοῆς προφυγόντα θαλάττης,
ναυηγὸν Λιβυκαῖς κείμενον ἐν ψαμάθοις,
οὐχ ἑκὰς ἠϊόνων, πυμάτῳ βεβαρυμένον ὕπνῳ,
γυμνὸν, ἀπὸ στυγερῆς ὅς κάμε ναυφθορίης,
ἔκτανε λυγρὸς ἔχις· τί μάτην πρὸς κύματ' ἐμόχθει,
τὴν ἐπὶ γῆς φεύγων μοῖραν ὀφειλομένην;

More may have been drawn to the epigram because it relates an event similar to what happened to Saint Paul (Acts 27:43–28:6).

221/5–6 **Dum . . . freto.** More probably did not intend "infesto fessus abusque freto" to mean "worn out by the hostile sea," for *abusque* cannot be used to indicate means. He seems to use a somewhat strained word order to signify "nudus et fessus iacet infesto abusque freto." The sailor is near the shore ("prope littora") but removed "from the hostile sea."

222/1–11 **DE CHIRVRGO . . . nihil.** As Charles Clay Doyle has pointed out ("Neglected Sources," pp. 7–11), this epigram is based on an Aesopic narrative (Perry, *Aesopica,* no. 57, pp. 343–44; Hervieux, *4,* 415). Mr. Doyle prints Latin versions by Rinucci de Castiglione and Odo of Cheriton, but the following version from a Greek and Latin Aesop printed by Johann Froben (Basel, January 1518) is somewhat closer to More:

> Mulier anus dolens oculos, conduxit medicum quendam mercede, conuentione facta si se curaret, pactam mercedem ei daturam, sin autem minime, nihil daturam. aggressus est igitur medicus curam. Quotidie uero accedens ad uetulam, et oculos ei ungens, cum illa nequaquam uidere posset ea hora ob unctionem, ipse uas aliquod ex domo auferens, quotidie discedebat. Anus igitur suam supellectilem uidebat singulis diebus minui, adeo ut tandem omnino liberatae nihil relinqueretur. At medico pactam mercedem ab ea efflagitante quasi pure iam uidente, & testes adducente, magis certe ait illa nunc nihil uideo. nam cum oculis laborabam, multa mea in mea uidebam domo, nunc autem cum me tu uidere inquis, nihil omnino ex illis uideo.
>
> Affabulatio.
>
> Fabula significat, prauos homines ex ijs quae agant, ignaros contra se ipsos argumentum afferre." [*Aesopi Phrygis vita et fabellae cum latina interpretatione* . . . , sig. h_5v]

222/5 **Quicquid . . . rapit.** To steal whatever is not "too heavy or too hot" was proverbial (Whiting, H316; Tilley, N322). Cf. Chaucer, *Canterbury*

Tales, "Friar's Tale," III, 1435–36: "I spare nat to taken, God it woot, / But if it be to hevy or to hoot."

222/8 **Mercedem . . . exacta.** See the Introduction, p. 32, n. 3.

222/11 **inde nihil.** The old woman uses "inde" instead of the more correct *eorum.* There are good classical precedents for *inde* in a partitive sense after *nihil* (*TLL* 7, 1119, lines 63–67), but not after a verb like *video.*

224/1–17 **DE HERODE . . . fides.** More's poem is closest to the version in Mark 6:17. Erasmus seems to have been influenced by this poem in his paraphrase on Mark (1523): "Quum igitur magno luxu fastuque instructa coena natalitia exhiberetur principibus, tribunis ac primatibus Galilaeae, quo plures haberet suae crudelitatis testes, ingressa est convivium puella Herodiadis ac Philippi filia, ut indecora lascivaque saltatione delectaret convivas. Quo turpius saltabat, hoc magis placuit convivis, ac Regi jam bis insano, ut qui praeter amorem incestae mulieris etiam vino incaluerat. Itaque Regali magnificentia dixit puellae: Posce a me quicquid voles, nihil enim frustra poposceris. . . . Hic mihi vide praeposteram Regis impii religionem. Quum nihil sit illis familiarius, quam omnia foederum ac religionum vincula dirumpere, hic religiosa religione stultissimi jurisjurandi constrictus est, praesertim quod tot testibus prodidisset. Itaque ne videretur parum bonae fidei, si quod forte per Regium diadema, aut genium suum, aut saltatriculae caput jurasset, non praestaret. . ." (*Opera omnia,* 7, 204–05).

224/5 **praetereaque.** Brixius claims that this word is a mere filler and that *–que* is not added to *praeterea* by classical poets (Appendix B, 540/22–32). On the second point he may (or may not) be right. But "praetereaque" marks the distinction between metaphorical drunkenness (Herod's passion for his wife and his luxurious living) and a literal drunkenness which is negligible by comparison.

224/12 **nouerca.** The malignity of stepmothers was proverbial (Otto, no. 1239 and Erasmus, *Adagia* 764, *Opera omnia,* 2, 323AB). See nos. 239, 241, and 258/9. Herodias was Salome's natural mother, but morally she was like a stepmother.

224/13 **Saltare . . . doces.** See *CW 12,* 279/18–25 and the Commentary thereon.

224/17 **Maius . . . fides.** In his discussion of perjury (*CW 6,* 764/5–6) More makes the point that one is not bound to keep a wrongful oath: "Alioqui qui se iurat occisurum quempiam peccaret, si non occidat." It is impossible to make grammar or sense out of this line if we accept the reading "quàm" for "quum" according to the errata of *1520*. Hence this "false" correction is presumably not More's. For the delayed connective, cf. "quam" in line 13.

225/5 **citior.** This word in the sense "earlier" seems to be unprecedented.

226/3 **Sanguine . . . Flaminij.** At a banquet Lucius Quinctius Flaminius (consul in 192 B.C.) complied with the request of a whore that he execute with an ax a criminal convicted of a capital crime (Cicero, *De senectute* 12.42). The accepted form of the name is now "Flamininus," but some manuscripts have "Flaminius."

227/4–5 **Corpora . . . patri.** The two brothers Atreus and Thyestes were rival claimants to the throne of Mycenae. Atreus killed the sons of Thyestes and served them to their father at a banquet. He revealed to Thyestes what flesh he had eaten by showing him the severed heads of his sons. The story is best known from Seneca's *Thyestes* (691–1006).

227/6–7 **Sic regi . . . Itym.** The Thracian king Tereus ravished Philomela, the sister of his queen Procne. The sisters took revenge by serving to Tereus the flesh of his and Procne's son, Itys. At the banquet Philomela hurled the severed head of Itys at Tereus. See Ovid, *Metamorphoses* 6.620–60.

228/1–4 **IN VEHEMENTER . . . quota est.** Translated from *AP* XI, 418. *Pl.* II, 13 (εἰς δυσειδεῖς), 17, sig. L_2.

> Ἀντίον ἠελίου στήσας ῥίνα, καὶ στόμα χάσκων,
> δείξεις τὰς ὥρας πᾶσι παρερχομένας.

228/4 **ostendas . . . est.** By adding "dentibus" More extends the parallel with the sundial: the nose is the pointer; the teeth, the marks on the disk. The Palatine reading is παρερχομένοις ("to all who pass by" rather than "the passing hours"). The edition of Johannes Lascaris (Venice, 1594) also reads παρερχομένας (sig. Λ_3).

229/1–4 **IN FVCATVM . . . emi?** Translated from *AP* XI, 310. *Pl.* II, 13 (εἰς δυσειδεῖς), 13, sig. L_2.

> Ἠγόρασας πλοκάμους, φῦκος, μέλι, κηρὸν, ὀδόντα.
> τῆς ἀυτῆς δαπάνης ὄψιν ἂν ἠγόρασας.

Cf. Martial 12.23.

229/3 **mel, ceraque.** Honey was used to cleanse the skin; wax, to soften it.

230/1–8 **IN HISTRIONEM . . . historiam.** Translated from *AP* XI, 254. *Pl.* II, 38 (εἰς ὀρχηστάς), 2, sig. M_5v.

Πάντα καθ' ἱστορίην ὀρχούμενος, ἓν τὸ μέγιστον
τῶν ἔργων παριδὼν, ἠνίασας μεγάλως.
τὴν μὲν γὰρ Νιόβην ὀρχούμενος, ὡς λίθος ἔστης.
καὶ πάλιν ὢν Καπανεὺς, ἐξαπίνης ἔπεσες.
ἀλλ' ἐπὶ τῆς Κανάκης ἀφυῶς, ὅτι καὶ ξίφος ἦν σοι,
καὶ ζῶν ἐξῆλθες, τοῦτο παρ' ἱστορίην.

230/6 **Capaneus.** The Greek shows that "Canapeus" in *1518* and *1520* is a misprint.

231/1–4 **IN HISTRIONEM . . . Nioben.** Translated from *AP* XI, 255. *Pl.* II, 38 (εἰς ορχηστάς), 2, sig. M_5v.

Δάφνην, καὶ Νιόβην ὀρχήσατο Μέμφις ὁ σιμός.
ὡς ξύλινος, Δάφνην. ὡς λίθινος, Νιόβην.

231/4 **Ligneus . . . Nioben.** This same line appears in a translation of this epigram wrongly attributed to Ausonius. The pseudo-Ausonian translation was first printed in Taddeo Ugoletti's edition of Ausonius (Parma, Angelus Ugolettus, July 10, 1499), which was reprinted in Venice in 1501. See *D. Magni Ausonii Opuscula,* ed. Karl Schenkl, *Monumenta Germaniae Historica, 5*/2 (Berlin, 1883), xxx–xxxi, 261.

232/1–4 **SOBRIOS . . . homo.** Translated from *AP* XI, 46. *Pl.* II, 47 (συμποτικὰ ἀστεΐσματα), 16, sig. N_4v.

Ἄνθρωποι δείλης, ὅτ' ἐπίνομεν· ἢν δὲ γένηται
ὄρθρος, ἐπ' ἀλλήλους θῆρες ἐγειρόμεθα.

233/1–4 **IN ANDREAM . . . repascis.** Charles Clay Doyle points out a parallel in Lucian's *Demonax* (35): "Again, when he was intending to make a voyage in winter, one of his friends remarked: 'Aren't you afraid the boat will capsize and the fishes will eat you?' 'I should be an ingrate,' said he, 'if I made any bones about letting the fishes eat me, when I have eaten so many of them.' "

236/1–6 **AD GALLVM . . . facis.** See note on 193/1–28. In a letter written at Ravensburg to Oswald Ulianus on November 30, 1523, Michael Hummelberg wrote a four-line Latin epigram against a plagiarist poet, pointing out that he was imitating this poem of More (Adalbert Horawitz, ed., *Analecten zur Geschichte des Humanismus in Schwaben 1512–1518* [Vienna, 1877], pp. 74–75).

237/1–5 **IN SCVRRAM . . . die.** As Charles Clay Doyle has pointed out ("Neglected Sources," pp. 5–7), this story was well known in the Middle Ages. It appears in *Mensa philosophica* (1475), a book on table manners which includes stories suitable for dinner conservation, in the following form: "Quidam histrio videns latrones in domo sua dixit, nescio quid vos hic potestis invenire in nocte: cum ego nihil invenire possim claro die" ([Cologne, c. 1480], fol. 76r). Bebel's *Facetiae* (*1*, no. 32, p. 18) gives the following version with the title "De histrione": "Quidam histrio cum noctu quosdam fures in domo sua deprehendisset, ait ad illos: 'Nescio, quid vos nocte hic invenire veletis, cum sereno die ego nihil invenire possim.'" Mr. Doyle ("Background," p. 61) also gives a version from *Scala Celi* (first published in 1476) by Johannes Gobius, who attributes the story to Jacobus de Vitriaco (d. 1240), though that telling does not seem to be extant. But there is a thirteenth-century version in the Syriac *Laughable Stories,* attributed to the Eastern Jacobite bishop John Abu'l-Faraj, known as Gregory Bar-Hebraeus (trans. E. A. Wallis Budge [London, 1897], p. 166, no. 658). Mr. Doyle has also provided the following versification of the story by Georgius Sabinus (1508–60) in his *Poemata* ([Leipzig, 1558], sig. T_8v):

Decoctoris Iocus

Cum sua decoctor subeuntem limina furem,
  Quaerere speratas nocte videret opes:
Nocte quid in nostris circumspicis aedibus? inquit,
  Hic ego nil media cernere luce queo.

The poem does not appear in the 1538 edition of Sabinus' poems. Cf. *AP* IX, 654 (*Pl.* IV, 14 [εἰς οἴκους], 6, sig. CC_5).

In *1518* More's poem is at the top of sig. K_1; the catchword at the foot of the facing page (sig. I_4v) is "De histrione." In *1520* the poem is at the top of sig. m_4v, and the catchword at the foot of the preceding page (sig. m_4) is "In curram." More must have originally entitled the poem "De histrione." During the printing of *1518* someone changed the title to "IN SCVRRAM PAVPEREM" in keeping with the first word of the poem itself, but left the catchword "De histrione" (Doyle, "Neglected Sources," pp. 5–7).

239/1–7 **IN PRIVIGNVM . . . fuge.** Translated from *AP* IX, 67. *Pl.* I, 49 (εἰς μητρυίαν), 1, sig. F_1v.

Στήλην μητρυιῆς μικρὰν λίθον ἔστεφε κοῦρος,
  ὡς βίον ἠλλάχθαι, καὶ τρόπον οἰόμενος.
ἡ δὲ, τάφῳ κλινθεῖσα, κατέκτανε παῖδα πεσοῦσα.
  φεύγετε μητρυιῆς καὶ τάφον οἱ πρόγονοι.

Erasmus quoted and translated this Greek epigram in *Adagia* 1195 (*Opera omnia, 2,* 481E). See note to 224/12.

240/1–4 **AD QVENDAM . . . tuus.** See note to 148/1–22. Charles Clay Doyle has pointed out an analogue in Plutarch's *The Education of Children, Moralia* 6F–7A:

> But to allow those who are still young to speak extempore stands responsible for the worst sort of rambling talk. They tell the story of a wretched painter, who, exhibiting to Apelles a painting, said, "This I have only this moment painted." Whereupon Apelles replied, "Even should you not say so, yet I know that it was painted hastily, and I only wonder that you have not painted more of like sort."

241/1–4 **IN NOVERCAS . . . potest.** Adapted from one of the following epigrams, probably the first: *AP* IX, 68–69. *Pl.* I, 49 (εἰς μητρυίαν), 2–3, sig. F_1v.

> Μητρυιαὶ, προγόνοισιν ἀεὶ κακόν. οὐδὲ φιλοῦσαι
> σώζουσιν. Φαῖδραν γνῶθι, καὶ Ἱππόλυτον.

> Μητρυιῆς δύσμηνις ἀεὶ χόλος. οὐδ' ἐν ἔρωτι
> ἤπιος. οἶδα πάθη σώφρονος Ἱππολύτου.

See note to 224/12.

241/3 **Priuigno . . . est.** See the Introduction, p. 32.

242/3–4 **Hispani . . . liber.** Martial 6.61(60).10: "Victurus genium debet habere liber."

242/6 **sine mente.** In no. 195 More makes Phoebus say that Brixius' *Chordigera* lacks "mens." A sidenote to More's *Letter to Brixius* makes the same point about Brixius' *Antimorus:* "Antimorus nomen libelli Brixi, quem sine mente nuper emisit" (see Appendix C, p. 632). Vergil says of the spectral image of Aeneas fashioned by Juno: "dat sine mente sonum" (*Aeneid* 10.640).

242/7–8 **ea est . . . suo.** Cf. no. 192 and Appendix C, Commentary at 602/17–19.

242/12 **qui caret ingenio.** In 6.61(60) Martial's interlocutor defends the writings of Pompullus: "Ingeniosa tamen Pompulli scripta feruntur" (line 5). But Martial replies that that is not enough for immortality.

242/14 **Genijs . . . malis.** Cf. no. 266.

242/15–16 **uati . . . bene est.** Martial 6.70.15: "Non est vivere, sed valere vita est." On *vivere* in the sense "live well" see Erasmus' *Moriae encomium, ASD 4/3,* Commentary at 194/276. In *Adagia* 2466 (*Opera omnia, 2,* 843C–D) Erasmus comments on the proverb "Vixit, dum vixit, bene":

"Est autem amphibologia in verbo *vivere,* quod interdum simpliciter vivere est, interdum genialiter vitam agere. . . ."

243/1–5 **DE CVPIDITATE . . . erit.** See *CW 4,* Commentary at 56/22 and 88/22.

244/1–8 **DE DEDITIONE . . . capi.** "Nervia" is the name of Nives, a small, little-known village in Luxembourg (*Orbis latinus, 3,* 15). Tournai is usually called "Tornacum" or "Tornacum Nerviorum" to distinguish it from two towns in France called "Tornacum" (*Orbis latinus, 3,* 501). More apparently uses "Nervia" to designate Tournai and the surrounding district. By comparison with the bloody victory of Julius Caesar over the Nervii (*De bello gallico* 2.15–28), Henry VIII's conquest of Tournai (September 21, 1513) might be called "sine sanguine." Apparently the inhabitants of Tournai did not find the English occupation advantageous, since large numbers of them abandoned the city from the time of the conquest until the city was returned to the French in October 1518. More visited Tournai in the summer of 1515. See Germain Marc'hadour, "Tournai-Doorijk: Comme là vit Thomas More," *Moreana, 46* (1975), 97–101; and C. G. Cruickshank, *Army Royal: Henry VIII's Invasion of France* (Oxford, 1969), pp. 127–85. Cf. *CW 6,* Commentary at 328/27.

245/1 **FABVLLA . . . ATTALO.** Martial applies the name Fabulla to a vain woman (1.64, 8.79), wearing powder and false hair (2.41, 6.12), who refuses her lover (4.81). He applies Attalus to a shabby busybody (1.79, 4.34).

246/2 **Febre . . . Hemitritaeo.** A semitertian fever, which returned every third day but remained longer and tended to grow progressively worse, was considered more dangerous than an ordinary tertian fever (Celsus 3.3.2).

246/3 **Sauromatae . . . medentis.** In his exile among the Sarmatians, Ovid complained that when he was sick he could not find adequate medical treatment (*Tristia* 3.3.3–12). At various times Sarmatia included most of Poland, eastern Russia, and parts of Rumania.

246/7 **Bitias.** He drank a deep draught at a banquet in the *Aeneid* (1.738–39).

247/1–9 **DE HESPERO . . . in deum.** More told a very similar anecdote in *A Dialogue Concerning Heresies* (*CW 6,* 234/8–14 and the Commentary thereon), where the penitent speaks a medley of French, Italian, and English. Since "Hesperia" was used poetically to mean Italy or Spain, the unusual personal name "Hesperus" may have Italian or Spanish overtones. Hesperus is also the same star as Lucifer and hence appropriate to a joke about devils. Jokes based on the confessional are frequent in Bebel's *Facetiae* (e.g., pp. 24, 25, 54, 57, 58, 62, 83, 88, 108, 112, 125, 147, 162).

247/6 **unquam.** As Garrod (p. 183) points out, the meter seems to require "nunquam." But only "unquam" appears in the early editions, and the slip may be More's.

247/7 **crediderat.** See the note to 94/3.

247/9 **in deum.** Brixius (Appendix B, 540/33–36) seems to think this is a patent barbarism, but More is obviously following the Credo of the mass: "Credo in unum deum." Cf. Augustine, *Sermo de symbolo* 1 (*PL 40*, 1190–91): "Non dicit, Credo Deum; vel, Credo Deo: quamvis et haec saluti necessaria sint. Aliud enim est credere illi, aliud credere illum, aliud credere in illum. Credere illi, est credere vera esse quae loquitur: credere illum, credere quia ipse est Deus: credere in illum, diligere illum."

248/1–14 **DE OCCASIONE . . . manus.** Translated from *AP* XVI, 275. *Pl.* IV, 13 (εἲς τὸν καιρόν), 1 (εἲς ἄγαλμα τοῦ Καιροῦ), sig. BB_6v.

Τίς; πόθεν ὁ πλάστης; Σικυώνιος. οὔνομα δὴ τίς;
  Λύσιππος. σὺ δὲ, τίς; Καιρὸς ὁ πανδαμάτωρ.
τίπτε δ' ἐπ' ἄκρα βέβηκας; ἀεὶ τροχάω. τί δὲ ταρσοὺς
  ποσσὶν ἔχεις διφυεῖς; ἵπταμ' ὑπηνέμιος.
χειρὶ δὲ δεξιτερῇ τί φέρεις ξυρόν; ἀνδράσι δεῖγμα,
  ὡς ἀκμῆς πάσης ὀξύτερος τελέθω.
ἡ δὲ κόμη, τί κατ' ὄψιν; ὑπαντιάσαντι λαβέσθαι.
  νὴ Δία τἀξόπιθεν, πρὸς τί φαλακρὰ πέλει;
τὸν γὰρ ἅπαξ πτηνοῖσι παραθρέξαντά με ποσσὶν,
  οὔτις ἔθ' ἱμείρων δράξεται ἐξόπιθεν.
τοῖον ὁ τεχνίτης με διέπλασεν εἵνεκεν ὑμέων
  ξεῖνε, καὶ ἐν προθύροις θῆκε διδασκαλίην.

In *Adagia* 670 (*Opera omnia, 2,* 289–90), Erasmus quotes the Greek and gives a less literal translation than More's. Erasmus also quotes an epigram of Ausonius (no. 33) partly based on the Greek. The Greek epigram, Erasmus' translation, and Ausonius' epigram do not appear under this adage in Aldus' edition of 1508 (sig. h_1), but they do appear in Froben's editions of 1520 (sigs. t_6v–u_1), 1523 (sigs. u_1v–u_2), and 1534 (sigs. x_5–x_5v).

250/1–2 **DE NVMMIS . . . SERVATIS.** Jerome Busleyden bequeathed 15 gold and 200 silver coins to his nephew Francis; because Francis died before his uncle, the coins came into the possession of Francis' mother (de Vocht, *Busleyden,* pp. 14, 63, 135). More himself had a coin collection (see 265/18–19). In July 1520 More gave two ancient coins to Francis Cranevelt (Allen, *4,* 350). Tunstall was also an enthusiastic collector of ancient coins (Allen, 2, 276).

250/7 **Caesareos . . . uultus.** More had a seal made in imitation of ancient coins; it contained the head of the emperor Titus (H. Meulon, "Une intaille antique," *Moreana, 10* (1966), 5–10; J. B. Trapp, "A Double 'Mise au Point,'" *Moreana, 11* (1966), 50–51).

251/2–3 **Ecquid . . . capsula?** Busleyden was very diffident about the value of his poetry; it was not published until 1950 (de Vocht, *Busleyden,* pp. 199–200, 205–55). See no. 279.

251/10–11 **An tibi . . . virginum?** Busleyden's collection contains no amatory or risqué poems; it consists of addresses to friends, epitaphs, religious and moral poems, and poems for his house.

251/14 **inflexilis.** This seems to be an unprecedented form for the usual *inflexibilis.* But it is an easy formation from *flexilis,* which is frequently used as a synonym of *flexibilis* (*TLL 6,* 905–06).

252/1–2 **AD BVSLIDIANVM . . . MECHLINIAE.** On Busleyden's new house, built about 1506–07, see de Vocht, *Busleyden,* pp. 50–65.

252/3 **contemplabar.** Writing to Erasmus around February 17, 1516, More described his visit to Busleyden at his new house during the summer of 1515: he was delighted during his embassy, he says,

> quod cum Buslidiano mihi intercessit amicitia, qui me pro egregia fortuna sua magnifice et pro animi bonitate comiter recepit. Domum tam singulari artificio excultam, tam eximia suppellectile instructam ostendit; ad haec tot vetustatis monumenta, quorum me scis esse percupidum; postremo tam egregie refertam bibliothecam, et ipsius pectus quauis etiam bibliotheca refertius, vt me plane obstupefecerit. (Allen, 2, 197)

See *CW 4,* Commentary at 20/11.

252/7–8 **illustres . . . manus.** An allusion to the Cretan labyrinth built by Daedalus (Ovid, *Metamorphoses,* 8.159–61).

252/9 **Apelles.** See note to 97/3 and cf. 276/23.

252/10–12 **Myronis . . . Praxitelem.** Cf. Statius, *Silvae* 2.2.63–67. Myron (fifth century B.C.) seems to have worked both in bronze and marble (*Paulys Real-Encyclopädie der classischen Altertumswissenschaft,* ed. Georg Wissowa et al. [Stuttgart, 1894–1963], 24 vols.; 2nd Series [1914–67], 9 vols.; *31,* 1124–30). But Lysippus (fourth century B.C.) was most famous for casting in bronze (Pliny, *Historia naturalis* 7.37.125 and 34.17.37). Pliny makes it clear that the Greek term *plastice* refers to modelling in clay, which was a preliminary step for casting in bronze (*Historia naturalis* 35.45.156). Though Praxiteles (fourth century B.C.) did some work in bronze, he was much more famous for his marble statues (*Historia naturalis,* 34.19.69).

252/13–14 **Disticha . . . Maro.** For the couplets Busleyden wrote for the paintings, windows, and furniture of his house see de Vocht, *Busleyden,* pp. 244–52.

252/15 **Organa . . . uoces.** Busleyden was very proud of his organ, which was probably built by the Nürnberg master Hans Suys. By the terms of his will it was moved to St. Rombaut's Church, where it was destroyed in 1580 (de Vocht, *Busleyden,* pp. 59–62). For *modulus* in the sense "pipe" see *TLL 8,* 1250, lines 32–38.

252/19–20 **At domus . . . senem.** Busleyden died at Bordeaux on August 27, 1517. Erasmus wrote two epitaphs for him (Reedijk, pp. 326–28). The Busleyden Palace in Mechlin, located in the Frederik de Merodestraat, now serves as the town museum for fine arts and archeology.

253/7–8 **Ille . . . ingenij.** The name "Agna" (ewe lamb) obviously suggests a docile disposition. "Philomenus" is derived from "Philomena," the medieval name of Philomela (lover of song), who was changed into a nightingale (see note to 227/6–7). But "Philomenus" (instead of "Philomelus") also suggests "lover of wrath" (φιλο-μῆνις), a personality not likely to be satisfied by Agna.

253/14 **cuculum . . . lupam.** Plautus uses "cuculus" to mean "adulterer" (e.g., *Asinaria* 923), but by More's time it also meant "cuckold" (see Erasmus, *Adagia,* 3484, *Opera omnia, 2,* 1072E; and *Moriae encomium, ASD 4/3,* Commentary on 95/421–22). Both meanings are applicable to Philomenus. *Lupa* meant not only "she-wolf," but also "prostitute" (e.g., Plautus, *Truculentus* 657).

254/1–9 **MEDICINAE . . . potest.** See Appendix D, pp. 699–701, below.

While More's epigram makes no pretense at loftiness, its scatology is not just a shocking irrelevancy. Rather, More was playing with a bit of medieval science: the notion that one evil smell can counteract another, and specifically that garlic and dung neutralize eath other. Whiting at S716 quotes two pertinent passages. One is from *Bartholemeus de Proprietatibus Rerum* [c.1398], trans. John de Trevisa (Westminster, W. de Worde, 1495; *STC* 1536), sig. JJ_8r: "And though noo good odoure be contrary to the other, yet some stenche is contrary to a nother stenche. For the stenche of Garlyk is contrari to the stenche of a dounghylle." The other is from Thomas Norton, *The Ordinall of Alchimy* [c. 1477], in Elias Ashmole, *Theatrum Chemicum Britannicum* (1652), p. 71: "This olde opinion you maie teach your Brother, [/] How noe good Odour is contrary to another; [/] But it is not soe of stinking smells. [/] For stinch of Garlick voydeth stinch of Dunghills." And, presumably, vice versa. For analogues from folktales recently collected see Vance Randolph, *Pissing in the Snow and Other Ozark Folktales,* annotated by Frank A. Hoffman (Urbana, Ill., 1976), pp. 130–31.

255/1–2 **NOVO . . . VERSO.** Erasmus' *Novum instrumentum* (Basel, 1516) contained the Greek text of the New Testament, a Latin translation, and a commentary. More's poem specifically concerns the Latin translation, which was the most widely accessible ("populis commoda," line 4) and immediately helpful ("commodiusue nihil," line 16).

255/4 **Prodit.** The present tense here dates More's epigram in the spring of 1516, when Erasmus' *New Testament* was published (Allen, 2, 183).

255/5–8 **Lex . . . situ.** More had made the same points in his letter to Martin van Dorp, dated October 21, 1515 (Rogers, pp. 57–59, lines 1033–1103; *SL,* pp. 43–45). In his letter to Dorp (May 1515), Erasmus comes even closer to what More says here: "Cur Hieronymus multa reprehendit et corrigit nominatim, quae tamen in hac [sc. vulgata] habentur aeditione? . . . At illud ipsa res clamitat, et vel caeco, quod aiunt, potest esse perspicuum, sepe vel ob imperitiam interpretis vel ob oscitantiam Graeca male reddita esse, sepe germanam ac veram lectionem ab indoctis librariis fuisse deprauatam, id quod cotidie videmus accidere, aliquoties mutatam a semidoctis parum attentis" (Allen, 2, 109).

255/5–10 **Lex . . . nitet.** These lines were designated to be expunged in the *Index librorum expurgatorum* printed at Madrid in 1584 by the order of the Inquisitor Gaspar Quiroga and reprinted at Saumur in 1601 from a copy of the 1584 edition obtained by Philipp Mornay du Plessis from the plunder taken from Cadiz by the Earl of Essex in 1596 (see F. H. Reusch, *Der Index der verbotenen Bücher,* 2 vols. [Bonn, 1883–85], *1,* 493). The lines are mentioned on sig. V_8 of the 1601 edition.

255/11–12 **Nec tamen . . . mediocre fuit.** The Latin translation in the 1516 edition is closer to the Vulgate than that in the second edition (1519), where Erasmus introduced his own original translation, made at Colet's instigation in England in 1505–06 (Allen, 2, 183). In his preface to the reader in the 1516 edition Erasmus explained that he departed from the Vulgate only when he thought it was clearly necessary, explaining his reasons in the annotations (Allen 2, 167).

255/13–14 **Quo fit . . . agi.** Because Erasmus stuck as closely as possible to the Vulgate, an inattentive reader might not notice important improvements.

256/1–5 **AD REVERENDISSIMVM . . . DATVM.** Thomas Wolsey became bishop of Lincoln in 1514, cardinal and lord chancellor in the fall of 1515. In a letter dated about June 21, 1516, More wrote Erasmus: "Dominus Cardinalis letissima fronte et litteras tuas et libros quos ante misisti recepit; ac perquam benigne pollicetur, quae spero praestiturum" (Allen, 2, 261). Among these books was almost surely a copy of Erasmus' recently published *Novum instrumentum.* Thus this poem can be dated in the late spring of 1516. In May 1519 Erasmus sent Wolsey a copy of the second edition of his New Testament (Allen, *3*, 575).

256/6 **Vnice . . . uirorum.** In 1519 Erasmus praised Wolsey as a great patron of learning (Allen, *3*, 588, 596).

256/8–9 **Cui populus . . . tuas.** More is probably thinking of the elaborate processions and ceremonies at Wolsey's installation as a cardinal in November 1515 (A. F. Pollard, *Wolsey* [London, 1929; reprint, New York, 1966], p. 56).

256/16–21 **Illa . . . tuis.** In August 1517 Wolsey said he intended to teach "the new law of the Star Chamber" (*LP*, 2/2, 1539, Appendix, no. 38). According to Pollard, "he meant a new dispensation of his own, new as distinct from the letter of the old testament of the common law, and instinct with the spirit of the new justice" (p. 73). As chancellor, Wolsey also presided in the Court of Chancery, primarily a court of equity designed to remedy grievances not provided for in common law. Wolsey himself later said of this court: "Therefore in his royal place of equal justice he hath constitute a chancellor, an officer to execute justice with clemency where conscience is oppressed by the rigor of the law. And therefore the Court of Chancery hath been heretofore commonly called the Court of Conscience because it had jurisdiction to command the high ministers of the common law to spare execution and judgment where conscience had most effect" (George Cavendish, *Life and Death of Cardinal*

Wolsey, in *Two Early Tudor Lives,* ed. R. S. Sylvester and D. P. Harding [New Haven and London, 1962], p. 121). In February 1516 More praised Wolsey's execution of the lord chancellor's duties (Allen, 2, 195).

256/23 **autori . . . faue.** In 1515 Wolsey was supposed to have granted Erasmus a prebend in the cathedral of Tournai, but it was eventually granted to someone else (Allen, 2, 149–50, note 15). More became involved in the somewhat delicate negotiations about this prebend (Allen, 2, 194). Erasmus received little but favor from Wolsey. As he himself wrote in 1524, "Cardinali Eboracensi, cui dedicauimus libellum Plutarchi, puto me nihil non debere ob singularem fauorem quo me iam olim prosequitur; et tamen hactenus ex illius munificentia non sum pilo factus ditior" (Allen, *1,* 43).

257/4 **Tanta . . . manu.** In 1512 William Warham, Archbishop of Canterbury, granted Erasmus an annual pension of £20 (Allen, *1,* 501). He also sent Erasmus a gift of 10 nobles on February 5, 1514 (Allen, *1,* 549). More helped Erasmus obtain payment of his pension from Warham's agent Maruffo (Allen, 2, 259–60, 344, 353).

257/6 **istud opus.** Like the preceding poem, these lines were almost surely designed to accompany a presentation copy of *Novum instrumentum.* In dedicating his edition of Jerome's letters to Warham, Erasmus tells him that he intended the dedication of *Novum instrumentum* to be shared by Pope Leo X and Warham (Allen, 2, 219). In June 1516, John Fisher wrote Erasmus to thank him for a copy of *Novum instrumentum;* Fisher immediately took the copy to Warham to show him the places where Erasmus had praised Warham (Allen, 2, 268–69).

257/11–12 **At partem . . . tuis.** In his dedication of *Novum instrumentum* to Leo X, Erasmus says he owes to Warham "quicquid illud est seu magnum seu pusillum, seu ludicrum seu saerium, quod huius ingenioli fundus produxerit" (Allen, 2, 186). The phrase "meritis imputat" suggests the language in which theologians discussed justification and grace. For Erasmus' commentary on *imputare* in Rom. 4:4–11 see *Opera omnia, 6,* 577F–578D.

258/1–16 **EPITAPHIVM . . . dabit.** For the text of this epigram, which More added to the prose epitaph he composed sometime between May 1532 and June 1533 (Allen, *10,* 31n. 258–61), I have collated not only *1518* and *1520,* but also the texts presented in the following four places:

1. More's letter to Erasmus of June 1533, as it appears in Erasmus' *De praeparatione ad mortem* (Basel, 1534), referred to in the variants as *Er.*
2. More's *Workes* of 1557 (sigs. XX_2v–XX_3), referred to as *1557.*

3. A manuscript in the Vatican collection, Codex Barberinus Latinus 2567, fol. 50, referred to as *Ba.* See Clarence H. Miller, "A Vatican Manuscript Containing Three Brief Works by St. Thomas More," *Moreana, 26* (1970), 41–44, and *CW 13,* cxliv.
4. The inscription slab of the tomb itself, now in Chelsea Old Church, as recorded in Harpsfield, p. 281, referred to as *T.* The lettering of the tomb was completely recut in the seventeenth (or perhaps the nineteenth) century.

The heading in *1557* says that More composed the epigram "XX yeres before," that is, in 1512 or 1513; but "XX yeres" is probably only approximate. It must have been written after More married his second wife, Alice, in 1511 (see note to 138/1–4). This is the last poem in *1518.* It is followed by a concluding formula (given in the variants) which may be translated: "The conclusion of the epigrams by the very famous and learned gentleman, Thomas More, citizen and undersheriff of London."

258/9–10 **priuignis . . . ulla suis.** See note to 224/12.

259/1–2 **AD SE . . . TEMPESTATEM.** In October 1515 More wrote that he had visited the universities of Louvain and Paris seven years before (Rogers, no. 15, lines 281–82). He was on a diplomatic mission to the Low Countries between May and October 1515. He was there again between August and December 1517 (Reynolds, pp. 99–100, 124–26), but the manuscript from which More's epigrams were to be printed was in Erasmus' hands before the mission of 1517 (see the Introduction, pp. 3–4).

259/5–6 **Talis . . . uices.** On August 19, 1517, shortly before leaving for Calais, More wrote Erasmus about an epidemic of the sweating sickness in England: "Nunc, vt audio, seuire Caleti incipit, quum nos eo extrudimur legatione functuri; tanquam parum sit in contagione vixisse, nisi sequamur etiam. Sed quid facias? Quod sors feret, ferendum est. Ego animum mihi in omnem euentum composui" (Allen, *3,* 47). See note to 246/2. The idea that life's joys are like the periods of relief between the attacks of an ague is stated by two early seventeenth-century writers as if it were a commonplace, but it does not appear in the usual collections of proverbs (Charles Clay Doyle, "John Webster's Echoes of More," *Moreana, 18* [1981], 51).

260/1–7 **IN PINGVEM . . . stulticia.** 1 Cor. 8:1. Cf. *Antibarbari* (*ASD 1/1,* 93), where (under the heading "ILLVD PAVLI SCIENTIA INFLAT, QVOMODO ACCIPIENDVM"), Erasmus begins: "Verum instant interim suo more et illud Paulinum constanter ingerunt. *Scientia inflat, charitas* *aedificat.* Non mentitur, inquiunt, Apostolus, *inflat scientia.* Nemo negat, sed inflat et inscitia." Although *Antibarbari* was not printed (in its revised form) until May 1520 and not published until August of that year (*ASD 1/1*, 14), manuscripts of an earlier version (containing the section quoted above) were in general circulation in July 1517 (Allen, *4*, 279). From a letter More wrote Erasmus on November 5, 1517, it is clear that Erasmus intended to introduce More himself as a speaker in the revised *Antibarbari* (Allen, *3*, 132–33), a plan he never carried out. In May 1517 Erasmus and Peter Giles commissioned a diptych by Quentin Metsys, which More received at Calais in October 1517 (Allen, *3*, 105–07; see no. 276, below). In the copy of Giles' portrait now at Longford Castle, his hand rests on a book labelled "ANTIBARBARON" ("*The King's Good Servant": Sir Thomas More 1477/8–1535*, catalogue of an exhibition at the National Portrait Gallery, ed. J. B. Trapp and H. Schulte Herbrüggen [London, 1977], no. 54, p. 42; *ASD 1/1*, 13).

260/5 **ample.** Ironically poised between the meanings "physically large" and "esteemed."

260/6 **gestas . . . uentrem.** Cf. *CW 14*, Commentary at 599/4.

261/1–3 **IN CHELONVM . . . philosophus.** It seems impossible to take "Chelone" as ablative with "hoc," referring to the Spartan sage Chilon. It seems better to take it as the vocative of "Chelonus," a name derived from χηλή (hoof) and ὄνος (ass). Hence, like *1563*, we have changed the heading from "IN CELONIVM" (*1518* and *1520*) to "IN CHELONVM." The philosopher (in a loose sense) who was great because of an ass is probably Apuleius, author of *The Golden Ass.* In *Lucius or the Ass* Lucian told the same story of a lively young man changed into an ass.

262/1–21 **DE FELE . . . fuit.** A remarkably realistic expansion of the proverb "As a cat plays with a mouse" (Whiting, C80; Tilley, C127). The escape of the mouse, which provides the ironical conclusion, is a departure from the usual proverbial outcome (the cat eats the mouse). The irony is marked by a sudden shift from the present to the perfect tense in line 17.

263/1–53 **GRATVLATVR . . . incolumen.** In *Dialogus de amoribus* . . . (Antwerp, [1551], sig. Ee_1v), Petrus Godofredus Carcasonensis gives a similar (and contrasting) anecdote from St. Ambrose: "Ad haec B. Ambrosius refert fabulis ferri, adolescentem quendam post amores meretricios peregre profectum, abolito amore, regressum postea veteri occurrentem dilectae, ne interpellasse quidam illam, ac cum ea mirata putaret non se agnitam, ideoque rursus obviam illi facta diceret: Ego sum[,] ipsum respondisse ego non sum ego" I have not been able to find the passage in St. Ambrose.

263/18–21 **Languidus . . . nouo.** Cf. Ovid, *Metamorphoses* 7.78–83.

263/21 **flamma uetusta.** Cf. *Aeneid* 4.23: "adgnosco veteris vestigia flammae."

263/24 **Lactea . . . colla.** Cf. *Aeneid* 8.660, 10.137.

263/26 **nostros.** More uses the plural here and at line 30 apparently because he was one of a group of boys at the dance. But in lines 15–17 More applies "mihi," "nostros," and "nostra" to himself alone.

263/48 **fuerat.** On the substitution of the pluperfect for the imperfect or perfect, see Kühner-Stegmann, *2/1*, 140–41.

263/49 **ipsa dies.** On the possible ambiguity of this phrase (the day of their first meeting or of their second), see Lee Cullen Khanna, "Images of Women in Thomas More's Poetry," *Albion, 10* (1978, Supplement), 81.

263/50–51 **At superos . . . tibi.** If we take "lustrum" as an exact period, twenty-five years have passed since More and Elizabeth fell in love. At that time More was sixteen years old (line 8). Therefore his long-delayed meeting with Elizabeth occurred forty-one years after his birth in 1477 or 1478, that is, in 1518 or 1519.

263/53 **contuar.** An archaism for *contuear.*

264/1–55 **T. MORVS . . . modo.** More may have sent Erasmus the manuscript copy for *1518* as early as September 1516, but Erasmus certainly had it by August 1517 (Allen, 2, 340 and *3*, 57). Hence More probably wrote this poem between the fall of 1517 and 1520, when it was first published. He might have written it during his visit to Calais between August and October 1517. But in 1518 and 1519 More often traveled on the king's business in England (see, e.g., Rogers, nos. 60, 77–79). Three prose letters More wrote to his daughters have reasonably been assigned to the years 1517 and 1518 (Rogers, nos. 43, 69, 70). But this poem has even closer affinities with a letter More wrote from court to his children's tutor William Gonell on the day before Pentecost, probably in 1518 (Rogers, no. 63). The last sentence of that letter is almost an outline of the poem: "Praeterea liberos meos, naturae primum iure charos, ac deinde literis et virtute chariores, efficies eo doctrinae ac bonorum incremento morum charissimos." Lines 20–39 of the poem detail More's natural paternal love; lines 40–49 show that love increased by the virtue and learning of the children; lines 50–55 predict that an increase in their virtue and learning will increase his love.

264/1–2 **MARGARETAE . . . IOANNI.** More's children by his first wife, Jane Colt, were born in the following years: Margaret, 1505; Elizabeth, 1506; Cicely, 1507; and John, probably 1509. See Rogers, no. 43; J. B. Trapp and H. Schulte Herbrüggen, *'The King's Good Servant': Sir Thomas More 1477/8–1535,* catalogue of the exhibition at the National Portrait Gallery (London, 1977), pp. 85–86.

264/3 **S. P.** That is, "Salutem plurimam [dicit]," echoed by "a patre missa salus" (line 5).

264/6 **peragratur . . . imbre.** "Peragratur iter" is unidiomatic and "pluuioque . . . imbre" is tautological.

264/7–8 **Dumque luto . . . carmen.** Here and in lines 16–17, More suggests that even when his horse's feet stumble or are stuck, his poetic feet continue.

264/23 **nodo . . . Herculeo.** A knot invented by Hercules, very difficult to untie, sometimes associated with the Gordian knot. In *Adagia* 1848 (*Opera omnia,* 2, 351), Erasmus cites Pliny, *Historia naturalis* 28.17.63–64 and Seneca, *Epistulae morales* 87.38.

264/41 **uidear.** Grammar and the parallel phrasing in lines 53 and 55 show that "uideor" in *1520* is a misprint.

264/42 **puerili . . . seniles.** The topos *puer-senex.* See note to 19/94–95.

265/9 **humilem . . . casam.** More lived in the Old Barge in Bucklersbury, London, until 1524, when he moved into a more splendid house in Chelsea (Reynolds, pp. 54, 179–92).

265/14 **Matrona.** The identity of this French lady (line 47) is unknown. Perhaps More is punning on her first name (Claire) in line 19. Between August and October 1518 a large French embassy, who had come to England to complete the Treaty of London, was lavishly entertained (*LP,* 2/2, nos. 4549, 4559, pp. 1393, 1395). See also *Calendar of State Papers and Manuscripts . . . Venice . . . ,* ed. Rawdon Brown and Allen Hinds, 38 vols. (London, 1864–1947), 2, no. 1074, p. 458.

265/18 **numismata.** See note to 250/1–2.

265/23 **ipso . . . stupor.** See Erasmus, *Moriae encomium, ASD 4/3,* Commentary at 95/434. Cf. *CW 14,* 115/6–7.

265/29 **genius . . . sinister.** Cf. Persius 4.27. See Erasmus, *Adagia* 72 (*Opera omnia,* 2, 55–56): "Genius malus."

265/31 **Surpueras.** Plautus and Horace use *surpui* for *surripui* (which More uses in line 53).

265/32 **Arte . . . Orpheus.** See Quintilian 1.10.9.

265/50–51 **Vulnus . . . opem.** Wounded by the spear of Achilles (who was from Thrace or Haemonia), Telephus learned from an oracle that his wound could be cured only by the spear which caused it. See Ovid, *Amores* 2.9.7–8; *Metamorphoses* 13.171–72.

265/52–54 **fabellae . . . fabellae.** The only precedents for the erroneous quantity "făbellae" seem to be a spurious and a genuine line from Avianus (6.14; 8.2).

266/1–8 **VERSVS . . . truci.** See Appendix B, 510/520–23.

266/16–17 **Vix . . . uanitas.** See 188/1–11 and Appendix C, 614/3–616/6.

266/20–23 **Vnum . . . furias.** For a similar ironic adaptation of the "Cretan liar" paradox see Lucian's *Vera historia* 1.4: ". . . though I tell the truth in nothing else I shall at least be truthful in saying that I am a liar."

266/21 **uero uerius.** See Erasmus, *Adagia* 3802 (*Opera omnia,* 2, 1145).

266/23 **Cingere . . . furias.** The dactylic substitution in the opening of the first dipody and the anapaestic in the opening of the second make the line strikingly irregular, especially in comparison with the preceding iambic lines.

267/1–3 **IN CHORDIGERAM . . . GALLI.** For Brixius' poem on the ship *Cordelière* see Appendix A. For Brixius' *Antimorus,* see Appendix B. Brixius entitled the poetic part of *Antimorus* "Sylva," meaning a collection of miscellaneous verse (as in Statius' *Silvae*).

267/7 **rate . . . furiae.** The phrase "rate sulticiae" refers to Sebastian Brant's *Narrenschiff,* which was first printed at Basel in 1494 and had been reprinted at least thirteen times before 1512. It was adapted into Latin (by Jacob Locher, Basel, 1497), Dutch (Lübeck, 1497), French (Paris, 1497; Lyons, 1498; Paris 1499), and twice into English (by Barclay, London, Pynson, 1509; by Watson, Westminster, Wynkyn de Worde, 1509). In 1505 Jodocus Badius Ascensius wrote his own independent *Navis stultifera.* See Aurelius Pompen, *The English Versions of The Ship of Fools* (New York, 1967), pp. 14–19. On the Furies in Brixius' *Antimorus,* see no. 266. "Furiae" here can mean "madness" as well as "the Furies."

268/1–5 **IN HVNC . . . protulisse.** In some extant copies of *Antimorus,* Brixius' line appears as More quotes it here, but it was corrected in the press so that in other copies it appears correctly: "Excussisse, forasque protulisse." See below, Appendix B, pp. 474–75.

268/11–12 **metiri . . . cubitis.** Cf. Erasmus, *Adagia* 589 (*Opera omnia,* 2,

255F–256B): "Tuo te pede metire." Cf. also Philostratus, *Vitae sophistarum* 525, on the eloquence of Polemo, a younger rival of Dionysius of Miletus: "Some think that from his lips flow springs, others measure his tongue by cubits, like the risings of the Nile."

269/2 **Germani.** See More's *Letter to Brixius,* Appendix C, p. 683, Commentary at 632/12.

269/6–7 **Nolo . . . sui.** See Appendix B, 488/120–25.

269/12 **coeli plagas.** The five are: two friged zones, two temperate, and one torrid zone between them. See Vergil *Georgies* 1.233–39 and *Aeneid* 7.225–27; *CW 4,* Commentary at 52/2.

269/14–17 **Ipse . . . ei.** See Appendix B, 510/542–45. More makes a similar humorous wager at *CW 8,* 643/36–644/3.

270/1–4 **IN FATVM . . . trahet.** Translated from *AP* X, 73. *Pl.* I, 13 (εἰς τὸν ἀνθρώπινον βίον), 9, sig. B_3.

> Εἰ τὸ φέρον σε φέρει, φέρε καὶ φέρου· εἰ δ' ἀγανακτεῖς,
> καὶ σαυτὸν λυπεῖς, καὶ τὸ φέρον σε φέρει.

See note to 259/5–6.

270/3 **ferris.** This form, instead of the usual *fereris,* seems to have been used only once by Ausonius (*Epigrammata* 112[114].2). See Alfonsus Traina, "Ad propositas quaestiones responsa: ferris an fereris?" *Latinitas, 3* (1955), 230.

271/1–9 **IN IACOBVM . . . nauiculam.** In 1510 Pope Julius II was preparing a "holy" league to unite Europe against France, his former ally, and drive her out of Italy. Louis XII planned to call a schismatic general council of the church to depose Julius. In October 1511, the Holy League was concluded by the Papacy, Spain, and England. The Empire joined in April 1512; Venice, a little later. Apart from Henry VIII, the members of the league were at best lukewarm belligerents. The league fell apart after the death of Julius II (February 21, 1513), and by 1514 peace was concluded between England and France. See Scarisbrick, pp. 26–40, and note to 184/4. This epigram was omitted from *1520* because by then England and France were again at peace (see note to 19/3).

271/2–3 **Dum . . . pontifici.** A royal proclamation of November 4, 1512, justified Henry VIII's invasion of France (and the taxes required for it) on the pious grounds of protecting the Pope and the church against the incursions of Louis XII (Hughes-Larkin, pp. 94–95). As James Tracy (p. 31) points out, in 1514 Erasmus expressed some doubt about these high motives: "Suscipiendi belli praetextus erat Iulius periclitans; sublata est causa belli [by Julius' death] nec tamen cessat bellum" (Allen, *1,* 553).

271/4 **Iacobus.** On the false quantity see note to 184/2.

271/10–11 **infans . . . manus.** At the age of fifteen James IV had been placed at the head of the rebels at the battle of Sauchieburn, where his father, James III, was killed on June 11, 1488 (*DNB*).

271/12 **perijt . . . suorum.** See note to 183/5–13.

272/1–2 **[VERSES . . . CLOTH].** More's pageant verses are introduced as follows in *1557:* "Mayster Thomas More in his youth deuysed in hys fathers house in London, a goodly hangyng of fyne paynted clothe, with nyne pageauntes, and verses ouer of euery of those pageauntes: which verses expressed and declared, what the ymages in those pageauntes represented: and also in those pageauntes were paynted, the thynges that the verses ouer them dyd (in effecte) declare, whiche verses here folowe" (*EW,* sig. ❡$_2$v). The subjects of the nine pageants were: Childhood, Manhood, Venus and Cupid, Age, Death, Fame, Time, Eternity, and the Poet. Except for the first, each figure overcomes its predecessor. See Robert A. Duffy, "Thomas More's 'Nine Pageants,'" *Moreana, 50* (1976), 21–23.

272/13 **Gaudia . . . honor.** The phrase is reminiscent of the opening line of a processional hymn for Palm Sunday in the Sarum rite (Dickinson, col. 260): "Gloria laus et honor." In *De tristitia* (*CW 14,* 367–69) More contrasted Christ's triumphal entry into Jerusalem with his arrest in the Garden of Olives to stress "assidue se uertentem humanarum rerum uicissitudinem."

273/1 **Morae.** Apparently More had not yet decided to Latinize his name in the second declension rather than the first. See 274/1.

273/1–2 **lucubraciunculas Holtiadae.** Numbers 273 and 274 first appeared at the beginning and end of John Holt's *Lac puerorum, Anglice Mylke for chyldren,* a Latin grammar written in English sometime before 1500 which survives only in later editions (see Introduction, pp. 65–66). John Holt was a fellow of Magdalen College at Oxford (1491–95), an usher at Magdalen College School (1494–96), grammar master of Cardinal Morton's boys at Lambeth Palace (c. 1496–1500), master of the Chichester prebendal school (1501–02), and the tutor of Prince Henry from 1502 till July 1504, when he died (Emden, 2, 953–54; Nicholas Orme, *English Schools in the Middle Ages* [London, 1973], pp. 28–29, 110). Whether or not he ever taught More at Oxford (as R. S. Stanier suggests in "Sir Thomas More's School Days," *The Times Literary Supplement,* January 1, 1954), he was on an intimate footing with More, as is shown by a letter More wrote from London (about November 1501) to Holt at Chichester (Rogers, no. 2). There is no evidence that he was related to

Nicholas Holt, who was very probably More's teacher at St. Anthony's School (see the correspondence on "Sir Thomas More's Schooldays" by J. O'Leary, R. J. Schoeck, L. Paul, and R. S. Stanier in *The Times Literary Supplement,* December 4, 18, and 25, 1953; and January 1, 1954). I have translated the patronymic "Holtiades" simply as "Holt," on the assumption that Holt chose it as a convenient Latin form (with a Greek ring to it, as in "Alcibiades") that runs easily into dactylic verse. Holt himself uses it in his epigram dedicating *Lac puerorum* to Cardinal Morton, though in the title of that epigram and at the end of the book he calls himself "Johannes holt." More uses the form "Holtus" in 274/21 and 30. John Leland called More's daughters "Moriades" in the title of a complimentary poem about them in his posthumously published *Encomia* (1589, *STC* 15447), reprinted in *De rebus britannicis collectanea,* ed. Thomas Hearne, 2nd ed., 6 vols. (London, 1770), *5,* 132. On More's association with John Holt and the possibility that More himself was granted the right to teach grammar by the University of Oxford in 1513, see Nelson, "Thomas More, Grammarian and Orator."

273/3 **pia furta.** More echoes Holt's dedicatory lines to Cardinal Morton:

> Hec equidem in varium breuiter collecta moretum.
> Ex multis rapui furta pudica locis. (sig. A_1v in *W*)

273/8 **Exiguum . . . opus.** Wynkyn de Worde's edition of *Lac puerorum* (ca. 1508) consists of forty-eight quarto leaves.

273/27–28 **Structa . . . erat.** The so-called long *Parvula* (*STC*[2] 23163.13) and the long *Accedence* (*STC*[2] 23153.4) associated with John Stanbridge, both Latin grammars in English, had been printed by 1495 (Orme, *English Schools,* pp. 108–09).

273/29 **tunsu.** More apparently coined the noun *tunsus* from *tundere* by analogy with such words as *tactus* from *tangere.*

273/31 **Ianua nostra.** Nelson ("Thomas More, Grammarian and Orator," p. 344) points out that "nostra" suggests More might have been concerned in the preparation of *Lac puerorum.* The figure of the door to a storehouse which begins in line 17 suggests that More was alluding to an extremely popular elementary grammar called *Janua,* attributed to Donatus and frequently printed after 1475. Its opening line is: "Ianua sum rudibus primam cupientibus artem." See Wolfgang Schmitt, "Die Ianua (Donatus)—ein Beitrag zur lateinischen Schulgrammatik des Mittelalters und der Renaissance," *Beiträge zur Inkunabelkunde,* Dritte Folge, *4* (1969), 50–54, 73–74.

273/32 **Ad digiti . . . sonum.** More refers wittily to two mnemonic diagrams (sigs. A_3v and A_5 in *W*) in *Lac puerorum:* one gives the declensions of *hic,* the other of *hic magister,* with the nominative, genitive, dative, accusative, and vocative from the thumb to the little finger and the ablative on the ball of the thumb. Perhaps the children were expected to drum their fingers ("sonum") as they recited the declensions.

274/2 **Macte puer.** Cf. Vergil, *Aeneid* 9.641: "macte nova virtute, puer: sic itur ad astra."

274/4 **Nec tibi . . . fructus.** Holt himself compared his book to a rustic salad ("moretum"); see note to 273/3.

274/6–9 **Carnis . . . sapor.** Cf. Heb. 5:12–14 and 1 Cor. 3:1–2.

274/14 **Sulpitii . . . mensa.** Johannes Sulpitius Verulanus (Giovanni Sulpizio da Veroli) was a fifteenth-century humanist who edited Frontinus, Lucan, Vegetius, and Vitruvius. His *De arte grammatica opus compendiosum* had been printed at least twelve times before 1500 (Ludwig Hain, *Repertorium bibliographicum* [Stuttgart and Paris, 1826–38], nos. 15143–51, 15154–56). It was also printed by Pynson (London, 1494 and 1498; *STC*[2] 23425 and 23426) and Wynkyn de Worde (Westminster, 1499, *STC*[2] 23427). But More also alludes here to Sulpitius' *De moribus puerorum carmen iuuenile* (also entitled *Stans puer ad mensam*), a poem on table manners (*STC*[2] 17030 and 23428–30). This poem was sometimes published as part of Sulpitius' grammar (e.g., sigs. a_4v–a_5v in an edition perhaps printed by Pincius about 1495, in the Beinecke Library at Yale, from which I quote in the following notes). The poem opens: "Quos decet in mensa mores seruare docemus" (sig. a_4v).

274/15 **Vtilibus . . . cibis.** The brief grammatical treatise of Phocas (fl. 300), *De nomine et verbo,* had been printed together with Diomedes' grammar at least nine times before 1500 (Ludwig Hain, *Repertorium bibliographicum* [Stuttgart and Paris, 1826–38], nos. 6214–16, 6218–23) and is available in Keil, 5, 410–39. In his preface Phocas says he has not striven to be original but rather to be brief and clear (Keil, 5, 410–11).

274/16 **Sepontini . . . Perotti.** Niccolò Perotti (1429–80), archbishop of Siponto, editor of Martial and Pliny, translator of Polybius, was perhaps best known for his *Cornucopia,* a linguistic compendium intended to elucidate Martial. In the 1540s at Ferrara his patron was William Grey, Henry VI's proctor to the papal curia (Giovanni Mercati, *Per la cronologia della vita e degli scritti di Niccolò Perotti,* Studi e Testi no. 44 [Rome, 1925], pp. 31–32). In 1468 at Viterbo he completed his *Rudimenta grammatices,* which was printed at least sixty times before 1500 (Mercati, p. 59).

274/17 **Diomedeis . . . cadis.** The grammarian Diomedes (fourth century after Christ) wrote a long treatise, *Ars grammatica,* which was printed at least nine times before 1500 (see note to 274/15). It is available in Keil, *1,* 297–529. The last part is a long discussion of scansion and verse.

274/19 **Dulcia . . . vtilibus.** Cf. Horace, *Ars poetica* 343: "omne tulit punctum qui miscuit utile dulci."

274/22–25 **Discenda . . . suis.** The core of Sulpitius' grammar consists of six sections: (1) the parts of speech; (2) the declension of nouns; (3) irregular nouns (heteroclites); (4) the gender of nouns; (5) the perfect tense and supines; (6) syntactical constructions, mainly of verbs. Since the student would already know the first two sections from Holt's grammar, More here gives the last four, echoing the language of a short poem in which Sulpitius lists the last five parts:

Nomina per casus nam te uariare docebo.
  Hinc sibi quod seruent nomina quaeque genus.
Post haec de uerbis & formis pauca locutus
  Praeteritis tradam iuncta supina suis.
Postremo ut uerbis deceat te iungere casus,
  Construere & partes foedere quasque suo. (sig. a_6)

(These lines do not appear in Wynkyn de Worde's edition, *STC*² 23427.)

274/26–31 **Sedulus . . . meis.** Sulpitius wrote a number of short metrical treatises, sometimes printed separately, sometimes with his grammar (as in Wynkyn de Worde's edition of the grammar, *STC*² 23427). *Ioan. Sulpitii Vetulani* [*sic*] *de versuum scansione. De sillabarum quantitate. De heroici carminis decoro & vitiis. De pedibus & diuersis generibus carminum precepta* (Venice, Joannes Tacuinus de Tridino, 24 September 1516, sig. F_2v) concludes with some lines by Sulpitius which More echoes here:

Me duce musarum choreas ingressa iuuentus
  Quae fingis dulci carmina docta sono.
Seu te meonio delectat ludere cantu,
  Siue per undenos nectere uerba pedes.
Seu quoscunque iuuat numeros contexere phoebo,
  Digna cane: obscenos non amat ille modos.
Et si non celebras me carmine: dicito saltem,
  Haec per Sulpitium plectra lyramque gero.

In Wynkyn de Worde's edition these lines appear out of place, at the beginning of the grammar (sig. a_2v).

275/1 **progymnasmata Linacri.** *Linacri progymnasmata Grammatices vulgaria* (London, John Rastell [1512]; *STC*[2] 15635), an elementary Latin grammar by Thomas Linacre (c. 1460–1524), was probably prepared at the request of John Colet for his new school at St. Paul's but was rejected as unsuitable (Allen, *1*, 467, 470). More's poem appears on the verso of the title page between twelve lines by Linacre and four lines by William Lily. Linacre tells his schoolboy readers that his grammar is experimental and advises their teachers that it contains innovations which will be justified in a later work; Lily points out that this is a correct edition of what had been issued in a corrupt form and under a false name. Writing to Colet on October 23, 1504, More called Linacre the director of his studies (Rogers, no. 3, lines 67–68). In 1515 More wrote Dorp that he had studied Aristotle's *Meteorologica* with Linacre some years before (Rogers, no. 15, lines 1297–1323). See Germain Marc'hadour, "Thomas More and Thomas Linacre," *Moreana, 13* (1967), 63–67.

275/4 **paruus.** The grammar consists of forty quarto leaves.

276/1–39 **Versus . . . tabellam!** In May 1517 Erasmus and Peter Giles commissioned Quentin Metsys to paint a diptych containing their portraits as a gift for Thomas More; after some delays caused by illness, Erasmus sent it to More at Calais on September 8, 1517 (Allen, *2*, 576; *3*, 33, 76). In July 1517 More was eagerly awaiting the paintings (Allen, *3*, 11–12). On October 7, 1517, he wrote Erasmus, thanking him heartily for this token of friendship and admiring especially the plastic, three-dimensional quality of the figures (Allen, *3*, 103–04). On the same day he wrote to thank Peter Giles, sending these epigrams and expressing his wonder at the skill with which Quentin imitated More's own handwriting in the letter Giles holds in the portrait (Allen, *3*, 105–07). Concerning the epigrams he remarked: "Versiculos quos in tabellam tam inscite feci quam illa scite depicta est, ad te perscripsi. Tu si digna videbuntur, Erasmo imparti; alioqui Vulcano dedas" (Allen, *3*, 105). On November 5, 1517, More wrote Erasmus: "Gaudeo versiculos meos in tabellam tibi placuisse. Tunstallus endecasyllabos plus satis laudauit, hexastichon moderate" (Allen, *3*, 133). The original paintings survive, somewhat modified by later hands, at Hampton Court (Erasmus) and Longford Castle (Giles). See Lorne Campbell, Margaret Mann Phillips, Hubertus Schulte Herbrüggen, and J. B. Trapp, "Quentin Matsys, Desiderius Erasmus, Pieter Gillis and Thomas More," *Burlington Magazine, 120* (November 1978), 716–25, from which the information in the following notes about the lettering and writing in the portraits is taken.

A manuscript in the British Library (Harleian 540), written in a sixteenth-century hand, contains a poem by William Lily on this diptych (fols. 223^{v}–224 [57^{v}–58]):

Guilielmi lilij in mori tabulam
continentem effegies erasmi & egidij /

pictam morus habet Quintino authore tabellam
continet effigies ista tabella duas
vna representat vultum scribentis erasmi
Altera virum clari nominis Egidium /
Illa aurum digito gestat quod morus Erasmo
Hac quas literulas miserat Egidio
Opposito tabule speculo consideret artes
Quilibet / Effigiem viuere vtranque putet /

(In the first two lines, the copyist miswrote "authore," "effigies," and "duas" as "ciuthore," "effigie," and "ducis." The mistake *ci* for *a* suggests copying from a manuscript written in an italic hand rather than from a printed copy or from a manuscript in a secretary hand.) The poem may be translated:

William Lily, on a painting belonging to More, containing
portraits of Erasmus and Giles

More has a painting executed by Quentin [Metsys]. This painting contains two portraits: one represents the countenance of Erasmus in the course of writing; the other, the famous gentleman Giles. One shows Erasmus wearing on his finger a gold [ring] sent to him by More; the other shows Giles with a letter sent to him by More. If one held up a mirror to the painting and considered its artistry, he would think both portraits are alive.

A list of Erasmus' money and rings, written by himself on April 9, 1534, includes four gold rings given to him by Thomas More: three with sapphires and one with a cameo in which the figure of a woman looking over her shoulder is engraved (*Bodleian Quarterly Record,* 2 [1917–19], Oxford, 1920, "Documents and Records I," p. 143). The cameo ring was mentioned in an inventory of Erasmus' possessions dated July 22, 1536; Erasmus had bequeathed it to Anna Lachner, wife of Hieronimus Froben (Emil Major, *Erasmus von Rotterdam,* Virorum illustrium reliquiae I [Basel, 1926], pp. 38, 48, 54). This may well be the ring Erasmus is wearing in the Metsys portrait; the design on the ring (clearer in the Rome copy than in the Hampton Court version) is the bust of a male or female figure (Campbell, Phillips, Herbrüggen, and Trapp, p. 724).

276/3 **Erasmum . . . Rhomanos.** On the recto page of the open book in which Erasmus is portrayed as writing appears:

(IN) EPISTOLAM (AD) RO
(M)ANOS PARIPHRASIS
ERASMI ROTERO
DAME

Paulus ego ille e Sau
lo factus, e turbulen
te pacificus, nuper obnox
(ius) legi mosaice. nunc
Moisi Liber(t)us. seruus au
tem factus Iesu.

On the facing verso page is "GRATIA." These words are written in a close imitation of Erasmus' own hand. (Letters in parentheses are no longer visible.)

276/4 **picti . . . suos.** The books on the shelves behind Erasmus are marked: "HIERONYMVS," "ΛΟΥΚΙΑΝΟΣ," "NOVVM TESTAMENT[VM]," and "HOR." The *H* of the last item was originally an *M* but has been falsely restored; the letters *OR* are not original and cover a paint loss. The original intention was probably "MOR[IAE] ENCOMIVM."

276/5 **Mori . . . effinxerat.** The letter Giles holds has been overpainted. What can now be made out is: V[iro] [illustrissimo?] Petro Egidio Am[ico charissimo] An[twerpiensi]. Because of the overpainting it does not help much to compare them with More's hand as preserved, for example, in the Valencia manuscript (*CW 14*). But More wrote Giles on October 7, 1517 that the imitation is so close that he is sure Quentin would make an excellent forger: "Mi Petre, cum omnia mirifice Quintinus noster expresserit, quam mirificum in primis falsarium videtur praestare posse! nam ita inscriptionem litterarum ad te mearum imitatus est vt ne ipse quidem idem iterum possem itidem" (Allen, *3*, 107).

276/11 **desyderio . . . absentis.** The form "absentis" can be either an objective genitive ([their] longing for the absent one) or subjective genitive (the absent one's longing [for them]); see *TLL 5*, 697, lines 73ff. The second couplet, which speaks of More's grief because of his absence from his friends, makes it more likely that "absentis" should be a subjective genetive referring to More.

276/16–20 **indicabit . . . libri.** See notes to 276/3–5.

276/23 **Apelle.** See note to 97/3.

276/40 **Quanti . . . tabellam!** The Giles portrait was sold in 1754 for 91 guineas (Campbell, Phillips, Herbrüggen, and Trapp, p. 717, n. 20).

277/5–6 **Tantos . . . inuicem.** See 276/7–8.

278/1–2 **conscriptum . . . oppeteret.** The publisher John Fowler thus dates the poem in 1532.

278/3–6 **Moraris . . . potest.** More puns on *mōror* ("to play the fool"), *mōrus* ("fool"), and *mŏror* ("to linger, stay"). For puns on More's name see Marc'hadour, "A Name for All Seasons," in *Essential Articles,* pp. 539–62, especially p. 556. Cf. Suetonius, *Nero* 33.1. More may also have had in mind μόϱος (death). Cf. Erasmus, *De praeparatione ad mortem, ASD 5/1,* 352/274–75.

278/9–10 **memor . . . mori.** The overtones of *memento mori* are inescapable. Ellis Heywood had already made the pun in his *Il Moro* ([Florence, 1556], sig. K_7v): the motto "memento mori" on a ring need not remind the wearer only of death but also of Thomas More: "parole . . . le quali potria anco intendere per un' altro stile, cioè che mi ricordassero non della morte, ma di uoi S[ignore] Moro." See Marc'hadour, "A Name for all Seasons," p. 555.

279/2–5 **Seu numeris . . . soli.** See notes to 251/2–3 and 252/3.

279/4 **Apolline scripsit.** The final *e* of "Apolline," which must be long by position, is metrically incorrect. It would have been simple and correct to write "Apolline panxit."

280/1–6 **Misisti . . . malorum.** In the Brailes flyleaf (see the Introduction, pp. 67–68 this poem is preceded by no. 278 (which Fowler in his heading said More wrote three years before his death) and is followed by two English poems (which William Rastell said More wrote while he was in the Tower; see *EW,* sig. XX_8v). Hence this poem also may have been written in the last three or four years of More's life. The unknown addressee of More's *Letter against Frith,* which is dated December 7 and was printed in December 1532, had sent More a manuscript of Frith's first treatise on the eucharist, which More returned together with a copy of his own *Letter against Frith:* "In my most hartye wyse I recommend me to you, & sende you by thys brynger the writing agayne which I receyued from you . . ." (*EW,* sig. G_5). Of Frith's treatise More also says: "Howebeit a worse than this is though the wordes be smoth and faire, the deuil (I trow) cannot make" (G_5). The riddling contrasts of the last two lines of the poem may refer to the "smoth and faire" words of Frith's treatise as opposed to his insidious denial of the real presence. For another poetic note to one of More's correspondents, see no. 200. The only other poem More wrote in hendecasyllabics is the second part of no. 276.

281/2–5 **A . . . adijce.** Tunstall says (*De arte supputandi* . . . , London, 1522, sig. s_4) that More supplied these mnemonic verses at his request. They apply to two methods of extrapolation to solve problems (which could be solved much more simply by algebra): (1) the method of more and less and (2) the method of differences. Tunstall's example is as follows: how can 100 coins be divided among three merchants so that the second receives 3 more than the first and the third 4 more than the second? We should choose two approximations (29 and 32), either of which may turn out to add up to either more (for example, 32 + 35 + 39 = 106) or less (for example, 29 + 32 + 36 = 97) than the required 100. By the method of more and less, if both approximations produce more or less than 100, one subtracts the smaller excess from the larger to produce a divider; multiplies the smaller approximation by the larger excess and the larger approximation by the smaller excess and subtracts the smaller of the two resultant numbers from the larger; and divides this difference by the divider to produce the correct figure. Thus approximations of 31 and 34 produce excesses of 3 and 12 and a divider of 9; cross multiplication produces 372 and 102; the difference, 270, divided by 9 produces the correct number, 30. But when the approximations produce one number above 100 and another below 100, the excess and the deficiency must be added instead of subtracted to produce the divider, and the dividend must be the sum and not the difference of the numbers produced by cross multiplication. Thus approximations of 29 and 34 produce a deficiency of 3 and an excess of 12 and a divider of 15; cross multiplication produces 348 and 102; their sum, 450, divided by 15 produces 30. The method of differences uses a proportion (the difference between the discrepancy from 100 to the difference between the approximations) to adjust the closer approximation to the correct number. More's verses apply to both methods: when both discrepancies produced by the approximations are either more or less than 100, the methods require subtraction ("deme," "subtrahe"); when one discrepancy is more and the other less than 100, both methods require addition ("coniungito," "adijce").

In his dedicatory epistle to More, Tunstall says he began working on his arithmetic book "ante aliquot annos" and worked on it intermittently over the years (Rogers, pp. 265–66). Hence More could have contributed his verses at any point in a long period of time, not necessarily at the time of publication.

APPENDIX A

The Chordigera *of Germanus Brixius*

EDITED BY STEPHEN MERRIAM FOLEY

APPENDIX A

The Chordigera *of Germanus Brixius*

ALTHOUGH GERMANUS BRIXIUS (Germain de Brie) is often remembered today as the object of Thomas More's scorn, he seemed to his contemporaries to deserve high praise as a humanist scholar and poet. He corresponded at length with Budé and Erasmus. As a leading member of the humanist circle in Paris, he was a friend of Guillaume and Jean du Bellay, of Baïf, Sadoleto, Macrin, Visagier, Longeuil, Bérauld, Bourbon, Vida, and Toussaint. Erasmus, even though he deplored the quarrel with More, admired Brixius' skill as a Hellenist, a poet, and a writer of Latin prose. Erasmus eagerly encouraged Brixius' translation of Chrysostom, and he praised Brixius without irony in the *Ciceronianus*, where Bulephorus describes Brixius as "a man of equal facility in both languages, whether he composes verse or writes an oration in prose, and no less gifted in his translations from Greek into the Latin tongue."[1] Salmon Macrin gives Brixius pride of place in a hymn to the poets of France:

> *Brixi, Dampetre, Borboni, Dolete,*
> *Vultei*que operis recentis author,
> Facunde numero elegante uates,
> Foelices animae atque honore dignae
> Queis et Gallia nostra gloriatur,
> Fidenter medium exerens et unguem
> Gentes Ausonias lacessit audax.[2]

De Brie, Dampierre, Bourbon, Dolet, and Visagier (author of a recent work, eloquent poet of polished verse), you happy spirits, worthy of honor, in whom France glories: confidently sticking out her middle finger, she boldly challenges the people of Italy.

---

[1]*ASD, 1/2*, 675–76. Brixius contributed an epitaph for Martin van Dorp to Froben's edition of the *Ciceronianus* (1528); see Allen, 7, 228n.

[2]*Hymnorum libri VI* (Paris, 1537), cited by D. Murarasu, *La Poésie néo-latine et la renaissance des lettres antiques en France, 1500–1549* (Paris, 1928), p. 139. For Murarasu's assessment of Brixius' poetry, see pp. 55–63.

Nicolas Bourbon, similarly, proclaims Brixius and Macrin the two best poets of a golden age.[1] And even the patriotic English antiquary John Leland, who knew More and his family, acknowledges that Brixius was a match for More in literary skill, if not in genius. He writes in his "Iudicium de Brixio et Moro":

> Brixius est nivei candoris plenus, et ille
> Judicii veri libera verba serit.
> Brixius aequavit mellito carmine Morum,
> Clarior ingenii nomine Morus erat.[2]

> De Brie is full of snow-white sincerity, and the other man exchanges frank words of sound judgment. De Brie equaled More in honey-sweet song, but More's reputation for genius was brighter.

Erasmus himself, even after publication of the *Antimorus*, insisted that More would have great respect for his opponent, if only they were better acquainted: "Is est, quem si nosses propius, hominis tum ingenio tum literis delectareris; neque quenquam alium facile reperies quem iudicares amore tuo digniorem."[3] When Brixius launched his counterattack in the *Antimorus* he was still a tyro—the *Chordigera* was his first major publication—and More was a man of international reputation. But Brixius was, nonetheless, a respected and promising man of letters. His quarrel with More was celebrated, embarrassing, and regretted, because it involved not merely one prominent humanist, but two.

Little is known about the early life of Germanus Brixius.[4] He is sup-

---

[1]*Les Bagatelles de Nicolas Bourbon*, ed. V. L. Saulnier (Paris, 1945), p. 48.

[2]*De rebus britannicis collectanea*, 2nd ed., Thomas Hearne, 6 vols. (London, 1774), 5, 97. Hearne reprints the first published edition of Leland's poetry, *Principium, ac illustrium aliquot et eruditorum in Anglia virorum, encomia* (London, 1589; *STC*[2] 15447).

[3]Allen, *4*, 241, lines 85–87.

[4]The best study of Brixius' life and literary career is that of Marie-Madeleine de la Garanderie: "Un Erasmien français: Germain de Brie," in *Colloquia Erasmiana Turonensia* (Paris, 1972), *1*, 359–79; this article is reprinted with minor alterations in de la Garanderie's *Christianisme et lettres profanes (1515–1535): Essai sur les mentalités des milieux intellectuels parisiens et sur la pensée de Guillaume Budé* (Lille, 1976). See also de la Garandarie's "Les Épitaphes latins d' Anne de Bretagne par Germain de Brie," *Annales de Bretagne, 74* (1967), 377–86. De la Garandarie relies principally on the work of two eighteenth-century historians: Jean Lebeuf, *Mémoires concernant l'histoire d'Auxerre* (Paris, 1743), 2, 501–503; and Philibert Papillon, *Bibliothèque des auteurs de Bourgogne* (Dijon, 1745). See also Scévole de Ste.-Marthe, *Gallorum doctrina illustrium elogia . . .* in *Scaevolae Sammarthani Opera*, 2 vols. in 1 (Paris, 1616), 2, sigs. A_6v–A_7; Louis Moréri, *Le Grand Dictionaire historique* (Paris, 1759), 2, 289; *Menagiana* (Paris, 1729), *1*, 130–33.

posed to have been born into a good family in Auxerre between 1488 and 1490 and to have received the degree of bachelor of laws before 1508. In 1508 he traveled to Venice, where he studied Greek under John Lascaris, and later to Padua, where he studied under Marcus Musurus. While in Italy, he met Pietro Bembo; Girolamo Aleandro, who wrote the prefatory letter to the *Chordigera;* and, most important, Erasmus, who was so impressed by Brixius' skill that he invited him to contribute to the *Adagia.* Two short Greek epigrams by Brixius and a longer poem by him in Latin stand at the head of the first Aldine edition of the *Adagia* in 1508.[1] In 1509 Brixius, now in holy orders, traveled to Rome in the service of Louis d'Amboise, bishop of Albi, nephew of the powerful cardinal Georges d'Amboise.[2] Brixius' patron, named cardinal by Julius II in January 1510 in an attempt to gain political leverage with Louis XII after the French victory over the Venetians at the battle of Agnadello, fell victim to the growing struggle between France and the papacy. In July 1510 he and four other French cardinals were forbidden to leave Rome; it was rumored that he was imprisoned at the Castello San Angelo. He died at Ancona in September 1510, perhaps poisoned, according to some French sources, by agents of the pope. Brixius, however, appears to have returned safely to France. Late in 1510 he was granted a position with Jean de Ganay, Chancellor of France. In November, after de Ganay's death, he was named Queen Anne's secretary. He retained his position in the royal household after Anne's death in 1514, and in 1517 he was appointed the king's almoner. While in the royal household, Brixius accumulated a rich collection of ecclesiastical benefices.[3] He was able to build himself elegant quarters in Paris, and in 1526 he became the proprietor of a country estate in Gentilly. In both his houses he enjoyed the rôle of the refined and lavish host—so much so that Budé even chided him for his attachment to the goods of fortune.[4] Brixius' literary reputation was based on his numerous epideictic works, both in prose

---

[1]See Allen, *1,* 447–48.

[2]On Louis d'Albi, see Denis Ste.-Marthe, *Gallia christiana,* 2nd ed., rev. Paul Piolin (Paris and Rome, 1856–99), *1,* 35–36; *4,* 422–23; corrected by Augustin Renaudet, *Le Concile gallican de Pise-Milan,* Bibliothèque de l'Institut Français de Florence, 1st Series (Paris, 1922), *7,* 3, 9; and also corrected by *Diarii di Marino Sanuto,* ed. Fulin Rinaldo et al. (Venice, 1879–1903) *9,* 9; *11,* 427.

[3]Archdeacon of Albi, 1512; canon of Auxerre, 1515–20; canon of Paris, 1519; he also received an income from the priory of St. Martin de Brétencourt, near Dourdan.

[4]Louis Delaruelle, *Répertoire analytique et chronologique de la correspondance de Guillaume Budé* (Toulouse, 1907), no. 103, pp. 156–57.

and in verse, and on his translations of five major works of Chrysostom.[1] He died on July 27, 1538.[2]

The event that thrust Brixius and More into controversy, the battle at sea between the *Regent* and the *Cordelière,* was one of the early encounters between England and France in the war of 1512–1514.[3] Erasmus, writing of this war to an Italian patron, described how it had disappointed his

---

[1]I list below the first editions of all the books by Brixius that I have been able to locate: *Chordigerae nauis conflagratio* (Paris: Josse Bade van Assche, 1513); *Diuersa epitaphia Annae Britannae Francorum reginae ac Britanniae ducis a Germano Brixio euisdem a secretis edita* (n.p. [Paris?] n.d. [1514]; *Antimorus* (Basel, Conrad Resch, 1519); *Poematia duo* (Paris, Nicolas de la Barre, 1520); *Chrysostomi quod multae quidem dignitatis sed difficile sit episcopum agere dialogus* (Paris, Simon de Colines, 1528); *Epistolae duae, Germani Brixii altera, altera Erasmi Roterodami, qua calumniam a suo Ciceroniano depellit, quam illi a quibusdam intentari ex Brixii literis intellexit, quasi scilicet Badium Budaeo, loco quodam, quod ad eloquentiam attinet, serio praetulerit* (Paris, Chrétien Wechel, 1528); *Germani Brixii epistolae gratulatoriae quatuor ad totidem viros, eiusdem epistolae quatuor ad totidem viros doctissimos, eiusdem versus aliquot ad Franciscum Galliarum regem* (Paris, Chrétien Wechel, 1531); *Diui Ioannis Chrysostomi in epistolam diui Pauli ad Romanos homiliae octo priores* (Basel, Jerome Froben and Nicolas Bischoff, 1533); *Epistolae duae lectu non indignae, altera ad reuerendissimum et amplissimum cardinalem Turnonium archepiscopum Bituricensem, altera ad reuerendum episcopum Parisiensem* (Paris, Antoine Augereau, 1534); *Comparatio regis et monachi,* in volume 5 of *Divi Ioannis Chrysostomi . . . Opera quatenus in hunc diem latio donata noscuntur omnia . . .* (Paris, Claude Chevallon, 1536). Perhaps just as important in establishing de Brie's reputation were the fugitive pieces that he published throughout his adult life: three poems in the first Aldine edition of Erasmus' *Adagiorum chiliades* (Venice, Aldus Manutius, 1508); preface and Greek poems in *Christophori Longolii civis romani perduellionis rei defensiones duae* (Paris, Josse Bade van Assche, 1520); Greek letters in Budé's *Epistolae posteriores* (Paris, Josse Bade van Assche, 1522); epitaph for Jean Bertauld in Cicero's *Opera philosophica* (Paris, Josse Bade van Assche, 1521); epitaph for Martin van Dorp in the first edition of Erasmus' *Ciceronianus* (Basel, Johann Froben, 1528); letter praising Erasmus in *Catalogi duo operum Des. Erasmi* (Basel, Jerome Froben and Nicolas Bischoff, 1537). Other miscellaneous poems may be most conveniently found in Jan Gruter's *Delitiae C. poetarum gallorum . . .* (Frankfurt, Jonah Rose, 1609) *1,* 720–66 and *3,* 1143: four elegiac poems on François Deloynes; two elegiac poems on Marcus Musurus; two elegies on Christophe Longeuil; a poem to Salmon Macrin; a poem to François and Claude Robertet; a series of verses on the statuary of Fontainebleau, addressed to Francis I; an epideictic poem addressed to Jean Visagier.

[2]Lebeuf (p. 503), following the register of Notre Dame de Paris, states that Brixius died in the village of Brezzoles on July 27, 1538. Scévole de Ste.-Marthe, curiously, reports that he died mad in the countryside near Chartres: "Sed inclinante iam aetate, postquam reprimi vitae feruor coeptus est, in atrae bilis incommodum incidit. Qua in aegritudine suspicionum, terrorumque plenus miserabile senium exegit: eaque tandem infestius vrgente, dum ab aula, quae tum apud Blaesios agebat, Lutetiam reuertitur, in agro Carnutensi extinctus est, eodem fere tempore, quo Budaeum, quicum illi ex studiorum coniunctione non vulgaris amicitiae vsus intercedebat, ereptum quoque luxit Gallia" (sig. A7v). Brezolles is about seventy-five kilometers northwest of Chartres. Budé died in 1540.

[3]For the background of the war, see H. A. L. Fisher, *The History of England from the Accession of Henry VII to the Death of Henry VIII, 1485–1547,* 2nd ed. (London, 1913), vol. 5

hopes for a golden age during the reign of Henry VIII: "I dreamt of an age truly golden and [of] fortunate isles—and then, to quote Aristophanes, 'up I woke.' . . . My other friends, and even the king himself, the parent of the golden age, were soon overtaken by the storms of war and torn from commerce with the Muses; with such a blast had Julius' famous trumpet roused the whole world to a passion for Mars."[1] Julius II, as Erasmus suggests, had brought together the Empire, England, Spain, the Swiss, and the Venetians in a Holy League against France.

In March 1508 France had joined with the pope, the Empire, and Spain in the League of Cambrai, which was intended to check the power of Venice, France's former ally. But Louis XII's great victory at Agnadello in May 1509 made Julius suspect his French ally's ambitions. In February 1510 Julius concluded a treaty with Venice; in March he made a treaty with the Swiss, who agreed to supply troops; and in July he persuaded Ferdinand to join him. After some defeats in the summer of 1510, Julius himself led his troops into battle, capturing Concordia and Mirandola in January 1511. But in May Julius suffered an embarrassing and dangerous loss when the French recaptured Mirandola and moved on to take Bologna, a papal stronghold. Louis also promoted a renewal of Gallicanism among the French bishops. In May 1511 a schismatic group of French cardinals called for a general council at Pisa. Julius in turn called for a Lateran council and appealed to the princes of Europe to join in a strong alliance, a Holy League, against the enemies of the church. In October 1511 he succeeded in uniting Spain, the Swiss, and the Venetians in the league. Meanwhile, Louis anxiously tried to prevent England from joining. He helped to settle disputes between Scotland and England; he overlooked provocation when Henry sent troops to the Netherlands to fight against a French ally, the duke of Gelders, in the summer of 1511; and he continued to make the semiannual payments to England specified by the Treaty of Étaples, concluded between Charles VIII and Henry VII in 1492 and renewed by Henry VIII and Louis in March 1510, just after Henry's accession to the throne.[2] Henry, however, was eager to prove his royal worth in battle, and his father-in-law, Ferdi-

---

of the *Political History of England,* ed. William Hunt and Reginald Poole, 12 vols. (London, 1905–10), pp. 164–92; J. D. Mackie, *The Earlier Tudors, 1485–1558* (Oxford, 1952), vol. 7 of the *Oxford History of England* (Oxford, 1934–65), pp. 267–85; P. S. Crowson, *Tudor Foreign Policy* (London, 1973), pp. 70–73; R. B. Wernham, *Before the Armada: The Growth of English Foreign Policy, 1485–1588* (London, 1966), pp. 77–88.

[1]Allen, 2, 70, lines 49–59; *CWE 3*, 89.

[2]*LP, 1/1*, no. 406, p. 186.

nand, was happy to encourage him. One army went to Gelders in 1511; another to Cadiz to help Ferdinand against the Moors; and an English fleet was dispatched to the North Sea in pursuit of Scottish privateers. In November 1511 England formally joined the Holy League. Henry also made a further agreement with Ferdinand to outfit a joint expedition to Guyenne, and to share the responsibility for naval operations against France. Ferdinand never fulfilled his part of the agreement, but Henry enthusiastically readied the army and the fleet for war.

In April 1512 an English fleet under the command of Sir Edward Howard set out from Portsmouth. For two weeks the English chased French fishing vessels and plundered merchant ships in the Channel. In May they put to flight a convoy of Scottish ships escorting home the French ambassador, who had just concluded a pact of mutual assistance between Louis and James IV. Later in May the English fleet was strengthened by the addition of two new landing barges and of the newly outfitted *Regent,* one of the two largest ships the English possessed, a 1,000-ton vessel built by Henry VII in 1486, carrying 400 soldiers and 300 mariners. In June, returning from a convoy of troops to Fuentarabia, Howard landed a raiding party at Bertheune in Brittany, stormed the garrison, and raided villages in the surrounding countryside. One party was sent to burn the town of Le Conquet and the estate of Hervé de Portzmoguer, the captain of the *Marie-la-Cordelière,* a 900-ton carrack that was the pride of the joint fleet of Brittany and France.[1] Additions continued to be made to the English fleet during the summer of 1512, and in July Thomas Knyvet, master of the horse to Henry, brother-in-law of Sir Edward Howard, and captain of the *Regent,* was charged with revictualling the entire fleet in preparation for a major assault. The French too strengthened their naval forces. Louis withdrew his ships from Genoa and sent them, along with his admiral in the Mediterranean, Prégent de Bidoux, to Brittany to bolster the fleet in the Channel.

The English fleet set out from Portsmouth for Brest as soon as the full French force was believed to have assembled. On the morning of August 10, Saint Lawrence's day, Howard sighted the French at anchor two or

---

[1]Anne of Brittany, wife successively of Charles VIII and Louis XII, put her fleet at the disposal of the French, although Brittany retained its independence until 1532; the name of the *Cordelière* recalls Anne's foundation of L'Ordre de la Cordelière, an order of Franciscan tertiaries for young ladies at court. For the naval campaigns of the war, see Alfred Spont, *Letters and Papers Relating to the War with France, 1512–13* (London, 1897). Spont includes (pp. 1–210) a collection of the primary sources for the study of the war and also provides a narrative summary (pp. vii–xlviii). See also William L. Clowes, *The Royal Navy: A History from the Earliest Times to the Present,* 7 vols., (London, 1897–1903), *1,* 450–58; Charles de la Roncière, *Histoire de la marine française,* 6 vols. (Paris, 1899–1932), *3,* 89–128.

three miles off the neck of the harbor at Brest. The *Cordelière* and a few other ships had just returned from the coast of Spain, and the night before, Saint Lawrence's eve, the ship had been the site of a large celebration. Several hundred local gentlemen (and some of their wives) had come out to join the party. Some remained on board. The battle between the two fleets lasted most of the day. All accounts agree that the most dramatic action occurred in the battle between the two most prized ships of the navies, the *Regent* and the *Cordelière*. A letter (August 26) from Thomas Wolsey to Richard Fox, bishop of Winchester and Lord Privy Seal, provides a vivid account of the struggle:

> And to assertayne yow of the lamentabyll and sorowfull tydyngis and chance wych hath fortunyd by the see, owr folkis, on Tuysday was fortnygth, met with xx gret shyppys of Frawnce, the best with sayle and furnyshed with artyllery and men that euyr was seyn. And aftyr innumerabyll shotynge of gunnys and long chasyng one a nother, at the last the Regent moste valyently bordyd the gret Caryke of Brest [the *Cordelière*]. Wherin wer fower lordis, ccc gentylmen, viij[c] solgers and marynes, iiij[c] crosbowe men, c guners, cc tonne of wyne, c pypys of befe, lx barellis of gonepowder and xv gret brasyn cortawdis, with to meruelose a nombyr of schot and other gunys of euery sorte. Owr men so valyently acquyt them sylf that within one ower fygth they had vtterly venquyshyd with schot of gonnys and arows the sayd Caryke and slayne moste parte of the men within the same. And sodenly as they war yeldyng them sylf, the Caryke was one a flamyng fyer, and lycke wyse the Regent within the turnyng of one hand. She was so ankyrryd and fastyd to the Caryk that by no meanys possybyll she mygth for hyr salfgarde depart from the same. And so bothe in sygth within thre owerys war burnt, and moste parte of the men in them. Sir Thomas Knyuet, wych moste valyently acquyt hym sylf that day, was slayne with one gonne; Sir John Carewe with dyuers others, whos namys be nat yet knowne, be lycke wyse slayne. I pray God to haue mercy on ther sowlys.[1]

Wolsey adds in a postscript: "The resydue of the French flete aftyr longe chassyng was by owr folkis put to flygt and drevyn in to Brest hauyn. Ther war vi as gret shyppys of the sayd flete as the Regent or Souerayn. Howbeyt as cowardis they flede."

The flight of at least some of the French fleet is confirmed by charges

[1]*Letters of Richard Fox, 1486–1527*, ed. P. S. Allen and H. M. Allen (Oxford, 1929), no. 37, pp. 56–58; *LP, 1/1*, no. 1356, p. 628, Spont. no. 30, pp. 49–50.

of cowardice and desertion brought against a French vice-admiral by one of his captains: "Thus it may be assumed that if [he] had stayed with us, we should have had victory over the enemy."[1] But all the surviving contemporary accounts of the battle differ greatly in detail.[2] The Florentine ambassador wrote from Paris (August 18) that the battle between the two fleets was a stalemate.[3] An Italian wrote from London (September 5) that the whole French fleet except the *Cordelière* turned back, and that the sailors on the *Cordelière* had finally fired their own ship.[4] Wolsey told a story slightly different from the one he told Fox, when he composed in Latin an elegant description of the battle for Cardinal Bainbridge. Here Wolsey reports that "a certain Frenchman," seeing that his ship had surrendered, decided that he would "rather die a heretic than a Christian," and set fire to the powder of his ship.[5] A Breton chronicler wrote in 1542 that at the end of the terrible battle between the two ships, "someone of the *Cordelière* who was on top of the mizzenmast threw fire down into the *Regent*," and that Hervé de Portzmoguer sought a Roman death, jumping fully armed into the sea.[6] Hall (1548) relates an entirely different sequence of events:

> . . . but when sir Thomas Kneuet whiche was ready to haue borded the greate ship of Depe, sawe that the Souereigne had missed the Caricke, which sir Anthony Oughtred chased hard at the starne, and bowged her in diuerse places, and set a fire her powder as some say, but sodainly the Regent crappeled with her a long boord and when thei of the Carick perceiued that thei could not depart, thei let slip and Ancre, and so with the streme the shippes turned, and the Caricke was on the wetherside, and the Regent on the lye side, the fight was very cruell, for the archers of the Englishe parte, and the Crossebowes of the Frenche part did their vttermoste: but for all

---

[1]Spont, no. 43, p. 66.

[2]Auguste Jal attempted to compare many of the sources, but his work raises more problems than it solves; see his "Marie-la-Cordelière (xvie siècle), étude pour une histoire de la marine française," *Annales maritimes et coloniales, 109* (1844), 993–1072. See also Jal's "L'Herveus de Germain de Brie: Errata pour 'Marie-la-Cordelière,'" *Annales maritimes et coloniales, 110* (1845), 717–30. Charles de la Roncière attempted a summary based on documents in Spont: "La Cordelière et le Régent," *Revue des questions historiques*, New Series, vol. 66 (1899), 200–10.

[3]Spont, no. 29, pp. 48–49.

[4]Spont, no. 33, pp. 52–55.

[5]Spont, no. 36, pp. 57–58.

[6]Alain Bouchart, *Les Grands Annales ou chroniques de Bretagne*, quoted by Spont, pp. xxvi–xxvii, n. 2.

The *Cordelière* and *Regent* in combat (reduced)

> that the English men entered the Caricke, whiche seyng a varlet Gonner beyng desperate put fire in the Gonne powder as other saie, and set the whole ship of fire, the flame wherof, set fire in the Regent, and so these twoo noble shippes which were so crappeled together that thei could not part, wer consumed by fire.[1]

The battle between the *Regent* and the *Cordelière* became a *cause célèbre* for the French. Brixius addressed his poem to Queen Anne in November 1512, just three months after the battle. His work was translated into French by Pierre Choque, a Breton who served as king-at-arms to Anne and who had sailed on an earlier voyage of the *Cordelière.*[2] Another epic poem, the *Herveis,* was composed by Humbert de Montmoret.[3] A folk song about the battle has survived to this day.[4] In England, the first reaction to the battle was shock. Henry was deeply shaken by the loss of the *Regent,* but he concealed his disappointment. Wolsey advised his correspondent Fox: "And my lorde, at the reuerens of God, kepe thes tydyngis secret to yowr sylf; for ther is no lyuyng man knowyth the same here but onely the kyng and I. Yowr lordeshyp knowyth rygth wel that yt ys exspedyent for a whyl to kepe the same secret. To se howe the Kyng takyth the matere and behauyth hym sylf, ye wold meruell, and myche allowe hys wyse and constant maner. I haue nat on my fayth seyn the lycke."[5] In the fall and winter of 1512–13 both the English and French strengthened their fleets in preparation for their next encounter, which would be an affair of honor for both sides. Emotions probably ran high in early 1513, when More wrote his epigrams on Brixius. Sir Edward Howard had vowed revenge. "Sir Edward," Wolsey wrote to Fox, "hath made hys voue to God that he wyl neuyr se the Kyng in the face tyl he hath reuengyd the dethe of the nobyll and valyant knygth sir Thomas Knyvet."[1] Howard's chance came on April 25, 1513, but it proved a further disappointment for the English. A squadron of galleys under Prégent de Bidoux was anchored off Brest. Howard led the attack in person from a small row-barge. He grappled and boarded the admiral's galley but was suddenly thrust overboard by pikes and drowned. The English fleet retreated in disgrace. Although the course of the war

---

[1]Hall, *Chronicle; Containing the History of England* (London, 1809), p. 534.

[2]Published by Jal, "Marie-la-Cordelière," pp. 1019–41.

[3]*Fratris Humbertani Montismoretani Herveis* (Paris, n.d.), *Inventaire chronologique,* 2, no. 625.

[4]The song is reprinted in *Moreana, 63/1* (1979), 48.

[5]*Letters of Richard Fox,* p. 58.

[6]*Letters of Richard Fox,* p. 58.

turned with Henry's victories at Therouanne and Tournai in August and September of 1513, his initial forays as a warrior prince were far from promising.

A Note on the Text

The text of the *Chordigera* given here is that of the first edition: *Chordigerae nauis conflagratio* (Paris, Josse Bade van Assche, January 15, 1513). Later in 1513 Josse Bade issued a second edition with the same date; for the distinction, see Phillipe Renouard, *Imprimeurs et Libraires parisiens du* XVIe *siècle* (Paris, 1969), 2, 106. A third edition was issued in Strassburg by Matthias Schürer in February 1514: *Chordigerae navis conflagratio, ex secunda recognitione.*[1] Donald Stone has published an edition of the poem with a complete textual apparatus (*Humanistica Lovaniensia,* 29 [1980], 177–193). The punctuation and capitalization of my text have been changed to make reading easier. Two misprints in the first edition have been corrected with readings from the second: "consecrandum" for "consecandum," 446/13; "praeconia" for "praecordia," 456/192. In three places (444/32, 446/5 and 32) "omnis" has been emended to "omnes." The sidenotes have been moved to the bottom of the page and final periods in the sidenotes have been silently omitted.

[1]Proctor and Isaac, part 2, sec. 1, no. 10219.

Hieronymvs Aleander Mottensis
Germano Brixio
Archidiacono Albiensi
et Francorvm Reginae a secretis. S.P.D.

Mirari non satis poteram dum adhuc in Italia essemus versatile tuum ingenium plurimamque graecae iuxta et latinae linguae eruditionem, qua non tuos solum gallos praestare, verumetiam italos ipsos, et eos non vulgares sed bonarum proceres literarum prouocare posses. Nunc vero vbi tuum poema legi quod in conflagrationem regalis nauis composuisti, coepi quamprimum sic mecum: Hem miseri homunciones, et conquerimur nunc nobis deesse ingenium, secordiamque nostram in saeculi inuidiam reiicimus. Quid hoc poemate grauius, elegantius, exactius. Quid epistola qua poema Reginae nuncupatur nitidius, purius, aut latinum magis. Vellem mihi per temporis spatium et epistolae terminos licere laudes huius libelli vberiore stilo exequi. Sed quemadmodum ii qui in parua tabella totum nostris oculis orbem delineant, ita si quis velit e breuibus verbis sententiam animi mei cognoscere, quantum ex isto poematio coniecto, sperare ausim te (modo pergas, et tibi per aulicarum curarum remissionem liceat) si non Ciceronem aut Vergilium (quos vt Achillem semper excipi apud literarum censores in confesso est) ex illis certe fore qui inter veteres possis merito connumerari. Mihi vero id etiamnum videris adsequutus quod paucis hactenus nouimus contigisse. Omnium enim nostrorum oratorum M. Tullius, Poetarum vero P. Maro facile primas obtinet. Et plaerique veterum, non nulli etiam recentiorum in vna quapiam re claruerunt. Sed illi iidem vbi aliud quidquam a sua arte attentare ausi sunt, Dei boni, quam ex eminenti illa curuli quodam veluti automato repente sibi subrepti in imo subsidunt. Adeo et antiquitus rarum fuit, et nostris temporibus adhuc rarius, aliquos inuenire qui iidem et carmine et soluta oratione excelluerint. Inter quos si quis te mi Germane non reponat, vel non sani iudicii, vel parum defaecati in te animi iure optimo existimabitur. Non immerito igitur tuum munus admirata augustissima francorum Regina Anna te sibi adsciuit a secretis et multis fauoribus multisque gratiis, quarum plenissima est, indies magis fouere pergit. Id autem quam prudenter fecerit praestantissima virago, cognoscunt ii qui tuam in rebus agendis dexteritatem, fidem, diligentiam, strenuasque operas non ignorant quas in Italia primum Ioanni

Girolamo Aleandro of La Motta to Germain de Brie Archdeacon of Albi and Secretary to the Queen of France Greetings

I could not sufficiently admire, while we were still in Italy, your versatile talent and great erudition in the Latin and Greek tongues alike; in this you could not only surpass your fellow Frenchmen, but challenge the Italians themselves—and not unlearned Italians, but the leading men of letters. But now, when I read your poem, which you composed on the burning of the royal ship, I immediately said to myself: Alas poor little men, we complain now that we have no talent, and blame our dullness on the unpropitious age in which we live. What could be more weighty, more elegant, more accurate than this poem? What could be more polished, more pure, more Roman than the epistle in which the poem is presented to the queen? Would that I were allowed a period of time and a letter long enough to pursue the praises of this little book in a more copious style. But just like those who might portray the whole world before our eyes in a small picture, so, if anyone wished to know the thoughts of my mind from some brief words, insofar as I can judge from this poem, I should venture to hope that (provided you persist and are allowed some respite from public responsibilities at court) you might be, if not Cicero or Vergil (who, as is well known, are in a class by themselves, like Achilles, according to critics of literature), then you might certainly be among those who can rightly be numbered among the ancients. Indeed even now you seem to me to have attained what we know few have ever achieved before. Marcus Tullius, of course, easily wins first place among all our orators, Publius Maro among our poets. And most of the ancients (and even some of the moderns) shone in some one genre. But when they dared to attempt something outside that genre, good Lord, how quickly they are catapulted from that lofty throne to the bottom. Thus it was rare in antiquity, and even rarer, until now, in our time, to discover any men who excelled in both verse and prose. If anyone, my dear Germain, does not place you among those who do, he will be thought to have either unsound judgment or a personal bias against you. Not without reason, therefore, did Anne, most august queen of the French, admire your gift. She appointed you her secretary. From day to day she continues to favor you with many gifts and rewards, with which she is most generous. How wisely this great heroine did this, is known to those who are aware of your cleverness, faith, and diligence in conducting public affairs, and of the difficult duties you executed—with the same skill you now devote to the service of the queen—in Italy, first for

Lascari regis christianissimi oratori viro vndequaque doctissimo, deinde cardinali Albiensi, postremo in Gallia Deganaeo cancellario nunquam satis neque a moribus neque a literis laudato, simili quo nunc apud Reginam functus munere exhibuisti. Proinde gaudere et gloriari non iniuria potes, et debes tanto huius Heroidos patrocinio. Gaudere et gloriari etiam ipsa potest tali suarum laudum praecone eodemque arcanorum fidelissimo et peritissimo ministro. Gaudere denique et gloriari saeculum nostrum vtpote quod per tuum ingenium et doctrinae excellentiam non multum priscis temporibus pateris inuidere. Vale. Lutetiae Parhisiorum. MDXII. Quarto Calend. Ianuarias.

AVGVSTISSIMAE FRANCORVM REGINAE BRITONVMQUE DVCI ANNAE GERMANVS BRIXIVS ALTISSIODORENSIS. FELICITATEM.

INGENS ILLA ANIMI tui beneuolentia, singularis fauor, atque exuberans quaedam benignitas qua Ioannem Deganaeum Franciae Cancellarium haud pridem vita functum dignata amplexataque fuisti, praestantissima Francorum Regina Anna, effecit sane vt ipse ego (qui me totum Deganaeo dedideram) eo statim extincto in te vltro conuerterim non eam modo obseruantiam omnem qua viuentem eum fueram prosecutus, sed vt tibi insuper vni dedicarem quidquid et venerationis et cultus habere vsquam poteram. Idque quandoquidem iampridem spectatum exploratumque nobis erat (si tamen mediocria sublimibus et deae heroa conferre phas est) quemadmodum quoscunque sui ordinis viros ille longo rerum earum quae ad tanti magistratus moderandam molem attinerent vsu atque experientia anteibat, ita et te vnam caeteras omnis aeui nostri viragines virtutum omnium laude facile praestare et longo post te interuallo relinquere. Erat nimirum Ioannes Deganaeus vir vt summa muneris quo fungebatur auctoritate, dignitatisque celsitudine hominum nostratium amplissimus, ita et corporis et animi raris eximiisque dotibus nemini nostra aetate (pace aliorum dixerim) secundus, vt tanti tui numinis tam profuso fauore tamque propensa mentis tuae benevolentia, si alius quisquam mortalis, is certe vnus maxime dignus censeretur. Atque equidem cum memor huius erga me benignae voluntatis (vtpote quem dum apud se a secretis habuit humanissime semper non sine aliqua nostri aestimatione fouit ac liberalissime vbique nemine id non vidente ornauit) tum vero conscius mihi, summi mei erga eum studii,

John Lascaris, ambassador of the Most Christian King, a man learned in every way, then for the Cardinal of Albi, and finally, in France, for the Chancellor de Ganay, who has never been sufficiently praised either for his character or for his literary attainments. Thus you may rightly rejoice and glory in the patronage of this noble lady, as indeed you should. And she herself may rejoice and glory in such a herald of her praises and a faithful and expert minister, likewise, of her private affairs. And finally our age may rejoice and glory inasmuch as you, through your skill and excellence in learning, will not suffer it to be too envious of ancient times. Farewell. Paris, 1512. December 29.

To the Most August Anne
Queen of France and Duchess of Britanny
From Germain de Brie of Auxerre
Felicitations

The great generosity, singular favor, and overflowing kindness with which you honored and embraced John de Ganay, the recently deceased chancellor of France, have brought it to pass, most excellent Anne, Queen of France, that I (who had devoted myself entirely to de Ganay) should, upon his death, not only transfer to you all the respect with which I served him when he was alive, but that I should also dedicate to you alone whatsoever veneration and obeisance I could ever possess. And I do this because I had long ago ascertained and determined (if one may compare ordinary things to lofty ones, and a hero to a goddess) that, just as he surpassed all men of his station because of his long exercise and experience in the affairs that are incumbent upon managing the burdens of high administrative office, so you too alone easily excel and outstrip by far all the great women of our time in the praiseworthiness of all your virtues. John de Ganay was without doubt (with all due respect to other opinions) a man second to none in our time, as much for his rare and outstanding gifts both of body and of mind, as for the supreme authority of the office he occupied and the loftiness of his position—the most honorable office and position among our countrymen—so that he alone, if any mere mortal could, should be judged most worthy of such abundant recognition under your command and of such ready favor in your thoughts. And of course, mindful of his kindly disposition towards me (whom he always supported most graciously—not without careful evaluation of me—when he employed me as his secretary, supplying my wants most generously, as anyone could see), and conscious too of my own high regard for him, of my utter faith, and

integrae fidei, singularisque obseruantiae vulgo quidem testatae atque omnibus spectatae, plane vt tantis vtriusque nostrum affectibus quantum in me erat satisfacerem, operaepretium esse duxi Deganaei de me optime meriti non modo memoriam dum viuam animo meo identidem recolere, sed et oculis quoque quodammodo meis ipsius effigiem et viuam quasi imaginem assidue repraesentare. Id vero ipsum nulla alia potius ratione assequi me posse intellexi quam si me ipsum totum tibi vni deuouerem, quam quidem sciebam excellentem illius integritatem et nullo vnquam aere corruptas manus (vt multiplicem cuiuslibet disciplinae peritiam caeterasque eximias eius virtutes subticeam) suspicientem admirantemque non ab re maximi semper fecisse eundemque prae aliis omnibus mira quadam indulgentia, immensaque benignitate fuisse prosecutam. Eo enim pacto fore speraui vt dum tibi addictus deuotusque teipsam contemplans admirarer, Deganaei quamquam mortui imago perinde ac viuentis praesentisque, quasi coram adesse oculisque nostris obuersari atque inhaerere videretur. Huc accedebat omnibus probitatis numeris absolutus animi tui candor et qua omnium animos demereris incredibilis humanitas, quae vtique cum in te tam viuidos virtutis suae igniculos ac (vt verius loquar) clarissimum lumen facemque ardentissimam excitarit, facit mediusfidius vt omnes aeque ad tui studium amoremque incendas atque inflammes. Nullusque usquam reperiatur ne beneficentiae quidem tuae expertium (quamquam quis expers est) quin te ob tantam istam optimo cuique obuiam atque expositam humanitatem vltro admiretur, obseruet, reuereatur. Praeterea et te sciebam bonis ingeniis fauentem Apollinisque et musarum sacra religiosissime colentem eos munificentissime fouere qui quidpiam seu soluta seu pedestri oratione [*sic*] quod vel ad tuam vel tuorum gloriam pertineret meditati essent. Esse enim haud falso dictitaris tam generosae tanquam diuinae mentis princeps foemina vt quemadmodum nemini nostrae aetatis principi viro cedis, nec magnitudine animi, nec liberalitate, nec prudentia caeterisve animi dotibus egregiis, ita plaerosque hac vna in re antecedis quod literas literatosque omnes honestissime exornas et perbenigne amplexaris. Nimirum arbitrata, idque saepenumero praedicas et crebris vsurpas sermonibus, magnum quoddam a deo optimo maximo beneficium in eos collatum esse qui bonarum literarum cognitione excelluerint hominesque ipsos doctrina atque eruditione alios aliis quammaxime praestare. O plusquam heroicum mulieris ingenium! O admirabile reginae iudicium! O raros! desuetosque (fatali quodam tempestatis nostrae contagio) et principis et foeminae mores! Vbi aliae pompas, luxum, delitias impensius diligentiusque curant, tu vna ingeniorum fautrix doctos studiosius foues,

of my singular devotion, which was seen publicly and acknowledged by all, I considered it important, in order to make just recompense (inasmuch as I was able) for the great affection we had for one another, not only to cherish the memory of de Ganay (to whom I owe so much) in my mind for as long as I live, but somehow to represent his likeness continually before my eyes, as if it were a living figure. I realized that I could accomplish this by no other means than by devoting myself totally to you alone, for I knew that you, esteeming and admiring his outstanding integrity, his hands uncorrupted by bribes (to pass over in silence his manifold expertise in every discipline and the rest of his preeminent virtues), had, not without cause, always set the greatest value on them, and had honored him before all others with a certain wondrous indulgence and limitless kindness. By this means I hoped that while I was your servant and gazed upon you in devoted and admiring contemplation, the image of de Ganay, even though he is dead, would seem just as lifelike and visible as if actually present before me, in close view and under the watchful gaze of my eyes. I was also prompted by the total integrity of your character, which includes all the elements of probity, and by the incredible generosity through which you put everyone in your debt; in any case it has awakened such lively sparks or rather such a bright beacon and such a gleaming torch of its virtue in you that it assuredly kindles all men alike to devotion and love for you. Among those acquainted with your benificence (although who is unacquainted?) no one will ever be found who does not admire, respect, and revere you for the kindness you show to all the best men. Furthermore, I knew that you, who reward fine talent and tend most devoutly the shrine of Apollo and the Muses, reward most munificently those who treat what pertains to the glory of you and yours, whether in prose or unversified discourse [*an error for* prose or verse?]. Indeed everyone says you are a princess of such noble and divine mind that, just as you yield to no prince of our age in either greatness of mind, or generosity, or prudence, or any other outstanding gift of character, so you excel most of them in this one thing: that you most kindly embrace and most nobly reward all literature and men of letters. Indeed you have thought—and frequently express the idea in speech—that a great benefit was conferred by the great and good God on those who excel in the knowledge of letters, and that the most important elements that rank one man above another are learning and erudition. O the more than noble nature of the woman! O the wondrous judgment of the queen! O rare and unusual (in the fatal pollution of our day) behavior for a woman and a prince! While other women excessively and eagerly care for pomp, luxury, and pleasure, you alone are eager to support the learned and nourish men of genius, withholding from them

honoribus cumulas, et nihil beneficentiae in eos non confers. Digna me hercule quam veluti bonorum exemplar morum expressissimamque verae virtutis effigiem principes tum viri tum foeminae omnes imitandam aemulandamve, aut (si id assequi non poterunt) saltem sibi admirandam proponant. Digna quae vna inter eas omnes quas ab huius regni primordiis nobis hactenus reginas habuisse contigit, siue quis corporis, siue animi bona spectet, primas parteis supremumque decus iure quodam tuo vendicare tibi possis. Digna quae (vt tua immensa liberalitate, humanitate, bonitate longum perfruamur) vel Nestoris vel Sybillae annos integra valitudine transcendas. Digna cui pro tot tantisque in genus humanum bene meritis perennes statuae decernantur perpetuique honores habeantur. Digna tandem in cuius laudes celebrandas nomenque ipsum immortalitati consecrandum vniuersus eruditorum chorus omnes ingenii vires certatim exponat, intendat, effundat. Quod ipsum tametsi pro virili nostra aggredi statuimus, certumque apud me est in te vnam meritis laudibus decantandam (modo tu mihi veluti quaedam ex alto fauens dea adsis) omnes Mineruae nostrae neruos intendere. Ne tamen cumulatissimas tuas virtutes, quas diffusior pleni operis campus vix capiat, hic me quispiam velle epistolari angustia complecti opinetur, finem epistolae nostrae faciens merita laudum tuarum praeconia in aliud tempus reiiciam. Interea vero vt quem tibi paulo ante dolorem tum Herueus Portimoger Nauarchus tuus tum chordigera illa tua toto oceano celiberrima nauis conflagratione sua inusserunt, eum nos aliqua ex parte deliniamus demulceamusque, atque eosdem eodem simul incendio absumptos tibi quodammodo posteritatique carminibus nostris restituamus, eorumque manes facta quasi parentatione euocemus, has veluti quasdam vigiliarum nostrarum primitias tibi praelibandas offerimus. Quas sane si ad stomachum istum facere, nec fastidio esse sensero, equidem et quammaximum fructum tum regiae tuae benignitatis tum nostri huiusce laboris causa tua suscepti me putabo percepisse, et nos certe si quos postea magis amoenos flores vberioresque fructus musae nostrae nobis benigniores reddiderint, eos omnes pleno copiosoque cornu vni tibi consecrabimus. Vale. Blesis decimo Kal. Nouemb. M.D. XII.

no reward. Worthy, by heaven, of being taken by all princes and princesses as an example of good morals and an exact image of virtue that should be imitated and emulated or (if this cannot be managed) at least admired. Worthy of claiming for yourself by a kind of inherent right the first place and the supreme honor among all the queens that we have had from the first origins of this kingdom until now, whether one considers the goods of body or of mind. Worthy of surpassing in the full vigor of health the years of Nestor or of the Sibyl (so that we may long enjoy your immense generosity, kindess, and goodness). Worthy of having everlasting statues commissioned of you and perpetual honors established in recognition of your many and great services to the human race. Worthy of having the entire chorus of learned men exert, pour forth, and expend all their powers of genius, rivalling one another in celebrating your praises and in making your very name immortal. I have resolved to pursue this very course to the best of my ability. And I am determined to devote all my literary powers to singing the deserved praises of you alone (if only you favor me with your presence, like a certain goddess from above). Lest anyone, however, think that I wished to include within the confines of an epistle all your most copious virtues, which even the more spacious range of a full-length work could scarcely contain, I shall bring my epistle to a close by putting off until some other occasion the well deserved celebration of your praise. Meanwhile in order that I may soothe and assuage the sorrow that both Hervé de Portzmoguer, your admiral, and the *Cordelière,* your ship, renowned beyond all others on the seas, burned into your heart just recently when they went up in flames, and in order that I may somehow in my songs restore to you and to posterity those taken from you in that same fire and call forth their shades as if at a funeral, I offer you these first fruits of my nightly labor as a foretaste. And if I feel that they are to your liking and do not displease your palate, I shall think that I have received the greatest fruition both of your highness's generosity and of this labor of mine, undertaken on your behalf. And certainly, if my Muses should afterwards be kind enough to grant me any more pleasant flowers and richer fruits, I shall dedicate them all to you alone in full and abundant measure. Farewell. From Blois, October 23, 1512.

GERMANI BRIXII. ALTISSIODORENSIS.
HERVEVS
SIVE CHORDIGERA FLAGRANS.

MAGNANIMVM aduersis ausum certare Britannis
Heruea et instantis posita formidine fati
Seruantem hostili patrios a clade penates
Chordigeramque cano mediis in fluctibus igne
Flagrantem indomito. Precor, aspirate canenti,
Nereides; vidistis enim et timuistis in atrum
Cuncta redire chaos miscerique aequora flammis.
Tu quoque, qui caecis heroum nulla tenebris
Gesta latere diu pateris, sed carmine vatum
Illustrans toti facis inclarescere mundo,
Huc adsis, Thymbraee, fauens et coepta secundes.
  Anglia felices oculis dum spectat iniquis
Successus, Lodoice, tuos lateque per omnem
Insubriam domitas armis victricibus vrbes,
Sanctam odium in saeuum pacem conuertit et audet
Sanguineas armare manus classemque parare
Aequoream et socio coniunctos foedere Gallos
(Infandum) iniusto periura inuadere bello.
  Iamque Calydonias admouerat vnda carinas
Littori Aremorico, populosque vrbesque propinquas
Terruerat passim venientis fama Brittani.
Iamque lares proprios patriaeque relinquere fines
(Vsque adeo mentes terror concusserat omnium)
Foemina virque sua trepidi cum prole parabant,
Cum subito hostilem contra stetit aequore classem
Chordigera inuectus parua comitante caterua
Bellipotens Herueus: Herueus cui provida classis
Anna vni Regina suae moderamen et omne
Imperium dederat. Non hunc numerosa carinae
Turba Calydoniae, non tectum classibus aequor
Terruit. Extemplo concurrere comminus hosti
Et lateri latus inferre et pugnare paratus,
In medios fluctus agit atque ostendit aperto

---

21 *Sidenote:* Anglorum aduentus in oram Britonum
29 *Sidenote:* Chordigera Reginae nauis Herueus eius nauarchus

HERVÉ, OR THE *CORDELIÈRE* ABLAZE
BY GERMAIN DE BRIE OF AUXERRE

STOUTHEARTED Hervé I sing, who dared to struggle against the Britons, casting fear of present death aside and saving hearth and home from destruction by the enemy, Hervé—and the *Cordelière,* ablaze in an invincible fire on the high seas. Favor this singer, I pray you, daughters of Nereus, for you saw everything and were afraid that all would return to dark chaos and the waters would be confounded with flames. Thou too, Apollo, who wilt not allow the deeds of heroes to lie hidden in shadows, but, enshrining them in poets' song, makest them grow in fame throughout the whole world, be present, and assist this undertaking.

When England beholds with envious eyes your happy successes, Louis, and cities far and wide throughout the duchy of Milan conquered by your victorious arms, she turns holy peace into fierce enmity and dares to arm her bloody hands, to prepare her naval fleet, and—oh unutterable—perfidiously to attack her sworn allies the French in an unjust war.

The arrival of the English on the coast of Brittany

The waves had just brought the Caledonian vessels to the Armorican shore, and the rumor that the English were approaching had frightened all the people and cities nearby. Fearful men and women, along with their offspring, were just preparing (so terrified were all) to leave behind their homes and the borders of their native land, when suddenly valiant Hervé took his stand against the enemy fleet at sea, sailing the *Cordelière* with a scanty crew—Hervé to whom alone Queen Anne had prudently given the tiller of her fleet and the general command. Neither the thronging crew of the Caledonian vessel nor the sea covered by ships brought terror to Hervé. Ready at an instant to engage the enemy, to turn gunwale to gunwale and fight, he steers into the waves and exposes the *Cordelière* to the open seas. She flies ahead

The Cordelière, *the queen's ship; Hervé, her admiral*

Chordigeram pelago. Volat illa ratesque sub altum
(Vt qu[a]eque occurrit) concussas mergit et vndis
Obruit. Hinc visam conuersa puppe Regentem
Praecipuam Anglorum nauem sequiturque fugatque.
Illa leues fugiens cursu praeuerteret auras;
Quae tamen insequitur validis impulsa lacertis
Ductorisque Heruei clamore adiuta fauenti
Ocyor est requiemque negat laterique Regentis
Imminet et raptam mordaci detinet vnco.
Sic vbi persequitur leporem canis, alter ut hostis
Effugiat rabiem morsusque eludat inanes
Praecipitante fuga per apertos evolat agros,
Alter ab inuenta dum non absistere praeda
Destinat, exertis tergo fugientis inhaeret
Dentibus et morsu leporem comprensat auaro.
  Tum bello videas animos flagrare suamque
(Quando fugae non est vsquam locus) agmine vtroque
Quemlibet audaci virtutem ostendere dextra
Et quas quisque habeat vires effundere in hostem,
Et nudare enses, pharetrisque expromere tela
Spiculaque extenso vibrare intorta lacerto
Agmen in aduersum cernas. It clamor ad astra.
Circumeunt vnum dextra laeuaque Britanni
Heruea. Tela volant brumali grandine plura
In caput vnius Heruei, quae fortiter heros
Excutiens clypeo contraria in agmina vertit.
Inter quae his comites dictis hortatur et inquit:
  "O quos perpetuo socii mihi foedere iunxi,
Quorum ego virtutem per ferrum saxaque et ignes
Expertus didici, quos ha[c]tenus vsibus istis
Communis patriae pro libertate tuenda
Seruatos numero dudum selegimus omni,
Nunc illos animos illasque effundite vires
Quas pelagi toties communia fata probarunt.
O iuuenum generosa manus, nunc pectore toto
Infensos vestris hostes defendite ab oris,
Extremamque omnes procul hinc depellite pestem,
Quam patriis inferre penatibus Anglica pubes
Iam parat. Aeternam hanc vestris auertite cladem

37 *Sidenote:* Regens praetoria Anglorum nauis

and smashes into the ships (whichever she encountered), plunges them into the deep, and buries them in the waves. Then, putting about, she catches sight of the *Regent,* the flagship of the English, follows her, and puts her to flight. Though the *Regent* outstripped the fleeting winds in her course of flight, the *Cordelière* follows fast upon her, propelled by mighty arms, and sustained by the encouraging cry of the commander Hervé. The *Cordelière* is swifter, and she gives no respite. She comes alongside the *Regent* and grapples her with a sharp hook. Thus when a hound chases a hare, the one, in order to flee the rabid fierceness of his enemy and elude his unsuccessful bites through swift flight, flies away through the open field; the other, resolving not to desist from the prey, once he has found it, catches the back of the fugitive with his fangs, and seizes the hare between his greedy jaws.

The Regent, *the flagship of the English*

Then you could see how in war spirits burn with rage, and everyone on both sides (when there is no place left to flee) displays his courage with a bold right hand, and each pours out what strength he has against the enemy. You could see swords unsheathed, arrows plucked from quivers, and javelins launched and hurled by outstretched arms against the enemy line. The battle cry reaches the stars. Left and right the Britons surround Hervé as he stands alone. Shaft upon shaft flies in a wintry hailstorm toward the head of Hervé alone, but the hero boldly shakes them off with his shield and turns them back against the other side. He rallies his comrades with a speech, saying:

"You whom I have bound to me in a perpetual covenant of comradeship, you whose courage I have seen proven through steel and shot and fire, who have been preserved till now (by such brave deeds) in order to defend the freedom of our common land, and whom, long ago, I selected from the ranks, now pour forth that spirit and that strength so often tested by the shared dangers of the sea. O noble band of youths, with all your heart now, repulse the raging enemy from your shores, and, all of you, scatter far hence this great plague that these English lads now make ready to inflict upon your homes. Turn back this everlasting

Verticibus, propriam vnanimes seruate salutem;
Cuius ni memores tangit vos cura tuendae,
At saltem patriae pietas et dulcis amoenae
Libertatis amor, saltem matresque patresque
Et suaves moueant cara cum coniuge nati,
Qui vestros seruant, imbellis turba, penates.
Et quae vos meritis omnes (vt caetera desint)
Vna mouere suis debet, qua principe laetos
Aurea felices per saecula ducitis annos,
Anna animos saltem vestros et pectora tangat,
Anna suam in vestra quae spem virtute locauit.
Nec vos pro patriae seruandis finibus ipsum
Detrectate animo fatum mortemque subite
Tela per et fluctus pro libertate decoram.
Sic vna quondam Fabios ex gente trecentos
Abstulit vna dies; sic Curtius impiger antrum
Insiliens, sic se Decii natusque parensque
Deuouere neci impauidi mortemque subire
Pro patriis laribus sanctumque piumque putarunt.
Pro patria ergo mihi nunc occumbere certum."
Dixit, et in medios ruit imperterritus hostes
Aduersamque premens versatque vrgetque Regentem,
Quem socii vnanimes clamore ad sydera misso
Intrepidis animis densa sunt mole secuti.
Distringunt gladios alii primosque trucidant;
Arcum alii tendunt et obumbrant aera telis;
Transtra per incursant alii contisque Regentem
Ferratis lapidumque intorta grandine vexant.
Bellica in aduersam vibrata vtrinque phalangem
Tartareum accenso mittebat sulphure fumum
Machina et inuentis atrox discrimine nullo
Corporibus passim dabat irreparabile lethum.
It coelo armorum strepitus gemitusque cadentum.
Ipse suos Herueus comites hortatur et instat,
Atque inter primos audax magno impete in hostes
Inuehitur. Ferit hos misso per tempora telo;
Transfigit huic gladio costas; huic ilia nudat;
Decutit his caput impacta per colla bipenni;
His latus, his humeros hasta perstringit acuta.
Qualis apud gelidi ripas vbi concitus Hebri
Bella ciet Mauors, rapidoque animosus in hostes
Fertur equo aduersos cursuque inimica fatigat

devastation from your heads, join forces to save yourselves; and, if concern for self-preservation does not enter your thoughts, let duty to country at least move you, and the sweet love of pleasant liberty, mothers and fathers and darling children, along with your dear wives, the unarmed keepers of your hearth and home. And beyond all these motives, she alone on her own merits should move you all—Anne, under whose rule you lead the happy and joyous years through this golden age, let Anne at least touch your hearts and minds—Anne, who places her hope in your bravery. Be willing—in order to protect the borders of your land—even to die, and submit to a fitting death through the spears and waves for the sake of freedom. Thus a single day once took from a single clan the three hundred Fabii. Thus Curtius who leapt readily into the pit, thus the Decii, father and son, who fearlessly dedicated themselves to destruction, thought that it is a holy and dutiful thing to suffer death for their native land. Therefore I myself am now resolved to lay down my life for my country." So he spoke, and unafraid he rushes into the midst of the foe. Bearing down hard against the *Regent,* Hervé charges the enemy forces and drives them back. His comrades fearlessly follow him in a dense swarm, sending with one voice a battle cry to the stars. Some unsheath their swords and cut down the front ranks; others bend the bow and darken the air with arrows. Some sally across the thwarts and vex the *Regent* with iron-tipped poles and a shower of flying stones. From both sides the engine of death is discharged against the adversary. Its burning sulfur sends forth hellish fumes, and it cruelly inflicts irreparable and random death as it strikes any bodies in its path. The clash of arms rings in the heavens, and so do the groans of the fallen. Hervé spurs his comrades on and himself presses forward. In the front ranks of a mighty attack, he drives boldly into the enemy. Some he strikes down with a javelin through the temples; through another's ribs he thrusts his sword; lays open the guts of another; with axe-blows to the neck he cuts off the heads of some, or wounds a flank or a shoulder with his sharp spear. Just as when Mars aroused rouses up war along the banks of the chill Hebrus and charges against the enemy on a swift steed, vexing the lines as he

Agmina, et hostiles passim prosternit aceruos,
Et pedibus victor congesta cadauera calcat,
Talis in instantes furit Herueus impiger Anglos.
Non impune tamen prosternit Brito Britannum.
Magnanimi contra insurgunt hostemque Britanni
Propellunt vi magna alacres caedesque suorum
Caedibus alternis et vulnus vulnere pensant.
Sanguinea excurrit Bellona vtrumque per agmen
Inflammatque animos renouataque praelia miscet.
Caesorum impletur madefacta cruore carina.
Anceps pugna diu fuit, et victoria longum
Incerta ambiguis volitans stetit aere pennis.
In mediae donec specula maiore Regentis,
Quam mali sustentat apex, nullo ordine nautas
Chordigera egressus librato aequaliter ictu
Sulphureus lapis excutiens descendere ab alta
Compellit specula attonitosque relinquere sedem.
Quam procul opposita Dholos vt conspexit inanem
Chordigerae e specula, correptis funibus audax
Corpore conscendens agili (mirabile visu)
Occupat. Hic silices duros, hic tela relicta
Repperit, aduersum quae mox conuersus in agmen
Intorquet Dholos et subiectos obruit hostes.
Deinde duas alias speculas, quarum altera proram
Vertice in excelsi mali regit, altera puppim,
Victor Aremoricus scandit summoque Britannos
Praecipitat solio et speculis dominatur in ipsis.
Et iam fessa Regens lassa ceruice lababat
Chordigeramque sequens inuisa ad littora passis
Vincta trahebatur palmis. Iam victa parabat
Terga Calydoniae dare caetera turba carinae,
Cum subito mediis procul exclamauit in vndis
Nescio quis vocem intendens paucisque Regentem
Alloquitur: "Spes nulla tibi, spes nulla salutis,
Nulla, inquam, spes est. Flammam vibrato coruscam
Chordigeramque incende." Regens non misit in auras
Vocem intellectam sed tota exaudiit aure.
Protinus ingentem volitante per aera gyro
Ardentis flammae bolidem violentius ictu

---

135 *Sidenote:* Dholos praefectus speculae Chordigerae

passes, striking his foes down, and victoriously trampling heaps of bodies underfoot, so too does the relentless Hervé rage against the English attackers. Yet Breton does not strike down Briton with impunity. The stouthearted Britons rise up and strike back swiftly and forcefully against their enemy, repaying slaughter with slaughter and wound with wound. Bloody Bellona runs through the troops on both sides. She inflames their spirits and brings them to the fray again and again. The ship is filled with the dripping gore of the dead. For a long time the fight was evenly matched, and uncertain victory long wavered in the air on fluttering wings, until, in the larger crow's nest amidships on the *Regent,* which was held aloft by the very top of the mast, a cannonball that issues from the *Cordelière,* aimed with great precision, forces the stunned sailors to leave their post and climb down from the crow's nest in a scramble. When Dholos from off in the *Cordelière*'s crow's nest on the opposite side saw that the *Regent*'s was empty, he boldly grasped the shrouds, and, boarding the *Regent* with an agility wonderful to see, he occupied the crow's nest. Here he finds some hard flints and arrows that were left behind. He hurls them back against the enemy line, overwhelming his enemy below. Then the Armorican victor scales the two other crow's nests—the one commanding the tall foremast, the other the stern—and dashes the Britons from this perch aloft, making himself master of the very crow's nests of the ship.

Dholos the commander of the crow's nest of the Cordelière

And now the weary *Regent* was starting to sink, her neck drooping, as she trailed behind the *Cordelière* and was towed in chains to the hated shores, begging for mercy. And the rest of the defeated throng of ships prepared to turn their backs on the Caledonian craft, when suddenly an unknown voice shouted out from afar across the waves, addressing a few brief words to the *Regent:* "There is no hope left for you, no hope of survival, no hope, I say. Fling forth the blazing flame, set fire to the *Cordelière.*" No voice could be heard in reply from the *Regent,* but she hearkened with all ears. And forthwith she hurls a ball of flaming fire in

Chordigeram in mediam librato torquet. At illa
Iniectam subito flammam pice concipit atra,
Quae simul ac laxas discurrens sentit habenas,
Transtra per et remos perque ipsa sedilia saeuit,
Nec vero heroum vires, nec flumina tantae
Certatim possunt infusa obsistere flammae,
Quive sub accensa Neptunus puppe supremum
Imperium tenet, et pelago dominatur aperto.
Ilicet ignis edax vdo sub robore vires
Colligit indomitas inuentaque stupa vaporem
Emittens tardum flammas irritat et auget.
Miratur trepidus Brito; miratur et Herueus
Attonitus subito casu, qui viribus altam
Vt vidit flammam non posse extinguier vllis
Nec superesse aliquam sociisque sibique salutem:
"Magnanimi o socii," dixit, "quos Anglica sensit
Victores hodie duro certamine classis,
Qui patriam et caros cara cum prole parentes
Seruili imperio vestra virtute redemptos
Linquitis assueta sub libertate, deorum
Credo equidem hanc nobis offeri munere mortem,
Quo simul edomitis victores hostibus igne
Excocti indomito vitiorumque vndique puri
Abstersis maculis supera ingrediamur ovantes
Astriferi conuexa poli aeternoque fruamur
Felices Iouis obtutu, immensumque per aeuum
Posteritas nomen colat indelebile nostrum
Obseruetque diem hunc memor et felicibus addat.
Sic quondam hac ipsa patienter luce beatus
Pertulit immoto ardentem Laurentius ignem
Corpore et aethaeream victor translatus in arcem
Praemia caelestis meruit sumpsitque coronae.
Hauriet Anna oculis tantae fastigia flammae
Stans solii augusti specula sublimis in alta,
Gallorum et summo regi regina marito
Illa suo ingeminans vestrae praeconia laudis
Nominibus dictis virtutem ad sydera tollet.
Et patriam vestris seruatam viribus ore
Iactabit memori memor et mandabit vt inter
Phoebaeos aliquis non aspernandus alumnos
Perpetuo celebret memorandum hoc carmine fatum.
Ergo agite, o socii, constanti corpore laetisque

a curved course through the air and strikes a resounding blow amidships, right into the *Cordelière*. And the black pitch kindles the fire that was flung aboard. As soon as it feels it could run unchecked, it rages through the thwarts, the oars, the very benches of the rowers, so that neither the heroic efforts of the men nor the streams of water that they zealously throw down can block the great flames, nor Neptune himself who holds dominion beneath the enkindled stern as master of the main. The greedy fire gathers its invincible forces below the waterline and stirs up and augments the flames as it catches on the oakum and throws out a thick smoke. The Bretons are astounded and alarmed. Even Hervé is astounded and stunned at this sudden turn, for he sees that no power can extinguish the high flames and that no way out remains for his companions or himself.

"O stouthearted comrades," he said, "you whom the English fleet has recognized as the victors today in bitter struggle, you who are leaving in their wonted liberty the native land, the dear parents and dear children that you reclaimed by your bravery from a servile rule, I verily believe that this death is offered to us by the gift of the gods. Through it we have been at once made victors over our conquered enemy and been refined by an unconquerable fire, so that, clear of all faults, cleansed of all spots, we may enter exultant into the starry vaults of highest heaven, and blessedly enjoy the everlasting vision of Jove, so that posterity may cherish our unperishing names through endless ages, observe this day reverently and add it to the calandar of blessed dates. Thus in the past on this very day Saint Lawrence patiently endured a searing fire without flinching; he was translated in victory to the heavenly citadel where he deserved and received the reward of a celestial crown. Anne shall take in the sight of the pinnacles of flame, as she stands aloft in the high watchtower of her august dominion. And to the great king of France, her husband, the queen shall repeat a roll call of your praise, calling out all your names, and exalt your valor to the stars. Mindful of you she shall boast to him, also mindful, of how you saved the country through your strength, and she shall command that one not to be despised among the disciples of Phoebus shall celebrate this memorable death in song. Stand firm in body, therefore, comrades, and vanquish these flames with joyful

Hos superate ignes animis; vos gloria Olympi,
Praemia vos aeterna manent." Sic fatus, at illi
Se flammam nihil horrere, et contemnere mortem
Impauidi exclamant. Reparant incendia vires;
Iamque fori et tabulae funesque et vela trabesque
Fraxineae et denso compacti robore mali
Sulphuraque admotis ardent viuacia flammis.
Ac veluti accensis lapidem fornacibus ignis
Concoquit et silice ex duro flammante fauilla
Amissa in cinerem vertit mutatque figura,
Non aliter medio heroes torrentur in igne,
Corporaque in cineres abeunt euanida adustos.
Ast animae sedes meliorisque atria Olympi
Felices adeunt, vbi viuunt munere diuum
Nectar et ambrosiam pastae summique tonantis
Aspectu et placida caeli statione fruuntur.
   Et tandem amplexans totam candente fauilla
Chordigeram effusis saeuit Vulcanus habenis,
Haud aliter quam cum ruptis praesepia vinclis
Effugiens quadrupes campoque potitus aperto
Liber agit cursus, et qua rapit impetus illum
Hac sine lege ruit nulloque inhibente furorem
Admisso expatians cursu sine fine pererrat.
Forte aliam coeli in partem perceperat Herueus
Inspirare notos solamque ardere Regente
Chordigeram intacta. "Sed non laetabere nostro,"
Dixit, "inulta malo," et verso in contraria clauo
Chordigeram obuertit sursum, qua ventus adactam
Vulcani rabiem mediae per transtra Regentis
Ferret et impleret transuersam flamma carinam.
Nec mora, suppositam inuadens lambensque Regentem
Ignis edax morsu totam depascit auaro.
Adduntur flammae flammis atque ignibus ignes.
Non sic foecundam cum forte furentibus Austris
Corripiunt segetem flammae, furit ignis et Euro
Inspirante leues stipulas incendit et omnem
Diffundens rabiem passim expatiatur et ipsas
Quas praetercurrit flammis absumit aristas.
Surgit in immensum geminatis ignibus atrox
Flamma rogum abrumpens nubes rapidoque volatu
Aethera conscendit. Collucent litora late et
Fulgorem emittunt, quamquam longinqua, coruscum,
Et rutilans splendore nouo coelum vndique fulget.

spirits. The glory of Olympus and eternal rewards await you." Thus he spoke. And they fearlessly cry out that they have no fear of the flames and scorn death. The fire gathers strength. Now the hatches and planks and ropes and sails and ashen timbers and stout masts of tough oak and the volatile sulfur blaze as the flames reach them. And just as when fire consumes a stone in a roaring furnace, the shape disappears and changes from hard flint into ash in the glowing coals, just so do the heroes roast in the midst of the fire and their evanescent bodies pass into burnt cinders. But their happy souls go on to the seats and courts of the real Olympus, where they live by the gift of the gods. Feasting on nectar and ambrosia they enjoy the vision of the great god of thunder and their peaceful abode in heaven.

Vulcan rages unchecked, surrounding the whole *Cordelière* in glowing embers, just as when a four-footed beast breaks its bonds, flees the stables, and runs free, gaining the open field, where, rushing aimlessly wherever his fancy takes him, he runs loose at full speed, his rage unreined, and strays endlessly. Perhaps Hervé had noticed that the winds were changing directions and that the *Cordelière* alone burned while the *Regent* remained unscathed. "You shall not rejoice in our misfortune without paying for it," he said. He turned the helm and shifted the *Cordelière* about so that the wind carried the driving rage of Vulcan across the thwarts amidships in the *Regent* and filled the ship alongside with flame. Invading the grappled *Regent* in no time, the gluttonous fire licks across her, and devours the whole ship in its greedy jaws. Flames breed more flames. Fire after fire breaks out. Fire does not rage with such might even when the winds by chance rage, and the flames destroy a fertile crop as the fire, driven by the wind, ignites the volatile stalks and spreads, dispersing its fury everywhere, and consumes even the very ears of grain which it merely brushes with flames. The blaze redoubles itself and the dread flame rises into an immense pyre, rending the clouds and climbing into the air with a swift course. The whole length of the shore glows brightly and even in the distance sends off a fiery glimmer. Everywhere the sky shimmers and gleams with new splendor. And now the

Mox vero immensum nigra caligine fumum
Atra fauilla vomit tenebrasque per aera densum
Exhalabat iners, piceaeque volumina flammae
Aethera densabant, veluti cum flumina opacas
Quandoque exhalant nebulas saeuamque mephitim.
Praeterea altisonis fremuit mare fluctibus ingens,
Et subitus summo fragor exauditus Olympo est,
Excelsos veluti si quis grauiore ruina
Corruere et subito montes subsidere lapsu
Audiat et tanto ingentis terrore fragoris
Horrescat pauidus stupidaque obtorpeat aure.
Inde alii effigiem coelo terrisque priorem
Antiquumque chaos mundo aduentare putabant;
Ast alii finem humanis imponere rebus
Velle Iouem et totum flammis absumere Olympum.
Qualiter exustis quando intonat Aetna cauernis,
Liquitur eque cauis magnos fornacibus ignes
Voluit et ingentes flammarum ad sydera tollit
Alta globos saeuoque ardens exaestuat igne.
Qualia Parthenopes felicia rura colonis
Attonitis quondam vidisse incendia narrant,
Cum subita emersit liquefacti flamma Vesaevi,
Oppidaque et colles conflagrauere propinqui;
Talem eructabant geminata incendia flammam.
Quae simulac totas fudere per aethera vires,
Hinc atque hinc late supraque infraque calorem
Ingentem spargunt, subitoque tepore calescunt
Sydera cum coelo cumque ipsis piscibus aequor.
Feruescitque mare, atque aestu miscentur harenae.
Effugiunt flammam nec iam super aequora pisces
Incuruo solitos audent dare corpore saltus.
Deformes fugiunt phocae, summumque sub aequor
Corpora non audent immania tollere cete.
Ipse pater Nereus nataeque et Doris et omnes
Aequoreae tepidis nymphae latuere sub vndis.
Forte caput summa paulum Neptunus ab vnda
Dum leuat ad tantae spectanda incendia flammae
Feruentesque auras velut e candente camino
Ore trahit, tepido perfusus tempora fumo,
Dum Phaetontei rediisse incendia currus
Formidat, summa effugiens velociter vnda
Vrget equos curruque celer dat lora volanti,
Aequoraque alta petens imas non deserit vndas.

dark embers disgorge an immense cloud of black smoke and sluggishly exhaled dark billows into the thick air. Wreaths of pitchy flame thickened the air just as rivers sometimes breathe out shady clouds and pestilent gas. The vast sea, moreover, raged with resounding waves, and suddenly a crash was heard in the heights of Olympus, just as if someone heard the mountains topple, crash, and sink down in sudden collapse, and he cowered with terror at so great a crash, standing stock still, his ears struck senseless. And then some thought that the former face of the heavens and the earth was returning, and that ancient chaos drew nearer to the world. And others thought Jove wished to impose an end to human life and to consume all Olympus in flames. Aetna flows in just such a way when it thunders from its charred caverns and spills great fires from its hollow furnaces, and lifts huge balls of flame up to the lofty stars and boils furiously with savage fire. Such fires the Neapolitans say their happy countryside once saw—to the shock of the farmers—when flame from erupting Vesuvius poured out unexpectedly, and the neighboring hills and villages went up in flames. In just such a way the redoubled fire belched out flames. As soon as it had poured forth all its strength into the air, it spread the enormous heat here and there, far and wide, up and down, and in a flash of heat the stars are inflamed along with the firmament, the ocean along with the very fish. The waters boil, and the sands are stirred up by the swell. The fish flee the flame, and do not dare to arch their bodies and make their accustomed leaps above the waters. The ugly seals flee, and the whales do not dare to lift their huge bodies to the surface of the water. Father Nereus himself, and his daughters, and Doris, and all the watery nymphs kept in hiding under the warm waves. When by chance Neptune lifts his head a little from the top of a wave to watch the burning of the great fire and draws the seething winds up in his mouth as if from a glowing forge, surrounding his temples with warm smoke, when he fears that the fire of Phaeton's chariot has returned, he urges his horses on, flees quickly from the surface, and gives his swift chariot free rein: he seeks the deep and does

Hunc senior Glaucus cumque Aegeone Palaemon
Inous summamque piger iam Phorcus adustus
Vndique caesariem et Triton Proteusque sequuntur.
  Ipse procul tantos miratur Iuppiter ignes
Celsior augusto e solio, qui terque quaterque
Concutiens caput horrificum, mare, sydera, terram,
Et totum attonitis superis tremefecit Olympum.
Nec minus expauit, quam cum superaddere montes
Montibus excelsos summumque inuadere coelum
Atque ipsis inferre deis fera bella gigantes
Tentauere suisque ipsum detrudere regnis.
Et metuit tanto ne forte accensus ab igne
Aetherque et summi regio flagraret Olympi.
Quippe esse in fatis reminiscitur omnia auaro
Igne cremanda olim et flamma absumenda voraci;
Qui medio postquam cognouit ab aequore flammam
Surgere et aethereos recta conscendere ad axes,
Hoc magis exardens dignas Ioue colligit iras.
Horret enim aequoreis ne fratrem forte sub vndis
Poeniteat regnique sui sortisque secundae;
Quem quoniam vidit caput exeruisse profundo,
Se contra hos ignes putat extruisse deumque
Loripedem simul arma ad coniurata vocasse.
  Protinus humentem caeli diuertit ad arcem
Vnde solet pluuias imbresque aspergere mundo,
Vnde ciet moestis nimbos et nubila terris;
Quam simul intrauit foribusque reclusit apertis,
Ecce graves vdo funduntur ab aethere nimbi
Praecipitesque ruunt liquefactis nubibus imbres.
Nuncia Iunonis velamina mille colorum
Induitur caelumque incuruo circinat arcu.
Hippotades summi iussu Iouis Aeolus Eurum
Terribilemque cauis Aquilonem claudit in antris,
Caeteraque effusos inhibentia flamina nimbos.
Emittitque aliis vnum indignantibus Austrum
Imbre grauem, pluuia stillantem nubila barba,
Horribilem tetra offusum fuligine frontem,
Et fluida vndosis aspersum tempora nimbis.
Qui simul explicuit rorantes humidus alas
Atque vtraque manu torsit pressitque madentem
Caesariem, densus ruit aethere nimbus ab alto,
Impellitque imbres imber grauis. Intonat aer;
Vndarum incursu sonat vnda; sonantibus vndis

not leave the bottom of the sea. Old Glaucus, Palaemon and Aegon, Inous, Triton, and Proteus follow, and sluggish Phorcus, whose hair is singed all over.

From afar Jupiter himself looks in amazement at the great fire, high above on his august throne; he shakes his awesome head three or four times and makes the sea, the stars, the earth, even all Olympus tremble, startling the gods. He was not less afraid than he had been when the Titans attempted to pile mountain upon tall mountain, to invade high heaven, to make fierce war against the gods themselves, and to oust Jupiter himself from his throne. And he feared lest perhaps the ether be ignited by the fire and the kingdom of high Olympus be set ablaze. Indeed he remembers that according to the fates all would someday be burnt by greedy fire and consumed by hungry flame. When he realizes that the flame was rising up from the midst of the ocean, and climbing straight up to the heavenly poles, it inflames him even more and he summons a wrath worthy of Jove. He shudders at the thought, indeed, that his brother under the waves may be dissatisfied with his realm and his second place, for he saw him lift his head up out of the deep, and thinks that Neptune has built this fire against him and called the lame god to a league of arms.

Forthwith he repairs to the watery stronghold whence he is used to sprinkle rains and showers upon the world, and whence he sends clouds and mists to the gloomy earth. As soon as he entered it and opened the gaping doors, behold, heavy rainstorms pour down from the wet air and the clouds turn to water, falling down in showers of rain. Juno's messenger dons her coat of a thousand colors and circles the sky with a vaulted rainbow. By Jove's command Aeolus, offspring of Hippotes, encloses Eurus and terrible Aquilo in hollow caves, along with the other winds that hold back the dripping clouds. And much to the displeasure of the other winds, he sends forth Auster alone, laden with rain, dripping clouds from his showery beard, his hideous face shrouded in foul mist, his temples sprinkled with billowing clouds. As soon as this wet wind has spread his bedewed wings, and has wrung and pressed his dripping locks with both his hands, a thick cloud rushes from high up in the atmosphere and waves of rain drive each other downward, and the air thunders. The wave resounds with the influx of waves, and when the

Aequora lata fremunt densique aspergine nimbi
Erigitur mediis et se mare nubibus infert.
Velle putes coelum latum descendere in aequor;
Velle putes aequor summum conscendere caelum.
  Combibit ignis aquas denso madefactus ab imbre,
Quasque modo in summum celer eructabat Olympum
Lentus agit flammas et iam caelestibus vndis
Inferior sensim vires amittit et ipsum
Sollicito terrore Iouem curaque grauatum
Alleuat ingenti. Qui protinus aethere toto
Discutiens imbres dispulsaque vndique nube,
Laetior ad magni redit alta palatia caeli.
Terrarumque alte deflectens lumina ad orbes
Marmoreo solio scaeptroque insignis eburno
Restituit vultum coelo terrisque priorem,
Admittitque diem discussa nube serenum.
Pontus et elati subsidunt aequoris vndae,
Conceptusque calor fugit emoriente fauilla,
Et gelidis linquit Neptunum, et Nerea in vndis.
  Neve iterum accensis vtroque ex agmine puppes
Quae superant animis pugnent, extinctaque surgat
Inducatque nouos animo noua flamma timores,
Iuppiter obscura latas caligine terras
Occuluit caelumque inducta condidit vmbra,
Et classem longo discriminat interuallo
Littoribusque suis acies vtrasque reducit.

Heruei Cenotaphium.

Magnanimi manes Heruei nomenque verendum
  Hic lapis obseruat, non tamen ossa tegit.
Ausus enim Anglorum numerosae occurrere classi,
  Quae patrium infestans iam prope littus erat,
Chordigera inuectus, regali puppe, Britannis
  Marte prius saeuo comminus edomitis,
Arsit Chordigerae in flamma extremoque cadentem
  Seruauit moriens excidio patriam.
Prisca duos aetas Decios miratur, at vnum
  Quem conferre queat nostra duobus habet.

Ex aedibus Ascensianis ad Idus Ianuarias M.D.XIII. ad calculum Romanum. Cautumque est priuilegio regio nequis praeter Ascensium in toto regno Franciae imprimere triennio proximo attentet.

waves resound, the ocean shudders far and wide, and its surface rises, driven by a dense shower of rain, and the ocean betakes itself to the midst of the clouds. You would think that either heaven was sinking down into the wide sea, or that the sea was climbing up to high heaven. The fire drinks in the water, soaked in the heavy rain, and the flames which it just now had belched swiftly to the top of Olympus it now emits more slowly and, weaker than the waves of the sky, it gradually loses its strength, to the relief of Jove himself, who was weighed down by vexing fear and overpowering anxiety.

Forthwith he disperses the rainstorm, scatters all the clouds, and returns in a happier mood to the lofty palaces of mighty heaven. Gazing down from on high upon the surface of the earth, seated on his marble throne, Jove, wielding the emblem of the ivory scepter, restored their previous countenance to both the heaven and the earth. He scatters the clouds and brings in a clear day. The main and the waves of the swollen sea subside, and the heat generated by the embers vanishes as they die down, and leaves both Neptune and Nereus in chill seas.

And lest anger flame out on both sides and set the remaining ships once more at odds, lest the extinguished flame arise anew and bring new fears to their hearts, Jupiter concealed the wide earth with a dark mist, and hid the heavens in shadow. And he separates the ships by a great distance, and brings both fleets back to their own shores.

The Cenotaph of Hervé

This stone commemorates the shade and redoubted name of greathearted Hervé; it does not, however, cover his bones. He dared to challenge the huge fleet of the English, which had approached right up to our shores, invading the homeland: he sailed the *Cordelière,* a royal ship, and after defeating the Britons in fierce war and hand-to-hand combat, he burned in the flames of the *Cordelière,* and dying saved his falling fatherland from final extermination. The former age looked in wonder at the two Decii, but our age has one man whom it may compare to two.

From the publishing house of Ascensius on the Ides of January [January 13] 1513 according to the Roman reckoning. Be advised that by royal privilege no one except Ascensius may print this book anywhere in France for the next three years.

APPENDIX B

The Antimorus *of Germanus Brixius*

EDITED BY DANIEL KINNEY

APPENDIX B

The Antimorus *of Germanus Brixius*

In his midseventeenth-century survey of illustrious poets, the Danish scholar Oluf Borch describes Germanus Brixius as "more celebrated for nothing today than that he came to grips with so celebrated an adversary"—that is, Thomas More.[1] Sixteenth-century Frenchmen in general had a much higher opinion of Brixius; according to some, Brixius actually won his poetic encounter with More. In midcentury, Scévole de Ste.-Marthe writes: "Brixius . . . having been atrociously and outrageously insulted in virulent verses by Thomas More, the most learned of the Britons, emerged from that contest the clear victor in the judgment of all learned men."[2] In the 1580s the erudite Claude du Verdier gives a

---

[1]Cf. Olaus Borrichius, *Dissertatio academica de poetis* . . . (Frankfurt, D. Pauli, 1683), p. 113: "Germanus Brixius . . . nulla hodie re celebrior, quam quod celeberrimo se commiserit aduersario [sc. Thomae Moro]." Borch's contemporary Thomas Pope Blount affords several complementary perspectives on the quarrel with Brixius in his *Censura celebriorum authorum: Editio nova* (Geneva, 1694), p. 562. In particular, Blount cites the balanced assessment of G. J. Vossius (*De historicis latinis*, Leiden, 1627, p. 614), in whose view More himself is most certainly to blame for the oversights listed by Brixius, oversights which, however, Vossius finds pardonable in a man with more serious business than smoothing hexameters. For more recent discussions of Brixius and his quarrel with More, see R. P. Adams, *The Better Part of Valor* . . . (Seattle, 1962), pp. 76–78, 182–84; M.-M. de la Garanderie, "Les Épitaphes latines d'Anne de Bretagne par Germain de Brie," *Annales de Bretagne, 74* (1967), 377–86; and "Un Erasmien français: Germain de Brie," in *Colloquia Erasmiana Turonensia* (Paris, 1972), *1*, 359–79, substantially reprinted in *Christianisme et lettres profanes (1515–35): Essai sur les mentalités des milieux intellectuels parisiens et sur la pensée de Guillaume Budé* (Lille, 1976), *1*, 171–204; and finally G. Lavoie, "La Fin de la querelle entre Germain de Brie et Thomas More," *Moreana, 50* (1976), 39–44. Two eighteenth-century accounts not consulted by these authors (*Menagiana* [Paris, 1762], *3*, 115–18, and *Le Grande Dictionnaire de L. Moréri* [Paris, 1759], 2, 289) add a detail or two to our knowledge concerning the *Antimorus* itself, but are otherwise now superseded.

[2]*Gallorum doctrina illustrium . . . elogia*, in *Scaevolae Sammarthani opera* . . . 2 vols. in 1 (Paris, 1616), 2, sig. A_6v: "Brixius . . . a Thoma Moro Britannorum doctissimo . . . versibus virulentis atrociter et improbe lacessitus, ex illo certamine doctorum omnium iudicio facile victor euasit." A different view of the two poets' relative merits seems to have been held by Leodegarius à Quercu (Duchesne), who in his *Flores epigrammaton ex optimis quibus-*

similar verdict: "Thus, More challenged Brixius, but beyond doubt succumbed in the unequal struggle."[1] Clearly not all of Brixius' contemporaries, at any rate, viewed his contest with More as a meaningless, one-sided feud; certain Frenchmen among them took pride in what they held to be a significant victory for the cause of French learning.

While French verdicts concerning More's clash with Brixius undoubtedly reflect some confusion about the actual facts of the case—after all, More quite generously suppressed his extended rebuttal of Brixius—and some measure of chauvinist prejudice, we cannot deal so lightly with the numerous contemporary testimonies to Brixius' poetic stature which have little directly to do with his role as a champion of French national pride against More.[2] For Lascaris, Erasmus, and Jerome Aleander, not to mention Budé, Brixius' bellicose patriotism had little bearing on his

---

que authoribus excerpti, 2 vols. (Paris, 1555–60), printed only a few poems by Brixius (including the *Antimorus,* in the second volume) but a greater number of More's epigrams than of anyone else's (see Appendix D, pp. 698, 716–17). Rabelais, who according to the *Menagiana* (*3,* 118) was personally acquainted with Brixius, alludes to the *Chordigera* as a celebrated example of poetic eulogy but gives no hint of how he himself rates it; cf. *Les faits et dits héroïques du bon Pantagruel,* 4.21.

[1]Cf. Claudius Verderius, *In auctores pene omnes antiquos potissimum censio* (Lyons, B. Honoratus, 1586), p. 163: "Morus itaque Brixium prouocauit, sed in impare pugna procul dubio succubuit."

[2]Nicolas Bourbon (*Nicolaii Borbonii Vandoperani nugarum libri octo* [Paris, Vascosan, 1533], sig. e5v; reprinted in *Les Bagatelles de Nicolas Bourbon,* ed. V. L. Saulnier [Paris, 1945], p. 48) ranks Brixius with Macrin as the two most illustrious poets brought forth by "this golden age." Claude Guilliard, canon of Autun (1493–1551), ranks Brixius with Budé as "Galliarum in re litteraria principes" (Lebeuf, 2, 502; cf. M. Pellechet, "Catalogue des livres d'un chanoine d'Autun," *Mémoires de la Société Eduenne,* New Series, 18 [1890], xxxi–xxxviii). Macrin himself begins his hymn to the poets of France with the name of Brixius (*Salmonii Macrini Iuliodunensis . . . hymnorum libri sex* [Paris, 1537], p. 37; cited in I. D. McFarlane, "Jean Salmon Macrin," *Bibliothèque d'Humanisme et Renaissance, 21* [1959], 322). McFarlane himself further states, "Comme on le sait, Macrin, Germain de Brie et [Jean] Dampierre constituent comme le triumvirat de la poésie néo-latine en France vers 1530" (p. 79). For Brixius' role as a mentor to Joannes Vulteius (Jean Visagier), see Ranutius Gherus [Janus Gruterus], ed., *Delitiae C. poetarum gallorum . . .* (Frankfurt, J. Rose, 1609), *3,* 1143–44. Brixius' own verse, including the *Chordigera* and the Latin of the *Antimorus* (*Sylua*), fills many pages in Gruter's first volume.

Finally, one eulogist (Gilbertus Ducherius, *Epigrammata* [Lyons, Gryphius, 1538], p. 150) ventures to set Brixius' gifts on a par with Erasmus', though without any reference at all to Brixius' strictly secular writings:

Germani Brixii Tumulus

Hipponi antistes, multo sanctissimus ille,
  Augustinus ubi est Brixion intuitus,
Brixion ad manes missum, haud aetate uieta,
  Subtristis misso talia uerba facit:

appeal as a humanist.[1] He epitomized one conception of what the New Learning should seek to achieve, a conception which More himself was unwilling to accept. In his *Letter to Brixius* (1520) More attempts to establish that Brixius' own notion of humanism is a sinister travesty that all good humanists ought to deplore. Not all good humanists were ready to do so.

Brixius' noted vigor and charm as a celebrant of a ceremonious and grandiloquent humanism made him perhaps the most flamboyant standard-bearer for a movement eventually bound to provoke More's revulsion. For More, the vainglorious humanism of men like Brixius represented an irresponsible defection from the cause of committed New Learning.[2] More stressed truth to the spirit of ancient historical and poetic models in the service of piety, prudence, and citizenship, whereas

---

Orbi tene Atropos inuidit pessima: sanctis
  Vsqueadeo scriptis utilem, et appositum?
Inuidit pridem et doctrinae lumen Erasmum,
  Et uirtutis item praenitidum speculum.
Porro quid miseris fiet mortalibus, atri
  Quos omni quatiunt Haeresiarchae opera?
Quando huc uenisti coelesti denique iussu,
  Et tibi nobiscum est denique parta quies:
Laetis te excipiet noster Chrysostomus ulnis,
  Ingenij adsertus nobilitate tui:
Et te dilectum dilecto iunget Erasmo:
  Vt paribus iunctos conuenit esse pares.

For another tribute to Brixius as a translator, see H. de Vocht, ed., *Literae . . . ad Fr. Craneveldium* (Louvain, 1928), pp. 527–30.

[1]Brixius' friendship with Janus Lascaris lasted from 1508 till Lascaris' death. Even immediately after the publication of the *Antimorus*, Erasmus is able to assure More that "is [sc. Brixius] est, quem si nosses propius, hominis tum ingenio tum literis delectareris; neque quenquam alium facile reperies quem iudicares amore tuo digniorem" (Allen, *4*, 241, lines 85–87). In 1528 Erasmus singles out for his praise Brixius' "iudicii . . . rectitudinem et ingenii suavitatem" (Allen, 7, 489, lines 248–49). Aleander compares Brixius' eloquence in the *Chordigera* to that of both Vergil and Cicero (Appendix A, p. 440). Budé exchanged a large number of letters with Brixius. There are two Latin letters, one Greco-Latin letter, and eleven Greek letters from Budé to Brixius in Budé's *Epistolae* and *Epistolae posteriores* (Paris, J. Badius, 1520 and 1522), along with two letters in Greek from Brixius to Budé, none of which seems to have any new light to shed on Brixius' clash with More. In Budé's *Opera omnia* (Basel, N. Episcopius, 1557; reprint, Farnborough, England, 1966), Brixius' letters and some of Budé's to Brixius have been silently dropped from the canon.

Brixius also figures in the correspondence of Jacopo Sadoleto during the 1530s; see *Epistolae familiares*, 4. 8–10, in *J. Sadoleti opera quae exstant omnia* (Verona, 1737), *1*, 84–91.

[2]For Brixius as a poetic votary of courtly and secular *gloria*, see F. Joukovsky, *La Gloire dans la poésie française et néolatine du* XVI*e* *siècle* (Geneva, 1969), pp. 145, 217.

to More Brixius seemed to stress mere mechanical truth to the letter of classical learning in the service of factional elitism. Erasmus delayed his own tactfully critical response to this sort of form-obsessed humanist heresy, the *Ciceronianus,* until late in the 1520s. More, predictably, moved much more swiftly.

Brixius' *Chordigera* appeared in manuscript in 1512 and in print in early 1513. More soon obtained a copy, more or less by chance, and responded with a series of epigrams (nos. 188–95, 209), taxing Brixius with a flagrant distortion of facts, a poor sense of dramatic plausibility, an unpleasant habit of stealing fine phrases from classical poets, and an overall lack of "intelligence" and "spirit" (*mens* and *cor*).[1] More nowhere resorts to crude insult, but the cumulative effect of his comparatively restrained rebukes in these verses is greater than each epigram, read by itself, might bring one to anticipate. From the fairly abstract charge that Brixius, through subverting the basis of history in fact, has "chronicled badly a deed performed well," More proceeds to adduce, ostensibly in order to justify Brixius' factual lapses, a concrete example picked out to discredit the *Chordigera* not only as history, but also as coherent fiction: Brixius' own account of the battle he celebrates had left no one alive to inform him what actually happened.[2] More's next two epigrams pursue the absurd implications of one particular rhapsodic extravagance in a work which has already been shown to be wholly a product of rhapsodic whimsy. In his fifth, More ostensibly labors to furnish Brixius with a source for his unnatural narrative, seeing that no mortal man could have provided it: it must have been Phoebus, enlisting the frenzied Brixius as his privileged prophet. More's sixth epigram arraigns Brixius for piecemeal thievery of phrases from classical poets, while his next derides a stolid simile likening the captain and crew of the *Cordelière* to the Decii brothers of Rome just because they all perished unnaturally. More's final two epigrams resume the oracular conceit of his fifth: "Phoebus" states in a number of ungainly puns that Brixius' polysyllabic extravagance falls short of success by two quite indispensable syllables, *mens* and *cor* ("intelligence" and "spirit"). Once again More insinuates that Brixius is a dunce by design, more at ease with fine phrases that signify nothing than he is with the subtler mechanics of telling the truth in an eloquent way.[3] By

---

[1]See Appendix C, 604/18–19: ". . . ipse [sum] casu tuum nactus librum / haud scio an etiam tum excusum typis. . . ." For More's own inventory of his poems against Brixius' *Chordigera* see Allen, *4,* 219–20.

[2]See no. 188/5 ("Nam tibi scripta mala est res bene gesta fide") and no. 189/10–11 ("Sed de chordigera vatem qui vera doceret, | Quiuit adhuc reducem nemo referre pedem").

[3]Cf. More's later remark to Brixius on the *Antimorus* itself: ". . . quis non assentiat illis uersiculis / quibus lectorem . . . promittis . . . paruo e carmine sedulo legenti magnam

the end of the series we have a clear sketch of Brixius as a prodigious victim of personal and national vainglory, the same sketch which More's *Letter to Brixius* fills in so unflatteringly.

More correctly supposed that his epigrams on Brixius were the likeliest of all to engender ill feeling. In a letter of September 3, 1516, More requested Erasmus to judge whether these poems might as well be excluded from any projected edition of More's complete epigrams. For some reason Erasmus neglected to strike out the Brixius epigrams. Brixius naturally placed all the blame for this insult on More. Having brooded fully two years on his injury, he was delivered of the *Antimorus* at the beginning of March 1520.[1]

The earliest reference we have to Brixius' intention of writing against More is in a letter dated 1518 in which Erasmus rather feebly attempted to dissuade him. Allen wishes to redate this letter to mid-1517 for a reason which I find inadequate.[2] The mid-1517 date would make it appear that Brixius planned the *Antimorus* as a reprisal for poems which were then extant only in manuscript. Certainly neither the poetry nor the prose of the *Antimorus* as it was published bears any apparent relation to an unpublished text of More's *Epigrams*: Brixius bases his entire case on More's poetry as printed.[3] In all likelihood Brixius plotted the *Antimorus* as a response to the first printed edition of More's *Epigrams* (March 1518).

---

demum uoluptatem fore? Erit haud dubie / nisi quis adeo sit agelastos / ut ne ad id quidem rideat / quo uno fere mouent risum hi / quibus natura negauit ingenium: nempe nihil ut dicant quod consistat secum. . ." (Appendix C, 636/1–7).

[1]According to Allen, *4*, 128, the *Antimorus* could have been printed as early as November 1519 or as late as March 14, 1519/20. These boundary dates are established by settling that November 1519 is the earliest date at which Brixius could possibly have looked at a certain book to which he refers, Erasmus' *Farrago nova epistolarum* (Froben, October 1519), whereas March 14, 1519/20 is the date of the earliest reference to the *Antimorus* in final published form. I suspect that the *Antimorus* appeared not long before March 14, for the following reasons. First, the *Antimorus* is the sort of book calculated to stir up a good deal of ephemeral excitement; there are no definite references to its publication before March 14 but at least two just after; it seems unlikely that there was an earlier flurry of publication announcements which has left no trace at all in the letters we have. Second, More makes a particular point of the speed with which he has prepared his rebuttal, the *Letter to Brixius* (Allen, *4*, 230, lines 528–33; Appendix C, 596/15–18); it would make little sense to insist on how prompt one has been in responding to a short text which has been out for months; the *Letter to Brixius* had only lately begun to be sold when More received Erasmus' letter of April 26 (Allen, *4*, 253, lines 119–21).

[2]See Appendix C, p. 564, n. 4.

[3]Brixius even insists that a second, "restored and emended" edition of More's poems is imminent; see 508/472–75. All the lapses which Brixius imputes to More are cited from Froben's first edition.

Salmonius Macrinus implies, in his hendecasyllables enjoining Brixius to send off his retort ("libell[o]s / Quos in Mori epigrammata exarasti," 482/19–20) to the printer, that Brixius had been merely polishing his verses in the eight or nine months before publishing them (482/22–26). Meanwhile, Brixius had probably also completed his two-part prose attack on More's Latin scansion and syntax, the "Lapsus Inexcusabiles in Syllabarum Quantitate" and the "Mori Soloecismi ac Barbarismi Aliquot Foedissimi" which were eventually appended to his versified "Sylua." *Antimorus* and *Sylua* are in fact interchangeable titles for Brixius' verse. According to one modern scholar the "Lapsus" was printed in 1519 and the *Antimorus* itself a year later; while this scholar affords no hard evidence to back up his claim, it is tempting, as we shall soon see, to suppose that Brixius did conceive of the "Lapsus" and "Sylua" quite separately.[1] According to Brixius' own account the *Antimorus* was already in large measure printed when Erasmus' epistle condemning the project finally reached Brixius by chance in late 1519 or early 1520 (Allen, *4*, 129, lines 23–26), too late to dissuade him from carrying out his intentions. As More points out, nothing prevented Brixius from suppressing the work even then: he was reasonably well-to-do and could certainly afford to absorb all the printer's expenses (Allen, *4*, 253, lines 111–15). As it was, the text (poetry and prose) came out in Paris no later than March 14, 1519/20, and reached Basel and London soon afterward (see Allen, *4*, 128).

Though it may have been polished at leisure, Brixius' text was undoubtedly printed in haste. At the end of the work he added a list of corrections which itself introduces a number of faulty readings and a few quite redundant adjustments.[2] Making fun of Brixius' not entirely successful attempts to exclude printer's errors, More states at one point that Brixius stood over his printer and reset the type of the *Antimorus* every time an error presented itself; this procedure would yield a whole spectrum of variants for Brixius' single press-run.[3] One variant especially

---

[1]See Hubert Elie, "Chrétien Wechel, Imprimeur à Paris," *Gutenberg Jahrbuch, 29* (1954), 182: "Peu auparavant, en 1519, il [sc. Christian Resch] avait . . . fait les frais de l'impression par Vidoue de l'ouvrage de polémique de Germain Brice contre Thomas Morus intitulé *Thomae Mori lapsus inexcusabilis in syllabarum quantitate,* puis, l'année suivante, de l'*Antimorus.*"

[2]Brixius failed to note in his list of errata that one leaf of his manuscript was printed somewhat out of order. The words "in eadem pagina" of 516/30 refer not to the "pagina 191" of the paragraph which ends at 516/29 but rather to the "pagina 204" of the paragraph which ends at 518/26. The correct way to order the text between 516/11 and 520/8 would be 516/11–29, 518/17–26, 516/30–518/16, 518/27–520/7. A lesser confusion ("pagina sequenti") results from a last-minute insertion at 526/19–30.

[3]See Appendix C, Commentary at 624/10–16.

calls for attention: in line 58 of the *Antimorus*, part of Brixius' hendecasyllabic reply to Macrinus, where most copies have the quite unexceptionable reading "Excussisse, forasque protulisse," at least two copies have a thirteen-syllable travesty of Brixius' chosen meter, "Excussisse, hominumque in ora protulisse."[1] Two of More's later epigrams (nos. 268 and 269) lay the blame for this travesty on Brixius, and indeed it is hard to see how Brixius' printer could have misread a manuscript text to produce this distortion. The reply to Macrinus may well have been one of the last sections written. Brixius seems to have lost control of his meter and then noticed his blunder too late to remove every trace of it in the first sheets of his verses to come off the press. Otherwise he is reasonably strict in his scansion, as indeed he must be if he hopes to be thought a just critic of More's.[2] Even three or four personal lapses like this one, however, are sufficient to make the punctilious Brixius fair game for More: despite Brixius' protests to the contrary, it may be that of all the mistakes he attributes to More few are actually More's mistakes.[3]

---

[1]The thirteen-syllable version appears in the copy belonging to the Newberry Library, Chicago, and in one of the copies belonging to the Bibliothèque Mazarine, Paris (shelf no. 11399).

[2]Brixius' other most noteworthy errors in scansion are these. At 492/197, 494/242 and 502/387 he scans "mercator," "inquis" and "Martis" with long final syllables. At 496/279 and 498/281, 289 he produces inadmissable hiatus in the middle of Greek pentameters (William Godwin, A Greek Grammar, Boston, 1910, ¶1670). At 506/463 he splits an elegiac pentameter in the middle of the word "uni." Unless we substitute the shortened form *dis* for "diis" at 500/344 that line too will be unmetrical. The seemingly irregular scansion of 504/420 has a close precedent in Ovid, *Metamorphoses* 1. 193, from which Brixius borrows most of his own line. Though he tries to avoid the unmetrical *condere,* "to store," by employing the kindred verb *condire,* "to season," at 496/259, only *condere* makes really adequate sense in the context, a close imitation of Vergil, *Georgics* 4.140–41, where the verb used is *cogere,* "to collect." Finally, at 496/264 and 500/348 he scans "modo" (the adverb) and "nisi" with the last syllables long; these are scansions found only in Plautus. Nor is Brixius entirely innocent of the unclassical diction he censures in More: neither *effigiare* (498/311) nor *altiloquus* (502/360) was current before early medieval times, while "reflagitator" (482/28, 484/54; cf. Catullus 42.6, "reflagitemus") and "Aone" as a singular adjective (508/488; cf. Vergil, *Eclogues* 6. 65, "Aonas in montes") do not seem to appear anywhere outside the *Antimorus.* On the interesting history of the verb *caespitare* (544/10), which remained fairly popular with humanists despite the late date of its first attestations, see Jozef IJsewijn, "De vocabulis adunatim et caespitare apud Fortunatianum episcopum," *Latinitas, 11* (1963), 224–29, and "Nova quaedam caespitandi verbi testimonia," *Latinitas, 12* (1964), 67–70.

[3]See Appendix C, Commentary at 630/10–11. There are other significant faults in More's scansion and phrasing besides the ones Brixius lists. On the basis of Brixius' own list, however, and in view of his own faulty scansion, he seems to have had little cause to brand More a mere *versificator* (488/116) while casting himself as a metrically expert *poeta* (536/10–12). See Brixius' own comments on this sort of double-edged criticism at 500/344–51.

Brixius' work abounds with appeals to the stylistic standards of other famed humanist writers. Very clearly he hopes that his work will be read as an authoritative apology for orthodox humanism. Even the rather pedestrian prose of the "Lapsus" includes an extravagant assault on More's failure to heed the example of Pontanus and Marullus, "Though our age . . . has only these two whom it justly may rank with the ancient poets" (542/14–15). Beatus Rhenanus, who ventured to prefer More's *Epigrams* to the works of these poets on account of More's sound moral stance in his poems, is the nameless recipient of Brixius' most impetuous abuse in this passage; otherwise, Brixius seems more inclined to win over More's friends than to censure them.[1] Brixius' "Sylua" can boast the endorsement of a truly great neo-Latinist, Salmonius Macrinus ("l'Horace français"), who years later, perhaps on maturer reflection, would celebrate More's verse, as well.[2] Brixius claims—quite unfairly—that More's verses could never have borne up underneath the intelligent scrutiny of humanist friends such as Tunstall, Pace, Linacre, and chiefly Erasmus, whom Brixius singles out at one other point for the ultimate flattery, "divine" (500/352–502/359, 498/286). His own works, Brixius claims, "were not wont to circulate publicly" before winning the sanction of men like Budé, François Deloynes, the great jurist and member of Francis I's parliament, and the Hellenist Janus Lascaris (502/367–77). Brixius falsely implies that the two great French humanists, Budé and Deloynes, likewise sanction his work against More; once again he associates himself with a clan of renowned modern writers.[3] In a lengthy "poetic extravagance introduced by way of digression" (504/410–506/439), Brixius sketches the idyllic life of the renowned bard of Cremona, Hieronimo Vida, as a specimen of honorable and well-deserved literary leisure, the same leisure of which More deplores his own lack in the letter to Giles introducing *Utopia*.[4] By the end of the "Sylua," where Brixius says disdainfully to More, "But while I mull over

---

[1]See 74/51–58 and 542/7–13.

[2]On Macrin see I. D. McFarlane, "Jean Salmon Macrin," *Bibliothèque d'Humanisme et Renaissance, 21* (1959), 55–84, 311–349; 22 (1960), 73–89, and the introduction in J. Salmon Macrin, *Le Livre des épithalames (1528–31): les odes de 1530 (livres I et II)*, ed. G. Soubeille (Toulouse, 1978); on Macrin's poems praising More see G. Soubeille, "L'amitié de Thomas More et de Salmon Macrin," *Moreana, 54* (1977), 11–21.

[3]More insists that Brixius actually defied his friends' counsel in printing the *Antimorus*; cf. Allen, *4*, 228, lines 437–39 and 251, lines 16–20.

[4]For Girolamo Vida, whose *Christias* furnished a model for Milton, see Mario A. di Cesare, *Bibliotheca Vidiana: A Bibliography of Marco Girolamo Vida* (Florence, 1974). Brixius wrote a letter to Vida included in a volume of 1531 (*Germani Brixii Eleemosynarii epistolae quattuor* [Paris, C. Wechel]).

the old poets, you should mull over the new ones" (512/549), Brixius' point is quite clearly that More himself has yet to learn what the New Learning stands for before he can even aspire to contend with Brixius and his like in real mastery of classical antiquity. Brixius fails to perceive that More's eminent humanist friends give him, too, a legitimate claim to be championing the spirit of humanism.

The prose sections of the *Antimorus* loosely conform to a reasonably well-represented genre of Renaissance scholarly writing, the amicable *castigatio* of one humanist's style in his unrevised works by another humanist. When Macrin composed such a private *castigatio* for the *Poemata* of Theodore Beza (Paris, C. Badius, 1548), Beza gratefully adjusted his verse in accord with Macrin's observations and attested his thanks in a verse letter shortly thereafter.[1] By publishing his own *castigationes* of More, especially with two such unflattering titles ("Lapsus Inexcusabiles . . . ," "Soloecismi ac Barbarismi . . . Foedissimi"), Brixius of course showed that his own motives were anything but amicable. Nonetheless, till he added his versified "Sylua," Brixius could still count on generic convention to make his pretense of a friendly and Christian concern for More's own reputation seem to some degree plausible. The more petulant and virulent tone of the "Sylua" made his pretense of friendly and Christian solicitude for More in the "Lapsus" appear more than faintly absurd. Brixius' "Lapsus" and "Sylua" may thus have been written quite separately.

In his versified "Sylua," Brixius seeks to move beyond petty prosodic criticisms and to discredit More's implicit theories of how poetry ought to be written. Like Beatus Rhenanus, Brixius here assumes that More's poems must be judged on the basis of their moral effectiveness; the main question is how subtly and cogently More's poems discriminate between what men should praise and what they should detest. Using More's own criteria, Brixius tries to establish that More's poems are failures. Brixius' "Sylua" is really an "Art poétique contre More": the Horatian epistle on praising great men (*Epistles* 2.1, *ad Augustum*) and especially the *Ars poetica* itself afford sources for many of Brixius' most serious reproaches.[2] Brixius' libelous allusions to More's scheme for praising his prince ("ad regias laudes"), allusions based mainly on More's coronation ode (no. 19), provoked and distressed More intensely. He devotes fully two hundred

---

[1]See McFarlane, "Jean Salmon Macrin," pp. 343–47, for a transcript of Macrin's *castigatio* with commentary.

[2]Cf. 492/178–85, *Epistles* 2. 1. 229–44; 492/186–91, *Ars poetica* 309–22; 494/220–21, *Ars poetica* 38–40; 504/408, *Ars poetica* 25; 510/527, *Ars poetica* 79; 510/547, *Ars poetica* 269; 512/554, *Ars poetica* 445–52.

lines in the *Letter to Brixius* to refuting the general notions of praise on which all these allusions are based, and indeed would gladly have withdrawn from the clash altogether, as Erasmus at one point insists, if Brixius had not made the "pernicious" claim that More somehow slandered Henry VIII by contrasting his reign with his father's.[1] Brixius counters More's emphasis on *fides,* or objective credibility, with an unswerving emphasis on *splendor,* a strictly subjective impression of majesty, as the primary concern of all authentic poets who praise kings.[2] While according to More only praise that is "faithful" can validate temporal authority, Brixius seems to think temporal authority validates even "unfaithful" praise. In his final confrontation with Henry VIII, when More could have saved his own life just by paying lip service to Henry's new order of "splendor," More was willing to die to uphold his first duty to "fides," to the "good faith" which he then as always construed as an ethical imperative as well as a matter of theological dogma. We should not be surprised at the vehemence he shows in opposing the rival account of legitimate praise on which Brixius bases his challenge.

Although Brixius' work is indebted thematically to Horace's didactic epistles on how to write poetry, his main formal debt is to Ovid. Ovid's *Ibis* is by far the finest representative in classical Latin of a genre devoted entirely to poetic "curses," a genre called ἀραί in Greek and *dirae* in Latin.[3] Ovid wrote his own *dirae* in the elegiac meter which is generally reserved for love poetry and lament; Brixius took over not only Ovid's meter but also Ovid's apology for using it in this unorthodox way.[4]

What distinguishes Brixius' work from its Ovidian model is the highly topical and circumstantial character of Brixius' invective. Ritual curses are almost all formulaic. Brixius' highly derivative verses are of course in their way formulaic as well, but he wishes at least to establish that More's personal literary sins have made him a particularly suitable target for

---

[1]More addresses himself to Brixius' libelous comments "ad regias laudes" in Appendix C, 638/4–648/23. For Erasmus, see Allen, *4,* 326, lines 10–17.

[2]See esp. 488/130–490/145, 492/208–494/231. In the first passage cited, Brixius mounts a straightforward attack on More's standard of *fides.*

[3]We find a poem titled *Dirae* in the *Appendix Vergiliana;* the grammarian Valerius Cato wrote another such work, which is now lost. At *Ibis* 85 Ovid calls his own work "dira carmina." Ovid's principal model is the lost elegiac poem *Ibis* of the Alexandrian poet Callimachus. Callimachus like Ovid disguised the true name of his enemy under the name of a bird the Egyptians considered both sacred and sinister. See further the essay in Ovid, *The Art of Love and Other Poems,* ed. J. H. Mozley (London and Cambridge, Mass., 1962), pp. 359–72.

[4]Cf. *Ibis* 45–54 and 512/568–74. For other echoes of the *Ibis,* cf. *Ibis* 85 and 504/420; *Ibis* 209–14 and 490/152–55; *Ibis* 643–44 and 512/558–63.

ritual curses. The title of Brixius' work sets it in the tradition of formal rhetorical invective; Caesar's *Libri Anticatones* against Cato the Younger (Juvenal 6. 338) provide the main classical precedent for the title which Brixius coined. Caesar's title *Anticatones,* like Erasmus' *Antibarbari,* is often treated as an adjectival noun in the masculine plural; Brixius' "Antimorus" is normally treated as an adjectival noun in the feminine singular, probably meant to agree with the word *sylua* or "miscellany" as its implied subject (488/101).[1] The targets of *dirae* were generally unnamed; by conflating the *dirae* tradition with that of rhetorical invective Brixius brings into being a particularly versatile kind of libel.

Remarkably, the first imitator of Brixius' libel was More's friend William Lily. Lily and William Horman had become embroiled in a bitter grammatical rivalry with Robert Whittinton, Poet Laureate of Oxford. Under the pseudonym "Bossus," Whittinton had distributed libelous epigrams against his two rivals. Lily and Horman responded in 1521 with two pamphlets, each called *Antibossicon.*[2] Lily actually sticks closer than Horman to the tradition of epigrammatic invective: Lily's book is replete with short epigrams against "Bossus" by fictitious authors, and even Lily's extended elegiac rebuttal is punctuated with couplets by Whittinton. Horman's work on the other hand includes a sustained elegiac invective which is followed by a prose exposé of Whittinton's inferior Latinity; this exposé may well be modeled on Brixius' "Lapsus." It appears that the pungency of Brixius' attack was not lost on his English contemporaries.

A Note on the Text and Translation

The Latin text of the *Antimorus* is taken from the copy in the Beinecke Library at Yale University. Two sidenotes (p. 542) have been added from a copy in the Bibliothèque Mazarine, shelf no. 11399. Occasionally I have silently dropped a comma or substituted a colon for a comma or period in order to make the sense more immediately clear. I have also expanded abbreviations (except in references to titles and parts of books), regularized the use of capital letters, and silently omitted the pilcrows employed in the copy-text. Page numbers, which Brixius gives in roman

---

[1]Compound Greek adjectives ending with –ος could be masculine or feminine, e.g., φιλόσοφος.

[2]Both these pamphlets were printed by Pynson in 1521. For further discussion of the quarrel see Wolfgang Mann, *Lateinische Dichtung in England vom Ausgang des Frühhumanismus bis zum Regierungsantritt Elisabeths* (Halle/Saale, 1939), pp. 15–19, and Nelson, *John Skelton,* pp. 148–57.

numerals, are changed to arabic. Quotations of verse or longer passages of prose which are given without interruption in the copy-text are here set off by indentation. Sidenotes to the verse text have been set as footnotes; periods at the ends of sidenotes have been silently omitted. At 498/285 I have retained the epithet παντοδαμεῦς (corrected from παντοδαμσῦς in the list of errata), which Brixius seems to have coined as an equivalent to the genitive πανδαμάτορος. The title page calls the work *Antimorus,* not *Antimωrus,* a form which highlights the pun on μωρός, "fool." But Brixius himself reserves the spelling *Antimωrus* for some parting shots (538/26, 542/31, 544/28, 546/9 and 24), and his distinction has been preserved here. In the translation I have tried to preserve the many Greek and Latin puns on More's name, but some defy lucid translation. Apart from μωρός, Brixius also links More's name with words like *mors* ("death"), *mora* ("delay"), and μόρος ("fate").[1]

---

[1]See Marc'hadour, "A Name for All Seasons," *Essential Articles,* pp. 539–62.

GERMANI BRIXII ANTISSIODORENSIS ANTIMORVS

[A_2] Salmonii Macrini ad Germanum Brixium Christianissimae Reginae a Secretis Hendecasyllabi

SIC TE CASTALIAE rigent puellae,
Toto gurgite Phocidis canentem.
Sic Cypri dea quicquid est leporis
Vsquam, versibus Antimorianis
Vbertim inferat, eque delicato
Cesto munditias profundat omneis.
Sic castis tibi blandiens labellis,
Chloris basia tot ferat, sereno
Clara quot numerantur astra coelo,
Chloris de numero puellularum
Vna illustrius adsecuta nomen [A_2v]
Tuis hendecasyllabis disertis,
Extremam lepidis manum libellis
Quos in Mori Epigrammata exarasti
Imponas, precor, hosque lectitandos
Flagitantibus hinc et inde amicis
Edas ocyus. Heus, quid immoraris?
Quid causas piger usque et usque nectis?
Cui non octo satis nouemve menses
Paucis carminibus repumicandis,
Huic vix secula sint satis Sibyllae.
Tecum haec liberius diserte Brixi,
Fortasse obstreperus reflagitator,
Consuetudine fretus, atque amore,
Qui nos glutine mutuo ligauit,
Sed non tam obstreperus reflagitator
Quam tu durus, et improbus negator. [A_3]

Germani Brixii Hendecasyllabi ad Salmonium Macrinum

Et Stentor mihi Homericus, Macrine,
Idem et Nestor es. Optimum poetam

conflagration of the *Cordelière* and the *Regent,* the former a French ship, the latter British; bearing an olive branch in the midst of the battle, my muse challenged no one. Foul-mouthed More, quite unique in assuming the mask and the speech of a moron as well as a Momus, lashed out at my poem unprovoked, though I knew him no better than he knew himself as a poet. Even though (as you, candid reader, may judge easily enough from the indiscreet fellow's impudence) he, like a feeble bitch, can do no more than bark, and cannot bite or wound, and even though insults launched by the tongues of bad men less often diminish the fame and renown of good men than enhance and perfect them (just as a palm tree borne down with a burden will strain up against the obstruction and soar even higher); nonetheless, I saw fit to respond, my sole sources of confidence being your fairness of vision, your purity of hearing, and the soundness and strength of my cause.

GERMANI BRIXII ANTISSIODORENSIS IN THOMAM MωRVM ANGLVM CHORDIGERAE CALVMNIATOREM ANTIMORVS, SYLVA

ME NIMIVM veteres dicis redolere poetas.
  Nimirum hoc de te dicere nemo potest.
Nam quae effutisti, nisi fallor, carmina vates
  Hos redolent, tua quos protulit Vtopia.
Quam bene quae breuis est, tibi fit producta canenti?
  Et quae longa tamen, syllaba curta tibi est?
Has tibi praescribis, qui scribis carmina, leges?
  Vsurpas tales belle poeta modos?
In media cursor quando vnquam vincat harena,
  Qui toties pedibus claudicet ipse suis?
Quae te multa pedis latuere errata Latini,
  Inuenies libri calce notata mei.
Sunt quoque plura eadem, quae nunc intacta relinquo,
  Nam criticum in nugis me pudet esse tuis. [B_1v]
Versificatorem quis te non dixerit Anglum?
  Cui numerus numero pangitur absque suo?
Vt sileam et foedos lapsus, quos nulla Latinae
  Sustinuise queat regula grammaticae.
Quippe soloecismis passim tua carmina abundant
  Pluribus, exundet quam mare fluminibus.
At numerare tropos, et schemata barbara, quaeque
  Scommata nil Graium, nil Latiale sonant,
Tam facile est, quam si numeres vel gramina Veris,
  Vel folia Autumni, poma vel Alcinoi.
Chordigera excussa, si quid me tale monebis,
  Debebo monitis tempus in omne tuis.
Hic te vnum offendunt versus mendacia nostri,
  Lectorem offendit menda pudenda tui.
O lepidum caput! Haud sua dat figmenta poetis,
  Atque hos carceribus continet historicis.
Ecquid Vergilius, vel vatum gloria Homerus
  Troianae historiae seruat vbique fidem? [B_2]
Num quae de Aeneae Didusque ardoribus ille
  Luserit, esse putas omnia veridica?

---

105 *Sidenote:* Vtopiam scripsit Morus, id est, rempublicam quae nusquam extat

THE *ANTIMORUS* OF GERMANUS BRIXIUS OF AUXERRE AGAINST THOMAS MORE THE ENGLISHMAN, SLANDERER OF THE *CHORDIGERA:* A MISCELLANY

YOU SAY I am too reminiscent of ancient poets; certainly no one could say this about you. The poems you prated out—unless I am mistaken—are more reminiscent of poets indigenous to your Utopia. How well short syllables stretch when you sing them! How well long ones shrink! Are these your personal canons of versification? You elegant poet, is this the right way to use meters? Has there ever been one winning runner who tripped over his own feet as often as you do? Many of the faults which escaped you in your Latin feet you will find recorded at the end of my book; there are more of the same sort which I leave untouched for the present, since I am ashamed to play critic concerning your trifles. Who could call you anything but an English versifier, since the meter you write is not really a meter? To say nothing of those vile mistakes insupportable by any rule of Latin grammar; indeed, your poems abound with more solecisms than the ocean redounds with its streams. But to number your barbarous figures and tropes and your taunts with no basis in Greek or in Latin is as easy a task as to number the grasses of spring, the leaves of autumn, or the fruits of Alcinous.

More wrote Utopia, that is, a republic which exists nowhere

I will be forever in debt for your comments should you, after examining the *Chordigera,* call any fault such as these to my notice; as it stands, the falsehoods in my verse offend none but you, while in yours shameful faults give offense to the general reader. O soul of wit! He begrudges the poets their fictions and shuts them up close in the bounds of historical truthfulness. Tell me, does Vergil or Homer, the glory of poets, stick faithfully to the history of Troy? What the former made up about the passions of Aeneas and Dido—do you think that is all the plain truth?

Hic quoque dum errores varios confingit Vlyssei,
Obligat historica num sua scripta fide?
Si nescis, bone vir, sua sunt figmenta poetis,
Quae si sustuleris, nulla poesis erit.
Heruea dum canimus tamen, e mediaque feroces
Chordigera Anglorum sustinet ille manus,
Dum seruat patrios praesenti a clade penates
Victor, et hostiles vexat agitque rates,
Haec, quae vera tuae testantur funera gentis,
(Vsque adeo es mωrus) falsa fuisse putas.
Proin de me quia quae voluisti dixti, age de te hic
Quae nolis audi, si potes, et patere,
Vt te quae subiit, male dum loquerere, voluptas,
Illa eadem te, audis dum male, destituat.
Mωre, scio, velles intra oris septa tenere,
(Septa tamen mωrus si qua pudoris habet) [B_2v]
Quae, Veneris sine, quae Phoebi sine numine, Musis
Auersis, latices fonte negante sacros,
Quae neruo sine, quae sine sanguine carmina, vere
Crimina, vulgasti mille premenda magis.
O lepidos versus, o splendida carmina, per quae
Principis extollis mentem, animumque tui?
Carmina quae cedro non sint indigna, quibusque
Luculli ornari bibliotheca queat.
Hic tamen, hic te Mωre diu insudasse putandum est,
Ingenii et vires applicuisse tui.
Durum Marcelli miserandi Octauia fatum,
Dum lugentem audit carmine Vergilium,
Quoslibet attonita ad numeros, sestertia vati
Imperat actutum munere dena dari.
Viginti accaepto donasse talenta libello
Nicoclem Isocrati scripta vetusta ferunt.
Scilicet Henricus numerosi carminis ergo,
Donauit Mωro mille talenta suo. [B_3]
Ten decet, o, tibi inaccessum conscendere pontum?
Credereque ignotis vela ratemque vadis?

---

141 *Sidenote:* Herueus Chordigerae nauarchus

156 *Sidenote:* Ironia

168 *Sidenote:* Ironia

Does the latter, as well, when he contrives the various wanderings of Ulysses, bind himself to write with historical accuracy? In case you do not know, my good man, fiction rightly belongs to the poets; take it away, and there will be no more poetry. When we sing of Hervé, nonetheless, as he holds off the fierce bands of Englishmen amidships on his *Cordelière,* and as he by his victory rescues the hearths of his homeland from imminent calamity and routs and harries the enemy's vessels, you suppose all of this to be false, such a moron you are, though your countrymen's funerals vouch for its truthfulness.

Hervé, the commander of the Cordelière

Since you spoke what you would about me, steel yourself now to hear (if you can) certain thoughts about yourself which you would rather not hear, so that the pleasure you garnered from speaking ill will abandon you now that you are hearing ill spoken. More, I know you would have liked to hold within the confines of your teeth—if, that is, any moron retains any confines of shame—the myriad songs, rather sins, which you published, though you should have withheld them instead, songs composed without Venus' grace, and without that of Phoebus, with the Muses averse to it all, and with Hippocrene denying you its sacred draught—songs both nerveless and bloodless.

O most elegant of lines, O most splendid of verses, wherein you extol both the mind and the heart of your prince! Verses not unworthy of cedar oil, and fit to embellish the library of a Lucullus! Here, at least, More, we must suppose that you toiled long and hard; here you must have applied the full strength of your talent. Octavia, when she heard Vergil mourning in verse the fate of the hapless Marcellus, marvelled at some of his verses and ordered at once that the poet be given a prize of ten thousand sesterces. Ancient tomes say Nicocles conferred twenty talents on Isocrates as a reward for one book; Henry doubtless bestowed fully a thousand on More for his well-measured verse.

Irony

Irony

Is it fitting for you to embark on a sea with which you have no acquaintance or trust sails and ship to that sea's unknown courses? Don't you

Ignoras pelagi mediis impingere saxis,
Qui nescit fragilem qua regat arte ratem?
Qui si forte putas cuiuslibet esse, poema
Pangere, et Aonias ore sonare deas,
Falleris: altisona non sunt nisi voce canendae.
Nec nisi Peliden Pelias hasta decet.
Quod si adeo Henricus (Latiae cui cura camoenae)
Gustasset fontis pocula Castalii,
Carminis vt posset dignoscere crimina, rebus
Esset consultum quam male Mωre tuis?
Contusumque caput pugnis tot Cherylus olim,
Inculti ob numerum carminis haud habuit,
Quot rex iste tuum contunderet. Ecquis enim rex
Qui sapiat, vatem tam ferat insipidum?
At non verba (inquis) debet, sed sensa poeta
Quaerere, Socraticis eruere eque libris. [B_3v]
Scilicet inspectus scopus hic fuit, haec ratio vna
Cantanti Henricum Mωre tibi vsque placet.
Nam cur non placeat? cum te sapientius vno
Laudandi partes nullus obire queat?
Ecquid enim Henricum dum vis extollere Olympo,
Laudibus et laudes accumulare putas?
Tum demum Henrici infamas, lacerasque parentem?
Vt cui aequi, ac legum non fuit vllus amor?
Anglia quo regnante iugum seruile subiuit?
Per quem et mercator aduena seruus erat?
Idque agis, Henricum affatus, quo scilicet aurem
Titilles nati valdius, atque animum?
Suauidice o vates, ten rhetorices Maro partem hanc
Aeneam Anchisae dum canit, edocuit?
An vel Meonius scriptor, dum cantat Vlyssem?
Vel dum Pelidae magnanimi acta refert?
Magna pio est nato (si nescis Mωre) voluptas,
Cum se patre audit progenitum esse bono. [B_4]
Nec melius natum possis laudare, parenti
Quam si addas laudes, attribuasque suas.
At formidasti, puto, ne praeconia patri
Addita, de nati nomine detraherent.

---

188 *Sidenote:* Ironia

192 *Sidenote:* Mori impudentia, dum filium laudare instituit, patrem vituperantis

know that the man who lacks skill in the steering of his fragile ship comes to grief on some rock in mid–ocean? If you think that just anyone can spin out a poem or give voice to the Aonian goddesses with his lips, you are deceived; they may be sung only with the voice of grandiloquence. The spear of Achilles befits only him.

If Henry, who shows some concern for the muse of the Latins, had ever drunk deeply enough from the Castalian fountain to distinguish the difference between songs and sins, what a sorry day, More, that would be for you! Choerilus' pate was the target of fewer blows on account of the meter in his ragged verse than the blows which the king would rain down on your pate. What king with any discretion could bear such an indiscreet poet?

You say that the poet ought rather to look to his sense, quarried out of the Socratic texts, than to strain for fine wording. Doubtless this was the object that you had in view; no doubt this is the one plan which pleases you, More, in your singing of Henry. For why should it not please, since no one can be wiser than you—you alone—when it comes to performing the duties of praise?

Irony

Indeed, when you set about exalting Henry to the heights of Olympus, do you think you are piling up praise upon praise? It is then that you defame and excoriate Henry's sire as one who bore no love for equity and the law, in whose reign England took on the yoke of servility, and through whom even foreign merchants were enslaved. And do you do this in your address to Henry so as to flatter more roundly the ears and the soul of the son? O honey-tongued bard, was it Vergil who taught you this element of rhetoric when he sings of Aeneas, the son of Anchises? Was it the Maeonian writer, perhaps, when he sings of Ulysses, or when he is recording the deeds of the magnanimous son of Peleus?

More's impudence in slandering the father as he sets out to praise the son

In case you are blind to it, More, every dutiful son takes great pleasure in hearing that he is the scion of a virtuous father; there is no better way to praise a son than to ascribe and attribute his praises to his sire. But you were frightened, I imagine, that the honors ascribed to the father would

O laudatorem condum, minimeque profusum,
Cuius ab ore cadunt pauca, sed apta tamen?
Iure etenim, oranti quondam quae munera Homerus
Atridae tribuit, sunt tribuenda tibi,
Facundo potius quam quae concedit Vlyssei,
Cui paria Hybernae verba fuere niui.
Pellaeus vetuit ne se, nisi solus Apelles
Pingeret, hoc studium corporis ille habuit.
Tune animum Henrici depingere magnanimi audes?
Regiaque incesta sceptra sacrare manu?
Materiam ingenio prudens quam deligit author
Comparat, aequa humeris pondera fertque suis.
Haud alios quam consimiles tibi Mωre poetas
Exturbare sua debuit vrbe Plato, [B_4v]
Quorum carminibus non arrisere sorores,
Nec dea praestiterit, nec deus vllus opem.
Magnus Alexander felicem acclamat Achillem,
Maeoniam nactus quod foret ille tubam.
Principis Henrici fatum heu lachrimabile, cuius
Virtutem efferri contigit ore tuo.
Eleuat elumbis vates quos tollit, et addunt
Splendori tenebras carmina, si mala sunt.
Quam metuo tibi Mωre. Etenim si senserit ille,
Frigida quam in laudes sit tibi musa suas,
Ilicet, actutum mediis te expellet ab Anglis,
Et migrare tuam coget ad Vtopiam.
Nec misero exilium continget tale poetae,
Quale olim summo contigit historico,
Expulsum patria quem mox reuocasse feruntur
Linguae admirati munera Cecropidae.
Praetereo et titulum, quo (dum offers carmina regi)
Mωre tuam excusas ingeniose moram. [C_1]
Versiculos (inquis) hos illustrissime princeps
Quam deceat, fateor, serius exhibeo,

---

212 *Sidenote:* Iliados Γ vbi Antenor Helenam alloquitur

229 *Sidenote:* Efferri significanter dictum, ac si dicas, sepeliri, ad sepulchrum ferri

237 *Sidenote:* Thucydides

242 *Sidenote:* Verba haec fere omnia desumpta sunt ex ea epistola quam Morus premittit carminibus suis ad Henricum regem scriptis

detract from the renown of the son; you stingy, ungenerous eulogist, from whose lips issue "few words, yet apt ones"! In all fairness, your rhetoric earns you the tribute which Homer once granted to Atreus' son; not, however, the tribute he pays to the fluent Ulysses, whose words fall from his lips "like the snow-flakes of winter."

Iliad *3, where Antenor is speaking to Helen [lines 214, 222]*

The Macedonian prince forbade all but Apelles to paint him, so great was his care for his outward appearance. Do you dare to portray, then, the heart of the great-hearted Henry, to consecrate his regal scepter with your impure hand? The prudent author suits every theme he selects to his talent, and takes up burdens meet for his shoulders.

It was poets no different from you, More, that Plato should have expelled from his city, those "poets" on whose compositions the Nine Sisters frowned, for which no god or goddess afforded his aid. Alexander the Great hails Achilles as blessed since his fame found its trumpet in Homer. Alas for King Henry's lamentable fate, that his greatness should have to be borne off on your lips! Nerveless poets detract from the ones they exalt, and poems which are no good cap off glory with darkness. How I fear for you, More! If he ever comes to perceive how enfeebled your muse is in singing his praises, right then and there he will expel you from England and force you to move to Utopia. The exile of this wretched poet will bear no resemblance to that of the greatest historian, whom the Athenians, having expelled him, are said to have soon summoned home out of reverence for his gifts of language.

Efferri *[to be borne off] is a verb with suggestive associations, as one might say "to be buried," "to be borne to one's tomb"*

Thucydides

Likewise, I will pass over the address wherein, as you offer your poems to the king, my ingenious More, you excuse your delay in producing them; "Most illustrious of princes," you say, "I am issuing these verselets less promptly than I should. I admit it. I turned them over to a painter to have them embellished, but he had scarcely begun painting when his

Almost all these words are taken from the letter that More prefixes to his poems addressed to King Henry

Pictori ornandos dederam, ast vbi pingere coepit,
Huic mox corripuit seua podagra pedem.
Inuentum o lepidum, et regalibus auribus aptum?
Daedalus hoc tene, an Mercurius docuit?
At, puto, pictorem nunquam esset adorta podagra,
Is nisi tractasset carmina Mωre tua,
Quae simul ac tetigit (quoniam passim illa lababant,
Vt quibus aegri essent inualidique pedes)
Actutum nocuit morbi contactus, et illum
Compedibus vinxit dira podagra suis,
Quod si qua me forte mei (dum carmina canto haec)
Poplite succiduo destituere pedes,
Carminis ipsa tui dedit hoc contagio, quamquam id
Non nisi supremis contigerim articulis.
Quinetiam et Graecos potis es traducere versus,
Et condire istis Attica mella fauis. [C_1v]
Quam bene sit mensura pedis tibi cognita Graii,
Nimirum e Latiis arguis ipse modis.
Nam reliqua vt sileam vocis commissa Pelasgae,
Insula Cretensis non tibi facta breuis?
Cum non longa modo, sed et haec hecatompolis olim
Extiterit, veri si quid Homerus habet.
Haud tamen abiicere hic animum te Mωre iubemus.
Errare, humani scilicet ingenii est.
I, sequere, et miserare inopes, quos Graecia linguae
Indignos opibus censuit esse suae,
His non inuideas diuina poemata vatis
Maeonii, numeris facta Latina tuis,
Vt miseris per te liceat cognoscere tandem
(Quod nondum licuit) quantus Homerus erat,
Quamque omnes longo praeuertitur interuallo,
Graecia quos peperit, quos peperit Latium, [C_2]
καὶ σὺ μὲν, ἐκτελέσας τόδε ἔργον ἀθέσφατον, οὐ δὴ
μωρὸς ἐν ἀνθρώποις ἔσσεαι, ἀλλὰ σοφὸς,
καὶ μέγα σοι δώσουσι γέρας, καὶ κῦδος ᾿Αχαιοὶ
σύμπαντες, καμάτου εἵνεκα θεσπεσίου.

---

258 *Sidenote:* Traducere significanter dictum, ac si dicas, infamare

262 *Sidenote:* Morus corripuit primam huius nominis, Creta, quae et Graecis et Latinis producitur

268 *Sidenote:* Morum hortatur per ironiam ad traducenda Homeri poemata

foot was seized with a severe attack of gout"—oh, a pretty invention, and fit for the ears of a king! Was it Daedalus or Mercury who taught you this? I suspect that the painter would not have contracted that gout without handling your poems, More; as soon as he touched them—for they were continually stumbling, since *their* feet were weak and infirm—the contagion immediately seized him and cruel gout bound him tight in her fetters. And if it has chanced, as I sing these lines, that my feet have given way beneath tottering knees, I have caught this infection from your poem, even though I have touched it with only the tips of my fingers.

And then there are your versions, I mean your subversions, of Greek verse, where you store up, in those hives of yours, Attic honey. Your acquaintance with Greek prosody may be gauged from your own Latin metrics; not to mention your other affronts to the Hellenic language, did you not try to shorten the island of Crete, though that island was not merely long, but at one time (if Homer is trustworthy) the location of one hundred cities? Do not lose heart, though, on that account, More, since to err is but human. Proceed! Pity those poor souls whom Greece has adjudged unworthy of the wealth of her language. Do not begrudge them the divine poems of the Maeonian seer. Make his poems Latin poems in your numbers. Let these poor wretches finally know (what up till now they could not know) how great Homer was, and by how large an interval he outstrips all the scions of Greece and the scions of Rome.

Traducere *[to translate] is a verb with suggestive associations, as one might say "slander"*

More shortens the first syllable in "Crete," it being long in both Greek and Latin

He ironically urges More to "traduce" the epics of Homer

Having finished this ineffable labor, you will no longer be a moron but a sage among men. Greeks one and all will concede you the palm and the prize for your

τῷ σε χρὴ τοῖον χερσὶν πόνον ἐμβάλλεσθαι,
  εἴ τιν' ἔχεις βιότου ἵμερον ἀθανάτου.
οὐ γὰρ πώποτ' ἀμαυρώσει μωρὸν μόρος, ἣν τὸ,
  βάρβαρος ὢν, τελέσῃς πάντοθεν ἀδύνατον.
καὶ τότε δὴ μωρὸς, καὶ κάμμορος ὤν περ ἀοιδὸς
  παντοδαμεῦς μοίρας ἄμμορος οἷος ἔσῃ.
οὐ νοέεις οἷον κλέος ἔλλαβε θεῖος Ἔρασμος,
  ἵρ' ἐπανορθώσας βιβλία; καὶ σὲ τὸν αὖ
δεῖ ζηλοῦν, ἵνα τίς σε καὶ ὀψιγόνων εὖ εἴπῃ
  ἀνθρώπων γενεῇ ἶσα χαρισάμενον.
Parce, precor, quisquis lectorem te mihi praebes,
  Miscuit hic Graios si mea musa modos. [C_2v]
Fecit id Argolicae nulla ostentatio linguae,
  Cantanti adspirent sic mihi Pegasides.
At propugnantem pro gentis honore Pelasgae
  Armauit telis Graecia grata suis.
Namque ea praesentem ad pugnam magis apta putauit,
  Quam quae essent Latios facta per artifices.
Mωre tibi poteras bene consuluisse, dicasses
  Harpocratis sacris si tua scripta dei,
Necnon Rheginas imitatus gerro cicadas,
  Sancta admisisses dogmata Pythagorae.
Tu vero licet illa scias tecum emoritura,
  (Tam longam poterunt si tolerare moram)
Hoc tamen in praesens stupidis imponere gaudes
  Nomine, gloriolae captus amore leuis,
Et tibi permagnum est, vulgi venarier auram
  Interea, et fumos combibere aure leues.
Si saperes, saperent correptos mordicus vngues
  Et pluteum caesum carmina Mωre tua. [C_3]
Vrsa tibi exemplo est, catulos quae lambere, et illos
  Hoc studio informes effigiare solet.
Maturanda quidem est, non praecipitanda camena,
  Debet et autumnos haec tolerare nouem.
Sunt quae et nugamur, sunt et quae ludimus, et sunt
  Quaeque facit risus carmina, quaeque iocus.
Non nisi quae bona sunt, bonus euulgare poeta
  Curat, cui famae est curaque, amorque suae.

---

286 *Sidenote:* Laus Erasmi

300 *Sidenote:* Rheginae cicadae mutescunt

godlike achievement. You ought therefore to take up a task such as this if you have any longing for everlasting life. Mortality will never mar this moron if, barbarian that you are, you complete this utterly impossible task; and then, no matter that you are a moron, and however morose your poetic prognosis, you alone will be party no more to all-conquering mortality. Do you not know what renown the divine Erasmus has earned for emending the holy Bible? You, too, in your turn, ought to emulate him, so that someone will praise you for having enriched even future generations of mankind with a gift equalling his.

Praise of Erasmus

Pardon me, please, you who do me the courtesy of reading me, if my muse interposed Grecian lines here. It was not done to show off my Greek—may the Muses who lend me their breath be my witness!—but Hellas was pleased to equip me with arms of her own as I went forth to champion the fame of the Pelasgian race; she considered these arms to be apter for my present contest than those wrought by craftsmen of Latium.

You would have been well advised, More, to have dedicated your writings to the cult of the god Harpocrates; prattler that you are, you should have imitated the cicadas of Rhegium and accepted the sacred teachings of Pythagoras. But although you yourself know that those writings of yours will die with you—if they can endure even that long—nonetheless for the moment you delight in deceiving dolts under this title, taken in as you are by your love for a fleeting and trivial glory; meanwhile, for you, it is a very great feat to go courting the breath of the rabble and drinking in fleeting acclaim with your ears.

The cicadas of Rhegium are silent

If you had any sense of good taste, then your poems, More, would savor of fingernails gnawed to the quick, and a much-battered desktop. The she-bear provides you a model; she is wont to lick her unformed cubs and by this effort shape them. Your muse should be ripened, not rushed; she should wait out nine autumns. There are poems which we strike off while idling and poems which we play at; some poems have their origin in laughter, and some in a joke. It is only good poems that a good poet cares to publish, any poet who has any care or esteem for his

Adde quod authori sua conseruare volenti
singula, depereunt omnia scripta simul.
Carminis, et nitor, et numeri praestantia, vati
Adiiciunt famae nomina, non cumulus.
Marsus Amazonidos numerosa volumina scripsit,
Persius exiguis versibus egit opus.
Hic tamen arctato cum codice viuit, at illum
Gloria tam magni est nulla secuta operis.
Qui sapiunt, hominum reliquum genus, ordine viuunt,
Sint sine quo ad primum cuncta reducta Chaos. [C_3v]
Nam prius ediscunt formare, et fingere vocem,
Et bene compactis verba referre sonis,
Ausint quam prodire palam, et vulgare loquendo
Errorem linguae, barbariemque suae.
Communem ad normam tibi viuere displicet, et qui
Omnibus est vnus, non placet ordo tibi.
Pangere vis versus, et fingere carmina inepte,
Nondum perdoctus carminis effigiem.
Ad sacra Mauortis non est accedere tutum,
Cui non sint habiles ad fera bella manus.
Palladis, et Phoebi sacra sancta, nouemque sororum,
Anne tibi censes esse verenda minus?
Vulgasset si quis Cereris mysteria, crimen
Purgabat capitis non nisi supplicio.
Non vulgas modo, corrumpis mysteria Phoebi.
Quae tua delicto huic poena satisfaciat?
Atque adeo, si diis placet, emunctissime vates,
Ausus es Andream carpere nescio quem, [C_4]
Qui dum perstringit numeroque, et carmine fastos,
Se neget adstringi carminis ad numerum.
Id tamen errati tecum est commune, nisi quod
Conscius ille sui est, nescius ipse tui es.
O sine fronte hominem? Tene exprobrare sodali
Crimina, quae redeant in caput ipsa tuum?
Non commisisses tam foeda piacula, amicis
Si commisisses ante legenda tuis.
Tunstallus, Paceusque tibi, tibi Linacrus, et qui
Ante alios Mωrum curat, Erasmus erat,

---

344 *Sidenote:* Mori impudentia, in aliis sua ipsius vitia damnantis

354 *Sidenote:* Tunstallus, Paceus, Linacrus, Erasmus

fame; and indeed, when an author intends to preserve every one of his writings, all perish together. The polish of his poems and the excellence of his meter are what confer fame on a poet, not the bulk of his output. Marsus wrote many volumes of his *Amazonis;* Persius finished his work in a few verses. The latter still lives with his one compressed tome, while no glory fell to the former for his work on so grand a scale.

Men of good sense, that is, all the rest of mankind, live by order, without which all things would be drawn back to primeval chaos. They learn how to shape and to pattern their voice, and to utter words fashioned of well-composed sounds, before they risk exposing openly and in public any barbarous wavering in their speech. It displeases you to live by the common rule, and the orderly plan to which all men uniquely accede is not pleasing to you. You want to compose lines and to pattern poems, blunderer, before you have learned what a poem's pattern is.

None may safely engage in the rites of Mars if he lacks hands which are apt for fierce fighting; do you think that the holy rites of Minerva, Phoebus, and the nine sacred sisters deserve any less reverence from you? Whoever divulged the mysteries of Ceres atoned for that crime with nothing less than his life. You do not merely divulge, you corrupt the mysteries of Phoebus; with what penalty, then can you expiate this violation?

More's shamelessness in condemning his own faults in others

And then, by all that is holy, O most fastidious of poets, you have dared to carp at a certain Andreas who touched on the feast days in metrical verse, yet refused to be bound by strict meter. Yet in fact you and he share the same fault, except that he is aware of his and you are not of yours. O the brazenness of it! Do you hurl reproaches at the failings of your fellow only to have them come back to fall on your own head?

Tunstall, Pace, Linacre, Erasmus

You would not have committed such odious crimes against taste if you had committed them first to your friends for their scrutiny. You had Tunstall and Pace; you had Linacre, and Erasmus, who takes special care of his moron; the first three are the three brightest

Trina Caledoniae tres illi sydera gentis,
Quartus Rhenani lumen, honosque soli,
Culti omnes doctique viri, quorumque decebat
Ad trutinam versus te reuocare tuos.
Nanque, nec altiloquum puduit quandoque Maronem
Iudicium Vari consuluisse sui,
Nasonique tuo recitasti saepe Properti,
Quos tibi dictarat Cynthia versiculos. [C_4v]
Quinetiam et tabulas pictorum gloria Apelles
Saepe reformauit iudicium ad populi.
Atque adeo, si parua licet componere magnis,
Olim etiam si quid nostra Thalia queat,
Haec vulgi non ante errare per ora sueuit
Quam sit amicorum subdita iudiciis.
Est mihi Budaeus, quo non praestantior alter,
Lingua Latina tibi, seu mage Graeca placet.
Est et Franciscus, per quem suprema senatus
Curia Parrhisii, tollit ad astra caput.
Illorum ad speculum sese componere nostra
Assolet, et vultus fingere musa suos,
Musa prius Veneti per amoenas gurgitis vndas
Auspice Mopsopios Lascare docta sales.
At vero tibi sunt vni tua pulchra, placentque
Plus, scio, quam possint illa placere bonis.
Sic proprios foetus plus simia, plus et asellus,
Vtraque deformis bestia, amare solent, [D_1]
Caetera quam soleant, quae sunt animantia passim,
Siue ea terra ferat, siue ea pontus alat.
Adde quod et proprios nonnunquam simia foetus,
Immodico amplexu dum fouet, ipsa necat.
Iusserat emoriens flammis Maro carmina dedi,
Horrida queis Martis arma, virumque canit.
Nempe verebatur doctus, sapiensque poeta,
Ne foret excultum non satis illud opus.
Id tamen et vixit semper, viuetque poema,
Donec erunt supero lunaque, solque polo.
Viuis et inuulgas morientia carmina, quaeque
Nec legit haec aetas, nec leget adueniens.

---

370 *Sidenote:* Budaeus

372 *Sidenote:* Franciscus Deloinus

377 *Sidenote:* Ianus Lascaris

stars of the Caledonian nation, the fourth one, the pride and the glory of the lands by the Rhine. All are men of culture and learning; on the scales of their judgment you should have weighed your own verses. Vergil for all his majestic eloquence was not ashamed sometimes to ask the judgment of his friend Varus. Propertius, you often recited to your friend Ovid the verses which Cynthia stirred you to write. Why, even Apelles, the glory of painters, often reordered his canvas in accordance with popular judgment; and futher—if I am allowed to match small things with great—my own Thalia's attainments in years gone by were not wont to circulate publicly before they had been submitted to the judgment of my friends. I have both Budé, than whom nobody is more competent whether in the Latin tongue or in the Greek, and I have François Deloynes, through whom the supreme assembly of the Parisian parliament uplifts its majesty to the stars. Our muse is accustomed to preen and compose her own features before these two, as if in a looking glass, she who was earlier schooled in the good taste of Attica by the beautiful waters of Venice's gulf under the auspices of Janus Lascaris.

Budé

François Deloynes

Janus Lascaris

But of course your own verses seem lovely and pleasing to you—not to anyone else; I am sure good men must find them less so. Apes and asses behave the same way; ill-shaped brutes that they are, they love their offspring more than all other beasts love theirs, whether land-born or sea-bred; consider besides that in some cases apes even kill their own offspring by cuddling them with immoderate zeal. Vergil asked on his deathbed that those verses be burned in which that poet sang of Mars' terrible "Arms and the man"; a wise, learned poet, he feared that his work still lacked polish. Nonetheless, his poem did live, and will live forever, as long as the moon and the sun will remain in the heavens above. You, who are alive, publish poems on *their* deathbed, which neither this age nor the next either reads or will read.

At puto formidas, coepto ne forte labore
Praeuortat numeris mors inopina tuis,
Contingatque illis, Veneri quod contigit olim,
Quae fuerat Coae coepta labore manus,
Aut (quod credo magis) ne post tua funera, vates
Carmina forte aliquis vendicet ista sibi: [D_1v]
Quam foret, o, Mωrus, si quis succedere Mωro
Vellet, et ingenii semina habere tui.
Si numeros sibi diuiderent tua pignora nati,
Non etiam nummos, te moriente, tuos,
Illis vel laqueo mors acceleranda, vel esset
Emendicatis vita trahenda cibis.
Ni forte allapsus caelo Pisistratus, audax
Maeonii assertor carminis, adueniat,
Atque tuos versus, delusus imagine, Homeri
Esse ratus, precio vendicet ille dato.
Si nondum audisti, Vidae Leo Tuscula summus
Proxima Romanis rura habitanda dedit,
Hic vbi Phoebeius diuina poemata vates
Cantat, et illustrat carmine Maeonio.
Cantanti reliquae inspirant Helicona sorores,
Dictat perpetuos Calliopea modos.
Concedit tripodas Phoebus, laurosque virentes,
Concedit sacre plectra canora lyrae. [D_2]
A dextra circumsiliunt, leuaque Napeae,
Nymphaeque, et Dryades, et Venus, et Charites,
Faunique, Satyrique, et capripedes Syluani,
Cumque his pastorum Pan deus, et nemorum,
Qui simul ad cytharae numeros, vocemque canentis,
Euanteis renouant laeta per arua choros.
Ipsa etiam ad cantus agitari arbusta putares,
Ventilat arboreas tam leuis aura comas.
Valle sub vmbrosa tenui cum murmure labens,
Irriguae excurrit riuus amoenus aquae.
Cantantem excipiunt, admiranturque poetam,
Vndique vicinis concita turba locis.

---

396 *Sidenote:* Venerem quam Apelles imperfectam reliquit post eum nemo repertus fuit qui iisdem limam emptis absolueret

410 *Sidenote:* Hieronymus Vida, Cremonensis vates

414 *Sidenote:* Luxuries poetica per digressionem facta

But perhaps you fear your sudden death will catch up with your verses when they are still only begun and that they will share the fate of the Venus begun long ago by the hand of Apelles, or (what I think more likely) that after your funeral some other poet will lay claim to your poems as his own. Oh, how moronic that poet would be if he wanted to be More's successor and heir to the seeds of your talent! If your children divided your verse, not your purse, as their legacy once you had died, they must needs either hasten their deaths with a rope or else drag out their lives with begged nourishment. Their sole hope would be this—that Peisistratus, bold champion of the Maeonian's verse, would happen in out of the blue and, misled by their look, take your verses to be Homer's, and buy them.

No one was found who, on the same terms, could put the finishing touches on the Venus which Apelles left behind him

Have you heard about this, More? Pope Leo gave Vida a farm to reside on near Rome, where this Phoebean bard tunes his heavenly lays with the brilliance of Maeonian verse. As he sings, all the rest of the Muses breathe Helicon on him; Calliope dictates his free-flowing lines. Phoebus gives him his tripods, green laurels, and the sonorous plectra of his sacred lyre. To his right and his left trip the nymphs of the dell, spring, and grove, Venus, the Graces, fauns, satyrs, and goat-foot Sylvani, and with them Lord Pan, god of shepherds and groves; in time with the strains of the lyre and the voice of the singer, they take up again and again Bacchic dances in the flourishing pastures. You would think that even the groves sway to his strains, such a gentle breeze stirs in the treetops. Through the shadowy vale, slipping by with a delicate murmur, a blithe freshet flows. All are rapt by the song of the poet and marvel

Hieronimo Vida, a poet from Cremona

A poetic flourish inserted by way of digression

Pone latet Momus, qui quod mordere canentem
Non valeat, labrum mordet vtrumque sibi.
Taliter in syluis quondam Rhodopeius Orpheus
Ad doctae cecinit fila canora lyrae.
Debueras pridem tua Mωre poemata, Summi
Pontificis doctis exhibuisse oculis. [D_2v]
Nam simul istius sensisset vocis honorem,
Audissetque oris classica tanta tui,
Scilicet exploso Vida Leo maximus, vni
Tuscula sanxisset rura habitanda tibi.
Hoc quoque nunc faceres, nisi quod praestantia, visque
Ipsa tui ingenii, non tibi nota satis,
More frementis equi, qui si cognoscere posset,
Vis sibi quanta insit corporis, atque pedis,
Sessore excusso indomitus, ferretur aperto
Aequore, et assereret libera terga sibi.
Magnus Alexander fuso, victoque Dareo,
Scriniolum arcanas repperit inter opes
Auratum, et multis radians hinc inde smaragdis,
Asseruans succos Regis odoriferos,
Atque aliis alios vsus monstrantibus, et quod
Non nisi victorem tale deceret opus,
Vnus Alexander, tua sit custodia (dixit)
Scriniolum, et libros seruet Homere tuos. [D_3]
At si te Magni genuissent secla, fuisset
Persica vel viuo capsa habitanda tibi.
Causidicos olim Galli docuere Britannos,
Hoc tribuunt illis scripta Latina decus.
At vero, tibi iam tritum si forte licebit
Ire iter, et coeptam continuare viam,
Nec linguam impediat tibi cura domestica vtramque,
At peragat cursus, illa vel illa suos,
Debebunt Graii, Latii, Gallique, Britannique
Eloquium Mωre vni tibi, et ingenium,
Quique bonas artes vlla nondum arte retectas
Edoceas populos quatuor, vnus eris.
Vnus eris, per quem Demosthenis, ac Ciceronis
Facundo incipient Rhetores ore loqui.

---

430 *Sidenote:* Momus

436 *Sidenote:* Ironia

460 *Sidenote:* Ironia aperta

before him; the crowd there assembled spreads out on all sides. Momus lurks in the background; unable to snap at the singer, he gnaws at his own lips. Even thus, in the greenwood, Rhodopean Orpheus once sang to the sonorous strains of his learned lyre. Long since, More, you should have presented *your* poems to the Pope's learned eyes; for as soon as he noted the dignity of that voice, and heard the grand trumpeting ring of your speech, doubtless Leo the Supreme Pontiff would have thrown Vida out and have offered his Tusculan retreat up for your sole possession. You would do this even now, if the preeminence and power of your talent were not insufficiently known to you, in the style of a high-mettled steed, who, if he could but learn how much power inhabits his hooves and his body, would cast off his rider, fly forth unsubdued over open terrain, and lay unchallenged claim to a burdenless back.

Momus

Irony

Alexander the Great, after Darius' disastrous defeat, found a casket of gold, all resplendent with emeralds and charged with the king's odorous gums, in the midst of his best-guarded treasures. As various persons proposed various uses and said that a trophy like this suited only the victor, Alexander himself said, "Let this casket be your safekeeping and care for your books, Homer." If you had been born in the age of that prince, then you would have had to spend your days living inside that Persian bookchest.

In times past, Frenchmen instructed British lawyers. Latin books credit them with this distinction. But if you may proceed along that beaten path, and continue the journey in progress, and if your domestic concerns do not keep you from pursuing your studies in both classical tongues until they run their course, then Greeks, Latins, French, and British alike will owe you—you alone—all their eloquence and talent; you alone will instruct four peoples in liberal arts which no art hitherto could disclose to them. You alone will teach orators to speak with the eloquent voice of a Cicero or a Demosthenes; you alone will teach poets' hearts, filled with poetic

Patent irony

Vnus eris, per quem vatum praecordia, facta
  Enthea, spirabunt numen Apollineum.
Felices nimium, quibus hunc aduexerit olim
  Splendidus aurato Phoebus ab axe diem. [D_3v]
Iam video, admonitus, quotquot potes, vndique mira
  Per te dispersos colligis arte libros,
Hosque repurgatis curas excudere mendis,
  Chalcographo impingens crimina, quae tua sunt.
Si potes imponas aliis, imponere doctis
  Non potes, has maculas non nisi scriptor agit.
Me penes atque alios prima exemplaria semper
  Extabunt lapsus exhibitura tuos.
Fac mone quod potes, haud poteris te abstergere, non si
  Tota eat in sordes unda Britanna tuas.
At tibi ne graue sit cunctos percurrere naeuos,
  Diluat errores vna litura tuos.
Consilium, hoc melius nullus praescribere possit,
  Qui tibi non ficto pectore amicus erit.
Dixisset tua si legisset scripta Catullus,
  Nulla in tam magno corpore mica salis.
Ac spes nulla quidem est olim fore, vt Aone aperto
  Per iuga Pegaseo sacra veharis equo. [D_4]
Cui semel Aoniae clauserunt templa sorores,
  Huic non vllo vnquam tempore aperta patent.
Si nescis, faciunt geniusque, et musa poetam,
  Mula tua ingenium, non tibi musa dedit.
Ante et Arabs Thamesim bibet, ante Britannia Nilum,
  Iusta sacri accrescat quam tibi forma pedis.
Quod si alia in vulgus meliore poemata lima
  Forte olim emittas nomine Mωre tuo,
Maiorem excutiet risum cornicula, quae se
  Emendicato picta colore tegat.
Haud tamen inficier genus esse epigrammatis, in quo,
  Si quisquam vatum de grege, Mωre vales,
Id vero sit quale genus, qui scire laborat,
  Quaerat ab Henrici carmine Abingdonii.
Regius hic cantor, per te suauissime vates,
  Rege tuo maius nomen habere potest.
Hic iacet Henricus. Veneres in carmine si quis
  Vult legere vno omnes, totum epigramma legat. [D_4v]

---

506 *Sidenote:* Hemistichion Moriani carminis

elation, to breathe forth the grace of Apollo. What a blessing for all to whom glorious Phoebus will one day convey this new dawn from the heavens' golden axletree!

Now I see; I am told that with marvelous skill you are gathering together as many as you can of the volumes which you have disseminated; you are planning to print them in corrected form, thus blaming your sins on your printer. Fool the rest if you can; you cannot fool the learned; blots like these must derive from the writer. Copies of your first edition remain in my hands, and in others'; they will always be there to exhibit your lapses. Say and do what you can, you can never be cleansed, no, not even if all Britain's waters converged on your foulness. But lest you find it burdensome to make your way through all your blemishes, let an unbroken sweep of the sponge wash your blunders away. No one who is your heartfelt friend can give you any better advice than this. If Catullus had read through your writings, he would say that there is not one speck of wit in that oversized body. There is no hope that you will ever open up the Aonian domain and traverse its sacred heights riding your Pegasus; once the Aonian maidens have closed off their temples to anyone, he will never again find them open. In case you do not know, a man's muse and his genius are what make a poet; your mule, not your muse, lent you your talent. Arabia will drink up the Thames, or else Britain the Nile, before the right shape for a poetic foot will occur to you. If at some point you publish some other less ragged verse in your name, More, the crow will be mocked all the louder for tricking himself out in borrowed plumage.

I will not deny, though, that there is one type of epigram in which you excel, More, if anyone does among the whole flock of poets. If anyone is eager to know what type that is, let him find it out by looking at your poem on Henry Abyngdon. This singer of your king may win more renown than your king does through you, O most delicate of poets. "Here lies Henry" [no. 160/1]—if anyone wishes to con every charm in one poem, let him read the whole epigram. Blessed poet, if only Apollo would dictate a

A half-line from a More poem

O te felicem, si vel modo carmina centum
Hoc genere, hoc numero, dictet Apollo tibi.
Id si vel genius dederit, vel cura pararit,
Mωre eterna tuum fama loquetur opus,
Ac minus Aeneis, longe et minus Ilias, illa
Vergilio, haec peperit laudis Homere tibi,
Quam Mωro paritura olim sint carmina centum,
Quae tamen aut risus, aut iocus excutiet.
Illa etenim, scio, te ridente excussa fuisse
Carmina, queis canitur cantor Abingdonius.
At tu ne ignores quae sit tua gratia, vates
Ridiculus bonus es, serius at malus es.
Haec mihi dictanti adstabant dirae auribus omnes,
Et furiae infernis concita turba vadis,
Alecto, et sacris caput irretita colubris
Tisiphone, et terrens ore Megaera truci.
Quas nisi frenassem, ad te omnes vno agmine adibant
Laturae Stygii dira flagella lacus, [E_1]
Mulsuraeque tuas non his concentibus aures,
In rabiem Archilocus, sed quibus actus erat.
Ac nisi Franciscus, cui paret Francia Regi,
Henricusque Angli Rex animosus agri,
Ambo pares aetate, pares virtutibus ambo,
Antiquae extinctis ignibus inuidiae,
(Spirabant patrium quanquam illis pectora Martem,
Pectora Cecropiae numine plena deae)
Sanctam iurassent ventura in secula pacem,
Iungere quae populos debet amore pari,
Pax mihi non tecum, nisi cum balantibus agnis
(Dum premit arcta fames) quae solet esse lupis.
Quin hic sensisses (sensus tibi si tamen insit)
Quale meo offensi fulmen ab ore cadat.
I modo, et antiquos dic me expilasse poetas,
Vt responderem morsibus ipse tuis. [E_1v]
Euoluas veterum, quaecunque volumina vatum,
His etiam authores, si vacat, adde nouos,
Deque illis carmen si me prompsisse, vel vnum
Arguis, hoc oculos erue Mωre mihi.
Non tamen inficior veterum me carmina vatum
Versare assidua nocte, dieque manu.

---

518 *Sidenote:* Nota scomma

hundred poems to you in this genre, in this meter! Whether your genius vouchsafed you this poem, or your own study wrought it, eternal renown, More, will celebrate your achievement. His *Aeneid* won far less praise for Vergil, or your *Iliad,* Homer, for you, than a hundred of More's poems may one day win for him, though he may strike them off in a moment of laughter or mirth. I know, More, that the verses wherein you sing the singer Abyngdon were struck off as a jest. But, lest you fail to note your appeal, you are fine as a laughable bard; as a serious one, you are a failure.

Notice the taunt

While I have been saying this, all the spirits of revenge and the Furies flocked around my ears, a band brought from the infernal shoals. Alecto was there, and Tisiphone, her head wreathed with dire snakes, and Megaera, who terrifies men with her hideous features. Unless I had restrained them, they all would have sped to attack you, en masse, bringing with them the cruel lashes of the Stygian lake, and soothing your ears, not with these, but with those songs which once drove Archilochus mad. If Francis, the king to whom France pays allegiance, and Henry, the stouthearted king of the English domain, alike in their years, and alike in their virtue, had not quenched the embers of long-standing grudges—though their bosoms, infused with the might of Minerva, breathed out the same martial resolve as their forebears—if they had not pledged sacred peace for the centuries to come which should join the two races they rule with like amity—there would be no more peace between us two than that which is wont to ally bleating lambs with wolves hard pressed by hunger. Then, indeed, you would have sensed—if you are not altogether insensate—what a thunderbolt falls from my lips when I am offended.

Go on and accuse me of pilfering from ancient poets so that I can personally rebut your aspersions. Leaf through all the tomes of the ancients; add the moderns, too, if you have leisure; and if you find that I have put forth even one line of theirs as my own, More, use it to pluck out my eyes. But I will not deny that I study the poems of the old poets

Me iuuat illorum studio impallescere, sed dum
  Voluo mihi veteres, tu tibi volue nouos.
Proin, si cura tui, aut patrii tibi nominis vlla est,
  Mωre tace, aut Latio discito more loqui,
Sicque tuos inter morari desine Mωre,
  Versusque, et mores indue Mωre nouos,
Nec tibi tam leue sit nugas effundere, quarum
  Authorem pudeat, poeniteatque suum.
His ego carminibus, volui proludere tecum,
  Dum cytharae tracto plectra remissa meae. [E_2]
Quod me si cupis hos lusus iterare, placetque
  Saepe tibi his similes excipere aure sonos,
Haecque eadem exoptas, per carmina nostra vagari
  De te, de ingenii delitiisque tui,
Fac modo saepe istis radens latratibus aurem hanc,
  Fila meae intendas desidiosa lyrae.

Finis [E_2v]

Ad lectorem

Ne lector tibi (quaeso) sit molestum
Legisse hos numeros, licet molesto, et
Auerso genio datos. Coegit
Mωri insania sponte prouocantis,
Nostram de pharetra insolente musam
Telum promere, seque dum tuetur,
Et dum cuspide cuspidem retundit,
Hostili oblinere cruore molles,
Imbellesque elegos, sibi perennem
Pacem, non etiam arma praeparantes.
Atque hoc nomine sperat impetrare
Sese abs te veniamque, gratiamque.
Nam quanquam sibi sciret haud decorum
Mωri versiculis inepti ineptis
Respondere, tamen silere visum est
Longe turpius, et mage indecorum.

Finis [E_3]

---

562 *Sidenote:* Allusit aduersus Mori artificium, qui iam olim inter rabulas primas obtinuit

assiduously, both night and day. I am glad to grow pale studying them; but while I mull over the old poets, you should mull over the new ones. Then, if you have any regard for your own name or that of your fatherland, keep quiet or learn to speak Latin. Stop fooling around, More, among your own ilk; adopt new morals, More, and a new sort of verses. Do not think it so light an offense to pour out shabby trifles which bring shame and remorse to their author.

These verses of mine were intended as merely a practice session with you, dashed off as I heedlessly strum on my lyre. But if you crave a rematch and want to hear more of the same, if you long to have these same assessments of you and your delightful talent borne still further abroad in my verses, go ahead, grate on my ears with some more of your barking; tighten the indolent strings of my lyre.

He is taking a swipe at More's trade, More having long since achieved the first place among litigious wranglers

The End

To the Reader

Reader, please do not be vexed to have read through these lines, although they were composed when my genius was vexed and averse. The sheer madness of More in provoking me without motive left my muse little choice but to draw forth her dart from her quiver, and, as she defends herself and returns blow for blow, to stain with the blood of her enemy her unwarlike and soft elegiacs, intending an unbroken peace, not more war. On this basis she hopes to secure your indulgence and favor; while she knew it to be hardly decorous for her to answer unseemly More's unseemly lines, she considered it far more indecorous and shameful to maintain her silence.

The End

THOMAE MωRI LAPSVS INEXCVSABILES IN SYLLABARVM QVANTITATE

In elegia ad Henricum Octauum Anglorum Regem pagina 186 in iis codicibus quos impressit Frobenius Basileae extant hi Mori versus:

Castalio quem fonte nouem lauere sorores,
Imbuit et monitis philosophia suis.

Dii boni quale monstrum hoc? inclusisse nomen id philosophia in carmen elegiacum? Enimuero quo authore id fecerit Mωrus non video, nisi forte vel Sidonio, vel si quis Sidonio deterior est.

In eadem elegia pagina 188:

Illa est quae Priscas vincat pietate Sabinas,
Maiestate sacras vicerit Heroidas.

Age o bone Mωre, qui tueri hic te poteris? correpta abs te secunda syllaba huius nominis Herois? Graecis satis constat productam esse, est enim ω si nescis. Ac sane mirum est te, qui totus es in traducendis epigrammatis Graecis (id quod quam egregie, ac potius quam inepte praestes, nemini docto non palam est) non animaduertisse carmen illud vulgatissimum inter Graecanica epi[E$_3$v]grammata Καλλιόπη σοφίην ἡρωΐδος εὗρεν ἀοιδῆς, qua in re si et Latini poetae testimonium requiris, en tibi Propertius lib. II:

Et tibi Maeonidas, interque Heroidas omnis
Primus erit nulla non tribuente locus.

Verum iam habeo quid tibi imposuerit, eo sane nomine, quod vocalis sit ante vocalem, correptam credidisti. Ea est inueterata versificatorum haeresis, abs qua longe difficilius fuerit illos reuocare, quam Aethiopem, vt dicitur, dealbare.

In eadem pagina:

Illa tibi felix populos, hinc et inde potentes.

Palam est carmen hoc claudicare, atque in eo syllabam vnam abundare, quae exempta, ne omnino pereat, reponenda erit in carmen illud

MORE'S INEXCUSABLE MISTAKES IN THE QUANTITY OF SYLLABLES

In more's elegy to King Henry VIII of England, page 186 in the edition printed by Froben at Basel [No. 19/118–19], these verses by More may be found:

Castalio quem fonte nouem lauere sorores
  Imbuit et monitis philosophia suis.

Good lord, what an outrage is this—to include the noun *philosophia* in an elegiac verse? For I do not see whose precedent More is following here, unless perhaps it is Sidonius or even some worse author.

In the same elegy, page 188 [no. 19/166–67]:

Illa est quae priscas vincat pietate Sabinas,
  Maiestate sacras vicerit Heroidas.

Well, More, how can you defend yourself here, where you have shortened the second syllable of the noun *Herois?* It is clear that the Greeks always lengthened it; in case you do not know, it is spelled with an omega. Indeed, it is amazing that you, while you are wholly absorbed in translating Greek epigrams (though it is obvious to everyone with any learning how egregiously or rather worse than ineptly you do it), should never have noticed that well-known Greek epigram, Καλλιόπη σοφίην ἡρωΐδος εὗρεν ἀοιδῆς [*AP* 9.504.1]. But if you need the example of a Latin poet as well here, consider this couplet from the second book of Propertius [28.29–30]:

Et tibi Maeonidas interque Heroidas omnes
  Primus erit nulla non tribuente locus.

But now I know what has misled you: you thought that it ought to be short on the ground that a vowel is preceding a vowel here. That is the inveterate heresy of certain versifiers, which it is much harder to make them renounce than to "whiten an Ethiop," as the saying goes.

On the same page [no. 19/180]:

Illa tibi felix populos hinc et inde potentes.

It is clear that this verse scans unevenly, and that it comprises one syllable too many; lest that syllable go altogether to waste, once it has been removed from this line it ought to be used to fill out another verse by the

eiusdem authoris, pagina 220, quod quidem Frobenii codices sic excusum habent:

> Quotquot viuimus hic sumus omnes Organa, quae
> Viuificis animat flatibus aura leuis.

Quo loco liquet deesse postremam heroici versus syllabam. Atqui erratum hoc vtrumque in typographum reiicerem, nisi quod non invenio in Graeco epigrammate (quod hic Latine reddit Mωrus) quicquam, quo carminis hiatum hunc complere possim. Sic enim habent versus Graeci:

> πάντες ὅσοι ζῶμεν κατὰ τὸν βίον ὄργανα δ' ἐσμὲν,
> αὔραις ζωογόνοις πνεύματα δεχύμενοι. [E_4]

Pagina 191:

> Sic et Philolaum, quondam occidere Cretenses.

Placuit hic Mωro syllabam corripere, quam et Graeci, et Latini omnes producunt. Ita enim Vergilius:

> Creta Iouis magni medio iacet insula ponto:

et Homerus Iliados, β;

> ἄλλοι θ' οἳ Κρήτην ἑκατόμπολιν ἀμφενέμοντο;

et alibi. Praeterea mille in locis. Magna est vero Mωri lepiditas, qui dum Graeca ad nos transfert, in Graecarum vocum quantitate identidem foedissime labatur, vt hic interim omittam duplicem lapsum commissum in dictione Philolaum, in qua dictione i produxit, a corripuit, a Graeco interim authore, quem traducendum suscipit, deficiens, cuius versus est eiusmodi:

> οὕτω καὶ Φιλόλαον ἀνεῖλε Κρότων ποτὲ πάτρη.

Quo ex carmine liquet, vt hoc etiam attingamus, Mωrum Cretensibus falso tribuere, quod Graecus poeta Crotoniatis tribuit, quum tamen hi in continenti, illi in medio mari iaceant. Poterat autem versus Graecus verti in haec verba:

> Sic Philolae Croto te patria sustulit olim.

In eadem pagina:

> Sudat in alueolo, mel alii comedunt. [E_4v]

Mel produxit Mωrus, cum tamen vna cum fel et similibus natura corripiatur.

Pagina 208:

> Abluat vt vino mucronem aeger obsecrat, absit.

same author, on page 220 [no. 130/4–5], which the Froben edition prints thus:

> Quotquot viuimus hic sumus omnes organa, quae
> Viuificis animat flatibus aura leuis.

It is obvious that the hexameter lacks its last syllable. I would blame each of these errors on the printer except that I find nothing in the Greek epigram which More translates here that I can use to fill this lacuna. The Greek verses read thus:

> πάντες ὅσοι ζῶμεν κατὰ τὸν βίον ὄργανα δ' ἐσμὲν,
> αὔραις ζωογόνοις πνεύματα δεχύμενοι.

Page 191 [no. 25/5]:

> Sic et Philolaum quondam occidere Cretenses.

More chooses to shorten a syllable which all Greeks and all Latins alike scan as long, as in Vergil's [*Aen.* 3.104],

> Creta Iouis magni medio iacet insula ponto

and Homer's [*Il.* 2.649],

> ἄλλοι θ' οἳ Κρήτην ἑκατόμπολιν ἀμφενέμοντο

from the *Iliad,* Book II, and a thousand other passages besides. More's elegance is immense: as he translates Greek poems, he trips up in Greek scansion disgracefully, to say nothing of his double mistake in the word *Philolaus,* where he both lengthens the *i* and shortens the *a,* diverging from the author he sets out to translate, whose words are as follows:

> οὕτω καὶ Φιλόλαον ἀνεῖλε Κρότων ποτὲ πάτρη.

It is clear from this line (to mention still another point) that More falsely asserts of the Cretans what the Greek poet asserts of the Crotoniates, although the latter dwell on the mainland while the former dwell out in the middle of the sea. The Greek verse could have been rendered thus:

> Sic, Philolae, Croto te patria sustulit olim.

On the same page [no. 76/10]:

> Sudat in alueolo; mel alii comedunt.

More lengthened *mel,* though this word (like *fel* and the like) is naturally short.

Page 208 [no. 90/14]:

> Abluat vt vino mucronem aeger obsecrat, absit

Mωro tam placeat breuitas, non tantum syllabas natura, sed et diphthongo quoque longas corripienti, veluti in hac dictione aeger, cuius primam syllabam, qui animo, ac sensu aegri non sunt, longam vbique apud poetas esse facile deprehendere possunt.

Pagina 211:

> Nicolaus nomen medici est. Qui conuenit? inquis;

ac paulo post:

> Huic medico vero est nomine Nicolaus.

Qui Graece sciunt poetae Nicoleos scribunt Attice.

Pagina sequenti:

> Audit vt in populo hoc vates iam serio verum est.

Vltimam in hoc aduerbio serio corripit Mωrus, quum doctis, ac seriis poetis longa sit. Hoc ipsum fecit in hoc quoque aduerbio denuo, cuius vltimam passim corripit. At quo authore recaepto id faciat non video, qui si quem forte habet, proferat, vt hoc ipsum eo docente discamus, neque [F_1] enim pigebit discere, quod plane ignoramus.

Pagina 192:

> Sors illos copulat similis, claudum vehit alter.

Debebo tibi Mωre authorem recaeptum adferenti, cui correpta sit prima syllaba verbi huius copulo. Nasoni sane longa est:

> Copula detrahitur canibus . . .

Pagina 204:

> Vt lampas oleo deficiente perit.

Mωro vltima huius dictionis lampas longa est, quae tamen et Graecis (est enim mera vox Graeca) et Latinis quoque nusquam non breuis est, neque vero hic caesura excusare eum debet.

Pagina 213:

> Quem mordent pulices, extinguit Mωrio lychnon.
>   Non me inquit cernent amplius hic pulices.

It is amazing how More likes brevity: he shortens not only those syllables which are naturally long, but also the ones which are long on account of a diphthong—this word *aeger* ("sick"), for instance, the first syllable of which all not sick in the head can easily perceive to be long everywhere it appears in the poets.

Page 211 [no. 96/4, 9]:

> Nicolaus nomen medici est; qui conuenit? inquis;

And a little after that,

> Huic medico vero est nomine Nicolaus.

Every poet who knows Greek writes *Nicoleos* like the Athenians.

On the following page [no. 101/10]:

> Audit vt in populo hoc vates iam serio verum est.

More shortens the last syllable in this adverb, *serio,* though all learned and serious poets scan it as long. He does the same with another adverb, *denuo,* the last syllable of which he repeatedly shortens [nos. 5/13, 17/9]. I don't know what accepted author he is following; if he has one, then let him bring him forward, so that we may learn this very thing from him, for there will be no shame in learning what we clearly do not know.

Page 192 [no. 31/4]:

> Sors illos copulat similis; claudum vehit alter.

I will be in your debt, More, if you cite me any accepted author who shortens the first syllable of this verb, *copulo.* Ovid certainly scans it as long [*Met.* 7.769]:

> Copula detrahitur canibus . . .

Page 204 [no. 75/9]:

> Vt lampas oleo deficiente perit.

More scans the last syllable of *lampas* as long, though both Greeks—for the word is pure Greek—and Latins consistently scan it as short; nor should the caesura excuse him here.

Page 213 [no. 106/3–4]:

> Quem mordent pulices extinguit Morio lychnon;
> Non me (inquit) cernent amplius hic pulices.

Grauibus, ac recaeptis authoribus, prima syllaba huius dictionis pulex longa est. Columella,

Paruulus aut pulex irrumpens dente lacessit,

et Martialis,

. . . vel si quid pulice sordidius.

Neque enim carmen illud triuiale, parue pulex, et amara lues, Oui[F_1v]dianum est, sed spurium, cuiusmodi sunt plurima.

Pagina 215:

Tunc ignaue iaces trunco non impar inani.

Item pagina 244:

Sic elephas illi dentibus impar erat.

Et hic quoque more suo Mωrus longam corripuit. Impar enim nullo pacto habere potest vltimam breuem, nisi omnino antiquorum poetarum regulas antiquare velimus. Horatius:

Ludere par, impar, equitare in arundine longa;

alibi in Epistolis:

Scribere te nobis, tibi nos, ac credere par est.

quod si Horatius tibi non satisfacit, Mωre, audi Lucretium li. II:

Hoc etiam mage ad haec animum te aduertere par est.

Ibidem:

Cum facere instituas cum primis quaerere par est.

Ouidius, li. XIII Meta.:

Sunt quoque par etas aliis in ouilibus agni;

et lib. XIIII:

Par animi formae, nec adhuc spectasse tot annos.

Pagina 221:

Nec sinit vt foenum, qui cupit edat equus.

Serious, accepted authors lengthen the first syllable of this word *pulex;* Columella, for instance [10.321],

> Paruulus aut pulex irrumpens dente lacessit,

and Martial [14.83],

> . . . vel si quid pulice sordidius.

That trivial verse, "parua pulex et amara lues" ["De Pulice" 1, in *Poetae Latini Minores,* ed. N. E. Lemaire, 7 vols. (Paris, 1826), 7, 275], is not Ovidian but spurious, as are many of this sort.

Page 125 [no. 114/9]:

> Tunc ignaue iaces trunco non impar inani.

Likewise page 244 [no. 191/11]:

> Sic elephas illi dentibus impar erat.

Here, too, as is his custom, More has made a long syllable short. There is no way to take the last syllable of *impar* as short unless we resolve to supersede all the prosodic rules of the ancients. Horace gives us the following [*Sat.* 2.3.248]:

> Ludere par, impar, equitare in arundine longa;

and elsewhere, in his *Epistles* [1.15.25]:

> Scribere te nobis, tibi nos, ac credere par est.

But if Horace does not satisfy you, More, hear Lucretius, Book II [line 125]:

> Hoc etiam mage ad haec animum te aduertere par est,

and then, in the same book [line 849]:

> Cum facere instituas cum primis quaerere par est,

or else Ovid, in the thirteenth book of the *Metamorphoses* [line 827]:

> Sunt quoque par etas aliis in ouilibus agni,

or in the fourteenth [line 324]:

> Par animi formae, nec adhuc spectasse tot annos.

Page 221 [no. 135/4]:

> Nec sinit vt foenum, qui cupit, edat equus.

Hic vero quae passim tam Graecis, quam Latinis poetis breuis est producit Mωrus sua vnius authoritate fretus. Edo enim pro comedo, quae Graeca omnino vox est, primam corripit, vt apud Ho[F_2]merum, 'Οδυσσ. ε,

ἔσθειν καὶ πίνειν οἷα βροτοὶ ἄνδρες ἔδουσι,

et 'Οδ. ϑ,

ὅσσοι νῦν βροτοί εἰσιν ἐπὶ χθονὶ σῖτον ἔδοντες,

et alibi centies apud eundem authorem. Vbicunque enim sese Homerus ad conuiuia conuertit, in quibus frequentissimus est, nunquam non eo vtitur verbo. Atqui facile hinc coniicere est Mωrum nunquam versatum in Homerica lectione, cum tamen alioqui Graecanicam eruditionem traducto, ac potius tradito vno, et altero epigrammate Graeco sibi vendicet, atque adeo, si diis placet, hac vna in re maximopere vni sibi arrideat.

Pagina 222:

Et sibi opportunum crederet esse locum.

Quae longa est, vel positione corripuit Mωrus. Opportunum autem habere primam longam satis constat vel ex hoc Lucretii carmine li. III:

Vtilis inuenietur, et opportuna cluebit.

Quod si tu, o Mωre, recentioribus magis applaudis, vt omnino applaudis, en tibi Politianus in Rustico:

. . . non opportunus iniqui
Iudicio vulgi . . .

Nec vnquam aliter docti in carmine vsurparunt.

Pagina 239:

Ipse ait audebo leoninam tangere linguam.

In hac dictione leoninam corripuit o Mωrus, quod longum est, id quod tam vulgatum est, vt exemplo nihil opus sit, neque hic syneraesis Mωrum excusare debet. [F_2v]

Pagina 250:

Squalida lasciuam macerent ieiunia carnem.

With himself as his only authority, More here lengthens a syllable which Greek poets as well as Latins consistently scan as a short. *Edo* in the sense *comedo* ("I eat")—a distinctively Greek turn of phrase—has a short first syllable, as in Homer, Book V of the *Odyssey* [line 197],

> ἔσθειν καὶ πίνειν οἷα βροτοὶ ἄνδρες ἔδουσι,

and Book VIII [line 222],

> ὅσσοι νῦν βροτοί εἰσιν ἐπὶ χθονὶ σῖτον ἔδοντες,

and in a hundred other places in that same author. For whenever Homer turns to a feast—and he very often does—he never fails to use that word. This readily prompts the conjecture that More never spent many hours reading Homer, although otherwise, through his Latin versions, or rather subversions, of this or that Greek epigram, More lays claim to learning in Greek; and indeed, by all that's holy, he even takes his chief pride in this single achievement.

Page 222 [no. 167/3]:

> Et sibi opportunum crederet esse locum.

More shortens even a syllable which is long by position. It is clear enough that *opportunum* has a long first syllable from this line in Lucretius' Book III [line 207]:

> Vtilis inuenietur et opportuna cluebit.

But if you, More, esteem the moderns more highly, as you generally seem to, consider Politian's lines from the *Rusticus* [lines 34–35, *Poeti Umanisti Maggiori,* ed. L. Grilli, Città di Castello (1914), p. 27],

> . . . non opportunus iniqui
> iudicio vulgi;

nor has any learned poet ever made use of this word any otherwise.

Page 239 [no. 181/6]:

> Ipse (ait) audebo leoninam tangere linguam.

More shortens the *o* in the word *leoninam* although it is long; this is so generally known that it needs no example; nor ought synaeresis to excuse More here.

Page 250 [no. 203/8]:

> Squalida lasciuam macerent ieiunia carnem.

Primam huius verbi macerat corripuit Mωrus secutus videlicet leues quosdam, ac recentiores authores. Nam et Ouidius produxit:

> Maceror interdum, quod sim tibi causa doloris,

et Horatius:

> Quam lentis penitus macerer ignibus,

et Lucretius libro III:

> Macerat inuidia ante oculos illum esse potentem,

ibidem:

> Macerat inque metu male habet, curisque fatigat.

More shortens the first syllable of this verb *macerat,* following the example, no doubt, of certain inconsiderable authors of more recent times. Ovid lengthens it [*Her.* 20.125]:

> Maceror interdum quod sim tibi causa doloris,

as does Horace [*Carm.* 1.13.8]:

> Quam lentis penitus macerer ignibus,

and Lucretius, Book III [line 75]:

> Macerat inuidia ante oculos illum esse potentem,

and [3.876]:

> Macerat inque metu male habet curisque fatigat.

MωRI SOLOECISMI AC BARBARISMI ALIQVOT FOEDISSIMI

In elegia ad Henricum Regem, pagina 185:

Ad mercatores aperit mare, si quod ab illis
Durius exactum est ante, remisit onus.

Mare aperire mercatoribus, non ad mercatores vt dicamus Romanae linguae candor admonet. Verum hic vt multis quoque aliis in locis secutus est Mωrus non Romanum, sed vernaculum loquendi tropum. [F3]

Pagina 191:

Vtraque sed florem rosa iam coaleuit in vnum,
Quoque potest vno, lis cadit illa modo.

Coaleuit in praeterito dixit Mωrus pro coaluit. Neque vero hic aliter sese tueri protest, nisi quod ita metri necessitas vrgebat, quemadmodum et alio quodam loco a iuuo formauit praeteritum iuuauit, tametsi Latini grammatici iuuit forment. Verumenimuero quid impedit, quominus Morus, cui omnino constitutum est Latinam linguam (quae illi manca nimis est, ac ieiuna) locupletare, pro arbitratu suo, vt syllabarum legem innouare, ita et verborum formationes inuertere, atque innouare possit? Iuuauit autem pro iuuit bis vsurpauit, pagina 225:

Iam te iuuauerit
Viros relinquere;

et paulo post:

Iam te iuuauerit
Sermone bland[ul]o,
Docto tamen, dies
Noctesque ducere;

Vt nihil hic interim dicam de ea locutione, qua eo loci vsus est Mωrus, dum plectra personat, tametsi a Vergilio dictum sit

. . . cythara crinitus Iopas
· Personat aurata.

Pagina sequenti:

Claudipedem gestat coecis vicinus ocellis;

SOME OF MORE'S UTTERLY DISGRACEFUL SOLECISMS AND BARBARISMS

In the elegy to King Henry, page 185 [no. 19/100–01]:

Ad mercatores aperit mare; si quod ab illis
Durius exactum est ante, remisit onus.

The purity of the Roman language admonishes us to say *mare aperire mercatoribus,* not *ad mercatores.* But here, as in many other passages, More adopts a vernacular turn of phrase, not a Roman one.

Page 191 [no. 23/5–6]:

Vtraque sed florem rosa iam coaleuit in vnum,
Quoque potest vno lis cadit illa modo.

For the preterite More puts "coaleuit" in place of *coaluit;* there is no way for him to defend himself here except on the grounds that the needs of his meter demanded it, as in a certain other passage he forms "iuuauit" as the preterite of *iuuo,* though the Latin grammarians form it as *iuuit.* But what is to deter More—whose basic resolve is to enrich the Latin language, since for him it is too barren and scanty—from overhauling and modernizing the conjugation of verbs the same way that he modernizes the law for the scansion of syllables? He uses "iuuauit" in place of *iuuit* at two different points, on page 225 [no. 143/125–26]:

Iam te iuuauerit
Viros relinquere,

and a little thereafter [no. 143/138–41]:

Iam te iuuauerit
Sermone blandulo,
Docto tamen, dies
Noctesque ducere.

I'll say nothing, meanwhile, of the phrase which More uses at that point where he "personat plectra" ["makes the plectra ring," no. 143/131], although what Vergil said was this [*Aen.* 1.740–41]:

. . . cythara crinitus Iopas
Personat aurata

The following page [no. 27/2]:

Claudipedem gestat coecis vicinus ocellis;

et in epigrammate sequenti: [F3v]

Coecus claudipedem gestat prudenter vtrumque.

Mirum est quomodo hic Mωrus auersatus fuerit vocem hanc loripes, a Latinis omnibus vsurpatam, vt nouam nobis, ac recentem induceret, quum tamen, etiam si loripedem hic dixisset, stare nihilo minus carmen poterat.

Pagina 198:

Congaudete sacrae varios et pascite flores.

Hoc verbum congaudeo alibi etiam Morus vsurpauit pagina 282 [i.e., 182] in elegia ad Henricum Regem,

Congaudent omnes pariter, pariterque rependunt
Omnes venturo damna priora bono,

quum tamen id nec poeticum, nec plane oratorium sit, nisi forte, aut Lyranus poeta, aut Scotus orator sint, vt Mωro fortasse sunt. Latini autem tum oratores, tum poetae, illi gratulor, hi grator et gratulor quoque agnoscunt, non congaudeo.

Pagina 200:

Dum cuncta lustro deprehendi pridie.

Abusus est Mωrus hoc aduerbio pridie secutus infantissimum barbarorum errorem, quid autem [F4] significet pridie, ac quonam pacto ea dictione vtendum sit, qui ex Tulliana lectione nescit, legat Vallam.

Pagina 207:

Tornato bene, Mulciber,
Argento mihi poculum,
Iam nunc effice concauum,
Et quantum potes, imbibum.

Et hic quoque in hac dictione imbibum Mωrus vt alibi pluribus in locis Romanam linguam locupletare voluit. Nempe ante eum vocem hanc nemo ex authoribus quidem recaeptis, ac ne ex explosis quidem, arbitror, vsurpavit. Neque vero video quid Mωrum impulerit, eo loci ea vti dictione noua mehercule, atque insolenti, cum Graeci poetae versus, quos felicissime scilicet nobis Latinitate donauit Mωrus, id verbi non

and in the following epigram [no. 28/2]:

> Coecus claudipedem gestat prudenter vtrumque.

It is amazing how More here avoids the word *loripes,* employed by all speakers of Latin, so that he can foist on us this recent and late-coined alternative, although, had he said *loripedem,* the poem would still have scanned correctly.

Page 198 [no. 57/9]:

> Congaudete sacrae varios et pascite flores.

More employs this verb *congaudeo* elsewhere, as well, in his elegy to King Henry on page 182 [no. 19/34–35]:

> Congaudent omnes pariter, pariterque rependunt
> Omnes venturo damna priora bono,

even though the verb in question is used neither by the poets nor by the orators, unless perchance Nicholas of Lyra is a poet, or Scotus an orator, as maybe they are in More's reckoning. Latin orators admit in such contexts the verb *gratulor,* Latin poets both this verb and *grator,* but neither *congaudeo.*

Page 200 [no. 62/6]:

> Dum cuncta lustro deprehendi pridie.

More misuses this adverb *pridie,* concurring in one of the most infantile of the barbarians' errors in usage. Anyone who does not know from the reading of Cicero what *pridie* means, and how it should be used, should read Valla [*Elegantiae Linguae Latinae,* II, xxxii–xxxiii, *L. Vallae Opera Omnia,* (Basel, 1540, reprint, Turin, 1962), p. 66].

Page 207 [no. 89/13–16]:

> Tornato bene, Mulciber,
> Argento mihi poculum;
> Iam nunc effice concauum
> Et, quantum potes, imbibum.

Here, too, as in many other passages, More desires to enrich Latin speech with this word "imbibum." No writer, indeed, as I judge, whether authorized or even condemned, ever used this word previously; nor do I see what brought More, for that matter, to use this truly strange and outlandish word here, since the Greek poet's verses which More here endows with Latinity for us, felicitously indeed, include no such word,

habeant, nisi forte alium codicem nactus sit Mωrus, quam eum qui caeteris omnibus communis est, apud quem ita scriptum repperi:

τὸν ἄργυρον τορεύσας,
Ἥφαιστέ, μοι ποίησον
ποτήριον δὲ κοῖλον,
ὅσον δύνῃ, βάθυνον.

Concauum et profundum poculum dixit Anacraeon poeta Graecus cui Aulus Gellius versus eos tribuit, non autem imbibum, nec quod voci huic Mωrianae, hoc est barbarae, opponi possit.

Pagina 209: [F_4v]

Filtro, bireto, pileoque Gallico,
Et calceis, et subligare Gallico.

Philtron, et Latinis et Graecis, amatorium significat poculum cui contrarium est μίσητρον vox a Graecis solum non etiam a Latinis vsurpata. Hoc vero loco Mωrus philtron, nisi fallor, chlamydem appelauit, aut aliud quoddam saguli genus, tametsi id non minus barbare protulit, quam cum biretum dixit. Neque vero hic aliud esse potest, quod hominem excusare possit, nisi quod in eo toto carmine, in quo Anglum quendam insectatur Gallice omnia adfectantem, ipse quoque vt fabulae nihil deesset, omnia Gallice, id est illatine agere voluit tametsi philtrum pro chlamyde Italis magis quam Gallis vernaculum sit.

Pagina 216:

Ast Hermoclides obiturum prae patre solus
Dixit, sed dixit postquam obiisse videt.

Prae patre hoc loco Mωrus dixit, pro eo quod est priusquam pater, quod quam Latine dixerit, doctis iudicandum relinquo. Nam tametsi prae praepositio (praeter alia significata quae habet omnibus nota) nonnunquam etiam ante significet, tamen hic a Mωro vsurpatum sonare id non potest. [G_1] Prae patre enim doctis auribus nihil aliud sonat quam comparationem. Ouidius:

Est quae Callimachi prae nostris rustica dicat
Carmina;

id est nostrorum comparatione carminum. Neque item hic Graecus codex, vnde epigramma desumpsit Mωrus, quicquam habet, quod opponi

unless perchance More has acquired a text not the same as the one generally current. In that text, I read,

> τὸν ἄργυρον τορεύσας,
> Ἥφαιστέ, μοι ποίησον
> ποτήριον δὲ κοῖλον,
> ὅσον δύνῃ, βάθυνον.

The Greek poet Anacreon, to whom Aulus Gellius [*N.A.* 19.9.5] ascribes these lines, describes the cup as "concauum et profundum," not as "imbibum," nor as anything else which can be linked to this Morian, that is, barbarous, epithet.

Page 209 [no. 95/12–13]:

> Filtro, bireto, pileoque Gallico,
> Et calceis et subligare Gallico.

In Greek as in Latin, the word *philtron* stands for a love potion; its contrary, μίσητρον, is a word employed only by the Greeks, but not by the Latins. Unless I am mistaken, More here uses this word for a mantle or some other kind of cloak, even though he employs it as barbarously as when he says *biretum.* Nor is there anything else which may mitigate the man's offense here besides this—that throughout this poem, as he snipes at some Englishman affecting French customs in everything, More himself, likewise, to top off his narrative, endeavors to treat everything in French—that is, non-Latin—phrasing. But *philtrum* for a mantle is less properly French than Italian.

Page 216 [no. 118/5–6]:

> Ast Hermoclides obiturum prae patre solus
> Dixit, sed dixit postquam obiisse videt.

More says here "prae patre" for *priusquam pater;* I leave it to the learned to judge just how idiomatic this is. For even if this preposition, *prae,* among other meanings familiar to all, does occasionally stand for *ante,* nonetheless as More uses it here it cannot have that meaning, since to learned ears "prae patre" suggests nothing besides a comparison. Ovid writes, for example [*Am.* 2.4.19],

> Est quae Callimachi prae nostris rustica dicat
> Carmina;

that is, "nostrorum comparatione carminum." Nor, for that matter, does More's Greek text for this epigram include anything which may be

possit his duabus vocibus prae patre; ita enim Lucillius ait:

> ἀλλ’ ‘Ερμοκλείδης αὐτὸν μόνος εἶπε πρόμοιρον.

Nempe postremum hoc verbum πρόμοιρον opposuit poeta Graecus illi, quod ante dixerat, μακρόγηρων.

Pagina 222:

> Qui capit vxorem defuncta vxore secundam,
> Naufragus in tumido bis natat ille freto.

Ducere vxorem, non capere, et poetae et oratores Latini dicunt. Neque hic sane idioma Graecum Mωrum subleuat, ne se hic forte in huius epigrammatis traductione Graecanicam figuram secutum excuset. Ita enim habent Graeci versus:

> εἴ τις ἅπαξ γήμας, πάλι δεύτερα λέκτρα διώκει,
> ναυηγὸς πλώει δὶς βυθὸν ἀργαλεόν. [G_1v]

Nec video plane, quid impedierit, quominus dicere potuerit, qui vxorem ducit.

Pagina 229:

> Hic sacer Andreae cunctos ex ordine fastos
> Perstringit mira cum breuitate liber.

Hic vero quis non videt coniunctionem, cum, abundare, solumque additam esse ad carminis complementum, et, vt Luciani verbis vtar, πρὸς τὸ τοῦ μέτρου κεχηνός. Mωro autem si in mentem venisset praepositio, sub, soloecismum facile euitare poterat. Age vero quis hic Mωrum non maximopere rideat, Andream quendam damnantem in syllabarum quantitate lapsum, et ipsum tamen interim, perquam egregium Priscianomastiga?

Pagina 248:

> Rex est in primo semper blandissimus aeuo;
> Omni anno consul rex erit ergo nouus.

Vel plane hallucinor, vel hic Mωrus, vbi dixit omni anno, dicere voluit, singulis quibusque annis, quotannis, ita enim Caesar

> ii (inquit) centum pagos habere dicuntur, ex quibus quotannis singula millia armatorum bellandi causa ex suis finibus educunt.

Hominis vero lapsum hunc ex[G_2]cusarem carminis compedibus obstricti, nisi et in Vtopia quoque sua (quam Vdepotiam non Vtopiam, si quid

linked to More's two words "prae patre," for these are the words of Lucilius:

> ἀλλ' Ἑρμοκλείδης αὐτὸν μόνος εἶπε πρόμοιρον.

The Greek poet uses this final word πρόμοιρον as the contrary of that which he had used earlier, μακρόγηρων.

Page 222 [no. 138/3–4]:

> Qui capit vxorem defuncta vxore secundam,
> Naufragus in tumido bis natat ille freto.

Latin poets and orators say *ducere vxorem,* not *capere vxorem.* Clearly Greek idiom yields no support for More here, lest he try to evade our attack on the grounds that he followed the Greek turn of phrase in translating this epigram. The Greek verses read thus:

> εἴ τις ἅπαξ γήμας πάλι δεύτερα λέκτρα διώκει,
> ναυαγὸς πλώει δὶς βυθὸν ἀργαλεόν.

I see no reason why he could not have said *qui vxorem ducit.*

Page 229 [no. 148/7–8]:

> Hic sacer Andreae cunctos ex ordine fastos
> Perstringit mira cum breuitate liber.

Who can fail to discern that the linking word *cum* is redundant here, being included with no other aim than to pad out the verse and (in Lucian's phrase [*Timon* 1]) "as a metrical stopgap"? If the preposition *sub* had occurred to More, he could easily have avoided this solecism. But who can refrain from a good laugh here at More's expense as he carps at a certain Andreas for mistakes in the quantity of syllables while More himself blatantly breaks Priscian's head?

Page 248 [no. 198/16–17]:

> Rex est in primo semper blandissimus aeuo;
> Omni anno consul rex erit ergo nouus.

Either I am delirious or More wants to say *singulis quibusque annis* or *quotannis* when he says *omni anno.* Caesar puts it thus [*B.G.* 4.1.4]:

> ii centum pagos habere dicuntur, ex quibus quotannis singula millia armatorum bellandi causa ex suis finibus educunt.

I would pardon this lapse in a man so bound up in the fetters of meter if he did not use the same manner of speech in his *Utopia* as well (which he

volebat Graece recte formare, appellare debuit) vbi solutus est, ac liber, locutionem eandem vsurparet, pagina 78,

> Syphograntos (inquit) semper in Senatum duos adsciscunt, atque omni die diuersos,

pro quotidie. Neque enim hic omni die pro toto die vsurpauit, cum sensus ipse reclamet, ac ne sic quidem Romanae linguae candorem obseruasset.

Pagina 252:

> Cum spectaret aquas princeps in ponte resedit,
> Primoresque suos ante stetere pedes.

Merus hic est soloecismus in hoc relatiuo, suos, dicendumque fuit, eius. Atqui Mωrum, et hic quoque crederem lapsum fuisse metri necessitate (quamquam si eius dixisset stabat suis pedibus carmen) nisi et eodem relatiuo in uniuersum, in Vtopia, quae tota quantacunque est manifestariis soloecismis, ac barbarismis scatet, abuteretur, cuiusmodi illud est, lib. II, pagina 87,

> Si quando (inquit) vllas ex suis vrbibus aliquis casus eousque minuerit,

vbi Mωrum relatiuo vice pronominis vsum liquet, et pagina sequenti,

> Ab his, inquit, quilibet paterfamilias, quibus ipse, suique opus habent petit,

quo loco ipse, suique vsur[G_2v]pauit pro eo quod est ipse cum suis. Et libro item primo, pagina 50, vbi de quodam Mωrione Mωrus agit,

> . . . tam frigidis (inquit) dictis captans risum vt ipse saepius quam dicta sua rideretur,

vbi Romane loqui volenti dicta eius dicendum fuerat. Vt interim nihil hic agam de mellitissimo, atque adeo facundissimo illo dialogo vbi fraterculus quidam cum Mωrione disceptat, in quo sane dialogo enarrando, exornandoque Mωrus ingenii sui acumen, phraseos vim, ac iudicii integritatem facile explicat. Qui si, dum tam frequens relatiuis abutitur, Graeca ad nos forte transferret, atque interim troporum genera eiuscemodi non de Latinorum, sed de Graecorum quibus schema id genus peculiare est, fontibus coactus desumeret, esset nimirum, cur tam

should have entitled *Udepotia,* not *Utopia,* if he had the intention of coining a name in accord with Greek usage), where he wrote in the freedom of prose. On page 78 of the *Utopia* [*CW 4,* 122/27–28], he writes,

> Syphograntos semper in Senatum duos adsciscunt, atque omni die diuersos,

where he should have said *quotidie.* Nor can he mean *omni die* here for *toto die,* since the sense of the passage rules out this suggestion; even so he would have been neglecting the purity of Roman idiom.

Page 252 [no. 206/3–4]:

> Cum spectaret aquas princeps in ponte resedit,
> Primoresque suos ante stetere pedes.

There is a patent solecism here in More's use of the reflexive, "suos": he should have said *eius.* Here, too, I would suppose that More lapsed through the exigencies of his meter (though this line would still scan if he had written *eius*), except for the fact that he uses the same word improperly throughout the *Utopia,* a work which throughout its whole length is rife with obvious solecisms and barbarisms. Here is one example of this sort from Book II, page 87 [*CW 4,* 136/17–18]:

> Si quando vllas ex suis vrbibus aliquis casus eousque minuerit,

where it is clear that More uses the reflexive *suis* in place of the pronoun *eorum.* Similarly, on the following page [*CW 4,* 136/29–30], he writes,

> Ab his quilibet paterfamilias, quibus ipse, suique opus habent petit,

where he uses "ipse, suique" for *ipse cum suis;* likewise, in Book I, page 50 [*CW 4,* 80/25–26], where More speaks of a certain fool,

> tam frigidis dictis captans risum vt ipse saepius quam dicta sua rideretur,

where, if he had wished to speak Latin, he should have said *dicta eius.* I'll say nothing, meanwhile, of that sweetest and cleverest of dialogues wherein a certain friar carries on a debate with the fool; in the structure and ornamentation of this dialogue, it is clear that More effortlessly exhibits the keenness of his intellect, the power of his phrasing, and the soundness of his judgment. If More, in misusing the reflexive pronouns so frequently, were perchance rendering Greek, and were compelled in the process to take over those particular styles of phrasing from some Greek source—syntax of that sort is peculiar to Greek—and not from a

crebro soloecizanti homini facilior condonari venia deberet. Verum quis vsquam est tam patientis stomachi, iraeque tam retusae, qui aequo animo videre, ac ferre possit, tam foedos lapsus, eosque non coactos, hominis praesertim aliorum scripta tam temere suggillantis, ac literarum quoque, si diis placet, ingeniorumque veluti censorem agentis? Cum me hic interim suppudeat non tam Mωrianam detegere barbariem, quam patefacere studii, atque ocii mei leuitatem, qui ea persequor, quae sint vnicuique, qui vel tantillum bonas literas olfecerit, familiarissima, praesertim quum instituti [G_3] tantum nostri id sit, Mωri hic non orationem prosam excutere, sed versus tantummodo, vel obiter examinare. Nam quum ad poeticae modo palaestram is me haud aliter, quam εἰς πεδίον, φασὶ, τὸν ἵππον prouocauerit, vt turpe sane nobis fuisset ad equum iamdiu rescriptis, hostem non ex insidiis, sed aperto marte adorientem, et eum pariter equo vtcunque insidentem non propulsare, propositamque omnino pugnam deprecari, ita profecto imprudentis, ac quodammodo insolescentis fuerit, ab equo desilientem, aduersarium in diuersum, ac longe aliud quam oblatum sit palestrae genus trahere. Quanquam ne eam quidem harenam, etiam si mihi non perinde tritam, si proponatur detrecto, facto potissimum iam a nobis satis superque periculo, quid in ea aduersarii vires valeant, ac potius quam non masculae, quam effoetae, quamque imbecilles, atque infirmae sint, quanquam ne sic quidem vltro prouocare velim. Absit enim, vt quenquam ipse vnquam lacessere in animum inducam meum. Id quod mehercule tam a moribus nostris alienum est, tamque institutis contrarium, vt non nisi grauissime lacessiti ad duellum accingamur. Sed redeamus ad expurganda caetera Mωri nostri peccata, quae ipsa quo erunt per nos expurgatiora, eo sane de homine peccatore magis merebimur, fietque propterea, vt, (siquidem is minime ingratus, atque adeo si Christia[G_3v]nus est, vt omnino Christianum puto, eundemque bonum) plus nobis deinceps debere se inde fateatur, etiam si me iam non in amicorum, sed in hostium suorum album recensuerit, errantem tam amice admonentibus, ac turpiter labentem tam beneuole subleuantibus, quam caeteris suis amicis, in hominis lapsibus partim caecutientibus, partim conniuentibus, partim etiam palpantibus. Verum quid faceres (vt hic interim Mωri amicos excusem) quando id ingenii versificatoribus id genus, quos insanabile scribendi, edendique cacoethes tenet, natura inditum est, vt si quando te ad vig-

Latin one, there would indeed be some cause to grant pardon more readily to a man who speaks so very often in solecisms. But who is so slow to anger, or so backward in wrath, that he can perceive and endure unperturbed such disgraceful mistakes—quite gratuitous ones—on the part of a man, in particular, who is so brash in carping at other men's works and—by all that is holy—holding forth like a general censor of style and of talent?

Meanwhile, I am a little ashamed to be not so much exposing More's barbarism as revealing the levity of my study and use of my leisure time, since I am dealing with points which are commonplace for anyone who has had even the slightest taste of good literature, and especially because the whole sum of my project is not to review More's prose diction, but merely to look over his verse in passing. For since he challenged me exclusively to a poetic clash, and called me out like "a horse into the plain," as they say—just as it would certainly have been shameful for me, long scheduled for a battle on horseback, to call off the proposed encounter and refuse to drive off a foe who attacked me with open aggression, himself likewise charging (however ill mounted) on horseback, and not from an ambush—in much the same way it would be sheer imprudence and (in a sense) insolence on my part to leap down from my mount and challenge my foe to a contest very different from that which he offered me. Even so, I will not shun that field, either, should it be proposed, although that one is not so familiar to me, since I have already made ample trial of my enemy's prowess therein, or—to be more precise—of my enemy's unmanly weakness and sinewless frailty. Not that I would challenge him on my own initiative; no, far be it from me to desire to offend any foe. That particular impulse, in fact, is so foreign to me, and so contrary to my principles, that I do not gird myself for a contest unless I have myself been most grievously offended.

But now I will turn back to expunging the rest of our More's misdeeds. Quite clearly, the more I expunge them, the more thanks I have earned from the man who committed them; therefore, if he is not an ingrate, and certainly if that man is a Christian (as I reckon him to be, and a good one, at that) it will follow that he, in his turn, will acknowledge himself more indebted to me—even if he has already entered my name in his list, not of friends, but of enemies—for my amity in admonishing him when he strayed, and my benevolence in helping him up when he slipped so disgracefully, than to his other friends for either overlooking his slips, or conniving in them, or even admiring them. And yet—let me say this on behalf of More's friends—reader, what would *you* do, since versifiers of the sort who are possessed by that incurable passion for writing and printing are naturally of such a mind that whenever they ask you to

iliarum suarum examen aduocauerint, communicauerintque, ac iudicio etiam tuo submiserint, quod ipsi tamen iam omnino a sese ablegare, et quicquid id est quod pepererint, edere decreuerunt, ac tu interea aequi iudicis, syncerique amici partes praestare volueris, admonuerisque, Corrige sodes, hoc vitium sonat, minime pareant, planeque obaudiant, ac nisi quaecunque scripserint admireris vel frigidissima, ineptissimaque te iam non amare, sed vel hallucinari, vel odisse, vel inuidere etiam suspicentur, atque adeo non nisi conniuentes in viciis amicos exosculentur, eos omneis qui erratorum commonefaciunt auersentur. Id quod etiam plane sibi placere Mωrus adfirmat, in quadam epistola ad Thomam Ruthalum, quae quidem extat pro foribus quorundam Luciani dialogorum, quos Latinos facere [G_4] conatus est, quosque eo nomine Ruthalo nuncupare se scribit, quod illo nemo esset in amicorum erratis conniuentior. Eumque ingenii Ruthalici, si diis placet, candorem appellat, tam candidi ipse, ac potius tam deprauati ingenii, vt quod adulatorum est, quodque verae ac syncerae amicitiae sacrosanctae leges procul a nobis ceu vitium arcendum censent, id ipsum noua quadam hospitalitate in aedes suas ceu virtutem admittat. Atque equidem, eiuscemodi quum sit Mωrianum ingenium hoc est palponibus applaudens monitoribus asperum, atque aduersum, dispeream, nisi ipse deinceps hominem mihi longe omnium infensissimum, atque adeo hostem deuotissimum, iuratissimumque sim habiturus, ac quo nomine apud eum bene audire deberem, eiusque beneuolentiam, gratiam, amicitiam comparare, eo certe ipso male sim auditurus, inuidiam quoque, maleuolentiam, odium in me capitale conciliaturus, quando et hoc quoque tempore, vt Terentiano olim, apud plerosque omneis obsequium amicos, veritas odium parit. Concedis enim nobis lector optime, vt vel id vnum interim hic de Mωri erga nos animo auguremur, quod augurium, tametsi verissimum sciebam, tamen in admonendis Christiani hominis erratis (quod ipsum quam modeste, quamque citra conuicium faciam palam est) malui, Christianus [G_4v] item ego, officiosum, ac beneuolum me exhibere, quam in dissimulandis adulatorem, ac palponem agere, potissimum quum id hominum genus, ceu mutuae mortalium fidei aduersissimum, amicitiisque pestilentissimum meopte ingenio sim semper execratus. Neque vero parum me Mωro debere fatebor, erratis eius per me hic expunctis, si et ipse quoque par pari referat, si in lapsus nostros, si qui forte in Antimωro erunt, vt omnino esse possunt (neque enim tam mihi placeo, tamque arrogo, vt me ipsum ab omni plane errato liberare, atque eximere velim) animaduertat; dum is tamen exemplum nostrum secutus, nihil calumnietur, nihil comminiscatur non a me commissum, sed omnia ex fide, omnia ex historia ipsa agat. Mene vnquam pudebit, vel Mωro docente pruden-

examine the products of their sleepless hours, and submit to your judgment what *they* have in fact already resolved to send forth and publish, whatever it is they have created, and you try to hold up the part of an equitable judge and true friend, and you tell them, "Mend this, friend; this is faulty," they never pay heed, plainly turning a deaf ear to your words; unless you admire all they have written, however inept and insipid it is, they suspect you of raving, or of malice, or even of envy instead of affection. Indeed, they cherish none who refuse to connive in their faults, and shun all who would point out their errors.

More further avows in plain terms that this attitude has his approval in a certain letter to Thomas Ruthall [*CW 3/1,* 8/1–5] appearing before certain dialogues of Lucian which More tried to render in Latin. He dedicates them to Ruthall on no other ground than that no one could be more indulgent than he toward the faults of his friends. By all that is holy, More calls this attitude of Ruthall's "candor," himself being of so candid, or rather so twisted, a mind that he, with a strange hospitality, gladly welcomes flattery into his home in the guise of a virtue, a quality which all the sacrosanct laws of sincere, honest friendship decree should be shunned as a vice.

Indeed, since More's own bent is thus, both approving of flatterers and hostile toward well-meaning critics, I will bet my life that he will be my greatest ill-wisher and most devoutly sworn enemy hereafter, while what ought to have earned me his praise, goodwill, thanks and affection will surely elicit, on his part, abuse, envy, malice, and implacable hatred. Now, no less than in Terence's time, it is almost invariably true that "Indulgence wins friends, truth wins hatred" [Terence, *Andria* 69]. For you, generous reader, do not begrudge me here this one prophecy about More's feelings toward me. Even though I knew that my prophecy was sure to come true, nonetheless I, a Christian, chose rather to show myself solicitous and well-meaning in proclaiming the faults of a Christian—and it is clear that I do it modestly, without any insults—than to play the part of a toady and flatterer in dissembling those faults; especially since temperamentally I have always hated flatterers as the worst enemy of man's common trust, and the worst bane of friendship. I'll acknowledge myself to be much in More's debt if, once I have expunged all his faults, he returns me the favor and calls my attention to my mistakes in the *Antimorus,* if there are mistakes therein, as there may very well be (I am not so in love with myself, and am not so presumptuous, that I seek to be clear and exempt from every fault), provided he follows my example in misrepresenting nothing and fabricating nothing where I did not transgress, and in dealing with each point sincerely and factually. Shall I ever be ashamed to grow wiser, even with More as my teacher? Indeed, I hope

tiorem fieri? Quem etiam volo tam diligentem, tam oculatum, tam etiam acrem, ac seuerum in me Aristarchum agere, sic, vt seueritatis, acrimoniaeque obeliscos omneis in errata mea (quae tamen in criminationem venire digna erunt) exacuat, intendat, eiaculetur, nec quod mihi crimen, vel me etiam id deprecante, condonet. Sed iam redeo, vnde digressus sum. Soloecismus igitur, quo de initio agebamus, admissus in eo quod praeposuimus carmine,

Primoresque suos ante stetere pedes,

nulla ex parte a Mωro excusari potest, nisi forte et eum quoque lapsum chalcographo [H_1] adscribere velit, harum duarum vocum suos, et eius similitudine deluso, tam inter sese videlicet similium, quam vel cygnus coruo, vel asinus equo similis est.

Pagina 255:

Ventum erat ad vinum, quum sic sua lumina moestus
Affatur posito iam peritura mero.
Huc iter est, huc me fidi duxistis amici,
Hunc bibite, et dulces ambo valete duces.

Id pronominis hunc palam est referri ad alterum horum nominum, vinum, merum. Itaque dicendum fuit hoc. At vero delictum id chalcographi alioqui diligentissimi neglegentiae vna cum aliis quamplurimis (quae tamen authoris esse non chalchographi liquet) tribuimus.

Pagina 258:

Ebrius adfectu rex coniugis, ebrius illo
Fortunae luxu, praetereaque mero.

Et hic quoque altera duarum harum vocum, praeterea, que, addita est ad carminis hiatum complendum, nec vero est quisquam, cui domestica, ac familiaris sit veterum poetarum phrasis, qui e vestigio non olfaciat, quam inepte, ne dicam barbare, Mωrus ea locutione vsus fuerit. Quis enim vnquam poeta recaeptus quidem iunxit coniun[H_1v]ctionem que cum praeterea aduerbio. Verum haec in paedagogorum scholis non ediscuntur, assiduam antiquorum lectionem, longum in literis vsum, sagacem nasum requirunt.

Pagina 264:

Multo labore, vix adhuc credo in deum.

Si Musae Romanae loqui vellent, hanc hanc videlicet phrasin, hoc est Morianam hanc barbariem vsurparent. Sunt et infinita prope alia in Mori versiculis errata, tum in syllabarum quantitate, tum in soloecismis, ac barbarismis turpiter admissis, sed quae facile abs quolibet lectore de-

he will play such a diligent, keen-sighted, even harsh and severe Aristarchus where I am concerned that he will sharpen, aim, and discharge every one of his barbs of severity and harshness into my various faults (provided they merit his censure), not pardoning my crime even if I beseech him to do so.

But now I turn back to the issue from which I digressed. The solecism I started out to discuss in the line I set forth at the outset, "Primoresque suos ante stetere pedes," cannot be excused by More on any grounds at all, unless maybe he wants to lay that mistake, too, to his printer, as if he would have been led astray by the likeness of *suos* and *eius* (as like one another, of course, as a swan and a raven or a donkey and a horse).

Page 255 [no. 214/8–11]:

> Ventum erat ad vinum, quum sic sua lumina moestus
> Affatur posito iam peritura mero.
> Huc iter est, huc me fidi duxistis amici;
> Hunc bibite et dulces ambo valete duces.

It is clear that the pronoun *hunc* must have either *vinum* or *merum* as its antecedent. Thus More should have written *hoc*. But I attribute this offense, along with a legion of others (although it is quite clear that they are More's, not his printer's), to the negligence of a printer who is otherwise marvelously diligent.

Page 258 [no. 224/4–5]:

> Ebrius adfectu rex coniugis, ebrius illo
> Fortunaeque luxu praetereaque mero.

Here, too, the second of these two words, *praeterea* and *que,* has been added to pad out a verse; nor will anyone who is at home or familiar with the phrasing of ancient poets not sense in an instant how ineptly, or even barbarously, More uses this turn of phrase here. For what accepted poet, indeed, ever joined the conjunction *que* with the adverb *praeterea?* Such points are not learned in elementary school; they require sustained study of the ancients, much practice in literature, and critical acumen.

Page 264 [no. 247/9]:

> Multo labore vix adhuc credo in deum.

If the Roman Muses wished to speak, they would doubtless use this turn of phrase, that is, this Morian barbarism. There are virtually countless other faults in More's verses, both in his scansion and in his foully perpetrated solecisms and barbarisms, which can easily be caught by any read-

prehendi queant. Nos autem ea tantum secuti sumus, quae insignem aliquam notam, atque ineluibilem haberent, neque enim libuit in huiusmodi trichis multum operae collocare, idque, ne lectori delicato nauseam adferet tam ingens erratorum numerus, qui sane maior est, quam sit Graecarum nauium apud Homerum catalogus. Quo fit vt inter tam apertam, tamque manifestam balbutiem, inter tam insignem, tamque conuictam Latialis Musae deformitatem, quorumdam vel adulationem, vel, si ea plane adulatio non est, coecitatem, ignorantiamque

Pontanus, Marullus

demirari satis non possim Mωri versificationes, ac meras ineptias, Pontani etiam, ac Marulli carminibus impudentissime praeferentium, pronunciantiumque, ac veluti decreto statuen[H_2]tium nihil illorum esse scripta prae Mωrianis epigrammatis, tametsi aetas nostra (quod citra controuersiam doctis omnibus esse video) ambos eos solos habet, quos quidem iuste antiquis vatibus opponere possit. Ac profecto esset studiosis omnibus Graeci, Latinique nominis calamitas maximopere lugenda, si poetarum duorum tam illustrium fulgorem, quos nobis, vel post tot secula singulares tandem, tum Italia, tum Graecia (fuit enim Marullus natione Graecus) peperit, vnius Mωri eiusdemque Britanni tenebrae obscurarent, ac tam claris luminibus caliginem offunderent. Verum id quod diximus decretum, municipale tantum est, non Senatusconsultum, aut Imperatorum lex sacrosancta, quam non obseruare religio sit, vt facile admodum fuerit Musarum cultores omneis ab eo, quem ante dixi, luctu vindicare, nisi si cui forte Mωri soloecismi tam aperte conuicti, ac barbarismi tam putidi suauius oleant (vt omnino suauius olere iudicibus eiuscemodi puto) quam a Pontano, Marulloque expressa Romani sermonis fragrantia, puritas, elegantia, maiestas, vt omittam hic vtriusque poetae ingenium, quod sane quam rarum, quam felix, quam diuinum fuerit, aeterna illa, quae posteris multa reliquere poemata plenissime

Excusat se Brixius

arguunt. Proinde te lector candide obsecro: existimes adductum me ad Antimωri editionem, non quod aut Mωrum hominem [H_2v] prorsus mihi incognitum alioqui odissem, aut Anglorum quidquam genti, seu publico seu priuato nomine infensus essem, sed quod iudicaui retundendam esse hominis insolentiam, ac furorem reprimendum, nec committendum, vt qui passim toto corpore vlcerosus esset, impune alterius naeuum vnum aut alterum suggillaret. Tametsi mihi quod obiicit Mωrus poema ludenti, apud eum qui synceri sit in politioribus literis iudicii, virtutis magis quam vitii loco habetur, debeoque inde praeconium reportare, non etiam in vituperationem venire. Qui enim iustius poetam laudare possis? (quando

er. I have here dealt only with those which exhibit a striking and indelible blemish, since I did not wish to waste much time upon trifles of this sort, and feared lest so great a collection of faults, surely greater than Homer's whole list of Greek ships, should arouse the disgust of my delicate reader.

Therefore I cannot wonder enough at the adulation or perhaps rather blindness and ignorance of some of More's readers, the ones who, for all More's self-evident and manifest babbling, and for all the conspicuous and amply established deformity of his Latin muse, shamelessly prefer his attempts at verse, his manifest trifles, to the poems of such men as Pontanus and Marullus; the ones who pronounce and decree, as it were, that the writings of these two are nothing compared with More's epigrams, even though our own age (and in this I perceive all the learned concur) has these two alone whom it may justly compare with the ancients. And indeed it would be a most lamentable calamity for all who are zealous for fame among Latins or Greeks if the obscurity of More all alone—and a Briton, at that—were to blacken the glory of two such illustrious poets, conceived for preeminence even in this late age of ours, one by Italy, one by Greece (for Marullus was Greek by birth), and to drown two such bright lights in darkness. But yet, since the decree which I have mentioned is merely provincial, and neither an edict endorsed by the Senate nor yet a sacred law of the Emperors, which it is anathema not to abide by, it is easy to free the true votaries of the Muses from the sorrow which I have described, unless perhaps some find More's clearly exposed solecisms and unsavory barbarisms more fragrant (as I reckon all judges of this sort must find them) than the sweetness, the purity, the elegance, and the dignity of the Latin discourse expressed by Pontanus and Marullus. At this point I will not mention the genius of either, since the numerous immortal poems which they left to posterity demonstrate beyond a shadow of a doubt how rare, how felicitous, how godlike the genius of each was.

Pontanus, Marullus

Candid reader, I beg you, do not think that what drew me to publish my work against More was hatred of a man with whom I otherwise have no acquaintance whatever, or some private or public antipathy toward the whole English nation; rather, I felt obliged to put down this man's insolence, and check his insanity, and to prevent him, whose whole body is ulcerous, from reviling with impunity this or that minor flaw in another.

Brixius exonerates himself

Yet the features More blames in my poem, which I wrote merely as a

duo omnino haec sunt quae ceu capitalia in nobis delicta, ac velut lesae Appollineae maiestatis crimina insectatur adversarius) quam si eundem adfirmaueris, simul fictionibus, quae non nisi vatibus conueniunt, abundare, simul veteres poetas aemulari? eorum vestigiis inhaerere? ac veluti clauam (quod aiunt) ab Herculis dextra eripere? potissimum vbi nulla in parte poematis oeconomiam, elocutionemve crimineris? At vero quandoquidem homines sumus, hoc est ad lapsus procliues, nec quisquam esse potest mortalium tam absolutae doctrinae, tamque solidi iudicii, quin aliquoties hallucinetur, erretque, absit vt mihi ipse tam constantes pedes tribuam, tamque firmos gressus arrogem, vt me cespitare nunquam posse confidam. Tantum autem abest, vt non boni consulam, si quis titubantem me admoneat, vt admonenti, atque adeo [H$_3$] increpanti gratiam habeam non vulgarem. Verumtamen increpantis partes conuenire arbitramur ei qui nullis, aut saltem quam minimis vrgetur vitiis, non etiam ei qui totus vitiosus est, ac nulla sui parte non morbidus. Siquidem quod verissime simul ac disertissime Demosthenes ait

> οὐκ ἔστι πικρῶς ἐξετάσαι τί πέπρακται τοῖς ἄλλοις, ἂν μὴ παρ' ἡμῶν αὐτῶν ὑπάρξῃ τὰ δέοντα.

Mωri autem carmen passim vitiosum esse, ac plane putidum, nemo sane est, qui vel modice inter Musas versatus sit, etiam si id per me conuictum non foret, qui perfacile ex se olfacere non possit. Nec video prorsus quae res hominis poeticam arrogantis tam crassam ignorantiam excusare possit. Nisi eum forte dixeris de industria (quod plane suspicamur) ignorantiam simulare, atque adeo ex composito mωrari, insanireque, quo literarum reipublicae officiat, quemadmodum contra versute olim, ac callide Solon insanire se simulauit, homo alioqui sapientissimus, quo plus aliquanto Atheniensium reipublicae prodesset. Vale candide lector, et nostra aliquot alia poematia (si te Antimωrum nostram non fastidiisse sensero) breui expectato, quae ipsa eo certe lubentius emittam, vt Mωro per me deinceps spaciosior calumniandi campus, ac liberior suggillandi facultas praebeatur. 1519.

In Thomam Mωrum Brixii Tetrastichon
E Graeco

Sunt Furiae et Musis, quae te fecere poetam. [H$_3$v]
Hinc sine iudicio, carmina multa facis.
Plura ergo, precor, ede poemata, quando precari
Maiorem hac nequeo Mωre tibi maniam.

pastime, are deemed virtues rather than vices by anyone who has any true literary discernment, so that I ought to win new acclaim on that score, not fall subject to censure. For how can you praise any poet more aptly (since these are the two things, after all, which my censor assails as my capital crimes and treasonous deeds against the majesty of Phoebus, so to speak) than to say, first, that that poet is fertile in fictions (uniquely the province of poets) and, second, that he bids fair to rival the ancients, following close in their footsteps and, so to speak, making off with the club of Hercules; especially if, in the meantime, you nowhere find fault with the disposition or phrasing of his poem?

But since we are but human, that is, prone to mistakes, nor is anyone so learned or prudent that his mind never wanders and strays from its course, far be it from me to consider my footing so firm and my course so secure that I may be certain I cannot ever fall to the ground. I take no offense when someone warns me that I am staggering; far from it. I am exceptionally grateful for his warning and even for his rebuke. But I hold that the role of a rebuker suits one who is himself afflicted with no defects, or only slight ones, at any rate; certainly not one who is defective and unsound throughout, since, as Demosthenes [2.27] puts it so cogently and so eloquently, "We must not play harsh censors in judging the actions of others if we ourselves fall short in essentials."

But no one who has the slightest acquaintance with the Muses can fail to sense for himself that More's verses are defective and fetid throughout, even if I myself had not proven it amply. I see no means of pardoning such ignorance in a man who claims poetic competence, unless perhaps you press the claim (which I am assuredly tempted to credit) that he purposely counterfeits ignorance, indeed, plays the madman and fool by design, to confound the republic of learning; just as Solon, on the other hand, once shrewdly and cunningly counterfeited madness, a man otherwise great in wisdom, in order to do greater good for the republic of the Athenians.

Farewell, candid reader; if I perceive that you have not found my *Antimorus* utterly contemptible, look for a number of my other little poems in the very near future; I publish them all the more willingly to give More a more spacious field for his calumny and ampler occasion for insults. 1519.

A Quatrain by Brixius against Thomas More
From the Greek

The Muses also have their Furies, and these made you into a poet; therefore you write many poems with no judgment at all. I implore you to publish more poems, since I cannot implore for you, More, any greater insanity than this.

Tetrastichon hoc, tametsi Polliani Graeci poetae esse constet, Mωrus ceu inuentum a se, licet aliis verbis ad Latinos, seu potius ad Britannos transferens, inter epigrammata sua retulit, nempe vendicans sibi quod maxime omnium videbat suis ipsius moribus conforme epigramma, vt facile eo nomine homini ignoscas, nisi et ipsum quoque identidem alibi faceret, Graeca inuenta pro suis non sine plagii nota proferens.

Mωri ridiculum epigramma in obitum
Henrici Abingdonii Cantoris Regii, ad quod
Brixius in Antimωro circa finem allusit

[Here no. 160 by More is reprinted.]

[H_4] Hoc reperies inter Mωri epigrammata, pagi. 252 in libris impressis per Frobenium.

Errata in Officina Impressoria Admissa

Ne quis forte Mωro μωρότερος authori imputet ea quae properantes typographi errata admisere, libuit ea paucis subnectere, quo suum quisque codicem emendare possit. [Brixius' corrections have been silently incorporated wherever possible. But his list of errata refers to some passages that are already correct in our copy-text and omits any mention of others that still need correction.] [H_4v] Quod si quis forte in vitiosum exemplar incidat non prius damnet authorem, quam quae emendata sunt alia exemplaria consuluerit. Nam ex eiusdem typographi praelo, dum operae festinanter nimis opus vrgent, simul exiere emendata quaedam, quaedam non item.

Cautum est ne quis hanc Germani Brixii Antimωron in biennium proximum vel imprimat, vel alibi impressam huc importet.

[There follows Erasmus' epistle to Brixius, "Epistola tua, mi Brixi" (Allen, *3*, no. 620), with Brixius' reply to Erasmus, "Heri quum forte" (Allen, *4*, no. 1045).]

Though this quatrain is clearly by Pollianus the Greek, More includes it among his epigrams as his own composition [cf. no. 103], though the wording, of course, in his Latin—that is, his British—translation is different. He claims as his own the one epigram which most closely conforms to his own character, and hence one might easily pardon him had he not done the same thing with other poems, presenting Greek compositions as his own, not without the opprobrium of plagiarism.

More's Ludicrous Epigram on the Death of Henry Abyngdon, Singer in the Chapel Royal [no. 160], to Which Brixius Alludes in the Last Part of His *Antimorus*

[Here no. 160 by More is reprinted.]

You will find this piece on page 252 of More's epigrams printed by Froben.

Faults Introduced in the Printing House

Lest anyone, more of a moron than More, impute to the author the faults introduced by the printers in their haste, I saw fit to list these faults succinctly, in order that each may emend his own text. [Brixius' corrections have been silently incorporated wherever possible in our Latin. But his list of errata refers to some passages that are already correct in our copy-text and omits any mention of others that still need correction.] If anyone comes across a defective copy, let him not censure the author until he has consulted other copies which have been corrected. For from the same printer's press, since the workers pushed the work forward too hastily, some copies were issued corrected and some uncorrected.

All are warned not to print the *Antimorus* of Germanus Brixius for the next two years or to import copies printed elsewhere.

[There follows Erasmus' epistle to Brixius, "Epistola tua, mi Brixi" (Allen, *3*, no. 620), with Brixius' reply to Erasmus, "Heri quum forte" (Allen, *3*, no. 1045).]

APPENDIX C

More's Letter to Brixius

EDITED BY DANIEL KINNEY

APPENDIX C

More's Letter to Brixius

ONE USEFUL approach to More's *Letter to Brixius* is to consider it as More's *ars poetica.* The French court poet Brixius had published two long poems, the *Chordigera* and the *Antimorus,* which had grievously offended More's literary sensibility; More's *Letter to Brixius* sets out to say why, taxing Brixius' verse as mendacious, absurdly extravagant, and crudely derivative.[1]

The main problem with this approach is that More's *ars poetica,* unlike that of Horace, forms part of a bitter polemic in which personalities and personal prejudices are apt to loom larger than any substantive issues, literary or otherwise. The consensus of recent scholarship is that More's conduct in this controversy was partisan and rather petty, no less so than the conduct of Brixius.[2] Indeed, More's hasty suppression of the *Letter to Brixius* suggests that More himself soon regretted the violence of this

---

[1]For the *Letter to Brixius* as More's *ars poetica* see Richard S. Sylvester, "Thomas More: Humanist in Action," in *Essential Articles,* p. 469; the article is reprinted from *Medieval and Renaissance Studies,* ed. O. B. Hardison (Southeastern Institute of Medieval and Renaissance Studies), *1* (1966), 125–37. G. Marc'hadour, in "Croisade triomphale d'Angleterre," *Moreana, 35* (1972), 67, calls More's letter "art poétique en même temps qu'art de vivre."

Since the *Letter to Brixius* has generally received only passing attention it would be unproductive to catalog every scholarly work in which this letter happens to figure. My main interpretive debts are to the works cited in note 2 below. In checking my translation I have had the benefit of consulting an unpublished English translation by Marcus Haworth, S.J., and a French translation by Marie-Hélène Dublineau–Le Breton, "Lettre de Thomas More à Germain de Brie (avril 1520)," dissertation, Université Catholique de l'Ouest (Angers), 1980.

[2]For this verdict see among others T. E. Bridgett, *The Life and Writings of Blessed Thomas More,* 3rd ed. (London, 1904), p. 188; E. E. Reynolds, *Thomas More and Erasmus* (London, 1965), pp. 144–45; P. G. Bientenholz, *Basle and France in the Sixteenth Century* (Geneva, 1971), p. 195; and G. R. Elton, "Thomas More, Councillor (1517–1529)," in *St. Thomas More: Action and Contemplation,* ed. Richard S. Sylvester (New Haven and London, 1972), pp. 112–13. See also Harpsfield, p. 102. R. Adams, who offers a careful and partially convincing apology for the pacifist program of More's Brixius epigrams, himself falters when it is a question of defending the *Letter to Brixius* (Adams, pp. 183–84).

personal invective. Soon after publishing the letter, the most cogent defense that More can muster for its unkind handling of Brixius is that More is no saint and should not be required to behave like one;[1] in the letter itself, More appears to admonish his readers against taking it too seriously when he speaks of polemical exchanges like this one as "quarrelsome and utterly fruitless rebukes."[2]

More professes to regard Brixius' attacks on his syntax and prosody as the only substantive issues, with one chief exception, on which he feels the need to refute Brixius.[3] This exception, the question of who actually started the quarrel, is an issue on which even a scholar who praises this letter as More's *ars poetica* feels that More fails to carry his point.[4] More himself, on the other hand, feels that to carry this point is his sole unimpeachable motive for writing the letter at all.[5]

If his argument fails on precisely this point, meanwhile showering his poetic adversary with wanton abuse, it can scarcely redeem either More or this letter to call it More's own *ars poetica;* nonetheless he himself gives us many incentives to do so. He is far too self-conscious a master of argumentation to compose what aspires to be "an art of poetry as well as an art of living" in defense of a thesis which shamelessly distorts the real sequence of events in this controversy; he quite clearly believes that the thesis that Brixius started the quarrel is true and important and that he can show how it is true by explaining his theory of poetry. We should try to avoid special pleading, but we do have good reason to look for a sense in which More actually does show that Brixius, not More, was the "first to offend."[6]

---

[1]See Allen, *4*, 255, lines 180–89: "And yet it may well be that my own sense of injury makes a statement seem not at all bitter to me which someone who is not so involved in the matter will find rather harsh. Even if this should happen, I have enough confidence in my readers' fairness, Erasmus, to be hopeful that even in me (although your love assigns me so grave a demeanor, just as it always looks for great things in me)—to be hopeful that even in me, while I still dwell in this mortal abode, and have certainly not yet been entered in the number of saints (let me laugh at a laughable notion), humane readers will exhibit some tolerance for those human emotions which no man has ever been able to banish entirely." This and other translations for which I do not give a reference to *CWE* are mine. More here alludes to a passage in the *Letter to Brixius* where he mocks Brixius for showing Hervé unsuccessfully trying to burn away his mortal passions, "provoked, I suppose, by Saint Lawrence's example" (602/26–28).

[2]See below, 598/12–13.

[3]See below, 622/16–19.

[4]See Sylvester, "Thomas More: Humanist in Action," in *Essential Articles,* p. 467.

[5]See below, 598/17–20.

[6]See 598/20, 608/1–2, 608/28–610/1, 616/17–18, and 656/11–12.

Rhetorical Structure

While the main arguments of the *Letter to Brixius* are not altogether self-explanatory, the peripheral events in More's controversy with Brixius have proven to be even less so. Hence the most sensible way to begin is to undertake a schematic analysis of the *Letter to Brixius,* first outlining its arguments and then trying to furnish a plausible account of how these various arguments cohere. More arranges his arguments according to a seven-part scheme used in numerous formal orations. Traditionally each of these parts reinforces and supplements the others in a certain predictable way; it turns out that the various sections of the *Letter to Brixius* adhere fairly closely to this standard functional pattern. More's discussion of how poetry ought to be written is also designed to support his contention that Brixius' *Chordigera* was a crude and direct provocation addressed to the English at large. Every section of the *Letter to Brixius* defends and refines on the thesis that not More but Brixius himself is to blame for provoking the quarrel.

The seven-part scheme More employs in composing the *Letter to Brixius* consists of an introduction (*exordium*), a review of the principal facts of the case (*narratio*), a statement of principal theses (*propositio*), an outline of positive arguments (*divisio*), the positive argumentation itself (*confirmatio*), a rebuttal of contrary arguments (*refutatio*), and an elaborate conclusion (*peroratio*). In his introduction (596/2–598/20) More sets out to harden "good men" against Brixius and to win their goodwill for himself (*praemunitio* and *captatio benevolentiae*) by refusing to use language similar to that of his adversary, language which More describes as appropriate for one who possesses a shameless assurance that nothing can make him look worse to the world than he already does. More here also anticipates two of his principal theses: since Brixius chooses to identify himself so completely with the miserable poem More originally criticized, More cannot defend his own statements at all without stooping to personal rebukes; he would not be responding to the *Antimorus* at all if he did not feel bound to refute the suggestion that he and not Brixius had touched off their quarrel. In his review of the principal facts of the case (598/21–606/5) More avoids an invidiously protracted discussion of what actually happened in the bloody but quite inconclusive sea battle which gave rise to Brixius' *Chordigera.* Instead, he concentrates on the monstrous array of national insults, factual distortions, and literary extravagances with which Brixius himself sought to flesh out the poor tale he had chosen to tell. In his statement of principal theses (606/6–610/12), More suggests as a general principle of fairness that since Brixius was willing to issue a libel against all the English, under his own name, in wartime, and since the English assuredly had as much right to respond to such books as the French had to write them, Brixius should have been just as prepared to bear the brunt of an English reaction to his libel as he was to claim most of the credit for issuing the affront in the first place. Brixius' immoderate reaction to More's playful epigrams on the *Chordigera* shows that More never owed it to Brixius to "spare the person, but to lash the crime,"[1] because the person in this case perversely stakes his whole renown on the crime being lashed. More's elaborate comparison of Brixius with a vindictive and unseasonable wrestler caps off his description of how we should construe Brixius' tactless renewal of hostilities in his *Antimorus*. In his outline of positive arguments (610/13–19), More first makes a brief forward reference to his planned refutation of Brixius' charges and then outlines the charges against Brixius which More will proceed to develop at length (610/19–622/3), charges stating that Brixius' *Chordigera* is riddled with flaws on the levels of phrasing (*elocutio*), arrangement (*dispositio*), and marshaling of arguments (*inventio*). These in fact are the same charges More makes in his series of Brixius epigrams; evidently More feels that if these charges are accepted as valid, his view of the *Chordigera* as a crude and direct provocation must then be accepted as well. In his rebuttal of Brixius (622/4–654/11), More takes up the charges which Brixius makes in his *Antimorus* against More's own diction and artistic skill or *ingenium*. Brixius' trifling objections to More's scansion and syntax suggest that meticulous conformity to classical phrasing is a greater poetic achievement than the witty and decorous expression of timeless or modern-day truths; Brixius' philologically naive punctilio has made him forget that the scansion and syntax of even the best classical poets are frequently idiosyncratic. On the level of *ingenium*, More devotes well over 200 lines to defending the notion of poetic praise which is embodied in More's coronation ode (no. 19), a work Brixius had fiercely attacked; according to More, ". . . even contrary to the received impressions of the crowd, whose taste generally runs to the worst things in life, we should little by little instill proper values in men's hearts with the sweetness of verse."[2] In his conclusion (654/12–658/23), More broad-

---

[1]This formula imitates Martial 10.33.10, "parcere personis, dicere de vitiis." In Allen, *4*, 221, More implicitly grants that mocking a writer by name is a more serious business than mocking his works without mentioning his name, even though it is easy to make it plain who is being mocked without mentioning names. Brixius' personal stake in the virulent lies of the *Chordigera*, on which he has based a good deal of his own fame and fortune, deters More from extending to Brixius the nominal immunity More freely accords to innocuous hacks in nos. 147 and 148. See also no. 236.

[2]644/5–7; cf. More's second letter to Giles in *Utopia*, *CW 4*, 250/7–8.

ens the focus of his answer to Brixius to a somewhat more general consideration of the "letter which kills" and the "spirit which gives life." At one point Brixius even takes up the role of a preacher, and virtually bids More to do penance for his solecisms; More adds, "I suppose, since the Kingdom of God is at hand." He ends with a prayer that the saints will be generous enough to correct both men's faults, both More's vagaries of scansion and Brixius' vagaries of intellect. Even though he appreciates the perils of the humanists' frequently central concern with *scientia verborum,* the science of words which inflates, More here stands by his faith in what he and Erasmus regard as the surest of human correctives, the earnest wordplay of a critical and self-critical humanism.[1]

Both More's review of the principal facts of the case and his positive argumentation for the charges first leveled at Brixius in the ten epigrams on the *Chordigera* include many amusing, intelligent remarks on the difference between good and bad poetry. It is nevertheless not immediately clear what remarks such as these have to do with More's principal thesis: does the quality of Brixius' writing really have any bearing on who started his quarrel with More? What More wants to establish in these two discussions, however, is not only that Brixius writes miserable poetry but that miserable poetry of the sort Brixius writes has a real and pernicious effect on the health of a culture; it is poetry of a sort that a decent man ought to malign. Brixius' poetry is mere versified propaganda; it may be more respectable (and thus *more* pernicious) than some propaganda on account of its dignified form, but its motives and objects are just as dishonorable as those of the worst yellow journalism. More sets out to establish that all of Brixius' strictly poetic transgressions result from his shameless contempt for historical truth. Later, we will examine more closely the claims which More makes for the kinship of poetry and history. For now, it will suffice if we show that for More Brixius' *Chordigera* is merely a mendacious history and deserves condemnation as such.

More artfully arranges an accurate summary of *Chordigera* (600/18–604/17) so as to make it sound very much like the first and second catalogues of historiographical atrocities which Lucian presents in his short treatise, *Quomodo historia conscribenda sit.*[2] Brixius joins in himself all the vices of both the discreditable historians whom Lucian describes,

---

[1]Cf. no. 260. More's *Letter to Dorp* was aimed largely at confuting Dorp's damaging claims, based on Augustine's allusive conflation of 1 Cor. 8: 1 and 2 Cor. 3: 6 in *Confessions* 1. 18, that the humanists were guilty of spurning the charitable wisdom which edifies for the wordy rhetorical know-how which merely inflates; see especially Dorp's second letter to Erasmus, Allen, 2, 128–29, lines 80–92, and cf. 654/20–22, below.

[2]Lucian, *Quomodo historia conscribenda sit* 14–15.

the retailer of partisan lies on the one hand and the thief of a past age's beauties of phrase on the other. Like Lucian's liar, Brixius thinks that false history couched in fine phrases is poetic truth. Like Lucian's liar, Brixius sets out to aggrandize the commander of his own party and to belittle the opposing commander, naturally failing to see that his own hero would have seemed greater if he had been matched with a hero and not with a wretched impostor. Lucian's liar and Brixius both open their narratives with scurrilous insults; Brixius calls his opponents the "spiteful" and "treacherous" English, while for Lucian's liar the opponent is the "most villainous and damnable Vologesus." Brixius foists whole Vergilian and Ovidian episodes into his poem; Lucian's stylistic thief thrusts Thucydides' plague narrative into his Roman history for no other reason than to grace his own work with the charms of Thucydides' style, as if even Thucydides could cut a fine figure when dressed half like a Roman and half like a Greek. Indeed More omits several of Brixius' stylistic transgressions which he treated at length in the *Epigrams* in order to make this list resemble more closely the two lists in Lucian.[1] Echoes of Lucian's carefully organized satire add force to More's obvious suggestion that Brixius' stylistic malaise is pervasive, and not just a question of this or that casual distemper. Furthermore, Lucian's satire affords More a precedent for attempting to heal this malaise with a few timely jests before it spreads to other and better authors. When he criticizes Brixius' *Chordigera,* More is setting the historical record straight; Lucian's precedent allows him to claim that he has every right to be doing so.

In his positive argumentation More begins by discussing Brixius' notion of the right way to imitate the diction of classical authors. For Brixius, imitation amounts to appropriating whatever he finds to be especially striking in the diction or imagery of this or that classical poet; Brixius thrusts in his borrowings wherever he can, showing almost no sense of decorum or context (610/19–612/19). If a fine borrowed phrase has no bearing on the matter at hand, Brixius simply dreams up a conceit in which he can use what he has pilfered; in this sense the arrangement of Brixius' narrative as well as its diction is spoiled by his passion for glittering ornament and his gross disregard for decorum and context

[1]More plays down the outright contradictions in Brixius' account of Hervé's polymorphous pugnacity (see nos. 190 and 191), shifts the emphasis in his main attack upon Brixius' *imitatio* from faults of expression to faults of narrative economy (see no. 193), and bypasses the matter of Hervé's extravagant cenotaph altogether (see no. 194). It is worth noting here that a factitious funeral oration ridiculed later in *Quomodo historia conscribenda sit* (ch. 26) may well have given More the idea for composing this epigram as well as no. 188 (on a narrator worthy to share in the slaughter he prates about).

(612/20–614/2). Finally, More turns to the way Brixius marshals his arguments. For Brixius, poetic license means a license to utter preposterous lies about matters of historical fact where the truth can be known. Brixius' radical contempt for historical context accounts for his shocking abuse of rhetorical context. To discredit Brixius' notion of poetic license More mentions three other mendacious French chronicles, one in verse, two in prose, and then asks why their authors do not have as much right as Brixius to hide behind poetic license (614/3–618/30). If Brixius' false history is poetic truth, so is all yellow journalism. It does not redeem turgid, muddled, mendacious historical writing to describe it as poetry.

Personal Insult and National Partisanship

Neither More's epigrams against Brixius' *Chordigera* nor Brixius' *Antimorus,* not to mention the *Letter to Brixius* itself, would be viewed as a libel today, and the very notion of libel as a punishable offense was less clear for More, Brixius, and their contemporaries than it is for us.[1] The most abusive text of all in this controversy, More's long letter to Erasmus on Brixius (Allen, *4,* 217–32), written very soon after the *Letter to Brixius* itself, goes so far as to deem Brixius worthy of dire scatological correctives but still stops short of all patently libelous suggestions that Brixius, apart from his writings, is guilty of any indecent or criminal behavior.

Although none of the texts which make up this polemical exchange are demonstrably libelous in our sense, it is immediately apparent that Brixius' answer to More's very limited critique embodies far more than its share of malicious intent. More restricted his jokes to one poem, the *Chordigera;* Brixius ranged throughout More's printed works, aiming taunts at the sentiments expressed in More's preface to three dialogues of Lucian, at the diction of the *Utopia,* and at the prosody and the sense of the *Epigrams* taken as a whole.[2] The most damaging attack of all was on a passage in More's coronation ode (no. 19), where More praises Henry VIII for repealing unjust ordinances enforced under Henry VII. Brixius even added a sidenote to point out "More's impudence in slandering the father while praising the son." More repeatedly stressed his impression that this thrust was aimed at his "perdition" (*pernicies*), and on this point Erasmus agreed with him.[3] The worst injury that anyone could

---

[1]See P. G. Bietenholz, "Ethics and Early Printing: Erasmus' Rules for the Proper Conduct of Authors," *Humanities Association of Canada Review, 26* (1975), 180–95.

[2]See Appendix B, 538/9–18, 532/33–534/34, and 540/36–542/30.

[3]See 648/26, below, and the Commentary.

do to a man's reputation in More's day was to make his king start to resent him: *Indignatio principis mors est.*[1] Since it was, in fact, meant to make Henry resentful of More, Brixius' retort may in this sense correctly be viewed as a libel. Just how much had More done to provoke it?

Although personal insult and national partisanship both figure prominently in the earliest stage of More's quarrel with Brixius, the relation between these two polemical modes is inverse, not direct. Brixius' stridently partisan *Chordigera* wholly depersonalizes the Englishmen whom it belittles; as More twice notes, Brixius does not even bother to identify the English commander by name.[2] On the other hand, More, while avoiding all stridently partisan rhetoric, does not hesitate to tax Brixius by name in the *Epigrams* for his portentous poetic extravagances and historical distortions. Brixius accuses the English as a nation of spitefulness (*inuidia*), perjury, and the violation of solemn peace treaties. At the same time, he earnestly tries to establish that there was a species of sainthood awaiting the captain and crew of the *Cordelière* as they gave up the ghost in this rather improbable Holy War. In his *Epigrams* More mentions once, very briefly, the schismatic effect of the Scottish king James IV's league with the French against England and Pope Julius II in what Henry VIII asked his own people to view as a "glorious crusade"; this particular indictment of James, More declares, had no point but to override Brixius' arraignment of England's good faith.[3] In an epigram written to chastise an Englishman for trying to pretend he was French (no. 95), More makes fun of several French mannerisms; in another epigram (no. 244) he succinctly congratulates Henry VIII for capturing the city of Tournay from the forces of France. Among More's poems expressly directed against Brixius' *Chordigera* there is one (no. 194) which suggests that Hervé and his crew actually differed in one crucial respect from the Decian martyrs of Rome, to whom Brixius had likened them: the Decii died to save Rome, but Hervé and his crew died because they had nowhere to flee. Even here More does not indict Frenchmen in general: every sane man would flee, if he could, accidental cremation.[4]

---

[1]This adaptation of Proverbs 16:14 was quoted to More in the course of his final confrontation with Henry VIII; see Roper, p. 71.

[2]See 602/5–6, below, and the Commentary.

[3]Number 271; see Allen, *4*, 221, lines 182–86. More wrote two other poems against James IV (nos. 183 and 184) stressing only his perfidy against Henry VIII, his own brother-in-law. These were not suppressed in 1520; no. 271 was.

[4]Even nonpartisan Erasmus was not so discreet; he wrote one poem which states that the French in this war were all cowards. See Reedijk, p. 304. Marc'hadour ("Croisade triomphale," pp. 65–68) notes that Erasmus, former tutor to James IV's son, seemed more hostile toward the war effort of France, but less so toward the war effort of Scotland, than More himself was; see also *ASD 4/1*, 208/316–18, 213/452–53, and Commentary.

In the *Letter to Brixius* itself More continues to assert that the question of which party showed off its martial *virtù* more impressively in the battle which Brixius had chosen to commemorate is needlessly rancorous, potentially embarrassing to *both* sides (appalling bad luck harried both), and therefore quite irrelevant to what More had written against Brixius' impudent boast that the French were the manifest victors.[1]

More's relative restraint on the moot point of which nation's military prowess manifested itself more convincingly in the war of 1511–14 suggests that he hoped to address a more general issue in answering Brixius, the issue of why France and England should always be fighting so bitterly. More may well have looked forward to an English victory in Henry's "crusade" against Louis XII without ever thinking that this or indeed any war could produce lasting peace between England and France. Brixius' *Chordigera* furnished More with a rare opportunity to write in the service of patriotism and common sense simultaneously. Arguments which on another occasion might well be used to challenge the rhetoric of every offensive war effort in the name of nonpartisan pacifism were here given a specific patriotic application by Brixius' outrageous rhapsody of pro-French historical distortions.[2]

More accused Brixius of engaging in a shoddy chauvinistic invective in which all moral terms were employed as capriciously as the glittering phrases which Brixius purloined from the ancients. In assigning the blame for such shoddy invective to Brixius the individual, More actually avoided attributing it to the French as a nation: More's suggestion that "Brixius the German" (*not* "Germanus Brixius") had written incendiary lines on the conflagration of the French *Cordelière* helped More stress his own sense from the first that the French as a nation were no more to blame than the English for a feud which was really sustained by warmongers like Brixius.[3]

No one, not even Brixius himself, took More's lines as a national affront to the French. More's defense of his poems against Brixius boils down, then, to this: by the rules of ordinary fair play, More, an English-

---

[1]See 600/8–17, below. At 620/31–33 More offers to adduce eyewitness testimonies if Brixius opposes his claim that apart from the burning of two ships, one French and one English, everything Brixius wrote is a falsehood.

[2]Adams' defense of More's Brixius epigrams as a pacifist satire "directed against the idea that it is automatically glorious to die in battle" (Adams, p. 77) is cogent enough in itself, but I think it is wrong to suppose that More's satire directs itself chiefly against literary clichés "inherited from the degenerate world of romantic chivalry." The extravagant rhetoric of humanists like Brixius betokened a new kind of degeneracy, meticulously "humane" in the shallowest sense, inhumane in a deeper one.

[3]See the Commentary at 632/12, below, and 189/1.

man, has the right to attack France in writing if this or that Frenchman has written against England; surely, then, More has just as much right to cirticize one such Frenchman by name when his writings encourage both sides to persist in their bloodshed. Brixius challenged More personally in the sense that the crudely inflammatory tract Brixius published made More personally ashamed to keep silence. His far-ranging reflections on history as well as on rhetoric itself as a shaping historical force gave More cause to conceive of himself as uniquely equipped to strip away the glittering verbal disguise from the warmongering spirit which Brixius had masked in his epic, despoiling the most esteemed monuments of all humane authors to "put an honorable face" on his inhumane passion for war.[1]

Common prudence made most humanist authors reluctant to take the initiative in judging their peers at all harshly by name, lest they be judged in turn. It was a very different story as soon as a humanist could claim that someone had provoked *him* by name: Brixius' overreaction to More's terse rebukes had innumerable precedents from Valla on down to Erasmus.[2] The humanists usually associated their code of initial restraint with biblical precepts condemning all personal abuse; More himself was extremely attentive to these precepts, and although he did not hesitate to connect Brixius' name with ten critical epigrams, it is clear that he had serious doubts about his right to publish them, leaving this decision up to Erasmus.[3] It must nonetheless have struck More, as it often strikes us, that the humanists invoke their own code of initial restraint much more as a casual convention of self-serving professional courtesy than as a fixed principle of charity espoused for the general good of the "Christian republic." In practice the only real issue for many of the humanists in deciding what constitutes personal abuse was the issue of who "attacked" first: any breach of initial restraint, but not any intemperate response, could be called an abusive attack. To a certain extent, this pragmatic if logically suspect equation between personal abuse and an

---

[1]See 606/12–13. More's "defense and illustration" of rhetorical culture appears in the *Letter to Dorp.*

[2]See Bietenholz, "Ethics and Early Printing," pp. 180–95; M. P. Gilmore, "De Modis Disputandi: The Apologetic Works of Erasmus," in *Florilegium Historiale: Essays Presented to W. K. Ferguson,* ed. J. G. Rowe and W. H. Stockdale (Toronto, 1971), pp. 62–88; and Allen, *1,* 21–31 (Erasmus' own *catalogue raisonné* of his polemical writings).

[3]See More's *Letter to Dorp,* Rogers, no. 15, lines 503–20. For More's doubts about publishing the poems against Brixius, see Allen, *2,* 340, lines 20–28, and *4,* 221, lines 156–62. Significantly, in the *Letter to Brixius* itself, More never acknowledges any doubt about the propriety of the personal mockery directed against Brixius in the *Epigrams.*

unprovoked verbal "attack" corresponds to another pragmatic equation between personal assault and an unprovoked physical attack: despite statutes and biblical precepts alike, it is standard judicial procedure to sanction some violent reactions in cases of clear self-defense. On the other hand, justified criticism can scarcely be called unprovoked; even when it successfully "makes an example" of someone by calling attention to really egregious offenses, it is not to be lightly equated with personal abuse. Whether or not More was right to treat Brixius' rhetorical transgressions as really egregious offenses, it is clear that at least some rhetorical transgressions do merit such treatment even if some pragmatic convention does label it an unprovoked verbal attack. More's 1518 letter to Gonnell, his children's humanities tutor, shows unusual astuteness in stressing the disruptive power of an amoral humanist's eloquence.[1] More's historical candor, the same candor which brought him to judge several powerful figures severely by name in his *History of Richard III*, prompted him to name Brixius, too, for his prominent role in commending a pernicious system of values by means of his partisan humanism.[2] As a group, humanists lacked any standards or rules of procedure for the frank self-appraisal which should have prevented sophistical *mis*application of eloquent counsel. More set out to adapt to this critical task the strict standards of credible history.

Brixius claims that More's epigrams assail him with pure "imprecations" and "curses"; he, however, has skilfully managed to turn them all back against More in the form of innocuous jests.[3] When More defended his epigrams against Brixius in a long letter addressed to Erasmus, he rightly stated that only one of his poems contains anything even remotely approaching a curse: in the second of his epigrams against Brixius, he suggests that instead of padding the *Chordigera* with so many outrageous lies Brixius should have been present on that very ship which, according to one of his lies, sank without leaving any survivors.[4] Like a similar

---

[1]See Rogers, no. 63, lines 8–11: "While I esteem learning compounded with virtue above all kingly treasures, what else does literary fame not compounded with probity of morals confer but a prodigious infamy?" Cicero (*De oratore* 3.35.142) went only so far as to prefer "unspeaking wisdom" to "talkative folly."

[2]Before we dismiss More's harsh judgments of Richard III and his cohorts as primarily propaganda for the new Tudor régime, we must remember that More freely criticized Henry VII's policies in a poem More allowed to be published (no. 19), while the *History of Richard III*, though painstakingly revised over a period of several years, was never released in More's lifetime.

[3]Allen, *4*, 129, lines 39–48. This letter was originally printed along with the *Antimorus*.

[4]Allen, *4*, 219–20, lines 106–34, on no. 188, which Brixius too singled out as especially invidious.

passage in Lucian, this mock-imprecation is simply a clever device for exposing the rift which divides the historical world of hard facts from the dreamworld of Brixius' fictions.[1] More wishes that Brixius could have been on the *Cordelière,* from which Brixius insists that not one man survived, so that he could have learned all the facts of the mishap. While this looks like a crude invitation to "go to the devil," Brixius could not have learned the most crucial historical fact for the truth of his narrative—namely, that a great number of men *did* survive—if he were not himself a survivor. Thus More's "curse" is in fact a disguise for a multiple blessing: not only would Brixius live if More's wishes came true; he would also be cured of his lying. In these poems More says nothing to endanger Brixius' personal prestige as a courtier, or even as a poet of promise. Far from calling Brixius himself a fool, More does not even call his poem foolish except indirectly. Brixius utterly misrepresented the tone of More's poems to conceal the embarrassing fact that they all raise substantial, impersonal objections to his kind of writing. If More felt he had good civic reasons for directing a few terse rebukes at the saber-rattling of Brixius' *Chordigera,* it is scarcely surprising that More felt no qualms about even the much harsher rhetorical correctives he used for the virulence of Brixius' *Antimorus.*

Erasmus' Role in the Quarrel

Erasmus was More's principal literary adviser and advocate throughout the controversy with Brixius. The evidence suggests that even though Erasmus shared most of More's critical positions, he felt a good deal of responsibility for protecting the literary reputation and the general self-esteem of his most loyal French partisan, Brixius. More's most trusted adviser and advocate was caught in a conflict of interest, and More's cause was handled the worse for it. More deferred to Erasmus' decisions from the start of the quarrel to the finish. Only once, at a very late stage of the quarrel, did More flatly reject any part of Erasmus' advice: whereas Erasmus advised that More ought to suppress even his first series of Brixius epigrams, More not only republished the first but appended a second series. Throughout the controversy More clung to

---

[1]In *Quomodo historia conscribenda sit* 26 Lucian ridicules a factitious funeral oration the deliverer of which concluded by despatching himself on the tomb of the man he was eulogizing. Of this speaker's death Lucian exclaims, "By the god of destruction he was worthy to die long before, since he made such a speech . . . but I faulted him most for omitting, before he himself died, to do in the historian who engineered this melodrama." Cf. p. 556, n. 1. In Allen, *4*, 220, More cites an alternative antecedent in Martial to justify the mention of Brixius' own name in this mock malediction.

the gradually weakening conviction that Erasmus would never withhold or grant his *imprimatur* except as a way of expressing a frank critical verdict. Inadvertently, through settling at last on the only possible interpretation of the motives and issues at stake which would let him retain both men's friendship, Erasmus obscured the extent to which Brixius both exaggerated the force of More's personal insults and simply evaded the force of More's general criticisms in his first Brixius epigrams. More deferred to Erasmus more readily than Brixius did; for this reason Erasmus' "definitive" account of More's quarrel with Brixius has turned out to do less than justice to More.

In More's view, Erasmus had actively sanctioned the publishing of More's first Brixius epigrams. In 1516 More had written,

> If later on you publish my epigrams, please consider whether you think it best to suppress those in which I attacked Brixius, for there are some rather bitter things in them, though I might be thought to have been provoked by the abuse he leveled at my country. All the same, as I say, please give them some thought, and in fact all those that you think might give offense. If besides them any are actually feeble, deal with them as you may think will be best for me. Quintilian said of Seneca that he was the sort of man one would wish to use his own brains in writing, but be guided by someone else's taste; and I am the sort of writer who ought to use not merely someone else's taste but another man's brains.[1]

Erasmus had a very active role in the original campaign to publish More's epigrams; indeed, he twice assured More that he personally had sent Froben in Basel the copy text which would be used for More's poems.[2] In More's view, then, Erasmus himself had decided that there was no reason for More to be nervous about publishing his Brixius epigrams. As More points out, discreetly but firmly, in April 1520,

> when I learned that there were plans to publish my *Epigrams* at Basel, you yourself know what I did to have those I wrote against Brixius omitted, along with some others; for some did not seem to be serious enough, even though they are far from that obscenity which I see to be all that commends certain men's epigrams to certain readers. And at the same time I was reluctant to mock anyone the least bit by name, even for a just cause.[3]

---

[1]Allen, *2*, 340 (*CWE 4*, 67–68).

[2]Allen, *2*, 576, lines 15–16, and *3*, 6, lines 43–44; cf. Allen, *4*, 254, lines 132–35 and *CW 4*, 2/17–19.

[3]Allen, *4*, 221, lines 156–62.

What More took as an active endorsement of his Brixius poems and their serious content Erasmus described in late April 1520 as an oversight which was partly More's own fault:

> I know you do not value so highly that little collection of poems which you jestingly wrote against [Brixius] that you will not let them be struck from your text, as a favor to me. For if you had not advised it too late, you would have seen to this yourself long ago, since you were none too pleased when you heard that the book as a whole would be published.[1]

Erasmus had more than six months to consider the wisdom of striking the Brixius epigrams before sending the text off to Froben in May 1517. It would seem that he simply did not view More's poems as unduly offensive. Erasmus himself once expressed a powerful dislike for the bellicose, mendacious style of "historical" poetry in which Brixius' *Chordigera* was written.[2] He did so in a letter of 1513, when the nameless poem he was condemning may well have been Brixius' own. When Erasmus retained More's *Chordigera* poems in the text of the *Epigrams,* it was probably by choice and not oversight.

In mid-1517 or 1518 Erasmus wrote a brief letter to Brixius discouraging him from replying to More's epigrams about him.[3] Since this letter is presented as a response to a letter of ceremonious flattery from Brixius dated April 6, 1517, Allen reasons that Erasmus' own letter must have followed soon after—in mid-1517, *not* in 1518, though the letter has been dated 1518 ever since its original printing. There are a number of serious objections to Allen's redating.[4] Although he asserts that "[Eras-

---

[1]Allen, *4,* 241, lines 98–101. It may well be that More did send Erasmus a letter specifically meant to forestall publication of the Brixius epigrams and that this letter did in fact fail to reach Erasmus in time; that would still not explain why Erasmus did not pay any heed to the strong reservations expressed in the earlier letter from More we have cited. That letter accompanied the *Utopia* manuscript which Erasmus acknowledged on October 2, 1516 (Allen, *2,* 354).

[2]Allen, *1,* 545, lines 92–103. At the end of this letter Erasmus originally printed the anti-French poem mentioned above (see p. 558, n. 4, and p. 575).

[3]Allen, *3,* 41–43.

[4]The main difficulty is that Allen's redating implies Brixius was planning to answer More's poems with a "vicious little book," a *dentatus libellus,* while More's poems were still only in manuscript. Even Brixius saw that to justify his *Antimorus* he had to have some ground for claiming that he had been "challenged"; the only conceivable ground for advancing this claim to an audience outside the small circle of those who had access to More's poems in manuscript was the general diffusion of More's poems in print. If Erasmus is taken to refer to no more than a scheme for revenge conceived on the assump-

mus'] answer to Ep. 569 [Brixius' letter] cannot have been long delayed," ceremonious flattery very rarely cries out for a speedy reply. Are we forced to infer that there was no delay just because Erasmus omits to apologize for any delay? Brixius himself never hints that the slightest apology was owed him, and yet Brixius himself, we are told, never saw the response to his letter of 1517 until (at the earliest) late *1519*, when it appeared (dated 1518) in a printed collection.[1] All the hard evidence suggests that Erasmus wrote one casual letter to Brixius in mid-1518 discouraging him from replying to More's Brixius epigrams. There was no follow-up, and Erasmus, it seems, never bothered to find out for certain whether Brixius had even received the first letter.[2] Erasmus' respect for the threat posed by Brixius' resentment lagged far behind More's, both before and after More's poems were first printed. Erasmus showed considerably more circumspection when he urged in the strongest possible terms that More make no response at all to Brixius' *Antimorus.* More had reason to feel he showed too much.

On receiving the *Antimorus* in late March or early April 1520 More immediately set to work on the *Letter to Brixius.* He completed the letter very quickly, and even seems to have taken some pride in the haste with which he had managed to launch his initial retort: "'In an easy cause anyone may be eloquent.'"[3] Already, however, More was planning a much more ambitious reply, for which he would need somewhat more leisure; he planned to assemble the *Chordigera,* his own Brixius epigrams, the *Antimorus,* and a considerable quantity of historical annotation and other supplementary material in a single elaborate volume.[4] The very scale of this critical enterprise—More promises to edit the *Antimorus*

---

tion that More's poems would be published shortly, Allen's mid-1517 date for this letter would then make total nonsense of Erasmus' contention in April 1520 that he had been warned against publishing More's Brixius epigrams too late to exclude them from the *Epigrams* volume of March 1518. Further, the mid-1517 date is not easily reconciled with a passage by More in a letter of May 1520 where More states that a well-informed Parisian source of his own had first notified him of Brixius' plans for revenge "about two years ago" (Allen, *4,* 251). Finally, a mid-1517 date seems quite inappropriate for a letter including one phrase ("the most firmly sealed peace into which the two peoples have entered") which appears to refer very clearly to Wolsey's "Perpetual Peace," a definitive treaty negotiated between July and October of 1518; cf. Allen, *3,* 580, lines 33–35; Appendix B, 510/534; *Letter to Brixius,* 594/6 and 606/16–19; Allen, *4,* 217, lines 13, 23; 240, lines 44–45; and 294, line 61.

[1]See Brixius' response to this letter, Allen, *4,* 128–32.

[2]In Allen, *4,* 240, lines 70–72, Erasmus readily accepts Brixius' claim that the original copy of Erasmus' short letter of 1518 must somehow have gone astray.

[3]See 596/17–18, below, and Allen, *4,* 230, lines 528–35, 543.

[4]See 632/23–26, below, and the Commentary.

more carefully than Brixius himself did—yields additional proof of More's personal conviction that a careful dissection of Brixius' morbid creations could assist other humanists substantially in ensuring the health of their own. When the *Letter to Brixius* had already been printed More promptly despatched along with it a long letter to Erasmus restating his case against Brixius from a new, complementary perspective.[1] In the *Letter to Brixius* itself More expounds his own general theory of what constitutes a sound and responsible style; in the letter to Erasmus More systematically penetrates the cosmetic impostures of Brixius' style, taking up a succession of stylistic fine points to pierce to the morbid interior. More undoubtedly intended this letter, too, for eventual publication.[2] Perhaps he intended for Erasmus to publish it, or perhaps he intended to publish it himself at the end of his omnibus volume just as Brixius had published a letter to Erasmus at the end of the *Antimorus*. Since the *Letter to Brixius* was published at once, while the letter to Erasmus was transmitted in only one manuscript copy and the omnibus volume was wholly suppressed, it is fair to describe the three texts as expressions of three distinct strategies for countering Brixius' attacks.

Erasmus alone was responsible for More's sudden decision in early May 1520 to buy up and put into safekeeping all the texts of the *Letter to Brixius* which had not yet been sold. At the same time, it seems, More gave up the intention of publishing his long letter to Erasmus and abandoned his plans for producing a collected edition of all the main texts in the controversy. In a letter to More dated April 26, 1520, Erasmus states that he has "heard about" an answer to Brixius which More has "already in hand" ("iam in manibus"). Erasmus not only exhorts More to give up all his plans for refuting the *Antimorus* but also proposes that More, at this point, should strike out all his Brixius poems from the next edition of the *Epigrams;* in return, Brixius may be induced not to publish his libel a second time.[3] Erasmus endeavors to link the two latter proposals as if their quid pro quo ought in fairness to satisfy More, a suggestion which struck More as not at all fair. Brixius' libel had already done as much damage as it could be expected to do, given that More's Brixius epigrams were readily available to show just how much Brixius had exaggerated the force of More's personal insults; now Erasmus proposed that these poems be suppressed, giving Brixius' libelous railing the semblance of just indignation.[4]

---

[1]Allen, *4*, 217–32.

[2]More's words in this letter are sometimes quite definitely aimed at a large and in part hostile audience; see Allen, *4*, 225, lines 329–30 and 345–47, and 229, lines 467–72.

[3]Allen, *4*, 240–41, lines 63–64, 98–103; cf. *4*, 295, lines 112–15.

[4]Allen, *4*, 254–55, lines 124–32, 167–72.

In a preface dated June 1520, Brixius repeated his principal charges against More.[1] More retained his ten poems against Brixius' *Chordigera* and added four more on the *Antimorus* itself in the *Epigrams* of December

---

[1]Here is the pertinent passage of Brixius' preface to *Poematia duo* (Paris, Nicolas de la Barre, June 2, 1520), sigs. a2–a2v: "Proinde tuum erit lector optime / vtrunque carmen, qualecunque est, post recentem adhuc Antimori nostrae editionem / aequi, bonique consulere tantisper, dum tibi recensemus, deligimusque et nostra item aliquot alia poematia, quae edita studijs, spero, tuis nonnihil sint tum voluptatis, tum compendij allatura. Caeterum et hic quoque Morum Anglum, in cuius videlicet gratiam Antimorum ipsam, quam diximus, lusimus, vehementer etiam, atque etiam obsecramus, vt in hendecasyllabos hos nostros Momum mordacem, atque adeo, si id praestare potest, oculatissimum, acerrimumque agat Aristarchum, ac si quid in ijs obelisco dignum comperiat, id ipsum e-uestigio citra omnem criminis cuiuscunque condonationem / palam damnet, confodiat, iugulet. Quis enim recuset tam specioso ensi iugulum porrigere? Nobis nimirum dictu facile [*misprinted* faci-cile] non est, quantopere optemus artificij nostri specimina, rudimentaque omnia ad tam perfectum unguem, vt Horatiano vtar uerbo, castigari, atque adeo ad tam rectam, tamque absolutam amussim correcta / informari, sicque demum hominis quanquam incogniti, tamen in me, quod uideo, perquam beneuoli / beneficio, artificioque ad exactam aliquam, iustissimamque effigiem quadam veluti facta metamorphosi / reduci, renouarique. Id quod etiam si illum ultro factitaturum (tam rara est hominis in me charitas) perfacile suspicamur, Tamen conuenire etiam ducimus equum vel sua sponte currentem, / simul clamore hortari, simul tuba incitare, simul plausu prosequi, simul etiam calcaribus nonnihil urgere. Tametsi periculum, opinor, esse non potest, ne me hic Morus in Deloini, Erasmique hominum nunquam satis laudatorum / decantandis encomijs uersatum / mendacij reum agat (Id quod, si dijs placet, ob Chordigerae poema a nobis scriptum facere conatur) neu obstrepat / falsa me de utroque praedicas[a2v]se. Neque enim illum putamus causas ab omnibus vno ore confessas, ac studiosorum sane omnium suffragijs iam olim praeiudicatas / oppugnaturum, easdemque in controuersiam reuocaturum, perinde quasi illi a me non suis, sed alienis depicti fuerint coloribus. Nisi prorsus tam lippus, tamque lusciosus est, vt ad splendidissimi solis radios caliget, atque in re clarissima caecutiat. Nam quod ad alterum crimen pertinet, quod nobis ex eodem illo Chordigerae poematio homo facetissimus / obijcit, videlicet neminem esse, qui me ipso diligentius antiquos poetas excusserit, deque eorum uersibus hinc inde flosculos, et gemmulas (vtar enim illius uerbis) manu capaciori legerit, perficerent Musae cum suo Appoline, vti in scriptis nostris omnibus crimen hoc, qualecunque est, per me admissum / agnoscere uolens nolens cogerer, nec aliquod vnquam poema pangerem, nisi per veterum poetarum non hemistichia modo, sed mera holostichia, quorum lectionem vtinam sic mihi familiarem, sicque domesticam reddere possem, vt ex illis omnibus de rebus, quas collibuisset, recentia opera edere, ac veluti rhapsodias coaptare, centonesue consuere liceret, vt si quid ipse peccarem, id ipsum non cum recentioribus poetis (quos vt non damno, ita certe Moro citra omnem inuidiam euoluendos, aemulandosque relinquo) sed cum antiqui, ac vere aurei illius saeculi uatibus peccarem. Verumenimuero ne aures tuas diutius obtundam / bis eandem, aiunt, cantilenam emodulans, vt qui tecum hac de re in Antimoro nostra satis, superque egerim, finem hic uerbis facio. Itaque lector candide bene uale, et quod dixi, expecta haud ita multos post menses alia quoque ingenij nostri specimina / non admodum his dissimilia. Ex Lutecia. xij. Calendas Maias. MD. XX. [April 20, 1520]" Erasmus refers to this preface in Allen, *4*, 295, lines 114–16, and 326, lines 19–21, where he seems to suggest in a vague way that Brixius has made more than one new attack. For More's new Brixius epigrams, see nos. 266–69.

1520. Meanwhile he continued to press for the release of the *Letter to Brixius;* at Calais in early July 1520, Erasmus barely managed to restrain him.[1] More's new Brixius epigrams were sufficient to show that he felt not at all repentant for his earlier mockery and that Brixius' libel was scarcely the sort of rhetorical performance that could ever inspire any of Brixius' critics to repent. In this sense More was able to settle accounts in his quarrel with Brixius even though his main printed response was withdrawn on Erasmus' advice. In another, less petty and personal sense, the withdrawal of the *Letter to Brixius* contradicted and prejudiced More's whole endeavor to settle accounts. Too late for More's own good, Erasmus began to treat More's controversy with Brixius as strictly a pernicious personal feud.[2] More's withdrawal of the *Letter to Brixius* in compliance with this attitude toward the controversy made it soon come to seem the correct one.

When Erasmus wrote to More on April 26, 1520, that he knew nothing except by vague hearsay about More's printed answer to Brixius, he may well have displayed something less than his usual candor. In replying to this letter with several strong hints that Erasmus was trying to dissemble a firsthand acquaintance with the *Letter to Brixius,* More himself almost certainly displayed something less than his usual implicit trust in Erasmus' professions. It by no means reflects on Erasmus or More, or on their generous friendship, if Erasmus dissembled one fact to keep his diplomatic detachment intact—he had two friends to think of, not one—or if More, whether rightly or wrongly, suspected Erasmus of doing just that. Signs of strain in More's literary partnership with Erasmus are not necessarily signs of bad faith in their friendship. On the other hand, such signs of strain have a definite bearing on Erasmus' role in More's controversy with Brixius, and thus they require our attention.

More sent off a personal copy of the *Letter to Brixius* and a long personal letter addressed to Erasmus himself sometime early in April,[3] but there is no proof that Erasmus received either letter by April 26. On the other hand, Erasmus' own letter of that date includes various expressions and arguments with remarkable affinities to expressions and arguments

---

[1]See Allen, *4,* 443, lines 20–24. In Allen, *4,* 324, lines 14–16, and 326, lines 10–13, after his conference with More in Calais, Erasmus suggests that his efforts to make More suppress his rebuttal of Brixius have still met with only partial success. For More's continuing readiness to fight in mid-February of 1521, see also Allen, *4,* 443, lines 1–4.

[2]See p. 570, n. 5, below.

[3]Allen, *4,* 230, lines 524–28, and 253, lines 107–21, make it clear that More sent Erasmus a printed copy of the *Letter to Brixius* along with the long personal letter to Erasmus (Allen, *4,* 217–32).

used in the *Letter to Brixius* itself and the letter to Erasmus which accompanied it. In one twenty-line section, Erasmus sums up the most rankling distortions included in Brixius' libel and contends that they are all too transparent to require any rebuttal at all; this whole section resembles a composite abstract of More's own two letters.[1] It is almost as if in this section Erasmus exploits the rhetorical claim that More's arguments *should* be self-evident to suggest that they actually are, so that More has no call to defend them explicitly: the obvious does not bear discussing. If Erasmus *is* echoing More's principal arguments, he certainly does not lack a motive; to facilitate a personal, diplomatic solution, he wants to discount every substantive issue More might see fit to raise.

More begins his reply to this letter by wondering aloud why Erasmus has waited so long to discourage him from answering Brixius at all.[2] More then makes up two feeble excuses for Erasmus to use: maybe the *Antimorus* did not reach Antwerp as quickly as it reached London, or maybe Erasmus was sure that More would not consider the tract to be worth a response. But the first is implausible because Antwerp is so close to Paris, while the second is implausible because Erasmus is so sure of Brixius' worth as a writer. Thus it may be that Erasmus' decision to keep More from issuing any response was not made until he had seen the response More had already drafted and printed. More then cavils at Brixius' claim that the reason he failed to comply with Erasmus' advice against publishing the *Antimorus* is that Erasmus' letter reached him too late to influence a state of affairs which was already settled.[2] Erasmus appears to be making a similar claim for a similar reason: he hopes that his claim to be ignorant as yet of what More's letter actually says will

---

[1]In lines 33–56 of his letter discouraging More from responding to Brixius (Allen *4*, 239–41), Erasmus appears to be borrowing methodically from More's own two letters in an effort to turn More's major arguments back on themselves. While Erasmus' wording in this section is predictably closer to that of the *Letter to Brixius* itself than to that of More's long covering letter, the stress which Erasmus here places on stylistic fine points makes it seem that he hopes to deflect the main arguments of More's covering letter as well. For Allen, *4*, 239, lines 33–35, cf. 598/17–20; for Allen, *4*, 239; lines 35–36, cf. 596/12–15 and 630/4–7; for Allen, *4*, 239–40, lines 36–38, cf. 624/17–26; for Allen, *4*, 240, lines 40–42, cf. 624/30–32 and 628/30–630/7; for Allen, *4*, 240, lines 42–45, cf. Allen *4*, 217, lines 21–25; for Allen, *4*, 240, lines 45–47, cf. Allen, *4*, 219, lines 82–88; for Allen, *4*, 240, lines 47–54, cf. 638/4–13 and 640/12–14; and for Allen, *4*, 240, line 56, cf. 610/20–21. Other parallels in Erasmus' own phrasing are numerous but not as conclusive as these; the pattern these form is so much like the overall pattern of More's own reactions to Brixius' libel that Erasmus could scarcely have written these lines without having More's texts close at hand.

[2]Allen, *4*, 251.

[3]Allen, *4*, 252–53.

excuse him from taking it seriously when he has the chance. Finally, More dramatically calls on Erasmus' own eyes as his witnesses that the *Letter to Brixius* is already in print; he then barely softens this indirect challenge by adding, "for I have no doubt that the book reached you earlier than this letter."[1] More feels that the serious issues he raises in the *Letter to Brixius* deserve to be seriously discussed (there would be no *Chordigera* and no *Antimorus* if the truth about issues like these were as obvious as Erasmus makes out), while Erasmus evades them.

Erasmus worked hard in the following months to make Brixius desist. He wrote Brixius an unsparing letter on June 25 which was seemingly meant to shame him into silence (Brixius had been saying that Erasmus was willing to grant him the victory for his erudition if he would abandon his quarrel with More).[2] At the same time, Erasmus was testing virtually every other route—*via* Vives, Beraldus, Hermann, and Budé—which might bring the dispute to an end.[3] In this letter to Brixius, Erasmus did not choose to mention that he had already exchanged lengthy personal letters with More about Brixius' libel and about what More should do in response to it. Nonetheless, it is reasonably clear from Erasmus' own phrasing that by June 25 he had read at least one of More's letters.[4] When Erasmus asserts near the end of his letter that "as yet More has made no response" to the *Antimorus,* he must mean, as he does in his August 9 letter to Budé,[5] that as yet More has issued no *public* response: all of More's letters make it quite clear that the *Letter to Brixius* was printed and ready to issue. When Erasmus suggests in a letter to Budé, dated February 16, 1521, that Erasmus was first shown the *Letter to Brixius* at Calais the previous July, even after Budé had examined it,[6] it may or

---

[1]Allen, *4,* 253, lines 103–08.

[2]Allen, *4,* 292–95.

[3]See Allen, *4,* 292, 324, 326, 442–43. The letter of January 10, 1520, from Budé to Vives which Erasmus is talking about on the last pages cited shows that Vives worked hard to make sure that Budé would not slacken his efforts to pacify Brixius; see *Guilielmi Budaei opera omnia* (Basel, 1557; reprint, Farnborough, England, 1966), *1,* 327–30.

[4]The phrasing of Allen, *4,* 293, lines 40–41, and 294, lines 63–64, seems inspired by More's phrasing in Allen, *4,* 251, lines 7–9, and 253, line 94. Erasmus' contention in Allen, *4,* 294, lines 59–60, that not More but Brixius was first to offend ("Prouocauit te Morus, sed prouocatus") is a basic contention of the *Letter to Brixius* and the long letter More sent to Erasmus along with it; this contention does not figure at all in Erasmus' own earlier letter to Brixius (Allen, *3,* 41–43).

[5]Allen, *4,* 326, line 21. In line 3, Erasmus has already suggested that Brixius and More have *each* written a "virulent tract" on the other. Erasmus consistently speaks as though both these tracts minister to the same sort of vicious intemperance; see Allen, *4,* 293, lines 56–58; 324, lines 14–16; and 443, lines 20–25.

[6]Allen, *4,* 443.

may not be the case that Erasmus is telling the whole truth. It is certain at least that Erasmus tried hard to preserve diplomatic detachment and even to put it to use.

Budé, not Erasmus, eventually prevailed upon Brixius to give up his animosity toward More. In the latter part of January 1521, Brixius suddenly decided to abandon the quarrel. Budé congratulated him on January 28 for "as it were kindly retracting the *Antimorus*."[1] We can only conjecture what sort of retraction Budé's words imply or why Brixius made a retraction at all. Perhaps More's latest Brixius epigrams, included in the edition of December 1520, helped stir Brixius to make this decision; they undoubtedly made it quite clear that More's pen had lost none of its sting. More had apparently let Budé examine the *Letter to Brixius* while they were together at Calais in June 1520;[2] perhaps Budé described it to Brixius in a way that eroded his confidence still further. On January 10, 1521, Budé still thought Brixius to be quite intractable. In a letter which probably dates from the following September, Erasmus combined generous thanks to Budé with a long, mutually flattering comparison of More and that regal French humanist.[3] Though Erasmus at this point claimed none of the credit for ending the quarrel, his tireless appeals to men like Budé who were in a better position to win Brixius' ear doubtless helped to ensure their success.

Remarkably, many years later, when Erasmus' *Ciceronianus* (1528) had aroused the same sort of resentment in Budé and others that More's epigrams had prompted in Brixius, Erasmus enjoined Brixius to silence Budé as Erasmus had once silenced More:

> . . . when a bitter controversy had sprung up around Martin Dorp, and when Jerome Busleyden and Thomas More had written very

---

[1]"οἷον εἰ τὴν ἀντίμωρον ἐκείνην εὐγνωμόνως μεταθεμένῳ," *Budaei opera omnia, 1,* 414–15. In a 1527 letter to Erasmus (Allen, *7,* 58), Brixius still claims that More was the first to offend; this suggests that whatever retraction Brixius finally did make was a grudging one. For a neat summary of the sketchy reports about the end of the quarrel, see G. Lavoie, "La Fin de la querelle entre Germain de Brie et Thomas More," *Moreana, 50* (1976), 39–44.

[2]Allen, *4,* 443. Erasmus can scarcely be hinting that Budé saw the *Letter to Brixius* being publicly circulated in Paris, since the letter from Budé to Vives which prompted Erasmus' own letter suggests that the efforts of More's friends to forestall *any* public reaction on More's part have been wholly successful. For More's conference with Budé at Calais in June, see Rogers, nos. 96 and 97, and M.-M. de la Garanderie, "La Correspondance de Guillaume Budé et Thomas More," *Moreana, 19–20* (1968), 41–68. Brixius may be the slanderer whom More seeks to thwart by requesting Budé to delay publication of More's various letters addressed to him (Rogers, no. 96, lines 13–22).

[3]Allen, *4,* 575–80; for the reference to Budé's own role in concluding the quarrel see 580, lines 177–79.

> sharply against him, I laid the whole tumult to rest, diligently suppressing the tracts in which I was being both vindicated and praised. I did the same thing when the encounter between you and More seemed to be on the verge of implacable rancor; I suppressed all that More had written against you, even what had already been printed, and implored More in spite of his passion to defer in that matter to me. Was there no one among Budé's friends, then, who would stamp out the blaze as it started?[1]

Erasmus does not merely argue that Brixius owes him a favor; he argues that this sort of favor is a virtuous act in its own right. If it was virtuous to shield an opponent like Dorp from one's friends, runs the argument, it must also be virtuous to shield one friend from another. Erasmus was doing the virtuous thing when he shielded Brixius from More; Brixius too will be doing the virtuous thing when he shields Erasmus from Budé. In the first case he mentions, Erasmus himself was the first party injured and thus it was up to Erasmus alone to say who should forgive and forget. In the last case he mentions, Erasmus himself *gave* the injury; is it still up to him to say who should forgive and forget? Though Erasmus invited and at times even reveled in controversy, he was often too quick to treat all controversy as evil and all acquiescence as good when he could not take any firm stand on the issues at stake without losing some valuable personal ally in the opposite camp. More himself seems to hint that a man with as little forbearance as Erasmus displays in responding to Lee and Lefèvre d'Étaples can have no general license to preach rigid forbearance to others.[2] Erasmus repeatedly claimed for himself and for his favorite saint, Saint Jerome, the rare skill of discerning what kinds of ad hominem rebuke do befit a polemic of principle.[3] It is strange that he could not concede any of this skill to More.

Political Theory

More had fairly good cause to expect that Erasmus would sympathize with his reaction to Brixius' attack. Not only had Erasmus passed More's

---

[1]Allen, *9*, 35–36, lines 218–26.

[2]More immediately followed his letter to Erasmus on Brixius with a letter exhorting Erasmus to recall that, although Lee's libel lacks even that modesty "which lay writers [*idiotas*] would be ashamed to deny to each other," Erasmus' own innuendos may have given Lee good cause to express so much outrage (Allen, *4*, 234). For Lefèvre d'Étaples, see Allen, *4*, 228–29.

[3]See, p. 560, n. 2, above; for Saint Jerome, see the *Life of Jerome*, in *Erasmi Opuscula*, ed. W. K. Ferguson (The Hague, 1933), pp. 134, 174–75.

Brixius epigrams for publication; he also shared More's contempt for Brixius' mode of poetic invention.[1] Further, the political attitudes which Brixius attacked in More's poetry of praise coincided in many respects with the attitudes Erasmus aggressively strove to inculcate through his *Institutio principis christiani* of 1516. More himself may have wished to stress this concurrence: in defending his own "regal praises" More places a good deal of stress on occasionally paradoxical notions of statecraft which were similarly expressed by Erasmus.[2] Finally, More's individual retorts to the bellicose Brixius formed a stirring if modest manifesto for Erasmian pacifism not dissimilar to the one which emerged from the politic aphorisms of the *Institutio* itself. To the *vanus fulgor* of militaristic bombast More, like Erasmus, opposes the wholesome if humble lucidity of honest political accounting.

Another point of contact between More's letter and Erasmus' *Institutio* is More's witty likening of Brixius to Phaethon, the irresponsible incendiary par excellence whose own mythical sweep of destruction is windily imitated in Brixius' account of how one burning ship set the whole world ablaze. In a later allusion to the Phaethon myth More describes Brixius as "so head-over-heels in his blind rushing-on" that he unwittingly brands not only King Henry but also King Francis as hopelessly ignorant men.[3] The comparison between Brixius and Phaethon reveals more than a rationalist's suspicion of *furor poeticus*. As Erasmus affirms, Phaethon also betokens a wanton abuse of political influence: "The fable of Phaethon . . . is the image of a prince who is head-over-heels in the heat of his youth but is sustained with no wisdom; when he takes up the reins of the state, he subverts everything to his own and the whole world's misfortune."[4] The false praise of adulators like Brixius subverts the whole basis of praise in the rational good of the commonwealth generally. Although Brixius is not himself a prince, Brixius and others like him help to make a bad prince what he is. Erasmus' own stress on the critical importance of a good *institutor regis* makes it clear that the power of a bad one is equally critical. Like Empson and Dudley, the "serpents" of Henry VII's reign, Brixius has made his career at the public's expense as a "regal deceiver."

---

[1]See p. 564, n. 2.

[2]See the Commentary at 640/27–29, 644/6–7, 644/11–12, and 644/21–23, below. While Erasmus of course has no monopoly on such notions as these, their appearance in his *Institutio, ex professo* a practical compendium for instilling right values in rulers, makes these notions considerably more serviceable for More's purpose here than they are if construed as mere Stoic or Platonist school paradoxes.

[3]See 604/8–12, 646/9–12, below, and the Commentary.

[4]See *ASD 4/1*, 142/199–201.

It is clear that More largely miscalculated what Erasmus' reception of the *Letter to Brixius* would be. Compared with Erasmus, who scorned the very notion of "justified warfare" and felt that both treaties and marriage alliances were frivolous and treacherous substitutes for the implicit concord he sought in the "Christian republic," More took the part of a zealous political realist in endeavoring to vindicate Henry VIII's military and diplomatic morality when Brixius had shamelessly twisted the facts to impugn it.[1] More avoided suggesting that Henry's campaign in defense of the wretched Pope Julius II deserved ungrudging praise as a genuine crusade, but he did clearly feel that to make war on France in defense of the pope was a significantly more justifiable activity than to make war on the temporal domain of the pope and even seek to make off with his spiritual primacy in defense of French national pride.

From Erasmus' own ideal political perspective, the motives of both parties to the conflict of 1512–14 were ultimately indefensible. Julius II was himself a *foedifragus*, a betrayer of treaties with France, while King Louis of France was a ruthless imperialist.[2] Which party one backed was a matter of personal taste or convenience. Paradoxically, More's own political realism committed him all the more fervently to a personal ideal of consistent political engagement. For More it did make a real difference which system of statecraft, or for that matter which system of organized religion, was the best among all of the faulty but workable options, and More felt obliged to defend such a system devoutly. Erasmus' character made him disinclined to approve of so risky a campaign, much less to accept a main part in it.

More associated the problem of which workable system of statecraft is best with the problem of how and how far wisdom ought to court power. More's Hythloday in the *Utopia* suggests that the voice of reason will never be heard at the court unless it joins the chorus of flattering and unreasoning voices supporting whatever the monarch decrees; that is, it can be heard only by ceasing to be the voice of reason at all.[3] In an epigram probably written at about the same time as *Utopia* More arrives at an insight which shrewdly discredits Hythloday's own excuse for political aloofness: if from some people, somewhere, the voice of reason did

---

[1]See *ASD 4/1*, 206–19. The Utopians avoid and distrust treaties (*CW 4*, 196/14–198/28), but More presents treaties in the *Letter to Brixius* as the best warrants for peace men can hope for (606/15–19; 608/23–26; see also no. 184).

[2]For Julius II as *foedifragus*, see *Iulius Exclusus*, in *Erasmi Opuscula*, ed. W. K. Ferguson (The Hague, 1933), pp. 75–76; for Louis as an imperialist, see *ASD 4/1*, 208/282–84, 213/452–53.

[3]See *CW 4*, 86/13–98/8.

win an unquestioning hearing, there too it would cease to rely upon reason at all and instead would exert its authority by fiat, like any other ruling directive.[1] While More in the *Utopia* opposes to Hythloday's rational purism "another philosophy, more practical for statesmen, which knows its stage, adapts itself to the play in hand, and performs its role neatly and appropriately," in the *Letter to Brixius* More describes his own political vocation as "deferring and hearkening to reason alone, even if I saw that all the poets and all the masses saw things just the opposite way."[2] There is no room for rational purism in any real state, but within More's own *philosophia civilior* there may well be room for two quite different notions of how far wisdom can afford to compromise itself in the courtship of power. More's responses to Brixius afford a suggestive and rigorous defense of the notion that all narrowly timeserving humanists like Brixius defeat even their own short-range purposes.

Poetry, History, and Rhetoric

More's distrust of *furor poeticus* brings him to judge poetry according to the same set of standards he uses for rhetoric, a habit which may at first seem rather unfair to poetry. In his letter opposing the overwrought style of poetic invention, Erasmus displays the same habit:

> I take the greatest pleasure in rhetorical poems and in poetical rhetoric, such that one can sense poetry in the prose and the style of a good orator in the poetry. And whereas some other men prefer more exotic elements, my own special approval goes to your practice of depending for your effects on the subject matter itself and your concern for displaying the subject matter rather than your own cleverness.[3]

Since the first task of rhetoric is persuasion, a speaker who devotes less attention to expounding his subject persuasively than to showing off his inspiration and style may well seem to omit the essential. We may grant that this holds true for rhetoric while denying that it holds true for poetry, yet for some reason More and Erasmus seem to feel that one follows from the other.

More is certainly not just naive about poetic license or "poetic truth." In his *Letter to Dorp* (1515) he ironically affirms the traditional dismissal of

---

[1]See no. 198/28–31.

[2]See *CW 4*, 98/11–14, and 644/11–13, below.

[3]Allen, *1*, 545, lines 98–103 (*CWE* 2, 271, lines 116–21), written to Andrew Ammonius on the occasion of a historical poem honoring Henry VIII.

poets as liars and contrasts them with dialecticians, who never, of course, stray one inch from the truth: "Poets fabricate and lie; dialecticians never speak anything but the truth, even when they say this is most true, that a dead man can take part in Mass. . . ."[1] In the *Letter to Brixius* More begins with the Horatian precept that good poets mix truth with falsehood and goes on to assert that in Homer and Vergil this mixture leads us to accept what they narrate as at any rate substantially true.[2] Poets differ from orators in the degree to which the former are suffered to elaborate on unadorned truth, but in poetry, just as in oratory, any genre in which more attention is given to whimsical virtuosity than to painstaking persuasiveness lacks one crowning artistic essential. Brixius' worst offense, however, was not to write a poem which belongs to the display genre of poetry, but rather to claim even poetic truth for a poem of a sort which does not admit any truth at all.[3]

More and Erasmus were both very fond of declamation, the principal subgenre of display oratory, and had both had a good deal of practice in it by the time Brixius' *Chordigera,* essentially a verse declamation, ap-

---

[1]Rogers, no. 15, lines 418–21.

[2]See 600/18–20 and 614/13–26. Juan Luis Vives, like More, places various historical restrictions on poetic license in *Veritas fucata, sive de licentia poetica, quantum poetis liceat a veritate abscedere* (Louvain, T. Martens, 1522), reprinted in Vives' *Opera omnia,* ed. G. Majansius, 6 vols. (Valencia, 1745; repr. London, 1964), 2, 517–31. Among Vives' "conditions" for tolerable poetic license are the following prescriptions: although public opinion is given a plenary license to make up and remake the factual record however it pleases, the individual poet or maker should not fabricate a whole new set of facts like an impudent liar without even the sanction of common report; even though he is free to elaborate upon what is known of the very distant past, he should not contradict history or public consensus with regard to the major events (Vives thus upholds Vergil's account of Aeneas' encounter with Dido); he may adorn but not alter the historical record for the more recent past; he may intersperse falsehoods with truth if the falsehoods are fabulous borrowings from distant antiquity; and where his primary purpose is general moral instruction, as in the writing of fables, comedies, and dialogues, by a special concession he may fabricate plots without fear of reproach for mendacity (Vives, *Veritas fucata,* pp. 527–28). In his "eighth condition" (*Veritas fucata,* p. 529) Vives stresses the inevitable penalties for whoever transgresses these rules: "Si cum fucabitur *Veritas* non adsint negotio gerendo verisimile, constantia, et decorum, absona, inepta, ridicula, explodenda, exibilanda, rejicienda omnia, futurum." Vives' "conditions" are paraphrased and briefly discussed in William Nelson, *Fact or Fiction: The Dilemma of the Renaissance Storyteller* (Cambridge, Mass., 1973), pp. 45–48; even though he occasionally exaggerates the precision and thoroughness with which the rhetorical genres of fiction and history were finally distinguished in theory, at least, near the end of the Renaissance, Nelson generally confirms the close link between poetry and history in the period which I am discussing; see especially Nelson, pp. 2–7, 35–43, 106–08, 111–15.

[3]See 600/23–24, "mendacijs plusquam poeticis."

peared.[1] More and Erasmus knew the ground rules of declaiming, even if Brixius did not, and a number of More's criticisms of Brixius' excesses simply point out the things one cannot do in serious speeches but can do in declamations. Erasmus shows how important it is for one to distance himself from the views expressed in a declamation, when he defines a declamation as "a fabricated argument which is elaborated *pro* and *con* as a speaking exercise. . . . Whoever presents a declamation waives any claim to credibility ["ipse sibi fidem abrogat"], nor can he be challenged except on the score of ingenuity."[2] More, who knew that incredible (*adoxa*) theses often make for the best declamations, since those theses require great ingenuity in the declaimer to attain any credit at all,[3] also knew that a speaker who argued such theses in earnest would lose his own credit for good. Erasmus spells out a related objection to Cicero, "so zealously artful that he is closer to a declaimer than to an orator as he angles for the glory of artistry at the expense of his credit. . . ."[4] As More remarked once to Erasmus, Brixius seems to suppose that if he shows enough virtuosity as a declaimer he will never need to bother about telling the truth: "Where you and anyone else with a hold on the facts are concerned, [Brixius] thinks it sufficient if he achieves this sort of praise, 'If I did not know the case, I would think he was speaking the truth.' . . ."[5] In More's view, Brixius, like the senile Scholastics and Luther in their home preserve of theology, loves to play about with the most deadly-serious political topics, eroding the faith of the people in learned men's counsel in the same way the Scholastics and Luther erode

---

[1]See *CW 3/1*, xxxii–xxxvii, on More's Lucianic declamation in relation to his other works. Arthur F. Kinney, "Rhetoric as Poetic: Humanist Fiction in the Renaissance," *ELH, 43* (1976), 413–43, and *Rhetoric and Poetic in Thomas More's Utopia*, Humana Civilitas: Sources and Studies relating to the Middle Ages and the Renaissance 5 (Malibu, California, 1979), studies various formal connections between declamation and More's fictional dialogue. In the first study I think Kinney pays too little heed to the difference between declamation and serious oratory, which seeks not to circumvent truth but to ratify some reconstruction of probable facts where the truth is not certain. If the craft of persuasion is simply the craft of deception, "persuasive" and "truthful" are antonyms. For a judiciously appreciative response to these studies see E. McCutcheon's review in *Moreana, 69* (March 1981), 111–13.

[2]*Appendix de scriptis Iodoci Clithovei, Opera omnia 9,* 812 F–813 A, a terse summary of *Apologia pro declamatione matrimonii, Opera omnia 9,* 108 A–E.

[3]Allen *4,* 21, lines 251–52.

[4]*Ciceronianus, ASD 1/2,* 633/20–21. For the old theme of manifest artifice detracting from "credit" see also 618/34–619/4 and 625/28–32. H. Caplan gives much useful background information in his commentary on the pseudo-Ciceronian *Rhetorica ad Herennium* (Cambridge, Mass., 1954), p. 250, *ad* 4. 7. 10.

[5]Allen *4,* 219, ll. 79–81, citing Terence, *Phormio* 278.

faith in Christ.[1] More assails Brixius' dangerous breach of decorum in the same fervent way he assails the indecorous games of the false theologians. More's style here may be more uninhibited but his aims are substantially the same.

More's first epigram against Brixius (no. 188) asserts that he writes with ill credit ("mala . . . fide") of a deed well performed and so damns his own verses. He promises history in his poem, but as soon as a history is untrue it is no longer history. No one will believe histories as soon as they begin to indulge either hatred or partisanship. Not even Brixius' hero acquires any praise through his words, since he forfeits the credit of his subject matter ("rerum . . . fide").[2] Although Brixius mocks More for thoughtlessly confounding poetry and history in this epigram, it is clear that More knows what he is doing: although Brixius' own name associates him with the Germans, renowned for their truth and good credit,[3] and although the title of his poem refers its reader to a well-documented historical event against which Brixius' tale may be verified or discredited, even so Brixius plays the untruthful declaimer. Even in a historical argument, where the most impeccable credit is called for, Brixius flouts credibility to show off his wit and to gratify partisan sentiment.[4] But since history is written for careful review by posterity, Brixius has chosen the worst of all possible audiences for his partisan bombast. He defrauds his own hero of even that praise which is due to a popular legend.

Brixius' response made More consider more carefully the basis of *fides,* or credit, for all modes of writing. After all, Brixius' epic was clearly no typical history. In his long letter to Erasmus, More phrases in more general terms his objection to Brixius' lies: "In the first of my epigrams I clearly state that all writers will lose their credibility if they get in the habit, based on his example, of writing not according to what is credible but according to partisan sentiment. . . ."[5] In the *Letter to Brixius* More points out that poetry itself has nothing to gain by a general exemption from the claims of truthfulness: in poetry as well as in prose, credible

---

[1]See More's *Letter to Dorp,* Rogers, no. 15, lines 908–12; *CW 5,* 632/19.

[2]See no. 188. For a close antecedent in Cicero see p. 579, n. 2, below.

[3]For the proverbial meaning of *Germana fides* see references in Allen, *4,* 564, line 361n.

[4]Ovid's lines made the notion of *historica fides* proverbial; see *Amores* 3.12.41–42, "Exit in immensum fecunda licentia vatum. | Obligat historica nec sua verba fide." The basic idea was still older; see p. 579, n. 2, below. More makes an intriguing connection between *Utopia* and *historica fides* in *CW 4,* 250. D. R. Kelley develops a complementary perspective on *fides historiae* in his *Foundations of Modern Historical Scholarship: Language, Law, and History in the French Renaissance* (New York and London, 1970), pp. 22, 27, 65, 153, 174, and 177.

[5]Allen, *4,* 220, lines 135–38.

praise is worth more than incredible, so that the general exemption which Brixius demands would merely warn any recipient of poetic praise to seek better praise elsewhere.[1] As an experienced lawyer, More has great respect for the influence of precedents, good ones and bad. A fairly prestigious historical poem such as Brixius' *Chordigera,* all aglitter with antique rhetorical ornaments but empty of credible content, is a bad, irresponsible precedent for humanist political discourse, which needs to retain down-to-earth credibility if it is to help shape kings' policies and not just be shaped by them. More suggests that in some sense all serious genres of poetry and rhetoric are subject to the same rules that Cicero applies to legitimate history, a genre which is nothing if not a "monument for eternity": "it must dare no falsehood, and leave no truth undared; there must be no hint of partisanship in the writing, and no hint of malice."[2]

Judged according to Cicero's standards, More's own *History of Richard III,* casting Richard III as a portentous tyrant, may appear to fall short of impeccable *historica fides,*[3] a circumstance which ought to remind us that even in its most rigorous sense *historica fides* is not the same thing as the clinical objectivity for which many modern historians strive. For the humanists, history was a rhetorical genre depending on rhetorical proofs, and the difference between even the most scrupulous historian and the most unscrupulous controversialist came down to a difference of subjective and local priorities: the historian had everything to lose and nothing to gain by a shameless distortion of facts, whereas the controversialist might at least gain a short-lived strategic advantage.[4] More certainly had no reason to tell shameless lies about Richard III's motivation but, equally, he had no reason to suppress any personal animosity toward Richard III which he felt that the people's consensus was bound to corroborate. The respectful use Shakespeare and Jonson made of More's history long after the events it describes bears out More's own stylistic decisions as well as More personally could have wished.[5] On the

---

[1]See 616/1–6, below.

[2]On history as a "monument for eternity, not a prize-debate for here and now," see Thucydides 1.22.4 and Quintilian 10.1.31. For the passage from Cicero see *De oratore* 2.15.62.

[3]See *Richard III, CW* 2, Introduction, pp. lxv–lxx, lxxviii–lxxx.

[4]See N. S. Struever, *The Language of History in the Renaissance: Rhetoric and Historical Consciousness in Florentine Humanism* (Princeton, 1970). For More's sense of the difference between controversy and "faithful" analysis see *CW* 5, 804–10.

[5]Shakespeare's *History of Richard III* is largely based on More's own English version. Jonson cites More's history as a model of style fifteen times in his *English Grammar* (in *Ben Jonson,* ed. C. H. Herford and P. and E. Simpson, 11 vols. [Oxford, 1925–52], *8,* 531–53), and his portrait of a tyrant in *Sejanus His Fall* may be generally indebted to More.

model of a comment by Richard Sylvester, we might say that even as there is a good deal of history in More's concept of poetry so there is a good deal of poetry in More's concept of history.[1] We arrive at the truth about history by means of selecting and ratifying the most plausible myths.

For More as for Lorenzo Valla, this conception of rhetorical proof as a paradigm for all proof in the humanities at large was distinguished from whimsical subjectivism by the transcendent authority of *fides Christiana,* the essential consensus of Christian believers: "Truth does not exist, but rather that which is subjectively accepted as such, and our common belief ["la nostra fede collettiva"] is Christianity."[2] In his discussion of Lucian's *Philopseudes,* prefixed to his four Lucianic translations, More makes his own sense of the relation between *fides* and *fides Christiana* quite clear:

> I'm not much troubled by the fact that the author [sc. Lucian] seems to have been disposed to doubt his own immortality ["non satis immortalitati suae confideret"]. . . . For what difference does it make to me what a pagan thinks about those articles contained in the principal mysteries of the Christian faith ["in praecipuis . . . fidei Christianae mysteriis"]? Surely the dialogue will teach us this lesson: that we should put no trust in magic ["ut neque magicis habeamus praestigijs fidem"] and that we should eschew superstition. . . . I have often suspected that a large portion of such fables [sc. the fables in saints' lives] has been concocted by certain crafty, wicked wretches and heretics whose object was partly to

---

[1]Speaking of the relation between the *Letter to Brixius* and the *Letter to Dorp* ("Thomas More: Humanist in Action," pp. 467–68) Sylvester says, "One can begin to see that there is a great deal of 'poetry' in More's dialectic and an almost equal amount of 'dialectic' in his poetry."

[2]Charles Trinkaus, "Il pensiero antropologico-religioso nel rinascimento," in *Il rinascimento: Interpretazioni e problemi* (Bari, 1979), p. 140; my translation. Trinkaus is probably thinking of such statements as the one cited below on p. 581, n. 2, in which Valla begins by equating Christian *fides* with Christian *persuasio.* This and kindred statements are vindicated for Catholic orthodoxy by Mario Fois, S.J., *Il pensiero cristiano di Lorenzo Valla nel quadro storico-culturale del suo ambiente* (Rome, 1969), pp. 192, 589–94. For More's sympathetic recasting of Valla's rhetorical philosophy in the *Letter to Dorp* see my article "More's *Letter to Dorp:* Remapping the Trivium," in *Renaissance Quarterly, 34* (1981), 179–210. For More's concept of Christian consensus see further John Headley's introduction to the *Responsio ad Lutherum, CW 5,* 740–45, 756–74, and 811. For the meaning of Christian consensus to Erasmus and the humanists generally see J. K. McConica, "Erasmus and the Grammar of Consent," in *Scrinium Erasmianum,* ed. J. Coppens, 2 vols. (Leiden, 1969), 2, 77–99, and J. D. Tracy, *Erasmus: The Growth of a Mind* (Geneva, 1972), pp. 223–26 and notes.

> amuse themselves by the thoughtless credulity of the simple-minded . . . partly to undermine trust in the true stories of Christians ["fidem ueris Christianorum historijs adimere"] by traffic in mere fictions; since they often invent things so nearly resembling those in sacred scripture that they easily reveal that by playing upon those stories they have been ridiculing them. Therefore we ought to place unquestioning trust ["eis indubitata fides habenda est"] in the stories commended to us by divinely inspired scripture, but testing the others carefully and deliberately by the teaching of Christ (as though applying the rule of Critolaus), we should either accept or reject them if we wish to free ourselves both from foolish confidence ["inani fiducia"] and superstitious dread.[1]

According to More, in the Christian republic consensus both ratifies the formulations of any responsible writer and derives added strength from them. What protects this smooth traffic in truths is the teaching of Christ, though Christ's teaching itself warns the faithful that there will be times when this traffic in truths will be made difficult and perplexed as a test for the faithful. In a highly influential discussion, Valla points out the attractiveness of substituting the term *persuasio Christiana* for *fides Christiana,* "the Christian persuasion" for "the Christian faith."[2] In classical Latin, according to Valla, *fides* properly signifies "proof"; but the Christian religion is founded on something "more powerful than proof," on persuasion itself, through the working of which men and women not

---

[1]More's "Letter to Ruthall" in *CW 3/1,* 5–7. Appropriately, the rule of Critolaus (Cicero, *Tusculanae disputationes* 5. 17. 51) opposes spiritual goods to both external and bodily ones. Christian *fides* is the spirit which informs mundane *fides* and enables it to function veridically.

[2]Lorenzo Valla, *Elegantiae linguae latinae,* 5. 30, in his *Opera omnia* (Basel, 1540; reprinted as vol. I, Turin, 1962), sig. L6v: "Apud Quintilianum autem, caeterosque sui temporis dicitur persuasio, pro certa opinione, atque sententia quam nobis persuasimus, ut lib. I. Si qua publice est recepta persuasio. Quae (quantum ego quidem sentio) id significare uidetur, quod Christiani dicunt, fidem. Et si originem Graecam inquiramus, nescio an commodius dicamus persuasio, quam fides, praesertim re ipsa pro nobis faciente. Fides enim proprie Latine dicitur probatio, ut facio fidem per instrumenta, per argumenta, per testes. Religio autem Christiana non probatione nititur, sed persuasione, quae praestantior est, quam probatio. Nam saepe probationibus non adducimur: ut malus seruus, malus filius, mala filia, mala uxor, optimo consilio, quod confutare non potest, non tamen acquiescit. Qui persuasus est, plane acquiescit, nec ulteriorem probationem desiderat. Non enim solum sibi probatum putat, sed sese commotum ad ea exequenda intelligit. Sed quia fides etiam pro (ut sic dicam) credulitate accipitur, quale est, habeo tibi fidem, recte etiam nostra religio nominata est fides, sicut a Graecis πίστις."

only affirm Christian teaching "as proven" but devoutly go on to espouse it in practice as *persuasio* par excellence. In his opening remarks Valla counters the claims of *theologia disputatrix,* the "wrangling theology" which makes a profession of basing church teaching on rigorous proof. Once it serves its polemical purpose, however, Valla carefully qualifies his earlier suggestion that Christian devotion is merely a form of subjective rhetorical persuasion: "But since *fides* is also taken to mean belief ["credulitate"], so to speak, as in 'I believe you' ["habeo tibi fidem"], our religion is also rightly named *fides,* as it is named *pistis* by Greeks." The religion of Christians is founded not only on passive submission to persuasion but also on willed acts of faith. While Valla begins by opposing "I prove" (*fidem facio*) to "I persuade" and by describing the Christian religion as an expression of persuasion, not of proof, he ends by describing the Christian religion as an expression of an act which in classical Latin is strictly complementary to the act he calls proof: where you prove (*fidem facis*) I believe (*fidem habeo*).[1] For More and for Valla, the bounty of the Christian religion is such that it fosters and feeds belief even where no wholly rigorous proofs are forthcoming and so generally ratifies "proof" of the one sort rhetorical relativism admits. In classical Latin the very notion of a "faith" or a "creed," of a system of principles knowingly taken on faith, would have been well-nigh inconceivable. For most Evangelical humanists the unclassical term *fides Christiana* was itself a supremely rich testament.

More saw very early that the precious and versatile standard of Christian consensus was not an invulnerable legacy. More refers us to Lucian's satire against pagan retailers of portentous lies, the *Philopseudes,* as an appropriate antidote for the portentous lies of prevaricating Christian hagiographers, who injure the faith by abusing the credence of their hearers. To strain credibility with shameless impunity is to weaken the credit of all authors, both secular and Christian, since the maintenance of Christian consensus, or any other conceivable consensus, depends on the maintenance of enough critical sophistication to keep people from being seduced by pernicious new whimsies or even stultified by apparently harmless ones. The faith of the writer is put to the test every time that he puts pen to paper; he must write to the community as it is, but write for it as it is at its best, and must thus conscientiously risk pleasing neither completely. More's own earnest employment of Lucianic liberty in responding to those whom he saw as purveyors of impudent license, the stultifying Brixius and the seductive Luther among others, has antag-

[1]See R. Heinze, "Fides," *Hermes, 64* (1929), 141, based on Cicero, *De officiis* 2.33.ff., where *fides ut habeatur* and *ad fidem faciendam* are used interchangeably.

onized many from his day to ours.[1] His own preface to Lucian, composed long before either Brixius or Luther released his first work, is More's bill of good faith as a critic of divisive mendacity.[2]

One effect of More's stress on the relation of rhetorical *fides* and *fides Christiana* is to strengthen the connection already perceived by the classical rhetoricians between rhetorical *fides* and ethical *fides,* or commonplace good faith, the root meaning of *fides* itself. In the words of More's friend Vives,

> Two qualities in a counselor contribute especially much to his persuasiveness, an estimation for probity and an estimation for prudence. The second is a particularly powerful argument in counsels, whence that saying of Hecuba's to Ulysses, "Your authority is what will persuade them"; for the same things said by others would not have the same effect. But prudence separated from justice has no power at all to secure credence ["ad faciendam fidem"], as Plato declares, since it is reputed fraud and cunning. . . . A reputation for probity . . . is secured first by living and counseling honorably and piously, whence that old saw, "One's life is the surest persuader." . . .[3]

---

[1]The radical reformers were quick to attack More's polemical employment of Lucianic license or "poetry" on the score of irreverence and levity; see R. Pineas, *Thomas More and Tudor Polemics* (Bloomington, 1968), p. 27, and D. Duncan, *Ben Jonson and the Lucianic Tradition* (Cambridge, 1979), pp. 77–82. More's polemical earnestness, it goes without saying, proved to be a still greater liability among his contemporaries.

For some of the many points of contact between More's two long letters on Brixius and More's answer to Luther see the Commentary below and *CW* 5, 776–77. Perhaps the most telling is the similarity between More's opening charge in the *narratio* of the *Letter to Brixius* and the *Responsio*'s charge that the license which Luther usurps leaves each man free to "form a new faith at his whim"; see the Commentary at 600/18–20, below. In More's view, Brixius stands for a trend toward capricious grandiloquence which could generally discredit the techniques of humanist persuasion; Luther stands for a trend toward supplanting deliberate faith with the heady self-confidence (*fiducia*) of Luther's Elect which could generally subvert Christian consensus.

[2]Contrast Elton, "Thomas More, Councillor (1517–29)," pp. 110–19, who attributes More's ultimate vehemence as a polemicist to his frustration at not being included in any of his king's chief constructive political decisions.

[3]Ludovicus Vives, *De consultatione,* in his *Opera omnia in duos distincta tomos* (Basel, 1555), *1,* sig. o_1v, paraphrased by Ben Jonson near the beginning of his *Discoveries* in *Ben Jonson,* ed. C. H. Herford and P. and E. Simpson, 11 vols. (Oxford, 1925–52), *8,* 565–66; for Vives' Latin, see *Ben Jonson 11,* 215. More exploits the semantic connection between the three notions of *fides* in *CW 4,* 196/21–29, and Rogers, no. 83, lines 126–29. A comparison of the Latin and English versions of *The History of Richard III* reveals that *fides* is frequently translated as "trouth," the same virtue which figures so centrally in the poetry of More's contemporary Thomas Wyatt (*CW* 2, 23/5, 29/10, 40/20–21, 41/15; cf. 11/24, 41/7); sometimes *fides* is actively rendered as "trust" (42/5–6, 45/22, 31; cf. 29/10, 41/15); *fidem faceret* becomes "might show a proof" and *fideli relatione* "by credible information."

The collective good faith of responsible authors accredits rhetorical argument. The bad faith of licentious authors like Brixius will quickly discredit it. More characteristically sets out to prove that what holds true for licentious authors collectively holds true for them individually as well. Even separately plausible statements in their works discredit one another as these authors blithely belie themselves in every other line or on every other page.[1] Shameless rhetoric derives from a radically defective conception of what one person wishing to purchase the trust of another is bound to provide in exchange for it. Because Brixius, for instance, sees fit to forget either facts or his own sworn assertions, he thinks that by casting a spell, so to speak, he can render his audience equally oblivious.[2] Keenly scrutinized, such rhetoric will turn out to include enough casual and secondary self-contradictions, enough incidental expressions of reckless bad faith, to discredit the work even without reference to its suspect primary themes. When the critical faculties of the community are sound, no *vir malus* can pass for an orator.[3]

---

[1]On More's strategy of turning an opponent's own rhetorical weapons against him, "a favorite practice of More's," cf. Pineas, *Thomas More and Tudor Polemics*, pp. 21–22, and *CW 5*, 813. Notable instances in More's controversy with Brixius are More's two epigrams on the absurdity of chronicling Hervé's heroics when according to Brixius no one survived to attest them (nos. 188, 191) and his two epigrams on the absurdity of having Hervé fight with five weapons at once (nos. 189, 200). In the *Letter to Brixius* itself note More's treatment of Brixius' preface to the *Antimorus* and his unguarded swipes at King Henry (634/5–636/8, 646/9–19).

[2]Cf. Allen, *4*, 217, lines 2–4 (". . . Brixius . . . simulatque ipsi quicquam dissimulare libet, reliquos idem mortales omnes satis ⟨c⟩elatum putat") and 227, lines 423–24. For Brixius' lapses of memory see 602/13–17, 634/5–17, and 646/9–19, below.

[3]For the most influential defense of the notion that no morally flawed individual can be a great orator see Quintilian 12. 1. 1–23. By a striking coincidence, More, as Erasmus' close friend, is enlisted as a straw-man Erasmian spokesman for Quintilian's position in the virulent answer of Etienne Dolet to Erasmus' *Ciceronianus*, the *Erasmianus* (1535; see the facsimile reprint with commentary by E. V. Telle [Geneva, 1974], pp. 106–10). Dolet scoffs at the notion that ethical *fides* or probity is particularly useful even for orators, an attitude Telle finds refreshingly realistic and modern. Actually Dolet himself cannot bear too much reality; since he cannot refute, he dissembles the genuine point of the Erasmian passage he challenges (*ASD 1/2*, 618/34–619/4), where the stress is on how even a false reputation for probity requires less artificial and licentious rhetoric than we find in Cicero (cf. p. 577, n. 4, above). Dolet grants that a fop or a recognized cheat will be a less effective persuader than a reputed exemplar of good conduct; nonetheless he, like Brixius, wishfully conceives of the province of rhetoric as one in which simply by casting his spell on his audience a speaker can fashion himself a new reputation at will. Dolet can and does claim history leaves him no choice but to solace himself with this make–believe rhetoric, but the same claim was ready at hand for the declaimers of decadent Rome and is thus not distinctively modern. In despair of reopening the forum of the global "republic of learning" which was closed by the radical reformers, Dolet retreats to the declaimer's academy.

More castigates Brixius' extravagant style in much the same way that he castigates his extravagant content. Although Brixius himself may believe that his style can make falsehoods more vivid and convincing than truths, More acutely contends that his addiction to falsehoods perforce renders Brixius' style flat and lifeless. More may well be indebted to Gianfrancesco Pico della Mirandola, a principal opponent of servile literary imitation, for the principles that there can be no apt expression (*elocutio*) where there is no apt development of arguments (*dispositio*) and that there can be no apt development of arguments where there is no apt and historically self-conscious selection of arguments (*inventio*).[1] More's own stress on *historica fides* at any rate brings him to refine and elaborate upon these two principles until they serve to explain the whole progress of Brixius' stylistic bad faith.

Pico argues that the concerns of each later age differ substantially enough from the concerns of Cicero and his contemporaries that it would be pointless to try to exploit in a speech of today the same arguments that Cicero exploited. It would be even more pointless to try to develop arguments different from Cicero's in just the same way Cicero developed his own, and more pointless still to try to express these new arguments in exactly the same phrases that Cicero used for expressing his arguments. Although we must not slight Cicero's achievement, its usefulness for our age resides in the instructive contrast it yields for what we ourselves are uniquely equipped to achieve. Our achievement at best will incorporate our sense of this contrast and by way of this highly judicious assimilation will owe much of value to Cicero. If, on the other hand, we promiscuously appropriate phrases from Cicero or any other classical author, we can do justice neither to him nor to ourselves; we will merely be housing a stunted and immature modern mentality in the ravaged remains of antiquity. Cicero comes back to life more substantially in the mind's eye of those who have gained enough insight to place him in his proper historical surroundings than he does in the posturing of those who burlesque him in modern surroundings.[2]

---

[1]See *Le epistole "De imitatione" di Gianfrancesco Pico della Mirandola e di Pietro Bembo,* ed. G. Santangelo (Florence, 1954), pp. 32–34, and cf. especially 610/16–19, below. These letters were first printed by Froben in 1518.

[2]Gianfrancesco Pico, "De imitatione," in *Le epistole "De imitatione,"* pp. 71–73. On the expression of the humanists' sense of historical disjunction in their imitation of classical authors see esp. Thomas M. Greene, "Petrarch and the Humanist Hermeneutic," in *Italian Literature: Roots and Branches,* ed. G. Rimanelli and K. Atchity (New Haven and London, 1976), pp. 201–24. Also interesting and often acute are the articles of G. W. Pigman III, "Imitation and the Renaissance Sense of the Past: The Reception of Erasmus' *Ciceronianus,*" *Journal of Medieval and Renaissance Studies,* 9 (1979), 155–77, and "Versions of

At this point More's sarcastic arraignment of irresponsible hagiographers comes readily to mind: ". . . they often invent things so nearly resembling those in sacred scripture that they easily reveal that by playing upon those stories they have been ridiculing them ["adludendo lusisse"]."[1] Secular imitation also has its decadence, and More's preface to Lucian suggests that the threat which it poses to *fides* in general may differ not in kind, but merely in degree, from the threat posed by hagiographical decadence. Personal bad faith leads some authors to think that a specious invention will always have far more effect than a true one, even though the main task of invention is to discover which arguments bearing on this or that theme actually merit more credit than others.[2] Rather than looking to the truth or the spirit of the texts they have chosen as models, such authors go on to plunder the development and the phrasing of these texts for anything they think may make their inventions still more specious. The result, as More says about Brixius' poems, is an inky vacuity studded with alien rhetorical gems which do not at all brighten it, a mindless conceit dressed in sweet-sounding trifles which utterly fail to disguise it, a tissue of stolen fineries drawn together like scars to seal in an abysmal stupidity, or what must once have been a most handsome hero, now metamorphosed through the wrath of some god into a ridiculous monkey.[3] The last half of More's epigram on Brixius' plagiarism, no. 192, plays upon a conceit drawn from Pliny of "making old new" through the working of art: it suggests that whoever makes newness of oldness as Brixius does will by no stretch of art ever make his own new works survive to grow old. In art as in nature, preposterous hybrids die young.

More's critique of Brixius' predatory and historically myopic imitation is complemented by Hythloday's account of imitation in *Utopia:*

> . . . just as they [sc. the Utopians] immediately at one meeting assimilated ["fecerunt suum"] every good discovery of ours, so I suppose it will be long before we adopt anything that is better arranged with them than with us. This trait, I judge, is the chief reason why, though we are inferior to them neither in brains nor in resources,

---

Imitation in the Renaissance," *Renaissance Quarterly*, *33* (1980), 1–32. R. S. Sylvester and John Headley have a number of helpful remarks on More's theory and practice of imitation in *CW* 2, lxxx–civ, and *CW* *5*, 814–21.

[1] *CW* *3/1*, 7.

[2] Cicero, *Partitiones oratoriae* 2.5.

[3] See no. 193/1–14; 622/14–15, below; Allen, *4*, 219, lines 94–101; and 612/20–614/2 below.

> their commonwealth is more wisely governed and more happily flourishing than ours.[1]

The last sentence precludes the suggestion that the Utopians are merely superior learners by nature and brings us to ask what makes their imitation bear more fruit more quickly than ours. This passage appears shortly after Hythloday's defense of Utopian communism and purports to afford a concrete refutation for the claim of the interlocutor More that where the motive of personal gain is abolished everyone will grow slothful through trust in the industriousness of others ("alienae industriae fiducia").[2] Hythloday rejoins that the industriousness of the Utopians is far greater than ours and adduces as proof what they managed to learn from one castaway crew of imperial Romans and from Hythloday's own crew. The Utopians' industriousness amounts to an unprejudiced common delight in the practical application of truth. It is surely no accident that they who have no private possessions are said to be able to make all our useful inventions "their own" in a single encounter. An ideal consensus sustained by a perfect community of material interests is a basic presupposition of the Utopian commonwealth. This consensus enables the Utopians to penetrate directly to whatever is worth imitating in the alien culture of Europe. For all their industriousness they have no gift at all for the art of dialectical self-aggrandizement which is practiced by Europe's scholastics.[3] Hythloday's spurious "proof" leaves unsettled the question whether an absolute community of material interests enhances or hampers industriousness, but the emphasis which Hythloday places on the relation between true community of intellectual interests and the capacity for historically and locally self-aware imitation has resonances beyond the trite primary question at issue. In the *Letter to Brixius* More himself carefully points to a similar cultural commerce between public-spirited *fides* and a true "antique style" in his homage to Paulus Aemilius:

> . . . meanwhile [even as we bear with such calumnies as Brixius' *Chordigera*] we cherish the hope that at some point no less a historian than Paulus Emilius, so strict and impartial in shaping his narrative that one might suppose he was bound by an oath and so elegant that

---

[1]*CW 4*, 108/13–19. I have changed the translation of "fecerunt suum" from "appropriated" to "assimilated" on the basis of Seneca's discussion of imitation in *Epistles* 84.7, where he opposes merely taking over or appropriating what some other has invented to "digesting" or "making it ours." See the Commentary at 612/16–17, below.

[2]*CW 4*, 106/7.

[3]*CW 4*, 158/22–29.

> if he did not write of more recent events he would seem not the humblest of ancients, will report for posterity the deeds of both peoples, at least those in which both had a part, with an unalloyed credibility ["syncera fide"].[1]

Even cultural advance based on learning from alien cultures must be mediated by consensus and *fides*.

More's own phrasing in the *Letter to Brixius* is a rich and complex tapestry of original rhetorical ornament and borrowings which are, for the most part, very well assimilated indeed. His proverbs and apothegms generally serve either to give a satirical twist to the discourse, to align More's position with the dictates of plain common sense, or to counter one appeal to strictly literary authority with another more pointed one. More's most extended borrowing, from Lucian's essay *Quomodo historia conscribenda sit,* is not so much incorporated into More's catalogue of Brixius' stylistic atrocities as formally superimposed on it. Two absurdly long sentences, one which comprises More's borrowing from Lucian and another, at the end of the tract, which does for the *Antimorus* what the first sentence did for the *Chordigera,* drive home the suggestion that Brixius' stylistic absurdities are too numerous to keep track of.[2] At one point More builds an entire passage from the *Antimorus* into his own running commentary as a kind of poetic sampler; since this one passage amply establishes the incoherence of Brixius' thinking, More then feels entitled to abstain from long quotations in the rest of the pamphlet and so gives the whole work a racy vitality not present in some of More's later polemical responses.[3] His phrasing grows remarkably stilted in passages dealing with Henry VIII. The contrast between how More treats the same subjects in this text and in his jubilant coronation ode (no. 19) is

---

[1]620/2–7, below.

[2]See 600/18–604/27 and 654/24–656/29, below. Compare the effect of Hythloday's marathon sentences insisting on the numberless perils and pitfalls awaiting the good man if he enters politics, *CW 4,* 86/22–90/22, 90/22–96/31.

[3]634/5–636/8, below. On the dreary polemical procedure of answering one's opponent almost line by line in an effort to be wholly fair to his own chosen wording see *CW 5,* 804–10. More's projected edition with commentaries of all the main texts in his quarrel with Brixius would probably have resembled the *Responsio ad Lutherum* much more than either of More's surviving letters on Brixius does. It is thus rather striking that More never returned to the polemical scheme he intended to use against Brixius, first composing one or more racy and brief retorts and then providing a somewhat more tediously thorough rebuttal of his opponent's claims, line by line, in the manner of the *Responsio ad Lutherum,* to be used as we use scholarly footnotes.

both clear and disturbing. Already, it seems, More is bracing himself for the tempests of Henry's maturity.

The Influence of the *Letter to Brixius*

We would not ordinarily expect that any work which was as energetically suppressed as the *Letter to Brixius* was would exert any literary influence at all. Even though both Budé and Erasmus examined the work, the atmosphere in which they did so was none too conducive to leisurely and dispassionate consideration of More's central argument. On the other hand we have More's assurance that many of his friends in England, including a number whose literary judgment he valued considerably more than his own, had both read and approved of the work; some of these even felt that More answered Brixius' aspersions more courteously than they deserved.[1] In the ferocity of its invective, the *Letter to Brixius* is quite without parallel in More's work before 1520; had this letter not been written and read, More would probably not have been chosen to write the invective *Responsio* to Luther's attack on King Henry. In the *Responsio* More borrows extensively enough from this letter and its long companion addressed to Erasmus to make it quite clear that in 1523 More still found his retorts against Brixius' divisive mendacity well suited for such a headstrong adversary as Luther.

There is some reason to believe that More's acute exploration of rhetorical *fides* and all it entails in his various rebuttals of Brixius helped to shape the main argument of Erasmus' *Ciceronianus* (1528). One of Erasmus' most damaging objections to the affected imitation of Cicero is that this affectation detracts as much from the *fides* of a speaker as any more vulgar affectation, such as the licentious employment of metaphors.[2] In

---

[1]See Allen, *4*, 230, lines 527, 550–52; 252, lines 52–54; 253, lines 104–09.

[2]See *ASD 1/2*, 618/34–619/4, 625/28–32, and 633/20–21. G. W. Pigman III, "Imitation and the Renaissance Sense of the Past," pp. 155–79, attributes the furor stirred up by the *Ciceronianus* largely to the fact that most humanists were not ready to recognize the new rhetorical exigencies implied by historical disjunction as acutely as Erasmus himself did. Pico's letter stirred up no such furor despite his insistence that speech apt for our day could not be the same as the speech apt for Cicero's day. Dolet's case (see p. 584, n. 3, above) might suggest that the last straw for Cicero's admirers was Erasmus' quite plausible contention that what might have been credible expressions on Cicero's lips can by no means be credible on ours: our historical bad faith in posturing as Cicero bereaves even our expressions of *fides*. More is first to lay on this last straw in the *Letter to Brixius* (610/18–19): "omnia denique sic abs te narrata [sunt] / ut neque in rebus ueritas esset / neque in uerbis fides."

an argument verbally reminiscent of More's first Brixius epigram and his preface to Lucian, which Erasmus indeed seems to have imitated once elsewhere, Erasmus suggests that a history which lacks *fides* does not even merit the name history and then claims that the *fides* of scriptural histories transcends that of all other historical narratives.[1] The implicit conclusion, that it is the living consensus of our Christian age which determines how much *fides* we may accord to any rhetoric formed upon pagan antiquity, is not far from the conclusion that More himself reaches in studying Brixius as imitator. There is no reason why Erasmus could not have returned to the *Letter to Brixius* in the years following the quarrel itself and learned whatever More's text could teach him.

A Note on the Text

Whatever its stylistic merits, More's *Letter to Brixius* is by no means a carefully finished composition. More, who mocks Brixius for spending so long on the *Antimorus,* also stresses how little time he himself saw fit to give to his own formal counterblast:

> As for my hastening to print what I wrote, which it might have been more circumspect to have polished at leisure, particularly when it was going to be set before such a keen-eyed opponent, who sees a fault even where there is none, I have chosen to leave him many bones on which he can exercise, weary, or even shatter his teeth rather than let trifles like these occupy my attention for long.[2]

Thus we might well expect some anomalies of syntax, and there are in fact one or two. Where a puzzling or abnormal phrase is probably More's, it is retained.

More important from a textual standpoint, the letter is carelessly printed. In the 1520 edition, on which every other edition is based either directly or indirectly,[3] spelling variants repeatedly perplex the whole

---

[1] *ASD 1/2,* 645/2–646/16. Erasmus' "historia, si fidem detrahas, ne nomen quidem historiae meretur," is very close to the wording of More's no. 187/6–7. Craig R. Thompson (*CW 3/1,* 140) notes the resemblance between the introduction to Erasmus' *Life of Jerome* (1516) and More's preface to Lucian's *Philopseudes;* cf. *Erasmi Opuscula,* pp. 134–36, and *CW 3/1,* 5–7.

[2] Allen, *4,* 230, lines 528–33; for More's mockery of Brixius' drawn-out literary gestation, see 634/17–636/4. More's own *sprezzatura* contrasts with the stress on slow painstaking diligence he admires in historians like Paulus Aemilius (618/31–620/7); the right method of "hastening slowly" in one sort of writing may not be the right method in another. See also the Commentary at 628/2–3, below.

[3] The editor of *1947* states that she has used *1520* as her copy text. The editor of *1760*

sense: adverbs supplant adjectives; ablative plurals trade places with nominative singulars; in one instance, the conjunction *velut* supplants the verb *velit*. Further, the 1520 edition is very heavily and capriciously punctuated in a way which obscures both the sense and the style. Such errors have been emended, but the reading of *1520* is always given in the variants. I have chosen not to substitute commas for virgules even though virgules may strike us as strange or distracting, since the autograph text of More's Latin *De tristitia Christi* appears to use virgules almost exclusively.[1]

In Rogers's 1947 edition of this letter a significant number of readings are attributed to the 1520 text which do not actually seem to be present there.[2] Neither our copy text in the British Library nor the five other copies of the 1520 edition which I have examined provide any authority at all for these questionable readings.[3] I observed only one interesting peculiarity in any of these copies: in the copy belonging to King's College, Cambridge, the sequence of leaves at the end of the volume is f_1, [f_5], f_3, [f_4], f_2, and [f_6]. This gathering consists of three pairs of conjugate leaves; the middle pair, which would normally have the text of f_2 *verso* on the lefthand side and f_5 *recto* on the righthand side of its upper surface when the gathering lies open, has been turned over at some point, so that now when the gathering lies open the text of f_5 *verso* is

---

states that he has used *1642*. There are three points at which both *1642* and *1689* have a singular verb form where a plural is required or vice versa (598/10, 602/19, 618/1); this suggests that the unknown editor of *1689* also used *1642* as his copy text. Both *1689* and *1760* present a number of intelligent conjectural emendations; when these merely concur with the reading of *1520* I normally do not record them. There are three points at which *1642* reproduces a distinctive typographical flaw in *1520* (606/19, 630/3, 632/22); this suggests that the editor of *1642* used *1520* and not some lost manuscript as his copy-text.

[1]The autograph manuscript of the *De tristitia* is reproduced in *CW 14*.

[2]Rogers attributes to *1520* "Quam" for "Quod" (598/21 and 612/25); "cliperum" for "clipeum" (614/6); "deter" for "detur" (614/10); "totum" for "totam" (614/12); "adseruatam" for "adseruatum" (618/30); "obstupefacit" for "obstupefecit" (628/1); "comitiis" for "commitijs" (644/29–30); "quod" for "quid" (650/2); "Charitates" for "charites" (652/20); and "obprobiis" for "obprobrijs" (654/29).

[3]According to More himself (Allen, *4*, 253, lines 117–21), in compliance with Erasmus' entreaties he personally bought up and put into safekeeping all but seven copies of this edition; he had already sent one apiece to Erasmus and Giles, and the printer had already sold five. There are in fact at least eight extant copies of the *1520* edition. Cambridge University Library and Trinity College, Cambridge, each own two copies; the British Library, King's College (Cambridge), Caius College (Cambridge), and the Folger Shakespeare Library each own one. I have collated the British Library copy with the copy in the Folger Shakespeare Library and have used the four copies in Trinity College, King's College, and Caius College for quick spot-collations. For a bibliographical description of the 1520 *Letter to Brixius* see Gibson, no. 60.

uppermost on the left and the text of f_2 *recto* uppermost on the right. Very probably this half-sheet was turned over by mistake in the course of rebinding.

To summarize my procedure in handling More's text, I have preserved the eccentricities of the spelling and capitalization in *1520* except when they cause a serious ambiguity or an outright confusion of sense; in these cases a clear reading is placed in the text and the reading of *1520* is given in the variants. The variants record all significant verbal departures from *1520*, but normally where I have retained the *1520* reading in this edition I do not list the texts which retain the same reading: unless I attribute a different reading to a given text in the variants, that text gives the same reading that I do. Departures from the punctuation in *1520* require a less detailed report; here the text and variants give a complete record only of the punctuation in *1520* itself. All abbreviations except in the salutation have been silently expanded and double quotation marks have been inserted to set off all extended citations. Sidenotes have been italicized and indented at the appropriate place within the text itself; terminal periods in the sidenotes have been silently dropped. In the copy text paragraphs are marked only by blank spaces at the end of the preceding lines; here they are indicated by indentation.

The following sigla have been adopted in the textual apparatus:

1520 London, Pynson, 1520 (Gibson, no. 60)
1642 in *Erasmi epistolae*, London, Flesher and Young, 1642 (Gibson, no. 147)
1689 in *T. Mori Opera omnia*, Frankfurt, Gensch, 1689 (Gibson, no. 77)
1760 in J. Jortin, *Life of Erasmus,* 2 vols., London, Whiston and White, 1758–60[1]
1947 in E. F. Rogers, ed., *The Correspondence of Sir Thomas More,* Princeton, Princeton University Press, 1947

[1]There is a second edition of Jortin's *Life of Erasmus,* 3 vols. (London, J. White, 1808), which simply reprints the text of the *Letter to Brixius* from Jortin's first edition.

THOMAE MORI Epistola ad Germanum Brixium:
qui quum MORVS in libellum eius /
quo contumeliosis mendacijs incesserat ANGLIAM:
lusisset aliquot epigrammata annis ab hinc plus septem:
iam intra sesquimensem /
in summa Anglorum Gallorumque concordia /
sub ipsum conuentum principum /
aedidit aduersus MORVM libellum /
qui et ineptis et uirulentis iurgijs
suum infamat authorem.

Apud inclytam Londini urbem
.M. D. XX.

A letter of Thomas More to Germanus Brixius,
who once attacked England with shameful lies
in a tract which More made fun of in some epigrams
more than seven years ago,
and who now, not a month and a half ago,
in a time of the most perfect peace
between England and France,
on the very eve of the meeting between their princes,
published a tract against More
which defames its own author
with its pointless and virulent rebukes.

In the renowned city of London
1520.

T. MORVS GERMANO BRIXIO. S.

NON ADEO TENERE MIHIMET Brixi faueo / ut quod nemini unquam contigit mortalium / id dedigner ac doleam non contigisse mihi. Quis enim ullo unquam saeculo tam inoffense transegit uitam / ut ei nullus aliquando inimicus exoriretur / quum haberet amicos? Quamobrem quando illud mihi uideo communi mortalitatis sorte negatum / ut penitus inimico caream: gaudeo saltem fortunae beneficio / amicos mihi perquam egregios / inimicum uero contigisse talem / quem neque amicum quisquam uelit / neque inimicum curet / ut qui neque iuuare beneuolens / neque nocere possit iratus. Et tamen mihi certe succenserem / si uel talis merito me odisses meo. Nunc uero eo aequiore animo fero / quod non dubito quin omnibus inclarescat facile / ineptum istud ac plusquam muliebre iurgium non aliunde quam ex animi tui morbo natum. Quin eo quoque minus mihi displicet hoc certamen / quod ut nihil inde boni potest accidere / ita preter chartae iacturam et temporis / quorum ego neutrum statui multum perdere / nihil alioqui queat alterutri nostrum magni euenire mali: quando tales vterque sumus / ut neque mihi quicquam tu nocere [a$_2$v] possis neque tibi quisquam: quum sis eiusmodi / in quo nihil fieri detrimenti queat.

Qua una fidutia te impulsum uideo / ut quaqua uersus apud literatos omnes (si qui tamen tam nugaces nugas dignabuntur legere) libello illo tam elegante / tam egregio indolis tuae specimine / morumque tuorum tam graui teste temet ipse traduceres / ut qui ante satis docuisses / cuiusmodi poeta sis / nunc demum aedito in id libello / qualis etiam vir sies ostenderes. Ostendisti uero tam insigniter / ac temet ita depinxisti graphice / ut ego tot tantaque in te probra spargere / quam quibus tute temet totum

2 faueo /] faueo: *1520* 4 inoffense] in offense *1520* 5 uitam /] uitam: *1520;* exoriretur] exorietur *1642 1760* 7 negatum /] negatum: *1520* 9 talem /] talem: *1520* 10 uelit /] uelit: *1520;* curet/] curet. *1520* 11 succenserem/] succenserem: *1520* 13 fero /] fero: *1520* 14 iurgium] iurgium: *1520* 15–16 certamen /] certamen: *1520* 17 temporis /] temporis: *1520* 17–18 perdere /] perdere: *1520* 18 queat] queat / *1520* 19 sumus /] sumus: *1520* 20 eiusmodi /] eiusmodi: *1520* 22 Qua] *No para. 1520;* uideo /] uideo: *1520* 25–26 traduceres /] traduceres. *1520* 26 sis /] sis: *1520* 28 insigniter /] insigniter: *1520;* graphice /] graphice: *1520*

T. MORE TO GERMANUS BRIXIUS, GREETINGS

I MYSELF, Brixius, am not so fastidious or so self-indulgent as to be vexed or hurt because I have not been granted a thing which has never been granted to anyone among mortal men. For who has ever, in any age, lived out his days so untroubled that he not only had friends but never encountered an enemy? Therefore, since I see that the blessing of having no enemy at all is denied me by the common lot of mortals, I am happy, at least, that through fortune's beneficence I have been granted the best sort of friends and an enemy such that no one would want him as a friend or be troubled by him as an enemy, a man who is equally unable to gratify when he means well and to injure when he is irate. And yet I would certainly be angry with myself if I had given even such a person as you cause to hate me. As it is, I bear it with all the more equanimity since I am quite sure no one fails to perceive that this pointless and worse-than-effeminate quarreling of yours has no source but your own morbid feelings. Indeed, I am also less vexed by this strife since, though no good can come of it, I also see that apart from a loss of paper and time (and I choose to waste little of either) no great ill otherwise can befall either one of us. Each of us, in his way, is immune; you can not injure me, nor can anyone injure you, since your sort leaves no room for disparagement.

I see that your confidence in this fact alone has driven you to embrace the expedient of traducing yourself, far and wide, before all learned people (if any, that is, will see fit to read trifles so trifling as these) with so elegant and splendid a specimen of your natural gifts and so sober a testimony to your moral soundness as that latest tract of yours furnishes. Having already established quite clearly just what sort of poet you are, now no doubt you intend to show by publishing this tract what kind of man you are. Indeed you have shown it so distinctively and have portrayed yourself so graphically that I neither would, if I could, nor could, if I would, spatter you with so many and such grievous slanders as

oblinis / neque si uelim / queam / neque si queam / uelim. Et tamen ut eiusmodi laudibus te gestire doces / ea uideatur una atque unica uia placandi propitiandique tui / si quis in te foedis uelit probris debacchari. Verum ego non usque adeo tuam amicitiam ambio / ut non ea potius mihi dicta cupiam / quae uel uni placeant bono atque honesto uiro / quam quae trecentis Brixijs: eoque praeclaram illam ac diuitem probrorum tuorum suppellectilem / qua te sic ostentas ac iactitas / haud contrectabo: neque / quoad abstinere licebit / attingam: tantum si quid in ea fuerit iucundioris insaniae / quod qui perpenderint ridere possint / odisse non debeant / eo non grauabor lectoris leuare fastidium: quod [a3] necesse est multum subeat in legendis eiusmodi rixis ac nihil unquam profuturis iurgijs. Caetera uero / quibus te conspurcas foedius / aut prorsus ualere sinam / aut sicubi cogar attingere / sic attingam leuiter / ut omnibus faciam perspicuum / non minus libenter me tua probra contegere / quam tute Brixi detegas ac uelut insigne prae te feras. Nam quae uitio uertis mihi tam insulsae sunt calumniae / ut non fuissem dignatus rescribere / si non hoc unum dumtaxat diluere uisum esset / quod tu tam frequenter inculcas / quam nunquam probas / huius tui iurgij authorem esse me.

At istud non dicere Brixi / uerum docere debueras. Quod si eam rem satis declarare uidebantur epigrammata mea / ea saltem abs te tuo libello conueniebat adscribi: ne uel illis uidereris impudens / quibus meum carmen non esset in manibus. Et fecisses haud dubie / nisi sensisses e re non esse tua / meos uersus legi. Qui si cominus conferantur tuis / etiamsi cui uideantur alij / quod uidentur tibi / tuorum scilicet splendorem carminum reueerituri / hactenus tamen aduersariorum luce fruerentur / ut res redderetur illustris / et ipsos magis obiurgatos esse / quam uictos / et

1 oblinis /] oblinis: *1520;* queam / neque] queam: neque *1520* 2 doces /] doces: *1520* 5 ambio /] ambio: *1520;* cupiam /] cupiam: *1520* 7 diuitem] diuitem: *1520;* suppellectilem /] suppellectilem: *1520* 8 neque /] neque *1520* 9 attingam:] attingam. *1520* 10 insaniae /] insaniae: *1520;* perpenderint] perpenderit *1642 1689 1760;* possint] possit *1689;* possint /] possint: *1520* 10–11 debeant] debeat *1689;* debeant /] debeant: *1520* 13 uero /] uero: *1520;* conspurcas] couspurcas *1642* 14 sinam /] sinam: *1520;* attingere /] attingere: *1520* 16 detegas] detegas: *1520* 17 mihi] mihi: *1520* 17–18 calumniae /] calumniae: *1520* 19 esset /] esset: *1520* 20 probas /] probas: *1520* 21 At] *No para. 1520;* Brixi /] Brixi: *1520;* Quod] Quam *1642 1760* 23–24 impudens /] impudens: *1520* 26 tuis /] tuis: *1520* 27 reueerituri /] reueerituri: *1520* 28 fruerentur /] fruerentur: *1520* 29 illustris /] illustris: *1520;* uictos /] uictos: *1520*

you plaster all over yourself. And yet you display so much eagerness for that sort of praise, it would seem that the one and only way to placate and propitiate you is to savage you with disgraceful slanders. But I am not so ambitious for your amity that I would not rather speak words which may please even one good and honorable man than words which may please three hundred Brixiuses, and therefore I shall not take in hand that illustrious and rich stock of insults in which you take such vaunting and boastful delight; nor, so far as I can stay away from it, will I touch on it at all. Only if there is some slight admixture of amusing insanity which thoughtful observers may laugh at, and need not detest, will I not hesitate to use it to alleviate my reader's disgust, of which he must endure a great deal as he reads through such quarrelsome and utterly fruitless rebukes. But the other slanders with which you pollute yourself more disgracefully I shall either avoid altogether or else, where I am forced to touch on them, I shall touch on them so lightly as to make it clear to everyone that I am no less eager to conceal your slanders, Brixius, than you are to reveal them and wear them about you like a badge of distinction. For the charges which you lay against me are such insipid calumnies that I would not have seen fit to reply if I had not decided to wash away this single charge, which you constantly harp on, but never establish, that I started this quarrel of yours.

But you should have confirmed that, Brixius, and not just affirmed it. And if you thought that my epigrams sufficed to demonstrate that claim, you ought at least to have included them in your tract, so that you would not have appeared impudent even to those who had no access to my poems. And undoubtedly you would have done so if you had not perceived it was not in your interest that my lines be read. For if they are compared closely with yours (even if anyone else thinks, as you do, that my lines should be quite overcome by the splendor of your verses), mine would still benefit to this extent from the luster of their rivals, that the main issue would be made quite clear: my lines have been rather reviled than refuted, and they do not give you an adequate

tibi non satis commodam ansam nunc demum debacchandi rursus arreptam. Quae res / quo fiat dilucidior / quando te libenter obliuisci uideo / prae[a_3v]clari istius duelli caput tibi redigam in memoriam. Sed ita redigam / ut potius omittam quaedam / quae ad rem meam faciant / quam ut ob causae commodum attingam quicquam / quod absque gentis cuiusquam contumelia tangi non possit.

QVVM ergo tumultus esset olim Lodouico regi uestro cum rhomano pontifice / ac princeps noster inuictus Henricus / eius nominis octauus / ab illa sacrosancta sede rogatus / labantibus ecclesiae rebus ferre statuisset auxilium: naues aliquot emisit in mare / quae classem perquam potentem / quam Lodouicus adornarat / arcerent atque compescerent. Quae quum sibi mutuo occurrissent / reliquis omnibus utrinque bona fortuna seruatis / duae tantum (quae primo congressu protinus iniectis harpagonibus ita sunt colligatae / ut tabulatis igne correptis dirimi non potuerint / triste belli praeludium) perierunt.

Hanc naualem pugnam quum tu ita descripsisses uersibus / non ut uera falsis inuolueres / sed ut rem ferme totam meris mendacijs fingeres / atque ex arbitrio tuo concinnares nouam: quum regis nostri pietatem nomine deprauares inuidiae / Angliamque totam uelut foedifragam atque periuram maledictis falsis perquam petulanter incesseres: Quum Herueum plusquam Herculeum mendacijs plusquam poeticis [a_4] in mare deduceres: Quum nostras naues / quibus aequor instraueras / una tu inuectus Chordigera / parua comitante caterua / fretus Herueo bellipotente disijceres / ac ueluti muscas quocunque tibi libebat abigeres: plerasque uero / fluctibus / homo crudelis / immergeres / quas paulo tamen postea Neptunus misericors incolumes remisit domum: Quum Regentem nostram / lepusculi

Chordigera nauis erat gallica quae cum Regente naue britannica conflagrauit

2 dilucidior /] dilucidior: *1520* 3 caput] caput / *1520* 4 quaedam /] quaedam: *1520* 9 pontifice /] pontifice: *1520;* Henricus /] Henricus *1520* 12 mare /] mare: *1520* 14 seruatis /] seruatis: *1520* 15 harpagonibus] harpagonibus / *1520* 16 colligatae /] colligatae: *1520;* correptis] correptis / *1520* 18 Hanc] *No para. 1520*; pugnam] pugnam / *1520* 19 totam] totam / *1520* 21 pietatem] pietatem / *1520;* inuidiae /] inuidiae: *1520* 23 incesseres:] incesseres / *1520;* Herculeum] Herculeum: *1520* 24 deduceres:] deduceres / *1520* 25 Chordigera /] Chordigera: *1520* 31 remisit] demisit *1760;* domum:] domum / *1520*

pretext for launching another savage attack at this late date. To make this still clearer, since I see just how eager you are to forget it, I will refresh your memory about the origin of this splendid duel of yours. But I will do so in such a way as to omit certain points which might strengthen my own case whenever I cannot touch on a point in my favor without insult to this or that nation.

During the late disturbance between Louis, your king, and the Roman pontiff, our unvanquished prince Henry, the eighth of that name, at the request of that sacrosanct see, had decided to lend his assistance to the faltering cause of the church: he ordered several ships to put to sea to blockade and restrain the formidable fleet which Louis had equipped. When these two fleets engaged each other, all the ships on both sides were lucky enough to survive except two which were lost; for these two, at their first encounter, had immediately thrown out grappling hooks and bound themselves together so tightly that when their decks caught fire they could not be parted—a dismal prelude to the war.

When you described this sea battle in verse, you set out not to combine truth with falsehood but to fabricate practically the whole of your story from out-and-out lies, tailoring new facts according to your personal whim. You disparaged the piety of our king by calling it envy. With false maledictions and unsurpassed petulance you assailed all of England as pact-breaking and perjured. With lies which were more than poetic you led out to sea a Hervé who was more than Herculean. Charging in with the *Cordelière,* all by itself, and a small crew of helpers, relying on the doughty Hervé, you dispersed all our vessels, with which you had covered the main, and drove them away like flies in whatever direction you pleased. You sank most of them under the waves, you cruel man, though a merciful Neptune soon sent home the same ships unscathed. You raced with the *Cordelière* like a thoroughbred hound in pursuit of our *Regent,* which fled like a poor little hare. You

The Cordelière *was a French ship that burned up with the* Regent, *a British ship*

more fugientem / tu generosus canis insequereris Chordigera: Quum Chordigeram / cui remigij nullus usus erat / ualidis remigum lacertis impelleres / ne tibi periret operosum illud hemistichium / "Validis impulsa lacertis": Quum Heruei clamoso flatu proflares uela: Quum nauis aduersae ducem / uirum magni nominis et loci / praeterires tacitum / idque ex arte uidelicet: Quum Herueum ferme facticium caneres non fortiter modo / uerum etiam prodigiose pugnantem: Quum eum in Regentem / in qua nunquam pedem posuit / in medios hostes imperterritum intruderes: Quum Regentem / occupatis eius speculis / horrenda aedita strage / uictam uinctamque traheres: Quum e uicta naue non satis obseruatus in uictricem iaceres ardentis flammae bolidem (quae res fuisset uictis uinctisque difficilis): Quum Herueum adhuc in Regente relictum memoria lapsus (quae res mentientibus facile solet [a$_4$v] obrepere) subito uelut bicorporem in conflagrante Chordigera / medijs in flammis / faceres longis logis concionantem: non in aliud (opinor) mortem differens / quam ut interea te uidelicet alumnum Phoebi suis aliquando fatis uatem uaticinaretur futurum: Quum Heroes uniuersos in cinerem decoqueres / meritoque adeo decoqueres / qui maluerunt exuri quam in Regentem sese transferre quam coeperant / quam uictam uinctamque trahebant / passisque ad sydera palmis: Quum Herueum describeres / suis superstitem socijs: iam iamque euolaturum ad superos (nimirum quicquid mortale gerebat excocto flammis / maximeque mortalium perniciosis affectibus / cuiusmodi sunt ira cum primis et odium) / tum demum ita purgatum / diui opinor Laurentij (ad cuius exemplar fortissimi uiri pectus effinxeras) exemplo prouocatum / captam nauem fingeres /

1 fugientem /] fugientem: *1520;* Chordigera:] Chordigera / *1520* 2 Chordigeram/] Chordigeram: *1520* 3 impelleres /] impelleres: *1520* 4 lacertis":] lacertis / *1520* 5 uela:] uela / *1520* 6 loci /] loci *1520;* tacitum /] tacitum: *1520;* uidelicet: Quum] uidelicet / quum *1520* 7 facticium] facticium / *1520* 8 pugnantem:] pugnantem / *1520* 9 posuit /] posuit: *1520* 9–10 intruderes:] intruderes / *1520* 10 Regentem /] Regentem: *1520;* speculis] spiculis *1689;* speculis /] speculis: *1520* 11 traheres:] traheres / *1520* 12 bolidem] bolidem / *1520* 13 difficilis):] difficilis) *1520* 15 bicorporem] bicorporem / *1520* 17 differens /] differens: *1520* 18 te] te / *1520* 19 uaticinaretur] uaticinarentur *1642 1689;* futurum:] futurum / *1520* 20 meritoque adeo decoqueres] *om. 1760* 21 coeperant /] coeperant: *1520* 22 palmis:] palmis / *1520* 24 superos] superos / *1520* 25 maximeque mortalium] maximeque / mortalium / *1520* 26 odium) /] odium) *1520* 26–27 purgatum /] purgatum: *1520* 28 prouocatum /] prouocatum: *1520*

drove the *Cordelière* on with the strong arms of oarsmen, although it made no use of oars, so that you would not lose that laborious half-line, "driven on by strong arms." You puffed up the sails with Hervé's noisy huffing. You silently passed by the commander of the opposing ship, a man of great name and station, and of course thought it artful to do so. You sang of your well-nigh factitious Hervé fighting not merely stoutly but prodigiously to boot. You foisted him, dauntless, into the midst of his enemies on the *Regent,* on which he did not once set foot. Having taken the *Regent*'s crow's nests and staged that abominable massacre, you led her in tow, bound and vanquished. Unguarded as you were, you threw a bolt of blazing fire from the vanquished ship into the vanquisher (not an easy feat for a crew bound and vanquished). By a lapse of memory (a trap liars often slip into) you made Hervé, whom you had left in the *Regent,* turn up suddenly on the burning *Cordelière,* as if he had two bodies, to deliver himself, there in the flames, of a long-winded sermon. You chose to put off his death for no other reason, I suspect, than to have him sing, in the meantime, of your future election as a nursling of Phoebus to sing of Hervé's own demise. You roasted your heroes to ashes one and all, and had good cause to roast them, indeed, since they chose to burn up when they could have moved onto the *Regent,* which they had captured and which they were leading in tow, bound and vanquished, begging heaven for mercy. You described Hervé, who had outlived his comrades, right on the verge of flying off to the heavenly saints (for by then the fire had burned away everything mortal about him, especially the ruinous emotions of mortals, in particular anger and hatred), and right then, of all times, you pretended that he, though thus purified—provoked, I suppose, by Saint Lawrence's example (whom indeed you had made your exemplar in fashioning that valiant man's character)—was induced by pure envy and lust for revenge, having nothing to gain for himself, to cremate the ship which he had captured and all

et tot egregia deditorum corpora / per inuidiam atque uindictae libidinem / nullo suo fructu concremantem secum: Quum demum non homines tantum ac naues usque adeo deuorares ignibus / ut ne deus quispiam e machina (quod fieri solet in tragediis) unum saltem seruarit incolumem / qui te rei quam decantas ordinem doceret / uerum etiam flammis illis corriperes "sydera cum caelo / cumque ipsis piscibus aequor" / [b_1] nec illud breui hyperbole / sed pluribus uersiculis accuratissime stolidis / pulchre uidelicet emulatus Ouidium / hoc etiam uincens / quod quum ille ab Solis equis absque rectore deerrantibus orbis finxerit incendium / tu perquam scite scilicet / caelum / terras / ac mare comburas a conflagrante nauicula: Quum sic uicto Nasone ferox / Maronem quoque lacesseres / et quoniam is effinxerat demissam a Ioue pluuiam / quae flagrantem Aeneae classem respergeret atque seruaret / tu perditis iam atque consumptis incendio nauibus imbrem e caelo copiose deplueres / ne uelut aqua perennis e pumice scaturit / sic ignis ex aqua iugiter eructatus / flammas eiacularetur in caelum: Haec ita cum tractares / ipse casu tuum nactus librum / haud scio an etiam tum excusum typis / quum tam immania portenta uiderem / tam foeda / tam pudenda mendacia / fictiones tam absurdas / purpureos aliorum pannos / hinc atque inde insutos illi tuo crassissimo bardocucullo / quibus ne locus non esset / habitum totum in eam compositum formam / quam "non sani esse hominis non sanus iuret Horestes" / uno atque altero epigrammate me significaui in narratione tua fidem rerum / in poemate desyderare consilium / tum plures abs te congestos quam pro horrei tui modulo alieni farris aceruos.

Eodem [b_1v] tempore epigramma luseram in nostratem quendam / qui ut parum tempestiue / sic non admodum feliciter / affectabat gallicitatem. Quo in epigrammate / si quid est mordacius / id in ridiculum recidit affectatorem / non in Gallos / de quibus / ut maxime torqueas epigramma / non aliud excuties dic-

1 corpora /] corpora: *1520* 2 secum:] secum / *1520* 3 ignibus /] ignibus: *1520* 5 incolumem /] incolumem: *1520* 6 doceret /] doceret: *1520;* corriperes] corriperes / *1520;* caelo /] caelo *1520* 7 aequor" /] aequor: *1520* 10 deerrantibus] deerrantibus / *1520;* incendium /] incendium: *1520* 12 nauicula:] nauicula / *1520* 15 nauibus] nauibus / *1520* 16 scaturit /] scaturit: *1520* 18 librum /] librum: *1520* 21 absurdas] obsurdas *1520* 24 Horestes] Orestes *1689 1760* 25 significaui] significaui / *1520* 26 congestos] congestos / *1520* 28 Eodem] *No para.* *1520* 31 recidit] incidit *1760;* Gallos /] Gallos. *1520*

those fine prisoners' physiques along with him. On top of all this you were not content merely to consume men and ships in the fire so completely that (contrary to what usually happens in tragedies) no *deus ex machina* saved even one man to show you the factual foundation for the story you harp at, but with those very flames you then kindled "the stars with the heavens and with all the fish in it, the sea," and did so not in some brief hyperbole but in numerous lines of impressively painstaking dullness, a fine emulation of Ovid, of course, which in one respect even outdoes him: in his fabrication, the steeds of the sun, gone astray for the want of their driver, burn only the earth, whereas you, with egregious cunning, of course, enflame sky, land, and sea with just one burning boat. Having thus outdone Ovid, you fiercely challenged Vergil as well, and whereas he had imagined a rain sent by Jove to besprinkle and thus save the fleet of Aeneas when it was afire, you delayed till the ships were long gone and consumed by the blaze and then rained down a copious torrent from heaven, as if otherwise the fire which was belched inexhaustibly out of the water (as water perpetually springs from a pumice stone) might launch some of its flames into heaven. When you handled these things in this way, I happened to get a copy of your book, perhaps even before it was printed, and when I observed such portentous monstrosities, such disgraceful, such shameful lies, such absurd fabrications, and those patches of other men's purple you wore stitched all over your ill-woven bardic *surtout* (to make room for which you had arrayed your whole habit in a form which "Orestes himself, though insane, would swear was a form which no sane man would choose"), I indicated in a couple of epigrams that I found your narration wanting in material credibility and your composition wanting in sense, while the hoard you had gathered of other men's corn had exceeded the measure of your granary.

At the same time I had written an epigram making fun of one of my countrymen who was given to affecting French manners both inopportunely and clumsily. If there is anything in this epigram which is too biting, it recoils on the ludicrous fop himself, not on the French, against whom, torture the epigram as you

tum / quam quod heri sitis in ministros paulo duriusculi. Quod nec uos opinor admodum diffitemini / et ego sicut non insector in uobis / ita quum sui cuique genti sint mores / in illo nostrate displicuit / quod apud nos preter consuetudinem nostram durius tractaret uestratem.

Haec ego quum illa tempestate scriberem / qua belli fremitu flagrabant omnia / etiam si quid asperius mihi uenisset in mentem / non credidissem certe / nec tam iniquum quemquam / nec ipsum te tam improbe fauentem tibi / ut libris in nos debacchati tamen exigeretis a nobis / uti ne uersiculo quidem uicissim tangeremini. Quamobrem si ego prior in te scripsi / prouocasse conuincar: sin tu prius in nos / quid habes quod isti tam inhonesto facto possis honeste praetexere? Quum ipse librum epigrammate rependerim / tu rursus epigramma iocosum retaliaris mirum quam uirulento uolumine. Ad haec cum ego statim illa mea / rebus nondum pacatis / luserim / tu nunc tot annis postea / in summa [b_2] pace / arctissima necessitudine coniunctis regibus / mira concordia conglutinatis populis / post sancitam sanctissimis utrinque caeremonijs saluberrimam nunc exoriris denique / qui sopitas atque obliteratas simultates renoues / coalescentia diuellas uulnera / et obductas cicatrices refrices / qui nobis in os ingeras / foedas nostrorum fugas / dispersas et obrutas classes / inuidiam / foedifraga periuria / quas res ipse foede confingis.

Atqui haec abs te omnia uideri uis concinne fieri / quod me strenuus uidelicet nunc aggrederis / qui tecum sim olim aliquando luctatus. At cui non perspicuum est / quam ridicule sit facturus athleta / qui prodiens in palestram / semelque uniuersos prouocans / quum forte sit deiectus a quopiam / tandem soluto coetu dimissoque ludo / aliquot post annis redeat denique / atque rebus animisque omnium immutatis / et in quidlibet potius quam eiusmodi certamina uersis / inopinus assiliens / antagonistam / quocum olim luctatus est / de repente corripiat medium / pro-

1 heri] heri / *1520* 4 displicuit /] displicuit *1520;* nostram] nostram: *1520* 6 Haec] *No para. 1520* 9 tibi /] tibi: *1520;* debacchati] debacchati: *1520* 12 nos /] nos: *1520* 13 Quum] quum *1520* 14 retaliaris] retaliaris / *1520* 16 nondum] non dum *1520;* pacatis /] pacatis *1520* 17 necessitudine] necessitate *1760* 19 *blank space in all texts;* tranquillitatem *conj. 1760,* pactionem pacis *conj. 1947* (*see commentary*) 20 denique /] denique *1520* 23 periuria /] periuria: *1520* 25 Atqui] *No para. 1520* 28 athleta /] athleta: *1520* 31 quidlibet] quid libet *1520* 33 quocum] *1689,* quo cum *1520 1642 1947,* cum quo *1760*

may, you will exact no other accusation than that as masters you are a little too harsh to your servants. And that, I suppose, not even you will deny. Nor do I attack that propensity in you, but rather, since each race has its own code of conduct, it irked me that that countryman of mine should defy our conventions by treating your countryman too harshly.

Since I was writing these epigrams at the time when everything was ablaze with the tumult of war, even if it had occurred to me to write something more biting, I would certainly not have believed that anyone was so inequitable or that you yourself were so outrageously self-indulgent as to demand that we should aim not one line at you Frenchmen, though you had launched book-length attacks against us. Thus, if I wrote against you first, I will be guilty of having challenged you; but if you wrote against us first, then how can you put an honorable face on so dishonorable an action as that? While I myself repaid a book with an epigram, you in turn retaliated against a jesting epigram with an amazingly virulent volume. Further, I wrote these playful pieces of mine right away, before peace had been made; as for you, only now, so many years later, in the most perfect peace, with our princes conjoined by the closest affinity, with our peoples bound together in a wonderful concord, after the most salutary [of peace settlements] has been consecrated on your side and ours by the most sacred rituals, now, of all times, you spring up and renew old and long-buried feuds, tear apart mending wounds, and chafe open the scars drawn across them; now you cast in our faces our men's disgraceful flight, our fleets scattered and sunk, and our envy and pact-breaking perjury, charges which you disgracefully fabricate.

Yet you want it to seem that all this is entirely in order, namely that you should attack me now, vigorously, as you imagine, simply because I fought with you once in the past. But who fails to see how ridiculously any athlete would be acting if he entered the arena and challenged all comers, if one of them happened to overthrow him and the meet was then finally broken up and the contest concluded, and if he then showed up once again, some years later, and only then, when everyone had different interests and outlooks and paid no attention to that sort of strife, he pounced in unexpectedly and seized by the waist the antagonist with

uocatum etiamnum sese clamitans / quasi uel prouocet qui prouocanti respondeat / uel initum semel certamen duraret aeternum: quam ridicule sit inquam eiusmodi facturus athleta / cui non est perspicuum / etiamsi fors congressu fuerit superior? Quod si sic insiliens / cum huc atque illuc uerterit sese / brachiaque [b_2v] iactans ac tibias / alios eiectis pugnis / alios calcibus feriat / atque in his fortassis etiam prioris ludi agonothetas: denique ubi diu frustra sese torserit / quum prosternere non possit aduersarium / ne frustra processisse uideatur / in uultum conspuat / crapulaque ac sanie totum ebrio eiecta stomacho conuomat / itaque gestiens tanquam re praeclare gesta discedat / egregium scilicet triumphum in ganeis ac popinis acturus / hiccine palestrita coronandus? an dignus potius fuerit / cui talos aliquis et crura perfringat?

Iam quis non uidet Brixi quam tu sis huic athletae similis: quanquam hoc fortasse dissimilis / quod non athletico certamine / totam gentem nostram / sed hostilibus prouocasti conuicijs / nisi forte contendas periurium non habendum pro contumelia / quod simile est ac si disputes / asinum non habendum pro quadrupede. Qua in prouocatione / quum ego tecum uno atque altero telo / sed exarmato / non tam dimicarem quam luderem (Nam is uidebare quem non esset operae precium laedere) tamen nescio quo pacto (ut facile penetratur pustula) tanto cum dolore ictum recepisti / ut nunc demum tot elapsis annis / toties facta firmataque pace / tam multis modis constabilita concordia / tam necessaria iunctis affinitate principibus (quae res una debuit inter [b_3] utriusque populos pristinas omnes simultates tollere) tu tamen / tanquam neque prior prouocasses / et adhuc duraret bellum / in me repente rursus insurgas / et omnibus in amorem / amicitiam / societatem / ac iam quoque hospitalitatem mutuam intentis / hostilibus armis inuadas: et telis non acutis admodum sed (quod amplius est quam inter homines non omnino barbaros ac syluestres belli iura permiserint)

1 clamitans /] clamitans *1520* 2 respondeat /] respondeat: *1520;* aeternum :] aeternum *1520* 3 athleta /] athleta: *1520* 4 perspicuum /] perspicuum: *1520* 5 insiliens /] insiliens: *1520;* sese /] sese: *1520* 7 agonothetas:] agonothetas *1520* 8 torserit /] torserit: *1520;* aduersarium /] aduersarium: *1520* 10 gestiens] gestiens / *1520* 16 nostram /] nostram: *1520* 22 recepisti /] recepisti: *1520* 26 tamen /] tamen: *1520* 27 prouocasses /] prouocasses: *1520* 28 societatem /] societatem: *1520*

whom he had fought in the past and proclaimed himself challenged even now, as if a person who answers a challenge could be called a challenger or as if any strife, once begun, lasts forever; who, I ask, fails to see how ridiculously such an athlete would be acting, even if he should happen to win the fight? But what if he jumps in as you do and lashes out in all directions, flailing his arms and legs, bruising some with his outflung fists and others with his heels, and among these perhaps the sponsors of the preceding contest, and what if at last, when he has racked himself for a long time in vain, unable to throw his adversary, lest he seem to have sallied forth wholly in vain he then spits in his opponent's face and throws up all over him, heaving the toxic and distempered vomit from his drunken stomach, and what if then, swelling with pride as if he had given a splendid performance, he goes off to celebrate his extraordinary triumph in low dives and taverns? Does such a wrestler then merit a victory crown? Or does he deserve rather to have his shins and his ankles broken?

Who does not see by now, Brixius, how much like this athlete you are; though you may be unlike him in this one respect, that you did not challenge our entire nation to a sporting competition but provoked us instead with belligerent abuse, unless perhaps you contend that to charge us with perjury ought not to be classed as an insult—in much the same way, you might argue that a donkey ought not be classed as a quadruped. In response to this challenge I took up a couple of darts, of the blunt-tipped variety, and did not so much fight you as sport with you (since it seemed you were not worth the trouble of wounding). Nonetheless, for one reason or another, as a pustule is easily punctured, my stroke left you in such grievous pain that even now, after so many years have elapsed, after peace has so often been made and confirmed, after concord has been established in so many ways, after our princes have been joined in such intimate affinity (although this fact alone should have settled all long-standing feuds between the nations of both princes), all of a sudden you rise up once more against me, as if you had not given the first challenge and the war were still on; and when everyone else is intent upon love, friendship, and now mutual hospitality, you set upon me with the weapons of war and attack me with darts which, although none too sharp, are (despite the fixed martial conventions of all who are not

impetas uenenatis: non stupide minus quam improbe clamitans interim / te prodire prouocatum / tanquam responsurus esses ad ea / quae nos in te / dum tibi responderemus / iniecimus: quae certe fuerunt eiusmodi / ut ea respondendo non possis quantumlibet sudaris effugere. Quod quum uerum esse sensisses / sic instituisti libellum tuum / ut tuam defensionem timide ac uelut obiter attingens / totus in me confodiendum conuertereris / qua in re quum quicquid tibi uirium fuerit intenderis / quid aliud effecisti denique / quam ut effutitis infacetis facetijs / euomito furiali ueneno / me tandem quum non potuisti laedere / ne nihil egeris perspuisti? atque ita demum discessisti uictor ac triumphator egregius?

Verum in me quam lepide dicax fueris mox uidebimus. Interea pensitemus / isto tam operoso libello / in quo elaborando plures perdidisti dies / quam liber habet [b3v] uersiculos / quanto cum artificio quae tibi sunt obiecta dilueris. Ego igitur quum in te taxassem alia furto subrepta ueteribus / alia perabsurde tractata / omnia denique sic abs te narrata / ut neque in rebus ueritas esset / neque in uerbis fides: ad primum sic respondes tanquam ego sim criminatus quod tui uersiculi nimis redoleant antiquitatem: a quo ego crimine (ne quid excusando te torqueas) facile te absoluo. Nam quod idem crimen alibi rursus attingens obiter / rursus dissimulas obiectum furtum / rursus uelut obiectam aemulationem defendis / ac non contentus si reprehensione careas / laudem etiam ab re tam illaudata uendices / quod ita uidelicet ueteres aemulatus sis / quod eorum assidue uestigijs inheseris / quod Herculi denique clauam e manibus eripueris / non potui hercle sine risu legere / e facto tam pudendo tam magnifice uendicatam gloriam. Nam quum omnia pessime sis imitatus / quum aliorum uel hemistichia uel integros uersus / uno interdum uerbulo male commutato / interdum ne commutato quidem / passim usurpes pro tuis / hoc non est opinor aemulari Brixi / sed contaminare /

2 te /] te *1520* 3 responderemus /] responderemus *1520* 4 eiusmodi /] eiusmodi: *1520* 6 tuum /] tuum: *1520* 13 Verum] *No para. 1520* 14 pensitemus /] pensitemus *1520;* libello /] libello: *1520* 15 uersiculos /] uersiculos *1520* 16 obiecta] obiecta / *1520* 26 aemulatus] aemulatis *1642*

wholly barbarous and savage) envenomed. Meanwhile, you insist, no less stupidly than dishonestly, that you come forth to answer my challenge, as if you were prepared to respond to those darts which we launched against you in responding to your provocation. But those darts of ours were clearly such that, however much you sweat, you cannot escape them by any response. Knowing this to be true, you arranged your own tract so that you need not touch on your personal defense except timidly and in passing but could turn your whole effort toward skewering me; and although this offensive absorbed every ounce of your vigor and virulence, what else did you finally achieve but to blurt out your bumptious urbanities, to spew out your furious venom, and at last, since you could not really wound me, to do something at least by spitting all over me, after which you marched off an egregious victor and triumphant hero?

But how wittily pert you have proven against me we shall see in good time. Meanwhile let us consider how artfully you refute my objections in that toilsome tract of yours, which has cost you more days to perfect than the book contains lines. Now, whereas I arraigned you for purloining some elements of your poem from the ancients, for developing other elements very absurdly, and for narrating everything in such a way that there was neither any truth in your subject matter nor any credit attached to your words, you responded to the first point as if I had charged that your lines smack too much of antiquity, from which charge, lest you strain yourself too much in answering, I freely absolve you. For elsewhere you touch again on this same charge in passing; again you dissemble the theft you are charged with; again you attempt to defend it as if I had accused you of emulating the ancients, and indeed, not content to escape any blame, you even claim praise for your blameworthy deed; you claim you have emulated the ancients, followed assiduously in their footsteps, and, in a word, wrested the club out of Hercules' hands. But I had to laugh, by Hercules, as I read what grand and glorious claims you had based on so shameful an action. For you have imitated everything in the worst possible way. You do frequently take over either half-lines or whole lines from others as if they were yours, meanwhile making some small and inept alteration. But in my opinion, Brixius, this is not emulating the ancients but con-

foedare / polluere: hoc non est Herculi clauam ui eripere / sed repositam furto subripere. Quanquam negare non possum quin [b_4] hoc sit ueterum inherere uestigijs. Verum enimuero Brixi nimis inheres importune / quum sic inheres uestigijs / ut eorum decutias calceos / quibus tuos pedes haud quaquam aequales obuestias. Nec tibi satis patrocinij fuerit / si quid tale de se dixit VERGILIVS / quale tu de temet iactas. (Neque enim cuiusque est / Corynthum petere.) Ille de se dixit / quod abunde praestitit: tu de te gloriaris in eo / quod praestare non sufficis / nisi simile putes esse pereuntes ENNII uersiculos VERGILII poematis aeternum uicturis inserere / et aeternos VERGILII uersus tuis infulcire pereuntibus: illum aliorum carmina interclusisse melioribus / te splendidissima quaeque uetustiorum sordibus immiscuisse tuis: illum sic certare cum graecis ut ubique sese parem probet / plerumque / etiam superet / te cum latinis congressum non hoc agere / ut emuleris aut certes / sed ut ex insidijs aliquid auferas / quod in tuam suppellectilem conferas integrum / si clam fore furtum speres: alioqui / uelut equi furtiui caudam atque auriculas amputes / ut uel deformato possis uti potius quam careas.

Qua in re adeo te industrium praebes ac plane frugi furem / ut frequenter ne uel hemistichio alieno contineas [b_4v] manum / si quod tibi uideatur eximie bellum / mire absurda commenta / fictiones ineptissimas / quas locus aut res neque petit / neque patitur / a caelo ad terras usque / sed quae neque caelum (quod aiunt) neque terram attingant / accersas. Quod si in explicanda pugna / si tempestate repraesentanda / uel si quid aliud erit eiusmodi / ueterum quempiam proponas aemulandum tibi: sic illius uerba pleraque / sic uersus plerumque totos in uersus inculcas tuos / sic quicquid uariaris / immutas in deterius / ut si quis parteis conferat seorsum / hinc nihil illi similis / hinc ille ipse uidearis. Sin utrinque

1 polluere:] polluere / *1520* 4 importune] *1689, conj. 1760 1947,* importunae *1520 1642 1760;* uestigijs /] uestigijs: *1520* 5 aequales] aequales / *1520* 7 iactas.] iactas *1520* 7–8 est / Corynthum petere.)] est Corynthum petere) *1520* 10 uersiculos] uersiculos / *1520* 11 tuis infulcire] tuisinfulcire *1520* 11–12 pereuntibus: illum] pereuntibus. Illum *1520* 12 te] Te *1520* 13 tuis: illum] tuis. Illum *1520* 15 superet / te] superet. Te *1520;* agere /] agere: *1520* 16 certes /] certes: *1520* 17–18 speres: alioqui /] speres alioqui *1520* 18 amputes /] amputes: *1520* 20 Qua] *No para. 1520;* furem /] furem: *1520* 22 quod] qnod *1520* 23 ineptissimas /] ineptissimas: *1520* 24 usque /] usque: *1520* 25 attingant /] attingant *1520;* Quod] Quam *1642 1760* 26 repraesentanda /] repraesentanda: *1520* 28 totos] totos / *1520* 29 deterius /] deterius: *1520* 30 seorsum /] seorsum: *1520;* similis /] similis: *1520* 31 totum /] totum: *1520*

simul contempletur totum / tum uero uideri possit / ira quapiam
taminating, disgracing, and polluting them; this is not wresting Hercules' club away forcibly but furtively snatching it up when he has laid it down. Still I cannot deny that this is following in the footsteps of the ancients, but assuredly, Brixius, you follow a bit too relentlessly: you follow so closely in their footsteps that you knock off their shoes and then wear them yourself, though your feet hardly fill them. It was a poor defense for you to boast of doing much the same thing that Vergil claimed to have done (not everyone has any business to head for Corinth). He was more than able to make good on his claim; you lack any means to make good on your arrogant boast; unless you suppose it is the same sort of achievement for Vergil to engraft the transitory lines of Ennius into his poems, which will live forever, as it is for you to obtrude Vergil's everlasting lines into yours, which are already dying; for him to set off others' verses with better ones, as for you to commingle whatever is finest in ancient writers with your sordid rubbish; for him to compete with the Greeks so that he everywhere proved himself their equal, often even surpassing them, as for you to encounter the Latins not in order to rival or compete with them, but in order to sneak up and pilfer something which you may transfer whole to your store (if you hope that your theft will not be noticed) or else lop off its tail and its ears, as you would treat a stolen horse, since you would rather secure the use of it even by disfiguring it than not have it at all.

In this matter you prove to be such an industrious and indeed thrifty thief that often, rather than let even a single half-line of some other poet escape you if you think it is especially pretty, you import wildly absurd fantasies and the most pointless fabrications, which the context and subject at hand neither call for nor tolerate, fabrications and fantasies ranging from heaven to earth, but without any bearing on heaven or on earth, as the saying goes. And if, in setting forth a battle or representing a tempest or anything else of that sort, you choose any one of the ancients to emulate, you obtrude so many of his words and even whole verses into your verses, you so change for the worse all that you alter, that if anyone considers the parts separately, on the one side you look not at all like your model and on the other side you look just like him. But if anyone regards the whole from both sides at once, then indeed it may seem that some angry god, by a wondrous

superorum / mira methamorphosi pulcherrimus heros quispiam in ridiculum commutatus simium.

Ergo quum obiecta tibi tua furta ratione tam elegante nempe dissimulatione diluisses / ad tam pudenda mendacia (quibus Chordigera tua non aliter scatet quam cadauer uermibus) uelut Aiacis clipeum aut Palladis aegida poetices opponis priuilegium / quo uidelicet historica lege tradendae ueritatis eximitur. At ego profecto Brixi ut poeticen / augustam sane ac perquam liberam diuam / non adeo angustis limitibus obsepserim / quin ut uerborum / ita rerum quoque fingendarum detur licentia / mo[c_1]do sumpta pudenter / ita plane non patiar / ut quidlibet impudenter ementiens / idemque tractans absurde / totam rerum seriem / atque adeo summam inuertat atque demutet. Quam si alioqui statueris / omnibus prorsus historiae legibus tam absolute liberam / ut et debellasse cantitet / qui non conflixerint / et uicisse pronunciet / qui uicti sint / hostesque fugasse / qui fugerint: iam non Didonis tantum miseranda fata (quae tu pro fictis affers) irriserimus (quae nescio an satis confutata certe trahuntur in dubium non sat indubitate fidis authoribus) uerum etiam falsa esse bella omnia / falsa fictaque coniugia / aut Aeneam certe a Turno / Turnum a Pallante superatum / omnia denique contra gesta / quam sunt a Marone tradita / crediderimus. De Vergilio uidelicet accedentes tibi / de Homero uero Dioni / homini tam infenso poeticae / ut totum Troianum bellum contenderit / atque ipsam propemodum Troiam / figmentum esse Homericum / idque obstinate contenderit / infinitis uictus argumentis. Quod non alio consilio fecisse uidetur / quam ut id ipsum infensus ageret / quod agis nunc ipse propitius / hoc tantum diuersus / quod quam rem ille studio conabatur / ut nemo poetas haberet in precio / hoc tu procures imprudens / non faber fabro inuidens / sed arti prorsus [c_1v] ipsi suam inuidens gloriam / ipsique adeo tibi tuam / si quan-

3 furta] furta / *1520* 8 poeticen /] poeticen *1520;* liberam] liberam / *1520* 11 patiar /] patiar: *1520* 12 ementiens /] ementiens: *1520* 14–15 liberam /] liberam: *1520* 18 confutata] confutata: *1520* 19 indubitate fidis] indubitatae fidis *1520 1642 1760,* indubitata fidis *1689*, indubitatae fidei *conj. 1760 1947* (*see commentary*); authoribus] a uthoribus *1520* 23 tibi /] tibi: *1520;* Dioni /] Dioni *1520* 24 poeticae /] poeticae: *1520;* contenderit /] contenderit *1520* 25 Homericum /] Homericum: *1520* 26 uictus] *1642 1689 1760 1947*, uictis *1520* 30 inuidens /] inuidens: *1520*

metamorphosis, has changed some very beautiful hero into a ludicrous ape.

Such was the elegant method—dissimulation, that is—which you used to answer my charge of thievery. And when you come to the shameless lies which swarm throughout your *Chordigera* like worms in a corpse, then you brandish before me, like the shield of Ajax or the aegis of Pallas, the privilege peculiar to poetry, whereby, you think, she is exempted from the law of history which prescribes truthful reporting. But assuredly, Brixius, while I would not shut up poetry (an august and extremely free goddess, to be sure) in such straitened confines as to deny her the license to fabricate not only words but also incidents, provided it not be used shamelessly, even so I will simply not stand for it if she tells some shameless lie and elaborates it absurdly, if she twists and perverts a whole sequence of incidents and even their very outcome. If you have decided, on the contrary, that she is so absolutely free of all the laws of history, without exception, that she is permitted to sing that men fought to the death, though they never came to blows, and that those who lost, won, and that those who fled, routed their enemies, at that point we would not only laugh at the lamentable fate of Dido, which you adduce as a fabrication (and indeed, although I am not sure it has been altogether confuted, it is certainly called into question by authors whose own credibility is not altogether unquestionable); we would also be brought to believe that those wars were all falsehoods and those nuptials false fabrications, or that Aeneas was certainly overcome by Turnus and Turnus by Pallas, and in short that everything was done just the opposite way from how it is reported by Vergil; that is, we would leave Vergil to join up with you, and then by the same token leave Homer for Dio, a man so inimical to poetry that he argues that the whole Trojan war, and Troy itself, practically, is a Homeric fabrication, sustaining this argument obstinately despite countless proofs which refute him. He had no other motive for doing so, it seems, than to bring about with an inimical intent just the thing that you now bring about with a friendly intent. You two differ in just one respect: he was deliberately trying to keep anyone from esteeming the poets; you accomplish the same thing through heedlessness, not as one craftsman envying another but rather as one envying art its own glory, indeed envying yourself your own

tus haberi postulas tantus uere uates esses / cui an non praecipuam gratiam decusseris / si nemo sua facta dignabitur poeticis uersibus commendari memoriae? Nemo certe dignabitur / qui mentem habeat / qui quidem habeat persuasum / habenda pro fictis omnia / quaecunque poeta cecinerit / idque eo fatente ipso qui cecinit.

Caeterum hac in parte (ut uere tecum loquar ac libere) non unus es / qui res nobiscum gestas a uobis / si non falso recenseas (nam id dicere apud tam teneras aures religio est) / at certe nimirum recenseas libere. Prodijt opusculum Pillei Turonensis satis canoris uersibus. Nam reliqua libens praetereo / ne is quoque se prouocatum clamitet: cuius in libello tamen quisquis aduerterit / in re narranda quam passim utatur Brixiana poetice / quam honoratis titulis nostram exornet Angliam / quam uenerandis epithetis inclytas honestet Hispanias / is opinor certe iudicabit / si quis Pilleum / aut Hispanus / aut Anglus / non tantum epigrammate remorderit / nihil habiturum causae Pilleum / cur se quaeratur lacessitum esse / quum prior laeserit. Quod si quis tam iniquus esset usquam / ut contra sentiat / non dubitassem / uel ipse eam subijsse calumniam / si liber olim mihi [c_2] uenisset in manus. Nunc uero non est consilium antiquatis amicitia noua simultatibus tumultuari de integro. Quamobrem omisso libro / titulum tantum proponam / cum ut ex ungue liceat estimare leonem / tum ut si cui libeat legere / nomen habeat saltem / quo uestiget librum. Is ita inscriptus est. De Anglorum e Gallijis fuga / et Hispanorum e Nauarra expulsione. Quis non uel absque cribro diuinet facile / cuius farinae reliquus siet liber / quum istiusmodi furfuris legat titulum / qui cum reliquo libro tam concinne concinit / quam ab historia tota discordat? Nam quis non rideat / quod Anglos prelio iactat e Gallijs esse fugatos? quos opinor satis constat (ut nihil amplius dicam) certe non fugatos e Gallijs: quod si fugatos sentit

1 haberi] *conj. 1760 1947,* habere *1520 1642 1689 1760* 5 cecinerit /] cecinerit: *1520* 6 qui cecinit] *conj. 1760,* cecinit *1520 1642 1689 1760 1947* 8 uobis /] uobis: *1520* 9 est) /] est) *1520* 9–10 nimirum] nimium *conj. 1760 1947* (*see commentary*) 12 clamitet:] clamitet. *1520* 13 narranda] narranda / *1520* 14 titulis] titulis / *1520* 14–15 epithetis] epithetis / *1520* 17 remorderit] remorderet *1642 1689 1760 1947* 22 de integro] deintegro *1520* 23 leonem /] leonem: *1520* 26 cribro] cerebro *1689* 29 discordat?] discordat. *1520* 31 Gallijs:] Gallijs / *1520*

glory if you were in fact such a great poet as you would be thought; for do you not spoil your own principal source of prestige if, because of you, no one will deign to have his deeds memorialized in the lines of the poets? Certainly no one will do so who has any sense, at least not if he is convinced that everything a poet sings is to be taken for a fabrication, especially when the singer himself testifies to the fact.

On this point, moreover, if I may talk with you truthfully and freely, you are not the only one to recount your nation's dealings with ours, if not falsely (for I scruple to utter that word in the presence of such fastidious ears), then at least very freely indeed. A short work was issued by one Pilleus of Tours, in sufficiently melodious lines; for I willingly pass by my other objections, lest he too should proclaim himself challenged. In his tract, however, if anyone observes how frequently he employs the Brixian style of poetry in narrating his story, or with what venerable titles he adorns our England, or with what reverend epithets he dignifies glorious Spain, that observer, I think, will assuredly judge that if anyone, either English or Spanish, should snap back at Pilleus with even more than an epigram, Pilleus would have no reason to complain about being offended, since he was the first to offend. And if anyone on earth were so inequitable as to think otherwise, I myself would not have hesitated to submit to the calumny of that man if the book had come into my hands at some point in the past. But now that new friendship has rendered such feuds obsolete, it is not my intention to stir matters up all over again, and so I will leave out the book and adduce nothing more than the title, both to enable my readers to gauge the whole lion by its claw and to give anyone who is inclined to read the book a name, at least, with which he can track it down. It bears this inscription: *On the Flight of the English from the Territories of France, and the Expulsion of the Spanish from Navarre.* Who needs a sieve to guess what stuff the rest of this book must consist of, since the title he reads consists of such chaff and rings as true to the rest of the book as it rings false to history? For who will not laugh at Pilleus when he boasts that in battle the English were driven out of France? It is, I think, amply established (to say nothing further) that the English were certainly not driven out of France; and if he thinks that the English were driven out by the people of Aquitaine, how could they

ab Aquitanis / quomodo fugari poterant ab hijs / cum quibus nec eo uentum est / ut liceret congredi? At istud multo adhuc magis insigniter est ridiculum / quod Hispanos buccinet Nauarrae possessione depulsos / qui Nauarram tum ingressi / perpetuo post possederint / hodieque possideant.

Sed donentur ista poetice qua Pillei musa / quod ad fictiones attinet / ita belle refert tuam / ut nusquam terrarum sit simia simiae similior. Quin et is opinor hanc obtundet poeticen / per quem haud ita pridem [c_2v] Parisijs excusus est fasciculus temporum / uere comburendus fasciculus / ut in quem congesta sint ligna quaedam / quae nisi noster princeps tam bene sibi conscius esset / ut se suaque facta non dubitet clarius latiusque testata / quam ut sint obnoxia latratibus inuidorum / potuissent aliquem fortassis ignem inter duos populos accendere. Nam ei libello cum alia quaedam nuper indita sunt seditiosa mendacia / tum coronis adiecta multo seditiosissima: qua legitur princeps uester iam ab hinc biennio fuisse moturus aduersus turchas / nisi ei fuisset infidelitas regis Angli suspecta. Quis haec ferat / qui norit / neque de tali expeditione tum fuisse cogitatum uobis / neque quenquam aut minus fuisse suspectum principi uestro quam nostrum / aut qui minus commiserit / quare suspectari debuerit? Iam quid illo scriptore uel dici uel fingi potuit impudentius / qui uestra lingua perscripsit Iacobum Scotorum regem / interea dum rex noster in armis esset in Gallia / Britanniam ingressum / rebus feliciter gestis / ingente cum gloria sese recepisse domum? nec reueritus est scriptor improbus totius orbis conscientiam / qua satis superque cognitum omnibus sciret esse mortalibus / fusos fugatosque scotos / ipsum regem cum tota fere nobilitate peremptum / corpusque eius / quod mo[c_3]reretur christianae communionis expers/ insepultum iubente pontifice tot annos adseruatum.

Haec atque alia quaedam eiusmodi / quum huc subinde proficiscantur istinc / tamen postquam tam alta pax coaluit / ma-

1 poterant] poterat *1642 1689 1760;* hijs] iis *1642 1689 1760* 1 quibus] quibus / *1520* 6 Sed] *No para. 1520;* poetice] poeticae *1689* 7 sit] sit / *1520* 9–10 fasciculus temporum] *Fasciculus Temporum 1689* 10 fasciculus /] fasciculus: *1520* 11 ligna] lingna *1520* 12 esset /] esset: *1520;* testata /] testata: *1520* 16 uester] uester / *1520* 20 nostrum /] nostrum: *1520* 21 commiserit /] commiserit: *1520;* debuerit?] debuerit. *1520* 26 improbus] improbus / *1520;* conscientiam /] conscientiam: *1520* 29 eius /] eius *1520*

have been put to flight by a people with whom they did not even have an opportunity to clash? But it is even more remarkably absurd that he should trumpet the Spaniards' repulse from their holdings in Navarre, for they entered Navarre at that time, held it steadily thereafter, and hold it today.

But yet let us concede all these whimsies to poetry; for in poetry, at least in the province of fabrications, Pilleus' muse recalls your muse so prettily that nowhere on earth is there simian more similar to simian. And indeed, I guess that that other author will also belabor this sanction of poetry, the one who, not so very long ago, printed in Paris a *Short Sheaf of the Times,* a sheaf truly made to be burned, since its author had gathered within it a number of firebrands which might very well have been enough to touch off a new conflagration between our two peoples if our prince's insight had not given him ample assurance that he and his deeds, both so clearly and generally commended, were proof against the barking of envious men. For besides certain other seditious lies which have lately been inserted into that tract, a final flourish has been added, by far the most seditious avowal of them all, where we read that your prince fully two years ago would have gone out to ward off the Turks if he had not suspected that the English king was untrustworthy. Who would put up with such stuff if he knows that at that time your people had not planned any such expedition and that no one had been less suspected by your prince than ours, or had done less to merit suspicion? Now what could be said or imagined more shameless than what that other writer asserted in your language: that while our king was in arms in France, James, the King of the Scots, entered Britain and waged a successful campaign and then made his way home with great glory? Nor was this wretched writer at all disconcerted by what was common knowledge everywhere, even though, as he knew, common knowledge had given every mortal more than ample assurance that the Scots had been routed and driven to flight, that the king himself had been slain with almost all his nobles, and that since he had died excommunicate his body had been kept without burial for so many years in accord with a papal injunction.

Although writings like these often make their way over from your shores to ours, nonetheless, now that such a general peace has been achieved we have chosen rather to make no response

luimus conticescere / patique potius ingestas indies contumelias / quam cum aliqua animorum offensione regerere / simul sperantes fore / ut Paulus Emilius / tam sanctus et incorruptus enarrator historiae / ut iureiurando putes obstrictum / tam elegans ut nisi recentiora rescriberet / uideri possit haud infimus antiquorum / res utriusque populi (quas quidem inter se gessere) syncera fide sit aliquando traditurus posteris.

At tuus liber quando mihi iam tum in ipso rerum tumultu fuit oblatus / haud quaquam existimaui maioribus uictimis expiandum piaculum / si librum eum / qui et tam acerbus esset et impudenter mendax / epigrammate saltem per ludum iocumque perstringerem. Et tu tamen qui (ut es undique mire facetus) ludis in dominationem meam / nisi qui te attigerim / me uicissim tangi paterer / quum totam gentem meam et conuitijs improbis et mendacijs impudentibus prior exagitasses / tam indigne tulisti / uel ioco contra tangi sacrosanctam maiestatem tuam / ut annos aliquot / in hoc unum totus perdius ac pernox incubueris / [c3v] ut aliquando posses accurato uolumine cum epigrammate plusquam extemporali confligere. Qua in re quum duo tibi proposueris / primum ut tua defenderes / deinde ut inueherеris in mea / alterum tam praeclare praestitisti / ut ex his / quae tibi obiecta sunt / alia dissimularis / alia non intellexeris / illud uero / quod maius erat / quam ut praeterire / notius / quam ut dissimulare / uerius / quam ut euitare potueris / tamen diffinitione declinasti commode / ut quicquid ego te mentitum argueram / tu non mentitum quidem te / sed finxisse contenderes.

Quamobrem quum hoc congressu sentiam tam acutum esse te / ut tenedia bipenni fictum a falso disseces / hoc est / ita temet erroneo mendacio explices / ut implices ultroneo / haud amplius tibi molestus fuero / quin hac sane parte peruiceris: modo hoc unum inter nos conueniat / quod alioqui iuratis euincam testibus / qui abs te exusti / adhuc supersunt tamen / tuasque fictiones arguunt / atque derident: conueniat / inquam / excepto duntaxat

4 obstrictum /] obstrictum: *1520* 5 rescriberet] scriberet *1689*, describeret *conj. 1760* 8 At] *No para. 1520;* liber] liber / *1520* 16 tuam /] tuam: *1520* 19 proposueris /] proposueris: *1520* 20 primum] primum / *1520* 21 praestitisti /] praestitisti: *1520* 22 maius] magis *1642 1689 1760* 24 diffinitione] definitione *1642 1689 1760* 24–25 commode /] commode: *1520* 27 Quamobrem] *No para. 1520* 28 bipenni] bipenni / *1520* 31 testibus /] testibus: *1520* 33 derident:] derident / *1520;* conueniat /] conueniat *1520*

and to bear with such calumnies, which are growing in bulk by the day, than to throw them back at you with any offense to your feelings; at the same time we hope that hereafter no less a historian than Paulus Aemilius, so strict and impartial in shaping his narrative that one might suppose he was bound by an oath and so elegant that if he did not write of more recent events he would seem not the humblest of ancients, will report for posterity the deeds of both peoples, at least those deeds which concerned both alike, with an unalloyed credibility.

But since your book was set before me when our relations were at their most troubled, I certainly never thought I would have to expiate my offense with a blood-sacrifice if I chastised that book, which was so bitter and shamelessly given up to lies, with a mere epigram penned in play and in jest. You, on the other hand, marvelously witty as ever, joke about my lordly privilege should I forbid you to touch me in turn after I had touched you, and yet even though you took the initiative in assailing the whole of my nation with wanton abuse and shameless lies, you were so irked at my touching your sacrosanct majesty with even a jest that for several years, day and night, you spent all of your energy in preparing to combat my casually improvised epigrams with a carefully planned volume. In it you set up two tasks for yourself, first to vindicate your lines and then to inveigh against mine; and you performed the first so magnificently that out of the things with which I had reproached you you dissembled some and misunderstood others, while the one charge which was too great to sidestep, too commonly known to dissemble, and too true to evade, you conveniently deflected with that definition, according to which all that I had exposed as a lie you contended to be not a lie but a sheer fabrication.

Wherefore, since our confrontation brings me to realize that you are so keen as to split fabrication from falsehood with Tenedian precision, which amounts to the same thing as extricating yourself from a mistaken lie by implicating yourself in a deliberate one, I will not make any more difficulties for you about this matter. You can claim the victory provided that we agree on this one point (and if not I will then win the point with sworn witnesses, whom you burned to a crisp, but who live to this day to expose and mock your fabrications); let us agree, I repeat, that apart

hoc uno / quod unum poteras uno clausisse uersiculo / nempe quod duae naues incensae sunt / caetera quae uolumen tuum tanto decantat hiatu / esse abs te ficta omnia.

Nunc igitur a tuis castris ita reiectus / atque depulsus / impellor ad mea tutanda refugere. In quibus horreo / ne tam acrem hostem / tam indigne pro[c_4]uocatum / tam capitaliter offensum / tam recente uictoria ferocientem / ab suis usque munitionibus / a me tam ignauiter oppugnatis / ab illo defensis tam fortiter / ad mea usque castra me persequentem / quae ego tam effusa fuga repetiuerim / nequeam sustinere. Quod quo magis exhorream / machinae illae tuae me commouent / quibus in me tam ualide non ista torques minutula / quae quum conijcerentur in te / ne declinare quidem ferme dignatus es: ueterum compilatos uersus canoris nugis insertos / ingenij stuporem tenuibus uerborum bracteis (per quas pellucet totus) obductum / et (quam laudi quoque ducis tibi modo uocetur fictio) mendacissimam petulantiam: sed barbarismos / ac soloecismos / et non satis consistentes syllabas / res / bone deus / quam atroces / quam impias / quam (si cum illis conferantur) immanes. Nam quae re obiectas ista sunt: caeterum uerbis et conuiciis meris / stultum / insanum / furentem uocas / idque plusquam centies / sed ea conuicia sunt Mopsopij sales tui / in hoc adhibiti / ut insulsum per se libellum tali condimento reddas insulsiorem. At syllabis illis et soloecis omnino me fortiter oppugnas / ac stringis.

Sed est adhuc / Brixi / quiddam / quo me constringis durius: uerum tu profecto praeter aequum ac bonum durior / qui non oppugnasse contentus / postules praeterea / quo me armorum genere defendam / ipse praescribere. [c_4v] Ita pro imperio iubes / ne quid ex hijs / quae tu impingis mihi / reijciam in Frobenium. Qua in re uide quam sis inciuilis / atque adeo iniustus etiam / qui quum scires opus impressum esse Basileae / quum ipse morarer in Anglia / nec dubitare possis / quin eo tempore fuerim occupatior / quam ut mihi liceret / e Londino Basileam / quotidie bis transcur-

11 commouent /] commouent: *1520* 12 minutula] minutila *1520* 13 es:] es *1520* 14 insertos /] insertos: *1520* 15 obductum /] obductum: *1520* 17 syllabas /] syllabas: *1520* 18 res /] res *1520* 19 immanes] inanes *1642 1689 1760;* sunt:] sunt. *1520* 20 uocas /] uocas: *1520* 21 centies /] centies: *1520* 25 Sed] *No para. 1520;* adhuc / Brixi /] adhuc Brixi *1520* 26 durior /] durior: *1520* 28 defendam /] defendam *1520;* praescribere.] praescribere *1520;* iubes /] iubes: *1520* 29 hijs] iis *1642 1689 1760* 30 etiam /] etiam: *1520*

from this one point, which you could have summed up in one little line—namely, that two ships were burned—all the other things your volume sings of with such tragic clamor are nothing but your fabrications.

Now, then, since you have driven and beaten me back from your camp in this way, I am forced to retreat to defend my own camp; in which I quake with terror lest so fierce an enemy, so rudely challenged, so mortally offended, fired up by so recent a victory, chasing me all the way from his bulwarks, which I had assaulted so feebly and he had defended so stoutly, all the way to my camp, to which I returned in such wild disarray, should now overwhelm me. I quake all the more violently at this prospect because of those siege-engines of yours, which so forcefully launch against me not those trifling objections which you scarcely deigned to deflect when I cast them at you, namely, that you had engrafted lines stolen from the ancients among your melodious trifles, that you had covered over the imbecility of your talent with a flimsy veneer of words which in no way disguises it, and that you lied with outrageous impudence. You consider that praiseworthy provided it is called fabrication. No, you charge me instead with barbarisms, and solecisms, and syllables which do not scan quite consistently. Good Lord, what atrocious and impious infractions these are! If compared to those others, how monstrous! For those are your only material objections; the rest is mere verbal abuse, as you cry "fool," "madman," or "raving idiot" time and time again. Such name-calling is simply your seasoning of Attic wit, introduced as a condiment to render a book which is insipid in its own right still more insipid. With those syllables and solecisms, on the other hand, you assault and beset me most stoutly.

But yet, Brixius, there is one more way in which you hedge me in more ruthlessly still; and indeed, you are ruthless beyond all equity and justice, since you are not content to have assaulted me but you also insist on prescribing which arms I may use to defend myself. Thus you command imperiously that I must not attribute to Froben any of the errors which you impute to me personally. Observe how uncivil you are on this point, and inequitable, too: though you knew that my work was printed in Basel, while I stayed in England, and though you cannot doubt that I was too busy at that time to be able to cross over to Basel from London

rere / quicquid errati tamen inueneris in opusculo / potius quam excusori quicquam imputes / omnia improperare malis authori. Enimuero si legem / quam in me tulisti / ferre debes et ipse / futurum non dubito / quin si quid tuorum posthac excudatur uspiam / ubi tibi non sit accessus ad impressorum praelum / satis in te nobis huiusmodi ministrabis telorum / qualia nunc in nos tanquam uno quoque plane transfixurus intorques. Cuius rei satis insigne documentum hic ipse quoque libellus exhibet: quo mihi tam ferociter aliena impingis errata / ut interdum etiam impingas tua / qui quum excuderetur adsistente te / et subinde raptas a praelo formas reformante / tamen absoluto uolumine / si non aut tute librarij lapsus emendasses / aut alius quispiam tuos / futurum fuerat / ut errores neque pauciores / neque minus ferendos / tuus haberet liber / quam quibus nunc insulse sic insultas in [d_1] meo. Quanquam ne nunc quidem / ita repurgasti tuum / quin hinc atque inde neuos aliquot quouis foediores polipo reliqueris.

At ego hac in re sic meam causam tutari possum / ut nec in Frobenium quidem ullam culpam deriuēm / etiamsi ipse literis ad me datis / a suis cessatum operis fatetur / ac pollicetur sese diligentius excusurum denuo. At ego certe quicquid esset / etiamsi corrupta quaedam sine mea culpa uidebam / illi tamen protinus imputare non poteram / conscius exemplar a me nullum quod sequeretur accepisse Frobenium: neque enim eorum ego carminum / praeter ea / quibus regis auspicia ueneratus sum / eaque / quibus in te luseram / uel aedidi fere quicquam / uel aedere adhuc decreueram. Quod si uel amici mei / uel pueri sibi descripsere libellum / aut apud me seruatum negligentius / aut apud quempiam fortasse / cui non in hoc credideram / atque ita contigerit / ut quibus liber adriserit / putarint euulgandum / neque miri quicquam est / si aliquid mendarum substruxerit scriptor / aliquid adstruxerit typographus / exemplari uidelicet usus et corrupto non nihil / et fortasse perplexo / neque aequum ipse feceris / si

2 malis] malis. *1520* 3 Enimuero] *Para. 1520;* tulisti /] tulisti: *1520* 5 uspiam /] uspiam: *1520* 7 transfixurus] tranfixurus / *1520* 9 errata /] errata: *1520* 15 repurgasti tuum /] repurgasti / tuum *1520* 17 meam causam] causam meam *1760* 22 nullum] nullum/ *1520* 25 luseram /] luseram: *1520* 31 usus] usus / *1520* 32 perplexo /] perplexo. *1520*

twice daily, you still choose to throw up to the author whatever mistakes you discover in that little work and to ascribe none at all to the printer. If the same law which you applied to me ought to apply to you, I am sure that hereafter, if anything of yours is printed in any place where you do not have ready access to the press of your printer, you will furnish us with plenty of darts we can turn against you, much the same as those you now launch at us as if each by itself could transfix us. A clear confirmation of that point is yielded by this very tract, which you did oversee, in which you are so fierce in imputing mistakes generated by others to me that at times you impute to me even mistakes which you generated: though it was printed with you standing by and continually correcting the forms as the sheets were removed from the press, once the volume was finished, if you had not furnished corrections for your publisher's errors or some one had not furnished corrections for yours, then your book would contain neither fewer nor more tolerable faults than the ones which you now so insipidly sneer at in mine. But not even now have you thoroughly emended your book, since you left, here and there, some warts fouler than any tumor.

Indeed, I can defend my own cause on this point even without shifting any of the blame onto Froben, although he himself wrote me a letter confessing that his workers were careless in printing my book and promising to reprint it more diligently. And in any event, even if I saw that certain passages had been corrupted through no fault of mine, nonetheless I could not automatically place the blame on him, since I knew that Froben had not received any copy text from me; for the poems in which I celebrated the king's coronation and the poems in which I made fun of you are virtually the only ones which I myself ever published or had ever intended to publish. And if either my friends or my servants made themselves copies of my booklet when it was not guarded carefully enough—either by me or by someone to whom I had lent it (although not for copying)—and if it happened that people who liked my book thought that it should be published, it is not at all surprising that the copyist should have made some mistakes or that the typesetter should have added others, since he had to rely on a copy text which was somewhat corrupt and quite possibly difficult to make out. It is hardly fair for you to blame me for

uitio uertas mihi / quicquid alienus uspiam uel error uel incuria peruerterit / atque ex aliena imperitia me condemnes inscitiae. [d_1v] Nisi protinus pronuncies illiteratum / et doctis prorsus omnibus explodendum / si quis indiligentius occluserit literarum suarum capsulas.

Quod si dubitari non potest / quin alienis mendis infectus sit liber / utpote et excusus typis / et ante non ab uno transcriptus / haud facile adducor / ut credam / quin et ipse me tacitus absoluas apud te / de quibus apud alios tam aperta calumnia traducis: sin tibi penitus insederit fixa / atque offirmata sententia / quicquid inemendatum reperisti / uicio prorsus id contigisse meo / quid aliud / quam laterem lauem / si tibi me purgare contendero? Vide ergo / quam ciuiliter agam tecum. Etenim quanquam (ut uides) possum apud aequos optinere iudices / ut quae mihi impingis / eorum pleraque deriuentur in alios (nisi quae res nulli unquam libro contigit / nusquam ut typographus / nusquam scriptor errauerit / id nunc demum contigisse uideatur meo): Tu quanquam in quibus ut certissimis exultas maxime / in his te uel calumniari maxime / uel certe maxime falli / certissimis mihi liceat argumentis euincere / partim productis authorum testimonijs / quibus erit perspicuum recta esse plurima quae reprehendis / partim prolatis illis ipsis chartulis / quibus olim aedidimus pauca illa / quae diximus / quibus liquido constiterit / aliter a me [d_2] composita quaedam / et aedita / aliter post excusa Frobenio / siue id exemplaris cuiusdam perplexitate contigit / siue euenit incuria / siue a meo describenti libro placuit scriptori quidpiam / quod ipse interlito uersu mutaueram (quis enim satis diuinare possit / quam multis casibus irrepat mendum / aut qua fortuna propemodum omnibus obtingat authoribus / ut uetustis etiam collatis exemplaribus lectio nonnunquam uariet?): Quanquam haec ut dixi possum / ego tamen Brixi quandoquidem tu tam ciuiliter temet in te tuendo gessisti / ut in eam rem nihil fere prorsus attuleris / quod

2 imperitia] imperitia / *1520* 8 credam / quin] credam: quin *1520* 9 alios] alios / *1520;* traducis: sin] traducis / sin *1520* 11 meo /] meo: *1520* 12 contendero?] contendero. *1520* 14 iudices /] iudices: *1520* 17 meo):] meo) *1520* 18 quibus] quibus: *1520* 21 plurima] plurima: *1520* 24 Frobenio /] Frobenio: *1520* 25 contigit /] contigit: *1520;* incuria /] incuria: *1520* 26 libro] libro / *1520* 27 mutaueram (quis] mutaueram: quis *1520* 29 authoribus /] authoribus: *1520* 30 uariet?):] uariet? *1520* 31 tam] *1689, conj. 1760, 1947* iam *1520 1642 1760*

corruptions caused by the errors or inattentiveness of others, and to condemn me for ignorance based on someone else's lack of expertise—unless you will automatically declare a man illiterate and decree that he be hooted out of all learned men's company if he has been just a bit careless about keeping his letterboxes shut tightly.

And if there can be no doubt that the book is marred by faults not my own, since it was set up in type and, before that, transcribed by a number of hands, I can scarcely be led to believe that you yourself do not tacitly absolve me in private of the very same errors of which you accuse me in public with such blatant calumny. If, on the contrary, you do have a deep-seated, fixed, obstinate sense that whatever you found uncorrected ought promptly to be blamed on me, I can no more exonerate myself before you than I can wash the clay out of a brick. See, then, how civilly I will deal with you. For although (as you see) I can carry the point, before equitable judges, that many of the faults you impute to me should be assigned to others (unless something occurred in the printing of my book which has never occurred in the printing of any book at all, that is, that neither the typesetter nor the copyist ever made one mistake); although in the very instances which you belabor most exultantly of all as my surest infractions, I can prove with the surest of arguments that your own judgments are either most slanderous or at any rate most ill conceived, partly by bringing forth authoritative testimonies according to which it will be crystal clear that many expressions which you take to task are correct, partly by bringing forth those very pages in which I once published those few poems I mentioned, which will make it quite clear that what I composed and circulated is different from what Froben printed, whether it happened because of some illegible copy text, or because of inattentiveness, or because some copyist preferred something which I myself changed by cancellations in the first version (for who can adequately divine by how many accidents a flaw may steal in, or by what fortune it happens to almost every author that even among the earliest copies the readings occasionally vary?); although, as I said, I am able to do all these things, nonetheless, Brixius, since you displayed so much civility in defending yourself that you brought to bear almost nothing which had any real bearing on the case (whether some

quidem ad rem pertineat: seu te ingenuus quidam sic obstupefecit pudor / ut non posses cogitata proloqui / seu festinatione praepeditus es obiurgandi mei: statui tecum simili contra ciuilitate contendere et / quod ad errata pertinet huiusmodi / defensionem meam in presente praetermittere / utpote cum erga te inutilem / cui nullo posset unquam pacto satisfieri / tum erga caeteros omnes minime necessariam / quorum ego neminem fore suspicor / cui tu persuaseris / ea mihi prorsus imputanda / quae taxas: sed lector aequus haud dubito / quin quiduis potius comminiscatur ex sese / quam ut me praesumat tam insigniter inscium / ut neque positionem in carmine / neque solaecismum in sermone cognoscam. [d_2 v]

Quod si mei lapsus esse uincerentur maxime / tamen quando ipse librum non aedidi (quae res manifestior est / quam ut liceat tergiuersari uel tibi) quo iure possis obijcere / si quid adhuc meditanti subductum est atque uulgatum ei / qui dicere possit illud Ouidij: "emendaturus / si licuisset / eram"? Quo mihi uersu / si cuiquam alij / meritissime licet uti: Nam ego totum librum / preter ea quae iam olim aedideram / pressurus eram perpetuo / ut qui nec illa ipsa fueram aediturus / nisi literatioribus quam ipse sum / magis adrisissent quam mihi: cui nihil meorum unquam salsum uisum est admodum / nisi quod nunc ex tua bile sentio aliquid habuisse salis / quo frictus es. Quod si librum aliquando publicare statuissem / certe quaedam immutassem: non quod errorem syllabae tam ualde magni penderem / sed quod essent aliqua minus aliquanto seuera quam uellem. In syllabis uero si quid hallucinatus essem / quanquam non fuissem grauatus emendare / tamen in una fortassis et altera / non nimis anxie me torsissem / presertim sicubi commode mutare sine sententiae damno non possem: quandoquidem non eos duntaxat authores / qui tanto te doctrina superant / quanto tu illos superbe despicis / uerum uetustissimos quoque non usquequaque seruasse reperio eodem tenore semper easdem syllabas / qua ex re natus est nimirum [d_3] aceruus ille communium.

2 proloqui /] proloqui: *1520* 3 mei:] mei / *1520;* statui] statu *1689* 4 contendere et /] contendere: et *1520;* huiusmodi /] huiusmodi *1520* 5 praetermittere /] praetermittere: *1520* 13 Quod] *No para. 1520* 17 licuisset /] licuisset *1520* 18 librum /] librum *1520* 19 ea] ea / *1520;* perpetuo /] perpetuo: *1520* 24 immutassem:] immutassem / *1520* 25 sed quod] *1689, conj. 1760*, quod *1520 1642*, quam quod *conj. 1760 1947* 27 emendare /] emendare: *1520* 28 nimis] minus *1689* 31 despicis /] despicis: *1520* 32 reperio] reperio / *1520*

sense of shame struck you dumb, so that you could not utter the things you had thought of, or your hurry to vilify me kept you from it), I have decided to recompense you with a corresponding civility in arguing my own case. With respect to mistakes such as these, I shall simply defer my defense for the present. It would be useless to you, since you can never be satisfied, and unnecessary for others, since I doubt that you will have persuaded anybody at all that the things which you tax are directly ascribable to me. Indeed, I am sure that every equitable reader would imagine almost any explanation on his own rather than presume me to be so extraordinarily ignorant as to know nothing about either placement in a verse or solecisms in phrasing.

But even if your claim that these errors are mine did prevail, still, since I myself did not publish the book (a fact which is too manifest for even you to be able to sidestep), what right do you have to reproach a writer whose work was snatched away and published while he was still thinking it over, and who can fairly cite that line of Ovid's, "I would have emended if I had been given the chance"? If anyone has a right to use this line, I most certainly do. For apart from those verses which I had already published some time ago, I was going to suppress the whole book permanently, and I would not have published even those unless readers more literate than I had liked them more than I did. To me personally, none of my writings has ever seemed at all savory till now, when I see from your bilious response that there must have been some touch of salt in the mockery with which I have chafed you. But if I had at some point decided to make the book public, I would certainly have changed various things in it; not because I would think a syllabic mistake so important, but because several poems in it were somewhat more frivolous than I would have liked them to be. But if I went astray anywhere in my scansion of syllables, even though I would not have been reluctant to correct them, nonetheless in one or two places perhaps I would not have strained too hard to change them, especially where I could not readily make a change without damaging the sense, for I find that not only those authors who surpass you just as much as you pompously scorn them but also very ancient authors did not always scan the same syllables in just the same way, so that there are many syllables which may be either long or short.

Postremo uel eo minus haec me remordet cura / ne quis ea putet mea esse omnia / quae tu carpsisti / quod in his ipsis uideam nonnihil eiusmodi / ut quanquam non sit meum / tamen pro meo me non puderet agnoscere: Neque quicquam dubito / quin cuique inter legendum succurrant exempla / quibus eorum pleraque / quae tu pro soloecismis in nos adnotasti / reperiantur pure puteque latina. Porro futurum denique / ut si quid reprehendisti rectius / id in me tamen certe non possis impingere / qui nec aderam castigationi / nec exemplar / unde excuderetur exhibui / nec librum prorsus aedidi. Contra uero / in quibus ipse aut deciperis aut calumniaris ultro / quae sunt haud dubie supra dimidium / temet ipse traduxeris uel ignorantiae uel sycophantiae / utrobique certe insignis impudentiae / qui tam superbe / tam nulla causa / tam longo tibi expensa tempore ad eum scribens / quem iam secundo prouoces / atque ad inquirendum in te quoque arrogans ac securus excites / tamen tam multa / quae recta sunt / uel imprudens per inscitiam / uel per inuidiam prudens / reprehendas. At tu / quum hunc ad modum strenue mea omnia uelut uno deflauisti spiritu / de te securus / et meras efflans glorias / iubes ut excutiam uicissim tua / nimirum certus / ita tibi pulchre [d_3v] instructa omnia / ut ne Momus quidem uel syllabam possit inuenire / quam uellicet.

Ego profecto / Brixi / multo uelim libentius eos libros excutere / e quibus aliquid excuti possit boni. Quanquam et hunc tuum / etiamsi nihil inde frugis uel expectaui uel reperi / tamen quoniam in me scriptus est / eo legi studiosius / quod quae mutari conueniat / quae uel amicis interdum commendat amor / uel ne quid offendant / obticent / ea plerumque solet inimicus iratus effundere. Itaque sic attentus legi / ut quo tu me uocas (nempe uti in syllabis excutiendis essem curiosus) eo nusquam respexerim / si quid uero inesset rerum / id certe non indiligenter expenderim.

1 Postremo] *No para. 1520* 5 inter legendum] interlegendum *1520 1642* 12 traduxeris] traduxeris / *1520* 14 tempore] tempore / *1520* 15 arrogans] arrogans / *1520* 16 excites /] excites: *1520* 17 tu /] tu *1520* 19 glorias /] glorias: *1520* 20 pulchre] pulche *1520* 21 quidem] quidem / *1520* 23 profecto / Brixi /] profecto Brixi: *1520* 24 tuum /] tuum *1520*

Finally, this circumstance too lessens my grief at the thought that someone should imagine all the faults you carped at were mine: among these very faults I note some which are not mine, and yet I would not be ashamed to avow them; nor do I have any doubt that examples will occur to everyone, as he reads, which will show that many of the things which you called solecisms on our part are actually Latin through and through. Indeed, to sum up, even if you had better cause to criticize some points, you cannot with certainty impute them to me, since I neither took part in the proofreading nor provided a copy text to be used in the printing nor published the book at all; on the other hand, in those instances when your own judgments are either mistaken or wantonly slanderous, which undoubtedly make up more than half of the total, you have convicted yourself of ignorance or slanderous knavery, and in either case, certainly, of egregious shamelessness, since even as you write so insolently and so gratuitously, in phrases you pondered for such a long time and addressed to a man you now challenge a second time, a man whom you rashly and haughtily urge to scrutinize you in the same way, you still criticize so many things with which nothing is wrong, whether ignorance blinds you to what you are doing or envy makes you do it all too clear-sightedly. But even after you have displayed so much vigor of this sort by blowing down all I have written in a single breath, so to speak, smug and breathing an air of sheer glory you urge me to sift through your writings, in turn; doubtless you are quite certain that all of your writings are so finely wrought that not even a Momus can find a single syllable to pick at.

For my part, Brixius, I would much rather sift through books from which I might sift out something good. But still I did read this book of yours, though I neither expected nor found any fruitful material in it; and I read it all the more carefully since it was written against me, and since an angry enemy will often blurt out faults which ought to be remedied, but which love can occasionally endear to one's friends, or which they do not mention lest they injure his feelings. Thus, I did read attentively, but in the following way. While I never paid any heed to the task which you set me—namely, that I should be punctilious in examining your syllables—wherever you had anything substantial to say I assuredly pondered it with no little diligence. And yet, however

Antimorus nomen libelli Brixij / quem sine mente nuper emisit

Et tamen quantumuis abhorream ab eo / ut ociosus occuper aucupio syllabarum / certe monosyllaba illa mens / quam in Chordigera desyderaueram / in Antimoro quoque sedulo quaesita / nec mihi tantum quaesita / sed multis / adeo nusquam inuenta est / ut libelli titulus / etiamsi breuis / tamen uideatur omnibus dimidio longior esse quam debet: opusque tuum non Antimoron appellandum / sed Moron: eoque iustius / quo tu insulsius in meum nomen affectas haberi salsus / quasi non in Hermolaum Barbarum fortuna dederit hoc scurrandi genus uel impense barbaris / et in Thomae Mori nomen Germano Brixio / qui / uere germaneque Moro / sit uere germaneque germanus. [d_4] Eum ego librum quum perquam attentus inspicerem nihil aliud uidi quam delira conuicia / quae uel recte scripta reprehenderent / uel mihi alienos lapsus obijcerent / uel tuum caput recta repeterent. Porro multa tam belle competebant in me / ut potius quadrare uideantur in quemlibet. Latratus audio plusquam caninos / sed elatratos inaniter / morsus plusquam rabidos / sed qui temet unum mordeant / uirus plusquam uipereum / sed uni tibi noxium. Quae quum sint eiusmodi / non miror admodum uereri te / ne forte non sustineam legere / quae nemo certe durare queat ut perlegat nisi haec omnia (qui Brixij lepor est) amaenis condulcarentur deliriis. Quae mihi tam uehementer in Morico isto adrident Antimoro / ut quum primum mihi dabitur ocium sim curaturus / ut accuratius aliquanto / quam nunc excusus est excudatur denuo / fortassis et illustretur commentariis: tantum abest / ut isti gloriae tuae inuideam / qua tibi factus uidere deus / si Mori despuibile tibi nomen exsibiles / ac uenerabile nomen Brixij libro isto tam elimato / tam erudito / tam lepido / tam festiuo / tam sacro denique aeternae consecraris infamiae. Cuius libri dotes admirandae / ne quid oscitantem forte lectorem lateant / nos exempli causa

5 titulus /] titulus *1520* 6 breuis /] breuis: *1520* 8 appellandum /] appellandum: *1520* 10 dederit] de derit *1520;* genus] genus/*1520* 10–11 barbaris] barbarus *1520 1642 1689 1760 1947,* barbaro *conj. 1760* (*see commentary*) 11 qui /] qui *1520* 12 Moro / sit] Moro sit / *1520;* germanus] Germanus *1689* 13 librum] librum: *1520* 14 conuicia /] conuicia: *1520* 15 obijcerent /] obijcerent: *1520* 17 caninos /] caninos: *1520* 18 inaniter /] inaniter. *1520;* qui] quid *1520* 19 uipereum /] uipereum: *1520* 20 uereri te] uererite *1520* 21 queat] queat: *1520* 22 lepor est] *1947,* lepor ē *1520,* leporem *1642 1760,* lepores *1689, conj. 1760* 23 Antimoro /] Antimoro: *1520* 26 commentariis:] commentariis. *1520;* gloriae] glotiae *1520* 27 despuibile] *1689,* dispuibile *1520 1642 1760 1947* (*see commentary*) 30 aeternae] *1642 1689 1760 1947,* aeterne *1520*

much I abhor the thought of idling away my energies stalking syllables, certainly that monosyllable "mind," which I had found wanting in the *Chordigera,* also turned out to be so completely absent from the *Antimorus*—though I searched for it conscientiously, and not only I but many others too—that the title of your book, short as it is, still seems to everyone to be longer by a half than it should be: your work should be called, not *The Anti-Moron,* but *The Moron.* This new title seems all the more fitting in view of the way you witlessly affect a reputation for wit by punning on my name, as if fortune had not made it possible even for total barbarians to joke in this way about Ermolao Barbaro. To joke in this way about Thomas More's name is also possible for Germanus Brixius, a true and germane cousin-german to a work which is truly, germanely named *Moron.* While I inspected that book very attentively indeed, I found nothing else in it but mad allegations which either criticize things written correctly or reproach me with someone else's errors or directly recoil upon your head. Further, many of your abuses suited me so prettily that they appear to be just as well suited for anyone. I hear currish barking, but it is barked out in vain; rabid biting, but it lacerates you alone; viperish virulence, but it harms only you. Since this is the sort of thing you had to say, I do not wonder at all that you fear lest perchance I will not have the patience to read what no one could endure to read to the end unless (here we have Brixius' sole charm) all these things were sweetened with entertaining delusions. They afford me personally such a powerful incentive to smile at that moronic *Antimorus* of yours that as soon as I have the leisure I am going to see to it that it is reprinted, somewhat more carefully than it has been printed already, and maybe even elucidated with commentaries; note how far I am from begrudging you any of that glory which makes you a god in your own eyes when you hiss at the name More, which you find so despicable, and with that book of yours, with so polished, so erudite, so charming, so festive, and finally so inspired a performance, you consecrate the venerable name Brixius to immortal infamy. Lest the admirable gifts of this book should perchance elude the yawning reader, we will point out a few examples to

Antimorus *is the name of the mindless tract Brixius just issued*

quasdam indicabimus / ut his ueluti stimulis excitatus / penitius in librum penetret / atque aduertat attentius / quam lepidi ioci / sales / delitiae / mel / et saccarum / ac plane [d_4v] lacteum suadelae flumen ex amne gallo scaturiat.

Exordiar igitur / unde tu exorsus es / ab endecasyllabis illis / quos scripsisti Macrino. In quibus tanquam in operis frontispicio insignem stuporis tui titulum praescripsisti. Nam quum initio Macrinum stentorem tibi fecisses Homericum / eundem etiam Nestorem / olim poetam optimum / iam uero et oratorem derepente prodeuntem / tam uenustum / tam uehementem / ut sua suada / cui tot charites / tot lepores / Venus afflauerat / ita quolibet tuum perpelleret animum / ut illi reluctari non possis flagitanti / uti quam primum exiret Antimorus / eoque ipsius auspicijs uolumen emiseris / cuius hortatibus non ualuisti resistere: paulo post / oblitus tui / negas eum unquam flagitando atque orando extorquere potuisse / ut elephantis ille praeclarus partus aederetur ante completum nouennium. Verum ne Venus inuenti tui deperiret tibi / libellum tam uenustum subprimenti diutule / quando scommata / nisi statim retorta / non habent gratiam / coactus es properare / et quo libellus aduersus epigramma posset subito paucis annis exire / necesse tibi fuit / singulis fere biduis / singulos uersus absoluere. In quibus quum ne tantulum quidem tibi suffragetur ingenium / ut uel primam paginam potueris eo tenore progredi / quin [e_1] tibi statim tam insigniter excideres / ac memoria lapsus / ipse sic pugnares tecum / ut quem tam potentem oratorem feceras/ qui te in suam sententiam impulerit / eundem proximo fere uersu diceres nihil persuasisse: cuius impulsu librum te scripseras aedere / quando uidelicet non potuisti tam mellitae suadelae resistere / eum protinus affirmares nunquam tam commode potuisse dicere / ut librum tibi possit elicere: Quum igitur quod dicebam Brixi in ipsis offendas foribus / et tam diu limatis / ac relimatis uersibus / tam longo labore / non alia scribas deliria /

2 penetret /] penetret: *1520* 3 suadelae] suadele *1520 1947* 5 igitur /] igitur: *1520;* es /] es *1520* 10 uehementem /] uehementem: *1520* 12 possis] possis / *1520* 14 resistere:] resistere / *1520;* post /] post *1520* 16 elephantis] elephantinus *1689* 18 diutule /] diutile: *1520* 23 ingenium /] ingenium: *1520* 27 diceres] diceres / *1520;* persuasisse:] persuasisse / *1520* 29 affirmares] affirmares / *1520* 30 possit] posset *conj. 1760;* elicere:] elicere. *1520*

spur him on, as it were, to penetrate more profoundly into the book and observe more attentively what charming jests, witticisms, pleasantries, honey and treacle, and, indeed, what a milky torrent of persuasiveness streams forth from the Gallic headwaters.

I will begin, therefore, where you began, with the hendecasyllables you wrote to Macrin. In these, as if in the frontispiece of your work, you inscribed a distinctive announcement of your imbecility. For at first you made Macrin your Homeric Stentor, your Nestor to boot, long established as the finest of poets, but now unexpectedly sallying forth as an orator too, and an orator so comely and so vehement that his power of persuasion, which the comely one, Venus, had charged with such numerous graces and charms, could manipulate your feelings however he pleased; you could not stand firm against his insistence that the *Antimorus* should come out at once, and therefore you brought out the volume under his auspices, since you had not been able to withstand his urgings. Then, a little while later, forgetting yourself, you deny that for all his insistence and his oratory he could ever have compelled you to issue that splendid elephantine offspring before nine full years had elapsed. But so as not to let the comeliness of your invention go to waste by suppressing so comely a tract even a little too long—since taunts, unless hurled back at once, never win any acclaim—you were forced to hasten, and, in order that your tract against my epigram might come out lightning-quick, in just a few years, you were forced to dash off individual lines in approximately two days apiece. But since in these lines your talent does not even sustain you long enough to make it through your first page with a consistent pace, or without losing your train of thought so prodigiously and contradicting yourself so flagrantly through a lapse of memory that, although you at first made Macrin out to be a sufficiently powerful orator to force you to think the way he does, you now in almost the next line say he failed to persuade you at all; although you wrote at first that he forced you to issue your book, since supposedly you could not withstand so much honeyed persuasion, you immediately assert that he never could have spoken so deftly as to lure the book from you; thus, Brixius, since you trip up on the very threshold, as I was saying, and in lines so long polished and repolished, with such sustained effort on your part, you write the same sort of drivel

quam quae subito solent effutire moriones: quis non assentiat illis uersiculis / quibus lectorem tibi uelut uoluptatis illecebra concilians / promittis ei paruo e carmine sedulo legenti magnam demum uoluptatem fore? Erit haud dubie / nisi quis adeo sit agelastos / ut ne ad id quidem rideat / quo uno fere mouent risum hi / quibus natura negauit ingenium: nempe nihil ut dicant quod consistat secum / sed diuersa omnia / atque pugnantia / tanquam uigilantes somnient. Quanquam non dissimulabo esse quidem / qui putent non esse stultum istud / sed nasutum / tanquam lepide uolueris irridere Macrinum / quem tam dulcem oratorem / tam uehementem facias / ita denique tibi uim adferentem sua suauiloquentia ut quod [e_1v] unum tibi uenusta illa suada suadeat / persuadere non possit. Ego certe non ita suspicor. Nam et is uidetur Macrinus esse / qui tuo sit amore dignior / quam quem ridere debeas / et reliquus liber ad diuersam longe uirtutem propius quam ad eiusmodi uafricies accedit: eoque causa non erat cur arte sic laborares tegere / quam diu tibi tuus liber haesit in manibus: nam ut scommatibus gratiam deterit mora / sic istius generis omnia tempus et labor commendant admodum. Nam si quid dicas insigniter stolide / id quo maiore conatu parturieris / eo pepereris gratius.

Quin mire facetum et illud / quod ueritatem quoque tuis mendaciis asseris iterato mendacio / dum rursus Herueum seruantem facis patriam / rursus uictorem tua tuba buccinas / rursus nostras rates agitantem uexantemque decantas / quae tam uera sunt omnia quam tu. Iam uero probatio / quam adfers / mirifica est. Ais enim ea quae narras / Anglorum testata funeribus. Si aliorum funera loqueris / quam qui in Regente perierunt / tam uera sunt illa funera / quam uera fuit illa uictoria: sin eos exprobras peremptos / quos Regentis incendium absumpsit / non adeo stultus sum (quantumuis tu me stultum uoces) quin tuum istud acumen sentiam pistillo quouis obtusius / quo sic nobis exprobras exustam

5 agelastos /] agelastos: *1520* 7 secum /] secum: *1520* 8 quidem /] quidem: *1520* 9 nasutum /] nasutum *1520* 10 Macrinum /] Macrinum: *1520* 14 dignior /] dignior: *1520* 15 debeas /] debeas: *1520* 16 accedit:] accedit / *1520* 17 manibus:] manibus / *1520* 18–19 omnia] omnia / *1520* 28 perierunt /] perierunt *1520* 29 uictoria:] uictoria / *1520* 32 obtusius /] obtusius: *1520*

which morons blurt out on the spur of the moment, who can fail to agree with the lines where you try to win over your reader as if with a bribe of delight, where you promise that he will obtain great delight from your poem if he reads conscientiously? Obtain great delight he assuredly will, unless he is so stone-faced that he does not even laugh at the kind of performance, the only kind almost, through which those to whom nature denies any wit raise men's laughter, namely by talking sheer nonsense, in pure contradictions and paradoxes, as if they are lost in a daydream. Though I will not dissemble the fact that some think this is not a foolish caprice but a cunning one, as if you had set out to be witty in making a laughingstock out of Macrin, since you make him out to be so sweet and so vehement an orator, and finally so able to sway you with his suave address, that on the one point where his comely persuasion attempts to persuade you, it fails to persuade you. I, at any rate, have no such suspicion. For Macrin, it seems, merits more loving treatment from you than that you should be laughing at him, and the rest of your book approximates a very different kind of felicity more nearly than this sort of wiliness. Hence you had no reason for toiling so artfully to disguise how long you had hung on to your book; just as delay detracts from the acclaim which is given to taunts, even so time and labor set off your sort of wit to advantage. For whenever you say something that is egregiously obtuse, the more you travail in preparing it the more acclaim greets your producing it.

And that is another remarkable touch of urbanity, indeed, when you vindicate the truthfulness of your lies by reiterating a lie, where you once again make Hervé out to be saving his homeland, again take out your trumpet and sound him the victor, again harp on him harrying and troubling our fleet, even though all these claims are as truthful as you are. Now the proof you adduce here is wonderful indeed. For you say that the things you recount are attested by Englishmen's deaths. If you mean any deaths but those of the men who were killed in the *Regent,* those deaths are as truthful as that victory was. If, on the contrary, you are trying to reproach us with the deaths of the men who perished in the burning of the *Regent,* call me fool just as much as you like, I am not such a fool that I fail to perceive that on this point your acumen is as dull as a pestle, since you reproach us with the fact

nauem / quasi dum arderet nostra / [e_2] uestra interim alserit / aut quasi eo uictorem probes Herueum / quod etiam prior arserit. Hoc Brixianum acumen est. Haec est Brixiana uictoria.

Sed operae precium est uidere / quanto cum artificio tractes eum locum / in quo ego inter principis nostri laudes commemoro restitutam ab illo reformatamque rempublicam quorundam ante sceleribus / auaritia / rapinis / delatione / calumnijs deformatam. Ergo quum statuisses nihil meorum relinquere ab ineptis intactum calumnijs / in hunc locum praecipue tumultuaris ineptissime. Hunc miris merisque sycophantijs exagitas. In hunc praeclaras omneis atque admirabileis effundis ingenij tui uirulentias. Hic temerarius tibi uisus sum / qui rem tantam / meis uiribus tam longe imparem / sim ausus adgredi. Quasi mihi principis enarrandas laudes omneis desumpserim / ac non potius / quod erga superos quoque / citra culpam / pro suo quisque facit affectu / id ipse fecerim in uenerandis principibus / ut tam felicia principatus auspicia / primo statim die tam salutaria / quum idem certatim facerent omnes / ego quoque pro mea uirili qualicunque poteram carmine concelebrarem. Qua in re / ut nihil dubito / quin et uberius laudari potuissent a peritioribus et dignius a praestantioribus: ita neque meo satisfecisset officio / quod fecissent alii / neque mea carmina [e_2v] cuiquam obstiterunt / quo minus et alij fecerint / et quibus facere libuisset / licuerit. Denique quisquis iusserit a nullo nostrum laudari principem / nisi qui parem praestare sese tantae rerum moli possit / is admirationis praetextu regis uirtutibus inuidet / quas quum omnes praedicare debent / omnes semel iubet conticescere.

At hic Apellem nobis (si superis placet) reuocas ab inferis / quod quidem tibi facile est / si quemadmodum scribis / tam familiares habeas infernaleis furias / ipse tam egregius pictor interim / ut quum istud in primis ei sit curandum / quisquis os cuiusquam

4 Sed] *No para. 1520* 12 sum /] sum: *1520;* tantam /] tantam *1520* 14 ac] at *1642 1689 1760* 21 alii /] alii *1520* 25 praetextu] praetextu / *1520* 26 inuidet /] inuidet: *1520;* debent /] debent: *1520* 28 At] *No para. 1520* 30 interim /] interim: *1520*

that our ship was burned up as if yours felt a chill while ours blazed, or as if you could prove Hervé the victor because his ship was first to catch fire. So this is what Brixian acumen is! So this is a Brixian victory!

But it is worthwhile to observe with what artfulness you handle that passage in which I record among the praises of our prince how he had restored and reformed a commonwealth which had previously been deformed by certain men's crimes, avarice, depredations, incrimination, and calumnies. Even though you decided to leave none of my writings untouched by your own inept calumnies, against this passage you stir up the most pointless tumults of all. You worry this passage with wondrous and unalloyed slanders. On this passage you pour all the splendid and admirable virulence your talent affords you. Here I seemed overweening to you for attempting so weighty a theme, one so vastly exceeding my powers, as if I had taken it upon myself to relate all the praises deserved by our prince, and had not done the same thing in offering due homage to princes that everyone does, even toward the saints, without any reproach, in accord with his own inclinations. Others were competing to celebrate such a happy beginning of our prince's reign, so advantageous to us from the very first day, and I did the same to the best of my abilities, in whatever manner of verse I was able to write. In this regard I do not doubt that it could have been praised both more richly, by more expert writers, and more worthily, by more distinguished ones; even so, others' actions would not have absolved me of my personal duty, and my poems kept no one from doing as I did, or claiming at will the same liberty to do so. Most important of all, whoever decrees that our prince ought to be praised by no one who cannot sustain the whole weight of so great a theme envies our king's attainments under a pretext of admiring them: while everyone ought to extol them, he bids everyone to keep permanently silent about them.

But at this point, if the gods will allow it, you summon Apelles back up from the infernal regions, which indeed is no difficult feat for you, if, as you write, you are on such familiar terms with the infernal Furies. Meanwhile you yourself prove to be such a consummate master of portraiture that even though anyone wishing to paint a definitive portrait must take care, above all, to observe what features and what disposition are so characteristic of

pingendo uelit exprimere / uti eas parteis / eum respiciat situm / qui ita sit cuique proprius / ut is repraesentatus faciem reddat maxime cognobilem / tu sic depingi regem postules / ut amabile decus reuerendi uultus / idque adeo tam rarum / ipsique suum / quoque uno maxime possit agnosci / delere prorsus e pictura iubeas. Nam tibi caeco prorsus pictori uideor uel stipite plane stupidior / qui non praeuiderim / eas fuisse laudes omittendas / quas fere solas / uel publica causa / uel sua principem referebat audire / utpote tales / quas ut fateor non fuisse Brixiano more poeticas / qui nihil poeticum censet nisi fictum / ita nemo fuit Anglorum / qui non suo bono senserit esse ueras: nec quisquam adeo sine [e3] sensu uiuit / ut non sentiat esse uere regias / nisi tu nobis aliud inuenias magis regium / quam regnum ab omni parte fatiscens reficere / prosperumque rursus ac felix reddere.

At nec praesentis honor principis quicquam decessori detrahit: cuius aduersa ualetudo fuit in causa / ne annis aliquot ante mortem proximis uel publicis rebus posset / uel domesticis sufficere: eoque nec mirandum / nec ipsi certe imputandum / si quorundam perfidia / quibus ille nimis credidit / sit labefactata respublica quam filius eius fere collabentem / feliciter exortus erexit: idque tam celeriter / ut correptis coercitisque repente maleficis / quorum scelere calamitas illata fuerit / omnia reformarit illico / priusquam se pateretur insigniri diademate. Nec sibi uisus est / neque sano certe cuiquam contumeliosus in patrem / quod illius ualetudine / aliorum malitia labentem erigeret patriam / aut quod seuere animaduerteret in eos / quorum perfidia / in patriae perniciem / fefellerat patrem / aut quum quaedam etiam patris instituta / quanquam non incommoda populo / maiore tamen commodo rescinderet / bonumque mutaret in melius. Et tibi uidetur immanis impietas / si quod patris felicitati negauit morbus / hoc filij statim regia uirtus effecit / si patriae compilatores / deceptores patris / euersores legum / [e3v] in patriae bonum / in legum robur /

3 postules /] postules: *1520* 5 delere] *see commentary* 6 pictori] pictori / *1520* 9 audire /] audire: *1520;* ut fateor] (ut fateor) *1520* 14 fatiscens reficere /] fatiscens / reficere *1520* 15 At] *No para. 1520* 16 causa /] causa: *1520* 17 proximis] proximis: *1520;* sufficere:] sufficere. *1520* 20 erexit:] erexit. *1520* 25 labentem] labentem / *1520* 27 quum] *see commentary* 28 populo /] populo: *1520*

this or that subject that when these are set forth in a likeness they will render the countenance most recognizable, the way you insist that the king be portrayed prescribes that we simply leave out of the picture the crowning appeal of his reverend face, one so rare and distinctively his, although this alone renders him most recognizable. For to you, a completely blind painter, I clearly seem stupider than a stump since I did not foresee that I ought not to touch on those praises which in our prince's case were preeminently worth mentioning, whether for the people's sake or for his own; for although I concede that these praises are not poetic in the same way as Brixian praises (since you suppose nothing poetic except what is fabricated), even so there was no one in England who failed to sense through some personal benefit that these praises are true, nor is anyone living so senseless that he does not sense them to be truly regal, unless you can invent for us some feat more regal than to remake a realm which is everywhere crumbling and to render it once again prosperous and happy.

Nor does the honor we give to the present prince detract anything from his forebear's acclaim, whose ill health was the cause of his failure for several years before his death to show adequate vigor in either public or domestic matters. Therefore we have no cause to marvel, and certainly no cause to blame him, if through the perfidy of certain men whom he trusted too much the commonwealth declined; as it swayed on the brink of collapse, his own son rose propitiously to right it, and did so with such purposeful haste that he captured and curbed the felons whose crime had produced the calamity, and he immediately reformed the whole realm before letting himself be adorned with the crown. Nor did it seem to him, nor to any sane person, at any rate, that he injured his father in righting his fatherland when it had been bowed down because of his father's ill health and the malice of others, or in dealing severely with those through whose perfidy, mortally threatening his fatherland, his father had been led astray, or in rescinding some of his father's laws, although these were not disadvantageous for the people, for the sake of some greater advantage, changing good for the better. Even to you, does it seem a portentous impiety if the son's regal virtue quickly accomplished what sickness denied to his father's felicity; if, for the good of his fatherland, for the strength of the laws, for the honor of his

in patris honorem coercuit / aut si quid denique prudentissimo patre prudentior filius in administranda republica uidit acutius? Quae quum princeps ageret non ad praesentem tantum rerum statum feliciter / uerum in futurum quoque tam salutare sanciret exemplum / ut facile declararet sese principalium esse artium omnium principem / non fuissem profecto deterritus / quo minus ea laudassem / etiamsi culpa quaepiam recidisset in patrem: Nec a nobis unquam tantum patris impetrasset pudor / ut eius facti laudem subriperet filio / quo facto nullo unquam saeculo princeps ullus quicquam fecit laudatius / aut quod magis publicae interesset rei / commendari memoriae.

Nec fortunae unquam tribuissem tantum / ac ne naturae quidem / uti uanum alterutrius fulgorem tam inclytae uirtutis uerae praeferrem gloriae. Quibus enim parentibus nascamur illis in manu est. Virtus una uere commendat bonos. "Nam genus et proauos / et quae non fecimus ipsi / uix ea nostra uoco." Qua Nasonis sententia / neque Maro quicquam neque Homerus / quos opponis mihi / aut uerius unquam dixit / aut salubrius. Quorum etiamsi utrunque ualde suspicio: nunquam tamen hactenus apud me ualebunt / ut ambobus hac in parte tribuam / quantum uni tribuam Platoni: qui op[e_4]tabile quidem censet / quantaque potest cautione curandum / ut filij nascantur honestis parentibus / quod uelut seminarium quoddam indolis atque uirtutis indatur occulte nascentibus: et tamen / ut fortunatiores aliquanto censet bonos prognatos bonis / ita multo laudatiorem iudicat mali patris bonum filium / idque adeo merito. Nam si sit eo turpior / quo magis claro patre degeneret / an non uicissim conuenit / eo plus cuique laudis esse / quo magis in diuersum tractus improbi parentis exemplo / sua ipse uirtute benefactisque claruerit? Haec

2 filius] filius / *1520* 5 sese] sese / *1520* 12 Nec] *No para. 1520* 13 fulgorem] fulgorem / *1520* 16 proauos /] proauos *1520* 17 quicquam] quicquam: *1520* 19 suspicio:] suspicio. *1520;* nunquam] nun quam *1520* 20 ualebunt /] ualebunt: *1520* 22 curandum /] curandum: *1520* 24 censet] censet: *1520* 25 iudicat] iudicat / *1520*

father, he suppressed the despoilers of his fatherland, the beguilers of his father, the subverters of the laws; or if, finally, the son surpassed even that most prudent father in prudence and showed in one case more discernment in governing the commonwealth? Since our prince's actions respecting these matters not only had beneficial results in the context of current affairs but also afforded the future so wholesome a regal example, and thereby established him prince of all princely attainments, I would certainly not have been deterred from praising these actions of his even if some blame had been thrown back on his father; nor would we ever have deferred so completely to our sense of respect for the father that it could have preempted the praise which was due to the deed of his son, since in no age has any prince ever performed any deed which was worthier of praise or which it could be more in the public interest to memorialize.

Nor would I ever have assigned such importance to fortune, or even to nature, that I could have preferred the vain splendor of either to the true glory of such an illustrious virtue. Who our parents are is theirs to determine; a good man's only true commendation is virtue. "Our race and our forebears, whatever we have not obtained by ourselves, I scarce call those things ours." Neither Vergil nor Homer, whom you set against me, ever said anything either truer or more wholesome than this maxim taken from Ovid. However much I esteem both the writers you mention, they will never prevail on my judgment to such an extent that I will concede as much authority on this point to both put together as I concede Plato alone. He does actually consider it highly desirable, an aim which we ought to pursue with all possible care, that children should have honorable people for parents, since in this way, to speak metaphorically, a seedbed of good nature and virtue is secretly fostered in these children when they are born; nonetheless, while he considers the good offspring of good parents to be somewhat more fortunate than others, even so he supposes the good son of a bad father to deserve greater praise, and quite rightly. For if a person is all the more dishonorable if he degenerates from an eminent father, does it not hold, in turn, that more praise is due to someone who is drawn in the opposite direction by the example of a bad parent but has nonetheless grown eminent by his virtue and his good deeds? Thus,

igitur quum senserit / haud dubie non alium poetam "exturbare sua debuit urbe Plato" / quam tui palponem similem / qui uel a fortunae iubes / uel a naturae commodis adulari principibus / a uirtute laudare non sustines / quae uel cum dispendio popularis aurae laudanda sit: et contra uulgi receptos sensus / cui fere placent pessima / mellitis numeris essent opiniones bonae sensim inferendae pectoribus.

Quamobrem / ego quod dixi / etiam si qua culpae pars haesisset in patre / non reticuissem tamen filij laudes / quae tum fuissent eo certe ipso cumulatiores / quod paternum errorem emendare potius quam imitari delegisset: atque id ita fecissem / rationi uni [e_4v] parens atque obtemperans / etiamsi poetas omneis / si uulgus uniuersum sentirem longe sentire diuersa: tantum abest / ut nunc ea non obticuisse poeniteat / quorum reprehensio ad eos pertinet / qui patris fide ad suum quaestum et malum publicum sunt abusi / gloria uero et immensa et aeterna pertingit ad filium / qui tam celeriter affectis poena nocentibus / ac restituta republica / patrem simul et patriam pius in utrunque / uindicauit. At tu laudator egregius / quae potissima regiae laudis portio sit: quam et priuatim et publice / uelut omnium laudum principem / et ei principi in primis propriam / totus agnoscit populus: quae adeo patri nihil detrahit / ut praecipuum ei decus adijciat / quod pater sit eius principis / qui regnum uere regijs administret artibus: eam censoria uirgula iubes expungi / non ob aliud opinor / quam quod uera sit: adeo nihil tibi placet / nisi poeticum tuum / ex ficto falsoque conflatum totum. Nam poesis tua (testante temet) "id si sustuleris / nulla poesis erit." At princeps quum ea faceret / non in tenebris occulte / quasi benefacti puderet / sed in clarissima luce / in oculis tractaret omnium / in priuatis / publicis iudicijs / in commitijs / in amplissimo totius regni conuentu / cum plebe / cum

2 similem /] similem: *1520* 4 laudare] laudari *conj. 1760;* sustines / quae] sustines: quae / *1520* 5 sit:] sit / *1520* 7 inferendae] inserendae *conj. 1760* 13 diuersa:] diuersa / *1520* 15 quaestum] quaestum / *1520* 18 laudator] laudatot *1520* 19 sit:] sit / *1520* 21 populus:] populus / *1520* 25 sit:] sit. *1520* 28 puderet /] puderet: *1520* 29 publicis] in publicis *conj. 1760*

since these were his own views, undoubtedly the one sort of poet that "Plato should have driven from his state" was the flattering sort, like yourself, who command that we adulate princes according to the endowments of fortune or nature, and will not let us praise them according to virtue, which we ought to praise even if it costs us the windy esteem of the people; even contrary to the ordinary ideas of the masses, whose taste generally runs to the worst things in life, we should little by little instill proper values in men's hearts with the sweetness of verses.

Accordingly, as I have said, even if some blame had come to rest on the father I would not have suppressed the praise due to the son, which indeed he would have earned all the more richly by resolving to remedy the error of his father instead of to imitate it. And I would have proceeded in this way, deferring and hearkening to reason alone, even if I saw that all of the poets and all of the masses saw things just the opposite way. Note how far I am from regretting that I did not keep silent about those deeds the infamy of which falls on those who exploited the father's credulity and served their own profit through public misfortune, while a vast and an undying glory accrues to the son, since he so quickly punished the guilty and restored the commonwealth, and thus redeemed father and fatherland at once, making good his devotion toward both. But you, who are such an egregious praiser, brandish your censor's rod at the principal element of his regal praise, the same one that the whole of our people in public and private avows as the prince of all praises and that which befits England's prince best of all, one so far from detracting from his father's memory that it actually affords him his own crowning honor, since he himself fathered this prince who now governs the realm with the true regal arts, and you command that this praise be expunged, on no other account, I suppose, than because it is true. Indeed, nothing meets with your sanction apart from that poetic product of yours which is wholly conflated from fabrication and falsehood. For your poetry, as you assure us, "will cease to be poetry at all if you take that away." But since our prince did these things not in secret, by night, as if he were ashamed of his good deeds, but in the brightest daylight, in the sight of everyone, in private and public hearings, in councils, in the amplest assembly of the entire realm, and in accord with the commons as well as the

proceribus: quum omnis aetas / ordo / sexus / [f_1] rem tam illustrem uideret / tam salubrem sentiret / tam egregiam laudibus in caelum ueheret: ego uidelicet / quod potissimum praedicare debebam / solum solus omitterem? Vt / quod nunc dictum incessit Brixius / id indictum riderent etiam pueri / quibus ipsis uel stupidissimus si non sensissem / uel improbissimus si non probassem / uel inuidissimus si non laudassem / merito uideri poteram.

Et tamen hunc locum tu nescio ineptius exagites / an inuidiosius / adeo caeco praeceps impetu / ut te non sentias inscitiae propemodum notare principem nostrum / atque adeo / quum ei parem facias / paris inscitiae notare etiam tuum. Nec interea tamen (quod tibi certe perpetuum est) quicquam consistis tecum. Nam primum ita curam ei tribuis camoenae latiae / ut tamen leges ignoret carminis: mox adeo facis inscium / ut ne quid uerba quidem sibi uelint sciat: et tamen tuum regem cum eo copulas / ut ex aequo sint ambo "Cecropiae numine plena deae." Numnam haec pulchre cohaerent? sed non est istud nouum / ut altero quoque uersu excidas tibi.

At me condum laudatorem uocas et parcum / ipse laudator adeo non profusus / ut eam laudem / quam Vergilius tribuit pastoribus / tu quum uelles applicare principibus / aliquid tamen tanquam nimis sumptuosa foret abraseris / atque in de[f_1v]terius / quod semper imitando soles / immutaris. Nam quum illius uersus sic habeat in pastores duos / "ambo florentes aetatibus" / tuus habet in duos reges / "ambo pares aetate": atque ita Vergilius in illis exprimit aetatis florem: tua laudatio quum his aptetur principibus / qui uere florent aetate / tamen sic est anceps / ut duobus possit conuenire decrepitis ac silicernis senibus. Porro quam de uirtute quoque subiungis / non admodum prodiga laus: quandoquidem ita uirtutem utrique tribuis / ut tibi relinquas liberum /

1 proceribus:] proceribus / *1520* 2 sentiret /] sentiret *1520* 3 ueheret:] ueheret / *1520* 3–4 debebam /] debebam: *1520* 4 omitterem? Vt /] omitterem: ut *1520* 5 riderent] *conj. 1760 1947*, rident *1520 1642 1689 1760*, rideant *conj. 1760* 5–6 stupidissimus] stupidissimus: *1520* 7 inuidissimus] inuidissimus: *1520* 9 Et] *No para. 1520;* exagites /] exagites *1520* 9–10 inuidiosius /] inuidiosius. *1520* 15 carminis:] carminis / *1520* 16 uelint sciat:] uelint / sciat. *1520* 17 deae.] deae *1520* 20 At] *No para. 1520;* parcum /] parcum *1520* 23 deterius /] deterius *1520* 25 aetatibus" / tuus] *see commentary* 27 florem:] florem / *1520* 29 silicernis] silicerniis *conj. 1760 1947* 30 laus:] laus. *1520* 30–31 quandoquidem] quandoquidem / *1520*

nobles; since every age, order, and sex saw how splendid his policy was, sensed how wholesome it was, and praised to the heavens how noble it was; should I actually have been the one person to leave out the one thing which I should extol most of all? How even the youngsters would laugh at my not mentioning what Brixius now has attacked me for mentioning; for to these very youngsters I would rightly have seemed either the stupidest of men, if I had not perceived it, or the most malignant of men, if I had not admired it, or the most envious of men, if I had not praised it.

And yet it is hard to tell which is worse in the way that you worry this passage, your pointlessness or your invidiousness; you are so head-over-heels in your blind rushing on that unwittingly you very nearly brand our prince with ignorance, and indeed, since you make your prince our prince's equal, you brand yours with ignorance equally. Nor yet, in the meantime (though assuredly this is your style all the time), do your words show the slightest consistency. For at first you concede to our prince some concern for the Latian muse, but so little that he may not know the rules governing versification; soon you make him so ignorant that he does not even know what the words mean; and yet you couple your king with him, so that both kings are equally "filled with the genius of the Cecropian goddess." These statements cohere none too handsomely, do they? But this is nothing new, that in every other line you should lose your own train of thought.

Yet you call me a thrifty and stingy praiser, even though you yourself are such an ungenerous praiser that when you wished to apply to two princes the same praise that Vergil attributed to shepherds you pared away something, as if you supposed it too sumptuous, and (as you generally do to whatever you imitate) you altered his praise for the worse. For his verse reads as follows, describing two shepherds, "both being in the flower of their age," while your own reads, describing two princes, "both equal in age." In that way, Vergil aptly expresses in those shepherds age at its most flourishing; your praise, even though you appropriate it for princes like these, who are truly in the flower of their age, is nonetheless so ambiguous that it could befit two decrepit and cadaverous old men. Further, the praise you tack on about virtue is not at all generous, since the way you concede each king virtue

utrique simul ac libebit adimere. Nam quum pronuncias "pares uirtutibus ambos" / neutri tamen affirmas inesse: sunt enim pares (si nescis) tam qui pariter carent / quam qui pariter habent.

Nec tamen istud eo dico / quod in eam partem te sensisse censeam / sed ut ostendam / si quis ad eum modum tuas excutiat laudationes / quo tu calumniaris meas / quam facile locus reperiatur obnoxius. Nec ego tamen huc Apelles atque Alexandros euoco / non Cherilos / pugnos / exilia / neque taleis tibi moueo tragaedias / qualeis tu mihi cies. Quod si et res minus esset illustris / et princeps noster tam esset inscius / quam tu eum facis / in quantum fors periculi coniecisses me: quum uix fieri possit / ut qui uersatur in publicis negotijs / non aliquem habeat aliquando / qui libenter optet [f$_2$] calumniari / si uel res pateretur / uel ignoratione principis liceret abuti: praesertim si qui sint / qui rursum cupiant rerum statum in deterius trahi / ut quem nunc aegre ferant magis in summam prosperare publice / quam seorsum sibi. Verum hi / si qui sint huiusmodi / sic rem uiderunt ipsi non clancularis machinis / sed actam et tractatam publicitus / sic in suis artibus sentiunt praestare principem / qui iterum atque iterum prorepentes uiperas / ac uelut post hyemem nouo sole apricantes sese / et calumniae uetus uirus denuo tentantes effundere / denuo retudit / compressit / elisit / ut facile sentiant noxijs uotis suis nullam relictam spem.

At tu quum istiusmodi scribas Brixi / quae sint non absurda modo atque inepta / uerum scelesta quoque et (quoad per te fieri potest) perniciosa: tamen Deloinum / Budeum / Lascarem / uiros literarum et uirtutis gratia toti commendatos orbi (quorum nominibus maior debebatur honor / quam ut libello contaminares istiusmodi / tanquam gemmas collocares in luto) nominas / eosque tecum uelut in parteis attrahis: quos et castigatores praedicas / et consultores adhibitos inconsultissimis consiliis. At ego quanquam

1 utrique] utrique / *1520;* libebit] *1520,* libebat *1642 1689 1760,* libeat *conj. 1760 1947* 2 inesse:] inesse. *1520* 4 Nec] *No para. 1520* 4–5 censeam /] censeam: *1520* 8 Cherilos] cherilos *1520* 11 me:] me / *1520* 13 calumniari /] calumniari. *1520* 14 abuti:] abuti. *1520* 15 trahi /] trahi: *1520* 20 uiperas /] uiperas: *1520* 22 elisit /] elisit: *1520* 24 At] *No para. 1520* 25 quoque] quoque: *1520* 28 debebatur] debebarur *1520* 28–29 istiusmodi /] istiusmodi: *1520* 29 nominas /] nominas. *1520*

leaves you free to revoke it at will. For while you pronounce both to be "equal in virtues," you never affirm there to be any virtues in either; in case you have not heard, men are just as much equals who lack something equally as men are who equally possess it.

I do not say this because I think that was your meaning but rather to show just how easy it is to discover a vulnerable passage if anyone examines your praises in the same way that you slander mine. Nor yet do I here invoke any Apelles and Alexander, any Choerilus, beating, or exile, nor do I advance any such tragedies against you as you stir up against me. But if the action in question were any less widely appreciated and our prince were as ignorant as you make him out to be, what dire peril you might have brought down on me! For it is almost impossible for anyone who is involved in political business to forestall the appearance of someone, at some point, who would gladly seize any occasion for slander if either the action in question admitted his cavils or he could exploit any ignorance on the part of the prince, especially if there are some persons who would like the whole state of affairs to be violently changed for the worse, since they dislike the way that the present state of affairs is more prosperous for the public at large than for them by themselves. But these men, if there are any such men, themselves saw the way that the action in question was done and advanced, not with any clandestine machinery, but out in the public domain; they themselves perceive how much our prince excels them in their favorite arts, he who beat down, suppressed, and stamped out the vipers time and time again, every time that they crept out of hiding as if to lie basking in the new sun which follows a winter and to try to pour forth again their old venom of calumny; hence they themselves are quite aware that their own harmful longings have lost every hope of fulfilment.

And yet, Brixius, even though what you write is not just absurd and pointless, but criminal as well, and indeed as pernicious as you have been able to make it, nonetheless you name Deloynes, Budé, and Lascaris, men revered by the whole world for their learning and virtue (whose names deserved greater respect than that you should contaminate them with such a tract as yours, as if setting jewels in the mire), and force them to enlist, as it were, in your faction; for you claim that these men were brought in to review and to aid in the planning of your ill-planned plans. But

de syllabis illis ac soloecismis quos obiectas mihi non possum spondere quid sentiant (quorum / ubi me audierint / nec in illis quidem detrectabo iudicium) [f_2v] certe taleis esse eos persuasum habeo / et philosophicae rei scientia / et rerum prudentia publicarum / ut si tu cuiusquam eorum calculum hac sane parte possis extundere / quo se (quod ad regias laudes attinet) sentire testetur tecum / ego tibi et in reliquis concedam omnibus / et laudem ultro deferam / qui nunc aliud suspicari non possum / quam quod uidetur omnibus / illas inferni furias (quas scribenti tibi fateris adfuisse) tale tibi inspirasse consilium: quod / seu furorem spectes / seu uirulentiam / haud obscure tartaream refert originem.

At aliquando tandem / uelut per antrum Trophonium emergens ab inferis / exhilaratus / in iocum solueris / et risu canis irritati meam subsannas epistolam / qua libelli dilationem confero in pictorem / cuius podagra fecerat / uti serius aliquanto / quam statueram / ueniret ad regem. Haec tibi causa non placet: homo supersticiose poeticus ferre non potest / ut dicantur uera / et ciuilitate plusquam aulica deridet / si quis apud principem de re nihil obscoena uerbis utatur ijsdem / quibus utitur populus. Quis ita ridentem non rideat?

Porro quid illud sibi scomma uelit / non intellego / uidetur enim sapere nescio quid salis reconditi / quo significas meis officere studijs curam rei dome[f_3]sticae: quo dicto nescio an tuis arte uendices praerogatiuam / quasi tibi nulla sit domus / sed liber et expers curarum / alienas paropsides uelut parasitus obambules / eoque necesse sit tuum poema praecellere / quod otium et cibus excolat alienus. Ego certe de te sentiebam honestius hodieque sentio: quanquam libellus tuus (ut uere dicam) et Pyrgopolinicen refert et Artotrogon. Neque uideo quid ad rem pertineat exprobrare mihi / quod habeam domum / nisi tu domum non habeas. Nam alioqui iocus ille festiuus / et (ut Plautinus ait parasitus) dictum de dictis melioribus in te recideret.

2 quid] *1520, conj. 1760,* quod *1642 1689 1760 1947;* audierint /] audierint: *1520* 3 iudicium)] iudicium *1520* 10 consilium:] consilium / *1520;* quod /] quod *1520* 12 At] *No para. 1520;* Trophonium] Tryphonium *1520, 1642* 14 irritati] irritati / *1520;* dilationem] *conj. 1760 1947,* delationem *1520 1642 1689 1760* 16 regem.] regem *1520;* placet:] placet / *1520* 19 obscoena] obscoena / *1520* 20 rideat?] rideat. *1520* 21 uelit] uelut *1520;* intellego /] intellego *1520* 22 reconditi /] reconditi. *1520* 23 studijs] studijs: *1520;* domesticae:] domesticae / *1520* 24 praerogatiuam /] praerogatiuam: *1520* 30 mihi /] mihi: *1520* 31 festiuus /] festiuus: *1520*

though I myself cannot vouch for their feelings regarding those syllables and solecisms with which you reproach me (and even concerning these points I would not shy away from their judgment if they could hear me out), I am fully convinced that those men have such a thorough knowledge of philosophical principle and such a practical mastery of political principles that if you can extort an endorsement from any of them on this issue, at any rate—that is, if you can get him to attest his agreement with you on the subject of praising kings—I will give way to you on all the rest of the issues and freely surrender my praise; though at present I cannot help suspecting what everyone thinks, that those infernal Furies (who you confess stood by you while you were writing) were the ones who inspired such a plan in you; for whether you look at its fury or its virulence, it recalls very clearly indeed its Tartarean origin.

But once, at long last, while emerging from hell by Trophonius' cave, as it seems, you are cheered and break out into jesting, and with the laughter of an angry cur you snarl at my letter, in which I attribute the tardiness of my booklet to the illuminator whose gout had caused it to be given to the king somewhat later than I had intended. You do not like this plea; superstitiously poetic, the man cannot bear that the truth should be told, and outdoes any courtier's refinement in laughing at me for using, as I tell the prince of a thing which is not at all obscene, the same words that the people use. Who will not laugh at whoever laughs thus?

Further, I do not understand what that taunt means, although it seems to smack of some well-hidden wit, in which you indicate that my household concerns interfere with my studies. Perhaps you are advancing this saying as an artful expedient to win precedence for your own studies on the basis that you have no household, but free and untrammeled by cares you roam back and forth between other men's plates like a parasite, and thus your poem must needs be preeminent because it is nourished by leisure and other men's bread. I for one thought more highly of you, and I still do today, even though, to speak truthfully, your tract does recall both Pyrgopolynices and Artotrogos. And I fail to see how it pertains to the matter at hand when you reproach me for having a household unless you have no household, since otherwise that festive jest or that excellent *bon mot,* as one Plautine parasite puts it, would simply recoil on you.

Certe quemadmodum te persuadeo mihi non esse plane parasitum (quantumuis istud liber prae se ferat tuus) ita uere te suspicor Cynicae sectae philosophum / non a latratu tantum / uerum etiam quod ubique te uideo ad diuitias ludere / ubique ad mendicitatem / ubique ad famem applaudere. Nam ita ludis in liberos meos / ut eorum describas miseriam / si tantum uersus meos haereditate / ac non etiam numos essent habituri: quasi tui sint futuri solis paternis uersibus felices. At ego liberis tuis / si quos aut habes / aut habiturus es unquam / longe laqueos / longe mendicitatem deprecor / quae mala tu facete scilicet ominaris meis / atque ex animo precor / ut uberior eis af[f3v]fulgeat alicunde fortuna / quam ex uersiculis tuis / quorum ego neminem esse usquam tam insanum censeo / qui trecenta milia redimat teruncio / quae quidem huius generis sint / cuius effutiuisti hactenus.

Eiusdem salis et illud est / quod lupo temet assimilas famelico / tanquam nisi meo bono reges duo sanxissent pacem / me miserum agnellum semel deuorasses integrum: nunc uero nefas ducis facta pace litigare / eoque libellum istum nunc demum aedidisti blandulum. Sed illud demum diuinum fuit inuentum / quod diras omneis / ac bellas illas charites inferorum furias / tam formosulas amiculas adfinxisti tibi / quibuscum lusites atque ocium oblectes tuum / imitatus uidelicet quosdam non imperite ridiculos / qui quum esse sibi quaedam uel corpore deformia / uel moribus foeda sentiant / quae uel obnoxia dicterijs sint uel criminationibus / homines scurrandi solertes in sua uicia ludunt ipsi / ut quando euitare non possint obprobrium / ansam saltem carpendi praeripiant aemulis / ipsique potius de se triumphum ducant. Ita quum tu uideres Antimoron tuam non Moriam modo / sed Maniam quoque spirare / quando nemini futurum uidebas ambiguum / unde sit ille furor emissus / maluisti in tuas furias ipse praeludere / quasi eas ultro sese offerentes tibi / amico ui[f4]delicet tam necessario et iuratissimo mystae / fueris emissurus in me.

1 Certe] *No para. 1520* 4 ludere /] ludere: *1520* 4–5 mendicitatem /] mendicitatem: *1520* 7 habituri:] habituri / *1520* 8 futuri] futuri / *1520* 9 unquam /] unquam *1520* 12 fortuna /] fortuna *1520* 21 amiculas] amicas *1760;* quibuscum] quibus cum *1520* 22 tuum /] tuum: *1520*

At any rate, even as I persuade myself that you are not an out-and-out parasite (however your book may enforce that impression), I do truly suspect that you are a philosopher of the Cynical sect, not only because of your barking but also because I observe how you everywhere make fun of riches and everywhere applaud beggary and famine. For you joke at my children's expense and you write of their misery if they were to have for their legacy only my lines, and not also my coins, as if yours will be happy with nothing beyond the lines of their father. But for my part I pray that your children, if you have any or ever should have any, may never have any experience of the gallows or beggary, the ills which urbanely, of course, you forebode for my children, and I pray from my heart that some richer fortune may dawn for them from some other source than your lines, since no one is, I think, so demented that he would buy three hundred thousand of those for a threepence, at least not of the sort you have blurted out up to now.

That other jest smacks of similar wit when you liken yourself to a famished wolf, as if you would have swallowed me up all at once, like a wretched lamb, if the two kings had not ratified the peace for my benefit; but now that the peace has been made you consider it wicked to quarrel, and so now, at last, you have published that meek little tract of yours. But that was an utterly heavenly invention when you fabricated all those Baneful Spirits, and those pretty infernal Graces, the Furies, to be your darling girl friends, to play with and gladden your leisure. You seem to be imitating certain clever clowns who discern in themselves either physical deformities or moral depravities which are vulnerable either to scoffs or to scandals. These master-buffoons mock their own flaws: since they cannot circumvent disrepute they can at least outstrip their own rivals in seizing a pretext for carping and, rather than give up the game, hold a triumph at their own expense. Similarly, when you saw that the spirit which breathed through your own *Antimorus* was not only moronic but maniacal to boot, since you saw how apparent to everyone it would be from what quarter this furor was loosed, you chose rather to take the initiative by joking about your own Furies, feigning that they had spontaneously offered their services to you, since of course you are such a close friend to them all and the most firmly sworn of their votaries, and that you would then loose them upon me.

Illud / opinor / nemo leget unquam / qui non insignem ingenij tui notam iudicabit / et plane Brixianam facetiam / quod quum te dignis uersibus ad tuam ipsius me pinxisses effigiem / ueritus ne nondum satis expressisses te / "rabulam" adnotasti in margine / quod talem me diceres esse in patria. Ego Brixi qualis domi sim non dico / ne similis tibi sim / cuius gloriam / siue quam ipse tibi tribuis / non mereor / siue quam tribuunt alij / non affecto. Tu uero qualis domi sis effecisti tandem foris ut cognosci possis. Quem (quum te uideri uelis a secretis esse reginae) non pudet eiusmodi rabie rabire in consiliarium regis / qua nec in rabulam quidem quisquam rabit nisi rabula.

Et tu quum hunc in modum toto te libello gesseris / operaeprecium est uidere quomodo sumpta scilicet auguris persona / diuines fore / ut me pro hoc tam amico in me officio / sis habiturus inimicum / cuius tu pudendos lapsus pia cura tollas in authoris honorem / relaturus tamen ab ingrato malam gratiam / atque ita tractas istud admirabile atque ex intimis rhetorices penetralibus depromptum schema / ut fere concionantis quoque personam induas et iniecta frequentius mentione christiani / [f_4v] atque identidem peccatoris nomen inculcans / tanquam animae res agatur / propemodum soloecismorum uelis agam poenitentiam / quod appropinquet (credo) regnum caelorum. Ego certe Brixi tuum illud augurium de me non dubitabo fallere: qui nunquam tibi statui inimicus esse. Nec usque adeo sum inhumanus / ut tam amicum in me officium non agnoscam / hominis tam officiosi in famam meam / ut aeditis atque excusis in me famosis libellis / aliena errata pro meis mihi insusurret in aurem / tam indulgentis in honorem meum / ut potius quam me non impetat falsis calumnijs / suum ipse nomen ueris inhonestet obprobrijs / tam propensi in salutem meam / ut principem meum uel impietatis insimulet / uel inscitiae / ni me prorsus exterminet. Nec usque adeo sum stupidus ut non sentiam quanto precio redimendus sit eius uiri fauor / qui sit tam

1 Illud / opinor /] Illud opinor *1520* 3 uersibus] uersibus / *1520* 4 nondum] non dum *1520* 7 alij /] alij *1520* 8 foris] foris / *1520* 10 rabie] *1689*, rabia *1520 1642 1760 1947* 13 auguris] *1689*, *conj.* *1760*, augurijs *1520 1642 1760 1947* 14 fore /] fore: *1520;* officio /] officio *1520* 15 lapsus] lapsus / *1520* 24 Nec] Neque *1760* 28 meum /] meum: *1520* 29 nomen] nomen / *1520* 30 meam /] meam: *1520;* inscitiae /] inscitiae *1520* 31 stupidus] stupidus /*1520*

There is one thing that I suspect no one is ever going to read without judging that it is an outstanding mark of your ingenuity and a stroke of distinctively Brixian urbanity: after painting me in your own image, in lines which are worthy of you, you were worried that your self-portrait might not do you justice, and so, in a marginal note, you marked "litigious wrangler," since you wished to say that in my fatherland that is my status. Brixius, I do not say what my status at home is, lest I be like you; I deserve no such glory as you grant yourself, and I crave no such glory as other men grant you. But you have made it possible to recognize, even abroad, what your status at home is: you wish to be styled a queen's secretary, but you rant at a king's privy councilor with more rabid impudence than anyone would rant, even at a wrangler, unless he himself were a wrangler.

And since this is the way you conduct yourself all through your tract, it is worthwhile to observe how you take up the part of an augur, of course, and divine that henceforth in return for your own friendly service toward me I will act as an enemy toward you, even though you picked out my shameful errors with pious concern for the honor of their author, an ingrate, however, who you think will never repay you except with ill thanks. You handle that marvelous conceit, drawn from rhetoric's innermost shrine, with such zeal that you practically take on a preacher's part, too; you throw in the word "Christian," too often, and frequently harp on the title of "sinner," as if you were concerned with the health of my soul, and all but insist I do penance for my solecisms, I suppose since the kingdom of God is at hand. I myself, indeed, Brixius, will not be reluctant to render your augury concerning me false, since I never resolved upon being your enemy. Nor am I so inhuman as not to acknowledge such a friendly service toward me on the part of a man so desirous of serving my fame that in defamatory tracts, published and printed against me, he whispers of others' mistakes in my ear as if they were my own; a man so careful of my honor that before he will pass up the chance to inveigh against me with false calumnies he dishonors his own name with truthful disgrace; a man so intent on my welfare that he arraigns my prince for either impiety or ignorance if he does not simply exterminate me. Nor yet am I so stupid as not to sense just how indebted I am for indulgence like this from a man who is

prudens / ut altero quoque uersu obliuiscatur sui / tanquam lethaeum poculum interbiberit: tam generosa palma / ut non erigat modo se aduersus maledicta aliorum / uerum ipse quoque sese oneret suis: tam fortis et inuictus pugil / ut Herculi surrepta claua / perpetuo pugnet secum: tam oculatus ac lynceus / ut non uideat sua in se redire scommata: tam urbanus / ut insanum / stultum / furiosum / canem / rabulam / habeat in fa[f_5]cetijs: tam placabilis ac tranquillae indolis / ut fidefragos / perfidos / et periuros inclamans / tamen abstineat conuicijs: tantus adsertor poetices / ut eam contemni postulet / praemonens / ne quis ambiat ab ea laudari / quae sibi uetat credi: tam uehemens orator / ut defendat eum prouocare / qui responderit / prouocatum uero / qui prior laeserit: tam pulchre oliuam medijs gerens in armis / ut in media pace de bello litiget: tam aequus ut insaniat / quod ipsius liber uere sit taxatus mendacij / ab illo / cuius totam gentem eodem libro falsus insimularat ante periurii: tam fructuosus Encomiastes / ut principes a corporis dotibus laudari postulet / a fortunae muneribus ferat / a uirtute non sinat / nisi si quid dicatur in genere / sic ut dici possit in quemlibet: si quid uero factum sit eiusmodi / ut id uiri / mulieres / pueri / lapides prope collaudent / eius rei pythagoricum indicat silentium: tantus Apelles / ut (nisi tabula eius cum fauore spectetur) duos uideatur principes ex eadem propemodum denigrare fidelia: tam anxie christianus / ut nisi mihi duo reges ab illo (precibus opinor) impetrassent ueniam / nunquam potuisset obtinere Christus / quin acerbe olim debacchatus in nos / quoniam uno sit repercussus uerbulo / me misellum agniculum homo plus ullo lupo famelicus [f_5v] totum deglutiret: tam lepidus denique / tam festiuus / tam solers / et undique tam consummatae sapientiae / ut sibi ipse familiareis esse fateatur infernaleis furias.

Eas ergo quum habeas Brixi domesticas / ut sis fortassis ambiendus alijs / sicubi sint / quibus cum eiusmodi sodalibus libeat

1 prudens /] prudens: *1520* 2 interbiberit:] interbiberit / *1520* 4 suis: tam] suis. Tam *1520;* pugil /] pugil: *1520* 5 secum: tam] secum. Tam *1520* 6 scommata:] scommata / *1520;* urbanus /] urbanus *1520* 8 fidefragos] foedifragos *conj. 1760* 8–9 inclamans /] inclamans: *1520* 9 conuicijs:] conuicijs *1520* 11 credi: tam] credi. Tam *1520;* orator /] orator: *1520* 12–13 laeserit: tam] laeserit. Tam *1520* 14 litiget: tam] litiget. Tam *1520* 16 periurii:] periurii. *1520;* Encomiastes /] Encomiastes: *1520* 18 genere /] genere: *1520* 19 eiusmodi /] eiusmodi: *1520* 21 silentium: tantus] silentium. Tantus *1520;* Apelles /] Apelles: *1520* 23 fidelia: tam] fidelia. Tam *1520* 27 deglutiret: tam] deglutiret. Tam *1520* 28 sapientiae /] sapientiae: *1520* 30 Eas] *No para. 1520*; domesticas /] domesticas: *1520*

so circumspect that he cannot remember what he wants to say from one line to the next, as if he had just drunk up a draught out of Lethe; so noble a palm that he not only stands upright despite other men's maledictions but even weighs himself down with his own; so stout and unvanquished a pugilist that, using the club which he pilfered from Hercules, he is everywhere violently at odds with himself; so keen-sighted and Lynceus-like that he fails to perceive that his own taunts recoil on him; so refined that he counts "madman," "fool," "lunatic," "cur," and "wrangler" among his urbanities; of so placid and tranquil a nature than when he proclaims someone "faith-breaking," "perfidious," and "perjured," he abstains nonetheless from abuse; so great a champion of poetry that he orders that she should be held in contempt, warning all in advance not to covet her praise, since she suffers no one to believe her; so vehement an orator that he upholds the view that a man who responds to a challenge delivers the challenge, while the first to offend is the man who is challenged; so adroit at upholding the olive branch in the midst of hostilities that in the midst of peace he is quarreling about a war; so equitable that he goes mad because his book was truthfully taxed for its lying by a man whose whole people that same book, before then, had falsely indicted for perjury; so wholesome a praiser that he orders us to praise princes for their physical gifts, lets us praise them for fortune's endowments, but does not permit us to praise them for virtue except in a general way which we might use for anyone at all, and imposes a Pythagorean silence whenever men, women, and children, and even the stones, one might say, all praise some worthy deed; so great an Apelles that he would appear to be blackening two princes from virtually the same pot of paint if his canvas is not viewed indulgently; so careful a Christian that if two kings had not secured me his pardon (with prayers, I suppose), Christ could never have stayed the man, ravenous beyond any wolf, from devouring me whole, like a hapless lambling, simply because he had been stung with one word in reprisal for savaging us long ago; so clever, so genial, so artful, and so thoroughly and consummately wise that he himself tells us the infernal Furies are his familiars.

Thus, since that is the company you keep at home, Brixius, someone somewhere who likes to play games with such intimates

ludere / ego te profecto nec inimicum horreo / nec amicum expeto. Nam hostem tuum nihil timendum est / ne (quod tu minaris) unquam inuadant furiae / nempe trabalibus clauis arctius ferruminatae tibi / quam ut a tam charo capite queant auelli quoquam. Amicis uero ac familiaribus eiusmodi pestis possit nocere contagium. Contra inimicus ipse tibi non ero: neque enim eum odisse possum / cuius sic obsessi misereor: immo adamarem certe / ni uererer / ne me redamares mutuo / ut qui frequenter audierim / quam sit molestus ac noxius amor eiuscemodi spectrorum.

Proinde quoad licet / erga te sic neutro memet affectu geram / ut nec dignaturus unquam sim albusne sis an ater inquirere. Quanquam nec opus est istud inquirere: tam atrum enim tuum te atramentum reddidit quam carbo est. Tantum ne tam grati officij prorsus oblitus uidear / quo meorum uersuum mendas adnotasti sedulo / nec eas cuiusquam pateris errores haberi quam meos / diris interim tute ac furiis (si uera fateris) obnoxius / utrique [f6] nostrum supplex quod sit salubre comprecor / uti superi mihi tibique tam propitij sint / amborum uicia ut corrigant / ac mihi soloecam orationem castigent / tibi perpurgent soloecismos ingenij: mihi barbara uerba uelint e sermone tollere / tibi barbaros istos mores e pectore: denique benigni largiantur et mihi sanos pedes in carmine / et tibi sanum caput in corpore.

Londini in aedibus Pynsonis.

6 ero:] ero. *1520* 7 misereor:] misereor. *1520* 11 Proinde] *No para. 1520* 12 albusne] albus ne *1520* 13 inquirere:] inquirere. *1520* 16 cuiusquam . . . quam] *see commentary* 20 soloecam] solecam *1520* 20–21 ingenij:] ingenij / *1520* 22 pectore:] pectore / *1520*

as yours may well crave your acquaintance. I for one neither quail at your emnity nor covet your friendship. For no one needs to fear lest the Furies will attack your enemy, as you threaten, since they are too deeply attached to you, with the most secure rivets, for anything to tear them away from a head they love so dearly. Your friends and familiars, however, risk hurt by contagion from this sort of plague. Nor will I myself be your enemy, for I cannot hate anyone whom I pity for being thus afflicted; indeed, I would certainly come to love you if I did not fear you would come to love me in return, since I often have heard how annoying and harmful the love of such specters can be.

Accordingly, as far as possible, my feelings about you will remain neutral; in fact I will not so much as try to find out whether you are white or black. But then there is no need to find that out; your own black ink has stained you as black as a coal. Still, lest I should seem to have simply forgotten so gracious a service as yours was in carefully marking the flaws in my lines and refusing to let them be blamed upon anyone but me, at a time when (if you are telling the truth) you yourself were beset by the Banes and the Furies, I humbly pray for whatever shall serve to make each of us whole; that the powers above may be so propitious to me and to you that they remedy both our deficiencies, correcting my uncouth expression as they purge away your uncouth thinking; that they may be so kind as to pluck out the barbarous words from my speech and those barbarous morals of yours from your heart; and, at last, that they may be so good as to grant me sound feet for my verse and you a sound head for your body.

London, in the publishing house of Pynson

COMMENTARY

This commentary follows the principles of the commentary on More's poems (see p. 309, above) except that all notes on the *Letter to Brixius* are keyed to page and line numbers.

594/4 **lusisset . . . septem.** Since More's letter to Brixius was published not later than April 1520, this remark dates More's Brixius epigrams (nos. 188–95, 209) to between November 1512 and April 1513. At 604/18–19 More suggests that he read and reacted to Brixius' *Chordigera* (*editio princeps* January 15, 1513) at a time when it might not yet have been printed. Cf. Allen, *4*, 252, lines 39–40.

594/7 **sub ipsum conuentum principum.** Probably a reference to Henry VIII's imminent meeting (June 7, 1520) with Francis I at Calais, at the Field of Cloth of Gold; see 608/28–29; Allen, *4*, commentary at 269, line 93; and *CW 6*, commentary at 51/6.

596/5–6 **nullus . . . amicos?** Cf. Plutarch, *Moralia* 86 C, translated as follows by Erasmus in *ASD 4/2, 173*, lines 13–15: "Chilon ille sapiens, quendam dicentem sibi nullum esse inimicum interrogauit, an nullum etiam haberet amicum." The same saying is cited in Plutarch, *Moralia* 96 A, and *ASD 1/3*, 378, lines 99–100. No one who stands by his friends (or compatriots) can avoid making enemies.

596/8–11 **inimicum . . . iratus.** Cf. *Adagia* 1709, *Opera omnia, 2*, 641DE: "Semper me tales hostes insequantur," and *Adagia* 2218, *Opera omnia, 2*, 787B.

596/14 **plusquam muliebre iurgium.** Cf. Allen, 2, 93, lines 82–83: "parum generosi pectoris est dolorem suum foeminarum more conuitiis vlcisci." More repeatedly arraigns Luther for "whorish wrangling" ("meretricia iurgia") in the *Responsio;* cf. *CW 5*, 30/4, 58/31, 474/33–35.

596/20–21 **sis . . . queat.** Cf. Terence, *Hecyra* 233–34, and *Responsio, CW5*, 244/6 *sidenote:* "Vix fieri potest, ut peior euadat [sc. Lutherus]."

596/25–26 **traduceres.** Brixius plays on the double meaning of *traducere* ("translate" and "traduce") in discussing More's epigrams based on Greek poems; see Appendix B (*Antimorus*), 496/258 *sidenote.*

596/27–598/1 **Ostendisti . . . uelim.** Cf. *CW 8,* 481/11–18.

596/28 **temet . . . graphice.** Cf. *Adagia* 306, *Opera omnia, 2,* 153CD.

598/2–4 **ut . . . debacchari.** Cf. Appendix B, 488/126–27, 538/34–41.

598/4–6 **Verum . . . Brixijs.** Cf. Heraclitus, fr. 49, worded thus in *A.P.* 7. 128 and Diogenes Laertius, *Vitae philosophorum* 9. 16: εἷς ἐμοὶ ἄνθρωπος τρισμύριοι, οἱ δ'ἀνάριθμοι | οὐδείς ("One man for me is equivalent to thirty thousand and countless men are but as nobody"). There is another allusion to this *sententia* in Allen, *5,* 490, lines 97–98. Cf. *CW 8,* 832/14–18.

598/9–10 **iucundioris insaniae.** See *Moriae encomium, ASD 4/3,* 116–18, where Folly distinguishes between the pernicious "insania" inflicted by *dirae* or Furies and the pleasant "insania" brought on by "iucundus mentis error".

598/18–20 **non . . . me.** The question of who struck the first blow is the leading concern of the letter to Brixius; see 606/11–13, 606/27–608/2, 608/14–18, 608/26–610/2, 620/15, 630/13–15, 656/11–12, and *Adagia* 4039, *Opera omnia 2,* 1189A: "Qui prior laesit."

598/21 **At . . . debueras.** More directs the same charge at Tyndale many times in the *Confutation.* For a verbal equivalent see *CW8,* 283/7–8.

598/25–26 **Qui . . . tuis.** In Allen, *4,* 229, lines 472–88, alluding to Brixius' own statements in Allen, *4,* 130, lines 68–73, More complains that Brixius avoids any close-range debate [*cominus pugnare*] which might actually come to the point and instead tries to overcome More with impertinent abuse from afar [*eminus*]. What More wants is a straightforward contest judged according to the palpable merits of each party's case; cf. the *Letter to Dorp,* Rogers, no. 15, lines 211–17, and below, note to 620/6. In an earthier sense, personal abuse and irrational arguments very often strike home even more directly than hard factual proofs; for More's own vivid expression of this working paradox see 606/25–610/12. Though he shares Erasmus' esteem for dispassionate *collatio argumentorum* as the surest procedure for judging which case is the best one, More is far too experienced a pleader to think that all judges use such a procedure. Matching Brixius argument for argument, More must also match him taunt for taunt.

598/27 **tuorum . . . reuerituri.** Cf. Lucretius 2. 51–52.

600/3 **duelli.** In Allen, *4,* 129, line 44, Brixius claims that "by the law of dueling" (*iure duelli*) he is entitled to answer More's epigrams in kind. For More on the "laws of war" see 608/30–610/1 and note.

600/8–11 **QVVM . . . auxilium.** More refers to the "Holy League" of Pope Julius II, Emperor Maximilian, Ferdinand of Aragon, and Henry VIII, who himself joined in 1511, against Louis XII of France. In 1511 the French had given Pope Julius II a stinging defeat at Bologna and had summoned a council of "schismatic" cardinals at Pisa to controvert Julius' authority as pope; by this time, however, the Venetians and Spanish were already completely committed to salvaging Julius' war effort, and it seems that what Henry desired most of all was a share in the glory of victory. See Polydore Vergil, pp. 156, 158, and 160.

600/11–13 **naues . . . compescerent.** More's statement of the relative size of the fleets, ambiguous as it is, may be disputed; see Appendix A, p. 434.

600/13–17 **Quae . . . perierunt.** More's cameo history of the encounter which took place on August 10, 1512, between the *Regent* and the *Cordelière,* the largest ships in the English and French fleets, respectively, may again be disputed on some points of detail; see Appendix A, pp. 435–37. More, however, insists on his readiness to provide more elaborate proof in a longer rebuttal which was suppressed on Erasmus' advice (Allen, *4,* 239–41, 252, lines 54–56); see 620/30–33, 632/23–26. According to Polydore Vergil (p. 186), judged according to casualties (the English lost 600 men, the French 1,000) the battle was technically a victory for England. The *Cordelière,* though a Breton ship, sailed for the French because Queen Anne of Brittany was married to Louis XII of France. The ship's name is derived from the name of an order of Franciscan tertiaries which Anne herself founded for young ladies at court, l'Ordre de la Cordelière; see Appendix A, p. 434, n. 1. Naturally Anne showed a rather proprietary concern for the fortunes of this ship, and ultimately made Brixius her own official secretary as a reward for his poem on how this ship was lost; see 654/9.

600/18–20 **non . . . nouam.** More arraigns Luther in very similar terms for subverting traditional readings of Scripture: " . . . ut interpretetur e suo quisque sensu scripturam sacram: et sibi, quam libeat, fidem formet nouam" (*Responsio, CW 5,* 618/33–620/2). Cf. also Horace, *Ars poetica* 151–52, 338–39:

> Atque ita mentitur [sc. Homerus], sic veris falsa remiscet
> Primo ne medium, medio ne discrepet imum.
>
> Ficta voluptatis causa sint proxima veris,
> Nec quodcunque volet poscat sibi fabula credi. . . .

For More the admixture of general truths in *Utopia,* primarily a fabric of totally fictional details, makes it just such an artful composite of fiction and truth as both he and Horace approve of; cf. *Utopia, CW 4,* 250/5–8, where More jokingly says that if he *had* chosen to write theoretically about the ideal state and a story like that of *Utopia had* occurred to him then, he would not have shrunk from that fiction which might have made truth, as if smeared round with honey, flow more pleasantly into men's souls. Brixius' fiction lacks truth even in this sense.

600/20–604/24 **quum . . . Horestes.** More arranges his criticisms of Brixius' *Chordigera* to correspond to the mocking critique of two stolidly artful historians in Lucian, *Quomodo historia conscribenda sit* 14–15; see pp. 555–56, above. Though he may have known Willibald Pirckheimer's translation of this text by Lucian (Allen, 2, 151), More assuredly knew Lucian's Greek text as well. The name of the Polylerites in *Utopia, CW 4,* 74–78, is derived from an imaginary "city of Much Nonsense" (πόλις πολλοῦ ληροῦ) projected by one of Lucian's mendacious historians in *Quomodo historia conscribenda sit* 31.

600/21 **pietatem . . . inuidiae.** Cf. Appendix A, 448/15–16.

600/21–22 **Angliamque . . . periuram.** Cf. Appendix A, 448/20–21.

600/23 **Herueum plusquam Herculeum.** Hervé de Porzmoguer was the Breton commander of the *Cordelière.* For the phrasing cf. *Adagia* 641, *Opera omnia,* 2, 277F–278E.

600/25–27 **inuectus . . . disijceres.** Cf. Appendix A, 448/29–34; *CW 8,* 659/7–8; and *Adagia* 2660, *Opera omnia,* 2, 897A.

600/26 **parua comitante caterua.** Cf. *Aeneid* 2.40: "magna comitante caterua."

600/28–30 **plerasque . . . immergeres.** Cf. Appendix A, 450/37–39.

600/31–602/1 **Regentem . . . insequereris.** Cf. Appendix A, 450/46–51, based on Ovid, *Metamorphoses* 1.933-38. In calling Brixius himself "noble cur," More may well be alluding in this passage, as he does in 652/2–5, to Brixius' own "cynical" or "currish" practice of cravenly twisting the truth to delight likely benefactors. According to Diogenes Laertius, *Vitae philosophorum* 2. 66, Diogenes, prince of the Cynics, once hailed Aristippus, prince of the Cyrenaics, a timeserving hedonist sect, by the name "regal cur." More inverts the satirical thrust of this hare-hound comparison as he taxes the tergiversation of a more formidable adversary in *The Confutation of Tyndale's Answer, CW 8,* 801/32–34: " . . . Tyndale hath as ye have herde scudded in and out lyke an hare that had xx. brace of greyhoundes after her, and were a ferd at every fote to be snatched up." Cf. also no. 185/1–7 and the Commentary thereon.

602/4 **Validis . . . lacertis.** Cf. Appendix A, 450/42; Lucretius 4. 829; Ovid, *Metamorphoses* 9. 223. In *Aeneid* 5. 15 and 10. 94 Vergil has "validis incumbite remis."

602/4–5 **Heruei . . . uela.** Appendix A, 450/43–44.

602/5–6 **nauis . . . uidelicet.** More refers here and in no. 189/5 to Sir Thomas Knyvet, commander of the *Regent.* In *Quomodo historia conscribenda sit* 14, Lucian mocks a historian who hopes to exalt one commander by belittling his adversary, as if Achilles would win greater glory by defeating Thersites than he would by defeating Hector.

602/6–8 **Quum . . . pugnantem.** Cf. Appendix A, 450/59–62, 452/109–454/120.

602/9–10 **in . . . intruderes.** Cf. Appendix A, 452/96. "Imperterritum" is an epic word; cf. Vergil, *Aeneid* 10. 770. See also *CW 14*, Commentary 1 at 419/2.

602/10–11 **occupatis . . . strage.** Cf. Appendix A, 454/130–44.

602/11 **uictam uinctamque.** Cf. Appendix A, 454/147.

602/12 **ardentis . . . bolidem.** Cf. Appendix A, 454/156.

602/13–17 **Quum . . . concionantem.** Cf. Appendix A, 456/172–458/200.

602/14–15 **quae . . . obrepere.** Cf. *Adagia* 1274, *Opera omnia,* 2, 514AB.

602/16 **longis logis.** Cf. Plautus, *Menaechmi* 779.

602/17–19 **non . . . futurum.** Cf. Appendix A, 456/195–97; Allen, *4,* 220, lines 141–43; no. 192, above.

602/19–21 **Quum . . . coeperant.** Cf. Appendix A, 458/206–10; Lucian, *Quomodo historia conscribenda sit* 26; and p. 562, n. 1.

602/22 **passisque . . . palmis.** Cf. Appendix A, 454/146–47, where the reading is "inuisa ad littora passis . . . palmis." More's change links Brixius' phrase to Vergil, *Aeneid* 1. 93, "tendens ad sidera palmas. . . ." Cf *CW 4,* 230/8.

602/22–604/2 **Quum . . . secum.** Cf. Appendix A, 458/222–27.

602/24–26 **nimirum . . . odium.** Cf. Appendix A, 456/179–82.

602/27–28 **diui . . . prouocatum.** Cf. Appendix A, 456/185–88. August 10, the day of the battle, was also Saint Lawrence's feast day. Saint Lawrence was martyred by being roasted on a grill. See Réau, *3/2,* 787–92, for details and bibliography.

604/4 **deus quispiam e machina.** Cf. *Adagia* 58, *Opera omnia,* 2, 52EF.

604/4–6 **unum . . . doceret.** Cf. nos. 189/10–13, 192/7–11; *Adagia* 926, *Opera omnia,* 2, 375B.

604/6–7 **sydera . . . aequor.** Appendix A, 460/269.

604/8 **pluribus . . . stolidis.** Cf. Appendix A, 458/239–462/307.

604/8–9 **pulchre . . . Ouidium.** Cf. no. 147, where More speaks of a stupid poet, "Maronem pulchre scilicet imitatus," who inverts a superlative compliment from Vergil and unwittingly offers the king a superlative insult.

604/9–10 **ille . . . incendium.** For the story of Phaethon and the chariot of the sun, see Ovid, *Metamorphoses* 2, esp. 201–10.

604/12–14 **Maronem . . . seruaret.** For the rain sent by Jove to save Aeneas' fleet, see Vergil, *Aeneid* 5. 687–99.

604/15–16 **imbrem . . . deplueres.** Cf. Appendix A, 462/308–464/333.

604/16 **aqua perennis e pumice.** Cf. *Adagia* 375, *Opera omnia,* 2, 174E–175A. The proverb applies to someone who tries to get something from someone who does not have it. Pumice was considered the driest kind of stone.

604/17 **ignis . . . caelum.** Cf. Appendix A, 462/296–99.

604/18–19 **ipse . . . typis.** See note to 594/4.

604/21–22 **purpureos aliorum pannos . . . bardocucullo.** Cf. Horace, *Ars poetica* 15–16 and 622/13–15. More uses the Horatian line in a similar way against Luther (*Responsio, CW 5,* 666/15–16: "Gestio profecto uidere, quem pannum purpurae tanto praetexat ulceri"). The *bardocucullus* was a coarse Gallic cloak; *bardus* can mean either "bard," in our sense, or a thick-skulled incompetent. More here neatly dissolves the first sense of this word into the second. Cf. *Des. Erasmi Roterodami adagiorum chiliades iuxta locos communes digestae . . . et aliorum quorundam adagia* . . . (Geneva, 1606), p. 1714, where Gilbert Cousin (Cognatus), one of Erasmus' secretaries, relates both senses of *bardus* to βραδύς, or "stupidus."

604/22 **quibus . . . esset.** Cf. Horace, *Ars poetica* 19: "Sed nunc non erat his locus." More employs the same line against Luther, *Responsio, CW 5,* 252/31; cf. also *Utopia, CW 4,* 98/8.

604/23–24 **non . . . Horestes.** Persius, *Satires* 3. 118; also quoted in More's *Letter to Dorp,* Rogers, no. 15, lines 427–28, and *Responsio, CW 5,* 252/31.

604/24 **uno atque altero epigrammate.** Cf. nos. 188–95, 209.

604/25–27 **fidem . . . aceruos.** Cf. nos. 188; 195, 209; 193. For "pro horrei tui modulo," see *Adagia* 589, *Opera omnia, 2,* 255F–256A, based on Horace, *Epistulae* 1.7.98 and *Sermones* 1.3.78; for "alieni farris aceruos," cf. Vergil, *Georgics* 1.181–86, where the pilferings of weevils and mice are described.

64/28–30 **epigramma . . . gallicitatem.** See no. 95.

604/30 **gallicitatem.** This is apparently a new coinage by More.

606/3 **sui . . . mores.** Cf. Terence, *Phormio* 454: "Quot homines tot sententiae; suus cuique mos."

606/7 **flagrabant omnia.** Cf. Rogers, no. 83, line 1252: "Dum res flagrabat maxime. . . ."

606/19 **saluberrimam.** The fifteen-space gap which follows this word may have been left open for a Greek word which the printer forgot to insert. εἰρηνοποίησιν fits the space.

606/21 **obductas . . . refrices.** Cf. *Adagia* 580, *Opera omnia, 2,* 253A.

606/22–24 **foedas . . . confingis.** Cf. Appendix B, 490/140–45. Through a pun More suggests a connection between *foedifraga periuria* and *foede confingere.* Cf. Sallust, *Bellum iugurthinum* 43.1.

606/25–608/12 **Atqui . . . coronandus?** Cf. Allen, *4,* 223, line 242, where More speaks of Brixius' "animum gladiatorium" (*Adagia* 1497, *Opera omnia, 2,* 580F). For another comparison between disputation and wrestling see *The Answer to . . . the Poysoned Booke, EW,* sig. BB_2. More frequently has recourse to very similar incongruous and slighting athletic comparisons in his *Responsio ad Lutherum;* cf. *CW* 5, 390/11 "animo gladiatorio"), 400/14 ("aegregius palaestrita"), and 694/9–14. For a precedent in Galen see *Adagia* 879, *Opera omnia, 2,* 361AB. In his *Letter to Dorp* (October 1515, Rogers, no. 15, lines 213–14), More expressed his dismay at the way in which certain disputants contrive to enlist *bonarum artium peritia* itself, part and parcel, in the service of factional contentiousness, "vbi rationem clamor vincit, vnde conspuentes inuicem consputique discedunt." In this earlier letter, Scholastic contentiousness provides a neat contrast to genteel humanistic discussion; More can still employ decorous military analogies for the tactical aspects of humanistic debate (line 1249; contrast lines 316–20). In the letter to Brixius, More's athletic metaphors introduce the reader into a twilight region in which the mock battles of serious learned debate imperceptibly degenerate by way of pugilistic and gladiatorial metaphors into deadly serious battles begun on the most frivolous intellectual pretexts. Here, as in the *Responsio ad Lutherum*/

Luderum ("sportsmaster"), the implication is always that nothing besides hard-won practical wisdom, firmly based on a faithful regard for decorum and historic consensus, can secure any man against fatal confusion of sporting and seriousness, the letter and the spirit, or the metaphor and the reality. The fastidious Brixius doubtless conceives of himself as anything but a no-holds-barred wrestler, just as Luther, convinced of his transcendent license to shake men's complacency, doubtless conceives of himself as anything but a wantonly bloodthirsty gladiator. More's metaphors are intended to strip away such men's rhetorical pretensions to tact and sobriety and lay bare their anarchic insistence on victory at any cost. See also the note on 598/25–26.

606/25–27 **haec . . . luctatus.** Cf. Appendix B, 486/79–98; 512/566–81; 536/10–25.

606/29–30 **soluto . . . denique.** Cf. *Adagia* 1852, *Opera omnia,* 2, 674DE: "Sic est ad pugnae partes re peracta ueniendum."

606/33 **corripiat medium.** In *Adagia* 396, *Opera omnia,* 2, 180AB, Erasmus notes with regard to this phrase, "si quem [palaestritae] medium corripuerint, facile vincunt."

608/6 **pugnis . . . calcibus.** Cf. *Adagia* 2021, *Opera omnia,* 2, 722CD.

608/10–12 **tanquam . . . acturus.** Cf. More's *Responsio, CW* 5, 42/20–21: " . . . ut furoris obstinati triumphum tuto reportaret domum ad compotores suos."

608/12–13 **dignus . . . perfringat?** The breaking of legs was a commonplace punishment in Rome for a variety of serious offenses; cf. Plautus, *Poenulus* 886; Cicero, *Pro Roscio Amerino* 20. 56–57, *Philippica* 13. 12. 27, Suetonius, *Vitae Caesarum* 2. 67, 3. 44; John 19:31. Cf. also *Adagia* 675, *Opera omnia,* 2, 292AB, where a man who habitually lies about his leg being broken ends up duly punished.

608/17 **periurium.** Cf. Appendix A, 448/20–21.

608/18 **asinum . . . quadrupede.** Cf. *Adagia* 2624, "Asinus auis," *Opera omnia,* 2, 889CD. More's phrase is of course equally reminiscent of medieval Scholastic sophismata, of which *asini* were often the subject; cf. *Responsio, CW* 5, 122/31, 224/9–10, 225/11, 316/1–2, and 326/3.

608/22 **facile . . . pustula.** Cf. *Adagia* 1248, *Opera omnia,* 2, 500A: "Homo bulla," and no. 59/3, where More translates μεγαλοφροσύνη as *tumor.*

608/23–25 **tam . . . principibus.** Wolsey's "Perpetual Peace" of 1518 included an official agreement that Henry VIII's daughter Mary would eventually be married to the dauphin of France. Cf. Scarisbrick, pp. 71–72.

608/26–27 **prior prouocasses.** See note to 598/18–20.

608/29 **hospitalitatem mutuam.** See note to 594/7.

608/30–610/1 **telis . . . uenenatis.** "Sylvestres" or "savage" alludes to the title of Brixius' "Sylua," the versified portion of the *Antimorus;* cf. no. 267. For Brixius' "poisoned darts," cf. Lorenzo Valla, *Dialecticae disputationes,* Book 3, pref. (*Opera omnia,* Basel, 1540; reprint, Turin, 1962, sig. Zz_6) on the captiousness of medieval sophists: " . . . sophistarum, qui noua quaedam uocabula ad perniciem aduersariorum confinxerunt, relicta ueterum consuetudine loquendi, non alia malignitate quam illi qui in praeliis spicula ueneno tingunt, aut forte etiam maiore." In his letter to Bugenhagen, Rogers, no. 143, lines 1099–1102, More likens the Lutherans' subversion of value terms commonly held to denote polar opposites, terms like *evil* and *good, sin* and *virtue,* "contra communem omnium tot seculorum sensum," to the preparation of a "venenatum spiculum." In his *Oratio pro Quinctio* 2. 8 Cicero describes as a "telum venenatum" a false accusation delivered in a way which does not let the accused counteract its effects. In his *De iure belli et pacis* (1625) 3.4.16, Hugo Grotius cites a large number of classical and medieval sources to prove that *ius gentium,* in Europe, at least, prohibits the use of poisoned weapons; see Grotius, *De iure belli et pacis libri tres,* ed. W. Whewell, 3 vols. (Cambridge, 1853), *3,* 87–88. On *ius gentium* see also *CW 4,* Commentary at 8/5–8.

610/4–5 **quantumlibet sudaris.** Cf. no. 193/27; *Responsio, CW 5,* 466/15 and n.; and Terence, *Phormio* 628: "sudabis satis."

610/5–7 **sic . . . conuertereris.** Cf. Allen *4,* 222, lines 210–13.

610/9–11 **ut . . . perspuisti?** We expect a subjunctive verb form here, e.g., "perspueres." *Perspuere* is in none of the lexicons and is apparently a coinage of More's own.

610/9–10 **furiali ueneno.** More's first references to Brixius' "pretty little playmates," the Furies; see 652/27–32, above. In his *Responsio, CW 5,* 672/22–23, More attributes "furiale uenenum" to Luther as well.

610/13 **dicax.** *Dicacitas* was an inferior grade of humor contrasted with *festiuitas.* See *CW 14,* Commentary at 298/6.

610/19 **in uerbis fides.** On the notion of words themselves meriting *fides* ("credit" or "currency"), cf. Horace, *Ars poetica* 49–51. For the pairing "veritas in voltu" and "in verbis fides" see Terence, *Andria* 857.

610/20 **tui . . . antiquitatem.** Cf. Appendix B, 488/102.

610/22–27 **rursus . . . eripueris.** Cf. Appendix B, 510/540–45, 542/40–544/5. For "uestigijs inheseris" cf. *Adagia* 3932, *Opera omnia, 2,* 1169E. For "Herculi clauam eripueris," a saying of Vergil's about his borrowings from Homer, see *Adagia* 3095, *Opera omnia,* 2, 990CD, where Erasmus cites Macrobius, *Saturnalia* 5.3.16.

610/25 **illaudata.** Cf. *Adagia* 1834, *Opera omnia,* 2, 670E–671A.

612/1–2 **hoc . . . subripere.** Cf. *Adagia* 1535, *Opera omnia,* 2, 594D: "Herculi mos erat res alienas vi abducere, non dolo."

612/4–5 **sic . . . calceos.** On the related theme of impolitic lack of selectiveness with regard to historical subject matter, cf. Sir Walter Ralegh, *The History of the World,* pref.: "Who-so-ever in writing a moderne Historie, shall follow truth too neare the heeles, it may happily strike out his teeth." More is probably alluding to Plautus, *Mercator* 952: "[Eutychus] sequere sis. [Charinus] Sequor. [Eutychus] Clementer quaeso, calces deteris."

612/5–6 **tuos . . . obuestias.** Cf. *Adagia* 1446, *Opera omnia,* 2, 566D. The incongruous image of this or that modern-day writer attempting to "fill the shoes" of a classical writer is elaborated with a similar satiric effect in Gianfrancesco Pico della Mirandola's famous letters to Pietro Bembo on the subject of imitation; see *Le epistole "De imitatione" di Gianfrancesco Pico della Mirandola e di Pietro Bembo,* ed. G. Santangelo (Florence, 1954), pp. 32, 72. Gianfrancesco's two letters to Bembo, like More's letter to Brixius, place a good deal of stress on the naive or dishonest anachronism of attempting a bodily "revival" of classical stylists in a contemporary cultural context; Gianfrancesco, like More, satirizes the notion of "summoning Apelles back up from the shades" to provide a stylistic ideal for every modern-day writer or artist to imitate (*Epistole,* p. 73; 638/28). Pico's letters to Bembo were first printed by Froben in 1518. One of More's earliest works was a translation of Gianfrancesco's life of his uncle Giovanni; see Rogers, no. 4, introduction. According to Latham, the verb *obuestire* which More himself uses here does not appear before 1520.

612/6–8 **Nec . . . petere.** For Vergil's claim to have taken away "Hercules' club," see note to 610/22–27. For the proverbial perils and attractions of cosmopolitan Corinth see *Adagia* 301, *Opera omnia,* 2, 150DE.

612/15–17 **te . . . conferas.** Cf. Folly on plagiarists, *ASD 4/3,* 142, lines 322–25.

612/16–17 **ut . . . integrum.** Cf. Seneca, *Epistolae* 84. 5–7, on the right way to imitate:

> . . . quod in corpore nostro videmus sine ulla opera nostra facere naturam . . . idem in quibus aluntur ingenia praestemus, ut quaecumque hausimus non patiamur integra esse, ne aliena sint. . . . Hoc faciat animus noster: omnia quibus est adiutus abscondat, ipsum tantum ostendat quod effecit.

Erasmus incorporates these precepts in his own attack on servile imitation, in particular of Cicero (*Ciceronianus, ASD 1/2,* 652, 704). More's phrasing in this passage is also somewhat reminiscent of the language in which he arraigns Edward Lee and the medieval *summularii* for plundering the discourses of other less ephemeral thinkers; cf. Rogers, no. 75, lines 535–39, no. 83, lines 833–35, and (for a satiric allusion to Seneca's analogy of bees gathering honey) no. 15, lines 841–56.

612/17–18 **clam . . . speres.** Cf. *Adagia* 1614, *Opera omnia,* 2, 617 CD, where Erasmus cites Terence, *Adelphoe* 69–71:

> Malo coactus qui suum officium facit,
> Dum id rescitum iri credit, tantisper pauet;
> Si speret fore clam, rursus ad ingenium redit.

612/18–19 **uelut . . . careas.** In *Opera omnia,* 2, sig. *3^v, Erasmus uses a similar figure for those who plagiarize his *Adagia:* "Etsi quid paululum novent, an credunt illico bene dissimulatum furtum, si veteribus ollis novas affigant ansas?"

612/24–25 **a caelo . . . attingant.** Cf. *Adagia* 1495, 444, *Opera omnia,* 2, 500C, 199B. More uses the second of these adages against Luther as well; Cf. *Responsio, CW* 5, 214/28–29.

612/28–29 **sic . . . deterius.** Cf. Quintilian, *Institutio oratoria* 10.2.15–16:

> Nec vero saltem iis, quibus ad evitanda vitia iudicii satis fuit, sufficiat imaginem virtutis effingere et solam, vt sic dixerim, cutem. . . . Hoc autem his accidit, qui non introspectis penitus virtutibus ad primum se velut adspectum orationis aptarunt; et cum iis felicissime cessit imitatio, verbis atque numeris sunt non multum differentes, vim dicendi atque inventionis non adsequuntur, sed plerumque declinant in peius et proxima virtutibus vitia comprehendunt. . . .

612/30–614/2 **Sin . . . simium.** Cf. Horace, *Ars poetica* 1–9.

614/1–2 **heros . . . simium.** Cf. *Adagia* 2409, *Opera omnia,* 2, 830A.

614/4–5 **mendacia . . . uermibus.** Cf. *The Supplicacion of soules, EW,* sig. v_4: " . . . hys bil couched as full of lies as any beggar swarmeth full of lice."

614/6 **Aiacis . . . aegida.** For the shield of Ajax, see *Adagia* 2737, *Opera* *omnia,* 2, 913E, based on Homer, *Iliad* 8. 267–68; for the aegis of Pallas Athena, see Homer, *Odyssey* 22. 297.

614/6 **poetices opponis priuilegium.** Cf. Appendix B, 488/128–31, 490/138–39.

614/7 **historica lege tradendae ueritatis.** Conformity with this law, generally known as "historica fides," is jokingly claimed for the fictional *Utopia* in More's second letter to Giles, *CW 4,* 250/16, 22. See also no. 188.

614/8 **poeticen . . . liberam.** Cf. *Adagia* 2048, *Opera omnia,* 2, 727DE, based on Horace, *Ars poetica,* 9–13:

> Pictoribus atque poetis
> Quidlibet audendi semper fuit aequa potestas.
> Scimus et hanc veniam petimusque damusque vicissim,
> Sed non ut placidis coeant immitia, non ut
> Serpentes auibus geminentur, tigribus agni.

In religion and politics, as in poetics, More is ever anxious to distinguish the "quidlibet audendi potestas" of individual caprice from the free and responsible creative interaction of an individual with a historic continuum. In his letter to a monk (Batmanson), Rogers, no. 83, lines 1221–84, More has an account of a "fraterculus e coelo lapsus" (line 1235), a character prophetically like More's later conception of Luther, who promises plenary remission of sins for whoever adopts one particular mode of obeisance to God. The result is that all the worst malefactors rush the fastest to adopt this same mode of obeisance, "non alia mente, quam quod sponderent sibi, quiduis audendi licentiam." One of More's fundamental arraignments of Lutheranism in his *Responsio ad Lutherum* (*CW* 5, 296/31–298/1) bears on the way Luther's own hermeneutical teaching intentionally "enervates the scriptures, which, he says, alone should reign, and gives everyone license to dare the same thing" ("faciat cuilibet idem audendi licentiam"). The "quiduis audendi licentiam" illegitimately claimed by religious innovators in the practical and hermeneutical spheres is only a slightly more sinister expression of the same irresponsible passion for wishful thinking, or "faining," which produced Brixius' shameful distortions in the realm of historical fiction.

614/9–11 **ut . . . pudenter.** Cf. Horace, *Ars poetica* 48–51.

614/11–13 **non . . . demutet.** Cf. Horace, *Ars poetica* 151–52.

614/17 **Didonis . . . affers.** Cf. Appendix B, 488/134–35.

614/19 **indubitate fidis.** The *1520* reading at this point, "indubitatae fidis," is ungrammatical, while one obvious emendation, "indubitatae fidei," is implausible paleographically. This is not the only place where *1520* confuses "-ae" and "-e"; see the variants at 612/4 and 632/30. For this alternative history of Dido, cf. Justinus, *Historiarum epitome* 18. 6, and Servius, *Commentarii in Vergilium* on *Aeneid* 1.267 and 4.459.

614/20–21 **Aeneam . . . superatum.** Vergil has just the contrary; *Aeneid* 10. 439–509, 12. 887–952.

614/23 **Dioni.** More refers to Dio Cocceianus Chrysostomus (c. 40–c. 120 A.D.), a late sophist; his *Eleventh Discourse,* in which he attempted to discredit the legend of Troy as pure lies, figured often in Renaissance quarrels on the value of poetry. This discourse was translated in the mid-fifteenth century by Francesco Filelfo.

614/30 **faber fabro inuidens.** Cf. *Adagia* 125. "Figulus figulo inuidet, faber fabro," *Opera omnia,* 2, 80Ef, taken from Hesiod, *Opera et dies* 25.

616/2–3 **nemo . . . memoriae?** Cf. More to Erasmus, Allen, *4,* 220, lines 108–11, on no. 190: " . . . adieci dignum fuisse Brixium qui fuisset in ipsa naue, vt suis oculis rem videret quam scriberet, ne ad eum modum tam turpiter mentiri cogeretur, et falsa pro veris commendare memoriae."

616/3–6 **Nemo . . . cecinit.** Cf. More, no. 188; More to Erasmus, Allen, *4,* 220, lines 135–38.

616/9 **teneras aures.** Cf. Persius, *Satires* 1. 107–08: "Sed quid opus teneras mordaci radere vero | Auriculas?" More has in his *Responsio* (*CW* 5, 58/2) "asininas auriculas coepit radere vero."

616/9–10 **at certe nimirum.** While the phrasing of the *1520* text seems redundant, emending to "at certe nimium" would alter the sense for the worse: More pretends here to be at great pains not to stir Brixius up with the charge that his telling of history is false, and the charge that his telling of history is *overly* free would here scarcely prove less of an irritant. Instances are not uncommon in which More himself set down two alternative expressions for the same meaning in a manuscript and his printer or copyist then retained both, to create a redundancy not unlike this one; cf. *Richard III, CW* 2, xli–xlii, and 626/26–27, above. We might then accept either "at certe" or "nimirum" as More's favored reading. Not knowing for certain which reading More favored, however, we here retain both. In any case, "nimirum" (*ni mirum,* "without doubt"; cf. Terence, *Eunuchus* 508) is not wholly synonymous with "at certe."

616/10 **opusculum Pillei Turonensis.** Cf. *Guilelmi Piellei de anglorum e* *galliis fuga et hispanorum e nauarra expulsione* (Paris, A Bonnemere, 1512 [February 1513]), *Inventaire chronologique,* 2, no. 429. By altering Pielleus' name to "Pilleus," More may intend a satirical stress to be placed on the meaning of this word in everyday Latin ("cap" or "cowl"); cf. no. 95/12, "pileoque Gallico." The change might also be merely a slip by More's printer. There is a brief discussion of Piellé's poem in the *Biographie universelle ancienne et moderne,* 84 vols. (Paris, 1811–55), 77, 171.

616/18 **prior laeserit.** See note to 598/18–20.

616/23 **ex ungue . . . leonem.** Cf. *Adagia* 834, *Opera omnia,* 2, 347D–F; Rogers, no. 75, line 244.

616/26 **uel absque cribro diuinet.** Cf. *Adagia* 903, *Opera omnia,* 2, 307CD.

616/27 **cuius farinae . . . istiusmodi furfuris.** Cf. *Adagia* 2444, *Opera omnia,* 2, 839DE, "nostrae farinae"; Rogers, no. 15, lines 490–91, "huius farinae, imo istius furfuris"; *Responsio, CW 5,* 18/6, "eiusdem furfuris."

616/30–618/5 **quos . . . possideant.** Near the end of the hostilities between England and France, after Pielleus' book was already in print, the English captured and held Therouanne and Tournay; see the Commentary at no. 244/1–8. The earlier English expedition to Aquitaine (1512) had ended in failure on account of disease and bad organization; for this expedition and for the bloodless capture of Navarre by the Spanish see Polydore Vergil, p. 180.

618/7–8 **simia simiae similior.** In his *Responsio* (*CW 5,* 436/10–11) More sets Luther alongside a hypothetical fool who believes he has learned how to vanish. More concludes by asserting, "Non simius, simio similior est: quam isti stulto stultus et stulte stultifex Lutherus." This proverbial phrasing finds no precise parallel in the *Adagia;* for "more alike than two eggs," see no. 94/6 and the Commentary thereon. Apes were noted of course for mechanical mimicry, so that this passage is not without bearing on More's distaste for Brixius' own *imitatio;* cf. no. 95/49–50 and the Commentary.

618/9–10 **fasciculus temporum.** This was the title of a popular universal chronicle written by the German, Werner Rolevinck (1425–1502), and first published in 1474. It was frequently brought up to date by less prominent writers. More refers here to *Fasciculus temporum omnes antiquorum cronicas succincte complectens* [*cum pluribus additionibus . . . vsque ad annum M. d. xviii*] (Paris, Jean Petit, 1518), fol. xciii verso (*Inventaire chronologique,* 2, no. 1941): "[sub anno M. DXV.] Leo parat & prouocat quoscunque christianos principes potissime franciscum in thurcas. Cui non adhesit Anglus infidelitatis suspectus. Fertur enim insidias moliri in regnum Francie: praestolans regis in thurcas egressum." For this excerpt we are indebted to Hubertus Schulte Herbrüggen.

618/10 **comburendus fasciculus.** For a similar pun see Rogers, no. 15, lines 913–14.

618/15–16 **coronis adiecta.** Cf. *Adagia* 3520, *Opera omnia, 2,* 1080B–E.

618/16–18 **qua . . . suspecta.** In 1518 Leo X tried unsuccessfully to enlist various kings in a Turkish crusade (Polydore Vergil, p. 250); this project may well have provided the pretext for the rumor which More here derides.

618/21–25 **Iam . . . domum?** More may well be referring to the supplement of Pierre Desrey which was frequently printed along with the French version of Robert Gaguin's *Compendium super francorum gestis,* otherwise known as the *Annales.* According to More's *Letter to Dorp* (Rogers, no. 15, lines 293–97), Gaguin's history shows a definite bias against England. The French translation by Nicole de la Chesnaye with the supplement of Pierre Desrey bringing the history up to 1514 was first printed in 1514 (*Les Grandes Croniques . . . des tresillustres . . . roys de France . . .*) and reprinted in 1516 and 1518, before More wrote his letter to Brixius; see *Inventaire chronologique, 2,* nos. 840, 1351, 1823. Cited according to a 1527 edition, here is Desrey's whole account of James IV's campaign in England:

> Durant ce Conflict [entre Angleterre et France] et enuahissement dessusdict Le tresnoble roy Descosse descendit au pays. Dangleterre / comme pretendant droit en icelluy Pays a cause de sa femme. Tant quil fut victorieux en certaines battailles demonstrant sa noble prouesse lan de grace Mil cinq cens et treze le vendredy .iii. iour de Juing. (Robert Gaguin, *La Mer des Croniques et Miroir Historial de France . . . Additions de Plusieurs . . .* [Paris, Jean de St. Denys, 1527], sig. P_2)

Desrey says nothing about James IV's "glorious" return to Scotland, but mistaken reports that the Scottish king had survived his disastrous defeat in the Battle of Flodden (September 9, 1513; see the Commentary at nos. 183–84, 271) were widespread for a while after the battle; see Marguerite Wood, ed., *Flodden Papers: Diplomatic Correspondence between the Courts of France and Scotland, 1507–17* (Edinburgh, 1933), pp. 85–90. For "uel dici uel fingi" cf. Plautus, *Curculio* 594, "neque dici nec fingi."

618/27–30 **fusos . . . adseruatum.** More himself wrote some rather cruel epigrams, one of them suppressed in *1520,* on the subject of James IV's invasion of England and his subsequent mortal defeat; see nos. 183–84,

271. In Allen, *4,* 221, lines 187–88, More declares that no. 271, like his verses against Brixius, had been printed against More's intention.

620/3–7 **Paulus Emilius . . . posteris.** Paulus Aemilius (c. 1460–1529) was a Veronese humanist who wrote a history of France to the time of Henry II under the patronage of Charles VIII and Louis XII, the *De rebus francorum.* In a note to Allen, *1,* 315, line 1, Allen suggests that this work and the *Compendium super francorum gestis* of Robert Gaguin, criticized in More's *Letter to Dorp* (Rogers, no. 15, lines 296–97), embodied two rival approaches to historiography in general; see further the bibliography in E. F. Rice, ed., *The Prefatory Epistles of Jacques Lefèvre d'Étaples* (New York, 1972), no. 15, n. 6. Erasmus praises Paulus Aemilius highly in the *Ciceronianus* and notes that he neither has nor affects Ciceronian style (*ASD, 1/2,* 668); he writes very slowly and painstakingly (*Opera omnia, 4,* 315A). More's emphasis on this historian's *fides* ("credibility") corresponds very closely to the emphasis which Aemilius himself puts on *fides* in his preface to the *De rebus francorum;* see *De rebus francorum* (Basel, Henricipetri, 1601), sig. †3.

620/6 **syncera fide.** This phrase recurs in More's highly suggestive account, in the *Responsio* (*CW 5,* 44/23–46/2), of why serious disputations should be conducted in writing rather than in person: " . . . what he [sc. the controversial writer] will have brought forward in the most ordered fashion—whatever he is able to bring forward at his leisure in accordance with the merits of the case—that will with honest fidelity ["syncaera fide"] appear in public." In *Adagia* 1260, *Opera omnia, 2,* 508D, Erasmus uses *sincera fide* as a synonym for *bona fide.*

620/9–10 **maioribus . . . piaculum.** The phrases *maioribus uictimis* and *maioribus hostiis* occur very often in Livy; they are used to distinguish propitiatory sacrifices, for which mature animals were generally used, from divinatory and other routine sacrifices, for which younger animals were used. See especially Livy, 22.1.15, 27.23.2, 42.20.3, and Servius, *Commentarii in Vergilium* on *Aeneid* 12. 170: " . . . in rebus quas volebant finiri celerius, senilibus et iam decrescentibus animalibus sacrificabant: in rebus vero quas augeri et confirmari volebant, de minoribus et adhuc crescentibus immolabant."

620/12–13 **ludis in dominationem meam.** Cf. Allen, *4,* 130, lines 73–78; Appendix B, 490/146–49.

620/15 **prior exagitasses.** See note to 598/18–20.

620/16 **sacrosanctam maiestatem tuam.** More uses the phrase "sacrosanctam maiestatem principis" with a serious intent in *Richard III, CW 2,* 62/64.

620/17 **perdius ac pernox.** Cf. *Adagia* 324, *Opera omnia, 2,* 160CD.

620/24 **diffinitione declinasti.** Cf. Quintilian 3. 6. 38, where Quintilian considers a case in which a man charged with *sacrilegium,* or stealing from a temple, must attempt to escape the indictment by defining his crime as plain theft, since he robbed not the temple itself but an ordinary citizen inside the temple. Cf. also *Moriae encomium, ASD 4/3,* 146, lines 392–94, and Rogers, no. 83, lines 1531–34.

620/25–26 **quicquid . . . contenderes.** Cf. Sir Philip Sidney, *An Apology for Poetry,* ed. G. Shepherd (London, 1965), pp. 123–24; "Now, for the poet, he nothing affirms, and therefore never lieth . . . though he recount things not true, yet because he telleth them not for true, he lieth not . . ." Brixius tries to escape by appealing to the letter of "poetic license" at the same time that he violates its spirit. For the classical, Scholastic, and Renaissance background of Sidney's assertion see Shepherd's invaluable notes.

620/28 **tenedia . . . falso.** For the double-edged axe of the king of Tenedos, as keen in his legal decisions as Solomon with his sword, see *Adagia* 829, *Opera omnia, 2,* 345F, and More's *Responsio, CW 5,* 212/18, 594/18. *Falsum fictumque* ("false and fabricated") is a commonplace pairing; see 614/20, 644/25–26, Cicero, *De divinatione* 2. 11. 27; Rogers, no. 83, line 1543; *Responsio, CW 5,* 660/8; and *A Dialogue Concerning Heresies, CW 6,* 98/22. As the past participle of *fallere, falsum* can mean "mistaken"; see *De tristitia Christi, CW 14,* 403/9–10, "falsa fallendi spe."

620/29 **explices . . . implices.** More uses a very similar figure against Luther; cf. *CW 5,* 54/27. In the letter to Giles introducing *Utopia* (*CW 4,* 40/28–29), More distinguishes between a falsehood and a deliberate lie: "potius mendacium dicam quam mentiar, quod malim bonus esse quam prudens." See also More's *Debellation, EW,* sig. T_8v. For the "truthfulness" of the *Utopia,* see the note to 600/18–20, above. What More means by asserting that Brixius extricates himself from an inadvertent lie by implicating himself in a deliberate one is that Brixius *admits* having fabricated an account of a significant historical event: when it comes to reporting of basic historical facts, any author can only be right, inadvertently wrong, or deliberately deceitful. More's Utopian persona naively condemns all deliberate falsehood alike; More himself has no qualms about dealing in poetic falsehood where no basic historical truth is at stake. He can claim the same sanction Boccaccio does in distinguishing the falsehood of poetry from the eight kinds of hurtful lies criticized in Augustine's *De mendacio* 14, *PL 40,* 505:

> . . . fictiones poetice, ut plurimum, non sunt nedum simillime, sed nec similes veritati, imo valde dissone et adverse. Et dato species

> fabularum una, quam videri potius hystoriam quam fabulam diximus, sit veritati simillima, antiquissimo omnium nationum consensu a labe mendacii inmunis est, cum sit consuetudine veteri concessum ea quis uti posse ratione exempli, in quo simplex non exquiritur veritas, nec prohibetur mendacium (Book 14, chapter 13, of Giovanni Boccaccio, *Genealogie deorum gentilium libri,* ed. Vicenzo Romano, 2 vols. [Bari, 1951], 2, 718).

Since Brixius' aim is to falsify rather than to illustrate, he lacks the same sanction. His transgression is made all the worse by the claim that the lies that he tells in his poem are the sort of misrepresentation that could never be made inadvertently.

620/29–30 **haud . . . fuero.** Buckingham in More's *Richard III* (*CW* 2, 76/1–2) makes a similarly sarcastic use of this phrase: "haud amplius molesti vobis hac de re [sc. regno Ricardi] futuri."

622/1–2 **hoc . . . sunt.** More himself compresses a poetic account of a ship's burning into just four lines in no. 36.

622/3 **tanto . . . hiatu.** These words form a new half-hexameter. Cf. Horace, *Ars poetica* 138; Juvenal, 6. 636; *CW 5*, 54/20–21.

622/4–10 **Nunc . . . sustinere.** For this humorously overwrought battle imagery cf. Book 2, chapter 36, of L. Valla, *On Pleasure/De voluptate,* trans. and ed. A. Kent Hieatt and M. Lorch (New York. 1977), p. 196:

> Et de omnibus que causa voluptatis desiderabat dixisse confido. Veruntamen videre videor hostes quasi in acie et iusto bello superatos in fugamque versos se in castra recepisse, atque inde e vallo vociferantes et victoribus probra ingerentes: suam esse vitam contemplativam, suam mentis securitatem. Hec bona solius esse honestatis et quidem sibi cum diis immortalibus communia. Nos vero vilissimam quandam sequi voluptatem refertam ac redundantem turpitudine, fastidio, penitentia. Debellemus igitur hos contumaces hostes, et ipsis etiam castris exuamus, que ipsi appellant duo secreta animi bona.

622/11 **machinae.** Cf. *Adagia* 3472, *Opera omnia,* 2, 1070A, *ASD 4/3*, 113, line 792, and Commentary.

622/14 **canoris nugis.** Cf. Horace, *Ars poetica* 322; *Adagia* 2598, *Opera omnia,* 2, 868D.

622/14–15 **ingenij . . . obductum.** Cf. *Adagia* 366, *Opera omnia,* 2, 172E.

622/15–16 **quam . . . fictio.** Cf. Appendix B, 542/40–544/4.

622/23 **soloecis.** For a passage defending this word against the more common "soloecismus" see Aulus Gellius 5.20. 3–7.

622/26 **aequum ac bonum.** For the significance of this phrase, and "equity" in general, in More's thought and writings, see the Introduction to More's *Responsio, CW 5,* 754–56. More is probably alluding to Terence, *Adelphoe* 64.

622/26–28 **non . . . praescribere.** Brixius, quick to appeal to the "law of dueling" when it suits his own purpose (see note to 600/3), disregards the same law when it comes to allowing More free choice of weapons.

622/28 **pro imperio.** Cf. *Responsio, CW 5,* 276/27–28; Terence, *Phormio* 196.

622/32–624/1 **eo . . . transcurrere.** Cf. the similarly mordant reminder of what should be obvious to anyone, in More's answer to Luther's denial of a universal papacy (*Responsio, CW 5,* 348/23–24): "longius absunt Indi, quam ut possint, ob quoduis negotiolum Romam currere."

624/3 **legem . . . ipse.** In *Adagia* 315, *Opera omnia,* 2, 186F–187A, Erasmus cites this as a "iureconsultorum regula," "Patere legem, quam ipse tulisti." Cf. Publilius Syrus, *Sententiae* 2, "Ab altero exspectes alteri quod feceris," cited in *Adagia* 699, *Opera omnia,* 2, 301A; Rogers, no. 85, lines 91–93; and no. 19/99, above.

624/6 **in te . . . telorum.** Cf. *Adagia* 51, *Opera omnia* 2, 48D–49A.

624/10–11 **qui . . . reformante.** For one certain instance of stop-press revision in Brixius' *Antimorus* see Appendix B, introduction, p. 475. A thorough collation of several copies (*Inventaire chronologique,* 2, no. 2004, lists thirteen surviving copies not including the Yale copy) might well reveal more such revisions.

624/13 **neque minus ferendos.** We expect "neque magis ferendos."

624/16 **foediores polipo.** Cf. Horace, *Epodes* 12. 5, where a nasal polyp is mentioned to stand for the very worst kind of disfigurement. For the errors to which More is referring here see Appendix B, introduction, p. 475 and notes.

624/18–20 **ipse . . . denuo.** This letter seems to be lost. In Rogers, no. 67, a dedicatory epistle prefixed to Ulrich von Hutten's *Aula,* Froben makes no mention of More's *Epigrams.*

624/23–26 **neque . . . decreueram.** More publicly issued (*edidit*) only those poems which he wrote for the king's coronation, nor had he ever (*adhuc*) resolved to issue publicly any poems but the ones for the king and the ones against Brixius. In suggesting that he had resolved to issue publicly his poems against Brixius, More may be referring to his plan for reprinting in one volume Brixius' *Chordigera,* More's own pertinent epigrams, the *Antimorus,* and very possibly a polemical commentary, a plan which anticipates the format of More's own *Responsio ad Lutherum;* cf. 632/23–26 and n. Earlier More had been very dubious about whether his Brixius poems should be published and may even have taken various last-minute steps to suppress them; see Allen, 2, 340, lines 20–28, and *4,* 221, lines 156–62 and 241, lines 98–101. After the *Antimorus* appeared, however, More declared that his Brixius poems, recommended by Brixius' abuse, had become his own favorites; see Allen, *4,* 221, lines 163–65, 254, lines 132–43, and 628/21–23, above. All the *1518* poems against Brixius reappeared in *1520* along with four new ones, nos. 266–69.

626/9–11 **sin . . . meo.** More uses a similar phrasing in bringing to a close his own lengthy defense of Erasmus against Edward Lee (Rogers, no. 75, lines 615–16): "Sin tibi penitus insederit tam generosus ardor gloriae, ut potius quam cum illo non dimices, malis genuinum frangere. . . ." For "fixa atque obfirmata sententia," cf. Rogers, no. 15, line 1010; *Richard III, CW* 2, 79/29.

626/12 **laterem lauem.** Cf. *Adagia* 348, *Opera omnia,* 2, 169E, from Terence, *Phormio* 186.

626/12–13 **Vide . . . tecum.** For a similar example of More's exaggerated courtesy in dealing with an obstinate adversary, see *A Dialogue Concerning Heresies, CW 6,* 170/21–22: "But syth I am so gentyll to graunt you so many thynges, I trust ye wyll graunt me this one. . . ." Cf. also *CW 8,* 556/19–36.

626/18–24 **certissimis . . . Frobenio.** For points at which Brixius' criticisms are simply mistaken see note to 630/10–11, below. For discrepancies between *1518* and the text of the poems written for Henry VIII which More himself issued see 624/23–26 above and nos. 19/168, 172, 180, 194, and 20/9, where the manuscript text is superior.

626/25–27 **siue a meo . . . mutaueram.** For More's practice of cancellation and interlineation see *De tristitia, CW 14,* 745, 751.

628/1–2 **ingenuus . . . proloqui.** Cf. Terence, *Phormio* 282–84.

628/2–3 **festinatione praepeditus.** Cf. *Adagia* 1001, 397C–401D ("Festina lente"), 2460, 842A–E ("Qui nimium properat, serius absolvit"). His rash invective gets Brixius nowhere.

628/17 **emendaturus . . . eram.** Ovid, *Tristia* 1. 7. 40.

628/22–23 **aliquid . . . frictus es.** Cf. *Adagia* 1252, *Opera omnia, 2,* 506D, where Erasmus quotes Horace, *Sermones* 1. 10. 3–4.

630/6–7 **pure puteque.** Cf. *Adagia* 3930, *Opera omnia, 2,* 1169CD, and Plautus, *Pseudolus* 989.

630/10–11 **in quibus . . . dimidium.** Brixius levels thirty-nine specific criticisms against More's scansion, vocabulary, and phrasing, including three criticisms directed against *Utopia* (Appendix B, 532/33–534/26). One of these three criticisms is debatable, and the other two are simply wrong; see Commentary at *CW 4,* 112/1–2, and nos. 198/17 and 206/4, above. Of the criticisms Brixius directs against More's *Epigrams* (*1518*), at least four attack forms of expression which have a clear precedent in "received" Latin authors of the first century after Christ or before; see the Commentary at nos. 138/1–4, 148/8, 198/17, and 206/4. Another nine criticisms attack More for casual and easily corrected mistakes which are almost certainly scribal errors; see the Commentary at nos. 19/100, 19/180, 23/5, 25/5, 31/4, 62/6, 76/10, 130/4, and 214/11. An additional six criticisms attack More for using phrases or words which were generally accepted in the Latin of his own day or for using less common forms or arrangements of good classical words; see the Commentary at nos. 19/34, 95/12, 143/125, 167/3, 224/5, and 247/9. Thus twenty-one of Brixius' thirty-nine criticisms may fairly be classed as "mistaken or wantonly slanderous." Of the remaining seventeen criticisms directed against *1518,* two attack instances of irregular scansion which might have resulted from casual inversion of word order (nos. 75/9 and 90/14); ten attack instances of unclassical scansion or phrasing which have distant analogies in classical writers or close precedents in writers like Ausonius, Prudentius, and Priscian (nos. 5/13, 19/119, 25/5, 101/10, 106/3, 114/9, 118/5, 143/131, 181/6, and 203/8); two attack coinages apparently original with More (nos. 27/2, 89/16; cf. 614/7–11, above) and three attack scansions which are clearly unjustifiable (nos. 19/167, 96/4 and 135/4). More changed some of these passages in *1520* and left others intact, caring more for the sense than for phrasing or scansion (628/23–34).

630/14–15 **ad . . . prouoces.** See note to 598/18–20, above.

630/19 **meras efflans glorias.** Aulus Gellius 1. 2. 6 describes an arrogant young Stoic as "inanes flans glorias." Cf. *Responsio, CW 5,* 76/25, where More describes Luther as "furiosas efflans glorias." For "uno deflauisti spiritu" cf. Plautus, *Miles gloriosus* 17.

630/21–22 **ne Momus . . . uellicet.** Cf. *Adagia* 474, *Opera omnia, 2,* 210B–211A.

630/26–29 **quae . . . effundere.** Cf. Horace, *Ars poetica* 450–51 and Appendix B, 536/27–538/9. *Obticere* ("to keep silent") is far less common in classical Latin than the perfect tense of *obticescere* ("to fall silent"); see Terence, *Eunuchus* 820 and *Heauton timoroumenos* 938. More freely uses both of these verbs (see also 644/14) as well as *conticescere* (620/1, 638/27) in a transitive sense without any clear classical precedent for the latter except Valerius Flaccus 3. 302. For the difference in meaning between various compounds of *tacere* see Donatus, *Commentarii in Terentium* on *Eunuchus* 820: "Tacemus consilia . . . , reticemus dolores . . . , obticemus, quorum nos pudet."

632/1–2 **quantumuis . . . syllabarum.** Cf. the *Letter to Dorp,* Rogers, no. 15, lines 321–28:

> . . . ut in Grammatica suffecerit eas obseruationes didicisse, quibus possis et ipse Latine loqui, et quae ab aliis Latine scripta sunt intelligere, non autem anxie innumeras loquendi regulas aucupari, itidem in Dialectica satis esse crediderim . . . Dialecticam protinus, velut instrumentum ad caeteras disciplinas accommodare.

Brixius' humanism confounds form with substance as thoroughly as the Scholasticism which More assails in the *Letter to Dorp.*

632/2 **mens.** Cf. no. 198 and the Commentary at no. 242/6. In the ancient scholium on Aristophanes, *Aves* 1392, we are told that the speech of the dithyrambic poets is more copious than anyone else's, whereas their sense, or their νοῦς, is inferior to everyone's, whence the proverb, "Minus habes mentis quam dithyramborum poetae" (*Adagia* 1131, *Opera omnia,* 2, 458B).

632/5–8 **libelli titulus . . . Moron.** Brixius carps at More's title for *Utopia* in Appendix B, 532/34–534/1, and builds much on a number of unflattering Greek and Latin puns on More's name; see Appendix B, 486/82–83, 496/276–498/289, 498/302, 512/552; and Germain Marc'hadour, "A Name for All Seasons," in *Essential Articles,* pp. 539–62. For another quip based on a syllable count, see *Utopia, CW 4,* 54/28–29.

632/9–11 **in Hermolaum Barbarum . . . barbaris.** More is probably not talking about any specific assailants of Barbaro, who indeed uses this pun against himself more than once; see, e.g., the famous correspondence between Barbaro and Giovanni Pico della Mirandola "de barbaro dicendi genere philosophorum" in *Prosatori Latini del Quattrocento,* ed. E. Garin (Milan, 1952), pp. 804–22, 844–63, esp. p. 844. The letters were accessible to More in Angelo Politiano's *Opera omnia* (Venice, 1498) and in a collection entitled *Illustrium virorum epistule ad Angelum Politianum . . .*

printed in Lyons and Paris by J. Badius several times before 1520. As More's editors have recognized, a dative is needed in place of the nominative "barbarus" which we find in the *1520* text. Since "barbaro" would have been hard to mistake for "barbarus," we should probably read "barbaris" (consider the similar confusion in the *1520* text between "uictis" and "uictus" [614/26]). For More's own word play based on proper names see also the Commentary at no. 96/5.

632/12 **germanus.** The prominent placement of this word at the end of a series of puns gives us cause to suspect that there may be a pun hidden in this word, as well. Germans were proverbially noted for both honesty and ferocity; the former connotation of the adjective *Germanus* allows More to make a neat pun in the title to his first epigram against Brixius, no. 189 ("IN BRIXIVM GERMANVM FALSA SCRIBENTEM . . ."), while the second connotation allows More to parallel "germanus" with "barbaris" here. For the *sylvestre ingenium* or "savage temperament" frequently ascribed to the Germans, see Allen, *3*, 533, line 11; *4*, 11, lines 64–65; 280, lines 64–67; 372, line 29; 401, line 10. At one point Erasmus deplores the way Reuchlin, the great German humanist, "satis Germanice debacchatur in aduersarios" (Allen, *3*, 589, lines 76–77). Barbaro similarly describes all barbarous Scholastics as "Teutones" in his letter to Pico; see Garin, p. 844. For another sort of pun on *germanus*, in the sense of "close relative," see Allen, *4*, 223, line 281. In *Moriae encomium, ASD 4/3*, 96, line 445, Folly ("Moria") says that Self-Love ("Philautia") is "like a sister to me" ("mihi . . . germanae est vice").

632/13–15 **nihil . . . repeterent.** Cf. Livy, 36.29.8; Rogers, no. 83, line 967; and *The Confutation of Tyndale's Answer, CW 9*, 176/26–27: "For all that he [sc. Tyndale] hath hytherto pored out and called myne errours be but hys owne, and tourne uppon hys owne toppe euerychone."

632/16–17 **Porro . . . quemlibet.** Cf. Allen, *4*, 229, lines 475–81, and note to 598/25–26, above. Brixius' praise is as vague and impertinent as his abuse is; see 646/20–648/3 and 656/16–19, above.

632/23–26 **Quae . . . commentariis.** More again mentions his plans to reprint the *Antimorus* along with the *Chordigera* and More's own pertinent epigrams in Allen, *4*, 219, lines 88–93, and 252, lines 60–63, where the plan is attributed to More's concerned friends. It would seem that this plan was abandoned when More's followed Erasmus' advice in suppressing the letter to Brixius.

632/23 **Morico.** More uses this word the same way in Allen, *4*, 223, line 268. Cf. *Adagia* 1801, *Opera omnia*, 2, 662F–664B ("Stultior Morycho");

Allen, *4,* 231, line 581, 252, line 46. More's friends used *moricum* as a synonym for "Moreanum," "pertaining to More"; see Rhen. Pref. 74/31, above; Rogers, no. 67, line 25; Allen, *4,* 294, line 83; *10,* 180, line 48. Apparently More combined this word with *Morychus,* an irreverent epithet for the "foolish" god Bacchus, to generate the meaning which "Morico" has here. According to Latham, *moricus* in the sense "foolish" is first used as a punning allusion to the surname More and does not appear before 1520. Vives formed the adjectives "Vivicus" and "Forticus" from the names Vives and Fortis (*In pseudodialecticos,* ed, Charles Fantazzi [Leiden, 1979], p. 55).

632/27–30 **qua tibi . . . infamiae.** Cf. Rogers, no. 63, lines 8–11: "Nam vt doctrinam, quae cum virtute coniuncta sit, vniuersis regum thesauris antepono, ita si morum probitatem seiunxeris, quid aliud affert fama litterarum, quam celebrem et insignem infamiam?" For the ambivalent meaning of "sacro," see the Commentary at no. 195/4; for "tibi factus uidere deus," cf. *Utopia, CW 4,* 168/13–14, and *Adagia* 499 and 3944, *Opera omnia,* 2, 219F–220C and 1171D. The original reading "dispuibile" at 632/27 is unattested in any of the lexicons and yields no satisfactory sense even etymologically.

634/4 **amne gallo.** A drink from the river Gallus in Phrygia caused madness; cf. no. 95/51–53 and the Commentary thereon.

634/5–30 **endecasyllabis . . . elicere.** Cf. Appendix B, 482/35–484/68. More's parody here is a close one.

634/6 **Macrino.** Brixius' friend, Salmonius Macrinus, later honored as "l'Horace français," contributed a liminary poem to the *Antimorus* exhorting Brixius to hasten its publication. In the mid-1520s Macrinus wrote several poems praising More highly; see G. Soubeille, "l'Amitié de Thomas More et de Salmon Macrin," *Moreana, 54* (1977), 11–21.

634/8–9 **stentorem . . . Nestorem.** Cf. *Adagia* 156 and 1237, *Opera omnia,* 2, 92BC and 496BC.

634/13 **ipsius auspicijs.** Cf. *Adagia* 3931, *Opera omnia,* 2, 1169D.

634/15 **oblitus tui.** Cf. *Des. Erasmi Roterodami adagiorum chiliades iuxta locos communes digestae* (Geneva, 1606), p. 916, where "Tui es oblitus" is presented under the locus–heading "Inconstantia et versutia." More repeatedly glances at Luther's short memory as well; see *Responsio, CW 5,* 40/9–10, 48/10, 240/29–30, 242/2, 539/10–11, 544/21.

634/16 **elephantis . . . partus.** See *Adagia* 811, *Opera omnia,* 2, 336DE, where Erasmus cites Pliny, *Historia naturalis* pref. 28 (cf. 8. 10. 28) on the ten-year gestation of elephants. In Appendix B, 484/55–58, on the other hand, Brixius alludes to the Horatian injunction to wait nine years before issuing a poem (*Ars poetica* 388).

634/21–22 **singulis . . . absoluere.** This statement is probably hyperbolic. See Appendix B, p. 473.

634/31 **in ipsis offendas foribus.** Cf. *Adagia* 477, *Opera omnia, 2,* 211EF.

634/31–32 **limatis . . . uersibus.** Cf. *Adagia* 458, *Opera omnia, 2,* 205BC, and Appendix B, 482/24–26.

636/1 **quam . . . moriones.** Cf. Erasmus, *Moriae encomium, ASD 4/3,* 74, lines 51–56.

636/1–4 **illis . . . fore?** Cf. Appendix B, 484/74–76. More gives a similar satirical twist to this commonplace claim in his poem on the poet Andreas who flouted strict meter, no. 148/21–22. For another example of this commonplace, see Desmarais to Giles, *Utopia, CW 4,* 28/7–9.

636/5 **agelastos.** Cf. *Adagia* 971, *Opera omnia, 2,* 387BC.

636/6–8 **nihil . . . somnient.** Cf. *Moriae encomium, ASD 4/3,* 194, lines 259–60; Horace, *Ars poetica* 6–9; and, for "uigilantes somnient," *Adagia* 1062 and 2281, *Opera omnia, 2,* 430C and 799CD. More uses this reproach very frequently against Luther (*Responsio, CW, 5,* 314/5–6, 462/21, 484/19, 572/6, 666/13, 678/5–6).

636/12–13 **quod . . . possit.** For the phrasing cf. *Adagia* 474, *Opera omnia, 2,* 211B: "Istud ne Pitho quidem ipsa persuaserit" and "Iste ne Fidei quidem ipsi fidem habeat."

636/22–638/3 **Quin . . . uictoria.** Cf. Appendix B, 490/140–45.

636/32 **pistillo quouis obtusius.** Cf. Rogers, no. 15, lines 732–33; *Responsio, CW 5,* 222/33; *Adagia* 2521, *Opera omnia, 2,* 852A, based on Jerome, *Epistles* 69. 4, in *PL* 22, 657.

638/4 **operae . . . uidere.** A favorite phrasing of More's. In his *Richard III, CW* 2, 45/25, the loose English equivalent of "Operae pretium est cognoscere" turns out to be "A merueilouse case it is to here. . . ."

638/5–7 **inter . . . deformatam.** For the wrongdoing and subsequent punishment of Richard Empson and Edmund Dudley, Henry VII's extortionary "fiscal judges," see no. 19/96–99 and the Commentary thereon, as well as Polydore Vergil, pp. 128–30, 150–52.

638/14–19 **quod . . . concelebrarem.** More is probably thinking of the variety of hymns used to celebrate saints' "coronation days," the days on which Catholics commemorate the triumphant entry of this or that saint into heaven. See the specimens assembled by Mone, *3*, esp. nos. 647–60 (hymns to John the Baptist), nos. 662–70 (hymns to the Apostles). On the other hand, Ovid makes much the same point by comparing Augustus to Jove; see *Tristia* 2. 73–76.

638/19–23 **Qua . . . licuerit.** This argument is inverted in John Lyly, *Euphues and his England* (1580) in *Lyly's Euphues,* ed. M. W. Croll and H. Clemens (London, 1916), pp. 234–35: ". . . Alexander must be painted of none but Apelles, nor engraven of any but Lysippus; nor our Elizabeth set forth of everyone that would in duty, which are all, but of those that can in skill, which are few."

638/28 **Apellem.** Cf. Appendix B, 494/216–17. Apelles was traditionally treated as a consummate master of honorific court-portraiture (see Horace, *Epistles* 2. 1. 234–41), whence his prominence in this controversy. In no. 97 More seems to associate Apelles with the practice of combining elegant details from many painters' subjects to produce a portrait a good deal less faithful than flattering; Erasmus too speaks of Apelles as a pictorial flatterer by trade in *Institutio principis christiani, ASD 4/1,* 177. For Brixius as "painter" see also the Commentary at no. 186/1–7.

638/29–30 **quemadmodum . . . furias.** Cf. Appendix B, 510/520–27.

638/31–640/3 **quum . . . cognobilem.** Cf. Horace, *Ars poetica* 316–18 on this same kind of poetic portraiture.

640/3–6 **tu . . . iubeas.** Cf. Plato, *Republic* 2. 378D.

640/5 **delere.** Perhaps we should read "deleri."

640/6–7 **stipite . . . stupidior.** Cf. *CW 14,* 115/6–7, and Otto, no. 1695. In his *Responsio, CW 5,* 576/25–27, More declares that Luther "non est . . . certe stupidus et insensatus stipes: sed homo sensus eximij planeque dignus, cuius tam sensatum caput sentiat insensatos stipites."

640/15–642/11 **At . . . memoriae.** Cf. Appendix B, 492/194–209.

640/19–20 **labefactata . . . erexit.** Here More himself employs a metaphor dear to court flatterers. Cf. the Duke of Buckingham's ceremonious petition to the usurper in *Richard III* (*CW 2,* 78/14–15): "[vt] procumbenti in se unum patriae subiiceret humeros, rempublicam prope dirutam ac proculcatam erigeret. . . ."

640/20–23 **idque . . . diademate.** See note to 638/5–7, above.

640/27 **quum.** Perhaps we should read "quod."

640/27–29 **quaedam . . . melius.** Cf. no. 19/112–15 and *ASD 4/1*, 200, line 27. In the *Utopia, CW 4*, 58/8–10, Hythloday arraigns the conservatism of convenience espoused by malicious and timeserving courtiers: "tanquam magnum sit periculum, si quis ulla in re deprehendatur maioribus suis sapientior." More stresses the prudence of Henry VII in no. 19/152 as well; in Allen, *4*, 222, line 225, More repeats his present claim that ill health and not imprudence accounted for England's misfortunes in the last years of Henry VII.

642/12–14 **Nec . . . gloriae.** See the Commentary at no. 19/56–58.

642/15 **Virtus . . . bonos.** Cf. Walther, no. 17016.

642/15–16 **Nam . . . uoco.** Ovid, *Metamorphoses* 13. 140–41.

642/17 **neque . . . Homerus.** Cf. Appendix B, 492/200–03.

642/21–26 **Platoni . . . merito.** Cf. Plato, *Republic* 3. 415A–C.

644/1–2 **exturbare . . . Plato.** Appendix B, 494/222–23. Plato banishes the poets in *Republic* 2. 378D–385E, and 10. 595A–608A.

644/2–4 **uel . . . sustines.** See 642/12–14 and n.

644/4–5 **popularis aurae.** Cf. Horace, *Carmina* 3.2.20; Appendix B, 498/306.

644/6–7 **mellitis numeris . . . pectoribus.** Cf. Plato, *Republic* 3. 401D–402A, and *ASD 4/1*, 136, line 31. More elsewhere frequently stresses the importance of instilling right attitudes from earliest infancy; see, for example, Rogers, no. 63, lines 3–99, and *Utopia, CW 4*, 58/2–5, 210/18–19. For "mellitis numeris," see also the "melle circumlitum uerum" in *CW 4*, 250/8.

644/11–12 **rationi uni parens atque obtemperans.** Cf. *ASD 4/1*, 194, lines 862–64. In More's own *ciuitas philosophica*, in which living according to nature is the cardinal ethical principle, the Utopians hold nature's guidance to be indistinguishable from that of reason: " . . . eum . . . naturae ductum sequi quisquis in appetendis fugiendisque rebus obtemperat rationi" (*CW 4*, 162/21–22).

644/15 **patris . . . abusi.** Cf. More's description (*CW 2*, 43/25–26) of how the Duke of Buckingham decided to join Richard III's seditious conspiracy: " . . . malumque publicum . . . , quando nequiret corrigi, quam maxime posset in suum bonum vertere."

644/21–23 **adeo . . . artibus.** Cf. *ASD 4/1*, 138, lines 64–66.

644/23–24 **censoria uirgula.** Cf. *Adagia* 3726, *Opera omnia,* 2, 1128DE.

644/26–27 **id . . . erit.** Cf. Appendix B, 490/139.

646/2–3 **in caelum ueheret.** Cf. *Adagia* 500, *Opera omnia,* 2, 220C–E.

646/5 **id . . . pueri.** Cf. *Responsio, CW* 5, 674–34, and *Adagia* 1042, *Opera omnia,* 2, 422C: "Et puero perspicuum est."

646/10 **adeo . . . impetu.** For satiric effect, More allusively here likens Brixius to the ungoverned steeds drawing the chariot of the sun from its natural course in the fustian Ovidian story of earth's conflagration, a story which Brixius has "imitated"; see 604/8–12, above, and Ovid, *Metamorphoses* 2. 202–07:

> Exspatiantur equi . . .
> . . . quaque impetus egit,
> Hac sine lege ruunt . . .
> . . . .
> Et modo summa petunt, modo per decliua, viasque
> Praecipites spatio terrae propiore feruntur. . . .

The suggestion is surely that Brixius' extravagant poetics and his irresponsible politics rush on hand in hand. For a similar interpretation of the figure of Phaethon see *ASD 4/1,* 144. Cf. also Plato, *Phaedrus* 248A, 254A, on the ungoverned rush of the "steed" which is irrational passion.

646/14–15 **Nam . . . carminis.** Cf. Appendix B, 492/178–81.

646/15–16 **mox . . . sciat.** Cf. Appendix B, 494/232–35.

646/16–17 **tuum . . . deae.** Cf. Appendix B, 510/533.

646/20 **At . . . parcum.** Cf. Appendix B, 494/210.

646/23–24 **in deterius . . . immutaris.** Cf. 612/28–29 and n.

646/24–26 **Nam . . . aetate.** Vergil, *Eclogues* 7. 4; Appendix B, 510/530.

646/25 **aetatibus" / tuus.** Perhaps we should read "aetatibus' / sic tuus."

646/27 **aetatis florem.** More uses the same phrase in his description of Jane Shore, *Richard III, CW* 2, 55/25–26; cf. also *Utopia, CW 4,* 240/10, and *Adagia* 2767, *Opera omnia,* 2, 917D.

646/29 **silicernis senibus.** Cf. Rogers, no. 83, line 1260, and *Adagia* 1052, *Opera omnia,* 2, 427D, where Erasmus cites Terence, *Adelphoe* 587.

648/1–2 **pares uirtutibus ambos.** Cf. Appendix B, 510/530.

648/4–7 **Nec . . . obnoxius.** Cf. Rogers, no. 15, lines 553–61.

648/7–9 **Nec . . . cies.** Cf. Appendix B, 492/178–494/235, based on Horace, *Epistles* 2. 1.

648/20–21 **post . . . sese.** Cf. Shakespeare, *Julius Caesar*, act 2, scene 1, lines 14–15: "It is the bright day that brings forth the adder / And craves wary walking." The comparison of seditious vainglory to a serpent is commonplace; cf. *Richard III*, *CW* 2, 12/21–23, *Utopia*, *CW* 4, 242/31. The serpent-image is developed very similarly at *CW* 8, 362/5–6, where the serpents are not traitors but heretics.

648/26 **perniciosa.** This charge recurs several times in other letters which bear on this controversy; cf. Allen, *4*, 230, line 545; 255, lines 195–96; 294, lines 65–67; 326, lines 10–17.

648/26 **Deloinum / Budaeum / Lascarem.** Cf. Appendix B, 502/370–77. François Deloynes (c. 1468–1524) and Guillaume Budé (1468–1540), both close friends of Brixius in Paris, were principal figures in the circle of "legal humanists" who along with Jacques Lefèvre d'Étaples and his circle of Evangelical humanists dominated the progressive intellectual scene in early sixteenth-century France. Deloynes was a member of the Parliament of Paris and in 1522 became "Président aux Enquêtes." Brixius claimed to have a very close friendship with Deloynes as early as 1517 (Allen, 2, 536, lines 209–11) and addressed a number of poetic encomia to him in the years which followed; see Appendix A, p. 432, n. 1. For more information on Deloynes, see Allen, 2, 405. Budé, who exchanged many letters with More and Erasmus as well as with Brixius, was a principal mediator between More and Brixius in the months following the appearance of Brixius' *Antimorus;* in September 1521 Erasmus gave Budé full credit for laying the quarrel to rest (see pp. 570–71, above; for additional details on Budé, see Rogers, nos. 65, 66, 68, 80, 96, 97, 102, 154, 156, and accompanying notes, as well as the Commentary at *CW 4*, 4/2). Joannes Lascaris (c. 1445–1535), a Greek born in Constantinople, was tutored and patronized by many of the most prominent figures in midfifteenth-century Italy, including Cardinal Bessarion, Demetrius Chalcondylas, and Lorenzo de' Medici. When Charles VIII of France invaded Italy, Lascaris transferred his allegiance to France. Under Louis XII Lascaris was made royal librarian and then royal ambassador to Venice, where he tutored Brixius in 1508 (Allen, *1*, 447, line 212n.). After Venice joined Julius II against France in 1509, Lascaris left the city; Leo X summoned him to Rome to preside over the Greek College in 1513 (cf. Rogers, no. 15, lines 269–71), where Lascaris remained with few interruptions for the rest of his life. Brixius and Lascaris remained on close terms; see further Allen, *1*, 523, line 51n., and *6*, 378, 382. According to More (Allen, *4*, 228, lines 438–39; 251, lines 17–20) Brixius actually published the *Antimorus* against the advice of the three men he here names as advisers.

648/29 **gemmas . . . in luto.** Cf. Otto, no. 997.

650/5 **calculum.** Cf. *Adagia* 455, 460, *Opera omnia, 2,* 203C–E.

650/6 **ad regias laudes.** On the "topics" of regal praise, see the Commentary at no. 19/56–58 *sidenote.*

650/9 **furias . . . adfuisse.** Cf. Appendix B, 510/520–27, and nos. 266–67.

650/12 **antrum Trophonium.** Cf. *Adagia* 677, *Opera omnia, 2,* 292F–294B; *Moriae encomium, ASD 4/3,* 71, line 13. Persons returning from the cave of Trophonius normally never smiled again. We would regularly expect "antrum Trophonii," but Τροφώνιος is used now and then as an adjective in Greek; see Julius Pollux, *Onomasticon* 1.37 s.v. τὰ Τροφώνια.

650/13–14 **risu canis irritati.** Cf. *CW 5,* 438/4–5; *CW 8,* 199/1–2; and Plautus, *Captivi* 484–86.

650/14–15 **meam . . . pictorem.** Cf. p. 96, More pref. 8–12, above; Appendix B, 494/240–496/257. More himself attacks Luther in similar terms (*Responsio, CW 5,* 464/25–27): "Credo profecto omnes articulos tuos concepisse chiragram, et podagram, ex frigore illius unius articuli. . . ."

650/19–20 **Quis . . . rideat?** Cf. "Deridens alios non inderisus abibit" (Whiting, M612, S92); Erasmus, *Opera omnia, 5,* 11D; and *Responsio, CW 5,* 94/21–22.

650/22–23 **quo . . . domesticae.** Cf. Appendix B, 506/458–61. Actually More is all too likely to feel the thrust of this taunt: the prefatory letters to *Utopia* are full of laments about More's domestic concerns and how they interfere with his studies (*CW 4,* 2/15–17, 22/14, 26/17, 38/22–40/9). By 1520 it was probably quite clear that More never again would be able to claim even so much leisure for study as the "minus fere quam nihil temporis" in which he had written *Utopia.*

650/25 **alienas . . . obambules.** Cf. Aristophanes, *Equites* 744–45, translated thus in *Adagia* 341, *Opera omnia, 2,* 168B: "Ego obambulans ab officina longius / Alio coquente, ollam paratam sustuli."

650/26–27 **otium . . . alienus.** Cf. *Adagia* 1234, *Opera omnia,* 2, 494F–495B; Terence, *Eunuchus* 265.

650/28–29 **Pyrgopolinicen . . . Artotrogon.** A blustering bully and a parasite in Plautus' *Miles gloriosus.*

650/32 **dictum . . . melioribus.** Cf. Plautus, *Captivi* 482.

652/3–5 **Cynicae . . . applaudere.** An apothegm of Diogenes the Cynic—"Currosopher"—underlines all three qualities More relates here to Brixius' own "cynicism," namely beggary, parasitical mores, and bestial abusiveness: "Being asked what he had done to be known as a 'cur,' he said, 'I fawn on those who give gifts to me, bark at those who give none, and bite rascals'" (Diogenes Laertius, *Vitae philosophorum* 6. 60). Cf. no. 43; *Adagia* 1334, *Opera omnia,* 2, 534E; and *Responsio, CW* 5, 180/24–25, where More scores Luther's indecorous abusiveness: "[qui] quaelibet in quemuis eiaculetur opprobria, more Cynicorum, si quis uel ausit hiscere contra eius placita, etiam absurdissima," and 464/6 *sidenote,* "Cynicus Lutheri mos." Lucian, *Parasitus* 53–54, attributes these same "cynical" properties to parasites. Cf. also Plautus, *Persa* 123: "cynicum esse egentem oportet parasitum probe."

652/5–8 **ita . . . felices.** Cf. Appendix B, 504/402–05.

652/9–10 **laqueos . . . deprecor.** "Go hang!" is a proverbial way of dismissing one's enemies in Latin as well as in English; see *Richard III, CW* 2, xxxviii, and *Adagia* 1367, *Opera omnia,* 2, 544DE. By reversing this formula here More anticipates his still more insulting suggestion that Brixius is not even worthy of being viewed as an enemy (654/22–24).

652/11–12 **uberior . . . fortuna.** A high-flown phrase here employed for satiric effect; cf. Livy 27.28, 30.30, and More's *Richard III, CW* 2, 37/8–9: "donec spes aliqua affulserit meliorum."

652/15–19 **lupo . . . blandulum.** Cf. Appendix B, 510/536–37, and *Adagia* 310, *Opera omnia,* 2, 155C–E.

652/19–22 **diras . . . tuum.** Cf. Appendix B, 510/520–27. Cf. the grim irony of Richard III's contrived motive for dragging one heir to the throne from asylum to rejoin his brother (*CW* 2, 26/5–10): "[Principis] incolumitas haud mihi certe fulciri satis vlla victus cura videtur, nisi ludi quoque voluptas accesserit. . . . Blandus adhiberi collusor debeat. . . ." Cf. also the note to 656/31–658/1, below.

652/27 **de . . . ducant.** Cf. *Responsio, CW* 5, 76/27: "[Lutherus] buccinat magnificas ipse de se victorias." The same paradoxical notion appears in Justinus, *Historiarum epitome* 14.4.16: "Sequitur exercitus [sc. Romanus] prodito imperatore suo et ipse captivus, triumphumque de se ipso ad victoris sui castra ducit."

652/28–30 **tu . . . emissus.** Cf. *Responsio, CW 5,* 78/14–17, and 626/17–18: "Non tibi uidentur, lector, per istud os impium, inferae spirare furiae?"

654/2–3 **quod . . . effigiem.** Cf. no. 88 and *Adagia* 306, *Opera omnia, 2,* 153CD.

654/4 **"rabulam".** Cf. Appendix B, 512/562 *sidenote.* A *rabula* was an unlearned pleader who lived by abuse; see Cicero, *De oratore* 1.46.202. This swipe at More's forensic calling again has a basis in More's own *Utopia,* where laws are few and lawyers excluded entirely. Cf. *Utopia, CW 4,* 102/29–30, 194/6–19. Listrius mentions More's distinction as a lawyer in his commentary to *Moriae encomium, ASD 4/3,* 70, line 65.

654/9 **a secretis . . . reginae.** Cf. Appendix B, 482/4–5.

654/14–20 **ut . . . inculcans.** Cf. Appendix B, 536/25–32.

654/16 **relaturus . . . gratiam.** The phrase *referre gratiam* almost invariably means "to render thanks." The only ancient instance of *referre gratiam* with the meaning "to receive thanks" occurs in *Querolus sive Aulularia* (*editio princeps* 1564), an anonymous comedy of the third or fourth century after Christ, written in imitation of Plautus and falsely ascribed to him by several medieval authors; see *Querolus sive Aulularia incerti auctoris comoedia,* ed. Gunnar Ranstrand, Acta Universitatis Gotoburgensis, 57/1 (Göteborg, 1951), p. 4, line 23. Erasmus uses the phrase with the same meaning in Allen, 2, 218 line 252. More uses the phrase "fructum . . . retulerunt" with the meaning "they received the profit" in his *Letter to Lee* (Rogers, no. 75 lines 146–47).

654/21–22 **uelis . . . caelorum.** Cf. Matt. 3:2.

654/27 **insusurret in aurem.** Cf. *Adagia* 247, *Opera omnia, 2,* 131CD.

656/1–2 **lethaeum poculum.** Cf. no. 139/5; *Adagia* 1855, *Opera omnia, 2,* 675E, and Otto, no. 943.

656/2 **generosa palma.** Cf. Appendix B, 486/93–94; Allen, *4,* 230, line 518; *Adagia* 204, *Opera omnia, 2,* 112D–113A, citing Aulus Gellius 3.6. The palm tree was thought to possess such resilience that it not only never gave way to a burden but actually grew higher on account of it.

656/4 **Herculi subrepta claua.** Cf. note to 610/22–27.

656/5 **oculatus ac lynceus.** Cf. Appendix B, 540/1; *Utopia, CW 4,* 248/23;

Responsio, CW 5, 50/11, 526/20; *Adagia* 1054, *Opera omnia,* 2, 427F–428C; *Moriae encomium, ASD 4/3,* 148, line 410, 154, line 476.

656/7–9 **tam . . . conuicijs.** Cf. Allen, *4,* 218–19, lines 65–67: "Et tamen audet [sc. Brixius] praefari oliuam sese mediis in armis gessisse, homo nimirum sic affectus erga mendacia vt periurium quoque et foedifragium habeat in blanditiis."

656/11–12 **tam . . . laeserit.** See note to 598/18–20.

656/13 **oliuam . . . armis.** Cf. Appendix B, 486/80, and note to 656/7–9, above.

656/17 **a corporis dotibus.** Cf. 642/12–14, 644/2–4, 650/6, and notes.

656/18–19 **nisi . . . quemlibet.** Cf. 646/29–648/3. At 632/16–17 More suggests that Brixius' reproaches have equally little to do with the distinguishing traits of the person to whom they are addressed. Brixius' dedicatory epistle to Queen Anne of Brittany prefixed to the *Chordigera* is likewise a tissue of vague and impersonal tributes to the "virtue" of Brixius' patroness; see Appendix A, 442/11–446/32.

656/20–21 **lapides . . . silentium.** On the proverbial suggestion that something is so manifestly true that "even the stones" will proclaim it, see *Adagia* 4117, *Opera omnia,* 2, 1205F–1206A, where Erasmus cites Luke 19:14. For "Pythagorean silence" see no. 127; *Adagia* 3272, *Opera omnia,* 2, 1019E; Appendix B, 498/298–301.

656/21–22 **nisi . . . spectetur.** Cf. 648/4–9. On the principle of "reading [or viewing] with indulgence," see also Allen, 2, 106, lines 593–96; Rogers, no. 15, lines 558–61; and Rogers, no. 143, lines 954–56.

656/22–23 **ex eadem . . . fidelia.** Cf. *Adagia* 603, *Opera omnia* 2, 263AB: "Duos parietes de eadem dealbare fidelia."

656/23–27 **tam anxie . . . deglutiret.** Cf. Ps. 123 (124):1–3.

656/26–27 **me . . . deglutiret.** Cf. 652/15–19 and n.

656/29 **sibi . . . furias.** Cf. 652/19–22 and n.

656/31–658/1 **alijs . . . ludere.** Cf. the grim sarcasm of Edward IV's widowed queen in responding to Richard III's plot to "reunite," in his own clutches, Edward's two sons and heirs, to be "playfellows" (*Richard III, CW* 2, 38/14–17): " . . . tanquam nusquam reperiri possit qui iocetur cum principe . . . nisi frater (cui per valetudinem non lubet ludere) ex asylo, id est, extra munitiones suas, velut lusurus eliciatur."

658/3 **trabalibus clauis.** Cf. *Adagia* 848, *Opera omnia* 2, 351DE; Rogers, no. 75, line 252: "adamantinis uinculis"; Budé to Lupset, *Utopia, CW 4,* 10/12; Cicero, *In Verrem* 5. 53: "ut hoc beneficium, quemadmodum dicitur, trabali clauo figeret."

658/4 **tam charo capite.** Cf. Horace, *Carmina* 1. 24. 2.

658/12 **albusne sis an ater.** Cf. *Adagia* 598, *Opera omnia, 2,* 925B; *Responsio, CW 5,* 188/16–17, 260/26; Rogers, no. 75, line 190.

658/13–14 **tam . . . est.** Cf. no. 143/223 and Allen, *4,* 252, lines 51–52.

658/14–23 **Tantum . . . corpore.** For a similar expression of mock gratitude see Rogers, no. 83, lines 20–26.

658/16 **cuiusquam . . . quam.** We would normally expect "alterius cuiusquam . . . quam" or "cuiusquam potius . . . quam."

658/21–22 **mihi . . . pectore.** Cf. Pico's letter to Barbaro in defense of the *barbarum dicendi genus* used by the medieval philosophers (Garin, pp. 804–22):

> Sciebat tam prudens quam eruditus homo [sc. Cicero], nostrum esse componere mentem potius quam dictionem, curare ne quid aberret ratio, non oratio. . . . Laudabile in nobis, habere Musas in animo non in labris. . . . [p. 814]
>
> . . . quaeso, quis in dubium reuocet, vter [sc. Lucretius an Scotus] poeta melior, vter philosophus? Extra omnem est controuersiam tam rectius Scotum philosophari quam ille loquatur ornatius. Sed vide quid differant: huic os insipidum, illi mens desipiens. Hic grammaticorum, ne dicam poetarum, decreta nescit: ille Dei atque naturae. [p. 822]

658/23 **sanum caput in corpore.** Cf. Juvenal, *Satires* 10. 356 ("mens sana in corpore sano"). Juvenal presents this phrase as an epitome of all prudent prayers to the gods; naturally Brixius' rival formula ("sanos pedes in carmine") makes him seem to neglect the essential. More alludes to the same line in Rogers, no. 60, line 68.

APPENDIX D

Reprints, Translations, and Adaptations of More's Latin Poems in the Sixteenth and Seventeenth Centuries

BY CHARLES CLAY DOYLE

APPENDIX D

Reprints, Translations, and Adaptations of More's Latin Poems in the Sixteenth and Seventeenth Centuries

THIS APPENDIX is intended as an aid and a spur to research on the history, influence, and reputation of More's Latin poetry from 1518 through the end of the seventeenth century. It lists a highly miscellaneous assortment of publications. The variety of books and the range of uses to which they put More's epigrams reflect the variety among the epigrams themselves and also the many facets of More's fame during the centuries. His name frequently appeared in short lists of notable "modern" poets, and when he was mentioned as an eminent English poet, we must suppose that the designation sometimes meant "Englishman who wrote poetry" rather than "writer of English poetry."

Without doubt, the category of More's epigrams that figured most prominently in sixteenth- and seventeenth-century publications was his translations from the *Greek Anthology*. Upon those rested a great part of More's reputation as a humanist. Much of the history of the *Greek Anthology* in Renaissance and early modern Europe—including the history of More's translations—was written by James Hutton in his monographs *The Greek Anthology in Italy to the Year 1800* (1935) and *The Greek Anthology in France and in the Latin Writers of the Netherlands to the Year 1800* (1946). Regrettably, Hutton's planned study of the *Anthology* in England never appeared. As Hutton showed, the pioneering and most influential figures in acquainting Europe with the *Anthology* were two German scholars, Joannes Soter (Heyl) and Janus Cornarius (Hagenbut). They published extensive selections which included, along with the Greek poems, Latin translations by More and several others. Soter's *Epigrammata aliquot Graeca veterum elegantissima* had successively larger editions in 1525, 1528, and 1544. Cornarius' *Selecta epigrammata Graeca Latine versa* of 1529 expanded Soter's 1525 edition. The Frenchman Henri Estienne in his *Epigrammata Graeca, selecta ex Anthologia* of 1570 adopted the format of Soter and Cornarius and drew upon their contents; the Englishman John Stockwood in his *Progymnasma scholasticum* of 1597 enlarged Estienne's collection. In 1602 Hieronymus Megiser expanded the Soter-Cornarius collection for his *Anthologia, seu florilegium graecolatinum* (reissued in 1614). In 1608 an annonymous compiler, probably a Jesuit, founded his *Selecta epigrammata ex florilegio* (published at Rome) on Soter's 1544 edition. Elias Cüchler in 1618–19, Thomas Farnaby in 1629, and Andreas Rivinus (Bachmann) in 1651 published collections of the same kind.

Through such collections nearly all of More's epigrams from the Greek were disseminated—quite apart from the editions of the *Epigrammata* (1518, 1520, 1638) and the collected editions of More's Latin *Opera* (1563, 1565–66, 1689). As Hutton remarked, "Soter and Cornarius had published their select translations with the avowed purpose of setting examples to the young."[1] The same is true of their successors. Countless fledgling scholars in all parts of Europe were introduced to More's epigrams as models of Latin verse. Even beyond such volumes garnered from translators of the Greek, other academic collections reprinted many of More's epigrams: for instance, Levinus Linius' *Disticha aliquot* (1522), Léger Duchesne's *Flores epigrammaton* (1536, 1555), Johann Gast's *Scholae Christianae epigrammatum libri duo* (1539, 1543) and Carolus a Sancto Antonio Patavino's *De arte epigrammatica* (1650).[2] Records show that More's epigrams (in what version is not specified) were part of the curriculum for the fourth form at Eton College in 1560.[3] Whether or not that curriculum was typical—in England or elsewhere—it is noteworthy that two Englishmen who translated More's poems, Timothy Kendall (1577) and Sir John Harington (1596, 1615, 1618), attended Eton just after that time.

The other category of More's epigrams from which later books drew in large measure—a category that overlaps the translations from the Greek and other academically serviceable poems—might be designated "popular." These epigrams were found suitable for use in all sorts of miscellaneous collections published for the entertainment and edification

---

[1]*Anthology in Italy*, p. 43.

[2]Stapleton cited the large number of More's epigrams that Duchesne included (157 in the 1555 volume) as evidence of More's excellence in the art and, by implication, of his repute: ". . . in a collection of epigrams which he selected with great critical acumen from various writers, he inserted a larger number of More's compositions than of any other writer, in spite of the fact that very few of More's have survived in comparison with the very large number that have been published by others"; *Tres Thomae* (1588), tr. Phillip E. Hallett (London, 1928), pp. 7–8.

[3]The manuscript "Consuetudinarium" of the schoolmaster William Malim, 1560; see H. C. Maxwell Lyte, *A History of Eton College*, 4th ed. (London, 1911), p. 145.

of a wide readership: jestbooks, vernacular verse anthologies, compilations of old saws and pious sentences.

Since many of the epigrams embody proverbs, it is not surprising that some should have found their way into aphoristic collections. Probably the earliest reprinting of a poem from the *Epigrammata* appeared in an edition of Erasmus' *Adagia*—if in fact Erasmus' publication did not actually precede More's 1518 volume. Erasmus quoted no. 52, beneath the original Greek of *AP* XI, 251, in his discussion of the adage *Surdaster cum surdastro litigabat.*[1] Other aphoristic compilations also contained material from More's epigrams. Antonio Germano's *Giardino di sentenze volgari* (1630) reprinted no. 41, from *AP* XI, 166, on true and false riches. Number 157, from *AP* XI, 430 (which notes that if a beard made a philosopher, then a goat could be Plato), appeared, along with a German translation, in Johann Georg Seybold's bilingual *Viridarium selectissimis paroemiarum et sententiarum Latino-Germanicarum . . . adornatum* (1677). Jeremias Simon included no. 157 in *Gnomologia prouerbialis poetica* (1683), which also contains the whole or part of nos. 4, 32, 113, and 125. All of those except no. 113 come from the *Greek Anthology;* no. 113 alludes to the famous retort of the old woman who prayed for the tyrant Dionysius.

Epigrams and proverbs are near kin. Proverbs—especially those marked by prominent rhyme, alliteration, or meter—might be thought of as oral epigrams. Many epigrams, from every literary period, have versified, elaborated, or commented on proverbs.[2] It is possible that More's epigrams had some effect on the dissemination of proverbs in England. Such expressions as "Like lips, like lettuce" (no. 161), "There's many a slip 'twixt the cup and the lip" (no. 42), and "Happiness is like the good hours of an ague" (no. 259) were to become common in English, but not till after 1518.[3]

Number 254 calls for special note. It details a series of antidotes for

---

[1]See the Commentary at 52/1–8.

[2]An extensive collection was issued by More's kinsman John Heywood, *Two hundred Epigrammes, vpon two hundred prouerbes, with a thyrde hundred newely added* (1555). Late in the century Gabriel Harvey reported that "some of Heywood's epigrams are supposed to be the conceits and devices of pleasant Sir Thomas More" (*Gabriel Harvey's Marginalia,* ed. G. C. Moore Smith [Stratford upon Avon, 1913], pp. 233–34). The same point was made in the mid-seventeenth century by the antiquarian Anthony Wood (*Atheniae Oxonienses,* 3rd ed., ed. Philip Bliss, 4 vols. [1813; reprint, New York and London, 1967], *1,* 351).

[3]"Like lips, like lettuce" is Whiting L372 and Tilley L326, first cited in English in 1546. "There's many a slip 'twixt the cup and the lip" is Tilley T191, first cited in English in 1539. "Happiness is like the good hours of an ague" is not recorded by Whiting or Tilley; some instances are given by Charles Doyle in *Moreana,* 70 (1981), 51, the earliest (aside from More's) being 1608.

foul breath: from leeks to onions to garlic to feces. B. J. Whiting in his dictionary of English proverbs before 1500 gave some medieval antecedents of the idea (Whiting S716; cf. Tilley S556).[1] Whether the point should be called a proverb, a joke, a piece of medical or herbal lore, or just a bit of gratuitous scatology, the epigram struck the fancy of Elizabethan and Stuart writers. Timothy Kendall translated it into English verse in 1577, as did Richard Stanyhurst in 1582. Stanyhurst, however, removed the indelicate "point" of the last two lines:

> If that theese simples wyl not thee filthhod abandon,
> A *rose,* or else nothing that drafty infirmitye cureth.

Kendall had ended his version more faithfully:

> If after thou of Garlicke strong,
> the sauour wilt expell:
> A *Mard* is sure the onely meane,
> to put away the smell.

Sir John Harington, nephew, courtier, and scatologist extraordinaire of Queen Elizabeth, reprinted and translated the epigram in his *Metamorphosis of Ajax* (1596) to illustrate the respectability of indecency. He revised the translation for his *Most Elegant and Witty Epigrams* (1618), where it is gallantly titled, "Of Garlick, to my Lady Rogers," the poet's mother-in-law. Harington managed the ending of the poem by resorting to a euphemism that was not uncommon in the seventeenth century (though it is not recorded in the *OED* or its supplements):

> But against garlikes savour, at one word,
> I know but one receipt. whats that? go looke.[2]

The joke, of course, is that the reader supplies the missing rhyme. That

---

[1]See the Commentary at 254/1–9.

[2]Elizabeth Story Donno, in her edition of *A New Discourse of a Stale Subject, Called the Metamorphosis of Ajax* (New York, 1962), reported that "when Harington included this epigram in his presentation copy for Prince Henry in 1605, he took cognizance of the royal point of view by changing the last line to read, 'I know but one receipt, what's that? Tobacco'" (p. 99). That application of More's poem had been anticipated by some lines from Sir John Davies's Epigram 36, "Of Tobacco" (1598; *Poems,* ed. Robert Krueger [Oxford, 1975], p. 144):

> And though ill breaths were by it but confounded,
> Yet that vile Medicine it doth far excell,
> Which by Sir Thomas Moore hath bin propounded,
> For this is thought a gentleman-like smell.

version is probably what Edmund Gayton had in mind in 1656 when he included the following in his riddle book *Wit Revived:*

> *Q. What is the best receipt to take away the sent of garlick?*
> A. Go-looke.

In the meantime, Henry Buttes in a dietary treatise of 1599 used More's epigram to develop the point that "Garlick, Onion, and Leeks, are very holesome, but their sauour is passing loathsome and offensiue." He ends his prose paraphrase thus: "and if then Garlicke breath be strong, choke him with a piece of a *T.* with a *u.* with an *r.* with a *d.*" In 1608 Thomas Milles, in *The Custumers Alphabet and Primer,* ended his translation of the epigram thus:

> What helpes vs then? *Tabacco?* no, but at a word I think,
> There is a thing can *Vndertake* to make a viler stinke.

Milles proceeds with an elaborate allegorization of the poem in terms of commerce and finance, glossing *leekes* as "Customer," *Onyons* as "Controller," *Garlicke* as "Supervisors," *Tabacco* as "Farmers," and *thing can Vndertake* as "Undertakers." Such is the variety of uses to which one aphoristic epigram was put.

The other popular category that More's epigrams drew upon and, in turn, contributed to is the jest or "merry tale" or *facetia.* A scant six years after the publication of the *Epigrammata,* nine of the poems were reprinted (with attribution) in a jestbook, Ottmar Nachtigall's *Ioci ac sales mire festiui* (1524). One of the epigrams included was no. 254, on remedies for foul breath. More an aphorism or a quip than a proper jest, the epigram contains no narrative. Nevertheless, besides Nachtigall's at least two other jestbooks included it, without attribution: the Italian prose collection of Lodovico Domenichi (1564) and the English one compiled by Richard Head (1675). Five years after Nachtigall's collection thirty-three of More's epigrams were reprinted in *Iocorum veterum ac recentium libri tres,* by Adrianus Barlandus (1529). The 1526 jestbook *A C. Mery Talys* gave an English prose version of an epigram, and *Tales, and quicke answeres* [1532?] gave seven. Neither of the English collections credited More. Thenceforth More's epigrams had a secure, though usually anonymous, place in the vernacular jestbook tradition.

As we have seen, jests overlap the category of aphorisms; a jest, or its kindred form the apothegm, may simply furnish a minimal narrative frame for a witty saying—the "punch line." For instance, no. 218 directs a quip at a dandy who mortgaged his land to buy clothing and now sweats under the weight of the acreage. By the seventeenth century the point had become a commonplace. William Camden (1605) assigned the quip to a courtier who boasted to Cardinal Wolsey, "Am not I a mighty man, that beare an hundred houses on my backe?"[1] The proverb dictionaries record numerous aphoristic versions of the point, including some from Shakespeare.[2] Not recorded are the following instances. From Robert Chamberlain's *Conceits, clinches, flashes, and whimzies* (1639): "One said roaring Gallants were like Pedlers, because some of them did carry their whole estates upon their backs."[3] From Thomas Freeman's *Rubbe, and a great cast* (1614):

> *Superbus* sold a gallant Mannor place,
> Himself with a new-fashion'd sute to grace.
> Meant he himselfe an Elephant to make,
> In carrying such a Castle on his backe.

From John Manningham's diary, for June 1602: "'Roome! roome!' said one, 'here comes a woman with a cupboard on hir head' (of one that had sold hir cupboard to buy a taffaty hat)."[4] If More originated the notion of wearing an estate, such later sayings must have been related indirectly to More's epigram. This appendix includes only versions that seem reasonably close to More's. Thus two of Shakespeare's (1623), as well as Camden's, Freeman's, and Chamberlain's, are included; Manningham's and several cited in the proverb dictionaries are not.

An apothegm characteristically assigns a memorable saying to a specific historical or legendary figure. Occasionally an epigram by More entered the apothegmatic tradition with More himself as alleged protagonist. An example is a jestbook version of no. 228, which itself came from *AP* XI, 418. *A banquet of jests* (1632) reports, "Vpon one that had an exceeding long nose, and great, and gag'd teeth, standing some distance one from another, Sir *Thomas More* made this Epigram." The Latin distich is then quoted and translated:

> Gape 'gainst the Sun, and by thy teeth and nose,
> 'Tis easie to perceive how the day goes.

Several of More's epigrams echo ancient and later *facetiae* and *apothegmata,* many of which weathered the Middle Ages in compilations of

---

[1]See the Commentary at 218/4.

[2]Tilley L452. *Oxford Dictionary of English Proverbs,* 3rd ed., ed. F. P. Wilson (Oxford, 1970), p. 874.

[3]A lengthier form of the "peddler" variant appeared in *A banquet of jests,* 1640. Ordinarily, in the history of jests, the more abbreviated form is presumed to be the derivative one; so probably the Chamberlain version is not the source of the *Banquet* version.

[4]*The Diary of John Manningham of the Middle Temple,* ed. Robert Parker Sorlien (Hanover, New Hampshire, 1976), p. 70.

exempla for use in preaching. It is usually impossible to ascertain what independent influence More's poems had on subsequent recountings of such jests. For example, the story in no. 237, concerning a poor jester futilely visited by thieves, had occurred previously in at least three Latin prose versions, two of which belong to collections printed several times in the early 1500s and still being reprinted in the seventeenth century. Hence, when we discover Martin Luther in his *Das schoene Confitemini* (1530) telling the same joke, can we assume that he learned it from More's 1518 *Epigrammata,* which he had seen?[1] Or is it just as likely that Luther got the story from the often-reprinted jestbook of his countryman Heinrich Bebel, or from the widely accessible *Mensa philosophica,* or from some other source, written or oral? I have cited Luther's jest in connection with no. 257 and given some other similarly speculative entries, in the hope of being plausibly comprehensive.

There is peril in identifying echoes of an epigram when the sources of the epigram are not recognized. For example, no. 164 jokes about a physician, playing on *medicus* and *mendicus.* Recently I suggested that an epigram by the Welsh poet John Owen, which employs the same wordplay, may have adapted More's poem.[2] At almost the same time Germain Marc'hadour, quite by accident, discovered that More (and almost certainly Owen as well) was adapting a bit of dialogue from a comedy by Plautus.[3] In fact, though, the connection had been noted more than three centuries ago in the annotations to the academic anthology *De arte epigrammatica* (1650) by Carolus a Sancto Antonio Patavino, where the lines from Plautus are quoted after More's epigram.

Tracing a jest forward from More's epigrammatic telling may also reveal, if not an actual prototype, then at least a possible motivation for the wit of the jest. The jest about a dim-sighted tippler, who rejects medical advice that he abstain from wine, takes three variant forms in More's verse. The punch line of each expresses the patient's preference for wine over eyesight. In no. 199 he proclaims that he would rather ruin his eyes through drink than keep them for worms to eat; in no. 210 he affirms that he has seen enough but not drunk enough; in no. 214 he takes solace in the thought that the wine's lovely color is the only quality that he must forgo. An epigram by Martial (6.78) presented the story, but not a punch line.[4] Each of More's punch lines recurred in the jestbooks and verse miscellanies of the following generations. Some vari-

---

[1] *D. Martin Luthers Werke: Briefwechsel,* vol. 1 (1930; reprint, Weimar, 1969), p. 147.
[2] *Moreana, 67–68* (1980), 40–41.
[3] *Moreana, 67–68* (1980), 42. See the Commentary at 164/1–3.
[4] See the Commentary at 199/1–5.

ants offered still other punch lines. One that was often repeated apparently originated in the Italian jestbook of Lodovico Guicciardini (1583); it observes that it is better for the windows to be destroyed than for the whole house to fall down. Francis Bacon (1625) gave this slightly incoherent variation of the jest:

> A physician aduised his Patient, that had sore eyes, that hee should abstaine from wine. But the Patient said, *I think rather, Sir, from wine and water; for I haue often marked it, in bleare eyes, and I haue seen water come forth, but neuer wine.*[1]

A fourteen-line epigram by John Donne the younger (1662) follows More's no. 214 but changes the punch line; here is the ending:

> His taste and smell are gone, the colour quite
> Of Wine begins to fail, so doth his sight:
> Yet for this loss, it somewhat eas'd his minde,
> That he'd not left one drop of it behind.

In a mid-seventeenth-century version, the nose rather than the eyes is the seat of the affliction:

> Thom: Brewer . . . through his proneness to goodfellowshippe having attained to a very rich and rubicund nose; being reprov'd by a friend for his too frequent use of strong drinkes and sacke, as very pernicious to that distemper and inflammation in his nose, "Nay, faith," says he, "if it will not endure sack, it is no nose for me."[2]

What is essentially the same joke as the one in More's three epigrams persists to the present; often, though, sexual misconduct takes the place of excessive imbibing.[3] Only with the discovery of an analogue from John Bunyan (1680) did the implication of the jest in its sexual form become clear: blindness is the result of venereal disease, the punishment for fornication.[4] That realization, in turn, made it possible to recognize a jest of about 1470, told in Italian by Lodovico Carbone, as similar to the one in More's epigrams:

---

[1]The joke would work if the patient answered simply, "I thinke rather, Sir, from water. . . ."

[2]From the manuscript jest collection of Sir Nicholas l'Estrange (1603–54), in *Anecdotes and Traditions, Illustrative of Early English History and Literature, Derived from MS. Sources,* ed. William J. Thoms, Camden Society Publications no. 5 (London, 1839), p. 76.

[3]Some of the modern versions are given and discussed by Charles Doyle in *Moreana, 51* (1976), 145–47.

[4]The Bunyan analogue was pointed out by Ward S. Allen, *Moreana, 55–56* (1977), 64.

> Because of his excessive addiction to lust, Febo dal Sarasino was gradually losing his eyesight. When he turned completely blind, he said: "The Lord be praised; now I will be able to indulge all I want without fear of going blind."[1]

One could theorize that the form told by Carbone preserves the essential or "pure" form of the joke—that the others, including Martial's and More's, have substituted the misbehavior of alcoholic excess, thereby avoiding the social impropriety or psychological anguish of the sexual taboo.[2] Not everyone will wish to accept that theory.

As the case of the dim-eyed dissipator reveals, a single joke can assume many disparate forms. The researcher must eventually confront a basic though baffling question: What is an analogue? How widely can two texts vary before they cease to be versions of the same jest and become simply two narratives? Does More's no. 96, a joke about a physician who lays low more people more permanently than a general, have any connection with Timothy Kendall's epigram "To an vnskilfull Phisition"?

> *Achilles* with a sword did slaie his foes.
> Thou killest with a hearbe on ground that growes[.]
> Thee worthier then Achilles I suppose. (sig. Q_8)

Kendall evidently thought not, since he did not include the poem in a section of his book devoted to translations from More (sigs. K_4–L_2). On the same theme, but still more distantly related, is an anonymous eight-line epigram in the 1641 edition of *Wits recreations,* concerning a fencing master and a physician; the poem concludes:

> A Doctor standing by, cries, fencing foole,
> Both you and hee to me may come to Schoole,
> Thou dost but prate: deeds shall show my skill,
> Where thou hurt'st one, an hundred I do kill. (sig. K_2v)

---

[1]Charles Speroni, trans., *Wit and Wisdom of the Italian Renaissance* (Berkeley and Los Angeles, 1964), p. 75. The original Italian may be found in Carbone's *Facezie,* ed. Abd-el-Kadar Salza (Livorno, 1900), no. 100.

[2]Someone wishing to pursue a psychoanalytical interpretation might begin with Freud's 1910 report, "Psychogenic Visual Disturbance," in *Collected Papers,* vol. 2, trans. Joan Riviere (New York, 1959), pp. 105–12. One curious poem, a distich by Charles Cotton (1689), combines the venereal and bacchic strains, though the precise relation to More is obscure. The epigram is cryptically titled "De Luxu, & Libidine. Epig. *Tho. Mori*" (cf. no. 8):

> Let who would die to end his Woes,
> Both Wench, and Tipple, and he goes.

Neither of these English poems is listed in this appendix. But discovering the source of either (or both) might cast light on the background of More's epigram.

Most jestbooks and apothegm collections borrowed boldly from other such compilations, without giving any attribution. Occasionally, however, a compiler took cognizance of the Latin verse prototype of a vernacular prose text. The 1614 edition of *The philosopher's banquet,* translated and supplemented by one W. B., Esquire,[1] included a prose version of no. 133:

> A certaine conceyted Traueller being at a Banquet, where chanced a flye to fall into his cuppe, which hee (being to drinke) tooke out for himselfe, and afterwards put in againe for his fellow; being demanded his reason, answered, that for his owne part he affected them not, but it might be some other did.

That story had been in prose jestbooks at least since Domenichi's Italian collection of 1564 (where the protagonist is *vno Inglese*). The English compiler added a little scholarly epilogue: "There is extant to this Ieast, an Epigram of Syr Thomas Moore's, which I have here inserted as followeth"—whereupon he quotes More's Latin and gives a verse translation. Probably that association of More's name with the jest was conflated into the apothegmatic version of the same jest in *Poor Robin's Jests* (1667), attributed to William Winstanley, where it appeared among several other anecdotes concerning More:

> Sir *Thomas Moor* being once a drinking, spied a Flie in his Glass, wherefore with his knife he took it out, but having drunk put in again, saying, Though I do not love them in my drink, perhaps some others do.

By the end of the seventeenth century some jokes had appeared in so many collections that a hasty hack compiling yet another book would sometimes unwittingly borrow the same joke twice—presumably from two different sources. Thus in 1700 another compiler designated W. B. included in *Ingenii fructus: or the Cambridge jests* two prose versions, several pages apart, of no. 187:

> A Gentleman being at a Gossipping, kiss'd all the Ladies but one . . . the Gentleman said, he would have kiss'd her but that her

---

[1]This W. B. has never been identified. He may, however, be the same as the compiler of *A helpe to discourse* (1619), who is usually said to be William Basse. In any case, the two W. B.'s gave precisely the same three-part handling of no. 133.

> Nose was so long, he could not come at her Lips for it; Then, says she, you may Kiss my Bum, I am sure there is no Nose to offend you. (sig. H_3)

> A Young *Cambridge* Schollar following a Young Maid, he lik'd her very well behind, but looking in her Face, found she had a very large Nose: Well, says he to her, if I had liked you before, as well as I did behind, I would have Kissed you. Pray Sir, says she, Kiss where you like. But it is your Nose that I mislike: Why, in that place that I appointed you to Kiss, I have never a Nose there. (sig. H_5v)[1]

Neither version does justice to the trenchancy and brevity of the girl's retort in More's epigram. Perhaps the joke, which entered the jestbook tradition with *Tales, and quicke answeres* (1532?), had been told too often and at too many clumsy removes from the deftness of More's wit.

Besides More's epigrams from the *Greek Anthology* and the "popular" ones of a jesting or aphoristic character, many others appeared again and again in publications of the sixteenth and seventeenth centuries: the epitaph on More's *uxorcula* Jane (no. 258), the burlesque epitaph on Abyngdon the singer (no. 160), some of the satiric poems on Brixius (nos. 188–95, 209, 266–69), and others. No work except *Utopia* did more to establish More's European reputation than his Latin poems.

This appendix lists, in chronological order, printed works of the sixteenth and seveteenth centuries that contain material derived from More's *Epigrammata*. Arabic numerals within the entries refer to the numbers assigned to the poems in this edition.

Whenever possible, one of the editors or staff members or a trusted deputy has inspected a copy of the edition listed, locating the items by signature.[2] When inspection was not possible, the source of the citation is given. The main entry is the earliest edition known to contain the material. When earlier editions exist but have not been seen, or when an earlier edition is known not to contain the material, the fact is noted.

If More's Latin is not itself reproduced in the work cited, the text is

---

[1]The second version might better have stopped after "Pray Sir, says she, Kiss where you like." That is the punch line in the anonymous telling of *Mercurius jocosus* (1654). *London jests* (1685) also contains both the "where you like" and "where there is no nose" versions, told more skillfully than in *Ingenii fructus;* in *London jests* the equivalency of the two jokes is not so evident.

[2]The "deputies" who kindly assisted are Anthony S. Bliss of the University of California (Berkeley), Donald J. Greene of the University of Southern California, and Franklin B. Williams, Jr., of Georgetown University.

said to be either a *translation* or an *adaptation*—the difference being, of course, a matter of editorial judgment. The entries also specify the language of the translations or adaptations and whether they are verse or prose.

A text is assumed to derive from More's version of a poem in the *Greek Anthology* only if (1) the text gives More's Latin practically verbatim, or (2) the work identifies the text as coming from More, or (3) some peculiarity or distinctive feature of More's Latin appears in the translation or adaptation. The few exceptions to this procedure are noted.

The criteria for including other kinds of material are looser. Often there is no means of determining whether a jest or aphorism or English epigram derives immediately from More, has a common source with More, or adapts a subsequent analogue in prose or verse, written or oral. In such cases the principle has been to include in the appendix as much as plausibility permits, and leave it to individual researchers to discriminate.

Mere translations of works containing material from More's epigrams are not given separate entries, though they are usually mentioned in the entry for the work translated. Manuscript material not published before modern times is also excluded, except for the particularly interesting English verse renditions by Nicholas Bacon (before 1579) and Francis Thynne (c. 1600).[1] Modern editions, collections, or reprints have been mentioned only when necessary to solve problems about early editions. Many of the works listed here are available on microfilm.[2]

---

[1]See also the Commentary at 187/1–9 and 220/1–13. Several manuscript versions of isolated epigrams are listed by Peter Beal, *Index of English Literary Manuscripts* (New York, 1980–), vol. 1, pt. 2, pp. 349–50. Numbers 167 and 249 were transcribed in the sixteenth century by Cornelius Valerius ab Auwater, *Epistolae et Carmina,* ed. Henry de Vocht, *Humanistica Lovaniensia, 14* (1957). This appendix also excludes the reprinting of no. 258 in *EW* (sigs. XX_2v–XX_3) and More's English prose recounting of the jest of no. 247 in *A Dialogue Concerning Heresies* (see the Commentary at 247/1–9, and *CW 6,* 234/8–14).

[2]Since the series from University Microfilms International, "Early English Books, 1475–1640" and "Early English Books, 1641–1700," are indexed according to the original *STC* and Wing numbers, those numbers are included with the present citations (in parentheses, if they differ from the later *STC*[2] and Wing[2] designations). A third University Microfilm series containing a few of the works listed here is that of the British Library's Thomason Collection. That collection consists of pamphlets, broadsides, and books from the era of the English Revolution, assembled and bound by the London bookseller George Thomason between 1640 and 1661. The British Library symbol for Thomason publications is "E" followed by the volume number and (in parentheses) the item number within the volume. When applicable, the Thomason number is included for entries in this appendix.

Also available are several series of microfilms of early German, French, and Italian

The compiling of this appendix has benefited from the published work of several scholars: R. W. Gibson, Hoyt H. Hudson, James Hutton, Frank and Majie Padberg Sullivan, and others.[1]

---

books. Research Publications, Inc., of New Haven has microfilmed collections at Yale and Duke Universities. The series are titled "German Baroque Literature" and "German Baroque Literature: The Harold Jantz Collection." The first series follows Curt von Faber du Faur, *German Baroque Literature: A Catalogue of the Collections in the Yale University Library,* 2 vols. (New Haven: Yale University Press, 1958), to which there is an alphabetically arranged supplement, *Bibliography-Index to the Microfilm Edition of the Yale University Library Collection of German Baroque Literature* (New Haven: Research Publications, 1971). The second series is to be used with *German Baroque Literature: A Descriptive Catalogue of the Collection of Harold Jantz, and a Guide to the Collection on Microfilm,* 2 vols. (New Haven: Research Publications, 1974). In this appendix the designations "German Baroque" and "Jantz" refer to the numbering in the catalogues of those two collections. Other microfilm series, issued by the Erasmus Press of Lexington, Kentucky, are titled "German Books before 1601," "French Books before 1601," "French Books Printed 1601–1700," and "Italian Books before 1601." Many works listed in this appendix are included in those series, but no standard enumeration or system of reference exists for them.

[1]Works by Gibson, Hudson, and Hutton are given in the bibliography. Frank and Majie Padberg Sullivan, *Moreana: Material for the Study of Saint Thomas More,* 5 fascicles and a supplement (Los Angeles, 1964–77). Jerome Breunig, S.J., in his master's thesis, "An Edition of Thomas More's Epigrams" (St. Louis University, 1942), was the first to list some important English translations of the sixteenth and seventeenth centuries (pp. xx–xxi). Thomas Whipple, *Martial and the English Epigram from Sir Thomas Wyatt to Ben Jonson* (Berkeley, California, 1925; reprint, New York, 1970). Articles in the journal *Moreana:* Ward S. Allen, *55–56* (1977), 64; Dominic Baker-Smith, 7 (1965), 106–08; André Blanchard, *50* (1976), 66–72; Jackson C. Boswell, in press; Bob de Graaf, *23* (1969), 53–55 and *45* (1975), 29–36; Charles Doyle, *34* (1972), 47–55; *38* (1973), 13–20; *41* (1974), 11–18; *45* (1975), 53–60; *54* (1977), 79–81; Marianne Meijer, *38* (1973), 37–42 and *50* (1976), 5–10; Anne Lake Prescott, *59–60* (1978), 35–41; *70* (1981), 5–24; R. J. Schoeck, *73* (1982), 67–68; Malcolm C. Smith, *65–66* (1980), 23–31; Emile Telle, *18* (1968), 21–22; Franklin B. Williams, *15* (1967), 209–10; *27–28* (1970), 83–86.

1. Erasmus, Desiderius 1517 or 1518
[*Adagia*] *ex tertia autoris recognitione . . . Ioannes Frobenius studiosis omnibus S. D. accipito candide lector Erasmi Roterodami, prouerbiorum chiliadas . . .* , Basel, Johann Froben.

Reprints: 52 (Y_3).

Many later editions include the epigram; earlier ones do not. See the Commentary at 52/1–8.

2. *De generibus ebriosorum* [1518?]
De generibus ebriosorum et ebrietate vitanda . . . , Worms, Gregorius Comiander.

Reprints: 143

See the Commentary at 143/1–234. Another edition in 1599 (see Urceo 1519).

3. Urceo, Antonio 1519
Rhythmus Codri [Antonii Urcei] festiuissimus. Carmen Mori vrbanissimum. I. [sic] *Lvsvs Camicziani verissimvs . . .* , Leipzig, Melchior Lotter.

Reprints: 143 (A_3v–B_1v).

Another edition in 1599 (published with a 1599 Frankfurt edition of *De generibus ebriosum*).

4. Erasmus, Desiderius 1520
Enchiridion militis Christiani, Mainz, Joannes Schoeffer.

Reprints: 68, 125, 145 (a_2).

For later editions of the *Enchiridion* which include these three epigrams see *BB,* vol. 12.

5. Linius, Levinus, ed. 1522
Disticha aliquot illustrium poetarum videlicet P. Fausti Andrelini, Martialis . . . , Ghent, Pieter de Keysere. Nijhoff-Kronenberg no. 2790.

Reprints: 2 (D_1v), 4 (D_1v), 6 (D_1v), 7 (D_1v), 8 (D_1v), 17 (D_1v), 30 (D_1v), 35 (D_1v), 48 (D_1v), 74 (D_1v), 77 (D_2), 78 (D_2), 84 (D_2), 86 (D_2), 92 (D_2), 104 (D_2), 105 (D_2), 106 (D_2), 115 (D_2), 125 (D_2), 138 (D_2), 153 (D_2), 154 (D_2), 157 (D_2), 164 (D_2v), 165 (D_2v), 170 (D_2v), 172 (D_2v), 217 (D_2v), 228 (D_2v), 229 (D_2v), 231 (D_2v), 240 (D_2v), 241 (D_2v).

6. Nachtigall (Luscinius), Ottmar [1524]
Ioci ac sales mire festiui, ab Ottomaro Luscinio Argentino partim selecti ex bonorum utriusque linguae authorum mundo, partim longis peregrinationibus visi & auditi, ac in centurias duas digesti, [Augsburg].

Reprints: 33 (K_6), 38 (E_7v), 39 (E_8), 61 (A_8), 95 (I_1), 96 (F_1v), 117 (F_2), 133 (K_6v–K_7), 164 (B_1), 174 (I_6), 175 (I_1v), 254 (E_8).

The citations here are from a copy at the University of Illinois, Urbana. There was at least one other edition of approximately the same date, represented by the Folger Library copy. Subsequently Nachtigall's collection was included in two editions of *Mensa philosophica* (Leipzig, 1603, and Frankfurt, 1608).

7. *A C. mery talys* 1526
A C. mery talys, London. *STC*[2] 23663.

Adapts (English prose): 144 (D_1).

Another edition in 1548.

8. Soter (Heyl), Joannes 1528
Epigrammata aliquot Graeca veterum elegantissima, Cologne.

Reprints: 1 (N_6v–N_7), 2 (N_5v), 3 (I_1v), 4 (B_5v), 5 (B_5–B_5v), 6 (I_1v), 7 (C_2), 8 (F_5), 9 (G_2v), 10 (A_5v), 11 (N_8), 12A (C_3), 12B (C_3), 13 (O_2), 14 (F_5), 15 (H_5v), 16A (T_5), 16B (T_5), 17 (R_8), 24 (M_6v), 25 (Q_6), 26 (M_6), 27 (A_4v), 28 (A_4v), 29 (A_4v), 30 (A_4v), 31 (A_4v–A_5), 32 (A_5), 33 (A_5), 34 (G_7), 35 (G_6v–G_7), 36 (G_7), 38 (H_7), 39 (M_5), 40 (M_5v), 41 (N_5), 43 (N_8), 44 (P_5), 45 (P_3v), 46 (P_3v), 47 (I_2), 48 (I_2), 49 (I_3v), 52 (L_7–L_7v), 53 (X_5v–X_6), 54 (X_1v–X_2), 58 (K_8), 59 (I_3–I_3v), 70 (F_4), 76 (H_3), 85 (C_5v), 86 (C_5v), 87 (L_4), 88 (L_4), 89 (M_8v–N_1), 91 (K_7v), 99 (N_5v), 100 (K_8v), 102 (L_2), 103 (M_3), 104 (K_7), 105 (K_3v), 106 (K_5v), 118 (K_5v), 119 (F_4v), 122 (L_8–L_8v), 123 (I_1), 124 (H_7), 125 (G_4v), 126 (H_7v–H_8), 127 (H_8), 129 (F_6), 136 (F_2v), 137 (F_2v), 138 (C_5), 140 (M_5), 141 (M_4v–M_5), 142 (N_6v), 145 (B_4), 146 (A_6), 149 (K_5), 150 (K_5v–K_6), 151 (L_7v), 152 (M_7), 153 (N_4v), 154 (L_2), 155 (L_2), 156 (L_2–L_2v), 157 (N_7v), 166 (L_8v), 170 (M_4v), 171 (O_2), 172 (O_2), 173 (O_2v), 177 (P_5v–P_6), 221 (P_6), 228 (L_2v), 229 (L_2v), 230 (M_2v), 231 (M_3), 232 (M_8), 239 (G_4v–G_5), 241 (G_5v), 248 (T_7v–T_8), 270 (C_2v).

There was an edition of 1525, and a later one of 1544.

9. Barlandus (van Baerland), Adrianus 1529
Iocorum veterum ac recentium libri tres, Cologne, Eucharius Cervicornus (Hirtzhorn).

Reprints: 1 (f_3), 26 (f_3), 27 (f_3), 39 (f_3–f_3v), 60 (f_3v), 63 (f_3v), 86 (f_3v), 95 (f_3v–f_4), 99 (f_4–f_4v), 106 (f_4v), 154 (f_4v), 157 (f_4v), 164 (f_4v), 165 (f_4v), 175 (f_4v), 179 (f_6), 186 (f_6), 197 (f_6), 202 (f_6–f_6v), 204 (f_6v), 206 (f_6v), 207 (f_6v), 210 (f_4v–f_5), 215 (f_5), 216 (f_5), 218 (f_5), 222 (f_5), 228 (f_5), 233 (f_5–f_5v), 235 (f_5v), 236 (f_5v), 245 (f_5v), 246 (f_5v).

More's epigrams are not in the Louvain 1524 edition. There was also an Antwerp edition in 1529.

10. Cornarius (Hagenbut), Janus 1529
Selecta epigrammata Graeca Latine versa ex septem epigrammatum Graecorum libris, Basel, Johann Bebel.

Reprints: 1 (Q_6v–Q_7), 2 (Q_5), 3 (I_6), 4 (C_1v), 5 (C_1–C_1v), 6 (I_6), 7 (C_6v), 8 (F_6), 9 (G_3v), 10 (B_4v), 11 (R_2), 12 (C_7–C_7v), 13 (R_5), 14 (F_6v), 15 (H_7v), 16 (Aa_7v), 17 (Y_8), 24 (P_3v), 25 (X_3v–X_4), 26 (P_3), 27 (B_3v), 28 (B_3v), 29 (B_3v), 30 (B_3v), 31 (B_3v), 32 (B_3v–B_4), 33 (B_4), 34 (H_2), 35 (H_1v–H_2), 36 (H_2v), 38 (I_1), 39 (P_1v), 40 (P_2), 41 (Q_3v), 43 (R_1v), 44 (T_5), 45 (T_2v), 46 (T_2), 47 (I_6v), 48 (I_7), 49 (K_1), 52 (N_8), 53 (Dd_7v), 54 (Cc_6), 58 (L_6v–L_7), 59 (I_8v), 70 (F_4v), 76 (H_5v), 85 (D_2v), 86 (D_2), 87 (M_7), 88 (M_7), 89 (P_6v–P_7), 91 (L_5v–L_6), 99 (Q_5), 100 (L_7v), 102 (M_3), 103 (O_6), 104 (L_5v), 105 (K_6v), 106 (L_1), 118 (L_2v–L_3), 122 (O_1–O_1v), 123 (I_4v–I_5), 124 (I_1), 125 (G_6), 126 (I_2v), 127 (I_3v), 129 (F_7), 136 (F_1v), 137 (F_1v), 138 (D_1v), 140 (P_1v), 141 (P_1), 142 (Q_6v), 146 (B_5), 149 (K_8), 150 (L_3), 151 (N_8v), 152 (P_4v), 153 (Q_2), 154 (M_2v), 155 (M_2v), 156 (M_3), 157 (R_1), 166 (O_2), 170 (O_8v), 171 (R_5), 172 (R_5v), 173 (R_6), 177 (T_7), 221 (T_8), 228 (M_3v), 229 (M_3v), 230 (O_5), 231 (O_5v), 232 (P_6), 239 (G_7), 241 (G_7v), 248 (Bb_3), 270 (C_7).

11. Agrippa von Nettesheim, Henricus Cornelius 1530
Splendidae nobilitatis viri . . . Henrici Cornelij Agrippae ab Nettesheym De incertitudine & vanitate scientiarum & artium . . . , Antwerp, Ioannes Grapheus. Nijhoff-Kronenberg no. 49.

Reprints: 61 and 65, as a single poem ("hoc epigrammate perpulchro") (M_2).

Translated into Italian (1547), English (from the Italian, 1569; *STC* 204), French (1582), and Dutch (1651). There were many editions of the Latin and of the translations.

12. Luther, Martin 1530
Das schoene Confitemini, an der zal der CXVIII Psalm, Wittenberg.

Adapts (German prose): 237 (I_4).

See Luther's *Werke,* vol. 31, pt. 1 (Weimar, 1913), p. 150.

13. *Tales, and quicke answeres* [1532?]
Tales, and quicke answeres, very mery, and pleasant to rede, London. *STC*[2] 23665.

Adapts (English prose): 187 (A_3), 199 (H_4v), 201 (D_3v–D_4), 207 (D_4), 208 (F_1v–F_2), 222 (H_4v), 237 (H_3).

Another edition in 1567.

14. Volusenus, Florentius 1532
Enarratio in Psalmum nobis 50, Hebraeis vero 51, Paris, Ludovicus Cyanaeus.

Reprints: 68.

See Dominic Baker-Smith in *Moreana,* 7 (1965), 106–08.

15. *De Imitatione* 1535
De Imitatione eruditorum quorundam libelli quam eruditissimi puta Caelii Calcagnini ad Ioannem Baptistam Gyraldum . . . , Strassburg, Ioannes Albertus.

Reprints: 89 (h_3v).

See Bob de Graaf, *Moreana, 23* (1969), 53–55.

16. Duchesne (a Quercu), Léger 1536
Flores epigrammaton ex optimis quibusque authoribus selecti per Leodegarium de Quercu Rothomageum quibus accesserunt iocularia quae animi gratia confinxit, Paris, Prigentius Calvarin.

Reprints: 2 (B_2), 4 (lines 5 and 9; B_2v), 5 (lines 7 and 13–15, B_2v), 6 (B_2v), 7 (B_2v), 8 (B_2v), 9 (lines 16–19 followed by lines 13–14, B_2v), 12 (B_2v), 52 (B_4), 55–56 (printed as one, B_3), 74 (B_3), 107 (B_3), 115 (B_3), 125 (B_3), 138 (B_3), 156 (B_3), 157 (B_3), 164 (B_3), 165 (B_3v), 174 (B_3v), 175 (B_3v), 180 (B_3v–B_4), 228 (B_4), 229 (B_4).

Another edition in 1542. See also Duchesne 1555.

The section is headed "Quae sequuntur sunt ex thoma moro."

17. Gast, Johann, ed. 1539
Scholae Christianae epigrammatum libri duo, ex variis Christianis poetis decerpti in usum adolescentulorum . . . , Basel, [N. Brylinger].

Reprints: 4 (p. 322), 5 (pp. 284, 309), 7 (p. 362), 12 (both verions, p. 307), 59 (p. 348), 68 (p. 354), 69 (p. 358), 70 (p. 327), 71 (p. 289), 72 (p. 293), 73 (p. 358), 74 (p. 321), 75 (p. 360), 76 (pp. 257, 282), 79 (p. 328), 80 (p. 311), 105 (pp. 334, 367), 107 (p. 337), 108 (pp. 290–291), 109 (p. 351), 110 (p. 346), 111 (p. 265), 112 (p. 266), 113 (p. 268), 115 (p. 329), 119 (p. 359), 120 (p. 334), 121 (p. 322), 125 (pp. 300, 308), 127 (p. 349), 130 (p. 360), 132 (p. 294), 135 (p. 270), 137 (with a third line of verse added, p. 100), 139 (p. 346), 149 (p. 280), 145 (p. 308), 158 (p. 305), 162 (p. 260), 180 (p. 283), 198 (p. 335), 206 (p. 386), 207 (p. 387), 224 (p. 112), 232 (p. 285), 238 (p. 359), 270 (p. 290).

Another edition in 1541. See also Gast 1543.

Some epigrams are given twice. The source of the citations is André Blanchard, *Moreana, 50* (1976), 66–72.

18. Opsopoeus (Heydnecker), Vincentius 1540
In Graecorum epigrammatum libris quatuor, Basel, Nicolaus Brylingerus

Reprints: 24 (r_8v), 26 (r_8v), 44 (B_8), 136 (e_1v), 140 (r_7v), 141 (r_6v–r_7), 142 (t_6–t_6v), 153 (t_2v), 157 (t_8v), 170 (r_6v), 177 (C_5), 222 (C_6v)

A Frankfurt edition of 1600 also reprints 41 (δ_7). There was another edition in 1614.

19. Schottenius, Hermannus 1540
Vita honesta, siue virtutis: quomodo quisque viuere debeat, omni aetate, omni tempore, & quolibet loco, erga Deum & homines. Autore Herman. Schoten. Hesso. Cvi nouissime adiecimus Institvtionem Christiani hominis, per Adrianum Barlandum aphorismis digestam . . . , Antwerp, Joannes Steels. Nijhoff-Kronenberg no. 3869.

Reprints: 69 (F_8), 75 (F_7v), 130 (F_7v).

Also contained in the Antwerp reprints of this edition (1551, 1562; *BB* S281 and S283). Not in the 1530 edition. There were other editions in 1532, 1538, and 1563.

20. Vasolli, Venturino 1540
Epigrammatium sylva, Pavia, Ioannes Maria Simoneta.

Reprints: 157 (fol. 17v).

Citation from Hutton, *Anthology in Italy,* p. 209. According to

Hutton, More's epigram is also included in Vasolli's *Amoenissimum musarum viridarium,* Pavia, 1553, at fol. 38v.

21. Gast, Johann, ed. 1543
Epigrammatum libri II ex Christianis poetis collecti, Basel, N. Brylinger.

Reprints: same sequence as Gast 1539 but omits 59 and adds 32 (z_7), 39 (x_6v), and 201 (A_6–A_6v).

22. Curione, Celio Secondo, ed. 1544
Pasquillorum tomi duo, Basel.

Reprints: 202 (C_6–C_6v), 204 (C_6v).

23. Tiraqueau, André 1546
De legibus connubialibus, et iure maritali, Paris, I. Kerner.

Reprints: 11 (D_4), 15 (R_4v).

The epigrams are not in the 1524 edition. There were many later editions. Sometimes the book is cited by another part of its title, *Ex commentariis in Pictonum consuetudines sectio, De legibus connubialibus. . . .*

24. Alciati, Andrea 1547
Parergon iuris libri VII posteriores, Lyons, Sebastianus Gryphius.

Reprints: 124 (C_6).

Another edition in 1554.

25. Patten, William 1548
The expedicion into Scotlande of . . . Edward, Duke of Soomerset, London. *STC*[2] 19476.5 (*STC* 19479).

Adapts (English prose): 211 (O_3–O_3v).

See the Commentary at 211/1–5.

26. Domenichi, Lodovico 1549
La nobiltà delle donne [partly translated from Agrippa], Venice, Gabriel Giolito de Ferrari.

Translates (Italian verse): 61 and 65, printed as a single poem, as in the Latin of Agrippa 1530, which Domenichi translated in 1547. The same Italian translation of nos. 61 and 65 appears here (M_1v).

Another edition in 1551.

27. Dupuyherbault, Gabriel 1549
Theotimus, sive de tollendis & expungendis malis libris, Paris, Joannes Roigny.

Adapts (Latin prose) and quotes the last line of 210 (g_8).

28. Habert, François 1549
Le temple de chasteté, Paris, Michel Fezandat.

Adapts (French verse): 228 (F_8v).

29. *Effigies* [1553]
Effigies Des. Erasmi Roterodami literatorum principis, & Gilberti cognati Nozereni, eius amanuensis: una cum eorum symbolis, & Nozeretho cognati patria. Accesserunt et doctorum aliquot uirorum in D. Erasmi & Gilberti cognati laudem, carmina, Basel, Ioannes Oporinus.

Reprints: 276 (A_6v–A_7).

30. Ronsard, Pierre de 1553
Livret de folastries, Paris.

May have used 89 (H_2–H_2v) and 157 (H_3v) in his French verse translations (see Hutton, *Anthology in France,* p. 357, notes 48 and 50).

Another edition in 1584.

31. Duchesne (a Quercu), Léger 1555
Flores epigrammatum ex optimis quibusque authoribus excerpti . . . tomus primus, Paris, P. Beguin.

Reprints: 1 (x_2), 2 (x_2), 3 (t_8v), 4 (s_2), 6 (t_8v), 7 (s_2), 8 (t_3v), 9 (t_4v), 11 (x_2v), 12 (s_2–s_2v), 14 (t_4), 16 (y_5v), 17 (y_3v), 19 (E_7–F_2v), 20 (F_2v), 21 (F_2v–F_3), 22 (F_3), 23 (F_3v), 24 (v_8v), 25 (y_1v–y_2), 26 (v_8v), 27 (s_1v), 36 (t_6v), 37 (F_3v), 38 (t_7v), 39 (v_8), 40 (v_8), 41 (x_1v), 43 (x_2v), 44 (x_7), 46 (x_6), 47 (t_8v), 52 (v_6), 54 (z_3), 59 (v_1), 60 (F_3v–F_4), 61 (F_4), 65 (F_4), 66 (F_4), 67 (F_4), 68 (F_4v), 69 (F_4v), 70 (t_3–t_3v), 73 (F_4v), 74 (F_4v), 75 (F_4v–F_5), 76 (t_7), 77 (F_5), 78 (F_5), 79 (F_5), 80 (F_5–F_5v), 83 (F_5v), 84 (F_5v), 85 (F_5v), 86 (F_5v), 87 (v_4v, F_5v), 90 (F_5v–F_6), 92 (F_6), 93 (F_6), 94 (F_6), 95 (F_6–F_7), 96 (F_7–F_7v), 97 (F_7v), 99 (x_1v–x_2, F_7v), 100 (v_3v, F_7v), 101 (F_7v–F_8), 102 (v_4), 103 (v_7), 105 (v_2v), 106 (v_3), 109 (F_8), 110 (F_8), 111 (F_8), 112 (F_8–F_8v), 113 (F_8v), 114 (F_8v), 115 (F_8v), 116 (F_8v–G_1), 117 (G_1), 118 (v_3), 119 (t_3v), 120 (G_1), 121 (G_1), 122 (v_6v), 123 (t_8), 125 (t_6), 126 (t_7v), 127 (t_8), 128 (G_1–G_1v),

130 (G_1v), 132 (G_1v), 133 (G_1v–G_2), 134 (G_2), 135 (G_2), 136 (t_2v), 137 (t_2v–t_3), 138 (s_2v), 139 (G_2), 140 (v_8), 141 (v_8), 142 (x_2), 149 (v_2v), 150 (v_3), 151 (v_6), 152 (v_8v), 153 (x_1v), 154 (v_4), 156 (v_4), 157 (x_2v), 158 (G_2), 164 (G_2), 165 (G_2v), 166 (v_6v), 169 (G_2v), 170 (v_7v), 171 (x_3), 172 (x_3), 173 (x_3v), 174 (G_2v), 175 (G_2v–G_3), 176 (G_3), 177 (x_7), 178 (G_3–G_3v), 179 (G_3v), 180 (G_3v), 182 (G_3v), 185 (G_4), 186 (G_4), 187 (G_4), 196 (G_4–G_4v), 197 (G_4v), 198 (G_4v–G_5), 199 (G_5), 200 (G_5), 201 (G_5–G_5v), 202 (G_5v), 204 (G_5v), 210 (G_5v–G_6), 211 (G_6), 214 (x_1), 216 (G_6), 221 (x_7v), 222 (G_6), 223 (G_6), 224 (G_6v), 228 (v_4–v_4v), 229 (v_4), 230 (v_7), 232 (v_8v), 236 (G_6v), 237 (G_6v), 238 (G_7), 240 (G_7), 242 (G_7–G_7v), 243 (G_7v), 252 (G_7v–G_8), 253 (G_8).

32. Fries (Frisius Tigurinus), Johannes 1555
Breuis Musicae Isagoge, Ioanne Frisio Tigurino authore. Accesserunt priori aeditioni omnia Horatij carminum genera: item Heroica, Elegiaca etc. quatuor uocibus ad aequales, in studiosorum adolescentum gratiam composita, Zürich, Frosch.

Reprints: 70 (DD_4v), 76 (DD_4v), 223 (DD_4v), 238 (DD_6).

33. Tiraqueau, André 1555
Commentarii in L. Boves, Venice, Dominicus Lilius.

Reprints: 138 (E_3v).

There was a 1554 edition, and later ones in 1556 and 1588.

34. Doublet, Jean 1559
Elegies de Ian Doublet, Paris, C. Langelier.

Translates (French verse): 202 (O_2v–O_3).

The signature comes from a facsimile reprint published by the Société des Bibliophiles Normands (Rouen, 1869), pp. 54–55.

35. Lemnius, Levinus 1559
Levini Lemnii Zirizaei occulta naturae miracula, ac varia rerum documenta . . . , Antwerp, Willem Simon.

Reprints: 205 (without lines 12–17 and 19–22, B_1v–B_2).

Italian translation, Venice, 1560; French translation, Lyons, 1566, and a different one at Paris, 1567; German translation, Leipzig, 1572; English translation, London, 1658 (Wing L 1044). There were many other editions of the Latin and of the translations.

36. Estienne, Henri, ed. 1560
Pindari Olympia, Pythia, Nemea, Isthmia. Caeterorum octo lyricorum carmina . . ., [Geneva], Henri Estienne.

Reprints: 145 (CC_3).

Other editions in 1566, 1567, 1585–86, 1586, 1598, 1599, 1600, 1612, 1624, and 1626.

37. Landi, Costanzo 1560
Lettera . . . sopra una impressa d'un pino, Milan, G. degli Antonii.

Reprints: 34 (C_6), 35 (C_6v).

38. Domenichi, Lodovico 1564
Facetie, motti et burle di diversi signori et persone private, Florence, i Giunti.

Adapts (Italian prose): 133 (D_2v–D_3), 144 (D_3–D_3v), 187 (H_4v), 237 (D_4v), 245 (H_4v), 254 (H_4v–H_5).

Earlier editions lack the adaptations from More. Another 1564 edition was published in Venice, and there were many later editions.

39. Turberville, George 1567
Epitaphes, epigrams, songs and sonets, London. *STC*[2] 24326.

Translates (English verse): 102 (M_3).

Another edition in 1570.

Many other poems by Turberville that derive from the *Greek Anthology* may have been influenced by More's Latin. See T. K. Whipple, *Martial and the English Epigram* (Berkeley, California, 1925; reprint, New York, Phaeton, 1970), pp. 314–16; and H. B. Lathrop, "Janus Cornarius's *Selecta Epigrammata Graeca* and the Early English Epigrammatists," *MLN, 43* (1928), 223–29.

40. Estienne, Henri 1570
Epigrammata Graeca, selecta ex Anthologia. Interpretata ad verbum et carmine ab Henrico Stephano: quaedam et ab aliis. Loci aliquot ab eodem annotationibus illustrati. Eiusdem interpretationes centum et sex unius distichi, aliorum item quorundam epigrammatum variae, [Geneva], Henri Estienne.

Reprints: 3 (h_6), 5 (b_8v–c_1), 8 (f_7), 17 (o_1), 34 (g_5v), 36 (h_2), 41 (k_6), 54 (p_5–p_5v), 87 (i_5v), 88 (i_5v), 100 (i_1), 102 (i_4v), 106 (i_1), 122 (k_3), 125 (g_2v), 136 (e_4v), 137 (e_5v), 141 (k_5v), 146 (b_1v), 154 (i_4), 155 (i_3v), 177 (l_6v), 221 (m_1v).

41. Du Verdier, Antoine 1573
La prosographie ou description des personnes insignes, Lyons, Antoine Gryphius.

Translates (French verse): 61 and 65 as a single poem (k_4v), as in the Latin of Agrippa 1530.

Other editions in 1586, 1589, 1603, 1604, 1605.

42. Sanctius (Sanchez de Brozas), Franciscus 1573
Comment. in And. Alciati emblemata, Lyons, G. Rovillius.

Reprints: 127 (D_4), 146 (Ee_3).

43. Mignault (or Minoe), Claude, ed. 1574
Omnia Andreae Alciati V.C. emblemata. Adiectis commentariis & scholiis, in quibus emblematum ferme omnium aperta origine, mens auctoris explicatur, & obscura omnia, dubiaque, illustrantur; per Claudium Minoem, Antwerp, C. Plantin.

Reprints: 65 (S_4v), 134 (N_2).

Hutton, *Anthology in France,* pp. 142–43, gives information on some other editions. According to him, the 1574 edition is the first to contain the epigrams by More, and not all editions after 1574 contain them.

44. Gascoigne, George 1576
The steele glas. A satyre . . . Togither with the complainte of Phylomene, London. *STC* 11645.

Adapts (English verse): 218 in lines 21–24 of the epilogue to "The Steele Glas" (I_1v).

45. Herdesianus, Henricus Petreus 1577
Aulica vita . . . , Frankfurt am Main, Joannes Feyrabendt.

Reprints: 72 (R_6), 95 (R_5v–R_6), 107 (R_6v), 109 (R_6v–R_7), 110 (R_6v), 111 (R_8), 112 (R_7v), 113 (R_8), 114 (R_7–R_7v), 115 (R_7v), 120 (R_7), 121 (R_7), 145 (X_1v), 162 (R_7v).

Another edition in 1578.

46. Kendall, Timothy 1577
Flowers of epigrammes, out of sundrie the moste singular authours, London. *STC*[2] 14927.

Translates (English verse): 65 (K_4), 66 (K_4v), 85 (K_4v), 86 (K_4v), 93 (K_5), 99 (K_5), 107 (L_1v), 109 (K_5), 114 (K_5), 115 (K_5v), 117 (K_5v), 133 (K_6), 134 (K_6), 135 (K_6), 144 (K_8v), 151 (L_1), 164 (K_6v), 165 (K_6v), 174 (K_6v), 187 (K_7), 196 (K_7), 199 (K_7v), 201 (K_8), 202 (K_8v), 223 (K_8v), 243 (L_1v), 254 (L_1v), 261 (L_1).

47. Lambin (Lambinus), Denys 1577
In Q. Horatium Flaccum . . . commentarii . . . editio postrema, Frankfurt am Main, A. Wechel, 2 volumes.

Reprints: 2 (vol. 2, p. 132 D).

Earlier editions lack the epigram; there was a later edition in 1588.

48. *Selecta quaedam de moribus epigrammata* 1577
Selecta quaedam de moribus epigrammata, Paris, Jean Bienné.

Reprints: 9 (p. 9), 38 (p. 12), 76 (p. 12).

Citations from Hutton, *Anthology in France,* pp. 145–46.

49. Bacon, Nicholas before 1579
Manuscript poems printed in *Recreations of His Age,* Oxford: Daniel Press, 1919 for 1903.

Adapts (English verse): 175 (pp. 29–31), 249 (pp. 25–26).

50. Stanyhurst, Richard 1582
The first foure bookes of Virgil his Aeneis translated intoo English heroical verse, . . . wyth oother poëtical diuises theretoo annexed, Leiden. *STC*[2] 24806.

Reprints: 240 (A_4).

Reprints and translates (English verse): 160 (Q_1–Q_1v).

Translates (English verse): 144 (O_4), 175 (O_4–O_4v), 187 (O_4v), 247 (O_4v), 254 (P_1).

Another edition in 1583.

51. Guicciardini, Lodovico 1583
L'Hore di ricreatione, Antwerp, P. Bellero.

Adapts (Italian prose): 199 (or 210 or 214, G_5).

There were many other editions, not all of which have the adaptation from More.

52. Melanchthon, Philip 1583
Epigrammata Philippi Melanthonis selectiora, formulis precum, historiis, paraphrasi dictorum diuinorum, & sententijs grauissimis maxime insignia . . . ut pueris in pia institutione proponi & inculcari possint . . . collecta, a M. Petro Hegelundo . . ., Frankfurt am Main, Sigismund Feyrabendt.

Reprints: 111 (O_3), 112 (O_3v).

53. Scot, Reginald 1584
The discouerie of witchcraft . . ., London. *STC*² 21864.

Adapts (English prose): one of 61–65 (Q_3).

Other editions in 1651, 1654, and 1665.

54. Du Verdier, Claude 1586
In auctores pene omnes, antiquos potissimum censio, Lyons.

Reprints: 160 (X_2), 190 (X_2v), 191 (X_2v).

Another edition in 1609.

55. Whitney, Geffrey 1586
A choice of emblemes and other deuises, Leiden. *STC*² 25438.

Reprints: 65 (V_3).

56. Mazzoni, Jacopo 1587
Della difesa della comedia di Dante, Cesena, Bartolomeus Raverius.

Reprints: 34 (Dd_5), 35 (Dd_5), 228 (D_1).

57. Averell, William 1588
A maruailous combat of contrarieties, London. *STC* 981.

Adapts (English prose): 218 (B_4).

58. Stapleton, Thomas 1588
Tres Thomae, Douai, Ioannes Bogardus.

Reprints: 272 (a_8).

Other editions in 1612, 1620, and 1689.

59. Tamisier, Pierre 1589
Anthologie ou recueil des plus beaux épigrammes grecs, pris et choisis de l'Anthologie grecque. Mis en vers françois, sur la version latine de plusiers doctes personnages, Lyons.

Translates (French verse): 12 (G_7v), 85 (G_8v), 123 (I_1v–I_2), 154 (D_8).

Many of the other French translations from the *Greek Anthology* may have been based on or influenced by More's Latin. More is mentioned (A_5v) as one of the translators whom Tamisier relied on.

60. Fale, Thomas 1593
Horologiographia: the art of dialling, London. *STC* 10678.

Reprints: 228 (A_3).

Other editions in 1626, 1627, 1633, and 1652.

61. Capece, Scipione 1594
De principiis rerum libri duo . . . Et elegiae quaedam cum epigrammatis, Naples.

Reprints: 17 (K_6v).

A Venice edition of 1546 lacks the epigram by More.

62. C[opley], A[nthony] 1595
Wits fittes and fancies, London. *STC* 5738.

Adapts (English prose): 144 (V_1), 199 (or 210 or 214, Aa_1), 207 (T_4v), 237 (X_1–X_1v), 245 (M_1).

Other editions in 1596 and 1614.

63. [Harington, Sir John] 1596
A new discourse of a stale subject called the metamorphosis of Ajax . . . [containing] An anatomie of the metamorphosed Aiax . . . [and] An apologie. 1. Or rather a retractation. 2. Or rather a recantation . . . , London, R. Field. *STC* 12772–74, 12779–81.

Reprints and translates (English verse): 4 (N_2), 39 (D_1), 254 (C_8v).

Adapts (English verse): 133 (P_5v).

The citations are from what Elizabeth Donno took to be the first edition (not in *STC*), containing all three parts, which are also found separately in multiple editions, all dated 1596. Harington uses 4 and 133 in the *Apologie*, 39 and 254 in *A new discourse.* In Mrs. Donno's edition (New York, Columbia University Press, 1962), 4 is on p. 218, 39 on p. 100, 133 on p. 258, and 254 on p. 99. Mrs. Donno summarizes the history of the text on pp. 23–39. See also Harington 1618.

64. [Harvey, Gabriel] 1597
The trimming of T. Nashe, gentleman, London. *STC* 12906.

Adapts (English prose): 37 (F_4).

65. Stockwood, John 1597
Progymnasma scholasticum, London. *STC*[2] 23281.

Reprints: 3 (M_7v), 5 (D_5), 8 (K_1), 17 (X_1v), 34 (L_7), 35 (L_3v), 36 (M_2v), 41 (P_5–P_5v), 54 (Z_6), 87 (O_1v–O_2), 88 (O_2), 100 (N_4), 102 (N_8v), 106 (N_3v), 122 (O_8v), 125 (K_7), 136 (H_1v), 137 (H_3), 138 (D_6), 141 (P_4v [P_4 mismarked O_4]), 146 (C_3), 154 (N_8), 155 (N_7v), 172 (Bb_7v), 177 (R_3), 221 (R_7v).

66. Barckley, Sir Richard 1598
Discourse of the felicitie of man, London. *STC* 1381.

Reprints: 5 (Ii_1).

There were other editions in 1603 and 1631. The 1631 edition, titled *The felicitie of man* (*STC* 1383), includes an English verse translation of 5 (Mm_2v).

67. B[astard], T[homas] 1598
Chrestoleros. Seven bookes of epigrames written by T. B., London. *STC* 1559.

Adapts (English verse): 218 (E_5v).

68. Buttes, Henry 1599
Dyets dry dinner, London. *STC* 4207.

Adapts (English prose): 254 (H_7).

69. Camerarius, Philippus 1599
Operae horarum succisivarum, Nürnberg, Christophorus Lochnerus.

Quotes: 75, lines 4–5 (F_4v).

French translation 1610; English translation 1621.There were many later editions of the Latin and of the translations.

70. Weever, John 1599
Epigrammes in the oldest cut, and newest fashion, London. *STC*[2] 25224.

Adapts (English verse): 205 (C_2), 217 (D_4v).

71. R[owlands], S[amuel] 1600
The letting of humours blood in the head-vaine, London. *STC*[2] 21393.

Adapts (English verse): One of 61–65 or 67 (C_3).

Another edition of 1600 is *STC*[2] 21392.7. There were later editions in 1605, 1607, 1610, 1611, and 1613.

72. Thynne, Francis c. 1600
Manuscript poems printed in *Emblemes and Epigrames,* ed. F. J. Furnivall, Early English Text Society, Original Series no. 64 (London, 1876).

Translates (English verse): 65 (pp. 85–86), 174 (p. 59).

Adapts (English verse): 187 (pp. 70–71), 202 (p. 60).

73. Jonson, Ben 1601
Every man in his humor, London. *STC*[2] 14766.

Adapts (English prose): 144 (E_4v; act 3, scene 2 in modern editions).

74. Campion, Thomas 1602
Observations in the art of English poesie, London. *STC* 4543.

Adapts (English prose): 161 (A_7v) and quotes line 7.

75. Melander (Holzapfel), Otho, ed. 1603
Iocorum atque seriorum, tum novorum, tum selectorum, atque memorabilium, centuriae aliquot . . . , Frankfurt, Palthenius.

Reprints: 202 (F_{10}), 205 (B_{11}–B_{11}v).

Another edition in 1617. See Melander 1605, 1611, and 1626.

76. Tabourot, Estienne 1603
Les bigarrures du seigneur Des Accordz, Paris, Iean Richer.

Reprints: 160, lines 2, 3, 5 (altered), 7, 8, and 9 (P_3).

The epigram does not appear in the editions printed at Paris in 1583 or at Rouen in 1595. There were other editions in 1585, 1586, 1588, 1591, 1595 (Paris), 1599, 1608, 1609, 1614, 1616, 1625, 1626, 1640, 1648, and 1657.

77. *Pasquils jests* 1604
Pasquils jests, mixed with Mother Bunches merriments, London. *STC*[2] 19451.

Adapts (English prose): 187 (C_4v in 1609 edition; p. 41 in W. C. Hazlitt's edition of the 1604 text, in *Shakespeare Jest-Books* [London, Willis & Sotheran, 1864], vol. 3).

Other editions in 1629, 1632, 1635, and 1650.

78. Camden, William 1605
Remaines of a greater worke concerning Britaine, London. *STC* 4521.

Adapts (English prose): 218 (Ff_3).

Other editions in 1614, 1623, 1629, 1636, and 1637.

79. Melander (Holzapfel), Otho, ed. 1605
Jocorum atque seriorum, tum novorum, tum selectorum atque memorabilium liber tertius . . . , Lich, published by Wolfgang Kezel, printed by Johann Berners.

Reprints: 175 (N_3).

See Melander 1603, 1611, and 1626.

80. D[ekker], T[homas], and George Wilkins 1607
Jests to make you merie, London. *STC* 6541.

Adapts (English prose): 237 (D_1v).

81. J[ohnson], R[ichard] 1607
The pleasant conceites of old Hobson the merry Londoner, London. *STC*[2] 14688.

Adapts (English prose): 199 (E_3).

Other editions in 1610, [1634?], and 1640 [1649?].

82. Pontanus (Spanmüller), Jacobus 1607
Institutio poëtica, in Ioannis Buchler, *Thesaurus phrasium poeticarum,* Cologne, B. Gualtheri.

Reprints: 1 (T_{12}).

The earliest editions of Pontanus, *Poeticarum institutionum libri III* (Ingolstadt, 1594 and 1597) lack More's epigram, which appeared in the publication of *Institutio poëtica* as an appendix to Buchler's *Thesaurus.* There were many later editions of Buchler with Pontanus appended: besides several in Cologne, Amsterdam, Leipzig, and Antwerp, at least eleven editions were published in London, the first of which (1620) is *STC* 3993a, where the epigram appears at sig. Y_{12}v.

83. W[alkington], T[homas] 1607
The optick glasse of humors. Wherein the foure complections are succinctly painted forth, London. *STC*^{2} 24967.

Reprints: 199 (C_5v).

Other editions in 1631, [1631?], 1639, and 1664.

84. Milles, Thomas 1608
The custumers alphabet and primer . . . , [London?]. *STC*^{2} 17927.

Adapts (English verse): 254 (L_1–L_1v) and reprints lines 4–5 of the Latin.

Another edition in [1609?]. The same version of 254 appears in Milles's *The custumers apologie. To be read more at large,* London [1613?]. *STC*^{2} 17930.

85. Rowlands, Samuel 1608
Humors looking glasse, London. *STC*^{2} 21386.

Translates (English verse): 144 (A_4v).

86. *Selecta epigrammata ex florilegio* 1608
Selecta epigrammata ex florilegio et alia quaedam ex veteribus poëtis comicis potissimum Latino item carmine conversa. Rome, B. Zannettus.

Reprints: More's epigrams from Soter (See Soter 1528 in this Appendix).

According to Hutton, *Anthology in Italy,* pp. 255–57, the Jesuit collection of 1608 "was founded on the third (1544) edition of Soter's book." Hutton implies that *Selecta epigrammata ex florilegio* contains all of More's translations printed by Soter, though perhaps in a different order.

87. W[est], R[ichard] [1608]
Wits A. B. C., London. *STC*² 25262.

Adapts (English verse): 217 (E_3–E_3v).

88. Heath, John 1610
Two centuries of epigrammes, London. *STC* 13018.

Adapts (English verse): 216 (B_3).

89. Mariscotti, Agesilao 1610
De personis, et larvis . . . syntagmation, Bologna, Ioannis Rossius.

Adapts (Latin verse): 58 (K_2).

Other editions in 1639, 1690, and 1699.

90. Boys, John 1611
An exposition of the dominical epistles and gospels in our English liturgie . . . Summer part, London. *STC* 3459.

Quotes: 77, line 3 (Q_8).

Other editions in 1615 and 1638. See also Boys 1612.

91. [Davies, John, of Hereford] [1611]
The scourge of folly. Consisting of satyricall epigramms and others . . . , London. *STC* 6341.

Adapts (English verse): 61–65 (C_7v–C_8).

92. Melander (Holzapfel), Otho, ed. 1611
Jocorum atque seriorum cum novorum, tum selectorum atque memorabilium libri ii, Schmalkalden, Wolfgang Kezel.

Reprints: 1 (P_3), 11 (A_6v), 32 (A_6v), 58 (V_6), 60 (Q_2v–Q_3), 61 (Q_3), 68 (A_8v), 70 (O_7v), 74 (O_7v), 84 (Q_1v), 90 (G_8), 96 (X_1v), 99 (T_5), 101 (Q_2v), 104 (A_6), 106 (O_8v), 110 (D_1v), 111 (D_2), 112 (D_2), 114 (D_2v), 115 (D_2–D_2v), 116 (C_2–C_2v), 117 (C_2v), 120 (D_2), 133 (X_1v),

138 (D_6v), 143 (B_6–C_1), 158 (D_6v), 160 (Gg_5v), 163 (P_6), 164 (A_3v), 168 (D_6v), 176 (E_1), 179 (Y_4), 186 (E_1), 187 (D_6), 196 (V_5), 197 (E_1), 199 (B_4), 201 (Q_1v), 202 (Ss_2), 203 (Q_4v), 205 (Mm_5–Mm_5v), 206 (Q_1v), 207 (Y_4), 210 (Q_4v), 214 (D_6), 222 (Y_4v–Y_5), 223 (Y_5v), 225 (B_4v), 228 (X_4v), 234 (B_4v), 235 (V_5), 238 (D_6v), 245 (V_4v), 246 (V_1), 247 (A_4), 254 (A_4).

See Melander 1603, 1605, and 1626.

93. Boys, John 1612
An exposition of the dominical epistles and gospels in our English liturgie . . . Autumn part, London. *STC* 3459.

Reprints: 202 (B_4v).

Published with Boys 1611. Other editions in 1616 and 1639.

94. Drayton, Michael [1612]
Poly-Olbion, London. *STC* 7226.

Quotes: 64, line 9 (H_6v), introduced by a half-line tag from Vergil's *Eclogues* (2.69 and 6.47).

Other editions in 1613 and 1622.

96. Taylor, John 1612
The sculler, rowing from Tiber to Thames, London. *STC*[2] 23791.

Adapts (English verse): one of 61–65 (E_1v–E_2).

Another edition in 1614.

97. Canoniero, Pietro Andrea 1613
Flores illustrium epitaphiorum, Antwerp, Ioachim Trognaesius.

Reprints: 159 (Z_7), 184 (Z_7), 258 (Z_7v).

Another edition in 1627.

98. B., W., compiler and translator 1614
The philosopher's banquet, the second edition, newly corrected and inlarged, to almost as much more. By W. B. Esquire [from the late fifteenth-century *Mensa philosophica,* attributed to Michael Scott], London. *STC*[2] 22062.

Reprints, translates (English verse), *and adapts* (English prose): 133 (R_8–R_8v).

Adapts (English prose): 205 (O_2).

In a final section titled "Certaine Conceyts & Ieasts . . . Collected out of Scotus, Poggius, and others." The material from More is not in the 1609 edition of W. B.'s translation. There was a 1633 edition.

99. Freeman, Thomas 1614
Rubbe, and a great cast, London. *STC* 11370.

Adapts (English verse): 218 (B_2).

100. *Omnium horarum opsonia* 1614
Omnium horarum opsonia, Frankfurt, Johannes-Jacobus Porsius.

Reprints: 4 (G_1v), 5 (F_7), 6 (Ii_4), 7 (H_2), 15 (EE_7v), 24 (g_7), 25 (u_1v), 26 (g_6v), 28 (B_6), 29 (B_5v), 30 (B_6), 31 (B_7v), 36 (CC_2), 39 (g_5), 40 (g_5v), 43 (k_5), 44 (p_3v), 45 (c_5v, o_4), 47 (Hh_6v), 48 (Hh_7), 49 (Kk_4v), 52 (e_3v), 53 (ii_7), 54 (c_4, bb_5v), 57 (DD_1), 59 (Kk_3v), 76 (EE_2v), 79 (h_5v), 85 (I_3), 89 (h_4), 99 (i_6v), 100 (b_4v, c_4v), 104 (Mm_1v, b_1), 106 (a_4), 122 (e_6v), 123 (Ii_1), 124 (GG_1), 127 (Hh_6v), 129 (T_4), 137 (P_8), 140 (g_4v), 141 (g_4), 145 (F_5), 146 (D_1), 149 (a_1v), 152 (g_8v), 156 (c_5), 166 (e_8v), 170 (g_3v), 173 (l_6v), 230 (f_6), 232 (h_3v), 239 (Z_6v), 241 (Z_7), 248 (bb_4), 270 (H_3v).

According to James Hutton (*Anthology in Italy,* p. 273), this is a reprint of Hieronymus Megiser, *Anthologia, seu florilegium graecolatinum,* Frankfurt, 1602.

101. Hakewill, George 1615
The vanitie of the eie, 3rd edition, Oxford. *STC* 12622.

Reprints: 61 (I_7v).

Not in the two previous editions of 1608 nor in the later one of 1633.

102. Harington, Sir John 1615
Epigrams both pleasant and serious, London. *STC* 12775.

Adapts (English verse): 169 (E_3).

See Harington 1618.

103. Pontanus (Spanmüller), Jacobus 1616
Attica bellaria, Munich, Widow of [Adam] Berg [the Elder].

Reprints: 60 (Hh_4v), 67 (Hh_4v), 85 (Ccc_6v), 92 (Ccc_7), 96 (Hh_4v–Hh_5), 117 (Hh_5), 157 (Hh_3v), 160 (Hh_5), 174 (Hh_5v), 186 (Hh_5v), 199 (Hh_6), 210 (Hh_6), 268 (Hh_6–Hh_6v).

Other editions in 1617 and 1644. See Pontanus 1644.

104. [Davies, John, of Hereford] 1617
Wits Bedlam, where is had, whipping-cheer, to cure the mad, London. *STC* 6343.

Adapts (English verse): 245 (E_2).

105. Harington, Sir John 1618
The most elegant and wittie epigrams, London. *STC* 12776.

Adapts (English verse): 133 (F_1), a slight variant of the epigram in Harington 1596; 169 (D_4), a somewhat different version of the adaptation in Harington 1615; the earlier version is at E_6v in the 1618 collection.

Translates (English verse): 254, a slight variant of the translation in Harington 1596.

Other editions in 1625, 1633, and 1663 [i.e. 1634]. In Harington's *Letters and Epigrams,* ed. Norman E. McClure (Philadelphia, 1930; reprint, New York, 1977), the 1618 adaptation of 133 is on p. 199 (no. 37); of 169, on p. 179 (no. 81); and of 254, on p. 166 (no. 48).

106. Cüchler, Elias [1618–19]
Florilegium diversorum epigrammatum veterum in centurias distributum, Görlitz, Ioannes Rhamba.

Reprints: 4 (K_3v), 5 (K_2v), 7 (L_3v), 8 (Ii_2), 9 (Oo_2), 10 (D_4), 14 (Ii_3), 15 (Fff_3), 27 (D_1), 28 (D_1v), 29 (D_1v), 30 (D_1v), 31 (C_4v), 34 (Xx_4v), 35 (Xx_2v), 36 (Zz_1v), 70 (Gg_2v), 76 (Ddd_4v–Eee_1), 85 (N_4v), 119 (Gg_3v), 124 (Iii_2), 125 (Rr_2), 136 (Bb_1v), 137 (Bb_3v), 138 (N_2), 141 (Rr_3), 143 (Rr_4), 145 (I_4v), 146 (F_2), 270 (L_4v).

107. B[asse], W., and E. P. 1619
A helpe to discourse, London. *STC* 1547.

Reprints, translates (English verse), *and adapts* (English prose): 133 (L_1v–L_2).

Other editions in 1620, 1621, 1627, 1628, 1635, 1636, and 1638.

108. *A helpe to memory* 1620
A helpe to memory and discourse, London, Bernard Alsop. Should precede *STC* 13051.

Reprints and translates (English verse): 164 (F_2).

Other editions in 1621 and 1630.

109. Peacham, Henry 1620
Thalia's banquet, London. *STC*[2] 19515.

Adapts (English verse): one of 61–65 (A_6).

110. Thuilius, Joannes, ed. 1621
Andreae Alciati Emblemata cum commentariis Claudii Minois . . . Francisci Sanctii . . . & notis Laurentii Pignorii . . . , Padua, Petrus Paulus Tozzius.

Reprints: 27 (Vv_5), 61 (Ee_5), 65 (Ee_5), 127 (E_2), 134 (T_4), 146 (Ss_8).

Another edition in 1661.

111. Ferrand, Jacques 1623
De la maladie d'amour ou mélancholie érotique, Paris, D. Moreau.

Reprints: 61 (H_7v).

English translation in 1640 (*STC* 10829), reprinted in 1645.

112. Shakespeare, William 1623
The famous history of the life of King Henry the Eight. In *Comedies, histories, & tragedies* (first folio), London. *STC*[2] 22273.

Adapts (English verse): 218 (t_3v; act 1, scene 1, lines 83–85).

The life and death of King John.

Adapts (English verse): 218 (a_2v; act 2, scene 1, lines 69–70).

Other editions in 1632, 1663, 1664, and 1685.

113. Sweerts, Pierre François 1623
Epitaphia ioco-seria, Cologne, Bernardus Gualtherus.

Reprints: 177 (B_2v).

Another edition in 1645.

114. Heywood, Thomas 1624
Γυναικεῖον: *or nine bookes of various history, concerninge women,* London. *STC* 13326.

Translates (English verse): 187 (Z_6v–Aa_1).

See the Commentary at 187/1–9. Another edition in 1657.

115. Bacon, Francis 1625
Apophthegmes new and old, London. *STC* 1115.

Adapts (English prose): 199 (or 210 or 214, I_2–I_2v).

Another edition in 1626. See Bacon's *Works,* ed. James Spedding, 14 vols. (London, 1857–74; reprint, New York, 1968), 7, 138 (no. 88).

116. Melander (Holzapfel), Otho, and Denis, eds. 1626
Iocorum atque seriorum cum novorum, tum selectorum atque memorabilium, tomus tertius . . . , Frankfurt, Wolfgang Hofmann [bound together with *tomus secundus* of the same work. Jantz no. 1761].

Reprints: 1 (KK_7v), 11 (AA_6v), 32 (AA_6v), 58 (OO_3), 60 (LL_3v), 61 (LL_3v), 68(AA_7v), 70 (KK_4), 74 (KK_4), 84 (LL_2v), 90 (EE_8v–EE_9), 96 (OO_6v), 99 (NN_6), 101 (LL_3–LL_3v), 104 (AA_6), 106 (KK_5v), 110 (CC_2), 111 (CC_2), 112 (CC_2), 114 (CC_2v), 115 (CC_2v), 116 (BB_6–BB_6v), 117 (BB_6v), 120 (CC_2), 133 (OO_6v), 138 (CC_6v), 143 (BB_2–BB_5v), 158 (CC_6v), 160 (VV_{12}–VV_{12}v), 163 (KK_{10}v), 164 (AA_3v), 168 (CC_6v), 176 (CC_9), 179 (PP_5), 186 (CC_9), 187 (CC_6), 196 (OO_2), 197 (CC_9), 199 (AA_{12}–AA_{12}v), 201 (LL_2), 203 (LL_5), 206 (LL_2–LL_2v), 207 (PP_5), 210 (LL_5–LL_5v), 214 (CC_6–CC_6v), 222 (PP_5v–PP_6), 223 (PP_6v), 225 (AA_{12}v), 228 (OO_9v), 234 (AA_{12}v), 235 (OO_2), 238 (CC_6v), 245 (OO_1v–OO_2), 246 (NN_{10}), 247 (AA_4), 254 (AA_4).

Other editions in 1625 and 1643. See Melander 1603, 1605, and 1611.

117. P[arrot], H[enry] 1626
Cures for the itch, London. STC^2 19328.

Adapts (English verse): 165 (F_2v).

118. Taylor, John 1626
Wit and mirth. Chargeably collected out of tavernes, ordinaries, innes, London. STC^2 23813.5 (*STC* 23814).

Adapts (English prose): 199 (or 210 or 214, B_5).

Other editions in 1628, 1629, and 1635.

119. Farnaby, Thomas 1629
Ἡ τῆς Ἀνθολογίας Ἀνθολογία, *Florilegium epigrammatum Graecorum, eorumque Latino versu a varijs redditorum,* London. *STC* 10701.

Reprints: 1 (with alterations, G_3v), 4 (with alterations, F_8v), 7 (A_6v), 11 (G_7v), 28 (A_2v), 40 (F_2v), 44 (with alterations, D_5v); 49 (with alterations, G_3v), 58 (lines 2 and 4 are More's, the rest Velius's, B_6v), 70 (with alterations, D_3v), 76 (with alterations, F_3v), 103 (with alterations, F_4v), 122 (with alterations, E_3v), 138 (B_4v), 141 (with alterations, F_6v), 152 (C_4v), 157 (G_5v), 172 (with alterations, C_3v), 177 (E_7v), 228 (C_2v), 229 (with alterations, C_2v), 230 (with alterations, F_1v).

Other editions in 1650 and 1671.

120. *A banquet of jests* 1630
A banquet of jests; or change of cheare, London. *STC* 1368.

Adapts (English prose): 207 (C_7).

See also *A banquet of jests* 1632, 1633, and 1640.

121. Germano, Antonio 1630
Giardino di sentenze volgari e Latine di diversi auttori antichi e moderni, Rome.

Reprints: 41 (p. 308).

Citation from Hutton, *Anthology in Italy,* p. 261.

122. M[artin], J[ames], ed. 1630
Joshua Sylvester, *Panthea: or, divine wishes and meditations,* London. *STC*[2] 23580.

Reprints and translates (English verse): 258, lines 15–16 (C_3v).

123. Weever, John 1631
Ancient funerall monuments . . . , London. *STC*[2] 25223.

Reprints: 258 (Yy_4).

Another edition in 1661.

124. *A banquet of jests* 1632
A banquet of jests; or, change of cheare, [London, Richard Royston]. Should follow *STC* 1368.

Reprints and translates (English verse): 228 (K_8–K_8v).

Also reprints the prose adaptation of 207 from *A banquet of jests* 1630. See *A banquet of jests* 1630, 1633 and 1640.

125. *A banquet of jests* 1633
A banquet of jests: or, change of cheare . . . the second part newly published, London. *STC* 1372.

Adapts (English prose): 237 (C_8v).

Other editions, with varying contents drawn from both the first and second parts, in 1634, 1636, and 1639. See *A banquet of jests* 1630, 1632, and 1640.

126. May, Edward 1633
Epigrams divine and morall, London. *STC*[2] 17708.

Translates (English verse): 187 (C_2v), 237 (F_1–F_1v).

127. Nash, Thomas ("Philopolites") 1633
Quaternio or a fourefold way to a happie life, London. *STC*[2] 18382.

Reprints: 3 (lines 9–10, L_4v), 7 (Mm_2v), 40 (lines 3–4, Hh_3v), 49 (D_4v), 55 (Bb_4v), 119 (L_1v), 157 (Z_2), 212 (L_1), 224 (lines 16–17, Ff_4v), 238 (lines 4–5, L_4).

Other editions in 1636 and 1639.

128. Heywood, Thomas 1635
The hierarchie of the blessed angells, London. *STC* 13327.

Translates (English verse): 108 (T_4) and reprints first line of Latin.

129. Featley, Daniel 1636
Clavis mystica: a key opening divers texts of scripture, London. *STC* 10730.

Adapts and translates (English prose): 202, lines 6–7 (N_2).

130. Heywood, Thomas 1636
Loves maistresse: or, the queens masque, London. *STC* 13352.

Adapts (English prose): 187 (I_4).

Other editions in 1640 and 1662.

131. Uthalmus, Lerimos [pseud., perhaps Thomas Willmers] 1636
Fasciculus florum: or, a nosegay of flowers, translated out of the gardens of severall poets, London. *STC*[2] 24559.

Reprints and translates (English verse): 157 (D_1v), 228 (D_7v).

132. *A pleasant history* 1637
A pleasant history of the life and death of Will Summers, London. *STC*[2] 22917.5.

Adapts (English prose): 237 (D_1–D_1v).

Another edition in 1676.

133. Baudius, Dominique 1638
Amores, edente Petro Scriverio, inscripti Th. Graswinckelio, Amsterdam, Ludovicus Elzevirius.

Reprints: 143 (S_5–S_8v).

Another edition at Lyons in 1638.

134. Brathwait, Richard 1638
A survey of history, London. *STC* 3583a.

Quotes: 267, lines 6–7 (Pp_3).

135. Featley, Daniel 1638
Stricturae in Lyndomastygem, published with Sir Humphrey Lynde's *A case for the spectacles,* London. *STC* 17101.

Adapts (English prose): 164 (Cc_8v) and reprints line 4 of the Latin.

136. L., H. 1638
Gratiae ludentes. Jests from the universitie, London. *STC* 15105.

Adapts (English prose): 237 (I_6v–I_7).

137. [Chamberlain, Robert] 1639
Conceits, clinches, flashes, and whimzies, London. *STC* 4942.

Adapts (English prose): 218 (D_5v–D_6).

See also Chamberlain 1640.

138. *A banquet of jests* 1640
A banquet of jests; or, a collection of court, camp, colledge, city, country iests, London. *STC* 1371.

Adapts (English prose): 218 (M_5v–M_6).

Also reprints from *A banquet of jests* 1630, 1632, and 1633 the prose adaptations of 207 and 237, and the Latin original with English verse translation of 228. Other editions in 1657, 1660, and 1665.

139. [Chamberlain, Robert] 1640
Jocabella, or a cabinet of conceits, London. *STC* 4943.

Adapts (English prose): 199 (or 210 or 214, B_3).

Also reprints the English prose adaptation of 218 from Chamberlain 1639.

140. Opitz, Martin 1640
Florilegium variorum epigrammatum, Danzig, Andreas Hunefeldius. *German Baroque* no. 224.

Reprints: 136 (A_4v).

Another edition in 1644.

141. *Wits recreations* 1640
Wits recreations. Selected from the finest fancies of moderne muses, London. *STC*[2] 25870.

Translates (English verse): 61 (C_6v), 99 (C_1v), 102 (C_7v), 133 (C_1v–C_2), 199 (C_6v), 207 (C_6v–C_7), 220 (C_7), 237 (C_7), 249 (C_7v).

Adapts (English verse): 208 (B_8v–C_1), 211 (I_1v).

The collection of unattributed eipgrams (many of them translations) is sometimes associated with the name of Sir John Mennes—for no good reason. See also *Wits recreations* 1641, 1654.

142. Weckherlin, Georg Rudolph 1641
Gaistliche und Weltliche Gedichte, Amsterdam, Johann Jansson. *German Baroque* no. 164.
Adapts (German verse): 254 (N_8).

See also Weckherlin 1648.

143. *Wits recreations* 1641
Wits recreations, containing 630 epigrams, London. Wing W3222.

Translates (English verse): 187 (L_8v) and the epigrams in the 1640 edition.

Adapts (English verse): 165 (K_6) and the epigrams in the 1640 edition.

Other editions in 1645 and 1650. See also *Wits recreations* 1654.

144. Barlaeus (Baerle), Caspar 1643
Dialogi aliquot nuptiales [issued with, though signed separately from] *Faces Augustae, sive poematia, quibus illustriores nuptiae, a Jacobo Catsio . . . celebrantur,* Dordrecht, M. Havius.

Reprints: 138 (F_1).

Another edition in 1656.

145. Gryphius, Andreas 1643
Epigrammata. Das erste Buch, Leiden.

Translates (German verse): 99 (B_2).

A variant appeared in *Epigrammata oder Bey-Schriften* (1663) and in *Teutsche Gedichte* (1698).

See *Lateinische und deutsche Jugenddichtungen,* ed. Friedrich-Wilhelm Wentzlaff-Eggebert (Hildesheim: Georg Olms, 1961), p. 205; and *Oden und Epigramme,* ed. Marian Szyrocki (Tübingen: Max Niemeyer, 1964), pp. 162 and 195.

146. [Guillebaud, Pierre] 1643
Iardin des muses. Ou se voyent les fleurs de plusieurs aggreables poësies, Paris, Antoine de Sommaville et August Courbé.

Reprints: 10 (S_6v), 52 (T_2), 202 (L_2).

147. Pontanus (Spanmüller), Jacobus 1644
Attica bellaria, Frankfurt, Joannes Godofridus Schonwetterus.

Reprints: 101 (Hh_4v).

Also reprints the epigrams that appeared in Pontanus 1616.

148. *Florilegium epigrammatum* 1645
Florilegium epigrammatum ex recentioribus auctoribus, Lucca, Balthazar de Iudicibus.

Reprints: 9 (F_5v), 40 (F_6), 49 (F_6).

149. Fickaert, Franchoys [1648]
Metamorphosis ofte Wonderbaere Veranderingh' ende Leven van . . . Quinten Matsys, Antwerp.

Reprints and translates (Dutch verse): 276 (pp. 19–21).

See Lorne Campbell, Margaret Mann Phillips, Hubertus Schulte Herbrüggen, and J. B. Trapp, "Quentin Metsys, Desiderius Erasmus, Pieter Gillis, and Thomas More," *Burlington Magazine, 120* (November 1978), 720.

150. Weckherlin, Georg Rudolph 1648
Gaistliche und Weltliche Gedichte, Amsterdam, Johann Jansson. *German Baroque* no. 164a.

Translates (German verse): 54 (Mm_5v–Mm_6).

Also reprints the adaptation of 254 from Weckherlin 1641. Perhaps influenced by the misprint of *Graecia* as *gratia* in More's 1518 Latin (see the Commentary at 54/1–6), Weckherlin addresses the lines to Venus rather than to Greece.

151. Carolus a Sancto Antonio Patavino, Anconitanus [pseud.] 1650
De arte epigrammatica; sive, De ratione epigrammatis rite conficiendi, libellus, Cologne, Cornelius ab Egmond.

Reprints: 14 (C_5), 52 (K_8), 60 (K_4v), 75 (K_7), 110 (lines 2–7, with line 4 altered, I_6v), 138 (I_2v), 164 (K_4v), 179 (L_1), 186 (G_7v), 210 (G_5), 216 (K_4), 237 (L_1).

Adapts (Latin verse): 216 (K_4).

The *British Museum Catalogue* (vol. 212, col. 484) identifies the author as Carolus Mazaeus. James Hutton spells that name "Marzaeus" (*Anthology in Italy,* p. 369). Elsewhere Hutton refers to the author as "Patavinus" (pp. 52 and 68) and "Carolus Aconitanus" (p. 368). The *National Union Catalog* (vol. 505, p. 341, col. 2)—following the cataloguing of the library at the University of California (Berkeley)—identifies the author as Gian Vittorio Rossi (1577–1647).

152. Mercier, Nicolas 1653
De conscribendo epigrammate opus curiosum, Paris, J. de la Caille.

Reprints: 164 (V_3v), 175 (S_4v), 179 (S_4v), 180 (G_6), 187 (S_4v–S_5), 202 (M_6), 222 (S_5), 237 (H_4), 262 (P_6v–P_7), 277 (I_6).

153. *Mercurius jocosus* 1654
Mercurius jocosus, or the merry Mercurie. Bringing news of the best concets, News-sheet, for July 14–21, 1654 (London, Thomas Lock). Thomason E805(7).

Adapts (English prose): 144 (A_2).

154. [*Wits recreations*] 1654
[Wits recreations], Recreation for ingenious head-peeces, London. Wing[2] M1714.

Translates (English verse): 228 (C_2v) and the epigrams in the 1640 and 1641 editions.

Adapts (English verse): 260 (F_3v) and the epigrams in the 1640 and 1641 editions.

The translation of 228 is from *A banquet of jests* 1632. Other editions in 1663, 1667, and 1683.

155. C[otgrave], J[ohn] 1655
Wits interpreter, London. Wing[2] C6370. Thomason E1448.

Translates (English verse): 133 (Bb_7v).

Other editions in 1662 and 1671.

156. [Gayton, Edmund] 1656
Wit revived: or, a new and excellent way, London. Wing[2] G423, Thomason E1703(1).

Adapts (English prose): 254 (A_{11}).

The adaptation is from the verse of Harington 1596. Another edition in 1674.

157. [Edmundson, Henry] 1658
Comes facundus in via, London. Wing[2] E180.

Adapts (English prose): 218 (2 versions, C_9v–C_{10}).

158. Pecke, Thomas 1659
Parnassi puerperium; . . . Translation of six hundred, of Owen's epigrams; Martial de spectaculis, or of rarities to be seen in Rome; and the most select, in Sir Tho. More . . . , London. Wing P1040, Thomason E1861(1).

Translates (English verse): 21 (K_5), 23 (K_5–K_5v), 24 (K_5v), 25 (K_5v), 26 (K_5v), 32 (K_6), 34 (K_6), 36 (K_6), 37 (K_6–K_6v), 38 (K_6v), 40 (K_6v), 41 (K_6v), 42 (K_6v–K_7), 43 (K_7), 46 (K_7), 47 (K_7–K_7v), 49 (K_7v), 50 (K_7v), 60 (K_8), 65 (K_8), 67 (K_8), 70 (K_8v), 71 (K_8v), 72 (K_8v), 79 (L_1), 83 (L_1), 85 (L_1), 86 (L_1), 90 (L_1–L_1v), 93 (L_1v), 98 (L_1v), 101 (L_1v–L_2), 102 (L_2), 106 (L_2), 107 (L_2), 112 (L_2v), 115 (L_2).

159. Brome, Alexander 1661
Songs and other poems, London. Wing[2] B4852.

Adapts (English verse): one of 61–65, probably 63 (T_3v); 237 (S_5).

Other editions in 1664 and 1668.

160. Donne, John (the younger) 1662
Donne's satyr, containing 1. A short map of mundane vanity. 2. A cabinet of merry conceits. 3. Certain pleasant propositions, and questions. London. Wing[2] D1877.

Translates (English verse): 31 (E_8), 32 (E_8), 42 (D_3v), 55 (E_7v), 56 (E_7v), 85 (D_4v), 86 (D_4v), 88 (D_4), 93 (D_3v), 133 (D_6), 135 (C_5v), 146 (D_8v), 163 (G_1), 166 (E_1), 167 (D_8), 168 (F_2v), 169 (D_2v–D_3), 174 (D_4v), 175 (C_6–C_6v), 180 (E_5v–E_6), 187 (C_7–C_7v), 215 (E_5–E_5v), 218 (G_1v), 219 (E_2v–E_3), 220 (E_2v), 222 (F_8v), 223 (E_2v), 224 (D_4–D_4v), 225 (C_6), 226 (D_4), 237 (C_5v).

Adapts (English verse): 94 (D_3v), 214 (D_6v), 216 (E_1), 217 (E_1).

Some other epigrams that derive ultimately from the *Greek Anthology* may have been influenced by More's Latin.

161. Labbe, Philip 1666
Thesaurus epitaphiorum veterum ac recentium, Paris, Gaspard Maturas.

Reprints: 44 (Y_8–Y_8v), 159 (Bb_5v), 160 (Bb_5v), 173 (Z_4), 177 (Z_1v).

Another edition in 1686.

162. [Winstanley, William] [1667]
Poor Robin's jests, London. Wing P2885A.

Adapts (English prose): 133 (G_1v), 199 (or 210 or 214, F_5v–F_6).

There was an edition in 1653.

163. [Dryden, John] 1668
Sr Martin Mar-All, London. Wing[2] D2359.

Adapts (English verse): 60 (K_4).

Other editions in 1669, 1678, 1688, 1691, and 1697.

164. Hicks, William 1671
Oxford jests, London, 3rd edition (no record of first or second). Wing[2] H1891.

Adapts (English prose): 144 (E_4–E_4v), 165 (B_4), 187 (C_2), 207 (E_6v), 237 (F_3), 245 (E_8v).

Other editions in 1684, [1700].

165. W[instanley], W[illiam] 1672
The new help to discourse, London. Wing W3069.

Translates (English verse): 187 (M_3–M_3v).

There was a 1669 edition, and later ones in 1680, 1684, and 1696.

166. *Cambridge jests* 1674
Cambridge jests, London. Wing[2] C332.

Adapts (English prose): 133 (F_1–F_1v).

167. *The complaisant companion* 1674
The complaisant companion, or new jests, London. Wing[2] C5627.

Adapts (English prose): 165 (C_7), 199 (or 210 or 214, C_3v).

168. [?Head, Richard] 1675
Nugae venales, 2nd edition, London. Wing[2] H1266.

Reprints and translates (English verse): 254 (P_5v–P_6).

Another edition in 1686. The first edition, evidently, was the anonymous *The complaisant companion* 1674 (Wing C5627), cited above.

169. Regi, Domenico 1675
Della vita di Tomaso Moro, Milan, A. Malatesta.

Reprints and translates (Italian verse): 119 (L_7–L_7v).

Other editions in 1678 and 1681.

170. Hicks, William 1677
Coffee-house jests, London. Wing[2] H1884.

Adapts (English prose): 210 (F_2v–F_3).

Other editions in 1686 and 1688.

171. Seybold, Johann Georg 1677
Viridarium selectissimis paroemiarum et sententiarum Latino-Germanicarum flosculis . . . adornatum, Nürnberg. *German Baroque* no. 609.

Reprints and translates (German verse): 157 (Nn_3v).

172. Dillingham, William, ed. 1678
Poemata varii argumenti, partim e Georgio Herberto Latine (utcumque) reddita, partim conscripta a Wilh. Dillingham . . . , London. Wing[2] D1484.

Reprints: 95 (Q_6–Q_6v).

173. Bunyan, John 1680
The life and death of Mr. Badman. London. Wing[2] B5550.

Adapts (English prose): 210 (E_6).

Other editions in 1685, 1688, and 1696.

174. Borrichius, Olaus (Oluf Borch) 1683
Dissertationes academicae de poetis, Frankfurt.

Reprints: 159 and first line of 160 (U_1).

First edition in 1681.

175. Simon, Jeremias 1683
Gnomologia proverbialis poetica, Leipzig.

Reprints: 32 (lines 3–7, L_4v), 113 (lines 3–4, Aa_5v), 157 (Hh_5v).

Adapts: 4 (A_5), 125 (R_1v).

176. *London jests* 1685
London jests, London. Wing[2] L2897A.

Adapts (English prose): 187 (two versions, D_2v–D_3 and I_6v), 199 (or 210 or 214, B_8), 207 (F_8–F_8v), 237 (H_{12}).

There was an edition in 1684.

177. Casalicchio, Carlo 1687
L'utile col dolce, Naples, Giuseppi Roselli.

Reprints: 52 (Qq_2), 117 (Vv_2), 180 (Cc_5–Cc_5v [first signing]), 174 (Dd_3v–Dd_4), 210 (Dd_4v).

There was a Naples edition in 1671.

178. Cotton, Charles 1689
Poems on several occasions, London. Wing[2] C6389.

Translates (English verse): 138 (Rr_8v).

Adapts (English verse): 41 (Rr_8v), 199 (or 210 or 214, Rr_8).

179. Blount, Thomas Pope 1690
Censura celebriorum authorum, London. Wing[2] B3346.

Reprints: 159 and first line of 160 (Eee_3).

Cites Borrichius as source; see Borrichius 1683. Other editions in 1694 and 1696.

180. Almeloveen, Theodor Jansson van 1694
Amoenitates theologico-philologicae . . . subjiciuntur epigrammata et poemata vetera, ut & plagiariorum syllabus altero tanto auctior, Amsterdam, Janssonio-Waesbergius.

Reprints: 101 (Q_4, first signing), 193 (A_4v, third signing), 198 (K_3–K_3v, first signing), 236 (A_8v, third signing).

181. Bayle, Pierre 1697
Dictionnaire historique et critique, Rotterdam, Reinier Leers.

Reprints: 61, 65 ($FFFFfff_3$v), and, on the same page, du Verdier's 1573 French verse translation of 61 and 65 (printed as a single poem).

182. M[iege], G[uy] 1697

Delight and pastime, London. Wing[2] M2008.

Adapts (English prose): 117 (E_6–E_6v).

183. B., W. 1700
Ingenii fructus: or the Cambridge jests, London. Wing[2] B214.

Adapts (English prose): 187 (two versions: H_3, H_5v).

184. Boyer, Abel 1700
The wise and ingenious companion, French and English, London. Wing[2] B3918.

Adapts (English and French prose, on facing pages): 144 (N_6v–N_7), 237 (M_7v–M_8).

APPENDIX E

Table of Corresponding Numbers:
More's Latin Epigrams (1953),
Edited by L. Bradner and C. A. Lynch,
and the Yale Edition

APPENDIX E

Table of Corresponding Numbers

	Numbers in Bradner-Lynch	*Numbers in Yale Edition*
Progymnasmata	1	1
	2	2
	3	3
	4	4
	5	5
	6	6
	7	7
	8	8
	9	9
	10	10
	11	11
	12	12
	13	13
	14	14
	15	15
	16	16
	17	17
	18	18
Epigrammata	1	19
	2	20
	3	21
	4	22
	5	23
	6	24
	7	25
	8	26
	9	27
	10	28
	11	29
	12	30
	13	31

Numbers in Bradner-Lynch	*Numbers in Yale Edition*
14	32
15	33
16	34
17	35
18	36
19	37
20	38
21	39
22	40
23	41
24	42
25	43
26	44
27	45
28	46
29	47
30	48
31	49
32	50
33	51
34	52
35	53
36	54
37	55
38	56
39	57
40	58
41	59
42	60
43	61
44	62
45	63
46	64
47	65
48	66
49	67
50	68
51	69
52	70
53	71

Numbers in Bradner-Lynch	*Numbers in Yale Edition*
54	72
55	73
56	74
57	75
58	76
59	77
60	78
61	79
62	80
63	81
64	82
65	83
66	84
67	85
68	86
69	87
70	88
71	89
72	90
73	91
74	92
75	93
76	94
77	95
78	96
79	97
80	98
81	99
82	100
83	101
84	102
85	103
86	104
87	105
88	106
89	107
90	108
91	109
92	110
93	111

Numbers in Bradner-Lynch	*Numbers in Yale Edition*
94	112
95	113
96	114
97	115
98	116
99	117
100	118
101	119
102	120
103	121
104	122
105	123
106	124
107	125
108	126
109	127
110	128
111	129
112	130
113	131
114	132
115	133
116	134
117	135
118	136
119	137
120	138
121	139
122	140
123	141
124	142
125	143
126	144
127	145
128	146
129	147
130	148
131	149
132	150
133	151

Numbers in Bradner-Lynch	*Numbers in Yale Edition*
134	152
135	153
136	154
137	155
138	156
139	157
140	158
141	159
142	160
143	161
144	162
145	163
146	164
147	165
148	166
149	167
150	168
151	169
152	170
153	171
154	172
155	173
156	174
157	175
158	176
159	177
160	178
161	179
162	180
163	181
164	182
165	183
166	184
167	185
168	186
169	187
170	188
171	189
172	190
173	190

Numbers in Bradner-Lynch	*Numbers in Yale Edition*
174	190
175	191
176	192
177	193
178	194
179	195
180	196
181	197
182	198
183	199
184	200
185	201
186	202
187	203
188	204
189	205
190	206
191	207
192	208
193	209
194	210
195	211
196	212
197	213
198	214
199	215
200	216
201	217
202	218
203	219
204	220
205	221
206	222
207	223
208	224
209	225
210	226
211	227
212	228
213	229

Numbers in Bradner-Lynch	*Numbers in Yale Edition*
214	230
215	231
216	232
217	233
218	234
219	235
220	236
221	237
222	238
223	239
224	240
225	241
226	242
227	243
228	244
229	245
230	246
231	247
232	248
233	249
234	250
235	251
236	252
237	253
238	254
239	255
240	256
241	257
242	258
243	259
244	260
245	261
246	262
247	263
248	264
249	265
250	266
251	267
252	268
253	269

	Numbers in Bradner-Lynch	*Numbers in Yale Edition*
Appendix I	1	270
	2	271
Appendix II	1	272
	2	273
	3	274
	4	275
	5	276
	6	277
	7	278
	not in *Bradner-Lynch*	279
	not in *Bradner-Lynch*	280
	not in *Bradner-Lynch*	281

INDEX OF FIRST LINES

INDEX OF FIRST LINES

References are to the poem numbers in this edition.

INDEX

INDEX